COMPETITION LITIGATION IN THE UK

AUSTRALIA
Law Book Co.—Sydney

CANADA and **USA**
Carswell—Toronto

HONG KONG
Sweet & Maxwell Asia

NEW ZEALAND
Brookers—Wellington

SINGAPORE and **MALAYSIA**
Sweet & Maxwell Asia
Singapore and Kuala Lumpur

COMPETITION LITIGATION IN THE UK

TIM WARD
Barrister, Monckton Chambers

and

KASSIE SMITH
Barrister, Monckton Chambers

LONDON
SWEET & MAXWELL
2005

Published in 2005 by
Sweet & Maxwell Limited of
100 Avenue Road, London, NW3 3PF
Typeset by YHT Ltd, London
Printed and bound in Great Britain by Cromwell Press Ltd, Trowbridge

No natural forests were destroyed to make this product,
only farmed timber was used and replanted

A CIP catalogue record for this book is available from the British Library

ISBN 0421 893 400

FOREWORD

By Sir Christopher Bellamy QC

It is with some diffidence that I agreed to write this foreword, since some of
the subject matter of this excellent new work inevitably touches on the role
of the Competition Appeal Tribunal, under the Competition Act 1998, as
amended, and the Enterprise Act 2002. However, the scope of this book
ranges much wider than that, and its appearance is, in my respectful view,
timely indeed.

The landscape for competition litigation in the United Kingdom has
changed out of all recognition in the last few years. Some of us still
remember the difficulties and frustrations of the 1970s and 1980s, when the
domestic competition scene consisted of the largely moribund restrictive
trade practices legislation, on the one hand, and administrative intervention,
on public interest grounds, on the other hand. At European level, there was
no Court of First Instance, and the European Commission did not seem
overly enthusiastic about complaints, preoccupied as it still was with
clearing the backlog of notifications. Apart from the occasional "Euro-
defence", there was virtually no "competition litigation" in the conventional
sense. Indeed, there was hardly any procedural framework in which such
litigation could take place.

Today, the situation is transformed. The establishment of the Court of First
Instance in 1989 marked the beginning of more focused litigation in the
competition law field. Domestically, the 1998 Act has brought competition
policy within a framework of legal principles and procedural norms, to be
gradually established on a case by case basis. That process has been taken
further under the Enterprise Act 2002 with decisions by the OFT and
Competition Commission on mergers and market investigations being largely removed from Ministers and brought within the ambit of judicial
review before the CAT. The new cartel offence, introduced by that Act, also
brings the criminal law explicitly into the picture, for the first time.

In addition, from May 1, 2004 the national authorities and courts of the
European Union have been given the power directly to apply Articles 81 and
82 of the EC Treaty, including Article 81(3). The last redoubt of

administrative discretion, the monopoly of the European Commission to grant exemption under Article 81(3), has thus fallen, sweeping away with it the notification system that had stood for 40 years.

In those circumstances, a new book on competition litigation is to be warmly welcomed. Covering briefly the substantive provisions, *Competition Litigation in the UK* concentrates mainly on the role of the OFT, the practice and procedure of the CAT, the cartel offence, judicial review in competition causes, actions for damages, litigation concerning state aid, practice and procedure in Europe, EC competition law in UK courts, and arbitration proceedings. A final chapter usefully sketches out key concepts regarding economic evidence in competition cases.

The developments over the last few years have brought together law and economics in a single procedural framework. At long last there is a real chance that those two great disciplines, law and economics, will flow coherently in a single stream. I am sure this book will greatly assist that process.

Christopher Bellamy

February 14, 2005

PREFACE

Ten years ago, a book on competition litigation in the UK would have been a slim volume. But a series of important changes in the law, both domestically and at European level, have fundamentally changed the landscape. The Competition Act 1998 and the Enterprise Act 2002 introduced powerful new mechanisms for competition law enforcement into domestic law for the first time, as well as a specialist tribunal to hear the disputes which its application has generated. Community competition law has also undergone recent fundamental reform, or "modernisation". The practical effect has been to shift the emphasis of competition law enforcement from the Community institutions to the national authorities and courts. Moreover, the European Court of Justice has recently recognised the possibility that private competition law enforcement through the courts may yield an award of damages. As a result of these changes, competition litigation is becoming ever more important in practice.

This book aims to provide a comprehensive overview of practice and procedure in domestic competition litigation, whether in the Competition Appeal Tribunal, the courts or in arbitration. The regime it describes (derived from Community law, the Competition Act 1998 and the Enterprise Act 2002) applies across the UK. Thus, it is hoped it will be of value to practitioners throughout the UK, even though it does not comprehensively address the rules of domestic law which are particular to Scotland or Northern Ireland.

The book is the product of the expertise of ten of our colleagues at Monckton Chambers, all of whom are competition litigators. It also benefits from the specialist contributions of Clair Dobbin, a barrister who practices criminal law and Paul Reynolds, a professional economist. We have sought to ensure that the chapters retain the individual stamp of their authors. Nevertheless we have also aimed to provide a complete survey of the field.

The law is stated as at February 1, 2005, although references to later authorities have been included so far as possible.

Tim Ward and Kassie Smith
Monckton Chambers
Gray's Inn
London

February 2005

ABOUT THE CONTRIBUTORS

Daniel Beard

Daniel Beard is a barrister at Monckton Chambers specialising in EU, competition and public law/human rights law. He acts for a wide variety of private clients, regulators and government departments in all areas of competition work and has appeared before a variety of courts ranging from the Court of First Instance in Luxembourg to the Haverfordwest County Court. He is a standing counsel to the OFT.

Michael Bowsher

Michael Bowsher has been a member of Monckton Chambers since 2001. He has been practising in London since returning in 1992 from a period with Cleary Gottlieb in Brussels. He is also called to the Bar of Northern Ireland and is a Chartered Arbitrator and Accredited Mediator.

Clair Dobbin

Clair Dobbin is a criminal practitioner at 3 Raymond Buildings who specialises in international criminal law, public law and regulatory offences. She is a member of the Treasury C Panel. Recent cases include *Attorney-General's Reference (No.2 of 2001)* [2004] 2 A.C. 72, HL; *R. (Guisto) v Governor of Brixton Prison* [2004] 1 A.C. 101, HL; *Government of the United States of America v Montgomery* [2004] 1 W.L.R. 1909, HL.

Julian Gregory

Julian Gregory is a barrister at Monckton Chambers specialising in competition, public and regulatory law. He has appeared in both competition litigation in the CAT and judicial review applications in the High Court. He is a Committee member of the Administrative and Constitutional Law Bar Association (ALBA).

Josh Holmes

Josh Holmes is a barrister at Monckton Chambers, specialising in EC, competition law and regulation. He is also a visiting lecturer at Kings College London. From 1998 to 2001, he held a fellowship in law at New College Oxford and from 2002 to 2004 worked as référendaire in the cabinet of Advocate General Jacobs at the European Court of Justice in Luxembourg.

Anneli Howard

Formerly a solicitor at Freshfields and référendaire to Judge David Edward at the European Court of Justice, Anneli Howard is a barrister at Monckton Chambers, specialising in EU and competition law. Anneli represents private parties and regulators in appeals before the CAT, the European Commission, the CFI, the ECJ and the ECHR.

George Peretz

George Peretz is a barrister specialising in competition law at Monckton Chambers. He has wide experience of representing clients before the OFT and the CAT in cases including *Replica Football Kit, Lladro Comercial,* and *BCL Old v Aventis.* He also represented the OFT in *Claymore Dairies* and *OFT v X.*

Meredith Pickford

A former professional economist, Meredith Pickford is a barrister at Monckton Chambers specialising in competition, regulatory and public law. He is on the Attorney General's panel of Crown Counsel and acts for a wide variety of private and public sector clients. Cases include *Wanadoo v Ofcom, P&O v European Commission, R. (T-Mobile) v Competition Commission, FA Premier League* and *MasterCard.*

Ben Rayment

Ben Rayment is a barrister at Monckton Chambers. He specialises in all areas of European and UK competition law representing private and public sector clients in a wide range of sectors. For three-and-a-half years he was legal secretary (référendaire) to Sir Christopher Bellamy QC, President of the UK Competition Appeal Tribunal. He also specialises in public and administrative law.

Paul Reynolds

Paul Reynolds is a Principal with the economics consulting firm, Charles River Associates. He has consulted extensively on competition and regulatory issues and was previously a senior economist with the Australian Competition and Consumer Commission. Paul has a Masters Degree in economics with first class honours from the University of Melbourne.

Valentina Sloane

Valentina Sloane is a member of Monckton Chambers practising in EU and competition law. Her cases before the CAT include *Aquavitae v Director General of Water Services, ABI v OFT* and *Albion Water v Director General of Water Services.*

Christopher Vajda QC

Christopher Vajda is a member of the Bar of England and Wales as well as the Bar of Northern Ireland. He practises from Monckton Chambers in London. He has acted in many competition cases before the UK courts as well as before the ECJ and CFI in Luxembourg. He is the author of the State Aids chapter in Bellamy & Child, *European Community Law of Competition* (5th ed.). He is a bencher of Gray's Inn.

CONTENTS

5. THE CARTEL OFFENCE   *Clair Dobbin and George Peretz*

6. JUDICIAL REVIEW IN A COMPETITION CONTEXT Christopher Vajda QC and Julian Gregory

7. DAMAGES IN COMPETITION LAW LITIGATION
Daniel Beard

8. STATE AID LITIGATION IN DOMESTIC COURTS
Tim Ward

9. PRACTICE AND PROCEDURE IN EUROPE
Anneli Howard

10. MODERNISATION: USING EC COMPETITION LAW IN THE UK COURTS   *Josh Holmes*

11. ARBITRATION AND COMPETITION   *Michael Bowsher*

12. UNDERSTANDING ECONOMIC EVIDENCE
Meredith Pickford and Paul Reynolds

APPENDIX

TABLE OF CASES

TABLE OF STATUTES

TABLE OF STATUTORY INSTRUMENTS

TABLE OF EC LEGISLATION

ABBREVIATIONS

The following abbreviations are used throughout this book:

CFI:	Court of First Instance
Competition Act:	Competition Act 1998
CAT:	Competition Appeal Tribunal
ECJ:	European Court of Justice
Enterprise Act:	Enterprise Act 2002
Modernisation Regulation:	Council Regulation (EC) 1/2003 on the implementation of the rules on competition laid down in Arts 81 and 82 of the Treaty [2003] O.J. L1/1
OFT:	Office of Fair Trading

CHAPTER 1

OVERVIEW

Kassie Smith[1]

1. INTRODUCTION

Why? The past few years have seen fundamental reforms of UK competition law and policy. The powers afforded to the Office of Fair Trading ("the OFT") and other sectoral regulators have increased dramatically and, with them, the level of activity by those regulators. In 2003–2004, the OFT opened 1,140 complaint cases under the Competition Act 1998 ("the Competition Act"), of which 46 involved possible cartel activity. Formal investigations were launched into 41 cases where the OFT had reasonable grounds to suspect that an infringement of the Act had occurred. The OFT has issued a growing number of infringement decisions and imposed penalties of up to £17 million on individual companies.[2] In 2000, a specialist court, the Competition Appeal Tribunal ("the CAT"), was set up to deal with appeals from OFT decisions under the Competition Act.[3] Private actions for damages are now being taken in the CAT and in the High Court.

Businesses and regulators need to be aware of the risks and opportunities

1–001

---

[1] Barrister, Monckton Chambers.

[2] By Decision CA98/8/2003 of November 21, 2003, the OFT imposed penalties on Argos Ltd and Littlewoods Ltd of £17.28 million and £5.37 million respectively for infringing the Chapter I prohibition by entering into agreements and/or concerted practices which fixed the price at which certain toys and games manufactured by Hasbro would be retailed by Argos and Littlewoods for a period of 14 months. Hasbro's penalty was assessed by the OFT at £15.59 million, but, because Hasbro had approached the OFT with information that led to the uncovering of the infringement and obtained leniency, its penalty was reduced to nil.

[3] It was then known as the Competition Commission Appeal Tribunal. The CAT was created by s.12 and Sch.2 to the Enterprise Act 2002 ("the Enterprise Act") which came into force on April 1, 2003. The current functions of the CAT are:

    (1) To hear appeals in respect of decisions made under the Competition Act by the Office of Fair Trading (OFT) and the regulators in the telecommunications, electricity, gas, water, railways and air traffic services sectors.

    (2) To hear actions for damages and other monetary claims under the Competition Act.

that this change in legal and policy climate presents them. Businesses need to be prepared to deal with the possibility of investigation by the OFT, as well as being aware of the potential to use competition legislation to restrain the anti-competitive behaviour of others. The landscape is constantly changing as the UK and EC authorities issue new procedural rules and the courts interpret and apply the law. This book is intended to give practical advice and guidance in order to assist in dealing with procedure and practice before the OFT, the European Commission and the relevant courts and tribunals.

1–002 **Introduction.** This chapter provides an introduction to some of the core topics dealt with in more detail in the rest of this book. It also seeks to provide a basic route map through a number of practical questions and issues that will arise for undertakings[4] (and their advisers) when navigating their way through the requirements of the Competition Act and the Enterprise Act. This chapter will consider issues that arise for undertakings seeking to ensure that they comply with the requirements of the Acts; those that find themselves subject to complaints and/or investigation under the Acts; and those that wish to use the Acts to restrain the anti-competitive behaviour of others.

1–003 **The scope of this chapter.** This section contains an introduction to the relevant legislative provisions. Section 2 deals with how undertakings can seek to achieve effective compliance with the requirements of competition legislation. Section 3 gives a practical overview of issues arising for undertakings that find themselves under investigation by UK or EU regulatory authorities. Section 4 provides guidance for undertakings finding themselves affected by the anti-competitive behaviour of others and wishing to do something about it.

1–004 **The Competition Act: a summary.** Chapter 2 provides an outline of the substantive EC and UK competition law legislation, including the requirements of the Competition Act in the UK. For the purposes of this chapter, it is sufficient simply to give a short introduction to the main provisions of the

---

(3) To review decisions made by the Secretary of State, OFT and the Competition Commission in respect of merger and market references or possible reference under the Enterprise Act.

(4) To hear appeals in respect of decisions made by the OFT under the EC Competition Law (Arts 84 and 85) Enforcement Regulations 2001 (as amended) in respect of air transport services and international maritime tramp vessel services.

(5) To hear appeals against certain decisions made by OFCOM and the Secretary of State relating to the exercise by OFCOM of its functions under Pt 2 (networks, services and the radio spectrum) and ss.290 to 294 and Sch.11 (networking arrangements for Channel 3) to the Communications Act 2003 ("the 2003 Act").

The first three of these powers will be dealt with in some detail elsewhere in this book.
[4] Arts 81 and 82 of the EC Treaty and the Chapter I and Chapter II prohibitions under the Competition Act apply to "undertakings". The meaning of "undertaking" is considered in para.2–009, below.

Competition Act. In general terms, the Act outlaws any agreements, business practices or conduct which have a damaging effect on competition in the UK. More specifically, the Act prohibits:

- agreements between undertakings, decisions by associations of undertakings (such as trade associations) and concerted practices[5] which prevent, restrict or distort competition, or which are intended to do so, and which may affect trade within the UK (the Chapter I prohibition); and

- the abuse by one or more undertakings of a dominant position in a market which may affect trade within the UK (the Chapter II prohibition).

Articles 81 and 82 of the EC Treaty. The Chapter I and Chapter II prohibitions are modelled on EC competition law as set out in Arts 81 and 82 of the EC Treaty. Articles 81 and 82 EC prohibit anti-competitive agreements, business practices and conduct which may affect trade between Member States of the European Union.   **1–005**

Application of UK competition legislation. In the UK, under the Competition Act, the UK regulatory authorities have powers to investigate undertakings believed to be involved in anti-competitive activities and to impose financial penalties on them. Main responsibility for administering the Competition Act lies with the OFT. However, the sectoral regulators have responsibility for the cases in the sectors they regulate.[6] Third parties who consider that they have suffered loss as a result of any unlawful agreement or conduct may have a claim for damages in the UK courts.   **1–006**

Application of EC competition legislation. The European Commission, as well as and/or in close cooperation with the OFT, has the power to investigate and impose fines for infringements of Arts 81 and 82 EC, *i.e.* anti-competitive agreements, practices or conduct which may affect trade between Member States of the EU.[7]   **1–007**

Identifying the breach. The first issue for any concerned undertaking will be to identify the situations that could involve a breach of EC and/or UK competition law and to assess whether they do in fact involve such a breach.   **1–008**

---

[5] See para.2–010, below.

[6] The sector regulators are the Office of Communications (OFCOM); the Gas and Electricity Markets Authority (Ofgem) in Great Britain and the Directors General of Gas and of Electricity Supply for Northern Ireland in Northern Ireland; the Water Services Regulation Authority (commonly referred to as Ofwat) in England and Wales; the Office of Rail Regulation (ORR); and the Civil Aviation Authority (CAA): see paras 3–005–3–008, below. References in this chapter to the OFT should be taken also to include references to the sector regulators.

[7] See Chapter 9, below.

A detailed treatment of substantive EC and UK competition law is outside the scope of this book,[8] but, in order to set the scene for this chapter, it is useful to consider some possible scenarios.

1–009   Identifying the breach: possible scenarios.

- A retailer is told by its distributor to charge certain retail prices for the goods supplied by that distributor, or the distributor is refusing to supply that retailer with those goods unless the retailer agrees to take certain unrelated goods in the distributors' range.

- At a trade conference, an undertaking is approached by its competitors who are seeking its agreement to work towards an "orderly market" by not poaching each other's customers and/or by concentrating their marketing efforts on different geographical areas.

- An undertaking is trying to enter or to establish itself in a particular market, but finds that its prices are being seriously undercut by the only significant existing undertaking in that market, or that it is being effectively excluded from that market because the aforementioned undertaking has "stitched up" the market with a network of exclusive distribution agreements.

All of these scenarios could involve a breach of EC and/or UK competition law. Some breaches will be easier to identify than others. For example, an agreement between a distributor and retailer to fix retail prices or a "tie-in" requirement is likely to be held to be a breach of the Chapter I prohibition (the first scenario outlined above).[9] Similarly, an agreement between competitors to share markets (the second scenario outlined above) will in all probability be contrary to the Chapter I prohibition. Issues that are liable to arise in such situations will include evidential issues, such as whether communications between undertakings about prices or markets amounted to prohibited arrangements/concerted practices or whether they involved purely unilateral action.[10]

On the other hand, a complaint by a new entrant that it is being prohibited from effectively entering a market by being undercut by the only significant existing undertaking in that market (the third scenario outlined above) could be a breach of the Chapter II prohibition in that it could involve abusive predatory pricing by a dominant undertaking. The existence of a network of exclusive distribution agreements could be a breach of the

---

[8] Useful guidance on substantive EC and UK competition law can be found in Bellamy & Child, *European Community Law of Competition* (5th ed., Sweet & Maxwell, London, 2001) and Whish, *Competition law* (5th ed., Butterworths, 2004). Chapter 2 provides an introduction to Art.81 EC, the Chapter I prohibition and Art.82 EC, and the Chapter II prohibition.

[9] Subject to the rules on exclusion of certain vertical agreements: see paras 2–018–2–019, below.

[10] See para.2–010, below.

Chapter I prohibition insofar as it forecloses the market to competitors. Such matters are more difficult to assess and may require the use of economic evidence.[11]

2. COMPLIANCE

Achieving compliance. Any undertaking engaged in business in the UK and/or the EU will wish to ensure that it complies with the requirements of EC and UK competition law.[12] The dangers of non-compliance are potentially very serious: **1–010**

- investigation by the OFT or by the European Commission, which may require significant management input;

- a financial penalty of up to 10 per cent of the undertaking's turnover[13];

- agreements being void and unenforceable;

- adverse publicity;

- the possibility of being sued for damages by those harmed by the unlawful agreement or conduct.

Risk of infringement. Certain undertakings may be more at risk of infringing competition law requirements than others. The OFT has set out a number of questions to help undertakings assess the risk[14]:   **1–011**

- What is the undertaking's position in the market?

  (a) are any of its relations with others likely to have an appreciable effect on competition in any market in which it operates?[15]
  (b) Could it be said to have a dominant position in any market in which it operates?[16]

---

[11] See Chapter 12, below.

[12] The OFT has published a series of short guides for business which can be found on their website (*www.oft.gov.uk*) and which includes *How your business can achieve compliance: A guide to achieving compliance with the Competition Act 1998*, OFT 424. It should be noted, however, that these guides for business do not constitute statutory guidance under the Competition Act.

[13] See paras 3–078–3–097, below for details of how the OFT will go about setting penalties, and para.9–068, for the situation under EC law.

[14] OFT 424, see n.12, above.

[15] As a general rule, the OFT's view is that an agreement is unlikely to have an appreciable effect on competition where the combined market share of the parties involved is less than 25% in the market concerned. However, where the agreement fixes prices, shares markets, imposes minimum resale prices or is one of a network of similar agreements that have a cumulative effect on the market in question, it is generally capable of having an appreciable effect whatever the market share of the parties involved.

[16] Whether an undertaking is in a dominant position will largely depend on its size and strength in relation to others in the market, but as a general rule it is unlikely to be considered dominant if its market share is less than 40%. See paras 2–024–2–026, below.

- Is there scope for sales, purchasing or marketing staff to enter into arrangements which might infringe the Chapter I or Chapter II prohibitions without the knowledge of senior employees?

- Do employees or directors of the undertaking have regular contact with competitors, on a business or social footing? This may be particularly likely where the undertaking is a member of a trade association or similar body.

1–012 **Raising awareness among employees.** It is sensible for employers to ensure that their employees are aware, at the very least, of the provisions of the Competition Act (and equivalent EC law provisions) and the possible consequences of infringement. From the point of view of preventing infringements and avoiding the costly consequences outlined above, it is particularly important that those employees involved in sales, marketing and purchasing are made aware of these issues. Employees involved in other areas, such as research and development, distribution and after-sales service, should also be made aware. An additional benefit for undertakings which ensure their employees are aware of the implications of UK and EC competition law is that those employees will be able to identify and draw attention to the anti-competitive actions of other undertakings which may affect their company's interests.[17]

1–013 **A compliance programme?** Where an undertaking is in a dominant position or in a market where the opportunities for collusion are great, or where an undertaking is so large and diverse that it is difficult to monitor the activities of individual employees, the risks of infringement are significant. Therefore, it may be sensible for the undertaking to consider implementing a formal compliance programme in order to ensure that it conducts itself in compliance with competition law requirements. It may also enable an undertaking to detect any cartel activity at an early stage, so allowing it to take full advantage of the OFT's leniency regime.[18] The existence and observance of a genuine compliance programme is also a factor that may be taken into account in assessing the level of penalties to be imposed on an undertaking found to have infringed the prohibitions.[19]

1–014 **Content of compliance programme.** The OFT has made it clear that there is no standard compliance programme that can be applied in all cases. It must

---

[17] See paras 1–032–1–039, below.
[18] See para.1–027, and paras 3–098–3–106, below.
[19] The OFT reduced the penalty by 10% in *Arriva/First Bus* [2002] U.K.C.L.R. 322 at para.66 ("genuine compliance systems genuinely followed and adhered to"). Failure to comply with a compliance system has sometimes been regarded as an aggravating factor: *John D Bruce and Ors* [2002] U.K.C.L.R. 435 at para.123 (10% increase), and *Replica Football Kit* [2004] U.K.C.L.R. 6 at para.715 (10% increase on penalty imposed on Manchester United); but sometimes not (*Hasbro* [2003] U.K.C.L.R. 150 at para.92—although a reduction of 10% was granted to recognise subsequent training activity). In this regard, see para.3–091, below.

be tailored to the particular undertaking concerned. However, the OFT has indicated[20] that it takes the view that the following four general features must be included as a minimum in any compliance programme if it is to work effectively:

(1) support of senior management;

(2) appropriate policy and procedures;

(3) training;

(4) evaluation.

Support of senior management. Senior management support should be   1–015
visible, active and regularly reinforced. It can be achieved in a number of ways, including a personal message to staff from the most senior individual in the organisation that states his or her commitment to the programme; reference to the policy in the undertaking's mission statement or code of behaviour and ethics; and incorporating adherence to the programme into the overall objectives of the organisation. The OFT recommends that a particular member of the board or senior management team is designated to take overall responsibility for ensuring that the programme is functioning correctly and to report annually on how it has operated.

Appropriate policy and procedures. A compliance programme must be   1–016
more than simply a commitment to comply with the Competition Act. It must be implemented through an effective policy that contains at least the following elements:

- an overarching commitment to comply with the Act;

- placing a duty on all employees and directors to conduct their business dealings within this overarching policy and seeking a written undertaking from them to this effect;

- the likelihood that disciplinary action will be taken against employees/ directors who intentionally or negligently involve the firm in an infringement of the Act.

The policy should provide a framework to enable employees to seek advice on whether or not a particular transaction complies with the Act and to report activities that they suspect infringe the Act. The OFT advises[21] that the policy and procedures are set out in a compliance handbook or manual which includes, at the least, the following:

---

[20] OFT 424, see n.12, above.
[21] OFT 424, see n.12, above.

- a clear statement of the undertaking's policy towards compliance, including the consequences for employees of not upholding that policy;

- details of the legislation: an explanation of its main provisions, the investigatory powers of the competition authorities and the consequences for undertakings of infringing the rules;

- examples of the types of conduct that are illegal, or may be construed as such, making reference to the undertaking's particular circumstances, and areas where caution should be exercised; and

- clear details of the undertaking's compliance procedures.

1–017 **Training.** The OFT recommends that training is given on the law itself and on the undertaking's policy and procedures as regards compliance both as part of an induction programme for new staff and on a continuing basis to keep staff up to date on changes to the law. It also states that a record should be kept of any training given.[22]

1–018 **Evaluation.** A compliance programme needs to be regularly evaluated in order to ensure that the programme is working properly but also to enable areas of risk to be identified and addressed. The evaluation should include some or all of the following:

- testing knowledge of the law, policy and procedures of individual employees;

- adherence to the undertaking's compliance policy should be included as an objective against which an individual's and a department's performance are appraised;

- formal audits of sales and procurement processes, by appointment or unannounced, to check for actual or potential infringements; and

- mechanisms for reporting actual or potential infringements to senior management and taking steps to put right the problem and to limit the risk of recurrence.

3. INVESTIGATION

1–019 **Introduction.** A detailed account of the enforcement of UK competition law and procedure before the OFT is given in Chapter 3. Chapter 9 concerns practice and procedure before the EC Commission. In this chapter, the

---

[22] This is particularly important if an undertaking needs subsequently to rely upon the existence of a compliance programme as part of its mitigation to the imposition of a penalty: see n.19, above.

intention is to highlight some of the main issues arising for undertakings that find themselves under investigation by UK or EU regulatory authorities, and to investigate how the various processes—UK and EU, administrative and judicial, civil and criminal—fit together.

Investigation by OFT. Often the first that an undertaking will know of the fact that it is under investigation by the OFT will be an OFT request for information and/or documents or a "dawn raid". However, these steps will not take place until after the OFT has decided to open an investigation under s.25 of the Competition Act. **1–020**

Challenging the OFT decision to open an investigation. Under s.25 of the Competition Act, the OFT may decide to conduct an investigation if there are reasonable grounds for suspecting that anti-competitive behaviour in breach of the EC or UK provisions is taking or has taken place.[23] Such a decision is susceptible to challenge by way of judicial review.[24] As the law presently stands, however, it is unlikely that such a decision will be an "appealable decision" under s.46 of the Competition Act and thus appealable to the CAT.[25] **1–021**

Responding to an OFT request for information. The OFT may make an informal request for information from an undertaking that is subject to investigation. There is no requirement for the undertaking to provide the information requested, but if it does so and provides information that is false or misleading then it may be guilty of an offence under s.44 of the Competition Act. If, however, the OFT makes a formal request for information under s.26 of the Act, the undertaking involved is required to respond. The OFT has indicated[26] that it will send a written notice, by post or fax, to the undertaking involved. This will tell the recipient what the investigation is about, specify or describe the documents and/or information that are required, give details of where and when they must be produced and set out the offences that may be committed if the undertaking fails to comply. The OFT can ask for information that is not already written down. For example, a sales manager might need to use his knowledge or experience to provide estimates of market shares. The time limit for responding will depend on the amount and complexity of the material required, although it is likely to be days rather than weeks. In addition, past or present officers or employees of the undertaking may be required to give explanations of any documents produced. If it considers it to be necessary, the OFT can go back for further explanations and can make additional requests for documents and information. **1–022**

---

[23] See paras 3–009–3–012, below.
[24] See Sections 2 and 3 of Chapter 6, below.
[25] The case law on what constitutes an "appealable decision" is developing rapidly: see paras 3–043–3–045, below.
[26] *Under investigation? A guide to investigations under the Competition Act 1998*, OFT 426.

1–023 **OFT's power to enter premises.**[27] The OFT has power under s.27 of the Competition Act to enter a business premises in connection with an investigation if it has given the occupier of the premises two days written notice or it may enter without notice when the OFT has a reasonable suspicion that the occupier is party to the agreement or conduct under investigation. The OFT may enter and search a business or domestic premises without notice if authorised to do so under a warrant issued by the High Court under s.28 or s.28A of the Competition Act. So far, the OFT has tended to enter premises pursuant to a warrant issued by the court pursuant to a confidential without notice application. The power to enter premises will be executed by an authorised officer of the OFT.

1–024 **OFT guidance.** The OFT has given the following guidance to undertakings whose business is being investigated[28]:

- Remain calm.

- You may consult your legal adviser.[29]

- You are entitled to be treated with courtesy and respect at all times.

- You should answer questions truthfully, to the best of your knowledge.

- You should not:
  - hide, destroy or falsify documents; or
  - obstruct the investigating officer.

  If you do, you will commit a criminal offence.

- if you have any concerns, you should raise them with the investigating officer.

1–025 **Obstructing the OFT: criminal offences.** Employees of undertakings that are the subject of investigation by the OFT must be particularly careful not to engage in any of the following actions which might constitute criminal offences:

- failing, without reasonable excuse, to comply with a requirement imposed under the powers of investigation;

- intentionally obstructing an OFT official who is carrying out an on-site investigation without a warrant;

---

[27] See paras 3–020–3–028, below.
[28] OFT 426, n.26, above.
[29] See Rule 3 of the OFT's Rules and para.3–027, below.

- intentionally obstructing an OFT official who is carrying out an on-site investigation under a warrant;
- intentionally or recklessly destroying, disposing of, falsifying or concealing a document that has been required to be produced or causing or permitting this to be done;
- knowingly or recklessly providing information that is false or misleading.

Civil or criminal investigation? Moreover, it is important for an undertaking to establish at an early stage (and ideally by the stage of any "dawn raid") whether the conduct that is the subject of the OFT's investigation could fall within the definition of the cartel offence set out in ss.188 and 189 of the Enterprise Act.[30] It is likely that any criminal investigation into a cartel offence will begin life as an investigation under s.25 of the Competition Act. It is critical, however, that where a criminal offence is suspected the investigation is conducted having regard to the rules of admissibility in criminal proceedings. A failure to do so may render any evidence gathered as a result inadmissible in a future cartel offence trial. Where there are grounds to suspect a person of a cartel offence they must be cautioned before any questions are put to them about that activity in accordance with the requirements of Code C of the Police and Criminal Evidence Act 1984.[31] Furthermore, an undertaking will wish to consider carefully whether it should obtain separate legal representation for the particular individuals involved in any possible cartel offence; the interests of those individuals and the interests of the undertaking could well conflict.

1–026

Leniency. Undertakings that uncover evidence of cartel activities[32] as a result of implementing a compliance programme[33] or during an OFT investigation will want to consider making an application for leniency to the OFT. In the case of civil infringements, this could enable an undertaking to have its financial penalty reduced substantially or it could avoid a penalty altogether.[34] However, it should be remembered that a successful application for leniency does not extend to the other consequences of infringing the Chapter I prohibition, which include the fact that the unlawful agreement is void and cannot be enforced and the possibility that third parties who consider that they have been harmed by the agreement may have a claim for damages in the courts.

1–027

---

[30] See paras 5–010–5–018, below.
[31] Code C, the Code of Practice for the Detention, Treatment and Questioning of Persons by Police Officers.
[32] For this purpose, "cartel activities" are agreements, decisions by associations of undertakings or concerted practices which infringe the Competition Act and which involve price fixing, bid rigging (collusive tendering), the establishment of output restrictions or quotas and/or market sharing or market dividing.
[33] See paras 1–013–1–018, above.
[34] See the detailed treatment of the OFT's leniency programme at paras 3–098–3–106, below.

1–028 **"No action" letters.** Where it is considered that there is evidence of a cartel offence in breach of ss.188 and 189 of the Enterprise Act, the individual(s) involved will need to consider whether they should apply for immunity from prosecution in the form of a "no-action" letter as provided for in s.190(4) of the Enterprise Act.[35]

1–029 **What happens next?** If the OFT considers that it has uncovered evidence of a cartel offence in breach of ss.188 and 189 of the Enterprise Act then it may pass the investigation over to the Serious Fraud Office ("the SFO"). The investigation will have to continue to comply with the requirements of criminal procedure.[36] For civil infringements, the OFT will continue its investigation. The OFT will analyse the documents and information that have been obtained with a view to establishing whether or not either of the prohibitions in the Competition Act have been infringed. Undertakings may be asked to produce further documents and/or explanations. If the OFT takes the view in due course that an infringement of the Competition Act prohibitions has been committed, it will send the undertaking(s) concerned written details of its findings and reasoning in the form of a Rule 4 Statement of Objections and invite a response within a specified period. The undertakings concerned will also receive an opportunity to make representations at an oral hearing.[37]

1–030 **What if the OFT decides to close the investigation?** Much recent case law of the CAT has considered whether third parties are able to appeal to the CAT a decision of the OFT to close an investigation before it has made a formal infringement finding. The CAT has held that such decisions are appealable under s.46 of the Competition Act where the OFT has made a decision as to whether the Chapter I or Chapter II prohibition has been infringed, either expressly or by necessary implication, on the material before it.[38] Although it is still unclear exactly where the line will be drawn between appealable and non-appealable decisions in file closure cases, it is certainly the case that the ambit of what is an "appealable decision" under the Competition Act is being drawn far more widely than many commentators and practitioners had expected. If there is a right to appeal an OFT decision to the CAT, that decision cannot then form the subject of an application for judicial review.

1–031 **What if the OFT makes an infringement decision?** Those undertakings that are the subject of the infringement decision have a right of appeal to the CAT.[39] Practice and procedure before the CAT are set out in detail in Chapter 4. Third parties who have a sufficient interest in the outcome of the

---

[35] See paras 5–049–5–051, below.

[36] See paras 5–027–5–048, below.

[37] See paras 3–066–3–071, below.

[38] *Claymore v DGFT (Preliminary Issues)* [2003] CAT 3. See the discussion of this case and subsequent CAT case law on this issue at paras 3–043–3–045, below.

[39] s.46 of the Competition Act.

proceedings before the CAT may be able to intervene in the proceedings.[40] A third party undertaking that made the complaint leading to an OFT investigation is likely to have sufficient interest to intervene in an appeal.

4. COMPLAINTS TO THE OFT OR ACTION IN THE COURTS?

Identifying anti-competitive behaviour.   As indicated above,[41] there is a wide   **1–032** variety of anti-competitive behaviour that may affect undertakings. The first task of any undertaking that believes itself to be so affected is to identify the anti-competitive behaviour at issue.

Potential grounds for complaint.   The OFT has provided some indication of   **1–033** potential grounds for complaint.[42] Examples of behaviour that may indicate that a competitor, supplier or customer is breaching one of the Competition Act prohibitions are given as follows:

- A major supplier has suddenly decided, for no apparent reason, to discontinue supplying you with a product.
- You have received quotes from various suppliers that are surprisingly and unusually similar.
- A major supplier is refusing to sell you the product you want unless you also buy a separate and unconnected product.
- You approach a number of competing suppliers and find that only one is willing to supply the goods you want in your area.
- A supplier is preventing you from selling its products at a discount.
- A number of customers notify you at around the same time that they are prepared to pay you only a certain price for your product and these prices are surprisingly similar.
- You have recently entered a particular market and a major competitor has responded by charging extremely low prices that you suspect would not cover its costs.

The OFT rightly observes that the fact that an undertaking is engaging in any of the behaviour shown in the examples does not necessarily mean that it has committed an infringement. This will depend on the particular

---

[40] See paras 4–037–4–047, below.
[41] para.1–009.
[42] *Making a complaint: A guide to making a complaint under the Competition Act 1998*, OFT 427.

circumstances of the case.[43] In some cases, the behaviour in question may be a perfectly legitimate response to rigorous competition in the market.

1–034   **Cartels.**   The OFT has also provided some guidance[44] to purchasers of goods and services on identifying cartels. In its simplest terms, a cartel is an agreement between undertakings not to compete with each other. The agreement is usually verbal. Typically, cartel members may agree on output levels, prices, discounts, credit terms, which customers they will supply, which areas they will supply, and/or who should win a contract (known as "bid rigging").

1–035   **Why cartels?**   The OFT has indicated[45] that it considers cartels to be a particularly damaging form of anti-competitive activity. Their purpose is to increase prices and as a result they directly affect the purchasers of the goods and services concerned, whether businesses or private individuals. They also have a damaging effect on the wider economy as they remove the incentive for their members to operate efficiently. For the purchasers of the goods or services at issue, a cartel could mean higher prices, poorer quality and/or a lessening of choice. Detecting cartels and taking action against their members is therefore one of the OFT's top enforcement priorities under the Competition Act.

1–036   **Identifying cartel activity.**[46]   There are a number of signs that may indicate that a cartel is operating. Some examples are where suppliers:

- raise prices by the same amount and at around the same time;

- offer the same discounts or have identical discount structures;

- quote or charge identical or very similar prices;

- use give-away terms or phrases, such as:

    - the industry has decided that margins should be increased;
    - we have agreed not to supply in that area;
    - our competitors will not quote you a different price.

The presence of these signs does not necessarily mean that a cartel is operating. Some, such as simultaneous prices changes or similar prices, can be perfectly consistent with normal competitive responses in the market place. A purchaser should be particularly suspicious, however, where several of the signs are present.

---

[43] See the introduction to the substantive EC and UK competition law provisions contained in Chapter 2.
[44] *Cartels and the Competition Act 1998: A guide for purchasers*, OFT 435. It should be noted that this publication does not contain statutory guidance under the Competition Act.
[45] *ibid.*
[46] See OFT 435, n.44, above.

Likelihood of cartel activity. Cartels can occur in almost any industry and can involve goods and services at the manufacturing, distribution or retail level. Some sectors are more susceptible to cartels than others because of their structure or the way in which they operate, for example, where there are few competitors; the products have similar characteristics, leaving little scope for competition on quality or service; communication channels between competitors are already established; the industry is suffering from excess capacity or there is general recession. The fact that these conditions are not present does not rule out the possibility that a cartel is operating. Conversely, the fact that an industry shows some or all of these characteristics does not automatically mean that some form of cartel is operating, but purchasers should at least be aware of that possibility. **1–037**

Bid rigging.[47] Bid rigging is a form of cartel that may arise when contracts are awarded by competitive tender. Here, members of the cartel collude with each other on who should win a particular contract. The possibility of bid rigging will be particularly relevant to public sector purchasers, given their legal obligations to award certain contracts by competitive tender. Although bid rigging operations are often very sophisticated in order to avoid detection, there are certain signs that purchasers can look out for, particularly where they award contracts regularly. For example: **1–038**

- Do certain suppliers unexpectedly decline an invitation to bid?
- Is there an obvious rotation of successful bidders?
- Is there an unusually high margin between the winning and unsuccessful bids?
- Do all bid prices drop when a potential new bidder comes on the scene (*i.e.* who is not a member of the cartel)?
- Is the same supplier the successful bidder on several successive occasions in a particular area or for a particular type of contract?

Avoiding bid rigging. There are certain steps that purchasers can take to hamper the success of bid rigging operations or to reduce the likelihood that they will happen. For example: **1–039**

- Make any bid qualifications as broad as possible so that they can be met by the widest range of suppliers.
- Shop around for suppliers when inviting bids.
- Ask for bids to be broken down into as much detail as possible.
- Keep records of bids for comparison purposes.

---

[47] See OFT 435, n.44, above.

- Insist that the main contractors assign sub-contracts through a competitive process.

- Seek information from bidders about their associated companies and subsidiaries.

- Obtain a signed declaration of non-collusion from each bidder and make this a term of the contract.

1–040 **Next steps.** Identifying illegal anti-competitive behaviour is often easier said than done. Even if a major competitor has responded to an undertaking entering a market by charging extremely low prices, it may be difficult for that undertaking to establish that the competitor is dominant in the market in question and/or that the prices it is charging are predatory[48] in breach of the Chapter II prohibition/Art.82 EC. Undertakings that are engaging in cartel behaviour do not usually advertise that fact. However, once an undertaking has identified an infringement of competition law that is causing it harm, a number of choices will have to be made. Is the infringement something about which a complaint should be made to the UK or to the EC regulatory authorities? Should a complaint be made to the relevant regulatory authority or should the undertaking take private action in the national courts?

1–041 **Jurisdiction.** The question of whether an undertaking should complain to the UK or to the EC regulatory authorities will depend on whether the suspected infringement falls within the Chapter I or Chapter II prohibitions in the Competition Act or whether it falls within Arts 81 or 82 of the EC Treaty. These provisions are very similar in form, except that the Competition Act prohibitions apply to anti-competitive behaviour that may affect trade in the UK, while Arts 81 and 82 EC apply to anti-competitive behaviour that may affect trade between Member States of the European Union. A judgment will therefore have to be made as to the effect of the anti-competitive behaviour with regard to the extensive EC case law on effect on trade between Member States.[49]

1–042 **Benefits of proceeding under the EC regime.** If a case falls within the jurisdiction of the European Commission, there may be considerable advantages in making a complaint to the Commission rather than to the OFT. Any eventual Commission decision will have binding status on all national

---

[48] See Chapter 12, below on the use of economic evidence and key theoretical and empirical tools that economists often use to assess these sorts of issues.
[49] See, for example, Bellamy & Child, n.8, above, paras 2–128 to 2–140. See, further, Chapter 10, below.

competition authorities and national courts in all 25 Member States.[50] However, the Commission is not required to accept all complaints submitted to it and will take account of the alternative enforcement options available to the complainant as part of its admissibility assessment. At the outset, the complainant should address the respective merits of a complaint to the Commission *vis-à-vis* complaining to one or more national competition authorities or lodging a claim for injunctive or monetary relief before the national courts and be prepared to justify its position.[51]

Different procedures. The procedure applicable to complaints to the OFT   1–043
in the UK is set out in some detail in Chapter 3. That applicable to complaints to the European Commission is dealt with in Chapter 9. The OFT's investigation and enforcement powers, and its procedural rules, derive much of their inspiration from, and in many cases closely resemble, similar powers enjoyed by, and procedures followed by, the European Commission. Moreover, following the CAT's decision in *Pernod-Ricard v OFT*,[52] it appears that the CAT will take the view that UK procedural rules should be interpreted so as to accord with the EC rules unless there is a "relevant difference" between the UK and EC rules justifying a difference in interpretation.[53] There may therefore be little by way of practical difference as regards procedure for an undertaking taking a complaint to the OFT or to the European Commission.

Investigation or private action? An undertaking will then have to consider   1–044
whether it is preferable to proceed by way of a complaint to the relevant regulatory authority or by way of proceedings for injunctive relief or damages in the national courts[54] or by a combination of both. Much will depend on the undertaking's objectives. Does the undertaking want to stop the infringement as soon as possible? Does it want to obtain damages but is prepared to wait?

Benefits of the investigatory route. The OFT is keen to receive and inves-   1–045
tigate valid complaints. It has referred to complaints as an extremely

---

[50] Case C–344/98 *Masterfoods* [2000] E.C.R. I–11369 at para.58 and paras 8, 11–14 of the Commission Notice on the co-operation between the Commission and courts of the EU Member States in the application of Arts 81 and 82 EC [2004] O.J. C101/54 ("the Notice on co-operation with national courts"). Moreover, in the UK, by virtue of ss.47A and B of the Competition Act, the Commission's infringement decision will bind the CAT in any subsequent proceedings for monetary compensation.

[51] See paras 9–018–9–025, below. As regards proceedings for injunctive or monetary relief before the national courts see paras 1–050–1–053 and Chapter 7, below.

[52] [2004] CAT 10.

[53] However, the OFT has stated that it disagrees with the CAT's view in *Pernod-Ricard* on the application of s.60 of the Competition Act to procedural matters, although it decided not to appeal the decision: OFT press release July 1, 2004, *www.oft.gov.uk/News/Press+releases/Statements/2004/Bacardi-Martini.htm*. See paras 3–002–3–003, below.

[54] Proceedings will be commenced in the national courts: see paras 7–008–7–011, below.

important source of information for the OFT.[55] The OFT is likely to be in a better position than a private undertaking to obtain the information that will be necessary to establish an infringement, for example, using its powers under ss.26–28 of the Competition Act to obtain information and/or documents from undertakings that are the subject of the complaint proving their involvement in cartel activity, or obtaining market information and commissioning research to establish relevant markets and dominance. Therefore, there are considerable advantages in terms of cost and resources for an undertaking if the OFT undertakes an investigation: it will be the OFT who does the bulk of the work rather than the undertaking making the complaint.

1–046 **Complainant's role.** However, the OFT has indicated[56] that a complainant should provide as much information as possible to back up its complaint:

> "This should include details of any relationship between you and the undertaking(s) complained of, notes of any telephone conversations, copies of any correspondence, or anything else you might consider relevant. Where possible you should also provide details of the market or markets concerned, including an explanation of the relevant goods or services, of the area in which the undertaking complained of operates, and an indication of its position in the market—for example, whether it is the leading player and how many other players there are.
>
> In making your complaint you should note that to be effective the OFT needs evidence rather than mere suspicion of wrongdoing."

1–047 **Form of complaints to the OFT and/or the European Commission.** There is no set format for making a complaint to the OFT. All that is asked is that a complainant outlines the nature of the complaint and provides as much information as possible to back it up (as outlined above).[57] Although an undertaking may make an informal complaint to the European Commission, it will only be entitled to the benefits of the procedural safeguards afforded to complainants under EC law and procedure if it lodges a formal complaint with the Commission under Art.7(2) of Regulation 1/2003 ("the Modernisation Regulation").[58]

1–048 **Basis for subsequent claim.** Another great advantage of proceeding by way of a complaint to the relevant regulatory authority is that the resulting decision by the OFT or by the European Commission will have binding

---

[55] OFT 427, p.1, see n.42, above. A former Director of Competition Enforcement at the OFT has said that complaints are the main way in which the OFT uncovers anti-competitive behaviour: Bloom, "Key challenges in enforcing the Competition Act" [2003] Comp. Law 85.

[56] OFT 427, pp.4–5, see n.42 above.

[57] See paras 3–034–3–041, below.

[58] [2003] O.J. L1/1. See paras 9–018–9–025 and Form C at para.9–087, below.

status. Under ss.58 and 58A of the Competition Act, a decision of the OFT that there has been an infringement will bind the national court[59] in proceedings in which damages or any other sum of money is claimed in respect of such an infringement. As indicated above,[60] a decision of the European Commission will have binding status on all national competition authorities and national courts in all 25 Member States. The binding nature of the OFT's and/or Commission's regulatory decisions means that a complainant who relies upon such a decision is saved the uncertainty and expense of proving dominance or the distortion of competition and can restrict the issues in any private litigation to causation and quantum of loss.

Disadvantages of the regulatory route. Neither the European Commission nor the OFT are obliged to open an investigation in response to a complaint.[61] A decision not to proceed may be on the basis that there are no reasonable grounds to suspect an infringement, in which case a complainant may be best advised to drop the complaint, or may be on the grounds of administrative priorities. In the latter case, a complainant may decide that it would be worthwhile to pursue the complaint in the courts. Moreover, a complaint to the European Commission or to the OFT will often take some time and the complainant will have little, if any, control over the progress of the investigation.[62] **1–049**

Interim measures. Another potential disadvantage of proceeding by way of a complaint to the relevant regulatory authority is the availability (or otherwise) of interim relief. Complainants to the EC Commission are not supposed to request interim measures as part of a formal complaint under Art.7(2) of the Modernisation Regulation.[63] The Commission will only award interim measures acting on its own initiative where the following conditions are met: **1–050**

- there is a case of urgency;

- there is a prima facie finding of infringement; and

- there is a risk of serious and irreparable damage to competition (not competitors or consumers).[64]

The OFT has power to make interim measures directions under s.35 of the Competition Act.[65] However, it has shown little enthusiasm for exercising

---

[59] Subject to the right of appeal to the CAT. A decision of the CAT on appeal will similarly bind the courts.

[60] para.1–042.

[61] See paras 3–034–3–041 and paras 9–018–9–025, below.

[62] For the rights of complainants during an OFT investigation, see paras 3–034–3–041, below. For the role of complainants in a Commission investigation, see Chapter 9 below.

[63] Complaints notice, para.80: see para.9–037, below.

[64] Art.8 of Regulation 1/2003, n.58, above.

[65] See paras 3–046–3–051, below.

this power and, even if it were to do so, it is likely that a decision to make such directions will take a matter of weeks rather than days. In cases of extreme urgency, therefore, it may be advisable for a complainant to make an application for interim relief to the national courts who will be able to deal with it much more quickly.

1–051 **Benefits of proceeding before the national courts.** An application to the national court to restrain a breach of competition law can be made quickly and without notice. In *Network Multimedia v Jobserve*,[66] an interim injunction was obtained to restrain an anticipated breach of Art.82 EC in a matter of days. However, as this case showed, there are risks inherent in obtaining interim injunctions, particularly those obtained without notice. The applicant has a duty to explain to the court all the relevant law and facts on a "full and frank" disclosure basis. If it does not, then the court may well discharge the injunction and order costs against the applicant. In competition cases, where the number of relevant facts may be large and legal points may be complex, this is a potentially weighty burden to discharge.

1–052 **Disadvantages of private actions.** In the past, the ability and/or the willingness of the national courts to deal with the potentially complex issues arising in competition law cases may have been in some doubt.[67] Recently, however, national courts have started to engage more confidently with issues of competition law and damages in particular.[68] The amendments made by the Enterprise Act to the Competition Act have also made it potentially easier for undertakings to obtain damages by way of private actions in the national courts. As well as the provisions providing for the binding nature of decisions of the OFT and EC Commission,[69] s.47A of the Competition Act provides that where the OFT or the EC Commission has found an infringement, the parties affected can bring damages actions before the CAT (with its specialist knowledge of the particular issues arising in competition cases) rather than the ordinary courts.[70]

1–053 **A combination of regulatory action and action in the courts.** As already indicated, a sensible and practical approach for an undertaking that wishes to obtain damages as a result of the anti-competitive behaviour of a competitor, supplier or customer and which is not required to act with utmost

---

[66] [2001] U.K.C.L.R. 814.

[67] See para.7–070, below and the comments of Ferris J. during the hearing in *Premier League* [1999] U.K.C.L.R. 258.

[68] See, for example, *Crehan v Inntrepreneur* [2004] EWCA Civ 637 and *Arkin v Borchard Lines Ltd and Ors (No. 4)* [2003] EWHC 687 (Comm).

[69] See para.1–048, above.

[70] Furthermore, s.47B of the Competition Act provides that bodies specified by the Secretary of State, such as the Consumers' Association, can bring "consumer actions" on behalf of those found by OFT to have infringed the Act. Such consumer actions would be brought on behalf of named individual consumers who have suffered loss and who have consented to the bringing of the action. The damages are to be paid to the individual or, with his consent, to the specified body on his behalf.

urgency would be to make a complaint to the OFT or the European Commission which generates an infringement decision and to then commence a "piggy back" damages claim in the national courts or CAT. The major drawback of such an approach is the availability or otherwise of interim measures.[71] However, it appears that it would be possible to go to court in order to obtain an interim injunction; following which a complaint can be made to the OFT and the court can then be asked to stay the proceedings pending an OFT decision.[72]

---

[71] See para.1–050, above.
[72] *Synstar v ICL* [2001] U.K.C.L.R. 585; [2002] I.C.R. 112.

CHAPTER 2

INTRODUCTION TO THE SUBSTANTIVE PROVISIONS OF EC AND UK COMPETITION LAW

Valentina Sloane and Julian Gregory[1]

1. INTRODUCTION

2–001   **The purpose of this chapter.** The purpose of this chapter is to provide a brief introduction to the main substantive EC and UK competition law provisions. Providing a full explanation of these provisions is a task to which several books are dedicated, and is outside the scope of this chapter.[2]

2–002   **The structure of this chapter.** After this introductory section, Section 2 provides an overview of the substantive provisions, explains how the EC and UK provisions relate to each other, and outlines the recent changes to the way in which these provisions are to be enforced. Section 3 provides a summary of Art.81 of the EC Treaty and Chapter I of the Competition Act 1998 ("Chapter I"). Finally, Section 4 provides a summary of Art.82 of the EC Treaty and Chapter II of the Competition Act ("Chapter II").

2. OVERVIEW

2–003   **The origins and structure of competition law in the EC and UK.** The origins of the current EC and UK competition law provisions may be found in the 1957 Treaty of Rome establishing the European Community. Subsequently, it was Arts 85 and 86 of the Treaty of Rome, by then re-numbered as Arts 81 and 82 EC, which the UK adopted as a basis for its reform of competition law that culminated in the Competition Act 1998. The result is that the main EC and UK provisions are virtually identical. Both Art.81 EC and Chapter

---

[1] Barristers, Monckton Chambers.
[2] For a full account, see Bellamy & Child, *European Community Law of Competition* (5th ed., Sweet & Maxwell, London, 2001) (hereafter "Bellamy & Child") and Whish, *Competition Law* (5th ed., Butterworths, 2004) (hereafter "Whish").

I prohibit anti-competitive agreements between two or more undertakings. Both Art.82 EC and Chapter II prohibit abusive conduct by dominant undertakings. Each provision requires that competition be assessed within a specified market, defined by reference to both products and geography.

The relationship between the EC and UK provisions. The jurisdictional **2–004** dividing line between the EC and UK provisions depends on the effect on trade caused by the agreement or conduct in question. The European provisions are applicable only if the agreement or conduct "may affect trade between Member States", whereas the UK provisions are applicable if the agreement or conduct "may affect trade within the United Kingdom" (it is therefore possible for both sets of provisions to be applicable).[3] However, with that jurisdictional exception, the wording of the UK and EC provisions is extremely similar. Further, when introducing the Competition Act, the UK government took the view that the application and development by the courts of the UK law should mirror that of the equivalent EC provisions. Section 60 of the Competition Act provides materially as follows:

"(1) The purpose of this section is to ensure that so far as is possible (having regard to any relevant differences between the provisions concerned), questions arising under this Part in relation to competition within the United Kingdom are dealt with in a mater which is consistent with the treatment of corresponding questions arising in Community law in relation to competition within the Community.

(2) At any time when [any court or tribunal] determines a question arising under this Part, it must act (so far as is compatible with the provisions of this Part and whether or not it would otherwise be required to do so) with a view to securing that there is no inconsistency between—

(a) the principles applied, and decision reached, by the court in determining that question; and

(b) the principles laid down by the Treaty and the European Court, and any relevant decision of that Court, as applicable at that time in determining any corresponding question arising in Community law.

(3) The court must, in addition, have regard to any relevant decision or statement of the Commission."

The Government stated that the concept behind s.60 was that European jurisprudence was to be followed unless the court was driven to a different conclusion by a provision in the Competition Act.[4] It was previously thought that s.60 applied primarily to the substantive provisions and that,

---

[3] See further paras 10–028–10–036, below.
[4] *Per* Lord Simon of Highbury, referred to in Whish, p352.

while it incorporated certain high-level principles of European law, it did not require the relevant UK bodies to adopt the same detailed procedures as their European counterparts.[5] However, in *Bacardi*,[6] the CAT suggested that s.60 was generally applicable in relation to the procedures adopted by the OFT in applying the UK provisions. That aspect of the CAT's judgment was controversial and the OFT issued a press release stating that, although it was not appealing the judgment because it accepted the result on its facts, it did not agree with the CAT's conclusions with regard to the application of s.60 to procedural matters.[7]

2–005   **The (modernised) enforcement of EC competition law.**   The way in which EC competition law is enforced has recently been fundamentally changed by the Modernisation Regulation.[8] Previously, the enforcement of Art.81 EC (explained in more detail below)[9] was based on a system of notification, as only the Commission had the power to grant exemptions to agreements that were caught by Art.81(1) EC but satisfied the terms of Art.81(3) EC. Now, however, both the Commission's exclusive jurisdiction and the notification system have been abandoned, and Art.1 of the Modernisation Regulation provides:

> "1.   Agreements, decisions and concerted practices caught by Article 81(1) of the Treaty which do not satisfy the conditions of Article 81(3) of the Treaty shall be prohibited, no prior decision to that effect being required.
>
> 2.   Agreements, decisions and concerted practices caught by Article 81(1) of the Treaty which satisfy the conditions of Article 81(3) of the Treaty shall not be prohibited, no prior decision to that affect being required.
>
> 3.   The abuse of a dominant position referred to in Article 82 EC of the Treaty shall be prohibited, no prior decision to that effect being required."

One of the purposes of abandoning the notification system was to allow the Commission to focus its resources on the most serious anti-competitive agreements and conduct. The Commission will therefore continue to carry out investigations of agreements and conduct and may impose fines where it takes a decision that an agreement or conduct infringes either Art.81 or 82 EC. In addition, Art.3(1) of the Modernisation Regulation provides that where national competition authorities, such as the OFT, apply national

---

[5]   Whish, p354.
[6]   [2004] CAT 10 at para.229.
[7]   *www.oft.gov.uk/News/Press + Releases/Statements/2004/Bacardi-Martini.htm.*
[8]   Regulation 1/2003 on the implementation of the rules on competition laid down in Arts 81 and 82 of the Treaty [2003] O.J. L1/1.
[9]   Paras 2–008–2–020. See further paras 10–018–10–025, below.

competition law to agreements or conduct to which European competition law applies, they must apply Art.81 or 82 EC. Article 3(2) provides that the application of national competition law must not lead to the prohibition of agreements that would be permitted under Art.81 EC. Member States remain free, however, to apply to unilateral conduct national laws that are stricter than Art.82 EC. Chapter 3 sets out more details in relation to the enforcement of Articles 81 and 82 EC at the administrative level by domestic competition authorities, and Chapter 9 elaborates on how individuals may rely in actions in national courts on the fact that an agreement or course of conduct is prohibited by Art.81 or 82 EC. Chapter 10 considers the powers of the Commission under the Modernisation Regulation.

Block exemptions and Commission Notices. In the light of its experience in applying Art.81 EC, the Commission came to recognise that certain types of agreement will not normally be anti-competitive. The Commission has therefore issued several Regulations, known as "Block Exemptions", that provide that agreements fulfilling specified criteria fall outside the scope of Art.81(1) and/or satisfy the exemption criteria of Art.81(3). These Regulations constitute "hard law", and bind European and national courts. One of the most important is the Vertical Restraints Block Exemption,[10] discussed further below. In addition, the Commission has published numerous Commission Notices, setting out guidance on the application of Arts 81 and 82 EC. These Notices are "soft law", and are expressly stated to be without prejudice to any interpretation that may be given by the European courts. Several of these notices are referred to below. **2–006**

The enforcement of UK competition law. The UK competition law provisions are enforced primarily by the OFT.[11] The OFT may carry out investigations of agreements and conduct and may impose fines where it takes a decision that an agreement or conduct infringes either Chapter I or Chapter II. Further details of the enforcement of UK competition law are provided in Chapter 3. The OFT publishes a large number of guidelines which explain how it applies the Chapter I and Chapter II prohibitions. As the OFT is also now under an obligation to apply Arts 81 and 82 EC, its guidelines also set out how it intends to apply the European competition law provisions. The OFT guidelines are available on its website.[12] As explained further in Chapter 9, individuals may rely in actions in national courts on the fact that an agreement or course of conduct is prohibited by Chapter I or Chapter II. **2–007**

---

[10] Commission Regulation 2790/99 on the application of Art.81(3) of the Treaty to categories of vertical agreements and concerted practices [1999] O.J. L336/21.
[11] And the sectoral regulators.
[12] *www.oft.gov.uk.*

3. ARTICLE 81 AND CHAPTER I

2–008 **The substantive provisions.**[13]   The EC Treaty and the Competition Act 1998 both prohibit, in certain circumstances, agreements between undertakings, decisions by associations of undertakings and concerted practices which have as their object or effect the prevention, restriction or distortion of competition. The prohibition is set out in Art.81(1) EC and the Chapter I prohibition contained in the Competition Act. The key difference between Art.81 EC and the Chapter I prohibition is their geographical scope:

- Article 81(1) EC applies to agreements which may affect trade between Member States and which have the object or effect of prevention, restriction or distortion of competition in the common market[14];

- the Chapter I prohibition applies to agreements which may affect trade within the United Kingdom and which have the object or effect of prevention, restriction or distortion of competition within the United Kingdom.

Article 81(1) EC and s.2(2) of the Competition Act each provide an identical non-exhaustive, illustrative list of agreements to which the prohibition applies, namely agreements which:

(a)   directly or indirectly fix purchase or selling prices or any other trading conditions;

(b)   limit or control production, markets, technical development or investment;

(c)   share markets or sources of supply;

(d)   apply dissimilar conditions to equivalent transactions with other trading parties, thereby placing them at a competitive disadvantage;

(e)   make the conclusion of contracts subject to acceptable by the other parties of supplementary obligations which, by their nature or according to commercial usage, have no connection with the subject of such contracts.

2–009 **Undertakings.**   The term "undertaking" is not defined in the EC Treaty or the Competition Act. It covers any natural or legal person engaged in economic activity, regardless of its legal status and the way in which it is

---

[13] For guidance on Art.81 and the Chapter I prohibition, see the following OFT guidelines: *Agreements and Concerted Practices*, OFT 401; *Vertical agreements*, OFT 419.
[14] See Commission Notice—Guidelines on the effect on trade concept contained in Arts 81 and 82 of the Treaty [2004] O.J. C101/81.

financed.[15] An agreement between a parent company and a subsidiary or between two companies which are under the common control of a third does not fall within Art.81(1) EC or the Chapter I prohibition if the companies form an economic unit within which the subsidiary has no real freedom to determine its course of action on the market.[16]

Agreements, decisions and concerted practices. The concepts of "agreement", "decision" and "concerted practice" overlap. Article 81 EC and the Chapter I prohibition are intended to apply to all forms of collusion between undertakings. The essential distinction is between unilateral conduct, which does not fall within the prohibitions, and collusion. Conduct which is apparently unilateral may infringe the prohibitions if it arises from an understanding, tacit or express, between undertakings.[17] Agreement has a wide meaning. It covers oral and written agreements, and includes agreements which are not legally binding (such as so-called "gentlemen's agreements"). The term "concerted practice" covers a form of co-ordination between undertakings which, without having reached the stage where an agreement properly so called has been concluded, knowingly substitutes practical co-operation between them for the risks of competition.[18] The concept of a "decision" by an association of undertakings includes the association's rules and its recommendations.[19]

2–010

The object or effect of preventing, restricting or distorting competition. In this context, the term "object" refers not to the subjective intention of the parties when entering into the agreement, but to the objective meaning and purpose of the agreement considered in the economic context in which it is to be applied. Where an agreement has as its object the prevention, restriction or distortion of competition, it is unnecessary to prove that the agreement would have an anti-competitive effect in order to find an infringement of Art.81 EC or the Chapter I prohibition. Where an agreement does not have as its object the restriction of competition, it is necessary to demonstrate that it has, or would have, a restrictive effect. The CFI has stated that in assessing the effect of the agreement, account should be taken of the actual conditions in which it functions, in particular the economic context in which the undertakings operate, the products or services covered by the agreement and the actual structure of the market concerned, unless it

2–011

---

[15] Case T–319/99 *Fenin v Commission* [2003] E.C.R. II–357; [2003] 5 C.M.L.R. 1.
[16] Case T–102/92 *Viho v Commission* [1995] E.C.R. II–17; [1997] 4 C.M.L.R. 469.
[17] See Case 75/84 *Metro v Commission (No.2)* [1986] E.C.R. 3021; [1987] 1 C.M.L.R. 118 but see also Case T–41/96 *Bayer AG v Commission* [2000] E.C.R. II–3383; [2001] 4 C.M.L.R. 4 and Joined Cases C–2/01 P and C–3/01 P *BAI and Commission v Bayer*, [2004] 4 C.M.L.R. 13 and *Unipart Group Ltd* [2004] EWCA Civ 1034.
[18] Cases 48/69 etc. *ICI v Commission ("Dyestuffs")* [1972] E.C.R. 619.
[19] See the OFT guideline, *Trade associations, professions and self-regulating bodies*, OFT 408.

is an agreement containing obvious restrictions of competition such as price-fixing, market-sharing or the control of outlets.[20]

2–012 **The *de minimis* doctrine.** An agreement will fall within the prohibition only if it has as its object or effect an appreciable prevention, restriction or distortion of competition. The European Commission's Notice on agreements of minor importance sets out, using market share thresholds, what is not an appreciable restriction of competition under Art.81 EC.[21] The thresholds do not apply to agreements containing any of the "hardcore" restrictions listed in para.11 of the Notice. The OFT has stated that in determining whether an agreement has an appreciable effect on competition, it will have regard to the Notice.[22]

2–013 **Examples of anti-competitive agreements.** Article 81 EC and the Chapter I prohibition apply to both horizontal and vertical agreements which have as their object or effect the prevention, distortion or restriction of competition.

2–014 *Types of horizontal agreement.* The following categories are examples of horizontal agreements which may infringe the Art.81 EC/Chapter I prohibition:

    (1) **Direct or indirect price fixing**—agreements which directly or indirectly fix purchase or sale prices or other trading conditions, between competing undertakings are prohibited by the Art.81 EC/Chapter I prohibition.[23] The prohibition covers not only fixing of prices in the narrow sense, but also the fixing of discounts, surcharges, margins, rebates and credit terms. Price fixing can also take the form of an agreement to restrict price competition, for example, an agreement not to quote a price without consulting potential competitors or not to charge less than any other price in the market.[24] The prohibition may also be infringed by price recommendations.

    (2) **Horizontal market sharing**—the prohibition is infringed if two or more suppliers agree to a territorial division of markets within the

---

[20] Cases T–374/94 etc. *European Night Services v Commission* [1998] E.C.R. II–3141 at para.136.
[21] Commission Notice on agreements of minor importance which do not appreciably restrict competition under Article 81(1) of the Treaty establishing the European Community (*de minimis*) [2001] O.J. C368/13.
[22] OFT Guideline, *Article 81 and the Chapter I prohibition*, OFT 401a at para.2.26.
[23] See OFT Decision CA98/8/2003, *Agreements between Hasbro Ltd, Argos Ltd and Littlewoods Ltd fixing the price of Hasbro toys and games* (Case CP/0480/01) and the appeals by Argos Ltd and Littlewoods Ltd to the CAT: *Argos Littlewoods v OFT* [2004] CAT 24; OFT Decision CA98/06/2003, *Price-fixing of replica football kit* (Case CP/00871/01) and the appeals to the CAT: *JJB Sports plc v OFT* [2004] CAT 17.
[24] See, for example, OFT Decision CA98/1/2004, *Collusive tendering in relation to contracts for flat-roofing services in the West Midlands* (Case CP/0001–02) and the appeals to the CAT by *Apex Asphalt and Paving Ltd v OFT* [2005] CAT 4 and *Richard W Price Roofing Contractors Ltd v OFT* [2005] CAT 5.

common market, in the case of Art.81 EC, or within the UK, in the case of the Chapter I prohibition. The prohibition is also infringed if two or more suppliers agree to a division of markets by sector or classes of customer.

(3) **Production quotas**—the prohibition applies to agreements which limit or control production, markets, technical development or investment.

(4) **Joint purchasing/selling**—an agreement between purchasers to fix (directly or indirectly) the price that they are prepared to pay, or to purchase only through agreed arrangements, can fall within the scope of the prohibition, as can an agreement between sellers, in particular where sellers agree to boycott certain customers.[25]

(5) **Information sharing**—whether the exchange between undertakings of price or non-price information has an appreciable effect on competition depends on the circumstances of each case. As a general principle, the OFT considers that there is more likely to be an appreciable effect on competition the smaller the number of undertakings operating in the market, the more frequent the exchange and the more sensitive, detailed and confidential the nature of the information which is exchanged.

Types of vertical agreement.[26] The following are the principal categories of vertical agreements which may fall within the scope of Art.81 EC and/or the Chapter I prohibition:

2–015

- **Resale price maintenance**—the agreement of fixed or minimum resale prices is a "hardcore" restriction which will almost always infringe the prohibition. Maximum prices and recommended prices may infringe the prohibition if, for example, they in fact fix prices or facilitate collusion.

- **Single branding agreements**—agreements which cause a buyer to purchase all or most of its requirements of products on a particular market from a single supplier may restrict inter-brand competition, in particular by foreclosing access to the market by other suppliers.[27]

- **Exclusive distribution agreements**—the grant by a supplier of exclusive distribution rights to a distributor for a particular territory may restrict intra-brand competition and partition the market.

---

[25] See *Institute of Independent Insurance Brokers v DGFT* [2001] CAT 4. For guidance, see Commission Notice—Guidelines on the applicability of Article 81 to horizontal cooperation agreements [2001] O.J. C3/2. The OFT has stated that in assessing joint purchasing/selling arrangements, it will have regard to the Commission's guidelines: OFT Guideline, *Agreements and Concerted Practices*, OFT 401 at paras 3.15 and 3.16.
[26] See *Crehan v Inntrepreneur* [2004] EWCA Civ 637.
[27] *ibid.*

- **Selective distribution agreements**—a selective distribution system, whereby the products may be bought and resold only by officially appointed distributors and retailers, may restrict intra-brand competition, foreclose access to the market and may facilitate collusion between buyers and sellers.

- **Franchising agreements**—franchise agreements commonly include potentially anti-competitive restrictions designed to maintain uniform commercial methods within the franchise system and to protect the intellectual property rights conferred on the franchisee by the franchisor.

- **Exclusive supply agreements**—an agreement which causes a supplier to sell its products only to one buyer within the market for the purposes of a specific use or resale may infringe the prohibition.

- **Tying agreements**—a tying agreement arises where a supplier makes the supply of one product conditional upon the buyer also buying a separate product.

Many vertical agreements will be exempt from Art.81 EC by virtue of the EC Verticals Block Exemption (see further para.2–018, below). The European Commission's Notice on Guidelines on Vertical Restraints sets out the principles for the assessment of vertical agreements under Art.81 EC, and in particular the application of the Block Exemption to vertical agreements.[28] Under domestic competition law, the exclusion from the application of the Chapter I prohibition for vertical agreements pursuant to the Competition Act 1998 (Land and Vertical Agreements) Order 2000 is repealed with effect from May 1, 2005.[29] However, vertical agreements which fall within the scope of the EC Verticals Block Exemption, or which would fall within its scope if they had an effect on trade between Member States, can benefit from a "parallel exemption" from the Chapter I prohibition under the Competition Act (see further para.2–018, below).[30]

2–016   **Exemption of agreements from the prohibition.**   An agreement which falls within Art.81 EC and/or the Chapter I prohibition may nevertheless be lawful if it satisfies the conditions set out in, respectively, Art.81(3) EC and s.9(1) of the Competition Act. If the conditions are satisfied, the agreement is not prohibited, no prior decision to that effect being required. The agreement is valid and enforceable from the moment the conditions are satisfied and for so long as that remains the case. The burden on proving the conditions are satisfied rests on the undertaking claiming the benefit of the

---

[28]   Guideline on Vertical Restraints [2000] O.J. C291/1.
[29]   The Competition Act 1998 (Land Agreements Exclusion and Revocation) Order 2004 (SI 2004/1260) repeals the Competition Act 1998 (Land and Vertical Agreements Exclusion) Order 2000 (SI 2000/310) with effect from May 1, 2005.
[30]   See competition law guidance, *Vertical Agreements*, OFT 419.

exemption. Article 81(3) EC and s.9(1) of the Competition Act set out four conditions which must be met for an agreement to be exempt from the prohibition, namely:

(1) the agreement must contribute to improving production or distribution or promoting technical or economic progress;

(2) it must allow consumers a fair share of the resulting benefit;

(3) it must not impose on the undertakings concerned restrictions which are not indispensable to the attainment of those objectives; and

(4) it must not afford such undertakings the possibility of eliminating competition in respect of a substantial part of the products in question.

The European Commission has issued a Notice, Guidelines on the application of Article 81(3) of the Treaty, to assist in determining whether an agreement satisfies these conditions.[31] The OFT has stated that it will have regard to the Notice in considering the application of Art.81(3) EC and s.9(1) of the Competition Act.[32]

Individual exemptions.   Prior to the entry into force of the Modernisation   **2–017**
Regulation and the parallel amendments to the Competition Act, an agreement could benefit from exemption only if it had been notified to the Commission (for exemption under Art.81(3) EC) or the OFT (for exemption under the Competition Act) and had been granted an "individual exemption" by that authority or if it fell within the scope of a block exemption for certain categories of agreement (see further para.2–018, below). Under the Modernisation Regulation it is no longer necessary for agreements to be notified to the competition authorities in order to benefit from exemption: if the conditions in Art.81(3) EC or s.9(1) of the Competition Act are satisfied, the agreement is not prohibited, no prior decision to that effect being required.[33] Individual exemptions granted by the OFT prior to May 1, 2004 are valid until their expiry date, although the OFT retains the right to cancel such exemptions. No individual exemptions will be renewed following their expiry. Agreements benefiting from individual exemptions granted by the European Commission prior to May 1, 2004 continue to be automatically exempt from Art.81 EC until the expiry date of the exemptions. The exemptions are binding on the OFT and the OFT will not apply Art.81 EC or the Chapter I prohibition to agreements benefiting from such exemptions. The OFT will consider comfort letters issued by the European Commission, but these are not binding on the OFT.[34]

---

[31] Guidelines on the application of Article 81(3) of the Treaty [2004] O.J. C101/97.
[32] OFT Guideline, *Agreements and Concerned Practices*, OFT 401 at para.5.5.
[33] Art.1(2) of the Modernisation Regulation. See further paras 10–018–10–025, below.
[34] OFT 401, n.32, above, at paras 5.17 and 5.18.

2–018 **Block exemptions.** Certain categories of agreement are automatically exempt from the Art.81 EC prohibition by virtue of European Community block exemption regulations, which exempt agreements on a generic basis. Where the parties to an agreement are able to show that the agreement falls within the scope of the block exemption, they are relieved of the burden of showing that the agreement satisfies the conditions in Art.81(3) EC. EC block exemption regulations currently in force include regulations applying to the following categories of agreements: specialisation agreements; research and development agreements; vertical agreements and concerted practices; vertical agreements and concerted practices in the motor vehicle sector; and technology transfer agreements.[35] Agreements which fall within the scope of an EC block exemption regulation, or which would fall within the scope of a block exemption regulation if the agreement had an effect on trade between Member States, benefit from a parallel exemption under the Competition Act.[36] These agreements are not prohibited under the Chapter I prohibition, no prior decision to that effect being required. The OFT may nevertheless impose conditions on the parallel exemption, or cancel the exemption following procedures set out in the OFT's Rules, if the agreement has effects in the UK (or a part of it), which are incompatible with the conditions in s.9(1) of the Competition Act. Domestic block exemptions may be made by the Secretary of State, acting on the recommendation of the OFT, where the OFT considers that categories of agreements are likely to fulfill the conditions in s.9(1) of the Competition Act. The only domestic block exemption currently in force is the Competition Act 1998 (Public Transport Ticketing Schemes Block Exemption) Order 2001 (SI 2001/319).[37]

2–019 **Exclusions.**[38] Under European Community competition law, certain categories of agreement are, in effect, excluded from the application of Art.81 EC. For example:

- Article 86(2) precludes the application of the competition rules to certain undertakings in so far as compliance with them would obstruct them in the performance of a task entrusted to them by a Member State.

- Article 81 EC does not apply if anti-competitive conduct if required of undertakings by national legislation, or if the latter creates a legal framework which itself eliminates any possibility of competitive activity on their part.[39]

---

[35] See Bellamy & Child at p.191–196 for a summary of current block exemption regulations.
[36] Para.10 of the Competition Act.
[37] See OFT Guideline, *Agreements and Concerted Practices*, OFT 401 at para.5.13.
[38] See, in particular, Whish at p.146 to 147 for a checklist of agreements that fall outside Art.81(1).
[39] See, for example, Case T–513/93 *CNSD v Commission* [2000] 5 C.M.L.R. 614 at paras 58–59.

- Article 81 EC does not apply to sub-contracting agreements.[40]

- Article 81 EC does not apply to restrictions directly related and necessary to mergers falling within the scope of the EC Merger Regulation.[41]

Under domestic competition law, Schs 1–3 to the Competition Act specifically exclude from the application of the Chapter I prohibition certain categories of agreement, including:

- an agreement to the extent to which it would result in a merger or joint venture within the merger provisions of the Enterprise Act 2002[42] or an agreement which would result in a concentration with a Community dimension and thereby be subject to the EC Merger Regulation;

- an agreement which is subject to competition scrutiny under the Financial Services and Markets Act 2000, the Broadcasting Act 1990 or the Communications Act 2003;

- an agreement made by an undertaking entrusted with the operation of services of general economic interest or having the character of a revenue-producing monopoly, insofar as the prohibition would obstruct the performance of the particular tasks assigned to the undertaking[43];

- an agreement to the extent to which it is made to comply with a legal requirement or an agreement which is required in order to comply with, and to the extent that it is, a planning obligation.

In addition to the exclusions set out in Schs 1–3 to the Competition Act, the Competition Act 1998 (Land Agreements Exclusion and Revocation) Order 2004 provides for the Chapter I prohibition not to apply to agreements relating to land, although the exclusion is subject to a withdrawal provision. A previous exclusion for vertical agreements is repealed with effect from May 1, 2005.[44]

Penalties for infringement. An agreement which falls within the scope of Art.81 EC or the Chapter I prohibition and which is not exempt under   **2–020**

---

[40] See the Notice on sub-contracting agreements [1979] O.J. C1/2.
[41] See the Notice on restrictions directly related and necessary to concentrations [2001] O.J. C188/5.
[42] See the Enterprise Act publication, *Mergers: substantive assessment guidance*, OFT 506.
[43] See the competition law guideline, *Services of general economic interest*, OFT 421.
[44] See the competition law guideline, *Land agreements*, OFT 420. The Competition Act 1998 (Land Agreements Exclusion and Revocation) Order (SI 2004/1260) repeals the Competition Act 1998 (Land and Vertical Agreements) Order 2000 (SI 2000/310) with effect from May 1, 2005.

Art.81(3) EC or s.9(1) the Competition Act, is void and unenforceable.[45] The OFT may impose a financial penalty on an undertaking which has intentionally or negligently committed an infringement of Art.81 EC and/or the Chapter I prohibition.[46] The maximum penalty is 10 per cent of the undertaking's worldwide turnover.[47] There is limited immunity from financial penalties for "small agreements", except in the case of agreements which infringe Art.81 EC or which involve price-fixing.[48] A "small agreement" is an agreement between undertakings whose combined annual turnover does not exceed £20 million.[49] The immunity relates only to financial penalties; it does not preclude the OFT from taking other enforcement action, nor does it preclude third parties from claiming damages for loss caused by the infringement.[50]

4. ARTICLE 82 AND CHAPTER II

2–021   **The provisions.**   As explained above, the wording of Art.82 EC and the Chapter II prohibition contained in s.18(1) of the Competition Act 1998 is, with the exception of the different jurisdictional tests, extremely similar. Article 82 EC provides:

> "Any abuse by one or more undertakings of a dominant position within the common market or in a substantial part of it shall be prohibited as incompatible with the common market in so far as it may affect trade between Member States."

Section 18(1) provides materially:

> ". . . any conduct on the part of one or more undertakings which amounts to the abuse of a dominant position in a market is prohibited if it may affect trade within the United Kingdom."

Both Art.82 EC and s.18 go on to provide a non-exhaustive list of examples of conduct which may constitute an abuse. They provide that conduct may constitute an abuse if it consists in:

> "(a)   directly or indirectly imposing unfair purchase or selling prices or other unfair trading conditions

---

[45] Art.81(2) EC and s.2(4) of the Competition Act.
[46] s.36 of the Competition Act. See more generally Chapter 3, below.
[47] See the competition law guidelines, *Guidance as to the appropriate amount of a penalty*, OFT 423 and *Enforcement*, OFT 407.
[48] para.39 of the Competition Act.
[49] See the Competition Act 1998 (Small Agreements and Conduct of Minor Significance) Regulations 2000 (SI 2000/262).
[50] See OFT Guidelines, *Agreements and Concerted Practices*, OFT 401 at para.7.3.

(b) limiting production, markets or technological development to the prejudice of consumers
(c) applying dissimilar conditions to equivalent transactions with other trading parties, thereby placing them at a competitive disadvantage
(d) making the conclusion of contracts subject to acceptance by the other parties of supplementary obligations which, by their nature or according to commercial usage, have no connection with the subject of the contracts."

The basic structure of the provisions. Each prohibition incorporates three basic elements. The first is that that an undertaking is dominant in a relevant market, and the second is that the undertaking has carried out conduct amounting to an abuse. Those two elements are discussed further in the following paragraphs. It is important to note that it is only the abuse of a dominant position, as opposed to dominance itself that is prohibited. However, conduct that would not be objectionable when carried out by a non-dominant undertaking may nonetheless be abusive when carried out by an undertaking that is dominant. That is because a dominant undertaking "has a special responsibility not to allow its conduct to impair undistorted competition on the common market".[51] The third basic element is that the conduct has an affect on trade, the requirements of which are discussed above.

2–022

Market definition. Market definition provides the framework for determining whether an undertaking is dominant and for competition analysis more generally. A Commission Notice[52] and an OFT Guideline[53] provide detailed guidance as to how to carry out market definition. As stated in the Commission Notice[54]:

2–023

"...the main purpose of market definition is to identify in a systematic way the competitive constraints that the undertakings involved face. The objective of defining a market in both its product and geographic dimension is to identify those actual competitors of the undertakings involved that are capable of constraining those undertakings' behaviour and of preventing them from behaving independently of effective competitive pressure."

The relevant market therefore has both a product and a geographic dimension. When defining the market, one looks at two of the main sources of competitive constraints on an undertaking, namely demand substitution

---

[51] Case C–322/81 *Michelin v Commission* [1983] E.C.R. 3461 at para.57.
[52] Commission Notice on the definition of the relevant market for the purposes of Community competition law [1997] O.J. C372/03.
[53] *Market Definition*, OFT 403.
[54] para.2.

and supply substitution. A key tool used when defining the market is the "hypothetical monopolist test", also known as the SSNIP test. The test seeks to analyse how the market would react if a hypothetical monopolist of a particular product introduced a small but significant non-transitory increase in price (hence SSNIP), of around 5 to 10 per cent. However, it should be noted that the test is no more than a helpful tool, as defining a market solely in accordance with its terms is rarely possible. That is the case partly because of the imprecise nature of the test, partly because the data necessary to apply the test may be difficult to attain, and partly because the test is unreliable in certain market conditions.

2–024 **Dominance.** The ECJ has defined a dominant position under Art.82 EC as[55]:

> "...a position of economic strength enjoyed by an undertaking which enables it to hinder the maintenance of effective competition on the relevant market by allowing it to behave to an appreciable extent independently of its competitors and customers and ultimately of its consumers."

The following paragraph sets out various considerations that are generally taken into account for the purpose of determining whether an undertaking is dominant. However, it should be noted that the test set out above remains the touchstone for assessing dominance and, occasionally, the unusual characteristics of a market may allow an undertaking to behave independently of competitive pressure even when dominance might not be obvious on the basis of a consideration of the usual criteria. Although the Commission has not published a notice on assessing dominance, the OFT has published a Guideline on *Assessment of Market Power*.[56]

2–025 **Considerations relevant to dominance.** The market share in the relevant market of the undertaking concerned is one of the most important considerations when assessing market power, although it is not conclusive. Obviously, the larger its market share, the more likely that an undertaking is dominant. The ECJ has stated that where an undertaking has held a market share of 50 per cent or more for a sustained period of time, it will be presumed to be dominant in the absence of exceptional circumstances pointing the other way.[57] Both the ECJ and the Commission have found undertakings to be dominant with market shares in the 40 to 45 per cent range, although the ECJ stated that, at that level, dominance must be determined having regard to the strength and number of competitors.[58] In addition, a range of other considerations may be relevant to an assessment

---

[55] Case C–322/81 *Michelin v Commission*, n.51, above.
[56] OFT Guideline, *Assessment of Market Power*, OFT 415.
[57] Case C–62/86 *AKZO v Commission* [1991] E.C.R. I–3359; [1993] 5 C.M.L.R. 215.
[58] Case C–27/76 *United Brands v Commission* [1978] E.C.R. 207 at paras 109 to 110.

of dominance, including barriers to entry, ownership of rights over intellectual property or land, the undertaking's conduct on the market, economies of scale, vertical integration and countervailing buyer power.

Collective dominance. Article 82 EC and the Chapter II prohibition prohibit conduct on the part of one or more undertakings which amounts to an abuse of a dominant position. As the CFI has stated: **2–026**

"There is nothing, in principle, to prevent two or more independent economic entities from being, on a specific market, united by such economic links that, by virtue of that fact, together they hold a dominant position vis a vis the other operators on the same market."[59]

The leading judgment on collective dominance is now that of the ECJ in *Compagnie Maritime Belge Transports v Commission*,[60] in which the court took the view that the concept of collective dominance under Art.82 EC was the same as that as under the EC Merger Regulation, and stated that legally independent undertakings may be collectively dominant if "they present themselves or act together on a particular market as a collective entity".

The concept of abuse. In *Hoffman-La Roche*,[61] the ECJ stated: **2–027**

"The concept of abuse is an objective concept relating to the behaviour of an undertaking in a dominant position which is such as to influence the structure of a market where, as a result of the very presence of the undertaking in question, the degree of competition is weakened and which, through recourse to methods different from those which condition normal competition in products or services on the basis of the transactions of commercial operators, has the effect of hindering the maintenance of the degree of competition still existing in the market or the growth of that competition."

Abusive conduct may be either exploitative or exclusionary. Exploitative conduct is conduct that exploits consumers or suppliers, the prime example of which is excessive pricing. Exclusionary conduct removes or weakens competition from existing customers, or establishes or strengthens entry barriers, thereby removing or weakening potential competition. Examples are predatory pricing and margin squeezing. Article 82 EC and the Chapter II prohibition contain no provision equivalent to that in Art.81(3) EC whereby harmful conduct may be exempted on account of the fact that it produces some sort of benefit. However, conduct may not constitute an abuse, even where it produces some sort of restriction on competition, if it is

---

[59] Case T–68/69 *Italian Flat Glass* [1992] E.C.R. II–1403; [1992] 5 C.M.L.R. 302.
[60] Case C–396/96 [2000] E.C.R. I–1365; [2000] 4 C.M.L.R. 1076.
[61] Case C–322/81 [1979] E.C.R. 461 at para.91.

capable of being objectively justified, and the conduct is proportionate to the justification. The requirement that a justification must be objective requires it to have some wider benefit, and not simply be of benefit to the undertaking itself. Objective justifications considered by the courts have, for example, included the need for goods to be safe for the public, and to avoid false and misleading advertising.

2–028 **Abuse in related markets.** The abusive conduct, and its effects, will often occur in the same market in which the undertaking is dominant. However, that need not be the case. The European case law makes it clear that conduct may still fall within the scope of Art.82 EC where: the abuse and dominance occur in one market, even though the effects of the conduct occur in another market[62]; and where the abuse and the effects of the conduct occur in one market, even though the abusive conduct occurs in another market.[63] Further, in *Tetra Pak II*,[64] the ECJ held that "in special circumstances", there could be an abuse of a dominant position "where conduct on a market distinct from the dominated market produces effects on that distinct market".

2–029 **Different types of abusive conduct.** The examples of abusive conduct expressly referred to in Art.82 EC and the Chapter II prohibition were set out above. However, those examples are not exclusive, and the following paragraphs set out some of the main types of conduct that are capable of constituting an abuse of a dominant position. Many of these types of conduct are considered in the OFT's Guideline on *Assessment of Conduct*.[65] It should be noted that the categories of abuse are not closed, and it is possible that new categories will be recognised as the law develops.

   (1) *Excessive pricing*.[66] Prices may be considered to be excessive where they bear no reasonable relation to the economic value of the product supplied. An example is the judgment of the CAT in *Napp*, in which it applied the European case law and found Napp to have priced excessively on the facts of the case.[67]

   (2) *Predatory prices*.[68] Predatory prices are prices set by a dominant firm with the primary intention of the elimination or substantial

---

[62] See, for example, Case C–7/73 *Commercial Solvents v Commission* [1974] E.C.R. 223; [1974] 1 C.M.L.R. 309, Case C–311/84 *Telemarketing* [1985] E.C.R. 3261 and *De Poste–La Poste* [2002] 4 C.M.L.R. 84.
[63] See, for example, Case C–310/93 *British Gypsum v Commission* [1995] E.C.R. I–865; [1997] 4 C.M.L.R. 238.
[64] Case C–333/94 P [1996] E.C.R. I–5951; [1997] 4 C.M.L.R. 662.
[65] OFT Guideline, *Assessment of Conduct*, OFT 414.
[66] See, in particular, Bellamy & Child, paras 9–073 to 9–075 and Whish, pp.688 to 694.
[67] *Napp Pharmaceutical Holdings Ltd v DGFT (No.4)* [2002] CAT 1; 64 B.M.L.R. 165.
[68] See, in particular, Bellamy & Child, paras 9–076 to 9–082 and Whish, pp.703 to 716.

weakening of a competitor. What needs to be shown to prove predation depends on the level of the price. The ECJ has stated[69]:

> "First, prices below average variable costs must always be considered to be abusive. In such a case, there is no conceivable economic purpose other than the elimination of a competitor, since each item produced and sold entails a loss for the undertaking. Secondly, prices below average total costs but above average variable costs are only to be considered abusive if an intention to eliminate can be shown."

(3) *Discriminatory and other harmful pricing practices.*[70] In addition, a dominant undertaking may infringe Art. 82 EC and the Chapter II prohibition if it prices in a discriminatory manner, *i.e.* charging prices to one customer than are higher than those charged to other customers, without any objective justification. However, the extent to which selective price cutting by a dominant firm will be abusive is controversial, as even dominant undertakings are generally allowed to reduce their prices in order to meet competition. A dominant undertaking may also commit an abuse by discriminating in favour of its own downstream operations, a practice known as margin squeezing.[71]

(4) *Exclusivity and fidelity rebates.*[72] A dominant undertaking may commit an abuse where it enters into agreements under which the purchaser is required to purchase all or a high percentage of its requirements from that undertaking. The same may be true where, although no express requirement exists, the dominant undertaking adopts pricing practices, such as loyalty rebates, that are intended to have the same effect.

(5) *Tying.*[73] A dominant undertaking may commit an abuse where it will supply a product (the tying product) only if the purchaser also purchases another produce (the tied product) from it. The same may be true where the undertaking prices its products in such a way as to produce a strong economic incentive for the purchaser to purchase both products.

(6) *Refusal to supply.*[74] It may be an abuse for a dominant undertaking to refuse to supply a purchaser. However, refusal to supply is a controversial topic, as the goal of promoting competition clashes directly with the general right of undertakings to choose for themselves the undertakings with which they enter into contractual

---

[69] Case C–333/94P *Tetra Pak II* [1996] E.C.R. II–755; [1997] 4 C.M.L.R. 726.
[70] See, in particular, Bellamy & Child, paras 9–083 to 9–085 and Whish, pp.710 to 721.
[71] The CAT considered the abuse of margin squeezing in *Genzyme v OFT* [2003] CAT 8.
[72] See, in particular, Bellamy & Child, paras 9–086 to 9–091 and Whish, pp.653 to 657 and 694 to 701.
[73] See, in particular, Bellamy & Child, paras 9–11 to 9–114 and Whish, pp.657 to 663.
[74] See, in particular, Bellamy & Child, paras 9–093 to 9–104 and Whish, p663 to 678.

relations. The position may be different as between existing and new competitors. The extent to which the owner of an "essential facility" may be required to supply purchasers is particularly controversial, and has been the subject of considerable debate over recent years.[75]

(7) *Discrimination.*[76] Selective discounting and the offering of loyalty rebates are both capable of being seen as examples of discriminatory behaviour. However, the application of dissimilar conditions to equivalent transactions is one of the types of conduct expressly referred to in the text of Art.82 EC and the Chapter II prohibition, and it is possible that other types of discriminatory behaviour by a dominant undertaking are capable of constituting an abuse (for example, discrimination on the grounds of nationality).

---

[75] See, in particular, Case C–7/97 *Bronner v Mediaprint* [1998] E.C.R. I–7791; [1999] 4 C.M.L.R. 112.
[76] See, in particular, Bellamy & Child, para.9–120.

CHAPTER 3

ENFORCEMENT AND PROCEDURE BEFORE THE OFT

George Peretz[1]

1. INTRODUCTION

Introduction. This chapter covers the powers of investigation and enforcement enjoyed by the OFT and other UK regulators charged with enforcement of the Competition Act 1998 and Arts 81 and 82 EC,[2] as well as the procedure before those bodies up until the conclusion of an investigation. This chapter also covers competition disqualification orders made against individuals whose undertakings infringe Art.81 or 82 EC or the Competition Act prohibitions. Appeals to the CAT against decisions taken by the competition authorities are covered in Chapter 4.

3–001

Impact of section 60 of the Competition Act. The OFT's investigation and enforcement powers, and its procedural rules, derive much of their inspiration from, and in many cases closely resemble, similar powers enjoyed by, and procedures followed by, the European Commission. Section 60 of the Competition Act requires "questions arising in relation to competition" under the Competition Act to be determined with a view to ensuring that there is no inconsistency with the principles applying to "corresponding questions" of Community competition law, save where there are "relevant differences" between the rules in question.[3] The question arises whether s.60 requires the domestic rules setting out the OFT's powers and procedures to be interpreted in accordance with the extensive EC jurisprudence on the Commission's powers and procedures. In *Pernod-Ricard v OFT*[4] the CAT had to decide whether a complainant: (a) had a right to be heard on a Rule 14 Notice (what is now a Rule 4 Notice) issued by the OFT

3–002

---

[1] Barrister, Monckton Chambers.
[2] In order to avoid constant repetition, references to the OFT in the context of the enforcement of the Competition Act and Arts 81 and 82 EC should generally be read as references to the OFT and the other regulators.
[3] See discussion of s.60, para.2–004, above.
[4] [2004] CAT 10; [2004] Comp. A.R. 707.

to the party about whose conduct it had complained; and (b) had a right to comment before the OFT decided to close the file on its complaint (after having received assurances from the third party as to its future conduct). Under the rules binding the Commission at the time,[5] the complainant would have had those rights; but in the UK the Director's Rules[6] made no provision requiring any consultation of complainants at all. The CAT held that s.60 applied to the question of whether under the UK rules, a complainant had the rights contended for:

"The 'corresponding question' under Community law is, in our view, what are the principles of administrative fairness which apply in relation to competition, i.e. in the sphere covered by the competition rules of the Treaty? Thus, although the question with which we are dealing does not relate directly to competition, as would for example a question covering the scope and meaning of the Chapter II prohibition, it seems to us that the question at issue does arise 'in relation to competition' within the meaning of section 60(1), at least indirectly, since it concerns the procedural principles to be applied in the application and enforcement of the competition rules. We add that complaints to the OFT and the EC Commission play a central role in both the Community and domestic systems of competition law, and may in many cases be the only means of detecting the abuse of monopoly power or illegal agreements. The procedures by which such complaints are handled have, in our view, a key bearing on how effectively the competition rules set up by Treaty, and adopted in the 1998 Act, are applied and enforced in practice. If that approach is correct, it would follow that we should, so far as possible, decide this case consistently with the corresponding provisions of Community law."[7]

It therefore appears that, in the view of the CAT, s.60 applies to any issue relating to the interpretation of the rules governing the OFT's procedures, since any such issue is likely to "concern the procedural principles to be applied in the application and enforcement of the competition rules" and give rise to the general question of "what are the principles of administrative fairness which apply in relation to competition?" The question in practice will therefore be whether there is any "relevant difference" between the UK and EC rules justifying a difference in interpretation. However, the OFT has

---

[5] Commission Regulation 2842/98 [1998] O.J. L354/18, Arts 6–8; equivalent provisions can now be found in Commission Regulation 773/2004 [2004] O.J. L123/18, Arts 6–8.

[6] Set out in the Schedule to the Competition Act 1998 (Director's rules) Order (SI 2000/293); now replaced by the OFT's Rules, set out in the Competition Act 1998 (Office of Fair Trading's Rules) Order (SI 2004/2751).

[7] *Pernod-Ricard v OFT*, n.4, above, at para.229. The tribunal went on (para.231) to refer, in support of its approach, to Ministerial statements during the passage of the Competition Bill through Parliament to the effect that the section imported "high level principles [of EC law], such as proportionality, legal certainty and administrative fairness" into the Act; see *Hansard*, November 25, 1997, col.961.

stated that it disagrees with the CAT's view in *Pernod-Ricard* on the application of s.60 to procedural matters, although it decided not appeal the decision.[8]

Other considerations. The last two sentences of the above quotation from **3–003** *Pernod-Ricard* suggest that, quite apart from s.60, the CAT is likely to be influenced in interpreting UK procedural rules by the consideration that, given the parallel enforcement of EC competition law by the OFT and by the Commission, it is undesirable for there to be procedural differences between them such that the law is potentially applied less effectively by the OFT than it would be by the Commission. The CAT also observed in that case that "whatever the strict interpretation of section 60, in deciding what would be a fair and reasonable exercise of the OFT's discretion, we think we are entitled to take into account how the EC Commission would proceed in similar circumstances."[9] The CAT further noted that the question might soon arise as to whether Community law, after the coming into force of Regulation 1/2003, now requires the OFT to follow Commission procedures in applying either Art.81 or 82 EC or domestic competition law.[10]

Article 6 of the ECHR. Article 6(1) of the European Convention on **3–004** Human Rights provides that:

"In the determination of ... a criminal charge, everyone is entitled to a fair and public hearing within a reasonable time before an independent and impartial tribunal established by law".

Article 6(2) provides for a presumption of innocence in favour of anyone charged with a criminal offence, and Art.6(3) provides that everyone charged with a criminal offence has certain minimum rights, including the right to have witnesses against him examined and to be informed promptly of the charges against him. It is plain that a criminal prosecution under s.188 of the Enterprise Act 2002 will be subject to Art.6(1) to (3); and the CAT has held that civil proceedings concerning the imposition of a penalty under the Competition Act 1998 are proceedings determining a criminal charge for the purposes of Art.6.[11] The OFT (and the CAT and any other court) is prohibited by s.6(1) of the Human Rights Act 1998 from acting in a way that is incompatible with Art.6 (or any other right under Arts 2–12 and 14 of the

---

[8] OFT press release July 1, 2004, *www.oft.gov.uk/News/Press + Releases/Statements/2004/Bacardi-Martini.htm*.
[9] *Pernod-Ricard v OFT*, n.4, above, para.238.
[10] *ibid.*, para.223. Regulation 1/2003 was not in force at the time of the decision subject to appeal in that case.
[11] *Napp Pharmaceutical Holdings Ltd v DGFT (No.4)* [2002] Comp. A.R. 13, following Case C–235/92P *Montecatini v Commission* [1999] E.C.R. I–4539 at paras 175–176 and the opinion of A. G. Léger in Case C–185/95P *Baustahlgewebe v Commission* [1998] E.C.R. I–8417 at para.3.

ECHR). The specific implications of Art.6 (and Art.8) will be explored below.

2. THE CIVIL PROHIBITIONS

(a) Bodies empowered to investigate and enforce the civil prohibitions

3–005   **The OFT.** The OFT plays the central role in the enforcement of the Competition Act, and is the central UK national competition authority charged with enforcement of Arts 81 and 82 EC. As far as most sectors of the economy are concerned, it is the only administrative body with powers to investigate and enforce the Act and (apart from the European Commission) Arts 81 and 82 EC. The OFT has sole responsibility for making the procedural rules that apply to all regulators,[12] and for issuing guidance.[13] Even in those sectors where other UK regulators have powers of investigation and enforcement, those powers are exercised concurrently with the OFT. Further, the OFT is the only competition authority with a role to play in investigating and (except in Scotland)[14] prosecuting the cartel offence, responsibilities which it shares (except in Scotland)[15] with the SFO. In order to avoid constant repetition, this chapter's discussion of Competition Act procedures refers only to the OFT, but references to the OFT can be read as references to other regulators in their various fields.

3–006   **Other regulators.** The other regulators with concurrent powers of investigation and enforcement of the Competition Act are[16]:

(1) The Office of Communications (OFCOM), insofar as the OFT's functions relate to activities connected with communications matters[17];

(2) The Gas and Electricity Markets Authority (often known as Ofgem), in Great Britain[18] and insofar as the OFT's functions relate to agreements and conduct relating to:

---

[12] Competition Act, s.51.

[13] *ibid.*, ss.31D (on acceptance of commitments), 38 (on level of penalties) and 52 (general guidance).

[14] In Scotland, prosecutions are conducted solely by the Lord Advocate.

[15] In Scotland, those responsibilities are shared with the International and Financial Crime Unit of the Crown Office.

[16] See para.2.1 of the OFT's Guideline, *Concurrent Application to regulated industries*, OFT 405.

[17] Communications Act 2003, s.371(2).

[18] In Northern Ireland, the Directors General of Gas and of Electricity Supply for Northern Ireland each enjoy similar powers under the Electricity (Northern Ireland) Order 1992 (SI 1992/231 (NI 1)) and the Gas (Northern Ireland) Order 1996 (SI 1996/275 (NI 2)).

(a) the carrying on of the activities of: conveying gas[19] through pipes to any premises, or to a pipe-line system operated by a gas transporter; supplying to any premises gas which has been conveyed to those premises through pipes; arranging with a gas transporter for gas to be introduced into, conveyed by means of or taken out of a pipe-line system operated by that transporter; and activities ancillary to those activities (including in particular the storage of gas, the provision and reading of meters and the provision of pre-payment facilities)[20]; and

(b) commercial activities connected with the generation, transmission or supply of electricity[21];

(3) As from April 2006 the Water Services Regulation Authority (until then the Director General of Water Services), in England and Wales[22] and insofar as the OFT's functions relate to commercial activities connected with the supply of water or the provision of sewerage services[23];

(4) The Office of Rail Regulation (formerly the Rail Regulator), so far as the OFT's functions relate to agreements or conduct relating to the supply of services relating to railways[24]; and

(5) The Civil Aviation Authority, so far as the OFT's functions relate to agreements or conduct relating to the supply of air traffic services.[25]

The Competition Act (Concurrency) Regulations 2004.[26] These Regulations make provision as to the allocation of cases between the other regulators and the OFT, and (in cases where more than one other regulator has jurisdiction) as between the other regulators. If a regulator (or the OFT) wishes to exercise its functions in relation to a matter in which the OFT (or another regulator, as the case may be) also has or may have jurisdiction, it must first inform the OFT (or other regulator), and they must then seek to reach

3–007

---

[19] As defined in s.48 of the Gas Act 1986, in essence natural gas.

[20] Gas Act 1986, ss.5(1) and 36A(3).

[21] Electricity Act 1989, s.43.

[22] The water industry in Scotland has not been privatised and the functions of the present economic regulator, the Water Industry Commissioner for Scotland, are not equivalent to those of the Water Services Regulation Authority. A Bill has been laid before the Scottish Parliament which does contemplate conferring on the Water Industry Commissioner additional functions broadly equivalent to the non-Competition Act functions of the Water Services Regulation Authority, notably in the price control and licensing areas. However, although the economic regulation of the water industry is a devolved matter under the Scotland Act 1998, competition policy is not a devolved matter and the Bill does not confer on the Commissioner any powers under the Competition Act.

[23] Water Industry Act 1991, s.31.

[24] Railways Act 1993, s.67; it may however not do so in relation to agreements or conduct entered into or engaged in by a rail link undertaker in connection with the Channel Tunnel rail link; s.22 of the Channel Tunnel Rail Link Act 1996.

[25] Transport Act 2000, s.86(3).

[26] SI 2004/1077.

agreement as to which of them will exercise their powers in the case.[27] In practice, decisions as to which regulator deals with a case will be taken on the basis of which of them is best placed to deal with it, having regard to such matters as: the detailed sectoral knowledge of the specialist regulators; previous contacts between the parties and the OFT or a regulator; and recent experience of dealing with similar issues. Agreement should usually be reached within a month and in practice is reached rather earlier.[28] Complaints may be sent either to the OFT or a sectoral regulator, but not both; the complainant will be told which authority is to deal with the matter.[29] In default of agreement, the Secretary of State decides which regulator is to exercise its powers in the case.[30] Until agreement (or a determination by the Secretary of State), no regulator can exercise its powers, and after an agreement or determination, only the regulator agreed on or determined may exercise its powers.[31] There is provision for the transfer of cases as between regulators after an investigation is under way.[32]

3–008 **Informal working arrangements.**   In addition to these statutory provisions, there are informal working arrangements between the OFT and the other regulators.[33] There is a Concurrency Working Party, on which the OFT and the other regulators are represented. Specific guidance has been issued as to how the OFT and Ofcom will work together.[34]

(b) Commencement of an investigation

3–009 **Power to begin an investigation.**   Section 25 of the Competition Act is, as amended,[35] a complex provision setting out a number of cases in which the OFT may conduct an investigation. Six cases are identified in which the OFT may conduct an investigation, the common element to each of them being "reasonable grounds for suspecting". The first two cases cover suspected current agreements[36] that: (i) may fall under s.2 of the Competition Act; or (ii) Art.81(1) EC. The third and fourth cases are where there are reasonable grounds for suspecting that there has been an infringement of Chapter II or Art.82 EC. The fifth and sixth cases are where there are reasonable grounds for suspecting a past agreement falling within s.2 or Art.81(1) EC.

---

[27] *ibid.*, reg.4.
[28] *Guideline on Concurrent Application to Regulated Industries*, December 2004, para.3.15.
[29] *ibid.*, para.3.20.
[30] SI 2000/260, reg.5.
[31] *ibid.*, reg.6.
[32] *ibid.*, reg.7.
[33] See the OFT Guideline, n.28, above, pt.3.
[34] *www.oft.gov.uk/NR/rdonlyres/5A75F852–4C48–4D12–8604–A7A85D504968/0/ofcom.pdf.*
[35] By the Competition Act 1998 and Other Enactments (Amendment) Regulations (SI 2004/1261).
[36] *i.e.* agreements, decisions of associations of undertakings or concerted practices; s.2(5).

Investigations into possibly exempt agreements.   The OFT may conduct an   **3–010**
investigation under Chapter I or Art.81 EC whether or not it considers or
suspects that the agreement may be (or may have been) exempt under s.9 of
the Competition Act or Art.81(3) EC. But it cannot conduct an investigation if it considers that the agreement is or was at the material time covered
(as far as s.2 is concerned) by a block or parallel exemption[37] or (as far as
Art.81(1) EC is concerned) by a Commission block exemption regulation,
unless, in the case of an existing agreement only, it has reasonable grounds
to suspect that it could withdraw the benefit of the exemption.[38]

Basis for conducting an investigation.   The material which forms the basis of   **3–011**
the reasonable grounds for suspicion may come from a variety of sources,
including press comments and information passed on by other Government
departments and foreign competition authorities. The OFT has emphasised
two sources of information.[39] The first is complaints, which the OFT has
referred to as an extremely important source of information for the OFT.[40]
The second is information obtained under the OFT's leniency programme.[41]

Discretion as to whether to open an investigation.   Section 25 provides that   **3–012**
the OFT *may* open an investigation once it has reasonable grounds for
suspecting an infringement, which raises the as yet unanswered question of
when the OFT is entitled to decline to do so. The OFT has not issued any
general guidance on the factors which it will take into account, although it
has given guidance as to the approach it will take when, as well as suggesting
a civil infringement, the evidence before it also suggests that the cartel
offence may have been committed.[42] A decision not to open an investigation
is in principle subject to judicial review in the High Court.[43] It may also be
subject to an appeal to the CAT if the decision is appealable under s.46 of
the Act.[44]

(c) Power to require the provision of documents and information

Informal requests.   The OFT may well proceed by informal requests for   **3–013**

---

[37] See para.2–018, above for an explanation of these terms.
[38] s.25(8)–(11).
[39] See, *e.g.* OFT Guideline, *Powers of Investigation*, December 2004, para.2.2.
[40] OFT Guideline, *A Guide to making a complaint under the Competition Act 1998*, OFT 427,
    p.1. A former Director of Competition Enforcement at the OFT has said that complaints are
    the main way in which the OFT uncovers anti-competitive behaviour: Bloom, "Key chal-
    lenges in enforcing the Competition Act" [2003] Comp. Law 85.
[41] See paras 3–098–3–106, below.
[42] See Chapter 5, below.
[43] Or the Court of Session in Scotland.
[44] For a discussion of the question of when a decision is appealable under s.46, see paras 3–042–
    3–045, below. The High Court is likely to refuse to entertain an application for judicial
    review if a decision is capable of appeal to the Tribunal.

documents or information rather than by using its formal powers.[45] There is no requirement to respond to such requests, though it may well be advisable to respond. If a response is made, it should be noted that it is an offence under s.44 of the Competition Act to provide false or misleading information to the OFT in connection with the exercise of its functions under Part I of the Act, and that section applies even to responses to informal requests.

3–014   **Use of material obtained during investigations of the cartel offence.**   The OFT is not precluded from using documents obtained under Enterprise Act powers in order to establish an infringement of the civil prohibitions by undertakings. Documents obtained by the SFO under its own powers can also be passed to the OFT for such use.[46] The OFT will not use information obtained from individuals in the course of compulsory interviews against their employers in Competition Act proceedings.[47]

3–015   **Regulation of Investigatory Powers Act 2000.**   In pursuance of its powers to investigate infringements of the Competition Act and Arts 81 and 82 EC, the OFT has been granted[48] powers under the 2000 Act to employ "directed surveillance" (essentially, monitoring of movements of people and cars)[49] and "covert human intelligence sources" (*i.e.* persons who will secretly report back what they observe to the OFT).[50] The OFT has stated that, as far as investigations under the Competition Act are concerned, authorisations for directed surveillance will be granted only in the case of suspected agreements to fix prices (including resale price maintenance), limit production or supply, share markets or rig bids.[51] Authorisation will be given only when the interference with privacy is necessary and proportionate[52]; account will be taken of the risks of intrusion into the privacy of third parties,[53] and of the risks of obtaining material covered by lawyer/client privilege, confidential personal information (relating to physical or mental health or spiritual counselling) or confidential journalistic information.[54] Authorisation may be given by the Director of Cartel Investigations within the OFT, but in cases where confidential information (in this case meaning

---

[45] n.39, above, para.2.4.
[46] Criminal Justice Act 1987, s.3(5)(a).
[47] OFT Guidance on powers for investigating criminal cartels, para.4.3.
[48] See the Regulation of Investigatory Powers (Directed Surveillance and Covert Human Intelligence Sources) Order 2003 (SI 2003/3171).
[49] s.26(2) of the 2000 Act defines "directed surveillance" as covert surveillance (*i.e.* carried out in a manner calculated to ensure that the persons subject to it are unaware it is taking place) undertaken for the purposes of a specific investigation, likely to obtain private information about a person, and otherwise than as an immediate response to events or circumstances.
[50] ss.28 and 29 of, and para.20B of Sch.1 to the Regulation of Investigatory Powers Act 2000. For the powers of the OFT under RIPA in the criminal sphere, see paras 5–032–5–041, below.
[51] Covert surveillance in cartel investigations, Code of Practice, August 2004, OFT 738, para.1.5.
[52] *ibid.*, para.2.4.
[53] *ibid.*, paras 2.6–2.7.
[54] *ibid.*, paras 3.1–3.11, where these terms are defined in detail.

information falling within the categories referred to in the previous sentence) is likely to be acquired, it will be given by the Chairman of the OFT or (in his absence) a designated deputy.[55]

Section 26.   Once it has opened an investigation, the OFT has power under   **3–016**
s.26(1) of the Competition Act to require any person to produce to it a specified document, or provide it with specified information, which the OFT considers relates to any matter relevant to the investigation. "Document" means, here and elsewhere under Part I of the Competition Act, information recorded in any form.[56] Section 26(2) requires that that power be exercised by notice in writing, and the notice must set out the document or information (or category of document or information) required.[57] The notice may also require the production or provision of the information or document at a particular time or place, or in a particular manner. The OFT has power to take copies of any document produced to it.[58] The OFT may also require the person on whom the notice is served (or any officer, employee, or former officer or employee of that person) to explain any document produced,[59] and will allow him to be accompanied by a legal adviser while he does so.[60] If the person concerned does not produce the document, the OFT may require him to state where (to the best of his knowledge and belief) it is.[61] Section 26 notices may be used after other powers have been exercised, for example in order to clear up outstanding matters after a s.28 investigation.[62] See paras 3–029–3–031 and 3–033, below for an account of lawyer/client privilege and of the extent to which recipients of a notice are entitled to invoke a privilege against self-incrimination. See also paras 3–058–3–065, below on confidentiality and the ability of the OFT to use the information and documents for other purposes or to disclose them.

Failure to comply with a section 26 notice.   Provided that the OFT has acted   **3–017**
in accordance with s.26,[63] it is an offence for a person[64] to fail to comply with a requirement imposed on him by the OFT under that section.[65] If he is required to produce a document, it is a defence for him to prove that the document was not in his possession or under his control and that it was not reasonably practicable for him to comply.[66] If he is required to produce information, it is a defence to prove that he had a reasonable excuse for

---

[55] *ibid.*, paras 3.1–3.2 and 4.8.
[56] s.59.
[57] s.26(3).
[58] s.26(6)(a)(i).
[59] s.26(6)(a)(ii).
[60] OFT 404, n.39, above, para.3.9.
[61] s.26(6)(b).
[62] OFT 404a, n.39, above, para.3.2.
[63] s.42(4).
[64] The offence covers both companies and individuals.
[65] s.42(1).
[66] s.42(2).

failing to comply.[67] It is also an offence, intentionally or recklessly, to destroy, dispose of, falsify, or conceal a document requested under s.26.[68] It is also an offence to provide, knowingly or recklessly, false or misleading information to the OFT.[69] Each of these offences carries a prison term of up to two years or an unlimited fine.

3–018   **Challenging a section 26 notice.**   There is no right of appeal to the CAT under s.46 of the Act in respect of the OFT's decisions under s.26. It is, however, possible to seek judicial review of such decisions on the usual grounds on which such decisions may be challenged in public law.[70] Further, any final OFT decision that relies on information or documents obtained *ultra vires* s.26 will to that extent be subject to challenge before the CAT.[71]

3–019   **Powers relating to exclusions.**   Certain categories of agreements and conduct are excluded from the Competition Act. In certain cases[72] the OFT can withdraw the exclusion and, in considering such withdrawal, is given power to require the provision of information in connection with the agreement. This is done by written notice, failure to comply with which within a certain period of time results in the OFT having power to withdraw the exclusion.

(d) Investigations on the spot

3–020   **Section 27.**   Section 27(1) of the Competition Act provides that an officer of the OFT who has been so authorised in writing by the OFT may enter any business premises[73] in connection with an investigation. At least two working days' notice must be given[74] unless either the OFT has a reasonable suspicion that the premises are occupied by a party to the suspected infringement being investigated, or all reasonable steps have been taken to give notice and they have failed. The officer is entitled to enter the premises, to take with him equipment as may be necessary, to require persons on the premises to give explanations of documents and where they may be found, to take copies of documents found, to require information on computer to be printed out in visible and legible form and to take necessary steps for the purposes of preventing interference with documents,[75] failure to comply with

---

[67] s.42(3).

[68] s.43. It is also an offence to cause or permit such destruction, etc.

[69] s.44.

[70] See para.6–008.

[71] *cf.* Case C–94/00 *Roquette Frères v Commission* [2002] E.C.R. I–9011 at para.49 and Case 46/87R *Hoechst v Commission* [1987] E.C.R. 1549 at para.34.

[72] *i.e.* mergers (Sch.1); agreements relating to agricultural products and farmers' co-operatives (Sch.3); land agreements and (until May 2005) certain vertical agreements.

[73] *i.e.* any part of premises not used as a dwelling; s.27(6).

[74] s.27(2).

[75] s.27(5).

which is a criminal offence. But the officer has no power under s.27 to force an entry or to search himself for documents. If the OFT is concerned that the undertaking may not be co-operative, it is likely to seek a court warrant under s.28. As to the ability to challenge OFT decisions under s.27, see para.3–018, above on s.26, *mutatis mutandis*.

Section 28: conditions.   Section 28 of the Competition Act gives the court[76]   **3–021** the power to issue a warrant giving certain powers to a named OFT officer and other persons to enter and search specified business premises. Under s.28(1), the court has power to issue such a warrant where it is satisfied that there are reasonable grounds for suspecting: (a) that there are on the premises documents which have been required to be produced under s.26 or 27 but which have not been produced; (b) that there are on the premises documents which the OFT could require to be produced under s.26 but that if they were required to be produced they would instead be concealed, removed, tampered with or destroyed; or (c) that there are documents that could have been required to be produced under s.27 on premises that an OFT officer has attempted to enter but has been unable to do so. In essence, therefore, the court has power to grant a warrant either when the OFT has tried to use its other powers to obtain documents which are reasonably expected to be on the premises but has been met with non co-operation or where the OFT has not used its other powers but reasonably suspects that attempting to do so would lead to interference with the documents.[77]

Terms of a section 28 warrant.   The terms of a warrant under s.28 are set   **3–022** out in s.28(2), with (in England and Wales) further relevant provisions being found in s.50 of the Criminal Justice and Police Act 2001. In England and Wales, the warrant will follow the template annexed to the May 2004 Practice Direction—Application for a Warrant under the Competition Act 1998. It will set out the subject matter and purpose of the OFT's

---

[76] In England and Wales, and in Northern Ireland, the High Court; in Scotland, the Court of Session. In England and Wales, the Practice Direction—Application for a Warrant under the Competition Act 1998 requires the application to be made to a judge of the Chancery Division in the Royal Courts of Justice (if available) (para.2.2).

[77] In *OFT v X* [2003] U.K.C.L.R. 785 at para.5 Morison J. said, in relation to the evidence in that case:

"The target companies, if they have been doing what the OFT suspect, are likely to have taken steps to make detection difficult and to be continuing so to act. The stakes are high, since the penalties if guilt is established are likely to be high. The entities being investigated include one of a substantial size, and whose reputation, apart from its financial position, may be damaged if incriminating material is found. There is, therefore, a strong inducement or motive for hiding the truth. The material which the OFT are most interested to see is relatively easy to conceal, given advance notice. For these reasons, I am satisfied that there are reasonable grounds for suspecting that the written material would be concealed or destroyed. It is in the public interest that if there has been wrongdoing it is uncovered and revealed."

investigation, and the offences committed by failure to comply with the warrant.[78] The warrant then enumerates the powers set out in s.28(2) and granted to: (i) the named officer[79]; (ii) other OFT officers authorised in writing by the OFT; and (iii) any other persons specified in the warrant.[80] They are empowered to enter the premises named in the warrant using such force as is reasonably necessary and to search the premises and take copies of any documents appearing to fall within the categories of document set out above ("documents of the relevant kind").[81] They are also empowered to: (i) take possession of documents, for up to three months,[82] that appear to be within of the relevant kind if that appears to be necessary to preserve them or because it is not reasonably practicable to take copies; and (ii) to require information stored in electronic form, which is accessible from the premises,[83] and which appears to be of the relevant kind, to be produced in a form in which it can be taken away and which is either visible and legible or from which a visible and legible form can be produced. They are also given powers to require any person to provide an explanation of a document appearing to be of the relevant kind or to state where, to the best of his knowledge and belief, it may be found.[84]

In England and Wales,[85] the warrant also empowers the persons conducting the search as follows: where it is not reasonably practicable to determine whether a document is a document of the relevant kind, to take a copy of it for the purpose of determining later and elsewhere whether it is such a document; and also, where a document of the relevant kind is comprised in a document which is not of the relevant kind but where it is not reasonably practicable to separate the documents which are of the relevant kind from those which are not, to copy all the documents.[86] The persons

---

[78] s.29(1).

[79] The OFT's practice—to which, apparently, the court has always agreed—has been to name at least two named officers, so as to ensure that there is cover in case of unexpected unavailability of the named officer.

[80] s.28(3A) allows the warrant to name persons who are not OFT officers; an example might be specialist IT investigators.

[81] In a case where the warrant is granted on the basis that were the OFT to seek the documents under its other powers there are reasonable grounds to suspect they might be interfered with, the warrant usually includes a provision entitling the OFT also to use its powers under s.28 in respect of documents relating to the investigation but where there is no reason to suppose that a risk of interference arises; s.28(3).

[82] s.28(7).

[83] This provision appears to cover documents in a database located outside the UK but which are accessible by electronic means from the premises.

[84] See paras 3–029–3–030, below for a discussion of the application of the rules relating to self-incrimination to this provision. Rule 3(3) of the OFT's Rules 2004 provides that a person made subject to such a requirement may be accompanied by a legal adviser.

[85] The powers referred to in this sentence are derived from s.50 of the Criminal Police and Justice Act 2001.

[86] One practical effect of this provision is to entitle the OFT to take copies of a whole database where it is not practicable on the premises to go through the database sorting the relevant from the irrelevant documents on it.

conducting the search are entitled to take such equipment with them as appears to be necessary.[87]

Responsibilities of the persons conducting a section 28 search. The named officer is required, when leaving unoccupied premises or premises where the occupier is temporarily absent, to secure them as effectively as he found them.[88] In England and Wales, the named officer must, in accordance with paras 6.2 and 8.1 of the Practice Direction, give the court a written undertaking to produce the warrant and an explanatory note (in a form annexed to the Practice Direction) on arrival at the premises and, as soon as possible thereafter, to personally serve a copy of those documents on the person appearing to be in charge of the premises. If there is no one at the premises when the named offer attempts to execute the warrant, he must take all reasonable steps to inform the occupier of the intended entry and, if he is informed, afford him or his representative a reasonable opportunity to be present when it is executed.[89] If the occupier is not informed, the named officer must leave a copy of the warrant in a prominent place at the premises.[90]   **3–023**

Execution of the warrant. In England and Wales, the warrant may, unless the court otherwise orders, be produced, and entry under it may take place, between 9.30am and 5.30pm Monday to Friday. Once they have entered, the persons named in the warrant may remain on the premises and re-enter the premises outside those times.[91] The warrant will however expire one month after it is issued.[92]   **3–024**

Procedural matters. In England and Wales, the application for a warrant is made without notice, and will be heard in private (unless the court otherwise directs).[93] The court file will be marked "not for disclosure", and no person may inspect it without first making an application (on notice to the OFT) to a High Court judge.[94] Further detailed provisions are made in relation to such matters as listing and the contents of the claim form in order to minimise any risk of "tipping off" the subject of the investigation.[95] The OFT must support its application with affidavit evidence, setting out all matters on which the OFT relies, including (in accordance with the strict duty of full and frank disclosure imposed on persons seeking without notice applications) all material facts of which the court should be made aware. In particular, the affidavit must set out the subject matter and purpose of the   **3–025**

---

[87] Examples might be tape recording equipment or CDs containing computer programmes designed to find deleted documents on a hard disc.
[88] s.28(5).
[89] s.29(3).
[90] s.29(4).
[91] Practice Direction, para.8.3
[92] s.28(6).
[93] Practice Direction, para.6.1.
[94] *ibid.*, para.3.
[95] *ibid.*, paras 2.3 and 5.

application, the identity of the undertakings suspected of having committed the infringement, the premises to be investigated and the connexion between those premises and the suspected undertakings, and the grounds for making the application.[96] The affidavit will set out all the evidence on which the OFT bases its suspicions of an infringement, and (in a case where the OFT has not sought to use its other powers) all matters relevant to the question of whether there is reasonable suspicion that the undertaking concerned might interfere with, or refuse to produce, the documents sought or (in a case where the OFT has used its other powers) particulars of non-co-operation with those powers.

3–026 Applications to vary or discharge the warrant. An application to vary or discharge the warrant may, in England and Wales, be made by the occupier or person in charge of the premises to the judge who issued it (if available). An application to stop the warrant being executed must be made immediately on service. The named officer must be informed of any application to vary or discharge the warrant.[97] The CAT has no power to review OFT decisions in exercise of its powers under s.28, although evidence obtained *ultra vires* s.28 is likely to be excluded on appeal to the CAT.[98]

3–027 Legal representation. There is no provision either in the Act or the Practice Direction that requires an occupier of premises to be given the opportunity to have his legal representative present during the investigation. However, Rule 3 of the OFT's Rules 2004 provides that, if an OFT officer considers it reasonable in the circumstances and subject to compliance with any appropriate conditions[99] he may impose, he shall grant a request by the occupier to allow a reasonable time for a legal representative to arrive before continuing the investigation.[1] The OFT will not agree any delay if there is an in-house lawyer on the premises.[2]

3–028 Section 28A: domestic premises. Section 28A contains almost identical[3] provisions, relating to "domestic premises" to those relating to business premises under s.28. "Domestic premises" are defined for these purposes as premises that are used as a dwelling and are either: (a) used in connection

---

[96] *ibid.*, para.4.

[97] Practice Direction, para.9. Applications under s.59 of the Criminal Justice and Police Act 2001 (applications in relation to property seized under s.50 of that Act and s.28 of the Competition Act) may be made to a judge of the Chancery Division under CPR Part 23 (para.10 of the Practice Direction).

[98] See para.3–018, above.

[99] Such as sealing of cabinets, allowing OFT officers to enter certain rooms, or suspending external e-mail communication; OFT Guideline, *Powers of Investigation*, para.4.11.

[1] *ibid.*, para.4.10.

[2] *ibid.*, para.4.11. It will be irrelevant that the in-house lawyer has no knowledge of competition law or procedure.

[3] The only material difference between the provisions of ss.28 and 28A is that there is no reference in s.28A, in the conditions for the grant of a warrant, to the situation where the OFT has attempted to exercise s.27 powers (which do not apply to domestic premises).

with the affairs of an undertaking or association of undertakings; or (b) premises where documents relating to the affairs of an undertaking or association of undertakings are kept. The description of the position in relation to s.28 warrants applies, *mutatis mutandis*, to s.28A.[4]

(e) Limitations on the OFT's powers to obtain documents and information

Self incrimination. The OFT has stated that it "cannot compel the provision of answers which might involve the admission [on the part of the party concerned] of the existence of an infringement, which it is incumbent on the OFT to prove".[5] The OFT is here referring to EC jurisprudence on similar powers enjoyed by the Commission, and in particular *Orkem v Commission*[6] and *Mannesmann v Commission*.[7-8] The *Orkem* principle can be seen as a restriction on the types of questions that may be asked, rather than on the matters about which questions may be asked.[9] An example of a question prohibited by the rule is a question requiring the recipient to state the purpose of a meeting which it attended (a suspected cartel meeting) and the nature of any decisions reached; such questions would compel the recipient to admit participation in an unlawful cartel.[10] However, the *Orkem* principle does not in any way restrict the extent to which the Commission (and by extension the OFT) may require the provision of pre-existing documents, no matter how incriminating they may be.

3–029

Self-incrimination and Article 6 of the ECHR.[11] In *OFT v X*[12] (an application to the High Court for a warrant under s.28), Morison J. discussed, in the context of s.28, the extent to which the OFT's powers to require the provision of documents and information was compatible with Art.6 of the ECHR, having regard to the jurisprudence of the European Court of Human Rights ("the ECtHR"):

3–030

(1) In dealing with the OFT's rights to seek documents, Morison J.

---

[4] The court is likely to insist, in any case where there is any reason to suppose that there is likely to be an unaccompanied woman on the premises, that at least one member of the OFT team is a woman; see Civil Procedure Rules, PD25 (Interim Injunctions), para.7.4(5), in relation to search and seizure orders.
[5] OFT Guideline, n.39, above, para.6.6.
[6] Case 374/87, [1989] E.C.R. 3283; [1991] 4 C.M.L.R. 502.
[7-8] Case T–112/98, [2001] E.C.R. II–729
[9] *Per* A.G. Gulmann in Case C–60/92 *Otto v Postbank* [1993] E.C.R. I–5683 at para.10. See, generally, Bellamy & Child, *European Community Law of Competition* (5th ed., Sweet & Maxwell, London, 2001) at para.12–022.
[10] *Mannesmann*, n.7, above, paras 71 and 73.
[11] For a full discussion, see Ward and Gardner, "The Privilege against Self-Incrimination under the ECHR" [2003] Comp. Law 200.
[12] [2003] EWHC 1042 (Comm); [2003] U.K.C.L.R. 785; [2004] I.C.R. 105.

discussed[13] the question of whether the power to require the production of pre-existing documents was compatible with the ECtHR's jurisprudence. In *Funke v France*,[14] the ECtHR found that the applicant's rights under Art.6 had been violated by a requirement upon him to produce documents for the purpose of a criminal investigation. However, in *Saunders v UK*[15] the ECtHR held, without seeking to reconcile its position with the reasoning in *Funke*,[16] that

> "the right not to incriminate oneself ... does not extend to the use in criminal proceedings of material which may be obtained from the accused through the use of compulsory powers but which has an existence independent of the will of the subject such as, *inter alia*, documents acquired pursuant to a warrant".[17]

In *OFT v X*, Morison J. noted this inconsistency in the Strasbourg case law,[18] but proceeded to find the OFT's powers to require the provision of documents[19] compatible with Art.6 on the basis that any interference in that respect with the right not to incriminate oneself pursued the legitimate aim of ensuring the application of the competition rules and thereby ensuring economic well-being,[20] and was proportionate to that aim[21] (noting in particular the right to challenge the OFT's exercise of its powers in the courts, the limitation imposed by the *Orkem* principle, the maintenance of lawyer/client privilege, and rights to obtain legal advice).[22]

---

[13] At paras 7–11.

[14] (1993) 16 E.H.R.R. 297.

[15] (1997) 23 E.H.R.R. 313.

[16] Although Martens J., dissenting, observed that *Saunders* implicitly overruled *Funke*.

[17] para.69.

[18] An inconsistency which has been exacerbated by the ECtHR's judgment in *JB v Switzerland* (judgment of May 3, 2001), where the ECtHR held that a fine imposed on the applicant for not providing copies of documents for the purposes of criminal tax proceedings violated his rights under Art.6; the ECtHR referred to *Saunders* but simply ignored the reference in that case to "documents" as an example of material that a suspect could be required to produce. See the criticism of *JB* in Ward and Gardner, *op.cit.* n.11, above, at 204–206.

[19] Under s.28, but the same reasoning applies *mutatis mutandis*.

[20] Following a similar analysis, in the context of Art.8 of the ECHR and the EC competition rules, by the ECJ in Case C–94/00 *Roquette Frères* [2003] 4 C.M.L.R. 1.

[21] In taking the view that the Art.6 privilege against self-incrimination is not absolute, but that the privilege can be restricted where that is necessary in pursuance of a legitimate aim and where the restriction is proportionate, Morison J. followed the Privy Council decision in *Brown v Scott (Procurator Fiscal, Dunfermline) and anor* [2001] 2 W.L.R. 817. See also Ward and Gardner *op.cit.* n.11, above, at 211, where they suggest that the inconsistent ECtHR case law on the application of Art.6 to powers to require the production of documents may be explicable on the basis of an (unarticulated) principle that intrusive requests for documents (involving, in the *Funke* case, a violation of Art.8) may be more objectionable than less intrusive requests.

[22] To which one might also add the point that any evidence obtained *ultra vires* is likely to be excluded on appeal to the tribunal; see para.3–018, above.

(2) He also applied the same approach to the question of whether the OFT was entitled to require the provision of explanations of documents under s.28, following dicta in *Mannesmann* to the effect that the *Orkem* principle provided sufficient protection and that an unrestricted right to silence

> "would have the effect of going beyond what is necessary to preserve the undertakings' rights of the defence and would constitute an unjustified hindrance to the accomplishment by the Commission of its task of ensuring respect for the competition rules in the Community."[23]

The same analysis would appear to apply in the context of requests for information under s.26.

Self-incrimination in relation to the cartel offence. Section 30A of the Competition Act provides that a statement made by a person in response to a requirement imposed under ss.26–28A may not be used as evidence against him on a prosecution for the cartel offence. The only exceptions are where, in giving evidence, he makes a statement inconsistent with the earlier statement, or where he himself adduces evidence relating to the earlier statement, or questions about the earlier statement are asked on his behalf. This provision is intended to avoid the contravention of Art.6 that is constituted by the use against a person in criminal proceedings of answers obtained from him by use of compulsory powers.[24]   3–031

Privacy and Article 8 of the ECHR. It is now settled that Art.8(1) of the ECHR extends to business as well as domestic premises; and in any event, s.28A provides for powers to enter and search domestic premises. That therefore raises the question of the extent to which the use of s.28 and 28A powers can be justified under Art.8(2). In *OFT v X*, Morison J. summarised the position as follows: 3–032

> "I accept that Article 8 may come into play even though the premises concerned are business rather than personal households.[25] The right to enter and search is potentially an interference with a person's right to be protected against arbitrary interference by a public authority. How far this goes is uncertain. This is not the occasion to try and interpret the limited jurisprudence on this topic. But it seems clear that the wider the Strasbourg Court interprets the words 'private life' and 'home' in Article 8(1) the wider it will interpret the justification provision in Article 8(2), in the sense that the test of what 'is necessary in a democratic society in the interests of the well being of the country' will more easily be satisfied

---

[23] para.12.
[24] *Saunders v UK*, n.15, above.
[25] See, *e.g. Niemietz v Germany* [1992] 16 E.H.R.R. 97.

where the premises are business rather than personal [see para.29 of the ECJ's decision in *Roquette*]. I can see no reason for concluding that any rights which the defendants may have under Article 8 will be unlawfully infringed. Again, the aim of the legislation is to avoid price cartels and for this purpose the OFT must carry out an investigation where that is justified, as here. Not to have the power to enter premises pursuant to a warrant would effectively emasculate the OFT's statutory functions. The safeguards are in place to protect the defendants. They can apply to have the order discharged and to seek appropriate relief in the event that the power is abused during the execution of the warrants. Access to the domestic court is quicker and more effective than access to the ECJ, for example. I conclude that the interference with any right under Article 8 is justified and proportionate."

Given the ability of the court to control the exercise of s.28 and 28A powers in advance, it seems unlikely that any use of these powers will be held to contravene Art.8.

3–033   **Lawyer/client and litigation privilege.**   Section 30 of the Act provides that a person cannot be required to produce a "privileged communication", that is to say, a document constituting a communication between a professional legal adviser and his client (lawyer/client privilege) or made in connection with or in contemplation of legal proceedings and for the purposes of those proceedings (litigation privilege), to the extent that such documents would be protected from disclosure in High Court proceedings on grounds of legal professional privilege.[26] This rule is more favourable to undertakings than the equivalent rule in Community law, which does not extend to in-house lawyers or non-EEA qualified lawyers.[27] However, the OFT accepts that the more favourable UK rules apply even when the OFT is applying Art.81 or 82 EC, whether on its own initiative or at the behest of the Commission or another national competition authority/[28] On the other hand, the OFT claims that it is entitled to use, in Competition Act investigations, documents that it could not have obtained itself because of s.30 but which are supplied to it by other national competition authorities whose law does not contain any such privilege.[29]

---

[26] Or, in Scotland, on the ground of confidentiality of communications in Court of Session proceedings.

[27] Case 155/79 *AM&S v Commission* [1982] E.C.R. 1575; [1982] 2 C.M.L.R. 264. The Community courts are currently being invited to revisit these issues in Cases T–125/3 and T–253/03 *Akzo Nobel and Ackros v Commission*.

[28] OFT Guideline, n.39, above, para.6.2.

[29] *ibid.*, para.6.3.

(f) Complaints

Importance of complaints. As the CAT observed in *Pernod-Ricard v OFT*[30]:

3–034

"... it is, we think, generally recognised that complaints have an essential role to play in bringing matters to the attention of the OFT, in stimulating investigations under the Act, and in securing the effective enforcement of the Chapter I and Chapter II prohibitions. Thus OFT 427, A Guide to making a complaint under the Competition Act 1998, refers to complaints as an extremely important source of information for the OFT (page 1). Margaret Bloom, then Director of Competition Enforcement at the OFT, has said that complaints are the main way in which the OFT uncovers anti-competitive behaviour (see 'Key challenges in enforcing the Competition Act' [2003] Comp. Law 85)."

Procedural rules regarding complainants. On the other hand, as the CAT also observed in the same passage:

3–035

"... apart from the right of appeal under section 47 [as to which, see para.3–043, below], the United Kingdom statutory provisions are virtually silent on the procedure for dealing with complaints".

The CAT contrasted this silence with the set of rights given to complainants under Community law.[31]

Complainants' rights as declared in *Pernod-Ricard*. In *Pernod-Ricard*, the CAT held, first, that UK law recognised the right to make a complaint to the OFT.[32] Secondly, the CAT held that it would "generally be proper, as a matter of fairness in administrative law"[33] for the OFT to disclose to a complainant which was sufficiently involved in the procedure before the

3–036

---

[30] [2004] CAT 10; [2004] Comp. A.R. 707, at para.197.

[31] In the tribunal's view (*ibid.*, para.225), those rights at Community level consisted of, at least, the rights: (i) To make a complaint to the EC Commission; (ii) If the EC Commission proceeded to issue a statement of objections, to receive a non-confidential copy of the statement of objections, and to make written (and usually oral) comments on the statement of objections; (iii) If the EC Commission came to the view that there were insufficient grounds for acting on the complaint, to be so informed in writing and be given an opportunity to make written comments before the complaint was rejected: Art.6 of Regulation 2842/98; (iv) To be given reasons if the Commission decided not to continue with the examination of a complaint, including the facts and legal considerations relied on, such reasons to be sufficiently precise and detailed to enable the Court of First Instance to review the Commission's use of its discretion to define priorities; and (v) To have the fate of the complaint settled by a decision of the EC Commission against which an action may be brought.

[32] n.30 above, para.226.

[33] Putting it another way, the tribunal said that "absent exceptional circumstances, we think the OFT's discretion should normally be exercised" in favour of disclosure (n.30, above, para.238).

OFT[34] a non-confidential version of a Rule 14 notice. Thirdly, again where the complainant had a clear interest in the case and had been closely involved in the investigation, the CAT held that:

"it would be a reasonable exercise of the OFT's discretion to give such a complainant the opportunity to submit its views to the OFT before a decision is taken not to investigate the complaint any further, in accordance with the consistent practice followed by the EC Commission. In the circumstances of this particular case, we think it was unfair not to do so".

The CAT summed up its approach as follows:

"it seems to us desirable that complainants should be afforded a structured opportunity to be heard by the OFT before decisions are taken, rather than having to raise matters for the first time before the Tribunal in circumstances where the complainant has been kept by the OFT largely at arms-length during the administrative process. If complainants are 'closely associated with the proceedings' as Article 27(1) of Regulation 1/2003 now requires, that in our view is likely to lead to fewer and less costly appeals, and better decision making."[35]

3–037 **OFT's Rules 2004 and complaints.** The OFT's Rules 2004 (made after the judgment in *Pernod-Ricard*) remain virtually silent on the subject of complainants. One change compared with the 2000 Rules is, however, that the OFT is obliged to give notice of a decision that there are no grounds for action in respect of an agreement or conduct to "any person whom it has undertaken to inform of the decision".[36]

3–038 **"Bare" complainants.** In *Pernod-Ricard*, the complainant had a plain interest in the outcome of the OFT's investigation and had played a full part in the investigation. Complainants who do not have such an interest (*e.g.* members of the public) or whose role in the investigation is more limited cannot assume that they will be entitled to similar rights.

3–039 **Super-complaints.** Section 11 of the Enterprise Act 2002 gives "designated consumer bodies" the power to make a "super-complaint" about features, or combinations of features of a market that appear to be significantly harming the interests of consumers. A "designated consumer body" is a body designated by the Secretary of State as appearing to him to represent

---

[34] Pernod-Ricard had been extensively involved in assisting the OFT and had a clear interest in the proceedings.
[35] n.30, above, para.241.
[36] The draft OFT's Rules had referred to "a complainant" at this point.

the interests of consumers of any description.[37] The OFT must respond to a super-complaint within 90 days setting out what action it proposes to take (or that it proposes to take no action). Action taken can include launching an investigation under the Competition Act, but can also include making a market investigation reference under Part 4 of the Enterprise Act. The OFT has issued guidance for designated consumer bodies on making super-complaints.[38]

Complainants' rights to obtain information from the OFT. As has already been pointed out, in contrast to the procedure in front of the Commission[39] there is no specific UK statutory provision giving complainants rights of access to information obtained by the OFT during its investigation.[40] Nor does it appear that complainants have any right to disclosure under Art.6 of the ECHR, since the OFT investigation does not determine the complainants' civil rights or obligations.[41] Complainants' rights of access therefore depend on the analysis adopted by the CAT in *Pernod-Ricard*. Those rights are, however, subject to the general restrictions on disclosure of information obtained by the OFT in the course of carrying out its statutory functions set out in Part 9 of the Enterprise Act 2002.[42]   **3–040**

Complainants' appeals to the CAT. A complainant may challenge certain decisions of the OFT before the CAT under s.47 of the Competition Act.[43] Where, however, a decision does not fall under s.47, it can only be challenged (if at all) by judicial review proceedings.   **3–041**

(g) Appealable decisions

What is a decision? The question of whether the OFT has taken a decision has presented few difficulties. The CAT has stated that "to take a decision in a legal context simply means to decide or determine a question or issue". It is irrelevant whether the decision is described by the decision-maker as such.[44] One potential area of controversy is whether, as the CAT has   **3–042**

---

[37] There is DTI guidance for bodies wishing to apply to be so designated: *www.dti.gov.uk/ enterpriseact/pdfs/superguide.pdf*.

[38] [2003] U.K.C.L.R. 1216.

[39] Art.8 of Commission Regulation 773/2004.

[40] Complainants enjoy the general right of access to information under s.1(1)(b) of the Freedom of Information Act 2000; but, as noted below, that Act does not assist in relation to material falling within the scope of Pt 9 of the Enterprise Act 2002 (which is likely to cover any information of assistance to a complainant).

[41] The contrary argument has been raised in *e.g. Claymore Dairies v DGFT* (*Preliminary Issues*) [2003] CAT 3, but the tribunal did not rule on the point.

[42] See para.3–058, below. Part 9 of the Enterprise Act does not apply to the Tribunal; for an analysis of the circumstances in which a complainant may obtain information from the OFT in the course of an appeal to the Tribunal, see paras 4–118–4–131, below.

[43] The Enterprise Act 2002 amended s.47 so as to remove the need for a complainant to apply to the OFT for a review of the decision in question before appealing to the Tribunal.

[44] *Bettercare Group v DGFT* (*Admissibility of Appeal*) [2002] CAT 6 at para.61.

observed *arguendo*, a failure to take any decision at all might be regarded as an "implied decision" to reject the complaint,[45] which could then be appealed. If developed by the CAT in future cases, this would create an appeal jurisdiction along the lines of the jurisdiction enjoyed by the Community courts under Art.232 EC to hear appeals against failure by the Commission to act.

3–043 **Appealable decision.** In contrast, much case law[46] has been generated by the question of whether or not a decision to close the file on, or to stop investigating, a complaint is appealable to the CAT under s.47 of the Competition Act. Under s.47, parties other than the person whose conduct or agreements are the subject of a decision, and who have a "sufficient interest" in the decision, may appeal against any decision of the OFT listed in s.46(3)(a)–(f). Section 46(3)(a) and (b) covers decisions "as to whether the Chapter I [or Chapter II] prohibition has been infringed". The question that has arisen is whether case closure decisions fall under s.46(3)(a) or (b), on the basis that the case closure is a decision that the relevant prohibition has not been infringed, so that a dissatisfied complainant may appeal to the CAT.

3–044 **The *Claymore* test.** In *Claymore v DGFT*,[47] the CAT set out the relevant principles as follows:

> "(i) The question whether the [OFT] has 'made a decision as to whether the Chapter II prohibition is infringed' is primarily a question of fact to be decided in accordance with the particular circumstances of each case (*Bettercare*, [24]).
>
> (ii) Whether such a decision has been taken is a question of substance, not form, to be determined objectively, taking into account all the circumstances (*Bettercare*, [62], [84] to [87], and [93]). The issue is: has the [OFT] made a decision as to whether the Chapter II prohibition has been infringed, either expressly or by necessary implication, on the material before [it]? (*Freeserve*, [96]).
>
> (iii) There is a distinction between a situation where the [OFT] has merely exercised an administrative discretion without proceeding to a decision on the question of infringement (for example, where the [OFT] decides not to investigate a complaint pending the conclusion of a parallel investigation by the European Commission), and a

---

[45] *Albion Water v DGWS* [2004] CAT 9, p.6; see also transcript of the CMC in *Wanadoo v Ofcom*, June 4, 2004, pp.8–9 (*www.catribunal.org.uk/documents/Tran1026Freeserve040604.pdf*).

[46] *Bettercare v DGFT*, n.44, above, *Freeserve v DGFT* [2002] CAT 8, *Claymore Dairies v DGFT* (Preliminary Issues) [2003] CAT 3, *Aquavitae v DGWS* [2003] CAT 17; *Pernod-Ricard SA v OFT* [2004] CAT 10. No application for leave to appeal against the Tribunal's decision was made in any of these cases.

[47] *Claymore*, n.46, above at para.122.

situation where the [OFT] has, in fact, reached a decision on the question of infringement, (*Bettercare*, [80], [87], [88], [93]; *Freeserve*, [101] to [105]). The test, as formulated by the Tribunal in *Freeserve*, is whether the [OFT] has genuinely abstained from expressing a view, one way or the other, even by implication, on the question whether there has been an infringement of the Chapter II prohibition (*Freeserve*, [101] and [102])."

The CAT went on to observe that:

"In our view a useful approach is to pose two questions: Did the [OFT] ask [itself] whether the Chapter II prohibition has been infringed? What answer did the [OFT] give to that question when making [its] decision?"[48]

Application of the *Claymore* test. A decision that one of the necessary **3–045** ingredients of an infringement of the prohibitions is missing, *e.g.* a decision that the body in question is not an undertaking, will amount to a decision that the prohibition has not been infringed.[49] A decision to close the file on the basis that, on the information available to the OFT, there is insufficient evidence to prove an infringement to the requisite standard is also appealable.[50] A decision to close the file on the basis that non-statutory assurances have been given by the subject of the investigation which remove the competition problem is also appealable, on the basis that it is a decision that the prohibitions will not be infringed if the assurances are complied with (the CAT attached little importance to the tense of the verb "has been infringed" in s.46(3)(a) and (b)).[51] On the other hand, a decision to close the file on the basis that future legislation was in prospect to deal with the problem was held not to be appealable[52]; and the CAT has itself given, in the extract from *Claymore* cited above, the example of a decision to close the file because the Commission has decided to take the case as another example of a non-appealable decision. It can, however, be predicted that application of the *Claymore* test will continue to cause difficulties, not least because file closure decisions may be based as much on considerations of administrative resources and priorities as on a view of the inherent merits of a case, and it is unclear where the line between appealable and non-appealable decisions is to be drawn in such cases.

---

[48] *Claymore*, n.46, above, at para.148.
[49] *Bettercare*, n.46, above.
[50] *Claymore*, n.46, above.
[51] *Pernod-Ricard*, n.46, above. However, as from May 1, 2004 there is a specific statutory regime governing the acceptance of commitments by the OFT; appeals against decisions to accept commitments may be made but the tribunal is required to decide them by applying judicial review principles, rather than on the merits; see para.3–057, below. It is unclear to what extent *Pernod-Ricard* would allow an alternative appeal to be made "on the merits" against a decision to accept commitments.
[52] *Aquavitae*, n.46, above.

(h) Interim measures

3–046 **Section 35 of the Competition Act and Article 5 of Regulation 1/2003.** Section 35 of the Competition Act gives the OFT power to give interim measures directions in any case where the OFT has begun a s.25 investigation but has not completed it (and still has power to conduct it). Article 5 of Regulation 1/2003 also gives the OFT power to give interim measures when applying Art.81 or 82 EC.

3–047 **Conditions.** Interim measures may be imposed only where the OFT considers that it is necessary to act as a matter of urgency in order either to prevent serious and irreparable damage to a particular person or category of persons, or to protect the public interest.[53] In cases under Chapter I or Art.81 EC, they may not be imposed where the person to be subject to the direction has produced evidence demonstrating, on the balance of probabilities, that the agreement meets the criteria for exemption under s.9 or Art.81 EC.[54] The OFT has said that the question of what amounts to "serious damage" is a question of fact and will depend on the circumstances of each case, but that it may be serious where the person or persons concerned may suffer "considerable competitive disadvantage likely to have a lasting effect on their position" and "is likely to include significant financial loss to a person as well as the proportion of that loss to the person's total revenue. Significant damage to goodwill or reputation might also constitute serious damage."[55] As to what is meant by "irreparable", the OFT has said that this "does not mean that a person must be threatened with insolvency, though this will generally suffice. Less extreme forms of serious damage may still be irreparable, in so far as they cannot be remedied by later intervention."[56] The damage must be shown to result from the putatively infringing behaviour.[57]

3–048 **Procedure.** Before giving such a direction, the OFT must give written notice to each person to whom it proposes to give a direction, informing them of the nature of the proposed direction and the reasons for it, and giving them an opportunity to make representations.[58] The addressee of the notice has a right of access to the file.[59] Although neither the OFT's Rules (made after *Pernod-Ricard*) nor its guidance provide for consultation of complainants, *Pernod-Ricard* plainly suggests that in most cases failure to

---

[53] s.35(2).
[54] ss.35(8) and (9).
[55] OFT Guideline, *Enforcement*, para.3.5.
[56] *ibid.*
[57] *ibid.*
[58] ss.35(3) and (4). There is no provision which specifically entitles them to make oral representations, but the OFT has said that the person concerned may request a meeting with OFT officials to elaborate on written representations; OFT Guideline, n.55, above, para.3.12.
[59] Rule 9 of the OFT's Rules; see para.3–069, below.

consult a complainant with a sufficient interest will be a procedural error.[60]

Contents. The OFT may impose such directions as it considers appropriate   **3–049**
for the purpose for which they are imposed.[61] In particular, they may require
the addressee to terminate, cease or modify the agreement or conduct in
question.[62]

Enforcement. Interim measures directions are enforced under s.34 in the   **3–050**
same way as final directions (see para.3–077, below).[63]

Appeals. The decision to impose interim measures may be appealed to the   **3–051**
CAT by the addressee or by a third party with a sufficient interest.[64] The
appeal does not suspend the measures unless the CAT orders to the contrary.[65] A decision not to impose interim measures may be appealed by a
third party with a sufficient interest.[66]

(i) Commitments

Sections 31A to 31E of the Competition Act and Article 5 of Regulation   **3–052**
1/2003. Sections 31A to 31E make provision for the giving of binding
commitments, before a final decision has been taken, in order to address the
OFT's competition concerns as identified during the investigation. Article 5
of Regulation 1/2003 empowers national competition authorities to accept
such commitments.

Circumstances in which commitments may be accepted. Commitments may   **3–053**
be accepted from any person the OFT considers appropriate,[67] at any time
between the beginning of an investigation and a decision that Art. 81 or 82
EC, or the Chapter I or Chapter II prohibition, has been infringed.[68] The
OFT has given guidance,[69] pursuant to s.31D, on when it may be appropriate to accept commitments. It is likely to do so only in cases where: (i) the
competition concerns are readily identifiable; (ii) they are fully addressed by
the commitments offered; and (iii) the commitments are capable of being
implemented effectively[70]; in particular, it will not do so if compliance with
the commitments, and their effectiveness, would be difficult to discern.[71] It

---

[60] See para.3–036, above.
[61] s.35(2).
[62] ss.35(6) and (7).
[63] *ibid.*
[64] s.46(2) and s.47(1)(d) and (2).
[65] s.46(4).
[66] s.47(1)(e) and (2).
[67] s.31A(2).
[68] s.31A(1).
[69] Annexe to OFT Guideline, *Enforcement.*
[70] *ibid.*, para.A14.
[71] *ibid.*, para.A16.

will only very exceptionally accept assurances in hard core cartel cases, or in cases of a serious abuse of a dominant position.[72] As to the timing of commitments, the OFT says that it is unlikely to accept commitments offered at a very late stage in its investigation, for example after the OFT has considered representations in relation to a Rule 4 notice.[73]

3–054 **Procedure.** It may of course be difficult, before a Rule [4] notice is issued, for the subject of an investigation to know precisely what the OFT's competition concerns are. To deal with that difficulty, the OFT will, at the request of the persons concerned and in a case where commitments may be appropriate, publish a summary of its concerns and of the main facts on which they are based (but not setting out the detail of the source of those facts).[74] Once commitments are offered,[75] the OFT may enter into discussions with the person concerned.[76] Before it accepts commitments, the OFT must give notice that it proposes to accept them.[77] The notice must either be published in such a way as the OFT thinks appropriate for the purpose of bringing it to the attention of those likely to be affected, or a copy must be sent to such persons as the OFT considers appropriate for that purpose.[78] The notice must state: that the OFT proposes to accept the commitments; the purpose of the commitment and the way in which it addresses the competition concerns; any other relevant facts; and the period in which representations may be made to the OFT (at least 11 working days from the giving of the notice). The OFT must consider those representations before accepting the commitments.[79] If the OFT then decides not to accept the commitments, it must give notice of that fact.[80] Alternatively, if it proposes to accept the commitments with modifications, it must give further notice of that fact, and give at least six working days for further representations.[81] Finally, if it accepts the commitments, it must publish them in an appropriate manner.[82]

3–055 **Effect of commitments.** Commitments have two effects:

(1) First, the OFT must terminate its investigation into, and may not make an infringement decision or give interim measures directions in respect of, the subject matter of the investigation insofar as it relates

---

[72] Annexe to OFT Guideline, *Enforcement*, para.A15.
[73] OFT Guideline, *Enforcement*, para.4.16.
[74] *ibid.*, para.4.17.
[75] The OFT will not use the offer of commitments as evidence in any subsequent decision on the matter; *ibid.*, para.4.20.
[76] *ibid.*, para.4.18.
[77] Sch.6A, para.2(1)(a).
[78] *ibid.*, para.8.
[79] *ibid.*, para.2.
[80] *ibid.*, para.4.
[81] *ibid.*, para.3; para.5 excuses it from doing so if it considers that the modifications are immaterial.
[82] *ibid.*, para.7.

to the concerns addressed by the commitments.[83] That restriction applies unless and until the OFT has reasonable grounds: (i) for believing that there has been a material change of circumstances; (ii) to suspect failure to adhere to one or more of the commitments; or (iii) to suspect that the information which led it to accept the commitments was materially false or misleading.[84] In such a case, the commitments remain in force until either a final decision or an interim measures decision.[85]

(2) Secondly, if the person bound by the commitments fails without reasonable excuse to comply with them, the OFT may apply to the court for an order requiring that person, or its officers, to make good the default.[86]

Termination and variation of commitments. Commitments will usually be entered into for a specified period of time.[87] The OFT may release a person from commitments when it is requested by the person who gave them to do so, or when it has reasonable grounds to believe that the relevant competition concerns no longer apply.[88] It may also accept substitute, or varied, commitments if those would address its current competition concerns.[89] Before it does so it must follow procedures which are, *mutatis mutandis*, essentially the same as those it must follow before accepting commitments.[90]   **3–056**

Appeals. The person whose agreement or conduct was the basis of the commitment may appeal to the CAT against a decision not to release those commitments on request, or a decision to release them on the ground that the competition concern no longer arises.[91] A third party with a sufficient interest may appeal to the CAT against a decision to accept, release, or materially to vary, commitments.[92] There is however no right of appeal by anyone to the CAT against a decision by the OFT not to accept commitments. In cases where an appeal may be brought, the CAT determines the appeal not on the merits (as is usually the case) but applying the same tests as would be used on judicial review.[93]   **3–057**

---

[83] s.31B(2) and (3).
[84] s.31B(4).
[85] s.31B(5).
[86] s.31E.
[87] OFT 407a, para.4.8.
[88] s.31A(4).
[89] s.31A(3).
[90] Sch.6A, paras 2–3 and 10–14; it need not do so if it considers the variation to be immaterial (para.1(b)).
[91] ss.46(3)(g) and (h).
[92] s.47(1)(c).
[93] para.3A of Sch.8 to the Competition Act. As to the way in which the judicial review test is to be applied in Tribunal appeals, see *IBA Health v OFT* [2004] EWCA Civ 142, dealing with similar provisions in relation to OFT decisions under Pt 3 of the Enterprise Act.

(j) Confidentiality and use of information for purposes other than the investigation

3–058   Scope of Part 9.   Part 9 of the Enterprise Act 2002 applies to all information which is obtained by the OFT (or the other regulators) under, *inter alia*, the Competition Act or most parts[94] of the Enterprise Act[95] and which either (a) relates to the affairs of an individual[96]; or (b) the business of an undertaking. Information not within Part 9 will in principle be subject to the right of access under s.1(1)(b) of the Freedom of Information Act 2000 (beyond the scope of this work); but information of which disclosure is prohibited under Part 9 is not subject to that right.[97]

3–059   General rule.   The general rule is that the OFT is not permitted to disclose information (unless it has already been lawfully disclosed) falling within the scope of Part 9 while the individual is alive or while the business is still being carried on[98]; and anyone who does so commits a criminal offence.[99]

3–060   Exceptions.   That rule is then subject to various exceptions:

(1) By consent of the individual or business concerned (and, if different, the person lawfully in possession of the information who gave it to the OFT)[1];

(2) In pursuance of a Community obligation[2];

(3) In order to facilitate the performance by the OFT of its statutory functions. This gateway allows the OFT to disclose information where to do so would, for example, allow a complainant or other third party to assist the OFT by providing comments on it. The complainant cannot, however, go on to use the information for any other purpose[3];

(4) In connection with the investigation of criminal proceedings, for the purposes of such proceedings, or the decision to start or end such disclosure[4]; and

(5) To overseas bodies under s.243 (discussed below).[5]

---

[94] That is to say, all parts save those parts (2 and 5) dealing with reforms to insolvency law and with the constitution of the Tribunal.
[95] EA, Sch.14.
[96] Disclosure of personal data remains, in addition, governed by the requirements of the Data Protection Act 1998 (s.237(4)).
[97] ss.2 and 44 of the 2000 Act.
[98] s.237(2).
[99] s.245.
[1] s.239.
[2] s.240.
[3] s.241.
[4] s.242.
[5] see para.3–063, below.

Balancing exercise before disclosure can be made. Even where a gateway applies, the OFT must, before it discloses information, consider the extent to which disclosure is necessary for the purpose being invoked, and balance that consideration against the need to exclude from disclosure information the disclosure of which could damage the public interest, and (as far as practicable) the need to exclude from disclosure information the disclosure of which could damage the legitimate business interests of the undertaking to which it relates (or significantly harm an individual). The OFT must inform the person supplying the information if it proposes to disclose any information identified as confidential, and give him a reasonable opportunity to make representations.[6]

3–061

Disclosure under Article 12 of Regulation 1/2003. Article 12 permits disclosure of information, including confidential information, as between national competition authorities and between them and the Commission. Under Art.12(2), the information may only be used for applying Arts 81 and 82 EC (and national law applied in parallel and leading to the same outcome). The OFT will have regard to the same three considerations as apply under the Enterprise Act before disclosing pursuant to Art.12, but will not inform the person supplying the information.[7]

3–062

Overseas disclosure. Sections 243(1), (2) and (12)(d), read with Sch.14, provide for disclosure by the OFT to foreign authorities other than EEA national competition authorities covered by Art.12 of Regulation 1/2003.[8] It may do so where disclosure would facilitate the exercise by those authorities of functions in relation to the investigation or enforcement of legislation appearing to the OFT to correspond to the Competition Act, the Enterprise Act, or other listed UK consumer protection and competition legislation. Before disclosing under this section, the OFT must, in addition to the matters set out in para.3–061, above, have regard to: whether the matter for the purpose of which disclosure is sought is sufficiently serious to justify disclosure; the protection offered by the foreign legal system with regard to self-incrimination; the protection offered by that system in respect of the disclosure of personal data; and whether there are mutual legal assistance arrangements in place between the UK and that country. As regards self-incrimination, the OFT's view is that any signatory of the ECHR, and the US by virtue of the Fifth Amendment to the US Constitution, will have sufficient protection against self-incrimination. As for protection of personal data, it considers that any EEA Member State will have sufficient protection

3–063

---

[6] OFT's Rules, Rule 6(1). The OFT may also require any person supplying information to it to identify what material should be treated as confidential, with reasons; Rule 6(3). A Rule 4 statement of objections will also require the addressee to identify confidential information in it; Rule 5(2)(b).

[7] OFT Guideline, *Powers of Investigation*, para.6.13.

[8] s.243 does not apply to information obtained under Pts 3 and 4 of the Enterprise Act (mergers and market investigations); s.243(1)(d).

of personal data by virtue of the EC Data Protection Directive; in the case of non-EEA States, the OFT will take into account whether the Commission has taken a decision under that Directive in relation to the adequacy of its data protection rules. In the case of the US, the OFT believes that the rules on subsequent disclosure that bind the US anti-trust authorities are sufficient to protect personal data.[9]

3–064 **Application of Part 9 to the CAT.** Part 9 does not apply to the CAT.[10] For a discussion of the CAT's approach to ordering disclosure of confidential material in the course of proceedings before it, see paras 4–118–4–131, below.

3–065 **Restriction on use of information in criminal proceedings.** Under s.30A of the Competition Act, the OFT cannot in general[11] use *information* obtained under its Competition Act powers in a prosecution of the person who provided the information for the cartel offence. But the OFT can in principle use *documents* obtained under its Competition Act powers in a prosecution for the cartel offence, providing that the chain of evidence is maintained in relation to those documents.[12] However, it is unclear to what extent the OFT can use information obtained by it while applying Arts 81 and 82 EC for the purpose of criminal proceedings, given the terms of Arts 12(3) and 28 of Regulation 1/2003, which respectively prohibit use of information exchanged between national competition authorities and the Commission for the purposes of criminal proceedings resulting in custodial sanctions, and restrict the use of information obtained by the Commission to the purposes for which it was acquired. In particular, given the broad principles enunciated by the CAT in *Pernod-Ricard*,[13] it appears to be arguable that similar restrictions on use of material in criminal proceedings should bind the OFT in respect of the use of information it obtains in the course of exercising its powers to apply EC competition law.

(k) Procedure leading up to an infringement decision

3–066 **Rule 4 statement of objections.** If the OFT proposes to make a decision to the effect that Art.81 or 82 EC, or the Chapter I or II prohibition, has been infringed, it must first give written notice to the persons whom the OFT considers to be a party to the agreement or to be engaged in the conduct in question.[14] The notice must state the facts on which the OFT proposes to

---

[9] OFT draft guidance on disclosure to overseas authorities, paras 4.6–4.19.
[10] s.237(5).
[11] The exception is where the defendant makes a statement inconsistent with the information or when evidence relating to the Competition Act information is adduced, or a question relating to it is asked, on his behalf.
[12] For an explanation of this distinction, see para.3–030, above.
[13] See para.3–002, above.
[14] s.31 and OFT's Rules, Rule 4.

rely, the matters to which it has taken objection, the action it proposes, and its reasons for the proposed action.[15] The OFT may not rely, in establishing its case, on anything that has not been disclosed to the defendant undertaking.[16] If the OFT later decides to rely on any further matters as against the defendant, it must serve a supplementary notice to that effect (see para.3–071, below). But if material is omitted and later relied on in a decision, the decision will be annulled only if the defence was affected by the defect, so that annulment would not follow if in fact the defendant was told informally of the new material and cannot show any prejudice as a result of the omission of the material from the notice.[16a] Where notice is to be given to a trade association, it may be given to an officer of that association.[17] If the notice is to be given to more than 20 undertakings who are members of a trade association, the OFT may give the notice to an officer of the trade association on their behalf.[18] If, particularly having regard to the number of undertakings concerned or the difficulty of identifying them, it is not reasonably practicable to serve a notice on each undertaking, a summary may instead be published on the OFT's website and a reference to it published in the London, Edinburgh and Belfast Gazettes and in at least one national newspaper.[19]

Documents relied on. The OFT may physically annex copies of any document relied on to the Rule 4 notice; but if many documents are relied on, it is likely simply to refer to the appropriate document on the file (to which the defendant will have access; see below).

3–067

Anonymous evidence. The OFT has stated that it may rely in a Rule 4 notice, and in any final decision, on evidence provided by complainants whose identities are not revealed to the defendant (steps being taken to anonymise any evidence emanating from them).[20] In deciding whether or not to rely on such evidence, the OFT takes the view that, even though proceedings resulting in a civil penalty under the Competition Act are to be regarded as criminal proceedings, at this stage in the procedure it is not bound to follow ECHR jurisprudence relating to the use of anonymous evidence in such proceedings, which requires that such evidence may only be

3–068

---

[15] OFT's Rules, Rule 5(2)(a).
[16] *Napp Pharmaceutical Holdings Ltd v DGFT (No.4)* [2002] Comp. A.R. 13 at para.138.
[16a] *Apex v Asphalt v OFT* [2005] CAT 4 at paras 92–110.
[17] OFT's Rules, Rule 17(1)
[18] *ibid.*, Rule 17(2).
[19] *ibid.*, Rule 18.
[20] *Lladró Comercial SA* [2003] U.K.C.L.R. 652, *e.g.* at para.2, n.2.

used where the rights of the defence can nonetheless be protected and where the interest being protected by the anonymity is legitimate.[21]

3–069 **Access to the file.** The OFT must give every addressee of the notice a reasonable opportunity to inspect the documents in its file that relate to the notice.[22] The OFT's practice is to prepare a list of such documents, marked according to whether, for reasons of confidentiality, they are to be wholly withheld or access given to them in redacted form.[23] Internal documents[24] need not be disclosed,[25] and will not be separately listed. It emerged during the *Replica Football Kit* appeals[26] that the OFT did not place documents relating to a failed leniency application by one of the parties—consisting of witness statements and correspondence relating to the application—on the file at all, and the documents concerned were not listed on the access to the file list made available to the other parties.

3–070 **Representations.** All addressees of the Rule 4 notice have the right to make representations to the OFT on the contents of the notice.[27] The notice will set a period within which written representations may be made; if none are made, then the OFT may proceed on the basis of the information before it.[28] The OFT must also give addressees a reasonable opportunity to make oral representations.[29] The OFT's practice is for hearings of oral representations to be chaired by a senior official not involved in the investigation. Hearings are in private, but in multi-party cases, the OFT has held joint hearings attended by all parties who wish to attend.[30] Parties may make their

---

[21] *ibid.*, paras.94–99.

[22] OFT's Rules, Rule 5(3). This right is equivalent to the fundamental right of access to the file in EC competition proceedings; Case T–30/91 *Solvay v Commission* [1995] E.C.R. II–1775; [1996] 5 C.M.L.R. 57, appeal dismissed Case C–288/95P [2000] E.C.R. I–2391; [2000] 5 C.M.L.R. 454. The availability of the file enables the undertaking to defend itself, notably by seeking exculpatory material; *Napp Pharmaceutical Holdings Ltd v DGFT (No.4)*, n.16, above, at para.138.

[23] Rule 5(3) provides that access need not be given to documents insofar as they are confidential. The OFT however has a discretion to disclose such documents; see para.3–060, above dealing with Pt 9 of the Enterprise Act.

[24] Defined in Rule 1(1) as documents produced by, or exchanged between, the OFT, a regulator or other public authority or produced by a person under a contract for services to such a body. *Quaere* whether this broad definition (which would appear to include, for example, a note taken by an OFT official of a conversation with a third party in which relevant, possibly exculpatory, information was passed to the OFT) is sustainable; it is strongly arguable that the right of defence must require access to such documents. It may be noted that the original draft of the OFT's Rules limited the exclusion for internal documents to documents on which the OFT could not rely as evidence and the disclosure of which could inhibit the free and frank exchange of views or prejudice the performance of the OFT's functions.

[25] Rule 5(3)(b). Again, the OFT has a discretion to disclose.

[26] *Umbro Holdings Ltd v OFT (Application for Leniency: Confidentiality)* [2003] CAT 26.

[27] s.31(1)(b).

[28] OFT's Rules, Rule 5(5).

[29] OFT's Rules, Rule 5(4).

[30] *Umbro Holdings Ltd v OFT*, n.26, above, [2004] U.K.C.L.R. 6.

representations through representatives or in person. The OFT may ask questions, but parties are not obliged to answer them.[31] A transcript will be made of the hearing. Once representations have been made, the OFT's general practice in multi-party cases has been to allow each party on request to see, and to make further representations upon the contents of, the other parties' representations, save to the extent that those representations are confidential.

Supplementary Rule 4 Notice. If as a result of representations made by other parties, further material coming to light, or further analysis by the OFT, the OFT wishes to make further adverse findings not previously covered in a Rule 4 Notice, it will need to issue a supplementary Rule 4 Notice. Such a notice gives rise to the same rights of access to the file and to make representations as did the original notice. **3–071**

(l) Final decision

Infringement decision. The OFT must give notice of any decision that one or more of the Chapter I or Chapter II prohibitions, or Art.81(1) or Art.82 EC, have been infringed to, as the case may be, the parties to the agreement or the person engaged in the conduct. The decision must state the facts on which it is based and the reasons for making the decision. The decision must be published.[32] There is a right of appeal to the CAT by the alleged infringer and by any other person with sufficient interest against any infringement decision.[33] **3–072**

Non-infringement decisions. Rule 7(2) of the OFT's Rules requires that notice of a decision that there are no grounds for action because there is no infringement of the Chapter I or Chapter II prohibitions, or Art.81(1) or Art. 82 EC (or, in the case of an agreement, that it is exempt under s.9 or Art.81(3) EC, or excluded from Chapter I) must be given to any person to whom the OFT has undertaken to give such notice and to any person in respect of which the OFT has exercised its powers of investigation. The decision must state the facts upon which it is based and the reasons for it. The decision may be, but does not have to be, published. Note that the fact that the OFT does not consider that a decision falls under Rule 7(2) does not necessarily mean that the decision is not appealable under s.47; but any decision that does fall under Rule 7(2) is likely to be regarded as an appealable decision.[34] **3–073**

---

[31] However, if a question is not answered, the OFT may (subject to the general limits on the exercise of that power) seek the information by a s.26 notice; see paras 3–016–3–019, above.

[32] OFT's Rules, Rule 7(1)(b).

[33] ss.46 and 47.

[34] See paras 3–042–3–045, above.

(m) Directions

3–074 Directions. Once the OFT has made a decision that: (i) an agreement is contrary to Art.81(1) EC or the Chapter I prohibition, and is not exempted or excluded; or (ii) conduct infringes Art.82 EC or Chapter II, it may give directions[35] to such persons as it considers appropriate.[36] Directions must be given in writing,[37] and the OFT must at the same time inform the person of the facts on which it bases the directions and its reasons for giving them.[38] Where the directions are given to an addressee of the infringement decision, the directions and the reasons for them are likely to be given as part of the infringement decision.[39]

3–075 Contents of directions. Directions may, in particular, require modification or termination of an infringing agreement or of the infringing conduct. But they may include any provision which the OFT considers appropriate to bring the infringement to an end,[40] and may include, for example, informing third parties that the infringement has been brought to an end or reporting to the OFT matters such as prices charged. The OFT has also referred to the possibility of imposing structural changes to the undertaking's business.[41] The CAT has applied the test of whether directions are "reasonably ancillary" or the "minimum necessary" to bringing the infringement to an end, and on that basis has upheld directions not to charge prices other than those set out in the directions without the [OFT's] consent, and not to enter into or engage in conduct to the same or equivalent effect.[42]

3–076 Appeal against directions. The alleged infringer may appeal against a decision imposing directions.[43] An appeal does not suspend the effect of the decision unless the CAT otherwise orders.[44]

3–077 Enforcement of directions. If the subject of directions fails without

---

[35] ss.32 and 33.
[36] Not necessarily the same as the parties to the infringement. The OFT may, for example, give directions to a parent company of the company responsible for the infringement; OFT 407a, para.2.2.
[37] ss.32(4) and 33(4).
[38] OFT's Rules, Rule.8(1).
[39] OFT Guideline, *Enforcement*, para.2.4; as the President of the CAT observed in *Napp Pharmaceutical Holdings Ltd v DGFT (No.1)* [2001] Comp. A.R. 1 at 34, complications arise in determining time for appeal if the directions become detached from the main decision.
[40] ss.32(1) and 33(1).
[41] OFT Guideline, *Enforcement*, para.2.3. *Cf.* Art.7(1) of Reg.1/2003, which gives the Commission power to impose "any behavioural or structural remedies which are proportionate to the infringement committed and necessary to bring the infringement to an end" but adds that "Structural remedies can only be imposed either where there is no equally effective behavioural remedy or where any equally effective behavioural remedy would be more burdensome for the undertaking concerned than the structural remedy". It is likely that similar conditions will be applied to any structural remedy imposed by OFT.
[42] *Napp Pharmaceutical Holdings Ltd v DGFT (No.4)* [2003] Comp. A.R. 13 at paras 553–554.
[43] s.46(3), tailpiece.
[44] s.46(4).

reasonable excuse to comply with them, the OFT may apply to the court[45] for an order requiring the default to be made good or, if the direction relates to the administration or management of an undertaking, requiring the undertaking or any of its officers to do it.[46] The court may order the defaulter, or any of its officers who is responsible, to pay the OFT's costs or expenses.[47] Failure to comply with such an order would amount to a contempt of court.

(n) Penalties

Power to impose a penalty. The OFT may require an undertaking which has infringed the Chapter II prohibition or Art.82 EC, or which is party to an agreement held to have infringed the Chapter I prohibition or Art.81(1) EC, to pay a penalty to the OFT.[48] The penalty is paid into the Consolidated Fund.[49] **3–078**

Procedure. Notice of a penalty must be given in writing (it will usually be given in the decision finding an infringement), and specify the date by which it is to be paid[50]; that date must be no earlier than the last date upon which the decision to impose the penalty may be appealed to the CAT.[51] The Rule 4 notice will not set out the amount of a penalty which the OFT intends to impose, although it will give an indication that it is intended to impose a penalty and discuss the seriousness of the infringement. **3–079**

Conditions. A penalty may be imposed only where the OFT is satisfied that the infringement has been committed intentionally or negligently.[52] The OFT does not need to decide which of the two mental states applies.[53] In order to establish intention, the OFT may consider internal documents of the undertaking, and regard deliberate concealment as strong evidence of intent.[54] In *Napp*,[55] the CAT gave the following guidance on the meaning of "intentionally": **3–080**

"As to the meaning of 'intentionally' in section 36(3), in our judgment an infringement is committed intentionally for the purposes of the Act if the

---

[45] *i.e.* the High Court in England and Wales and Northern Ireland and the Court of Session in Scotland.
[46] s.34(1).
[47] s.34(2).
[48] ss.36(1) and (2).
[49] s.36(9).
[50] s.36(6).
[51] s.36(7).
[52] s.36(3); *cf.* Art.23(2) of Reg.1/2003, which provides for the same requirement in respect of fines imposed by the Commission.
[53] *Napp Pharmaceutical Holdings Ltd v DGFT*, n.42, above at para.455.
[54] OFT Guideline, *Enforcement*, para.5.11.
[55] *Napp Pharmaceutical Holdings Ltd v DGFT*, n.42, above, at para.456.

undertaking must have been aware that its conduct was of such a nature as to encourage a restriction or distortion of competition: see *Musique Diffusion Français*, and *Parker Pen*, cited above. It is sufficient that the undertaking could not have been unaware that its conduct had the object or would have the effect of restricting competition, without it being necessary to show that the undertaking also knew that it was infringing the Chapter I or Chapter II prohibition: see *BPB Industries and British Gypsum*, cited above, at paragraph 165 of the judgment, and Case T–29/92 *SPO and Others v Commission* [1995] ECR II–289, at paragraph 356.[56] While in some cases the undertaking's intention will be confirmed by internal documents, in our judgment, and in the absence of any evidence to the contrary, the fact that certain consequences are plainly foreseeable is an element from which the requisite intention may be inferred. If, therefore, a dominant undertaking pursues a certain policy which in fact has, or would foreseeably have, an anti-competitive effect, it may be legitimate to infer that it is acting 'intentionally' for the purposes of section 36(3).''

The CAT also stated, in relation to "negligently" that: "In our judgment an infringement is committed negligently for the purposes of section 36(3) if the undertaking ought to have known that its conduct would result in a restriction or distortion of competition".[57] The OFT has said that an undertaking acting under pressure may nonetheless be acting intentionally or negligently—but its penalty may be reduced to reflect its unwillingness.[58]

3–081 **Limited immunity.** Section 39 of the Competition Act confers a limited immunity from penalty in respect of Chapter I infringements on parties to a "small agreement". The immunity does not apply if the agreement is a price-fixing agreement, *i.e.* an agreement by which one or more of the parties restrict their freedom determine the prices to be charged to a non-party.[59] A "small agreement" is one which falls within regulation 3 of the Competition Act 1998 (Small Agreements and Conduct of Minor Significance) Regulations 2000,[60] *i.e.* all agreements between undertakings the combined applicable turnover[61] of which for the business year ending in the calendar year preceding one during which the infringement occurred does not exceed £20 million. Section 40 confers a similar limited immunity from the Chapter II prohibition in respect of "conduct of minor significance", that is to say conduct falling within regulation 4 of those Regulations, namely conduct by

---

[56] In other words, as the OFT puts it in OFT 407a, para.5.10, the intention or negligence relates to the facts, not the law; ignorance that the conduct was illegal is no bar to finding an infringement.

[57] *Napp Pharmaceutical Holdings Ltd v DGFT*, n.42, above, para.457.

[58] OFT Guideline, *Enforcement*, para.5.13.

[59] s.39(1)(b) and (9).

[60] SI 2000/262.

[61] As determined in accordance with the Schedule to the Regulations.

an undertaking the applicable turnover[62] of which for the business year ending in the calendar year preceding one during which the infringement occurred does not exceed £50 million. Either immunity may be withdrawn, with prospective effect only, by the OFT if it considers, after investigation, that the agreement or conduct is likely to infringe Chapter I or II[63]; the OFT must have regard in setting a date for withdrawal to the amount of time the undertaking will need to secure compliance.[64] The OFT may not, in addition, impose a penalty if it is satisfied that the undertaking in question acted on the reasonable assumption that the immunity applied.[65] The immunity does not extend to Art.81(1) or 82 EC, although of course in those cases the agreement or conduct must be shown to have an effect on trade between Member States.

Exceptional cases where no penalty imposed. In *Lladró Comercial*[66] the OFT decided not to impose any penalty where the Commission had previously given the undertaking a comfort latter which the OFT accepted could be read as containing a favourable substantive competition assessment of the terms at issue and which could reasonably have led the undertaking to assume that the terms were not of a type that could infringe Chapter I. In *Northern Ireland Livestock and Auctioneers' Association*,[67] no penalty was imposed because the recommendations at issue were publicised and the circumstances (the severe effect of BSE and foot and mouth disease on the Northern Ireland cattle industry) were wholly exceptional. **3–082**

Statutory maximum. A penalty may not exceed 10 per cent of an undertaking's turnover.[68] For these purposes, turnover is calculated in accordance with the Competition Act (Determination of Turnover for Penalties) Order 2000.[69] The applicable turnover is that for the business year ending within the year leading up to the OFT's decision (or, if unavailable, for the year before that).[70] "Applicable turnover" is, for most undertakings,[71] defined as amounts derived by the undertaking from the sale of products and the provision of services falling within the undertaking's ordinary activities after deduction of sales rebates, value added tax and other taxes directly related to turnover,[72] and calculated in accordance with generally accepted accounting principles and practices.[73] **3–083**

---

[62] As determined in accordance with the Schedule to the Regulations.
[63] ss.39(4) and 40(4). The OFT must give each of the parties concerned written notice of its decision, which is not appealable to the Tribunal under ss.46 and 47.
[64] ss.39(8) and 40(8).
[65] s.36(4) and (5).
[66] [2003] U.K.C.L.R. 652 at paras 124–125.
[67] [2003] U.K.C.L.R. 433 at paras 72–73.
[68] s.36(8).
[69] SI 2000/309, as amended by SI 2004/1259.
[70] *ibid.*, art.3.
[71] *ibid.*, Schedule, makes special provision for credit institutions, financial institutions, insurance undertakings, and associations of undertakings.
[72] *ibid.*, Schedule, para.3.
[73] *ibid.*, para.2.

3–084   **The OFT's Guidance.**   The statutory maximum operates as a cap on the amount of penalty that may be imposed. As to how the penalty will be set below that cap, the OFT is required to publish guidance, approved by the Secretary of State, as to the approach it will take. It is required to take account of that guidance in setting any penalties imposed.[74] This guidance does not bind the CAT, which is not even obliged to have regard to it,[75] and has adopted a "broad brush" approach to assessing penalty.[76] Nonetheless, the CAT has stated that "it does not seem to us appropriate to disregard the [OFT's] guidance ... when reaching our view as to what the penalty should be".[77]

3–085   **The OFT's approach.**   The OFT's policy objectives are to impose penalties which reflect the seriousness of the infringement, and to ensure that the threat of penalties deters other undertakings from engaging in anti-competitive practices.[78] It also aims, through its leniency programme, to encourage undertakings to come forward with information about cartels in which they have been involved.[79] The OFT's Guidance[80] adopts a five-step approach.

3–086   **Step 1: starting point: seriousness.**   The OFT starts by fixing a starting point, determined by reference to the seriousness of the infringement and the "relevant turnover" of the undertaking. As to seriousness, the OFT regards price-fixing[81] (whether resale price maintenance or horizontal price fixing), market sharing and other cartel activities, and conduct by a dominant undertaking such as predatory pricing[82] which has a particularly serious effect on competition, as among the most serious infringements. The OFT will consider in that regard factors such as the nature of the product, the structure of the market, market shares, entry conditions, the effect of the

---

[74] s.38. The current guidance is the OFT's Guidance as to the Appropriate Amount of a Penalty, December 2004, OFT423.

[75] *Napp Pharmaceutical Holdings Ltd v DGFT*, n.42, above, at para.497. The tribunal also observed, at para.499, that the undertaking concerned was entitled under Art.6 of the ECHR to have its penalty reviewed *ab initio* by an independent tribunal unconstrained by the guidance, and that in any event the tribunal would fix a penalty with regard to the case as it stood at the end of the appeal.

[76] *ibid.*, para.535. The approach produced a similar result to that produced by applying the OFT's Guidance to the facts as found by the tribunal; para.539.

[77] *ibid.*, para.500.

[78] OFT 423, para.1.5.

[79] *ibid.*, para.1.5; see paras 3–098–3–106, below.

[80] n.74, above.

[81] In *Arriva/First Bus*, [2002] U.K.C.L.R. 322 at para.60, the OFT set the starting point at 10% (market sharing by allocating bus routes). In *John D Bruce and Others* [2002] U.K.C.L.R. 435 at para.97, the OFT stated that RPM would usually attract a 10% starting point, but in very special circumstances involving a small new entrant, the starting point as afar as the manufacturer was concerned would be 5% (8% for the distributors).

[82] Identified by the tribunal as a serious infringement in *Napp Pharmaceutical Holdings Ltd v DGFT*, n.42, above at para.519. In *Aberdeen Journals Ltd v OFT (No.2)* [2002] U.K.C.L.R. 740 at para.128, the OFT set a starting point of 10% of relevant turnover on the basis that the predation there was aimed at eliminating the undertaking's only competitor and would have created a monopoly; the tribunal ([2003] CAT 11) agreed that a substantial penalty was warranted but regarded the OFT's approach as being on the high side given that the infringement lasted only one month (paras 497–498).

conduct on competitors, third parties and—in particular—direct or indirect damage caused to consumers.[83] The starting point will then be determined by applying a percentage of up to 10 per cent to the undertaking's "relevant turnover"; if the agreement did not cover all products in that market, the OFT may reduce the percentage accordingly.[84]

Starting point: relevant turnover. The OFT takes as an undertaking's "relevant turnover" the turnover of that undertaking in the relevant product and geographic market in the undertaking's last business year, assessed in the way set out in the OFT's guideline on market definition.[85]   **3–087**

Step 2: duration. Penalties for infringements lasting more than one year[86] may be multiplied by not more than the number of years of the infringement.[87] Part years may be treated as full years for this purpose,[88] but in *Replica Football Kit*[89] the OFT decided to round up duration in the second year of the infringement to the nearest quarter, rather than the nearest whole year, in order to encourage undertakings to terminate agreements as soon as possible, and in *Argos v OFT (No.2)*[90] an agreement lasting 14½ months was dealt with by a multiplier of 1.2 rather than 2.   **3–088**

Step 3: adjustment for other factors: deterrence. The OFT may then apply a further substantial adjustment in order to secure the objective of deterring other undertakings which might be considering anti-competitive activities.   **3–089**

The OFT will at this stage take into account the OFT's objective estimate of any economic or financial benefit obtained from the infringement,[91] matters such as size and profitability of the undertaking, and gains that

---

[83] OFT 423, paras 2.4–2.5. In *Replica Football Kit* [2004] U.K.C.L.R. 6, the OFT regarded it as a relevant factor that the products were mass-market and that the agreements operated at peak selling times, and that the prices agreed allowed what the OFT regarded as significant mark-ups (para.576).

[84] *ibid.*, at (*e.g.*) para.581. In *Hasbro* [2003] U.K.C.L.R. 150 at para.76, the starting point was set at between 5 and 8% to reflect the less than 5% share of sales affected.

[85] OFT 423a, para.2.7; the market definition guideline is OFT 403. In the appeals in the *Replica Football Kit* case (forthcoming) a number of parties have argued before the tribunal that the OFT's approach to "relevant product market" in that case failed to apply this standard approach to market definition.

[86] The OFT states that the starting point may be *reduced* "in exceptional circumstances" where infringements last less than a year; OFT 423, para.2.10. See the Tribunal's observations in *Aberdeen Journals*, n.82, above.

[87] OFT 423, para.2.10.

[88] *ibid.*. No adjustment for duration beyond 1 year for an 18 month infringement was made in *John D Bruce and Others*, n.73, above, para.99.

[89] n.83, above, para.584

[90] Unreported, December 2, 2003, para.388; the extra 2 ½ months did not include the busy Christmas period.

[91] In *Napp Pharmaceutical Holdings Ltd v DGFT*, n.42, above, at paras.511 *et seq.*, the tribunal expressed considerable scepticism as to the appropriateness of trying to engage in the arithmetical calculation of a "gain" save in the clearest cases. It observed that such calculations: involved assumptions that were difficult to verify; and inevitably failed to deal with unquantifiable factors such as the deterrent effect of predatory pricing on entry to the market.

might accrue to the undertaking from the infringement in other markets.[92] The OFT's recent approach has been to apply a multiplier at this stage; in *Replica Football Kit*, multipliers of 2 and 3 were applied (the lower figure applying to an undertaking where the penalty already represented a significant part of its overall turnover, given that it derived a larger part of its business from the products in question than did other undertakings involved).[93] In *Aberdeen Journals*, the multiplier was 4.[94] The OFT may decide not to make any adjustment for deterrence to an undertaking found by it to have played a whistleblower role,[95] or where the penalty is already adequate to achieve deterrence.[96] The OFT may also take into account at this stage earlier assurances given by players in the industry not to engage in similar conduct.[97]

3–090 **Step 4: adjustment for other factors: aggravating factors.** Aggravating factors may include[98]: the role of the undertaking as leading in or instigating the infringement[99]; involvement of directors or other senior management[1]; retaliatory or other coercive measures against other undertakings to ensure continuation of the infringement; continuing the infringement after the start of the investigation[2]; repeated infringements by the undertaking or members of its group; and infringements committed intentionally rather than negligently.[3]

---

[92] OFT 423, para.2.11; see the OFT decision in *Aberdeen Journals Ltd v OFT*, n.82, above, para.130 (reputation for aggressive reaction to entry assisted the undertaking's group in other markets).

[93] n.84, above, para.587. Conversely, in *John D Bruce and Others*, n.73, above, para.121, a multiplier of 3 was applied to the one undertaking forming part of a large group to ensure that the penalty acted as a deterrent.

[94] The tribunal described this as being at the top end of the scale; [2003] CAT 11 at para.497.

[95] *ibid.*, para.752.

[96] *John D Bruce and Others*, n.73, above, para.100; *Argos/Littlewoods (No.2)*, n.82, above, paras 418 and 429

[97] *ibid.*, para.586; the point was also made in relation to certain parties who had not given the assurances in question.

[98] OFT 423, para.2.14.

[99] *Replica Football Kit*, n.83, above, paras 589, 614, 673, 713 (10% increase for pressurising supplier to stop discounting; 10% for putting pressure on retailer to stop discounting; 15% for organising a cartel meeting).

[1] Increases of 20% were made on this basis in *Replica Football Kit*, n.83, above, (involvement of chairman, CEOs and other senior directors); in *Arriva/First Bus*, n.81, above, para.65, a 10% increase was imposed as a result of the involvement of senior executives, including divisional directors; a similar increase in respect of senior management (below board level) was made in *Hasbro*, n.84, above, para.90.

[2] However, in *Napp Pharmaceutical Holdings Ltd v DGFT*, n.42, above, the tribunal observed at para.514 that the continuance of an infringement will properly be reflected in the penalty as a result of the adjustment for duration. Any additional adjustment should be confined to cases where an undertaking had been clearly warned that it was engaging in a plain and obvious infringement, which it blatantly ignored.

[3] *ibid.*, para.455.

Step 4: adjustment for other factors: mitigating factors. Mitigating factors   3–091
may include[4]: the fact that the undertaking is acting under severe duress or
pressure[5]; genuine uncertainty as to whether the agreement or conduct was
an infringement; maintenance of an adequate compliance system[6]; termination of the infringement as soon as the OFT intervened[7]; co-operation
which enabled speedier or more effective completion of the investigation.[8]

Step 5: adjustment to prevent statutory maximum being exceeded and to avoid   3–092
double jeopardy. The OFT will then adjust the penalty, if necessary, to
ensure that the statutory maximum is not exceeded.[9]

Cartel offence. The OFT regards the fact that individuals have been pro-   3–093
secuted for, or convicted of, the cartel offence as irrelevant to the calculation
of a penalty.[10]

Parallel application of UK and EC competition law. When assessing the   3–094
amount of a penalty for infringement of Art.81 or 82 EC, the OFT will take
into account fines already imposed under the Competition Act.[11] It will also,
with the permission of the national competition authority of the other
Member State concerned, take into account, in determining relevant turnover, turnover obtained in that Member State.[12–13] Conversely, the OFT
(and the CAT and, on appeal, the Court of Appeal or House of Lords) must
take into account in determining the amount of a penalty any fines or
penalties imposed in respect of the agreement or conduct in question by the
Commission or any court or body in another Member State.[14]

Tax position. The Inland Revenue takes the view that penalties under the   3–095

---

[4] OFT 423, para.2.15
[5] This does not include internal pressure on staff to achieve targets, or difficult market conditions; *Arriva/First Bus*, n.81, above, para.66.
[6] Reduction of 10% in *Arriva/First Bus*, n.81, above, para.66 ("genuine compliance systems
genuinely followed and adhered to"). Failure to comply with a compliance system has
sometimes been regarded as an aggravating factor: *John D Bruce and Others*, n.73, above,
para.123 (10% increase), and *Replica Football Kit*, n.281, above, para.715 (10% increase on
penalty imposed on Manchester United); but sometimes not (*Hasbro*, n.84, above, para.92—
although a reduction of 10% was granted to recognise subsequent training activity).
[7] Examples include: reduction of 20% in *Aberdeen Journals Ltd v OFT*, n.82, above, para.132;
20% in *John D Bruce and Others*, n.73, above, para.104; 10% in *Hasbro*, n.84, above, para.94
(in spite of a delay of nearly 2 months).
[8] Examples include: reduction of 10% in *Aberdeen Journals Ltd v OFT*, n.82, above, para.132;
John D Bruce and Others, n.73, above, paras 102–103 (10% each for co-operation and not
disputing the facts). No further discount will be given where undertakings benefit from the
OFT's leniency programme; *Arriva/First Bus*, n.81, above, para.66; *Hasbro*, n.84, above,
para.93.
[9] OFT 423, para.2.17.
[10] OFT 423, para.1.14.
[11] OFT 423, para.1.15.
[12–13] *ibid.*, para.2.6.
[14] s.38(9).

Competition Act are not deductible in computing trading profits under s.74(1)(e) of the Income and Corporation Taxes Act 1988.[15]

3–096 **Appeal.** Any person on whom a penalty has been imposed may appeal to the CAT under s.46(2)(i) against the decision to impose it or its amount. Third parties have no right of appeal under s.47 against a decision to impose, or not to impose, a penalty. The CAT has unlimited jurisdiction to quash the penalty or to impose a different penalty. An appeal will suspend the imposition of a penalty,[16] although if the CAT upholds all or part of the penalty, interest will be payable.[17]

3–097 **Enforcement of a penalty decision.** Once the period for payment of the penalty has expired, or any appeal has been determined, the OFT may recover it as a civil debt.[18]

(o) Leniency in cartel cases

3–098 **Policy.** The risk of large penalties could dissuade undertakings involved in seriously anti-competitive cartels from informing the OFT of their activities. Because of the secret nature of cartel activity, which may otherwise be difficult or impossible to detect, encouraging whistle blowing outweighs the usual interest in imposing large penalties to deter participation in such activity.[19] The OFT therefore operates a policy of granting immunity from, or a substantial discount from, penalties to undertakings who come forward with information about cartel activity in which they have been involved.

3–099 **Scope.** The policy extends only to "cartel activities", *i.e.* agreements which infringe Art 81 EC or the Chapter I prohibition and involve price-fixing (including resale price maintenance), bid-rigging, output restrictions, market sharing and market dividing.[20]

3–100 **The cartel offence.** The leniency policy may well overlap, in cases where individuals have committed the cartel offence, with the OFT's policy on no-action letters.[21]

3–101 **Multi-jurisdictional cases.** An application for leniency to the OFT is not to be counted as an application to any other authority which may deal with the

---

[15] OFT Guideline, *Enforcement*, para.5.15.
[16] s.46(4).
[17] see para.4–145, below.
[18] s.37.
[19] OFT 423, paras 3.1–3.2.
[20] *ibid.*, n.8 to para.1.5. For other types of infringement, co-operation with the OFT will be regarded as a mitigating factor; para.3–091, above.
[21] See paras 5–049–5–051, below. It may well be necessary for those acting for the undertakings and for the individuals involved to co-ordinate a joint approach to the OFT.

case, such as the Commission or the competition authority of another Member State. Undertakings involved in infringements which cover the territory of a number of Member States should therefore consider a simultaneous application to the relevant authorities.[22]

Case 1: undertaking is the first to come forward before the OFT begins an investigation.   There are three cases where the leniency programme may apply. The first is where an undertaking is the first to come forward with evidence of the existence and activities of a cartel before the OFT has begun an investigation. In such a case, provided that all the following conditions are fulfilled, the undertaking will be granted total immunity from a penalty.[23] The conditions are:

    3–102

(a) The OFT must not already have sufficient evidence to establish the existence of the cartel;

(b) The undertaking must provide the OFT with all the information, documents and evidence available to it regarding the cartel activity;

(c) The undertaking must maintain continual and complete cooperation with the OFT throughout the investigation and until the conclusion of any action arising as a result;

(d) The undertaking must not have taken steps to coerce another undertaking into taking part in the activity; and

(e) It must not continue to participate in the cartel, except as the OFT may direct.[24]

Case 2: undertaking is the first to come forward, but does so after the OFT begins an investigation.   In this case, the OFT has a discretion as to whether to grant total immunity. In order to fall within case 2, the undertaking must be the first to come forward with evidence of the existence and activities of a cartel, and it must also do so before service of a Rule 4 notice. In addition, it must comply with conditions (b) to (e) above.[25] In exercising its discretion as to whether or not to grant total immunity, the OFT will consider the stage at

    3–103

---

[22] OFT 423, para.3.7

[23] *ibid.*, para.3.9.

[24] The OFT might, for example, be concerned that a sudden and unexplained withdrawal might lead the other participants to start destroying evidence. It might also wish to employ staff of the whistleblower as covert human intelligence sources; see para.3–015, above.

[25] OFT 423, para.3.11.

which the undertaking comes forward, the evidence the OFT had in its possession at that time, and the evidence provided by the undertaking.[26]

3–104 **Case 3: undertakings which are not the first to come forward, or do not meet the other conditions.** Discounts of up to 50 per cent will be given to undertakings that are not the first to come forward or who fail to meet one of the other conditions, but which comply with conditions (b), (c) and (e) in para.3–102, above.[27] In deciding what, if any, discount to give, the OFT will consider the stage at which the undertaking comes forward, the evidence the OFT had in its possession at that time, and the evidence provided by the undertaking.[28]

3–105 **Co-operation in more than one cartel investigation.** If an undertaking obtains total immunity under either case 1 or case 2, and is involved in another cartel investigation, its co-operation will lead to a reduction in any penalties imposed in that other investigation.[29]

3–106 **Confidentiality.** The OFT will endeavour to keep the identity of undertakings that have applied for leniency confidential throughout the proceedings.[30] In *Argos v OFT (No.2)*, it refused on those grounds to disclose information relating to Hasbro's leniency application to the other defendants.[31] In *Replica Football Kit*, the fact of Umbro's failed leniency application, and documents and correspondence relating to it, were not disclosed at any time during the investigation and not revealed even in the version of the decision made available to the public or the other parties. The CAT however ruled that disclosure of that fact and those documents should be given, observing that the (conditional) promise by the OFT and Umbro's interest in confidential was outweighed by the other parties' rights of defence

---

[26] *ibid.*, para.3.12. In *Argos v OFT (No.2)*, n.82, above, para.11, it is recorded that Hasbro received total immunity in relation to agreements with retailers after an application made some 6 months after an investigation started into its agreements with distributors, some 4 months after the s.28 investigation into its distributor agreements, and after (in the course of that investigation) information was sought in respect of its dealings with retailers. Hasbro facilitated the OFT's obtaining of witness statements from staff concerned. In *Arriva/First Bus*, n.81, above, First Bus was granted leniency under case 2.

[27] OFT 423, para.3.13. In *Arriva/First Bus*, n.81, above, Arriva was granted leniency (36% discount) under case 3.

[28] OFT 423, paras 3.14–3.15.

[29] OFT 423, para.3.17.

[30] OFT 423, para.3.18.

[31] n.90, above, para.317; the OFT observed that

> "The desirability for confidentiality does not solely concern the identity of the party which has applied for leniency, but also the OFT's reasons for granting or refusing leniency. This is in the form of a private agreement between the OFT and the applicant and as part of the duty of full co-operation that is involved, the applicant is expected to enter into a dialogue with the OFT that in other circumstances it would be likely to regard as contrary to its commercial best interests and which could in many cases lead to reprisals against it or its employees from the other parties involved. In this case Hasbro was given assurances that any representations it made would be regarded by OFT as confidential."

(the material included, *inter alia*, previous undisclosed and to some extent inconsistent witness statements by witnesses on whose evidence the OFT sought to rely) and the difficulty of dealing with Umbro's appeal (which concerned the discounts it was given on the basis of its cooperation with the OFT) in any open way without disclosure of those matters.[32]

3. COMPETITION DISQUALIFICATION ORDERS

Nature of a competition disqualification order (CDO). A CDO, made by the High Court[33] under s.9A(1)–(3) of the Company Directors Disqualification Act 1986 as amended by the Enterprise Act 2002, disqualifies the individual to whom it applies from acting as a director of a company for a period of time not exceeding 15 years.[34] While a CDO applies to a person, it is an offence for him, without leave of the court, to be a director of a company, to act as a receiver of company property, to be in any way concerned in the promotion, formation or management of a company, or to act as an insolvency practitioner.[35] Any person involved in the management of a company in breach of a CDO is personally liable for the debts of the company.[36]   **3–107**

Conditions. The court must make a CDO where it is satisfied, first, that the company of which the person concerned is a director has infringed the Chapter I or II prohibitions or Art.81 or 82 EC. It should be noted that a director of a parent company of the infringing undertaking may be considered to be a *de facto* or shadow director of the undertaking. The court must, secondly, be satisfied that that person's conduct as a director makes him unfit to be a director of a company.[37]   **3–108**

Unfit to be a director. In considering the second question, the court must have regard to whether: **3–109**

(1) the person's conduct contributed to the breach of competition law (in which case it is irrelevant that he did not know that the undertaking's conduct constituted the breach)[38];

---

[32] *Umbro Holdings v OFT* (Application for Leniency: Confidentiality) [2003] CAT 26; [2004] Comp. A.R. 217.
[33] Or, in Scotland, the Court of Session; s.9E(3).
[34] s.9A(9).
[35] ss.1(1)(a) and 13 of the 1986 Act.
[36] s.15(1)(a).
[37] s.9A(1)–(4).
[38] s.9A(7).

(2) if the person's conduct did not so contribute, whether he had reasonable grounds to suspect that the undertaking's conduct constituted the breach and he took no steps to prevent it; and

(3) the person did not know but ought to have known that the undertaking's conduct constituted the breach.[39]

The court also may have regard to the person's conduct as a director in connexion with any other breach of competition law.[40]

3–110 **Procedure.** A CDO is made by the court on application by the OFT or a regulator.[41] The OFT may exercise the powers it has under ss.26 to 30 of the Competition Act in investigating whether it should make such an application.[42] Before it makes an application, the OFT must give notice to the person concerned and give him an opportunity to make representations.[43] The notice will, *inter alia*, set out the grounds for the proposed application and the evidence relied on, and set a date for the receipt of representations.[44]

3–111 **OFT policy.** The OFT's guidance on CDOs sets out the factors the OFT (or a regulator) will consider before applying for a CDO. First, the OFT will apply for a CDO only where an infringement by the undertaking has been established by decisions of the OFT, a regulator or the Commission, which have not been appealed or where any appeal has been concluded.[45] Nor will it apply for a CDO in respect of conduct before s.9A of the 1986 Act came into force (June 20, 2003). Secondly, the OFT will not apply for a CDO where no financial penalty has been imposed (or where the penalty has been quashed on appeal).[46] Thirdly, the OFT will not apply for a CDO where leniency has been granted to the undertaking under the leniency programme, unless the director was removed as a director for involvement in the infringement or for opposing the application for leniency.[47] Fourthly, the OFT will consider the director's responsibility for the infringement.[48] The OFT is likely to apply for an order where the director has been directly

---

[39] s.9A(5)(a) and (6).
[40] s.9A(5)(b). The court must not, under s.9A, have regard to various other matters set out in Sch.1 to the 1986 Act.
[41] s.9A(10); see para.3–006, above for a list of regulators.
[42] s.9C(2). For the OFT's powers under ss.26–30 of the Competition Act, see paras 3–016–3–028, above.
[43] s.9C(4).
[44] OFT guidance on CDOs, para.5.2.
[45] CDO guidance, paras 4.7–4.9.
[46] *ibid.*, para.4.10.
[47] *ibid.*, paras 4.11–4.14.
[48] *ibid.*, paras 4.16.

involved in the infringement,[49] quite likely to do so where the director improperly failed to take corrective action,[50] and does not rule out doing so where the director failed to keep himself properly informed of the activities which amounted to the breach.[51] Finally, the OFT will consider aggravating[52] and mitigating[53] factors.

Cartel offence. Where a director is convicted of the cartel offence, the convicting court has power to impose a CDO.[54] In such case, the OFT would use that route rather than s.9A.[55] The OFT will not apply for a CDO against the recipient of a no-action letter.[56]

3–112

Competition disqualification undertakings. Under s.9B, the OFT may accept a competition disqualification undertaking ("CDU") instead of applying for, or continuing an application for a CDO. A CDU is in the same terms as, and has the same legal effect as a CDO. The OFT will expect the period of the CDU to be proportionate to the seriousness of the conduct.[57]

3–113

---

[49] Examples given by the OFT are: taking steps to carry out the infringement, planning, approving or encouraging the infringing activity, ordering or pressuring those who engaged in the activity to do so, or to attend meetings to participate in or discuss the activity; attending meetings at which the infringing activity was discussed; and ordering or advocating retaliation against undertakings who were reluctant to participate in the infringement; *ibid.*, para.4.17.

[50] Examples given by the OFT are: approving the expenditure of funds used to finance infringing activity, knowing or having reasonable grounds to suspect that they would be used for such activity; failing to take reasonable steps to halt the activity when knowing or having reasonable grounds to suspect that persons were engaged in such activity; *ibid.*, para.4.20.

[51] The OFT will look at the director's role in the company, his relationship to those responsible for the breach, the knowledge and skill possessed by the director, and that which could have been expected of such a director, and the information available to the director. The OFT does not expect directors to have any expertise in competition law, but does expect them to appreciate that compliance with competition law is a crucial matter and that price-fixing, market sharing and bid-rigging agreements contravene competition law; CDO guidance, para.4.21.

[52] Including matters such as: past involvement in competition law infringements; involvement in destruction of documents to conceal the breach; obstruction of an OFT or Commission investigation; ordering or encouraging continued participation in the breach once the investigation has started; *ibid.*, para.4.23.

[53] Including matters such as: the fact that the undertaking was coerced by another undertaking; uncertainty as to whether the activity was a breach; taking prompt remedial action when the breach was drawn to his attention; taking disciplinary action against those responsible; the fact that the director was under strong internal pressure to be involved in, or to permit, the breach; *ibid.*, para.4.24.

[54] s.2 of the 1986 Act.

[55] OFT guidance on CDOs, para.4.26.

[56] *ibid.*, para.4.27.

[57] *ibid.*, para.3.4.

CHAPTER 4

PRACTICE AND PROCEDURE BEFORE THE
COMPETITION APPEAL TRIBUNAL

Ben Rayment[1]

1. INTRODUCTION

4–001 **Overview.** This chapter explains the procedural law and practice of the CAT in proceedings brought under the Competition Act 1998 ("the Competition Act") and the Enterprise Act 2002 ("the Enterprise Act").[2]

This chapter broadly follows the structure of the CAT's Rules. Section 1 provides a general introduction covering the composition of the CAT and the powers of the Registrar, the different types of proceedings which may be entertained by the Tribunal, the general philosophy behind the rules and the various sources on which the Tribunal may draw in determining procedural issues. Section 2 deals with the rules governing the commencement of appeal proceedings. Section 3 covers the response to appeal proceedings. Section 4 covers the questions of intervention, consolidation and forum. Section 5 covers the CAT's extensive case management powers. Section 6 deals with the way in which the CAT's procedures are modified in relation to the CAT's jurisdiction under the Enterprise Act, principally in relation to the review of decisions arising in connection with the control of mergers or market investigations. Section 7 outlines the CAT Rules applicable to claims for damages and other monetary claims. Section 8 covers practice and procedure in relation to hearings before the CAT. Section 9 addresses the CAT's approach to issues of confidentiality and disclosure. Section 10 deals with the rules relating to the decision of the CAT. Section 11 covers the CAT's rules on costs. Section 12 covers the question of a further appeal against a decision of the CAT. Section 13 deals with the making of

---

[1] Barrister, Monckton Chambers (former Legal Secretary to the Competition Appeal Tribunal).

[2] Proceedings under the Communications Act 2003 are beyond the scope of this chapter although in most respects the general procedural law and practice described will also apply to such proceedings.

references to the ECJ. Section 14 deals with the CAT's powers to make interim orders and measures. Section 15 outlines the manner in which the CAT's orders may be enforced.

The CAT.   The CAT is a specialist tribunal established under the Enter-   **4–002**
prise Act.[3] The CAT is a hybrid institution combining aspects of the traditional litigation model of English and American courts, with their emphasis on adversarial proceedings, oral evidence and extensive disclosure of documents with a more inquisitorial model placing greater emphasis on written procedure and not relying simply on the parties. The Court of First Instance of the European Communities has been an important influence on the CAT's design. Unusually for a statutory tribunal, the CAT exercises both an appellate public law jurisdiction as well as an original private law jurisdiction.[4] The CAT's jurisdiction extends throughout the UK.

Constitution of the CAT.   The CAT is presided over by its President.[5] For   **4–003**
the purposes of proceedings before it the CAT is constituted in panels of three. The panel must consist of a chairman and two other members.[6] The Chairman must be the President or a member of the panel of chairmen.[7] The other "ordinary" members may be chosen from either the panel of chairmen or the panel of members.[8] The "ordinary" members of the CAT combine relevant expertise in areas such as economics, finance, law, business and accountancy.[9]

The CAT Rules.   Proceedings before the CAT are governed by the Com-   **4–004**
petition Appeal Tribunal Rules ("the CAT Rules"), which came into force on June 20, 2003.[10] Appeals lodged prior to June 20, 2003, continue to be governed by the rules of the Competition Commission Appeal Tribunal Rules ("the 2000 Rules").[11] Cases decided under the 2000 rules continue to be relevant to the interpretation of the CAT Rules as in many cases there is little or no material difference between their provisions.

The CAT's Rules govern the following types of proceedings:

---

[3] ss.12, 14 and 15 and Schs 2 and 4. Section 14 of the Enterprise Act was brought into force on April 1, 2003: see SI 2003/766, art.2. The tribunal replaces the Competition Commission Appeal Tribunals ("CCAT") established under s.47(5) and Pt III of Sch.7 to the Competition Act 1998.

[4] For private actions for damages.

[5] s.12(2)(a).

[6] s.14(1).

[7] s.14(2).

[8] s.14(3).

[9] The President must arrange such training for members of the CAT as he considers appropriate: s.12 and sch.2, para.8 to the Enterprise Act 2002.

[10] SI 2003/1372, as amended by the Competition Appeal Tribunal (Amendment and Communications Act Appeals) Rules SI 2004/2068 made pursuant to s.15, and Part II of Sch.4 to the Enterprise Act 2002.

[11] See SI 2000/261, made under s.48 of the Competition Act (repealed); Rule 69 of the CAT's Rules.

- Appeals against certain decisions made under the Competition Act of the Office of Fair Trading ("the OFT"), the Civil Aviation Authority, the Office of Communications ("OFCOM"), the Director General of Electricity Supply and Director General of Gas for Northern Ireland, the Gas and Electricity Markets Authority, the Director General of Water Services, and the Office of Rail Regulation.[12] Appeals under the Competition Act may be made in respect of the following decisions:

  (a) as to whether the prohibitions in Chapter I or Chapter II of the Competition Act and Arts 81 or 82 of the EC Treaty, have been infringed[13];
  (b) as to the imposition or amount of any penalty[14];
  (c) whether to make a direction in relation to agreements or conduct[15];
  (d) whether or not to grant interim measures pending the outcome of an OFT investigation[16];
  (e) to cancel a block or parallel exemption[17];
  (f) to withdraw the benefit of an EC block exemption in the UK[18];
  (g) whether or not to accept the release or variation of commitments[19];
  (h) whether or not to grant interim relief pending the outcome of an investigation.[20]

- Appeals against the decisions of the OFT under the EC Competition Law (Arts 84 and 85) Enforcement Regulations 2001 (as amended) in respect of air transport services and international maritime tramp vessel services.[21]

- Applications for review, as the case may be, in respect of decisions under Parts 3 and 4 of the Enterprise Act of the OFT, Competition Commission and Secretary of State in connection with a reference or possible reference in relation to a relevant or special merger situation or market investigation.

- Appeals under the Enterprise Act against a penalty imposed by the Competition Commission for failure to comply with a notice issued by

---

[12] Established on July 5, 2004 by the Railways and Transport Safety Act 2003 (replacing the Office of the Rail Regulator).
[13] s.46(3)(a) to (d). "Whether" means "whether or not": see *Bettercare Group Ltd v DGFT (Preliminary Hearing: Jurisdiction)* [2001] CAT 6; [2002] Comp. A.R. 9.
[14] s.46(3)(i).
[15] s.46(3).
[16] s.46(3).
[17] s.46(3)(e).
[18] Under Art.29(2) of Regulation 1/2003: s.46(3)(f).
[19] ss.46(3)(g) and (h). Such decisions are challengeable only on the grounds of judicial review: Sch.8, para.3A.
[20] s.47(1)(e) of the Competition Act.
[21] SI 2001/2916 as amended by SI 2002/42.

the Competition Commission requiring the production of documents and information and the attendance of witnesses.[22]

- Claims made by individuals based on infringement decisions made by the OFT under the Competition Act or by the Commission of the European Communities under Arts 81 and 82 of the EC Treaty once any appeals against such decisions have been finally determined.[23]

- Appeals under the Communications Act 2003.[24]

General. The CAT's Rules reflect the CAT's hybrid nature and are mod-   **4–005**
eled partly on the Civil Procedure Rules ("CPR") and partly on the Rules of Procedure of the Court of First Instance of the European Communities ("CFI").[25] The CAT's guidance on the application of the CAT Rules is set out in the *Guide to Appeals under the Competition Act 1988* ("the Guide"). In addition to the CAT Rules the Guide is an essential reference document for the parties.[26] The CAT has observed[27]:

"We entirely appreciate the difficulties of the subject matter, the pressure of time, and the fact that all concerned are naturally on a learning curve as regards the procedures to be followed in appeals under the Act, but we hope that the principles of the Guide can be closely followed in future cases."[28]

The five main principles on which the CAT Rules are based are set out in para.2 of the Guide. They are:

- early disclosure in writing;

- active case management;

- strict time-tables;

- effective fact-finding procedures;

- short and structured oral hearings.

Other sources of potential relevance when considering questions of practice and procedure may include the following:

---

[22] ss.114 and 176(1)(f) of the Enterprise Act.
[23] s.47A of the Competition Act.
[24] s.192. Such appeals are beyond the scope of this work.
[25] Codified at [2001] O.J. C34/1.
[26] Both may be found on the tribunal's website: *www.catribunal.org.uk*. The current Guide was issued in relation to proceedings under the 2000 Rules. A new version of the Guide will be published in due course to take into account the amendments introduced by the 2003 Rules. Many of the rules remain materially the same; consequently the practical guidance contained in the Guide remains applicable and should be followed.
[27] *Napp Pharmaceuticals Holdings Ltd v DGFT (No.4)* [2002] Comp. A.R. 13.
[28] *ibid.*

- the position under EC competition law and the rules of procedure of the CFI[29];

- the position in other UK domestic jurisdictions[30];

- Practice directions issued by the President under Rule 68(2) of the CAT Rules[31];

- Practice directions applicable in civil litigation.[32]

(a) The Registrar

4–006   **General.**   The Registrar, who must be a qualified lawyer,[33] oversees the administration of the work of the CAT.

4–007   **Administrative functions.**   Acting in accordance with the instructions of the President, the Registrar is in particular responsible for:

- the establishment and maintenance of a register in which all pleadings and supporting documents and all orders and decisions of the CAT shall be registered[34];

- the acceptance, transmission, service and custody of documents in accordance with the CAT Rules[35];

- the enforcement of decisions of the CAT[36];

- certifying that any order, directions or decision is an order, directions or decision of the CAT, the President or a chairman, as the case may be.

Any administrative function of the Registrar may be performed on his behalf by any member of staff of the Competition Service whom the President may authorise for the purpose.[37]

---

[29] See s.60 of the Act. Familiarity with these provisions remains useful despite the fact that questions remain as to the exact scope of this provision in relation to procedural issues.

[30] For example, in *Napp Pharmaceuticals Holdings Ltd v DGFT (No.4)*, n.27, above reference was made in Napp's request for interim relief to the position in Scotland in relation to granting interim injunctions. Depending on the location of the proceedings (see below) other national rules may be relevant in relation to procedural matters: see Rule 19(2)(k) (disclosure), Rule 23(3)(b) (summoning or "citing" of witnesses) and Rule 55 (costs).

[31] The Guide is the main Practice Direction currently in existence. There is also a Notice on neutral citations of Tribunal's judgments of July 8, 2002 to be found on the CAT's website.

[32] In its final judgment in *Napp Pharmaceuticals Holdings Ltd v DGFT (No.4)*, n.27, above the CCAT indicated that regard should be had to *Practice Direction (Citation of Authorities)* [2001] W.L.R. 1001 which is not dissimilar in its guiding principle to para.11 of the Guide. This practice direction has subsequently been incorporated into the CAT's own Notice on the citation of authority.

[33] Rule 4(1).

[34] Rule 4(2)(a).

[35] Rule 4(2)(b).

[36] Rule 4(2)(c), pursuant to paras 4 and 5 of Sch.4 to the Enterprise Act.

Judicial functions.   In addition to his administrative functions the Registrar   **4–008**
may when authorised to do so by the President, consider and dispose of
certain interlocutory matters. Those are:

- make any order for consent, except where the CAT considers the
  proposed order may have a significant effect on competition[38];

- deal with extensions or abridgments of time limits, except a request
  for an extension of time for filing an appeal or application[39];

- deal with requests for confidential treatment[40];

- exercise the powers of the CAT in respect of the service of
  documents.[41]

(b) Representation

In proceedings before the CAT, a party may be represented by a qualified   **4–009**
lawyer having a right of audience before a court in the UK, or any other
person allowed by the CAT to appear on his behalf.[42]

2. APPEALS

(a) Commencing appeal proceedings

The time for commencing an appeal.   An appeal to the CAT must be made   **4–010**
by sending a notice of appeal to the Registrar so that it is received within
two months of the date upon which the appellant was notified of the disputed decision or the date of publication of the decision, whichever is the
earlier.[43] It is frequently the case that the OFT will publicly announce that it
has taken a decision via a press release published on its website before
making the full text of its decision publicly available. The full text of the
decision will generally on that date have been notified to the addressee of the
decision in order to permit the undertaking in question to make representations about the confidentiality of information contained in the decision
prior to its publication. A non-confidential version of the text of the decision
will then be published at a later stage. If the person seeking to appeal the
decision is not the addressee of the decision but a third party it is "extremely

---

[37] Rule 4(5).
[38] Rule 62(3)(a) read subject to Rule 57(4).
[39] Rule 62(3)(b).
[40] Rule 62(3)(c) (under Rule 53).
[41] Rule 62(3(d) (under Rule 63).
[42] Rule 7.
[43] Rule 8(1).

doubtful" whether the issue of a press release constitutes "notification" of the decision.[44] The issue of a press release is generally also highly unlikely to constitute "publication" of the decision. The date of publication of the decision is the date of the publication of the reasons for the decision and not the date of the announcement by the OFT of the fact of the decision.[45] Only when an appellant is in possession of the reasons for the decision is it in a position properly and fairly to assess whether or not to file an appeal. Any alternative approach might lead to appeals being brought on a precautionary basis which would be likely to lead to unnecessary costs being incurred in further applications for amendment or withdrawal once the full reasons become available. In this regard it is relevant that the CAT Rules require the appellant to annex a copy of the disputed decision to his notice of appeal.[46]

It is desirable in "normal circumstances" that directions consequent upon the decision[47] should be made in the same document as the decision to avoid complications over the time for lodging an appeal.[48]

The Guide urges parties to file the notice of appeal as early as possible and in any event not to wait until the last possible moment.[49] This is of general importance but particularly so in relation to cases where urgency is a specific ground for granting relief. In such cases waiting two months before lodging an application might well cast doubt on the urgency of the application.[50]

4–011   Extensions of time.   The circumstances in which the CAT may extend the time for the filing of the notice of appeal are extremely limited. The CAT Rules provide that the CAT may not extend the time for the filing of the notice of appeal unless it is satisfied that the circumstances are "exceptional".[51]

4–012   Contents of the notice of appeal.   The relevant provisions and guidance are contained in Rule 8 of the CAT Rules and the Guide. In particular the Guide gives detailed guidance on both the form and substance of the notice of appeal including as to the structure, format and length of the notice and the documents to be annexed. The requirements set out in the Guide reflect the CAT's emphasis on written procedure which is directed to assisting the CAT in determining often complex cases expeditiously and efficiently.

---

[44] *Federation of Wholesale Distributors v OFT* [2004] CAT 11, para.22. This case was decided under Rule 26 of the CAT Rules in relation to an application for review of a refusal by the OFT to refer a merger to the Competition Commission. Rule 26 is materially in the same terms as Rule 8(1).

[45] *Federation of Wholesale Distributors v OFT* [2004] CAT 11, para.23.

[46] Rule 8(6).

[47] Under ss.32 and 33 of the Competition Act 1998.

[48] *Napp Pharmaceutical Holdings Ltd v DGFT (No.1)* [2001] Comp. A.R. 1 at para.34.

[49] para.4.2.

[50] *e.g.* under s.47(1)(e) of the Competition Act 1998 (appeal against a decision by OFT not to grant interim relief pending the outcome of an investigation).

[51] Rule 8(2).

To assist the orderly and expeditious progress of proceedings the Guide emphasises:

- Each party's case must be fully set out in writing as early as possible, with supporting documents produced at the outset.[52]

- The notice of appeal should contain not only the grounds relied on for the appeal but a succinct presentation of each of the arguments supporting the grounds. The two month period for preparing the notice of appeal is in order to permit a written development of each of the factual and/or legal grounds of appeal so that the CAT is seized in writing from the outset with the substance of the case and any evidence not already presented during the administrative procedure. Direct comparison is made in the Guide with the form of a notice of application in appeals to the CFI.[53]

- All of the applicant's grounds of appeal should be set out in a closely argued and succinct notice.[54] Two months is provided in which to achieve this.[55] It cannot be assumed that if the CAT later decides to direct the filing of skeleton arguments a party will be free to use such a document to add new grounds to those already contained in the notice of appeal, or to reply to points made by the respondent unless the CAT's permission has been obtained.[56]

- A proper attempt should be made to distinguish between disputes of primary fact and disputes about the interpretation of those facts. Where primary facts are disputed the application should clearly identify which facts found by the OFT are contested and upon what grounds.[57]

- Case management issues should as far as possible be included in the application. This will facilitate the first case conference which will normally be held before the lodging of the defence.[58]

It is important that this approach is adhered to.[59] The CAT has commented that one of the reasons that an appeal did not go entirely according to the plan in the Guide was that the notice of appeal was not as focused as the CAT would have wished.[60] In certain circumstances in appeals against a penalty the CAT has permitted an appellant to file a "fairly exiguous" notice

---

[52] Guide, para.2.4.
[53] Guide, paras 5.4, 5.5.
[54] Guide, para.5.14.
[55] Rule 8(2).
[56] As to the possibility of amending the notice of appeal see paras 4–015–4–023, below.
[57] Guide, para.5.9.
[58] Guide, para.5.13.
[59] *Floe Telecom Ltd v Ofcom* [2004] CAT 7 at para.37.
[60] In *Napp Pharmaceutical Holdings Ltd v DGFT (No.4)* [2002] CAT 1; [2002] Comp. A.R. 13 at para.88.

of appeal, provided that the main points of the appeal are clear enough and it is clear that there will be no ambush at a later stage of the proceedings.[61] The position is not necessarily identical in relation to appeals by complainants in relation to the rejection of their complaint.[62] It should be noted that no further pleadings may be filed without the permission of the CAT.[63]

In complying with the requirement to provide a summary of the grounds of appeal in the notice of appeal an appellant should ensure that his summary does not contain confidential information. This is because the summary will form the basis of the summary of the notice of appeal which must be published as soon as practicable after the receipt of the notice of appeal.[64]

4–013   **Defective notices of appeal.** If the CAT considers that a notice of appeal does not comply with the CAT Rules, is materially incomplete, unduly prolix or lacking in clarity, the CAT may give such directions as may be necessary to ensure that those defects are remedied.[65] The CAT may, if satisfied that the efficient conduct of the proceedings so requires, instruct the Registrar to defer service of the notice of appeal on the respondent until after any directions given have been complied with.[66]

4–014   **The power to reject.** The CAT may after giving the parties an opportunity to be heard, reject an appeal in whole or in part at any stage in the proceedings if:

- it considers that the notice of appeal discloses no valid ground of appeal[67];

- it considers that the appellant does not have (or represent those who have) a sufficient interest in the decision in respect of which the appeal is made[68];

- it is satisfied that the appellant has habitually and persistently and without any reasonable ground:

  (a) instituted vexatious proceedings, whether against the same person or different persons[69]; or

  (b) made vexatious applications in any proceedings.[70]

---

[61] Case 1022/1/1/03 *JJB Sports plc v OFT*, unreported, October 23, 2003. In that case a schedule was filed in addition to the notice of appeal particularising matters in the decision with which the appellant took issue. That schedule was later described in the CAT's final judgment as "without practical utility": *JJB Sports plc v OFT* [2004] CAT 17 at para.213.

[62] *Floe Telecom Ltd v Ofcom*, n.59, above, at paras 39 to 40.

[63] Rule 19(2)(b).

[64] Under Rule 15.

[65] Rule 9(1).

[66] Rule 9(2).

[67] Rule 10(1)(a).

[68] Rule 10(1)(b).

[69] Rule 10(1)(c)(i).

[70] Rule 10(1)(c)(ii).

Save for the provisions dealing with vexatious appellants these provisions apply equally to the defence.[71]

An application to the CAT to strike out a pleading on the ground that it discloses no valid ground of appeal or defence should not be made except in the clearest cases.[72] Unlike the position in relation to claims for damages there is no rule specifically providing for summary judgment in appeals under the Act. Where preliminary issues arise involving a relatively discrete point of law whose determination might dispose of an appeal there is nothing to prevent such a point being decided as a preliminary issue in a manner akin to an application for summary judgment in the English civil courts.[73] The relatively complex factual and/or legal nature of appeals and applications for review before the CAT will frequently not be particularly suited to a summary judgment procedure.[74]

(b) Amendment

General. The notice of appeal may only be amended with the permission of the CAT.[75] Where the CAT grants permission to amend the notice of appeal it may do so on such terms as it thinks fit.[76] The form of a notice of appeal in appeals to the CAT is essentially the same as a notice of application in appeals to the CFI against decisions of the European Commission. Unlike a traditional English High Court pleading the notice of appeal is a detailed narrative presentation of factual and legal argument. Consequently the concept of "amendment" as traditionally applied to a pleading in the High Court cannot be directly transposed to proceedings before the CAT.[77] It will not normally be necessary to apply formally to "amend" simply to put into

4–015

---

[71] Rule 14(7).

[72] Guide, para.11.3. This statement was referred to by the CAT in its summary of the procedural law governing an interlocutory application to strike out and exclude evidence from its file in *Napp*, n.48, above.

[73] The CAT has determined a number of cases involving the jurisdictional issue of whether the OFT had adopted a decision which was appealable to the tribunal. That jurisdictional issue has been determined as a preliminary issue: see *Bettercare Group Ltd v DGFT*, n.13, above; *Claymore Dairies v DGFT (Preliminary Issues)* [2003] CAT 3; [2004] Comp. A.R. 1, *Aquavitae v DGWS* [2003] CAT 17; [2004] Comp. A.R. 117, *Pernod-Ricard v OFT* [2004] CAT 10. However, even this issue can be difficult to decide without at least a degree of inquiry into the facts which may in some cases make it less attractive to deal with such issues on a preliminary basis.

[74] In the different context of an application for an interim injunction the Court of Appeal has said: "In general, abuse of a dominant position is a complex question of mixed fact and law, which should be determined at trial on the basis of tested oral and documentary evidence and rival submissions, rather than in the summary setting of an application for an interim injunction." *Jobserve Ltd v Network Multimedia Television Ltd (t/a Silicon.com)* [2002] U.K.C.L.R. 184, CA, *per* Mummery LJ at para.12. See also *Intel Corporation v Via Technologies* [2002] EWCA Civ 1905 at para.96.

[75] Rule 11(1).

[76] Rule 11(2).

[77] Para.11.1 of the Guide.

different words the written submissions made in support of a ground of appeal which already figures in the notice of appeal.[78]

The CAT Rules applicable to amendments to the notice of appeal also apply to amendments to the defence[79] and any statement of intervention.[80]

4–016 **Permission to add a new ground of appeal.** In the case of a proposed amendment which adds a "new ground" for contesting the decision the CAT has no discretion to permit the amendment unless:

- the ground is based on matters of law or fact which have come to light since the appeal was made[81]; or

- it was not practicable to include such ground in the notice of appeal[82]; or

- the circumstances are exceptional.[83]

The CAT Rules are on their face more restrictive in relation to proposed amendments than those under the CPR.[84] However, it should be noted that the extent to which this is true in practice depends on how the distinction between a "new ground" and an argument in support of an existing ground is applied. The distinction is easier to state than apply in particular cases.

4–017 **A new ground?** Rule 11 of the CAT Rules is modelled on the equivalent rule in the Rules of Procedure of the CFI.[85] The CAT has explained that in European civil law jurisdictions "the ground" is the basic plea such as error of law, illegality, discrimination, procedural failure etc. to be distinguished from the arguments in support of the ground.[86] In *Floe Telecom Ltd v Ofcom*,[87] the appellant, Floe, contended in its original notice of appeal that it was an authorised "user" of certain wireless telegraphy equipment under s.1 of the Wireless Telegraphy Act 1949 ("WTA"). Floe sought to amend its notice of appeal to argue that on the true construction of "use" in s.1 of the WTA it was not in fact "using" the relevant equipment. In allowing the amendment the CAT held that the ground of appeal was to be categorised in general terms as an error of law in the interpretation of s.1 of the WTA. Defined in those terms the ground was not a new one and had been included in the original notice of appeal. The proposed amendment sought merely to advance an additional argument in support of Floe's contentions as to the correct construction of s.1 of the WTA and did not amount to a "new"

---

[78] *ibid.*
[79] Rule 14(7).
[80] Rule 16(10).
[81] Rule 11(3)(a).
[82] Rule 11(3)(b).
[83] Rule 11(3)(c).
[84] See CPR Pt 17.
[85] Art.48(2).
[86] *Floe Telecom Ltd v Ofcom*, n.59, above, at para.32.
[87] n.59, above.

ground for contesting the decision in the sense that an allegation of "predatory pricing", "excessive pricing" or "tying" would have been.[88]

Matters of fact or law which have come to light since the appeal was made. In *Floe* the CAT indicated that had it concluded that the amendment involved a "new ground" it would have been unlikely to conclude that it was one which had "come to light" since the appeal was made, that provision being primarily directed at the situation where previously unknown facts emerge or there is, for example, a new decision by the higher courts.[89]

4–018

Not practicable to include a new ground in the notice of appeal. Whether it was "practicable" to include a new ground in the notice of appeal may not necessarily be confined to whether it was "physically possible" to do so.[90] It has been stated in this regard that in a specialised field of law it cannot be assumed that it will always be "practicable" for those without access to legal advice to have included a ground in the original notice of appeal.[91]

4–019

Exceptional circumstances. In *Floe* the CAT was of the view that even if it had not been correct to conclude that the proposed amendment did not constitute a new ground it should have been allowed because the circumstances were exceptional. Particular factors relied upon by the CAT were as follows: failure to permit the amendment ran the risk that the correct interpretation of s.1 of the WTA might be decided on a false basis; the point would have been raised in a further complaint in any event; it was in the public interest to decide an apparently fundamental point at the earliest opportunity; the point did not involve a fresh investigation or disputed facts; the appellant was in administration and had not had access to legal advice in preparing its notice of appeal; the proposed amendment was raised at an early stage; and the respondent had not relied upon a submission that the argument had no reasonable prospect of success.[92]

4–020

Exercise of the CAT's discretion. The concept of the overriding objective in the Civil Procedure Rules will be relevant in the context of deciding whether to exercise the discretion to grant permission to amend.[93] Thus amendments which are likely to require further factual investigation, possibly of an extensive nature, which may affect third parties not party to the proceedings

4–021

---

[88] *Floe Telecom Ltd v Ofcom*, n.59, above, at para.52.

[89] *Floe Telecom Ltd v Ofcom*, n.59, above, at para.55. A decision of the EC Commission might also be a relevant matter.

[90] The tribunal referred at 56 of *Floe Telecom Ltd v Ofcom*, n.59, above, to employment cases such as *Parker v Southend-on-Sea BC* [1984] 1 All E.R. 945, where the words "reasonable practicable" have not been confined to what is "physically possible".

[91] *Floe Telecom Ltd v Ofcom*, n.59, above, at para.56.

[92] *Floe Telecom Ltd v Ofcom*, n.59, above, at para.57.

[93] See *Floe Telecom Ltd v Ofcom*, n.59, above at para.29, citing the observations of Peter Gibson L.J. in *Cobbold v London Borough of Greenwich*, unreported, August 9, 1999, CA.

may be refused as a matter of discretion even where they do not constitute a "new ground".[94] In applications for review of a merger decision under s.120 of the Enterprise Act it is likely to be the case that the CAT will be slow to give permission to amend.[95]

4–022 **Costs.** The costs of an amendment may well be left to be dealt with at the end of any substantive hearing.[96]

4–023 **The CAT's power to raise issues on its own initiative.** In *Floe* the CAT observed that even if it had not granted permission to amend it would have invited legal submissions from the parties on the correct interpretation of s.1 of the WTA, including the issues raised by the proposed amendment, under its case management powers to "invite the parties to make written or oral submissions on certain aspects of the proceedings."[97] This possibility is therefore an important one to bear in mind in considering the question of amendment.

(c) Withdrawal

4–024 **Notice of appeal.** An appellant may only withdraw their appeal with the permission of the CAT, or if the case has not yet proceeded to a hearing, the President.[98] Where the CAT gives permission to withdraw an appeal it may do so on such terms as it thinks fit and instruct the Registrar to publish notice of the withdrawal on the CAT website or in such other manner as the CAT may direct.[99] The CAT may publish any decision which it would have made had the appeal not been withdrawn.[1] Thus any attempt to withdraw an appeal in order to avoid an anticipated adverse ruling is unlikely to be successful if the CAT considers that it is in the public interest that it should issue a decision. The stage the proceedings have reached is likely to be a relevant factor in exercising this power.

Where an appeal is withdrawn two immediate consequences follow: first any interim order of the CAT other than an order for costs ceases to have effect,[2] and secondly no fresh appeal may be brought by the appellant in relation to the decision which was the subject of the appeal withdrawn.[3]

---

[94] *Floe Telecom Ltd v Ofcom*, n.59, above at para.60.
[95] *Federation of Wholesale Distributors v OFT*, n.44, above, at para.30.
[96] *Floe Telecom Ltd v Ofcom*, n.59, above at para.61.
[97] *Floe Telecom Ltd v Ofcom*, n.59, above at para.59, referring to Rule 19(3).
[98] Rule 12(1). See para.4–143, below on the question of costs of an application for permission to withdraw proceedings.
[99] Rule 12(2)(a) and (b).
[1] Rule 12(2)(c), inserted by para.1(b) of the Schedule to the Competition Appeal Tribunal (Amendment and Communications Act Appeals) Rules (SI 2004/2068).
[2] Rule 12(3)(a).
[3] Rule 12(3)(b).

Defence. There is no specific provision for the unusual situation in which a   **4–025**
respondent wishes to withdraw its defence, or, where it has yet to file its
defence, indicates that it does not intend to defend its decision. In such cases
the respondent may merely submit to an order setting the decision aside.
However, in order to obtain an order setting aside the decision in such
circumstances it may be necessary for the respondent to give undertakings as
to such appropriate action in relation to the case that the CAT may consider
is warranted.[4] Alternatively the parties could submit a consent order for the
CAT's approval. However, again an order is likely only to be approved if it
contains appropriate provision as to any further action by the respondent
that the CAT considers is warranted in the circumstances, whether or not
this is sought by another party.

(d) Initial procedure after the application is lodged

Once the notice of appeal is filed the following steps take place:

Checking the notice of appeal. The notice of appeal must comply with the   **4–026**
formal requirements of the CAT Rules.[5] Documents that do not constitute
appeals under the Competition Act, or appeals which are out of time, will
not be registered.

Defective notices of appeal. A notice of appeal which does not comply with   **4–027**
formal requirements of the CAT Rules or is "materially incomplete", "unduly
prolix" or "lacking in clarity" is defective. Where this is the case the CAT may
give such directions as may be necessary to ensure that those defects are
remedied.[6] If the efficient conduct of the proceeding requires it the CAT may
direct that service by the Registrar of the notice of appeal on the respondent
be deferred until any remedial directions have been complied with.[7]

Acknowledgment and notification. Upon receipt of a notice of appeal the   **4–028**
Registrar will send the appellant an acknowledgment of its receipt. A
properly constituted notice of appeal must be served by the Registrar on the
respondent that made the disputed decision.[8]

Publication of summary of the notice of appeal. A summary of the notice of   **4–029**
appeal must be published on the CAT's website as soon as practicable. The
purpose of the summary is to put potential interveners on notice as to the
existence of the proceedings.[9] It will be based on the summary included in

---

[4] *e.g.* Order of July 30, 2004 in Case 1036/1/1/04 *Association of British Insurers v OFT*
(Decision set aside in the light of the respondent's decision "not to contest the notice of
appeal". The CAT agreed to make the order sought, subject to an undertaking by the
respondent to consider what further action might be appropriate within 6 months in the light
of a list of issues indicated to it by the tribunal). As to the costs of such an application see
para.4–143, below.

[5] Rule 8 (see para.4–012, above).

[6] Rule 9(1).

[7] Rule 9(2).

[8] Rule 13(a).

[9] Rule 15(1), see below in more detail.

the notice of appeal which should therefore not contain any information in respect of which confidentiality is claimed.

4–030 **Constitution of the CAT.** The President will constitute the CAT to hear and determine the appeal. The parties are usually informed of the identity of the three members of the CAT at this stage.

4–031 **Listing of the first case conference.** The CAT will aim to summon the parties to the first case management conference no later than four weeks after the lodging of the appeal.[10] It is a particular feature of the CAT's procedure that this hearing is held before the service of the defence. Even at this relatively early stage of the proceedings the issues in the case are likely to be apparent from the notice of appeal and the decision under challenge. The CAT's usual practice is to send an agenda to the parties outlining the matters that may be dealt with at the first case management conference. The following issues are likely to arise[11]:

- whether any preliminary issue arises, for example, as to the CAT's jurisdiction[12];

- the question of forum and/or the location of the proceedings[13];

- whether the appeal should be consolidated or heard together with other appeals[14];

- whether any issues arise as to the confidential treatment of the notice of appeal;

- a preliminary identification of the main issues in the case and of the evidence likely to be relevant;

- the timetable for the case, including the date for the service of the defence, the timing of the main hearing[15];

- any directions which have been sought by the parties[16];

- any other issue regarding the preparation of the proceedings which can be conveniently and fairly addressed.

The CAT's practice is normally to hold case management conferences in public. The transcripts of such hearings are published on the CAT's website.[17]

---

[10] Guide, para.7.5.
[11] Some indication is given at para.7.6 of the Guide.
[12] See appealable decisions, below.
[13] See paras 4–050–4–051, below.
[14] See para.4–048, below.
[15] See Rule 21.
[16] Set out in Rule 19. See para.4–053, below.
[17] See *Umbro Holdings Ltd v OFT (Case Management Conferences Ruling)* [2003] CAT 30. This is despite the terms of Rule 20(3) which states that case management conferences are held in private.

3. RESPONSE TO APPEAL PROCEEDINGS

(a) The defence

Time for filing the defence.   The respondent must file its defence so that it is   **4–032**
received within six weeks of the date on which the respondent received a copy
of the notice of appeal. The possibilities for extending the time for the filing
of the defence are limited.[18] The asymmetry between the times for the filing of
the defence and the notice of appeal is explained by the fact that the principal
arguments relied upon by the respondent should ordinarily already be set out
in the challenged decision.[19]

Formal requirements.   The formal requirements of the defence are similar to   **4–033**
those which apply to the notice of appeal.[20]

The contents of the defence.   Much depends in this respect on the nature of   **4–034**
the case made by the appellant. In general, where the issues of fact and/or
law which form the basis of the appeal are dealt with in the respondent's
decision, the defence should avoid rehearsing the decision that has already
been taken, or rebutting arguments which have already been rejected.[21] The
respondent is not however precluded from responding to new arguments,
more developed arguments or new evidence put forward in the notice of
appeal for the first time.[22]

Documents to be annexed.   The CAT Rules require that a copy of every   **4–035**
document upon which the respondent relies be annexed to the defence.[23]
However, where those documents have been annexed to the notice of
appeal, duplication should be avoided and the possibility of using common
agreed working bundles explored. This is an issue that may be appropriate
to consider at the first case management conference.[24]

Witness evidence to be annexed.   The CAT Rules require "the written   **4–036**
statements of all witnesses of fact, and where practicable expert witnesses, if
any" to be annexed to the defence.[25] Insofar as the decision depends on

---

[18] See *Freeserve v DGFT* [2002] CAT 9 (extension of the time for the filing of the defence
following the determination of a preliminary issue).
[19] See *Napp Pharmaceutical Holdings Ltd v DGFT*, judgment of July 10, 2001, at p.3.
[20] Rules 14(2) to (6). As to the requirements imposed in relation to the notice of appeal see
para.4–012, above.
[21] *Napp Pharmaceutical Holdings Ltd v DGFT*, n.19, above.
[22] *ibid.*
[23] Rule 14(5).
[24] See Guide, para.8.3. Liaison with the Registry is advisable.
[25] Rule 14(5).

issues of primary fact the evidence relied on by the respondent should generally be contained in the decision.[26]

The CAT Rules governing defective notices of appeal, the power to reject and amendment also apply to the defence.[27]

4. INTERVENTION, CONSOLIDATION AND FORUM

(a) Intervention

4–037   **General.** A person who considers that they have a "sufficient interest" in the outcome of the appeal may make an application for permission to intervene in the proceedings in support of one of the parties to the appeal.

4–038   **Summary of the notice of appeal.** As soon as practicable, upon receipt of an appeal the Registrar must publish a summary of the notice of appeal on the CAT's website drawing the proceedings to the attention of potential interveners. The summary may also be published in such other manner as the President may direct.[28] The summary of the appeal itself must contain a statement indicating that an application for permission to intervene in the proceedings must be received within three weeks of the publication of the notice or such other period as the President may direct.[29]

4–039   **Timing of a request for permission to intervene.** An application for permission to intervene must normally be made within three weeks of the date of publication of the summary of the notice of appeal.[30] The emphasis is on the need for interveners to do so promptly without waiting until the end of the period allowed.[31] The earlier the intervention the more possibility the intervener will have of participating in the development of the case.[32] Experience suggests that most interveners are able to submit their requests to intervene in advance of the first case management conference. A prompt request for permission to intervene is particularly vital in relation to applications for review in merger cases.[33]

---

[26] It should be noted that the possibility for an appellant to introduce evidence not previously adduced at the administrative stage of the proceedings before the OFT is much wider than that open to the respondent. For the limited circumstances in which it may be permissible for a respondent to introduce further evidence at the stage of the defence in appeal proceedings: see para.4–061, below. As to the requirements of evidence, including expert evidence, submitted to the tribunal see paras 4–060, 4–063 and 4–064, below.

[27] Rule 14(7).

[28] This may be appropriate where some other means is particularly suited to bringing the appeal to the attention of persons who may have a sufficient interest in the outcome of the proceedings.

[29] Rule 15(2)(f).

[30] Rule 16(2).

[31] Guide, para.9.3.

[32] The general principle is that an intervener must accept the case as he finds it at the time of his intervention: *cf.* art.116(3) of the CFI's rules of procedure.

[33] Under s.120 of the Enterprise Act.

Requests to extend the time in which to make a request to intervene. The **4–040** CAT Rules provide that the CAT may make directions as to the abridgement or extension of any time limits whether or not expired.[34] No specific provision is made as to the grounds on which this power should be exercised in relation to requests to extend the time in which to make a request to intervene. In relation to extensions of time for the filing of the defence the CAT has held that fairness requires that it exercise its power to extend time on the same basis that an extension would be granted to an appellant in relation to the notice of appeal, that is to say only where the circumstances are "exceptional".[35] Parity of reasoning would suggest that a similar approach would be adopted in relation to an application to extend the time for filing a request for permission to intervene.[36]

Request for permission to intervene. Persons who consider that they have a **4–041** "sufficient interest" in the outcome of the proceedings may make a request to the CAT for permission to intervene.[37] The CAT Rules set out the formal requirements for such a request.[38] The request must set out a concise statement of the matters in issue in the proceedings which affect them.[39] The request must also identify the party in support of whom the request to intervene is made.[40] The Registrar must invite the observations of the other parties to the proceedings on the request within a specified period.[41]

Persons with a "sufficient interest". Persons should not make a request to **4–042** intervene unless they have a substantial interest in the outcome of the particular case before the CAT. Similarly there may be no need for an interested party to intervene if the interests of that party are already adequately protected by the position taken by another party.[42]

An undertaking whose activities have been the subject of a third party complaint to the OFT or other regulator will invariably have a sufficient interest in any appeal proceedings brought by the third party against a decision to reject its complaint.

It should not be assumed that a person who has a sufficient interest for the purposes of intervening in an appeal necessarily has a sufficient interest in

---

[34] Rule 19(1)(k).
[35] Rule 8(2).
[36] In *Albion Water v DGWS* [2004] CAT 9 the CAT indicated at a case management conference that it was minded to consider that where an unusual procedural situation meant that it was extremely difficult for a potential intervener to have deduced whether they had a sufficient interest to intervene from what was contained in the notice published on the CAT's website pursuant to Rule 16, and, if so, what the grounds of such an intervention might be, that might constitute "exceptional" circumstances.
[37] Rule 16(1).
[38] Rule 16(4).
[39] Rule 16(5).
[40] Rule 16(5)(b).
[41] Rule 16(3).
[42] Guide, para.9.4.

the decision for the purposes of bringing an appeal against it.[43] Complainants whose complaint is rejected are likely, assuming that the respondent has taken an appealable decision in closing its file on their complaint to be found to have a sufficient interest in the result of any appeal against that decision.[44] Participation in the administrative proceedings leading to a decision is not a necessary precondition of having a sufficient interest to intervene.[44a] It may be difficult to determine on an application to intervene in a complex case whether the issues sought to be raised by an intervener are outside the scope of an approval.[44b] The CAT has yet to consider a case where the complainant is a person whose position is no different from any other member of the public.[45]

4–043   **Discretion whether to grant permission.**   The CAT Rules provide that "[i]f the CAT is satisfied, having taken into account the observations of the parties, that the intervening party has a sufficient interest, it may permit the intervention on such terms and conditions as it thinks fit."[46] The CAT has refused permission to intervene without appearing to decide the question of whether or not the person seeking to intervene in fact had a sufficient interest where to grant permission would "over complicate" the proceedings.[47] The CAT has not been attracted to the idea of an intervener who had been the whistleblower in relation to a cartel acting as a "second prosecutor" to the OFT in an appeal against penalties.[48] Where permission is refused the position can be kept under review in the light of developments in the case. Where a person's interests are affected by the proceedings the requirements of fairness may be satisfied by giving them an opportunity to be heard on a particular matter without necessarily granting permission to intervene.[49] The presence of the OFT as a party may be sufficient in some cases to protect a person's interests, allowing their point of view to be

---

[43] Under s.47(2) of the Competition Act 1998. The CAT will be astute to ensure that attempts to appeal by persons with a less significant interest than another person are case managed in an efficient manner. This may mean rejecting the appeal where a person has an insufficient interest. Alternatives are that the appeal of the person with a lesser interest is stayed and the person can make an intervention in the case of the person more directly affected, or the two cases can proceed but subject to very tight control over the points that are to be argued (indications given at a case management conference): see *Albion Water v DGWS* [2004] CAT 9.

[44] Persons whose activities are not the subject of the decision may only appeal under s.47(2) if they have a "sufficient interest" in the decision with respect to which the appeal is made, or that he represents persons who have such an interest.

[44a] *Albion Water v DGWS* [2004] CAT 9 at para.67.

[44b] *ibid.*, at para.74.

[45] See *Pernod-Ricard*, n.73, above, at para.245.

[46] Rule 16(6).

[47] *Umbro Holdings Ltd v OFT (Permission to Intervene)* [2003] CAT 25.

[48] *ibid.*, at para.9.

[49] *ibid.*, at para.10. And see Rule 19(2)(n) (direction envisaged for hearing a person who is not a party to the proceedings where it is proposed to make an order or give a direction in relation to that person).

advanced without the need for a formal intervention.[50] Requests for intervention have generally come from persons closely associated with the OFT's administrative procedure, in many cases as a complainant. Accordingly there have been few if any heavily contested requests for intervention. The counterbalance to a relatively liberal approach to intervention is the CAT's power to control the scope of the intervention once permission is granted.

Granting a request for intervention. On granting permission to intervene the CAT shall give all such consequential directions as it considers necessary with regard to, in particular, the service on the intervener of the documents lodged with the Registrar and the submission by the intervener of a statement of intervention.[51] In making any decisions in connection with interventions the CAT must have regard to the need to protect confidential information.[52] The CAT will be astute to avoid duplication of arguments by the intervener of arguments already advanced by the party whose position the intervener seeks to support. If appropriate, the CAT may give directions for the submission by the principal parties of a reply to the statement of intervention. Depending on the case it may be more efficient to address points in the statement of intervention in the skeleton arguments rather than by means of a further round of formal pleadings.

4–044

The intervener's role. Once an intervention is made the intervener plays an "ancillary" role in the proceedings and is there to advance arguments in support of the position of the party on whose behalf he has intervened, not to raise new issues or evidence or to duplicate existing arguments.[53] This will be relevant to the ground to be covered by the statement of intervention and any evidence the intervener wishes to file. The CAT will act to ensure that interventions do not unduly delay proceedings.[54] It should not be assumed that because a person may have a sufficient interest in the substantive outcome of proceedings that they will necessarily be entitled to make submissions in relation to preliminary or interim issues.[55]

4–045

Competition authorities acting as *amicus curiae*.[56] Competition authorities of the Member States, acting on their own initiative, may submit written

4–046

---

[50] *ibid.*, it will certainly be cheaper.

[51] Rule 16(7).

[52] Rule 16(8). Claims in respect of confidential information under Rule 53 should ordinarily have been received by the Registrar before any copies of documents on the CAT's file are served on an intervener. The documents will generally be served on the intervener in redacted form. It will then be for the intervener to seek disclosure of any material it considers necessary for the preparation of its case.

[53] Guide, para.9.9.

[54] Guide, para.9.9.

[55] Compare *Bettercare Group Ltd v DGFT (Preliminary Hearing: Jurisdiction)* [2001] CAT 6; [2002] Comp. A.R. 9 and cases such as *Claymore Dairies v DGFT (Preliminary Issues)* [2003] CAT 3; [2004] Comp. A.R. 1 and *Freeserve v DGFT* [2002] CAT 8.

[56] Literally acting as a "friend to the court". Under the English CPR an *amicus* is now referred to as an "advocate to the court".

observations to the national courts of their Member State on issues relating to the application of Art.81 or Art.82 of the Treaty. With the permission of the national court in question, they may also submit oral observations to the national courts of their Member State.[57]

Where the coherent application of Art.81 or Art.82 of the Treaty so requires, the EC Commission, acting on its own initiative may submit written observations to courts of the Member States as an *amicus curiae*.[58] With the permission of the court in question, it may also make oral observations.[59]

The national competition authority or the Commission, as the case may be, may request the relevant court of the Member Sate to transmit or ensure the transmission to them of any documents necessary for the assessment of the case.[60-61]

4–047   No specific rules have been made to deal with the participation by a competition authority in proceedings before the CAT. Where a Member State has not yet established the relevant procedural framework, the national court must determine which procedural rules are appropriate for the submission of observations in the case pending before it. Such rules must be consistent with the general principles of Community law as to the fundamental rights of the parties involved in the case.[62] The rules selected also must not make the submission of such observations excessively difficult or practically impossible (the principle of effectiveness) or make the submission of such observations more difficult than the submission of observations in court proceedings where equivalent national law is applied (the principle of equivalence).[63]

The CAT Rules on intervention provide a clear mechanism to manage the participation of competition authorities in proceedings before the CAT although the CAT's permission would not be needed to submit written

---

[57] Art.15(3) of Regulation 1/2003. Art.15 sets out other forms of assistance which the Commission may provide to national courts, notably information and opinions concerning the application of Arts 81 and 82 EC (Art.15(1)).

[58] Commission Notice on the co-operation between the Commission and the courts of the EU member States in the application of Arts 81 and 82 EC [2004] O.J. C101/04, para.17. It should be noted that there is considerable divergence of practice as to the role and status of an *amicus curiae* in judicial proceedings. A memorandum on the circumstances in which the appointment of an *amicus* (now known as an "advocate to the court") may be appropriate and his role once appointed has been drawn up in relation to proceedings in England and Wales was published on December 19, 2001 by the Attorney General and the Lord Chief Justice. A potentially difficult situation may arise where one of the parties in a case is relying on a Commission decision in its defence to a claim for damages. If the Commission were to intervene in such a case there would be the appearance if not the reality of it becoming allied to the party seeking to uphold its decision and the potential for it to go beyond the traditional role of an *amicus* concerned solely to assist the court with the appropriate interpretation of the law in issue. An intervention by the EC Commission in a case such as *Crehan* might potentially raise such issues.

[59] *ibid.*

[60-61] *ibid.*

[62] Notice, para.35(a).

[63] *ibid.*, paras 35(b) and (c).

submissions. Permission to intervene would ordinarily entitle a person to submit both oral and written submissions, although this would go further than the minimum requirement under Community law which is to permit written observations. Although permission to submit written observations is therefore unnecessary in the case of a national competition authority or the Commission, the Commission's submission of its observations would nevertheless be subject to the CAT's case management powers as regards its intervention.[64]

Interventions by national competition authorities or the EC Commission are likely to be relatively infrequent before the CAT. In appeals involving Arts 81 and 82 before the CAT the relevant national competition authority will already be involved as the respondent. There may be cases where despite the involvement of the national competition authority the Commission considers it is necessary for it to exercise its right to submit observations, although this should be rare in practice. The right may also be exercised in relation to claims for damages. However, given the more limited scope of so called "follow on claims" under s.47A of the Competition Act and the fact that remedies are for the time being principally a matter for national courts such proceedings may rarely be expected to raise issues relating to the application to Arts 81 and 82 justifying the intervention of the national competition authority, let alone the Commission.

(b) Consolidation

General. Where two or more proceedings are pending in respect of the same decision or which involve "the same or similar issues" the CAT may on application or of its own initiative order that the proceedings be consolidated or heard together for any particular issue or matter raised.[65]   **4–048**

Consolidation has been directed where both applicants sought a variation on some separate and some overlapping grounds of a non-infringement decision resulting from a notification.[66]

(c) Forum

General. In relation to the question of the "forum" of the proceedings the CAT may be required to determine two questions. The first question relates to the "jurisdictional" issue of whether the proceedings are to be treated as proceedings in England and Wales, in Scotland or in Northern Ireland.[67]   **4–049**

---

[64] Provided that those powers are not exercised in a manner so as to make the Commission's participation unduly difficult.

[65] Rule 17(1).

[66] Under s.14 of the Competition Act (repealed): *IIB and ABTA v DGFT*, unreported, June 21, 2001.

[67] Rule 18(1)(a).

The second question relates to the "location" issue of where in the UK the CAT should physically sit for the purpose of the proceedings, or any part of them.[68]

4–050 **The "jurisdiction" question.** As regards statutory appeals against the decisions of the OFT and other regulators the principal significance of the determination of the jurisdiction question is as to whether an appeal from a decision of the CAT lies to the Court of Appeal of England and Wales, the Court of Session, or the Court of Appeal of Northern Ireland.[69] In principle the issue may also have to be determined in relation to other matters which arise in connection with the proceedings.[70] The CAT must take into account in reaching its determination as to which domestic jurisdiction the proceedings relate "all matters which appear to it to be relevant", but "in particular":

- the habitual residence or head office, or principal place of business of any individual party to the proceedings[71];

- the habitual residence, head offices, or principal places of business of the majority of the parties to the proceedings[72];

- the place where any agreement, decision or concerted practice to which the proceedings relate was made or implemented or intended to be implemented[73];

- the place where any conduct to which the proceedings relate took place.[74]

Without prejudice to the matters set out above, in making a determination as to the appropriate forum of the proceedings in the case of a claim for damages under s.47A or the Competition Act the CAT may also have regard to the law applicable to the claim.[75] Where the principal parties are both located in one particular jurisdiction of the UK and the events in question and effect on consumers took place in that jurisdiction then those factors are likely to be decisive in determining the jurisdiction of the proceedings.[76]

The fact that no point of Scots law as distinct from English law arises has been held to be of "no particular relevance" in determining the jurisdiction

---

[68] Rule 18(2).
[69] See s.49(3) of the Competition Act as substituted by s.21 and para.4 of Sch.5 to the Enterprise Act 2002.
[70] Rule 18(1)(b).
[71] Rule 18(3)(a).
[72] Rule 18(3)(b).
[73] Rule 18(3)(c).
[74] Rule 18(3)(d).
[75] Rule 18(4).
[76] *Aberdeen Journals Ltd v DGFT(Preliminary Hearing: Jurisdiction)* [2002] Comp. A.R. 1 at paras 4 to 10; *Bettercare Group Ltd v DGFT (Admissibility of Appeal)* [2001] CAT 6; [2002] Comp. A.R. 9; *Claymore Dairies v DGFT (Preliminary Issues)* [2003] CAT 3; [2004] Comp. A.R. 1 at para.195.

issue.[77] The fact that the proceedings raise a preliminary issue of law of importance to the whole of the UK does not justify determining a preliminary issue under the jurisdiction of one part of the UK when other issues have a closer connection with another.[78] The remote possibility of procedural complications raised by parallel judicial review proceedings initiated in one jurisdiction has been held to be an insufficient basis on which to determine that the proceedings before the CAT should take place in that jurisdiction.[79] Where an appeal is commenced with lawyers from one jurisdiction, the potential costs of having to instruct different lawyers for the purposes of an appeal is another factor unlikely to have much bearing on the jurisdiction question.[80]

The "location" question.   The determination of the second question, namely in which part of the UK the CAT should sit for the purpose of hearing the proceedings or any part of them is without prejudice to the determination of the jurisdictional question. Thus in determining the "location" question of where the CAT should physically sit, the CAT may determine the matter as it thinks fit having regard to the just, expeditious and economical conduct of the proceedings.[81]   **4–051**

As explained the jurisdictional and location issues are in principle distinct. However, "other things being equal" the answer to the jurisdiction question is a "powerful factor" towards physically holding the hearing in that jurisdiction.[82] Where the conduct in question took place may be relevant in considering the "just" conduct of the proceedings in relation to the location question, at least in relation to the final hearing.[83]

5. CASE MANAGEMENT

General.   The CAT has wide and flexible case management powers to enable it to deal with cases justly, in particular by ensuring that the parties are on an equal footing, that expense is saved, and that appeals are dealt with expeditiously and fairly. In particular, the CAT may at any time, on the request of a party or of its own initiative, at a case management conference, pre-hearing review or otherwise, give such directions as are provided for in the CAT Rules, or such other directions as it thinks fit to secure the just, expeditious and economical conduct of the proceedings.[84]   **4–052**

---

[77] *Aberdeen Journals Ltd v DGFT (Preliminary Hearing: Jurisdiction)*, n.76, above, at para.11.
[78] *Bettercare Group Ltd v DGFT*, n.76, above, at paras 10 to 16.
[79] *Claymore*, n.76, above, at para.197. The likelihood of parallel proceedings has been reduced by the CAT's approach to what is an appealable decision: see paras 3–042–3–045, above.
[80] *Claymore*, n.76, above, at paras 198 to 199.
[81] Rule 18(2).
[82] *Aberdeen Journals Ltd v DGFT (Preliminary Hearing: Jurisdiction)*, n.76, above, at para.12.
[83] *ibid.*
[84] Rule 19(1).

4–053 **Directions.** The specific matters referred to in the CAT Rules in respect of which the CAT may make directions are as follows:

- as to the manner in which the proceedings are to be conducted, including any time limits to be observed in the conduct of the oral hearing[85];

- that the parties file a reply, rejoinder or other additional pleadings or particulars[86];

- for the preparation and exchange of skeleton arguments[87];

- requiring persons to attend and give evidence or to produce documents[88];

- as to the evidence which may be required or admitted in proceedings before the CAT and the extent to which it shall be oral or written[89];

- as to the submission in advance of a hearing of any witness statements or expert reports[90];

- as to the examination or cross-examination of witnesses[91];

- as to the fixing of time limits with respect to any aspect of the proceedings[92];

- as to the abridgement or extension of any time limits, whether or not expired[93];

- to enable a disputed decision to be referred back in whole or in part to the person by whom it was taken[94];

---

[85] Rule 19(2)(a). See the hearing.
[86] Rule 19(2)(b). It is important to note that the filing of further pleadings is not automatic. See also Rule 39 in relation to damages claims.
[87] Rule 19(2)(c).
[88] Rule 19(2)(d). See the summoning and citation of witnesses.
[89] Rule 19(2)(e). See evidence.
[90] Rule 19(2)(f). See expert evidence.
[91] Rule 19(2)(g). See the hearing.
[92] Rule 19(2)(h).
[93] Rule 19(2)(i), read subject to rules on the time for filing the notice of appeal (Rules 8(2) and 29) and defence (Rules 14 and 29(2)); notice of application (Rules 26 and 27) and defence (Rule 28(4)) and statement of case (Rule 31) and defence (Rule 37).
[94] Rule 19(2)(j). It should be noted that the tribunal's powers to give directions to remit or refer a decision back to the person who made it vary depending according to the proceedings in question. In relation to appeals a decision is referred back in the context of a case in which the CAT has the power to make any decision or direction the competition authority could have made (see para.3 of Sch.8 to the Competition Act (Decisions of the Tribunal). These provisions were considered in *Argos v OFT (Case Management: Witness Statements)* [2003] CAT 16 (directions made in order to allow three witness statements containing new material not in the decision to be put to appellants as part of a supplemental rule 14 procedure). Directions made in connection with a referral back were made in *Aberdeen Journals Ltd v OFT (No.1)* [2002] CAT 4 (decision referred back in order to permit supplemental Rule 14 procedure on issues of market definition); *Freeserve v DGFT* [2003] CAT 15; (decision set aside with directions as to manner and time frame within which any further investigation and

- for the disclosure between, or the production by, the parties of documents or classes of documents[95];

- for the appointment and instruction of experts, whether by the CAT or by the parties and the manner in which expert evidence is to be given[96];

- for the award of costs or expenses, including any allowances payable to persons in connection with their attendance before the CAT[97]; and

- for hearing a person who is not a party where, in any proceedings, it is proposed to make an order or give a direction in relation to that person.[98]

The CAT may in particular, of its own initiative:

- put questions to the parties[99];

- invite the parties to make written or oral submissions on certain aspects of the proceedings[1];

- ask the parties or third parties for information or particulars[2];

- ask for documents or any papers relating to the case to be produced[3];

---

decision to be taken; direction as to time frame later extended: see [2003] CAT 22); *Association of British Insurers v OFT*, Order of CAT of July 30, 2004 (decision set aside with direction by consent for OFT to consider what further action to take in the light of a list of points raised by the tribunal).There do appear to be limits to the directions that can be given. In the context of a referral back the CAT has said, "In our view it is not appropriate for the Tribunal to seek to micro-manage the administrative procedure, or to attempt in any way to prejudge points that will inevitably be raised on the appeal." *Argos v OFT, ibid.* In the case of an application for review (including cases involving the acceptance of statutory assurances under s.31A of the Competition Act) the tribunal may only refer the matter back to the original decision maker with a direction to reconsider and make a new decision in accordance with the CAT's ruling (see s.120(5) of the Enterprise Act; and para.3A of Sch.8 to the Competition Act).

[95] Rule 19(2)(k). Non-compliance with an obligation imposed under this rule is an offence: Sch.4, para.17(1)(f) of the Enterprise Act.

[96] Rule 19(2)(l).

[97] Rule 19(2)(m).

[98] Rule 19(2)(n).

[99] Rule 19(3)(a).

[1] Rule 19(3)(b). See *Floe Telecom Ltd v Ofcom* [2004] CAT 7 cited in the context of amendments to the notice of appeal. Other examples include *IBA Health v OFT* [2003] CAT 27 (correct approach to s.33 Enterprise Act). *Argos v OFT* [2003] CAT 16 (failure by OFT to put certain evidence in the Rule 14 Notice). *Association of British Insurers v OFT*, n.94, above (Terms on which a matter should be remitted to the OFT). Some issues *e.g.* ones going to jurisdiction may be ones that the CAT must take on its own initiative.

[2] Rule 19(3)(c) *e.g.* in *Aberdeen Journals v OFT (No.2)* [2003] CAT 11 the CAT requested information regarding certain costs of the dominant undertaking, (at para.373).

[3] Rule 19(3)(d). *e.g.* in *Napp Pharmaceutical Holdings v DGFT (No.4)* [2002] CAT 1; [2002] Comp. A.R. 13, the CAT requested and received a number of internal documents relating to the company's pricing strategy in the market in question (see paras 311 to 333).

- summon the parties' representatives or the parties in person to meetings.[4]

4–054 **Requests for directions.** A request for directions must be made in writing as soon as practicable and shall be served by the Registrar on any other party who might be affected by such directions and determined by the CAT taking into account the observations of the parties.[5]

4–055 **Case management conferences.** Where it appears to the CAT that any proceedings would be facilitated by holding a case management conference or pre-hearing review the CAT may, on the request of a party or of its own initiative, give directions for such a conference or review to be held.[6] There is no clear distinction between a case management conference or a pre hearing review. The latter is more likely to be a short hearing held relatively close to the start of a main hearing to ensure the smooth progress of the proceedings.

Unless the CAT directs otherwise, a case management conference shall be held as soon as practicable after the filing of the appeal, whether or not the time for service of the defence has expired.[7] In practice the first case management conference is generally convened no later than four weeks after the filing of the notice of appeal and before the filing of the defence.[8] In principle the Respondent's decision should already provide an indication of its position on the main points in the appeal, even before the defence is filed. Accordingly an informed discussion about the further progress of the appeal is possible even at this early stage in the proceedings. An agenda is usually circulated to the parties in advance of the CMC containing the main points to be addressed.

The CAT's practice is to hold case management conferences in public.[9] According to the CAT Rules, the purposes of a case management conference is to:

- ensure the efficient conduct of the proceedings[10];

- to determine the points on which the parties must present further argument or which call for further evidence to be produced[11];

- to clarify the forms of order sought by the parties, their arguments of fact and law and the points at issue between them[12];

---

[4] Rule 19(3)(e).
[5] Rule 19(4).
[6] Rule 20(1).
[7] Rule 20(2).
[8] Guide 5.13, 7.5.
[9] Rule 20(3) actually provides that a case management conference will be held in private unless the tribunal directs otherwise. The CAT has indicated that the transcripts of such hearings will generally be published on the tribunal's website: see *Umbro Holdings Ltd v OFT (Case Management Conferences Ruling)* [2003] CAT 30.
[10] Rule 20(4)(a).
[11] Rule 20(4)(b).
[12] Rule 20(4)(c).

- to ensure that all agreements that can be reached between the parties about the matters in issue and the conduct of the proceedings are made and recorded[13];

- to facilitate the settlement of the proceedings.[14]

The CAT may authorise a person qualified for appointment to the panel of chairmen to carry out on its behalf a case management conference, pre-hearing review or any other preparatory measure relating to the organisation or disposal of the proceedings.[15]

Timetable for the oral hearing. As soon as practicable, the CAT shall: **4–056**

- set a timetable outlining the steps to be taken by the parties pursuant to the directions of the CAT in preparation for the oral hearing of the proceedings[16];

- fix the date for the oral hearing[17];

- notify the parties in writing of the date and place for the oral hearing and of any timetable for that hearing[18]; and

- if it considers it necessary for the expeditious disposal of the proceedings, send the parties a report for the hearing summarizing the factual context of the case and the parties' principal submissions.[19]

(a) Evidence

General. The strict rules of evidence do not apply in proceedings before the   **4–057**
CAT.[20] The CAT has said that it will "be guided by circumstances of overall fairness, rather than technical rules of evidence."[21] What is fairly needed by way of evidence to determine the issues in any particular case may vary widely. Appeals "on the merits" against penalties may involve issues of

---

[13] Rule 20(4)(d), *e.g.* an agreed statement of facts on technical issues.
[14] Rule 20(4)(e). This may be particularly appropriate where there are issues in the case which are not directly competition issues.
[15] Rule 20(5).
[16] Rule 21(a).
[17] Rule 21(b).
[18] Rule 21(c).
[19] Rule 21(d).
[20] The Civil Evidence Act 1995 does not apply to proceedings before the CAT as it only applies to civil proceedings before any tribunal in relation to which the strict rules of evidence apply as a matter of law. See Section 11, below. The definition of civil proceedings in the Civil Evidence (Scotland) Act 1988 is slightly different: "Civil proceedings" includes, "in addition to such proceedings in any of the ordinary courts of law ... any proceedings before a tribunal ... except in so far as, in relation to the conduct of proceedings before the tribunal ... specific provision has been made as regards the rules of evidence which are to apply."
[21] *Argos v OFT*, n.94, above, at 105. And see the CAT's comments in *Claymore Dairies v OFT (Observations)* [2003] CAT 18 and *Aberdeen Journals Ltd v OFT (No.2)* [2003] CAT 11 at para.126 (no hierarchy of evidence).

primary fact, necessitating oral evidence from witnesses of fact. On the other hand questions such as what is the relevant market, whether dominance can be established or whether abuse can be objectively justified, whether there is an effect on interstate trade are more likely to involve a more or less complex assessment of mainly economic data and perhaps expert evidence.

4–058 **Burden of proof.** Once the addressee of a decision finding an infringement puts that finding in issue by appealing to the CAT the burden is on the OFT to satisfy the CAT, on the evidence, that the infringement is duly proved.[22] It should be noted that in relation to some issues the legal burden of proving them rests on the appellant.[23]

4–059 **Standard of proof.** The standard of proof which must be met by the OFT in proceedings before the CAT is the civil standard, that is to say the balance of probabilities.[24] This standard applies to all proceedings which arise under the Chapter I and Chapter II prohibitions.[25] However the evidence needed to satisfy the CAT on the balance of probabilities must be commensurate with the seriousness of the infringement alleged.[26] In *Napp* the CAT said that the OFT must adduce strong and compelling evidence, taking account of the seriousness of what is alleged, that the infringement is duly proved, the undertaking being entitled to the presumption of innocence, and to any reasonable doubt there may be.[27] However, the CAT has cautioned that its remarks in *Napp* should not be used to re-introduce the criminal standard of proof "via the back door".[28] In another case the CAT said that it should approach the matter by asking itself the question "is the CAT satisfied that the [OFT's] analysis ... is robust and soundly based?"[29] What evidence is sufficient to prove the infringement will depend on the circumstances and the facts.[30] It should be noted that many cases involving questions of expert assessment do not involve "proof" of primary facts at all. The relevant

---

[22] *JJB Sports Plc v OFT* [2004] CAT 17 at para.164.

[23] *e.g.* under Art.2 of Regulation 1/2003 the burden of establishing the criteria for an exemption under Art. 81(3) rests on the person claiming to be entitled to an exemption.

[24] In *Napp Phramaceutical Holdings Ltd v DGFT (No.4)* [2002] CAT 1; [2002] Comp. A.R. 13.

[25] *ibid.*, at para.194.

[26] *JJB Sports Plc v OFT*, n.22, above, at para.190.

[27] *Napp Pharmaceutical Ltd v DGFT (No.4)* [2002] CAT 1; [2002] Comp. A.R. 13 at paras 108 to 109.

[28] *JJB Sports Plc v OFT*, n.22, above, at paras 203 to 204.

[29] *Aberdeen Journals (No.2) v OFT* [2003] CAT 11; [2003] Comp. A.R. 67 at para.125. This formula may be more appropriate when dealing with issues of economic evaluation where the concept of proof, in the sense of proof of primary facts, may not be apposite.

[30] *ibid.*, at para.205. The CAT referred to *Claymore Dairies v OFT (Observations)* [2003] CAT 18, where it had expressed the concern that its remarks in *Napp* were being interpreted in an unduly cautious manner by the OFT. In *JJB*, n.22, above, the CAT repeated those concerns notably in relation to cases involving the Chapter II prohibition. The CAT also referred to the undesirability of applying a standard of proof in domestic law which might be out of line with the approach applied by the CFI and ECJ: see *e.g.* Cases 204/00 etc. *Aalborg Portland v Commission*, judgment of January 17, 2004 at paras 55 to 57. The CAT also mentioned the difficulty of resolving issues such as whether an agreement delivers "economic progress" under s.9 of the Competition Act by reference to the criminal standard of proof (at para.193).

standard of proof elaborated by the CAT aims to take account of the wide range of different issues which the CAT may be called upon to determine.

Witness statements. The CAT Rules state that "As far as practicable" written statements of all witnesses of fact, or expert witnesses, if any, should be annexed to the notice of appeal.[31] The CAT may control the evidence by giving directions as to:

4–060

- the issues on which it requires evidence[32];

- the nature of the evidence which it requires to decide those issues[33]; and

- the way in which the evidence is to be placed before the CAT.[34]

The CAT may admit or exclude evidence, whether or not the evidence was available to the respondent when the disputed decision was taken.[35] This rule must, however, be read subject to the CAT Rules and case law on amendments to the pleadings and its case law on the admissibility of evidence.[36]

Penalty appeals. In proceedings against a penalty under the Competition Act the position is that an appellant may generally adduce any evidence, including expert evidence, not produced during the administrative proceedings before the OFT.[37] As regards a respondent, however, the discretion to admit such evidence will only be exercised "sparingly" in its favour.[38]

4–061

The circumstances in which a respondent's evidence may be admitted in appeals involving penalties were summarised by the CAT in *Argos*[39]:

"Turning to the principles to be distilled from the *Napp* cases and *Aberdeen Journals (No.1)*, we note the following:

(1) The Director should normally be prepared to defend the decision on the basis of the material before him when he took the decision. The decision should not be seen as something that can be elaborated on, embroidered or adapted at will once the matter reaches the CAT. It is a final administrative act which fixes the Director's position. An attempt to strengthen by better evidence a

---

[31] Rule 8(6)(b). For the procedural requirements as to evidence in claims for damages, see para.4–091, below.

[32] Rule 22(1)(a).

[33] Rule 22(1)(b).

[34] Rule 22(1)(c), this includes whether it should be oral or written: Rule 19(2)(e). As to the oral testimony of witnesses see The hearing, below.

[35] Rule 22(2).

[36] See paras 4–061 *et seq.*, below.

[37] See *Napp Pharmaceutical Holdings Ltd v DGFT (No.4)* [2002] CAT 1, at para.117.

[38] *Napp, ibid.*, at para.114.

[39] *Argos v OFT*, n.94, above at para.66.

decision already taken should not in general be countenanced: *Napp (preliminary issue)* at para.77.

(2) Were it otherwise, the important procedural safeguards envisaged by Rule 14 of the Director's Rules would be much diminished or even circumvented altogether. There would be a risk that appellants would be faced with a "moving target". The CAT would not be adjudicating on the decision as taken, but on a "bolstered version": *Napp: preliminary issue* at 78; *Aberdeen Journals (No.1)* at para.176.

(3) There is therefore a presumption against permitting the Director to submit new evidence that could have been made available in the administrative procedure: *Napp: preliminary issue*, at para.79; *Napp: substance*, at para.133.

(4) That presumption may be rebutted, notably, where what the OFT wishes to do is to adduce evidence in rebuttal of a case made on appeal, as distinct from evidence that is intrinsic to the proof of the infringement alleged in the decision: *Napp: preliminary issue*, at para.83; *Napp: substance* at para.119; *Aberdeen Journals (No.1)*, at para.169.

(5) On the other hand, where the new evidence goes to an essential part of the case which it was up to the OFT to make in the decision, the CAT will not admit evidence that was not put to the parties in the course of the Rule 14 procedure: *Aberdeen Journals (No.1)* at paras 169 to 178. This approach applies where the evidence in question goes to "an essential part of the case ... which it is up to the Director to establish", or is relied on "to support a primary finding in the decision", or is sought to be adduced "for the purpose of upholding an essential element in the decision": *Aberdeen Journals (No.1)*, at paras 170, 173 and 178 respectively.

(6) The CAT should resist a situation in which matters of fact, or the meaning to be attributed to particular documents, are canvassed for the first time at the level of the CAT, when they could and should have been raised in the administrative procedure and dealt with in the decision: *Aberdeen Journals (No.1)*, at para.177.

(7) If there is relevant evidence sought to be adduced on appeal which has not been the subject of the Rule 14 procedure, the CAT has power to remit the matter to the Director for the Rule 14 procedure to be followed, if satisfied that the interests of justice so require: *Aberdeen Journals (No.1)*, at paras 190 to 197."

In *Napp* certain witness statements were admitted by the CAT on the basis that they were introduced to rebut certain points in the notice of appeal which had not previously been raised. Internal company documents disclosed pursuant to a request of the CAT were also admitted on this basis taking into account also the fact that the company had had ample opportunity to comment on them during the hearing.[40] In *Aberdeen Journals (No.1)* and *Argos* the evidence sought to be introduced, although relevant to the question of infringement (market definition and agreement/concerted practice, respectively), did not go to any new point not previously raised at the administrative stage of the proceedings. In *Argos* the CAT characterised both *Aberdeen Journals (No.1)* and *Argos* itself as attempts by a respondent impermissibly to "bolster" its existing decision and "materially expand" on the evidence contained in the decision rather than a response to new points raised at the appeal stage.[41] It should be noted that it may be difficult for the CAT to determine at an early stage in the proceedings on which side of the line particular material falls.[42] Where the CAT determines that the evidence should be excluded it may nevertheless conclude in the interests of justice to remit the matter to the respondent in order for the correct administrative procedures to be followed.[43] The approach in *Argos* was followed by the CAT in *Allsports Ltd v OFT*.[44] In that case the CAT held that it was important that it should not artificially limit the development of the evidence at the appeal stage in the case where the appellant has not put forward evidence as part of its response to the Rule 14 notice. Fairness required that the OFT be given a "certain latitude" to develop its case in response to that new evidence, providing that the Rule 14 procedure has been properly observed. In the circumstances it would have been "artificial and disproportionate" to prevent OFT from bringing forward a new witness statement in response to material that the appellant had, for the first time produced on the appeal.[45]

"Complainants" appeals and applications for review. As mentioned above the nature of the proceedings will have an important impact on the type of the evidence that will be required fairly to determine the issues which arise. On an appeal by a party against the rejection of his complaint of an infringement of the Chapter I or Chapter II prohibition the CAT has indicated that generally speaking its primary function is to identify whether the OFT has made any material error of law, whether it has carried out a

4-062

---

[40] para.314.

[41] *Argos v OFT*, n.94, above, at para 72.

[42] In *Aberdeen Journals (No.1)* [2002] Com. A.R. 167 the need to remit was not identified until the main hearing, whereas in *Argos v OFT*, n.94, above, the matter was remitted at an interim (or interlocutory) stage before the main hearing. The various procedural options for remitting a decision to the respondent are discussed in *Argos v OFT*, n.94, above, at paras 86 to 103 and see also, [2003] CAT 24 on the relevant procedural mechanics (original decision not formally set aside at least until amended decision issued).

[43] e.g. *Aberdeen Journals (No.1)*, *ibid.* and *Argos v OFT*, n.94, above,. The procedural mechanism by which a matter may be remitted to the respondent is discussed further at para.4–053, above.

[44] [2004] CAT 1.

[45] *ibid.*, at paras 62 to 76.

proper investigation, whether its reasons are adequate and whether there are material errors in its appreciation.[46] This approach is also more akin to the inquiry undertaken by a court or tribunal on an application for review. Thus, ordinarily, it should not be necessary for such purposes to go in great depth into evidence comprising the underlying documents which would reveal, for example, the underlying data and calculations used by the respondent.[47] Generally in such cases the question is not whether conduct complained of amounts to an infringement but whether the respondent's approach is correct.[48] As far as the respondent is concerned, in applications for review the well-established principle in administrative law is that "the Court should at the very least be circumspect about allowing material gaps to be filled by affidavit evidence or otherwise"[49] However, there is nothing wrong with such evidence being admitted to "amplify" the reasons for the decision where this is not used as a means of concealing or altering the true grounds of the decision.[50]

4–063   **Manner in which evidence is to be given.**   The CAT may require any witness to give evidence on oath or affirmation or if in writing by way of affidavit.[51] The CAT Rules make additional provision for the way in which evidence may be given, for example by video link or other means. The CAT may dispense with the need to call a witness to give oral evidence if a witness statement has been submitted in respect of that witness.[52] To avoid any uncertainty it may be sensible to obtain an express direction from the CAT that a witness' statement will be treated as the witness' evidence in chief.

4–064   **Expert evidence.**   As regards expert evidence, the CAT takes into account the principles and procedures envisaged by CPR Part 35. Part 35, its accompanying practice direction and the Code of Guidance on Expert Evidence provide clear guidance as to what is expected of expert witnesses. As under CPR Part 35 it is the duty of the expert to assist the CAT on

---

[46] *Claymore v OFT (Disclosure: Confidentiality)* [2003] CAT 12 at 7; [2004] Comp AR 63 at 20. *Freeserve v Ofcom* [2003] CAT 5.

[47] It should be noted however that, at least in appeals under the Competition Act, the tribunal noted that further developments to this approach in other case presenting different circumstances could not be ruled out: see *Claymore Dairies Ltd v OFT (Recovery and inspection)* [2004] CAT 16 at para.111.

[48] *ibid.*

[49] *R. v Westminster City Council Ex p. Ermakov* [1996] 2 All E.R. 302 at 312E *per* Hutchinson L.J. (a case where statutory reasons were required). The same reasoning has been held to be part of the common law duty to give reasons: see *e.g. R. v Secretary of State for the Home Department Ex p. Lillycrop*, unreported, November 27, 1996, DC).

[50] *IBA Health v OFT* [2004] EWCA Civ 142 at [106] *per* Carnwath L.J. His Lordship stated that there was no statutory duty on the OFT under s.107 of the Enterprise Act 2002 to set out all the evidence in the decision letter, albeit "when a challenge is made, there is ... an obligation on a respondent public authority to put before the Court the material necessary to deal with the relevant issues ..." (see *R. v Lancashire CC Ex p. Huddleston* [1986] 2 All E.R. 941.)

[51] Rule 22(3).

[52] Rule 22(5).

those matters which fall within his own expertise. That duty overrides any obligation to the person by whom he is instructed or paid. An expert's report should, in particular, set out the material facts, and the substance of all material instructions, on the basis of which it was written. The report should contain, at the end: (i) a statement that the expert understands his duty to the CAT and has complied with that duty; and (ii) a statement that the expert believes that the facts stated in the report are true and his belief that the opinions expressed are correct. Expert evidence should be the independent product of the expert uninfluenced by the pressures of litigation. An expert should not assume the role of an advocate.[53]

A failure to comply with these requirements may not render the evidence inadmissible but may detract from the weight the CAT feels able to place on the expert's evidence.[54] In particular it will be important for the expert to be provided with all relevant material necessary for his report. The expert must request clarification of material provided where this is inadequate for the preparation of their report.[55] There is no reason in principle why an expert could not himself seek a direction from the CAT regarding the preparation of his evidence.[56] The report must be firmly grounded in the facts of the particular case.[57]

Expert evidence should be restricted to that which is reasonably required to resolve the proceedings and the CAT will exercise its case management powers to this end.[58] In order to focus on the main points in dispute the CAT may organise, prior to the hearing, a structured discussion in the presence of the CAT between the parties and their experts in an attempt to focus on the main points of dispute.[59] Other procedures may include putting written questions to experts, discussions between experts, the appointment of a single joint expert, or, where relevant, the CAT's own expert.[60]

Disclosure. The general approach to disclosure before the CAT is that it is not automatic and must be ordered by the CAT upon request by a party to the proceedings. Before it will order disclosure the CAT must be satisfied that the disclosure sought is "necessary, relevant and proportionate to determine the issues before it."[61] The need to show necessity, relevancy and proportionality can be particularly acute where the information concerned is

4–065

---

[53] CPR 35 PD, paras 1.2 and 1.3.

[54] *Aberdeen Journals v OFT (No.2)* [2003] CAT 11 at para.288.

[55] See *Leeds City Council v Watkins* [2003] U.K.C.L.R. 467 at para.88, where various failures to respect the requirements of CPR 35 were criticised in relation to the presentation of expert economic evidence.

[56] *e.g.* under Rule 19(2)(l).

[57] In *Napp Pharmaceutical Holdings Ltd v DGFT(No.4)* [2002] CAT 1; [2002] Comp. A.R. 13 at para.254. Difficulties with expert economic evidence were also noted in *Hendry v The World Professional Billiards and Snooker Association Ltd* [2002] U.K.C.L.R. 5 ("risk of not seeing the wood for the trees").

[58] Rule 19.

[59] Sometimes referred to in some jurisdictions (*e.g.* Australia) as a "hot tub".

[60] Guide, para.10.4.

[61] *Claymore Dairies Ltd v OFT (Recovery and Inspection)* [2004] CAT 16, at para.113.

commercially confidential and belongs to a direct competitor of the party seeking access to it.[62]

(b) Summoning or citing of witnesses

4–066 The CAT may at any time, either or its own initiative or at the request of any party, issue a summons,[63] or in relation to proceedings taking place in Scotland a citation, requiring any person wherever he may be in the UK to:

- attend as a witness before the CAT, at a time and place set out in the summons or citation[64]; and/or

- to answer any questions or produce any documents or other material in his possession or under his control which relate to a matter in question in the proceedings.[65]

A request for the issue of a summons must state:

- upon which facts the witness is to be questioned and the reasons for the examination[66]; and/or

- the documents required to be produced.[67]

A person may not be required to attend in compliance with a summons or citation unless:

- he has been given at least seven days notice of the hearing[68]; and

- he is paid such sum as would be recoverable by that witness in respect of his attendance in proceedings before the Supreme court of England and Wales, the court of Session or the Supreme Court of Northern Ireland.[69]

---

[62] *Claymore Dairies Ltd v OFT*, n.61, above, at para.114. Disclosure to a confidentiality ring, where appropriate, should be kept to the minimum necessary to do justice to the case (at para.115). Questions of disclosure and confidentiality are discussed in more detail at paras 4–118 *et seq.*, below.

[63] In civil cases witnesses are traditionally called only with the consent of one of the parties (*Re Enoch and Zanetsky, Boch and Co's Arbitration* [1910] 1 K.B. 327. In criminal cases a judge may call and cross examine witnesses himself in the interests of justice and notably where the jury request it: see *Chapman* (1838) 8 C & P 558; *Holden* (1838) 8 C & P 606. It has been said in the criminal context that the power to call witnesses would be exercised sparingly and with great care: *R. v Edwards* (1948) 3 Cox C.C. 82. See further: *Evidence and the Adversarial Process* (1998), p.87.

[64] Rule 23(1)(a).

[65] Rule 23(1)(b).

[66] Rule 23(2)(a).

[67] Rule 23(2)(b).

[68] Rule 23(3)(a).

[69] Rule 23(3)(b).

In an urgent case the CAT may direct that the period of time for the service of the summons be abridged.[70] The CAT may make the summoning or citation of a witness conditional upon the deposit with the Registrar of a sum determined by the CAT as sufficient to cover the costs of the summons or citation and/or the sum payable in respect of his attendance.[71] There is currently no fee payable for the issue of a witness summons. In practice the CAT is likely to direct the party issuing the summons to pay the witness's expenses of attendance to the witness rather than require the deposit of the sum with the Registrar. Where the CAT summonses a witness of its own initiative the Registrar must advance the sum payable in respect of the witness's attendance.[72] Ultimately the CAT may recover any sum it advances by making an appropriate order for costs.[73]

A person who fails to comply with a requirement to attend to give evidence and/or produce documents without reasonable excuse is guilty of an offence.[74]

Failure to comply with directions.   In addition to the offences which exist in relation to non compliance with certain obligations under the CAT Rules, the CAT, may if it considers that the justice of the case so requires, order that any party that fails to comply with any direction given in accordance with the CAT Rules be debarred from taking any further part in the proceedings without the permission of the CAT.[75]   **4–067**

6. PROCEEDINGS UNDER THE ENTERPRISE ACT 2002

Introduction.   Part III of the CAT Rules introduces a number of modifications of form and substance to the main body of the CAT Rules in connection with proceedings under the Enterprise Act. Thus as a matter of form, "the notice of appeal" becomes "the application", "the appellant" becomes "the applicant" and "the grounds of appeal" become "the grounds of review".[76] The changes of substance are set out in more detail below.   **4–068**

Time for making an application for a review of a merger decision.   An application for a review of a decision by the OFT or the Secretary of State in connection with a reference or possible reference in relation to a relevant merger situation or a special merger situation by a person aggrieved must be made within four weeks of the date on which the applicant was notified of the disputed decision, or the publication of the decision, whichever is the   **4–069**

---

[70] Rule 19(2)(i).
[71] Rule 23(4)(a) and (b).
[72] Rule 23(5).
[73] Rules 19(2)(m) and 55(5).
[74] Para.17(5)(a) of Sch.4 to the Enterprise Act 2002.
[75] Rule 24.
[76] Rule 28(1).

earlier.[77] The importance of respect for deadlines in appeal proceedings is likely to be of even greater significance in relation to applications for a review of merger control decisions.[78]

4–070   **Time for commencing an application for a review of a market investigation decision.**   An application for a review of a decision in connection with a reference or possible reference in relation to a market investigation must be made within two months of the date on which the applicant was notified of the disputed decision, or the publication of the decision, whichever is the earlier.[79] The time for commencing review proceedings under the Enterprise Act may only be extended if the circumstances are exceptional.[80]

4–071   **The notice of application.**   There is no prescribed form for a notice of application, however it must contain the matters set out in the CAT Rules which are essentially the same as those required in relation to a notice of appeal and follow the guidance set out in the Guide.[81]

4–072   **Amendment.**   Although the CAT Rules relating to the amendment of a notice of appeal apply to a notice of application the CAT has indicated that, in the context of an application for review, it is likely to be the case that the CAT will be reluctant to give permission to amend.[82]

4–073   **Power to reject.**   The CAT's power to reject appeals[83] is modified to include a power to reject an application for review if it considers the applicant is not a person aggrieved by the decision in respect of which the review is sought.[84]

4–074   **Person aggrieved.**   Applications for review under the Enterprise Act may be brought by the "person aggrieved" by the decision which it is sought to challenge. This is a different test of standing to the rules which govern appeals under the Competition Act[85] The precise scope of a person "aggrieved" has not to date been the subject of any analysis by the CAT. The term has its origins in the context of the rules on standing developed at common law in connection with applications for the prerogative writs. It

---

[77] Rule 26.
[78] *Hasbro UK Ltd v DGFT (Application for Time Extension)* [2003] CAT 1; [2003] Comp A.R. 59.
[79] Rule 27.
[80] Rule 28(2), by reference to Rule 8(2).
[81] Rule 28. Somewhat curiously an appeal against a decision by a respondent to accept statutory assurances under s. 31A of the Competition Act 1998 although to be determined in accordance with the same principles as would be applied by a court on an application for judicial review (Sch.8, para.3A(2)) is nevertheless made by a "notice of appeal" under Rule 8 rather than a notice of application under Rule 28.
[82] *Federation of Wholesale Distributors v OFT* [2004] CAT 11 at para.30.
[83] Under Rule 10.
[84] Rule 28(4).
[85] *i.e.* either the addressee of the decision or a person with a "sufficient interest" in it (ss.46(1) and (2); s.47(2)).

was superseded by the sufficient interest test which was introduced in 1977 to simplify rather than change the threshold for standing in claims for judicial review in the English High Court.[86] The term survives today in a number of provisions dealing with statutory appeals, notably in the planning field.[87] The sufficient interest test was adopted in the Competition Act which provides that an appeal may only be brought by an addressee of the decision or a third party having a sufficient interest in the decision challenged or who represents persons who have such an interest.[88] There appears to have been no authoritative resolution of whether there is any significant difference between a person "aggrieved" by a decision and a person having a "sufficient interest" in a decision.[89]

The House of Lords has held that the question of whether a person has a sufficient interest is a mixed question of fact and law. In determining the question it will be necessary to consider the powers or the duties in law of those against whom relief is sought, the position of the applicant in relation to those powers or duties and to the breach of those said to have been committed. Those matters cannot be considered in the abstract but must be considered in the legal and factual context of the case.[90] This may mean the issue is not an easy one to determine at a preliminary stage.

The sufficient interest test was introduced to simplify the test rather than change the threshold for standing which, as the House of Lords has pointed out, depends on the particular circumstances of the case. In those circumstances it is suggested that the general approach adopted by the House of Lords in relation to the sufficient interest test should be applied in the context of determining who is a person aggrieved for the purpose of applications for review under the Enterprise Act.

---

[86] Introduced into Order 53 of the Rules of the Supreme Court (now CPR Part 54) in 1977, and later put on a statutory footing in s.31 of the Supreme Court Act 1981. In Scotland the question of standing is dealt with by the common law rules on title and interest to sue. It has been said that Scots law in this area is "restrictive and confused". It has also been said that "The law is potentially highly restrictive in relation to petitions by business competitors, by third parties in planning and by pressure groups." Mullen, Pick & Prosser, *Judicial Review in Scotland* (1996) at p.53. However, there appears to have been some pressure for liberalisation of the law e.g. by the Dunpark Committee Report (1984) and some reported cases have reflected increasing liberality in practice, although this has apparently not been entirely consistent.

[87] See *e.g. Buxton v Minister of Housing* [1960] 3 W.L.R. 866; *Berkeley v Secretary of State for the Environment* [2001] 2 A.C. 603 (right of local resident to challenge a grant of planning permission on the grounds of potential harm to the river Thames).

[88] ss.46(1) and (2); s.47(2).

[89] The draftsman's use of a "person aggrieved" is unfortunate as the term has given rise to considerable confusion which was supposed to be resolved when Order 53 was introduced in 1977. Lord Wilberforce noted in the *National Federation* case that the courts have always reserved the right to be satisfied that the applicant had some genuine *locus standi* to appear before them and referred in that connection to old cases involving applications for prerogative orders which referred to "persons aggrieved" or with "a particular grievance". He noted that the move to a sufficient interest test in Order 53 (now CPR Pt 54) was merely an attempt to simplify the test. The new test did not mean that its application was the same in all cases regardless of the context.

[90] *Per* Lord Wilberforce in *R. v Inland Revenue Commissioners Ex p. National Federation of Self-Employed and Small Businesses* [1982] A.C. 617.

On the CAT's limited case law to date the following tentative conclusions may be drawn about which persons will have standing to bring applications for review under the Enterprise Act. The actual or proposed parties to a merger would qualify as persons aggrieved for the purposes of challenging a decision directly affecting their contractual arrangements. A third party competitor with a direct financial interest in the merger would also appear to be a person aggrieved.[91] An application by a trade association of wholesalers for a review of a decision by the OFT not to refer the acquisition of 45 convenience stores by a national supermarket chain to the Competition Commission was not opposed on the basis that the trade association was not a person aggrieved or did not represent any aggrieved persons.[92]

4-075 **Intervention.** Despite the differences in the test for standing between appellants under the Competition Act and applicants under the Enterprise Act, the test for standing under the CAT Rules for an intervener remains the same in both types of proceedings, namely that a proposed intervener must demonstrate a sufficient interest in the outcome of the proceedings.[93] Given the importance of expedition in such cases it may be sensible where possible to serve the notice of application on persons appearing to the applicant to have a sufficient interest in the outcome of the proceedings.[94]

4-076 **The defence.** In proceedings for a review of a merger decision the time for the filing of the defence is abridged to four weeks.[95] In the case of reviews of market investigation decision the period of six weeks applies as it does in relation to appeals under Part II of the CAT Rules.

4-077 **Case management.** The abridged time limits for the filing of the pleadings in applications for review in merger cases reflect the fact that such cases are generally of a particularly time sensitive nature. However, those already abridged time limits were shortened even further in *IBA Health v OFT*.[96] Thus within three days of the filing of the notice of application the CAT issued case management directions in writing granting permission to the parties to the proposed acquisition to intervene and the filing of skeleton arguments. Both the defence and the statement of intervention were dispensed with in favour of skeleton arguments. Although the period for making a request to intervene is not shortened in relation to review

---

[91] In *IBA Health v OFT* [2003] CAT 27, IBA's standing to bring the appeal was not challenged. It would appear its interests were directly affected as it had entered an exclusive distribution agreement in the UK with one of the parties to the merger, Torex.

[92] *Federation of Wholesale Distributors v OFT* [2004] CAT 11. It may be noted that there is no equivalent provision in the Enterprise Act to s.47(2) of the Competition Act which expressly refers to the position of a person who represent persons with a sufficient interest.

[93] Rule 16.

[94] *cf.* CPR Pt 54.7(b) in claims for judicial review, which requires the claim form to be served on any person the claimant considers to be an interested party.

[95] Rule 28(3).

[96] [2003] CAT 27; and also in *Unichem v OFT* (Case 1049/4/1/05).

proceedings by operation of the CAT Rules themselves, the time sensitivity of such cases may well require a shorter period to be specified for the filing of such a request as was the case in *IBA Health*. Any person intending to seek a review would be well-advised to notify those persons that can reasonably be considered likely to have an interest in such proceedings as soon as possible in order that they may make any request to intervene in as timely manner as possible.

Interim relief. The CAT's Rules apply to requests for interim relief made in connection with proceedings under the Enterprise Act.[97] An application for a review does not automatically suspend the effect of the contested decision.[98] Where it is possible to deal with applications as quickly as was the case in *IBA Health* it is unlikely that a separate application for interim relief will need to be determined.   **4–078**

Given the contractual uncertainty that may be created by review proceedings the summary of the appeal will be published by the Registry with minimal delay so that the parties to the transaction in question are able to ascertain their contractual position. Parties concerned as to whether a transaction has become unconditional should stay in close touch with the CAT's Registry.

(a) Appeals against penalties imposed by the Competition Commission

General. In conducting a merger or market investigation the Competition Commission may impose penalties for failure to comply with a notice issued by it requiring the production of documents and information and the attendance of witnesses.[99] Where it decides to impose a penalty the Commission must give written notice of the penalty.[1]   **4–079**

Time for commencing an appeal. An appeal against a penalty imposed by the Competition Commission must be made by sending a notice of appeal to the Registrar so that it is received within 28 days, starting with the day on which a copy of the notice imposing the penalty was served on the person concerned.[2] The notice must set out the matters giving rise to the penalty and, in the case of a penalty calculated by reference to a daily rate, the day on which the amount first starts to accumulate and the day on which it might cease to do so.[3]   **4–080**

---

[97] Rule 25.
[98] ss.120(3) (mergers) and 179(3) (market investigations).
[99] ss.109 to 117. See Competition Commission: Statement of Policy on Penalties (June 2003), issued pursuant to s.116 of the Enterprise Act. Experience of similar powers under the Fair Trading Act 1973 (repealed) suggests that such powers will be used rarely, if ever.
[1] s.112 of the Enterprise Act.
[2] Rule 29(1)(a).
[3] s.112(2).

Within 14 days of the date of service of a notice imposing a penalty on him, a person may apply to the Competition Commission to specify a different date by which the penalty or any portion of it is to be paid. Where a person avails themselves of this procedure, the time for appealing to the CAT is 28 days from the day on which the person concerned was notified of the Competition Commission's decision on their application.[4]

4-081   **The defence.** The Competition Commission's defence to such an appeal must be received by the CAT within three weeks of the date on which it receives a copy of the notice of appeal.[5] The slight asymmetry between the time for the filing of the notice of appeal and defence is explained by the fact that generally speaking the Competition Commission's case should already be set out in its notice and/or decision on an application to vary the starting date of the penalty.

4-082   **Intervention.** Interventions by third parties are not permitted in such appeals.[6]

7. CLAIMS FOR DAMAGES

4-083   **Introduction.** Infringements of competition law established by decision of the OFT or EC Commission may be the subject of so-called "follow on" or "piggy back" claims for damages before the CAT. Such claims may be made on the basis of decisions establishing infringements of the Chapter I and Chapter II prohibitions of the Competition Act 1998 and Arts 81 and 82 of the EC Treaty. Additionally, claims may be based on decisions under Arts 65(1) and 66(7) of the European Coal and Steel Treaty,[7] which correspond to Arts 81 and 82 respectively.[8]

4-084   **Applicable rules.** The rules applicable to claims for damages under ss.47A and 47B of the Competition Act are those principally set out in Part IV of the CAT Rules. Parts I and V of the CAT Rules also apply to claims for damages. Under Part II of the CAT Rules the CAT's case management powers applicable to appeals are also applicable to claims for damages.

4-085   **Civil procedure rules.** The CAT Rules governing claims for damages have been broadly modelled on rules to be found in the CPR. However, the CAT Rules are intended to be a coherent self-standing set of procedural rules governing the conduct of proceedings before the CAT. The CAT Rules are

---

[4] Rule 29(1)(b).
[5] Rule 29(2).
[6] Rule 29(3).
[7] The ECSC Treaty expired on July 23, 2002.
[8] s.47A(6) of the Competition Act 1998 (as amended).

intentionally more simply drafted than the CPR and are drafted in a more general and flexible manner than the procedural rules in the CPR. In particular, the CAT Rules are not designed in such a way that parties to proceedings before the Tribunal must constantly have recourse to the CPR (or any other set of rules governing civil litigation in the UK). Although analogies with other procedural rules such as the CPR may be useful such analogies cannot or should not be taken too far. This is because there are a number of areas of procedure as regards cost, time limits, the nature and content of written pleadings, amendment of pleadings and disclosure, to give only some examples, where the rules and practice of the CAT are deliberately different to the CPR. It should also be noted that in construing the CAT Rules it may sometimes by necessary to have regard to the position in Scotland or Northern Ireland.[8a]

(a) Time for filing a claim for damages

A claim for damages (or other monetary claim) may be made within a period of two years beginning with the "relevant date". The "relevant date" is the later of either: **4–086**

(i) the end of the period specified in s.47A(6) or (7) of the Competition Act in relation to the decision on the basis of which the claim is made; or

(ii) the date on which the cause of action accrued.

The period in (i) is the date on which an infringement has been established by decision of the OFT, of the CAT on appeal from the OFT, or of the European Commission. Unless the CAT grants permission, no claim may be commenced in respect of a decision which may still be the subject of an appeal (for instance an appeal to the CAT in the case of decisions of the OFT, to the Court of Appeal or the Court of Session in the case of CAT decisions, or an application to the CFI or European Court of Justice in the case of decisions of the European Commission) or a decision in respect of which appeal proceedings have been initiated but have yet to be determined.[9]

The period in (i) is likely to cover the majority of cases. The period in (ii) takes into account that in some cases there may be some delay between the relevant decision establishing an infringement and the occurrence of the damage in which case time only starts to run from the date on which the loss occurred.

The CAT may grant permission for a claim for damages to be initiated before the relevant period for an appeal against the decision has expired.[10] It

---

[8a] *BCL Old Co Ltd and Ors v Aventis SA and Ors (Limitation)* [2005] CAT 1 at paras 41–45.
[9] s.47A(6) of the Competition Act.
[10] *ibid.*, s.47A(5)(b).

may be appropriate in some cases to permit the claim to be commenced in order that preliminary matters can be dealt with, before they are then stayed pending the outcome of the appeal. Permission in such cases can only be granted once any proposed defendant has been given the opportunity to submit observations on the request for permission.[11]

The CAT has discretion to add parties to an action before it after the expiry of the limitation point.[11a] It will not be appropriate to exercise that discretion to allow a party to be added after the end of the limitation period without "good reason".[11b] The addition or substitution of the party must be in respect of the same claim for damages being pursued by the existing claimants.[11c]

(b) Manner of commencing a claim for damages under section 47A or 47B of the Competition Act

4–087 A claim for damages under s.47A of the Competition Act should be made by way of a claim form.[12] Section 47B of the Act also provides for a claim under s.47A to be begun or continued by a specified body on behalf of a group of individually named consumers.[13] The CAT Rules set out both the formal and substantive requirements of the claim form.

(c) Formal requirements

4–088 A claim form must be signed and dated by the claimant, or on his behalf by his duly authorised officer or by his legal representative and be verified by a statement of truth, and must contain[14]:

- the claimant's name and address, the name and address of his legal representative if any, and an address for service in the UK;

- the name and address of the defendant.

In addition a claim form in proceedings brought under s.47B should:

- contain the name and address of the specified body and a concise statement of the object or activities of that body;

- contain the names and addresses of the persons that the body seeks to represent;

---

[11] Rule 31(3).
[11a] Under Rule 35.
[11b] *BCL*, n.8a, above, at para.46.
[11c] *BCL*, n.8a, above, at para.43.
[12] Rule 32.
[13] The specified bodies are, the Consumer's Association; the National Association of Citizens Advice Bureau; and the National Consumer Council: see The Enterprise Act 2002 (Bodies Designated to make Super-Complaints) (Amendment) Order 2004 (SI 2004/3366).
[14] Rule 32.

- be accompanied by a document or documents, giving consent to the specified body by each of the individuals listed in the claim form to act on his behalf[15];

- indicate whether each individual listed in connection with the claim is a "consumer" for the purposes of s.47B of the Competition Act.[16]

(d) Substantive requirements

The claim form should contain a concise statement of the relevant facts, identifying any relevant findings in the decision on the basis of which the claim for damages is being made; a concise statement of any contentions of law which are relied on; a statement of the amount claimed in damages, supported with evidence of losses incurred and of any calculations which have been undertaken to arrive at the claimed amount; and any matters that may from time to time be specified by practice direction.[17] **4–089**

Annexed to the claim form should be a copy of the decision on the basis of which the claim for damages is being made and, as far as practicable, a copy of all essential documents on which the claimant relies.[18]

Unless the CAT otherwise directs the signed original of the claim form should be accompanied by ten copies certified by the claimant or his legal representative as conforming to the original.[19]

(e) The structure of the claim form

Although the formal and substantive matters that must be contained in the claim form are set out in the Rules there is no set format for the presentation of the claim form. What is vital is that the CAT is able fully to understand the claim from the moment of its receipt. **4–090**

It will normally be appropriate first to set out the background to the decision on which the claim is based. Parties should be careful to identify

---

[15] As required by s.47B(3).
[16] A claim under s.47B applies to goods or services which—

  "(a) the individual received, or sought to receive, otherwise than in the course of a business carried on by him (notwithstanding that he received or sought to receive them with a view to carrying on a business); and
  (b) were, or would have been. Supplied to the individual (in the case of goods whether by way of sale or otherwise) in the course of a business carried on by the person who supplied or would have supplied them." (s.47B(7)).

  A business includes: a professional practice; an other undertaking carried on for gain or reward; any undertaking in the course of which goods or services are supplied otherwise than free of charge (s.47B(8)).
[17] Rule 32(3).
[18] Rule 32(4).
[19] Rule 32(5).

concisely the facts found in the decision that are alleged have caused loss to the claimant.

Having identified the facts on which the claim is based the claim form should identify in a concise manner the grounds which entitle the claimant to recover the sums claimed. The arguments supporting those grounds should then be developed in a concise manner. Where various grounds overlap, it is sufficient to refer back to the arguments already developed. Any calculations relied on as to the amounts claimed and any interest thereon should be clearly set out, either in the body of the claim form or, if lengthy in nature, contained in a document annexed to the claim form.

In setting out the arguments in support of each ground, it is unnecessary to set out lengthy extracts from decided cases: short citations, accompanied by the case reference and para. number, will normally suffice. The CAT has indicated that regard should be had to *Practice Direction (Citation of Authorities)*.[20] The obligation on practitioners to comply with the Practice Direction has been stressed by the Court of Appeal.[21]

(f) Documents to be annexed

4–091   The claimant is required to annex to the claim form a copy of the decision on the basis of which the claim for damages is being made and all essential documents that he relies on.[22] Documents of only a peripheral nature should not be annexed. The claimant is not required to annex the statements of any witnesses he proposes to rely on. However, the claimant should in the claim form identify the nature of the evidence that he proposes to adduce in support of the grounds pleaded and where possible should include at the least the identity of the witness, or witnesses, concerned.

The provisions of the Guide dealing with the presentation of an appeal should apply to claims for damages unless the context requires otherwise.[23]

(g) Initial procedure after the claim form is filed

4–092   Once the claim form has been filed a similar process takes place to that followed by the CAT in relation to an appeal. The Registrar will check the claim form and send an acknowledgment of its receipt to the claimant. The CAT will be constituted to determine the claim.

In the case of a claim for damages the first case management conference will, unlike the position in relation to appeals, not generally take place until after the receipt of the defence.

---

[20] [2001] 1 W.L.R. 1001.
[21] *Napp Pharmaceutical Holdings Ltd v DGFT(No.5)* [2002] EWCA Civ 796.
[22] Rule 32(4).
[23] See para.4–012, above.

(h) The defence

Provided that the claim form complies with the CAT Rules the Registrar **4–093**
will serve the claim on the defendant. Within seven days the defendant must
acknowledge service by returning the form served by the Registrar with the
notice of claim.[24] Within 28 days of receipt of the copy of the claim form
from the Registrar the defendant shall send to the Registrar a defence setting
out in sufficient detail which of the facts and contentions of law in the claim
form it admits or denies and on what grounds and on what other facts or
contentions of law it relies.[25] The defence should condescend to the same
level of detail required in respect of the claim form and annex essential
documents relied on. Unless the context requires otherwise the provisions of
the Guide apply equally to the preparation and presentation of the defence.
The contents of the defence must be verified by a statement of truth.[26]

(i) Additional claims

A defendant may make a counterclaim against a claimant or a claim against **4–094**
any other person without the CAT's permission if he includes it with his
defence; or at any other time with the CAT's permission.[27]

(j) Amendment

A claim form may only be amended with the written consent of all the **4–095**
parties or with the permission of the CAT.[28]

(k) Power to reject

The CAT has the power to reject a claim for damages at any stage of the **4–096**
proceedings on the following grounds: where it considers that there are no
reasonable grounds for making the claim[29]; where it considers in a consumer
claim by a specified body that the body bringing the proceedings is not
entitled to do so or that an individual on whose behalf the proceedings are
brought is not a consumer for the purposes of that section[30]; if the claimant
is a vexatious litigant within the meaning of the CAT Rules; or where the

---

[24] Rule 36(2).
[25] Rule 37.
[26] Rule 37(2).
[27] Rule 38.
[28] Rule 34.
[29] Rule 40(1)(a).
[30] Rule 40(1)(b).

claimant fails to comply with any rule, direction, practice direction or order of the CAT.[31]

(l) Summary judgment

4-097   The CAT has the power to give summary judgment on a claim for damages.[32] The grounds for summary judgment are where the CAT considers that:

- the claimant has no real prospect of succeeding on the claim or issue[33]; or

- the defendant has no reasonable grounds for defending the claim or issue[34]; and

- there is no other compelling reason why the case or issue should be disposed of at a substantive hearing.[35]

Unlike the power to reject, the power to give summary judgment in claim for damages may not be exercised before the filing of the defence.[36] The CAT may give such directions as it considers appropriate for dealing with a request for summary judgment[37] and upon giving judgment may make any consequential order it considers appropriate.[38]

(m) Withdrawal of claim

4-098   A claimant may only withdraw his claim with the consent of the defendant or with the permission of the President or, if the case has proceeded to a hearing, the CAT.[39] Where a claim is withdrawn the CAT may make any consequential order it thinks fit and no further claim may be brought by the claimant in respect of the same subject matter.[40]

(n) Offers and payments to settle

4-099   **Payments to settle.**   Once a claim for damages has been commenced a defendant may make a "payment to settle" the claim either in whole or in

---

[31] Rules 40(1)(c) and 40(1)(d).
[32] Rule 41.
[33] Rule 41(1)(a)(i).
[34] Rule 41(1)(a)(ii).
[35] Rule 41(b).
[36] Rule 41(2).
[37] Rule 41(3).
[38] Rule 41(4).
[39] Rule 42(1).
[40] Rule 42(2).

part by serving a notice of such a payment on the claimant and on the Registrar.[41]

The claimant may accept a payment to settle at any time up to 14 days before the substantive hearing.[42] In that case the defendant will be entitled to his costs up until the date of acceptance of the notice of payment.[43] If the claimant does not accept the payment to settle and fails to better the payment to settle following a substantive hearing then the CAT will order the claimant to pay any costs incurred by the defendant after the latest date on which the payment or offer could have been accepted unless it considers it unjust to do so.[44] The offer must not be communicated to the members of the CAT hearing the case.[45] Only a payment made in accordance with the CAT Rules will count as a "payment to settle". Payments to settle made in accordance with the CAT Rules will be treated as made "without prejudice" except as to costs.[46]

Offers to settle. Under the CAT Rules any party may make an offer to settle.[47] This is an offer which does not comply with the requirements of Rules but may nevertheless be taken into account by the CAT in considering the question of costs.   **4–100**

(o) Case management

In determining claims for damages the CAT shall actively exercise the CAT's case management powers with a view to ensuring that the case is dealt with justly.[48] "Justly" is defined in the CAT Rules in similar terms to the "overriding objective" set out in Part 1 of the CPR.[49]   **4–101**

(p) Security for costs

A defendant to a claim for damages may by request seek security for his costs of the proceedings.[50] That request should be supported by written evidence setting out the basis on which security for his costs is sought.[51] The defendant's written evidence should address the question of why it would be   **4–102**

---

[41] Rule 43(3).
[42] Rule 43(5).
[43] Rule 43(6).
[44] Rule 43(7).
[45] Rule 43(8).
[46] Rule 43(9).
[47] Rule 43(10).
[48] Rule 44(1). The relevant case management powers are set out in Rules 17 (consolidation), 18 (forum), 19 (directions), 20 (case management conferences), 21 (timetable for oral hearings), 22 (evidence), 23 (witnesses) and 24 (failure to comply with directions).
[49] Rule 44(1).
[50] Under Rule 45(1).
[51] Rule 45(2).

just in all the circumstances for the CAT to make an order for security for costs. The circumstances which may make it just to order security for costs include the following:[51a]

(a) whether is appears that the application is made in order to stifle a genuine claim, or would have that effect whether or not that is the intention behind the defendant's application;

(b) the stage of the proceedings at which the application is made and the amount of costs which the claimant has incurred to the date of the application;

(c) the claimant's financial position, whether it is impecunious and if so why it is impecunious and particularly, whether the impecuniosity can be attributed to the defendant's infringement;

(d) the likely outcome of the proceedings and the relative strengths of the parties' cases, if that can be discerned without prolonged examination or voluminous evidence;

(e) any admissions by the defendant, open offers or the like, but the defendant should not be adversely affected in seeking security because it has attempted to resolve the matter using alternative dispute resolution; and

(f) the provisions of Rule 55 of the CAT's Rules as to orders for costs.

Orders for security for costs are likely to be rare in the CAT. In cases not involving a "passing on" defence the only issue will be as to quantum of damages and in such cases absent special factors such as payments into court or unreasonable or vexatious conduct the defendant will not normally be entitled to costs. In cases involving a passing on defence, until the availability of such a defence is established in actions under the Competition Act the burden of risk as to costs is likely to be left to be assumed by the defendant as a person already found to have infringed public law.[51b]

The defendant must also show that one or more of the conditions contained in Rule 45(5)(a) to (g) applies. Those conditions are all essentially matters which might make it difficult for the defendant to recuperate any costs he was held entitled to following a successful defence of the claim. The provisions of the CAT Rules in this area broadly follow those contained in the CPR.[52]

[51a] *BCL Old Co Ltd and Ors v Aventis SA and Ors (Security for Costs)* [2005] CAT 2 at para.27.
[51b] *BCL (Security for Costs)*, *ibid.*, at paras 40–43. The need to file evidence of the costs incurred and anticipated (at para.47). The CAT also said (at para.48) that it would be unlikely to order an automatic stay of proceedings pending payment where security has been ordered. Instead the claimant would be given a reasonable time to pay. To do otherwise might unduly delay or disrupt the preparation of the case for trial.
[52] Pt 25.

(q) Interim payments

The CAT may order a defendant to make an interim payment of damages.[53] **4–103** An interim payment is a payment on account of any damages that the defendant against whom the order is sought has admitted his liability to pay and where the CAT is satisfied that, if the claim were to be heard, the claimant would obtain judgment for a substantial amount of money (other than costs) against that defendant.[54] The CAT must not order an interim payment of more than a reasonable proportion of the likely amount of the final judgment.[55]

A request for an order for an interim payment of damages may not be made before the time for the filing of the defence has expired.[56] A claimant may make more than one request for an order for an interim payment.[57]

The request must set out the grounds on which the interim payment is sought and any directions necessary in the opinion of the claimant for the determination of the request.[58]

On receiving a request for an interim payment the Registrar shall send a copy to all the other parties to the proceedings and shall inform them of the date by which they may submit written or oral observations to the CAT.[59]

(r) Transfer of claims from the CAT

If at any stage of the proceedings the CAT considers, whether at the request **4–104** of a party, or on its own initiative, that the claim or any part of it could be more appropriately dealt with by another court it may direct that a claim for damages (other than a claim included in proceedings under s.47B of the Competition Act) be transferred to the High Court or county court in England and Wales or Northern Ireland or to the Court of Session or a sheriff court in Scotland.[60]

Where the CAT makes an order transferring proceedings to another court it shall notify the parties in writing of the transfer and shall send to the other

---

[53] Under Rule 46.
[54] Rule 46(4).
[55] Rule 46(5).
[56] Rule 46(2).
[57] Rule 46(3).
[58] Rule 46(6).
[59] Rule 46(7).
[60] It has been said "... It is not for this court to make trial management decisions in the proceedings before the court for the collateral purpose of affecting the course of proceedings before the tribunal or to preempt case management decisions by the tribunal which the tribunal is perfectly competent to make on its own." See *ICL v Synstar* [2001] U.K.C.L.R. 585 at para.18 (claim for injunction started issue whether case should be stayed pending an appeal to the CCAT in respect of a decision of the OFT in relation to the same conduct). It seems reasonable to assume that a similar approach is likely to be adopted by the CAT. In England & Wales the transfer will be to the High Court (Chancery Division), see n.61, below.

court a notice of the transfer containing the name of the case accompanied by the CAT's case file.

(s) Transfer of claims to the CAT

4–105   A claim for damages made under s.47A of the Competition Act may be transferred to the CAT from any court in accordance with rules of court or any practice direction.[61]

According to the CAT Rules, within seven days of the order of the court transferring the claim, the claimant must send to the Registrar a certified copy of the order of the court transferring the claim to the CAT; any pleadings and documents in support of the claim filed with the court in which the claim was begun and any directions sought for the further progress of the claim.[62]

Following receipt of the documents relating to the claim a case management conference will be convened.

4–106   **Transfer of section 47A claims to the CAT by the High Court.**   Under the Civil Procedure Rules, where the court orders a transfer it will immediately send to the CAT a notice of the transfer containing the name of the case and all papers relating to the case and notify the parties of the transfer.[63]

When the English Court considers whether to make an order to transfer the court shall take into account whether:

- there is a similar claim under s.47A of the Competition Act based on the same infringement currently before the CAT[64];

- the CAT has previously made a decision on a similar claim under s.47A of the Competition Act based on the same infringement[65];

---

[61] s.16(4) of the Enterprise Act 2002. Rules of Court have been introduced to implement this provision in Great Britain: see Civil Procedure Rules Pt 30, PD 8.1–8.8; Chapter 32A of the Rules of the Court of Session, inserted by the Act of Sederunt (Rules of the Court of Session Amendment No.5) (Miscellaneous) 2004 (SSI 2004/331). In England and Wales the transfer will be made by a judge of the Chancery Division of the High Court to which all claims involving competition law must be transferred: see CPR Pt 30.8. It is open to the Chancery Division judge to transfer with the case as the judges of the Chancery Division have all been appointed as chairmen of the tribunal.

[62] Rule 49(2).

[63] 30 PD 8.5. Unfortunately the current CPR Practice Direction, which was made some time after the CAT Rules were enacted does not dovetail very conveniently with Rule 49 which, while naturally not imposing any obligations on the High Court, merely envisages an Order for transfer and the transmission of the Court File to the party requesting the transfer for filing in the tribunal. A number of consequential orders upon transfer will need to be considered by the parties and the CAT, notably as to the form of the statement of case, documents lodged and the number of copies required. Where a number of similar claims have already been commenced in the CAT it may be that the transferred claim will look rather different in from those originally commenced in the CAT.

[64] 30 PD 8.4(1).

[65] 30 PD 8.4(2).

- the CAT has developed considerable expertise by previously dealing with a significant number of cases arising form the same or similar infringements.[66]

Although these are matters which shall be taken into account a number of other factors may also be relevant and are not excluded from consideration.

Transfers of section 47A claims to the CAT by the Court of Session. The Rules of Session provide that an application to transfer a cause to the CAT may be made by motion. Where the cause is transferred the Deputy Principal Clerk of Session shall, within four days after the interlocutor transferring the cause has been pronounced, transmit the process to the party on whose motion the transfer was made together with a certified copy of the interlocutor granting the motion.[67] Once the original process (the pleadings) have been transmitted to the party which requested the transfer, the process must then under the Rules be filed at the CAT within seven days accompanied by any directions sought as to the further progress of the claim.[68]   **4–107**

Transfer of other claims to the CAT. Section 16 of the Enterprise Act provides that the Lord Chancellor may by regulations make provision for the courts to transfer to the CAT for its determination so much of any proceedings before the court as relates to an infringement issue.[69]   **4–108**

8. HEARINGS

Hearing to be in public. The hearing of any appeal, review or claim for damages is to be held in public except for any part of the proceedings where the CAT is satisfied that it will be considering information which is, in its opinion, information of the kind referred to in para.1(2) of Sch.4 to the Enterprise Act. That is information the disclosure of which would be contrary to the public interest, divulge business secrets or the private affairs of an individual which would or might significantly harm the interests of the undertaking or individual concerned.[70]   **4–109**

Confidentiality. It should be noted that just because the CAT is "considering" information of the type described above it does not automatically follow that it must sit in private. It may be possible for the information to which reference is being made to be identified without the need for it to be   **4–110**

---

[66] 30 PD 8.4(3).
[67] Rule 32A.1(2) of the Rules of the Court of Session.
[68] Rule 49(2). The new Guide is likely to specify the number of copies which should accompany the transferred pleadings.
[69] The power provided for in this late amendment to the Act has yet to be exercised.
[70] Rule 50. Case management conferences are also generally held in public, see para.4–031, n.17, above.

actually stated in public. The CAT has developed a practice of ensuring that confidential information is clearly identified in the documents from which it, the parties and witnesses are working. In this way, a particular figure, for example, can be identified without being stated in public. In such cases the information in question is not confidential to professional advisers[71] and/or the parties themselves but is sought be kept confidential *vis-à-vis* the wider public as a whole.

4–111   **Procedure at the hearing.**   The hearing is opened and directed by the President or the chairman who is responsible for the proper conduct of the hearing.[72]

As far as appropriate, the CAT will seek to avoid formality in it is proceedings and shall conduct the hearing in such manner as it considers most appropriate for the clarification of the issues before it and, in accordance with its general case management philosophy, for the just, expeditious and economical handling of the proceedings.[73]

As far as possible the CAT holds short structured hearings based on the CFI model.[74] The CAT's approach to the nature of the hearing is heavily influenced by its largely written procedure, which reflects a model that in "broad overview" has been found to be a suitable model for the types of cases the CAT is asked to determine.[75] Given the written development of their cases the parties are expected at the oral hearing to focus on the principal written submissions already made and to respond to any questions the CAT may wish to ask. Indicative time estimates for submissions may be issued by the CAT.

Generally this procedure is particularly suitable method of proceeding in cases involving relatively complex assessments of fact and/or law heavily dependent on documents. In some cases where there are genuine disputes of primary fact and credibility, oral evidence and cross-examination will be permitted where this is necessary to determine the matters in issue. Whether oral evidence is really necessary to resolve matters in issue should be identified as far in advance of the hearing as possible. The CAT may limit cross-examination of witnesses to any extent or in any manner it deems appropriate.[76]

In cartel cases involving significant disputes of fact the practice has been for the OFT to call its witnesses for cross examination followed by the witnesses of the appellant(s). Closing submissions have been made first by the appellants followed by the OFT. The appellants have then had the last

---

[71] Through the use of a confidentiality ring, see para.4–129, below.
[72] Rule 51(1).
[73] Rule 51(2).
[74] Guide, para.12.7.
[75] *Floe Telecom Ltd v Ofcom* [2004] CAT 7 at para.30.
[76] Rule 51(4). The CAT has said that in appeals against penalties a certain latitude may be given to a party to explore commercially confidential matters in open court where this is necessary as a matter of fairness: *JJB Sports plc v OFT* [2004] CAT 17 at para.326.

word by way of reply.[77] This practice is still relatively underdeveloped given the limited number of cases of this type that have been heard by the CAT.

Witnesses. Unless the CAT directs otherwise, no witness of fact or expert shall be heard unless the relevant witness statement or expert report has been submitted in advance of the hearing and in accordance with any directions of the CAT.[78] It should be recalled that as far as practicable all documents including witness statements should be annexed to the notice of appeal, defence or statement of intervention.[79] The CAT's practice to date has generally been to permit witnesses to remain in court during cross examination of other witnesses.

4–112

Skeleton arguments. The fact that the CAT expects a detailed notice of appeal implies that in many cases it will not be necessary to file lengthy skeleton arguments.

4–113

Oral openings. Opening oral statements of any length should rarely be necessary as the parties' cases will have been set out in detail in their written submissions.

4–114

Report for the hearing. In cases to date the CAT has directed the filing of skeleton arguments rather than sending out a report for the hearing.[80]

4–115

(a) Quorum

Chairman unable to continue. If, after the commencement of any hearing, the chairman is unable to continue, the President may appoint either of the remaining two members to chair the CAT; and in that case the CAT shall consist of the remaining two members for the rest of the proceedings.[81] If the person so appointed is not a member of the panel of chairmen, the President may appoint himself or some other suitably qualified person to attend the proceedings and advise the remaining members on any questions of law arising.[82] A person is "suitably qualified" if he is, or is qualified for appointment as, a member of the panel of chairmen.[83]

4–116

Member unable to continue. If, after the commencement of any hearing, a member of the CAT (other than its chairman) is unable to continue, the

4–117

---

[77] *JJB Sports plc v OFT*, n.76, above, *Argos v OFT (Case Management: New Material)* [2004] CAT 24.
[78] Rule 51(3).
[79] Rule 8(6)(b), 14(5), 16(9)(c).
[80] Rule 19(2)(d), Guide, para.12.4.
[81] Rule 52(1).
[82] Rule 52(2).
[83] Rule 52(3).

President may decide that the CAT shall consist of the remaining two members for the rest of the proceedings.[82] Where the CAT consists of two members its decision must be unanimous.[83]

9. CONFIDENTIALITY AND DISCLOSURE

4–118   **General.**   In the course of an investigation the OFT (or other sector regulator) may obtain personal, commercial and other potentially sensitive information from a wide range of persons.[84] The complex set of obligations which govern the circumstances in which the OFT is either required or may be permitted to disclose such information to third parties is dealt with in paras 3–058–3–065, above. The way in which the relevant provisions are interpreted will inevitably have an influence on the frequency and nature of applications for disclosure to the CAT. Issues of disclosure are particularly likely to arise in relation to material in the OFT's possession which has not been disclosed because it does not "relate" to the Rule 4 Notice. Disclosure of such "unused" material may be sought by an appellant the defence (insofar as it is aware of the material's existence) in a case involving penalties on the basis that it is actually or may potentially be relevant to its defence.

4–119   **Third parties.**   Without prejudice to the statutory regime governing the disclosure of information to a person subject to a Rule 4 Notice it is axiomatic that a public authority remains under a duty to act fairly. The CAT has held that it will be generally proper, as a matter of fairness in administrative law, for the OFT in exercising its discretion, to disclose a non-confidential version of the Rule 4 Notice to a complainant who has been closely associated with the OFT's investigation. It has also held that such a person has a right to comment on the decision to reject a complaint.[85]

4–120   **Complainants' appeals.**   It should be noted that in most appeals against an OFT decision to reject a complaint the CAT's task is to identify whether the respondent has made any material error of law, whether he has carried out a proper investigation, whether his reasons are adequate and whether there are material errors in his appreciation. This is a similar exercise to that carried out by the CAT on an application for review. It should not, at least ordinarily, be necessary to go in great depth into the underlying documents in order to establish whether any of these grounds arise.[86] Such disclosure is accordingly "unlikely to be the norm".[87] Once an appeal has been filed a

---

[82] Rule 52(4).

[83] Rule 52(4).

[84] "Investigation" is here not confined merely to the situation where the OFT has concluded that there are reasonable grounds for suspecting that an infringement has been committed and has decided to open a formal investigation under s.25 of the CA 98.

[85] *Pernod-Ricard v OFT* [2004] CAT 10, at para.241.

[86] *Claymore (Disclosure: Confidentiality)* [2003] CAT 12 at p.7.

duty remains on public authority respondents voluntarily to assist a court or CAT with full and accurate explanations of all the facts relevant to the issue the court or CAT must decide, so far as that is compatible with the statutory regime.[90]

The CAT. The general restriction on disclosure imposed on the OFT under Part 9 of the Enterprise Act does not apply to the CAT.[91] In making applications for disclosure of such information to the CAT[92] it is important to bear in mind two preliminary questions: the first being, whether the material sought can be said to be potentially relevant to an issue in the case, and secondly, the extent to which the information relates to a legitimate business interest, or might cause harm to an individual, undertaking or the public interest. Only if both these questions can be answered in the affirmative does the need arise to consider the extent to which disclosure should be made. As will be seen below the CAT has given each of these questions close scrutiny before determining whether disclosure is necessary and proportionate.

4–121

Requests for confidential treatment of documents. The CAT Rules require a person requesting confidential treatment of a document or any part of a document filed in connection with proceedings before the CAT, to do so in writing within 14 days of the filing of that document, giving specific reasons for the request.[93] A request made outside the 14 day period shall not be permitted unless the circumstances are exceptional.[94]

4–122

Disputes. In the event of a dispute as to whether a claim to confidentiality should be maintained the CAT Rules state that the CAT shall under Rule 53(3) determine the matter taking into account the matters referred to in para.(2) of Sch.4 to the Enterprise Act.[95] That provision provides that in preparing the document which records a decision of the CAT, the CAT shall have regard to the need for excluding, so far as practicable:

4–123

- Information the disclosure of which would in its opinion be contrary to the public interest[96];

---

[89] *ibid.*

[90] *Aquavitae v DGWS* [2003] CAT 17; [2004] Comp. A.R. 117 at para.219 (where the Director voluntarily disclosed certain "internal" documents verifying what factors had been taken into account in reaching his decision), citing Laws L.J. in *R. (Quark Fishing Ltd) v Secretary of State for Foreign and Commonwealth Affairs* [2002] EWCA Civ 1409, [2002] All E.R. (D) 450 at para.50. In *Aquavitae* at para.219 the CAT said that such disclosure was unlikely to be the norm because of the limited evidential value of internal preparatory documents. This is one aspect of the duty to conduct public law litigation with all cards face up on the table referred to by the tribunal in *IBA Health v OFT* citing *R. v Lancashire CC Ex p. Huddleston* [1986] 2 All E.R. 941.

[91] s.235(5).

[92] Under Rule 19(2)(k).

[93] Rule 53(1).

[94] Rule 53(2).

[95] Rule 53(3).

[96] Sch.4, para.1(2)(a).

- Commercial information the disclosure of which would or might, in its opinion, significantly harm the legitimate business interests of the undertaking to which it relates[97];

- Information relating to the private affairs of an individual the disclosure of which would, or might, in its opinion, significantly harm his interests.[98]

The requirement to have regard to the need for exclusion from the decision of information falling into these categories is subject to the need also to have regard to the extent to which any disclosure of that information is necessary for the purpose of explaining the reasons for the decision.[99]

The interrelationship between the power to order disclosure under the CAT Rules and the terms of para.1(2) of Sch.4 to the Enterprise Act is slightly awkward as para.1(2) on its face only applies to the document recording the CAT's decision. However, in order to give meaningful effect to that requirement the CAT will take such steps to protect during the proceedings information that it would be likely to regard as confidential for the purposes of its judgment, subject to the overriding requirement of ensuring the fairness of the proceedings.[1] In the event of a conflict between the rights of the defence and other claims to confidentiality there is a presumption that the rights of the defence prevail.[2]

4–124   **Hearings *in camera*.**   The CAT has power under Rule 50 of the CAT Rules to conduct hearings in camera to protect the categories of information specified in para.1(2) of Sch.4 to the Enterprise Act.[3]

4–125   **Information whose disclosure would be contrary to the public interest.**   Under this category of information the OFT has sought to protect information provided to it in the course of an application for leniency. The CAT has accepted that there is a public interest in those undertakings who seek leniency being able to do so at least in the first instance, in confidence and should not be denied that confidence unless there are important countervailing reasons.[4] Parties who seek leniency and thereby expose wrongdoing should not be placed unnecessarily at risk of potential commercial retaliation in the market place.[5] This approach requires a balancing exercise to be

---

[97] Sch.4, para.1(2)(b).
[98] *ibid.*, para.1(2)(c).
[99] *ibid.*, para.1(3).
[1] *Umbro Holdings Ltd v OFT(Application for Leniency: Confidentiality)* [2003] CAT 26 (October 27, 2003) at para.23; *Argos v OFT*, n.77, above, at para.56 (the CAT specifically mentioned its role in this respect in the context of Art.6(1) ECHR).
[2] *ibid.*, at para.33.
[3] The Tribunal has said that in appeals against penalties a certain latitude may be given to a party to explore commercially confidential matters in open court where this is necessary as a matter of fairness: *JJB Sports plc v OFT* [2004] CAT 17 at para.326.
[4] *Umbro Holdings Ltd v OFT*, n.1, above, at para.34.
[5] *ibid.*

conducted by the CAT between the relevant public interest, such as the effectiveness of the OFT's leniency programme, on the one hand with other considerations, such as the rights of the defence, on the other. In some cases the CAT may be able to reach its conclusion as to whether or not to order disclosure without seeing the documents in question. In other cases the CAT may not feel able to conduct the exercise without at least a schedule and brief description of the documents. Where appropriate the CAT may need to inspect the documents itself in a manner somewhat akin to applications for public interest immunity. Such consideration may in the first instance take place *in camera*.

Information whose disclosure would harm a legitimate business inter- **4–126** **est.** Such information typically consists of information relating to market shares, revenues, costs and information regarding yields of various kinds.[6] Commercial information of this nature which was over three years old has been held to be too old to be capable of causing "significant harm" to the interests of the undertaking concerned, or that there would be any "legitimate" business interest that still required protecting.[7] In the absence of any evidence of possible harm being put forward, information two and a half years old has been held not to give rise to any legitimate interest deserving of protection.[8]

In *Umbro*[9] the CAT doubted whether an undertaking appealing on the basis of its failed application for leniency had any legitimate business interest within the meaning of Sch.4 to the Enterprise Act in maintaining the confidentiality in respect of the principal fact on which it relied on in its appeal, or that by the appeal stage there was any remaining confidentiality within the meaning of the Act.[10]

The commercial repercussions which may follow if competitors become aware that an undertaking which had obtained leniency had acted contrary to their business interests is not generally the sort of information that qualifies for protection under para.1(2)(b) of Sch.4 to the Enterprise Act.[11] Such an argument may be more appropriately advanced as a public interest ground for protecting certain information.[12]

It is important to note that there is no absolute guarantee of being able to maintain confidentiality indefinitely when an application for leniency is made to the OFT.[13] Thus while non-disclosure of such information at or

---

[6] *Aberdeen Journals Ltd v DGFT (Confidentiality of Judgment)* [2003] CAT 14.
[7] *Aberdeen Journals*, n.6, above. The tribunal doubted that there was a risk that the disclosure of turnover figures between 2 to 3 years could "significantly harm" an undertaking's business interests.: *Umbro Holdings v OFT(Disclosure: Terms of Confidentiality)* [2003] CAT 29.
[8] *Argos v OFT* [2004] CAT 5 at para.61.
[9] *Umbro Holdings Ltd v OFT*, n.1, above.
[10] *Umbro Holdings Ltd v OFT*, n.1, above at para.41.
[11] *Argos v OFT*, n.8, above, at para.64. On the facts the CAT concluded that it was "extremely unlikely" that commercial repercussions would follow if the information was disclosed
[12] See para.4–125, above.
[13] *Umbro Holdings Ltd v OFT*, n.1, above at para.42.

near the time of the application for leniency may be justified it cannot be assumed that non-disclosure will continue to be justified some years later at the stage of an appeal.

4–127   **Information necessary to explain the reasons for the decision.**   In *Replica Football Kit*, Umbro appealed to the CAT solely on the amount of the penalty on the basis that the OFT had taken insufficient account of its co-operation during the administrative procedure. Umbro resisted disclosure to the other parties of a failed application for leniency and documents which consisted of certain draft witness statements and accompanying correspondence. The CAT pointed out that Umbro's very appeal relied squarely upon the material in respect of which it sought to prevent disclosure. In those circumstances it would be "virtually impossible" to write the CAT's decision without referring to its application, the fact of which Umbro in any event accepted would have come to light during the appeal.[14] The CAT also referred to the fact that it would be "almost impossible" to conduct the public hearing without revealing the fact of the application. The difficulty of conducting the oral hearing in such a case in camera pointed to disclosure.[15] The CAT was also satisfied that the information might have a "horizontal" effect on the other parties who in fairness ought to have the information disclosed to them in order to determine whether, for example, they had been discriminated against in respect of the penalty,[16] or to assess the reliability of the evidence submitted by Umbro.[17] These considerations mean that turn-over information of an undertaking during the period of the infringement is likely to have to be disclosed as well as the OFT's starting percentage applied to the "relevant turnover" in calculating the amount of the penalty. It may be that by the time of an appeal the information in question will be too old to be covered by business confidentiality.[18] However, even if the information in question remained sensitive it would likely still have to be disclosed in the light of the considerations set out above.

4–128   **Privilege.**   It has been claimed that "settlement" negotiations between the OFT and a company under investigation, which led the OFT to close its investigation and accept assurances as to the company's future conduct, are protected from disclosure by "without prejudice" privilege. The CAT, without deciding the matter, considered this claim with some scepticism.[19] The non disclosure of the content of such negotiations may well be more appropriately argued on public interest grounds.

In civil litigation, notes made in connection with the preparation of witness statements and drafts of such statements may well attract privilege from

---

[14] *Umbro Holdings Ltd v OFT*, n.1, above at para.37.
[15] *Umbro Holdings Ltd v OFT*, n.1, above at para.38.
[16] *Umbro Holdings Ltd v OFT*, n.1, above at para.39.
[17] *Umbro Holdings Ltd v OFT*, n.1, above at para.40.
[18] *Umbro Holdings Ltd v OFT*, n.1, above at para.20.
[19] *Pernod-Ricard v OFT* [2004] CAT 3 at paras 73–74.

disclosure. It is unclear the extent to which privilege covers such material in the OFT's possession. In criminal proceedings such material is not privileged from disclosure. The position of the OFT in the context of proceedings under the Competition Act 1998 is clearly more akin to that of a prosecutor than a private party involved in civil litigation. The issue has yet to be determined by the CAT.

Disclosure on a limited basis.   In some situations the CAT may be prepared to contemplate the disclosure of confidential information on a limited basis. This may involve disclosure of the information in question to legal or other professional advisers subject to undertakings by those persons not to disclose the information without the permission of the CAT; a so called "confidentiality ring".[20]   **4–129**

The need for such an approach will not automatically be accepted by the CAT.[21] Such confidentiality arrangements also have the potential to put professional advisers in an extremely difficult position *vis-à-vis* their clients. In cases involving penalties such arrangements are generally inappropriate unless there are "very strong countervailing considerations".[22]

This approach has in some cases been adopted in the context of appeals against decisions of the OFT to reject a complaint.[23] This approach may assist to address the balance between the public interest in the exercise of litigation taking place with as full disclosure as possible and the need to protect the legitimate business secrets of the undertaking complained about which have been obtained by the OFT in the course of its investigation.[24] Where the parties can agree to such arrangements this may offer the practical advantage that work on the case can take place without the immediate need for contested interim applications concerning confidentiality which may affect the expedition, efficiency and cost with which the proceedings may be determined.

Interests of third parties.   It is vital that third parties potentially affected by applications for the disclosure of confidential information are notified as soon as practicable in order that they may be given an opportunity to make any observations they wish on the application.   **4–130**

---

[20] *Claymore v DGFT (confidentiality)* [2003] CAT 12. For an example of the terms of such a "confidentiality ring" of professional advisers see the CAT's order of June 9, 2003 in the above case available on the tribunal's website. *Genzyme v OFT (Disclosure of Confidential Information)* [2003] CAT 7. A similar approach is adopted in the Patent Court: see *Warner-Lambert Co v Glaxo Laboratories Ltd* [1975] R.P.C. 354, CA and *Roussel Uclaf v Imperial Chemical Industries plc* [1990] R.P.C. 45.
[21] "...confidentiality rings have disadvantages. There is undoubtedly scope for error. The amount of information disclosed within them should be kept to a minimum necessary to do justice in a case. They should not be overloaded." *Claymore Dairies v OFT (Recovery and Inspection)* [2004] CAT 16 at para.115.
[22] *Umbro Holdings Ltd v OFT*, n.7, above, at para.30.
[23] In particular see para.4–120, above as to when disclosure is appropriate in such cases.
[24] *ibid.*, at para.13.

4–131 **Information in the published decision.** Disputes may arise in relation to material that is to be contained in the published version of the OFT's decision. A decision of the OFT to publish material in its decision is not itself an appealable decision specified under the Competition Act.[25] However, under its powers to grant interim relief the CAT may suspend in whole or in part the effect of any decision which is the subject matter of proceedings before it and may grant any remedy on an interim basis which it would have the power to grant in its final decision where that is necessary to prevent serious irreparable damage. Given that the CAT has the power in its final judgment to give such directions or take such other steps as the OFT could itself have given or taken or make any decision which the OFT itself could have made this could also include the question of the confidentiality of the information included in the decision. Accordingly it is arguable that on an application for interim relief the CAT does have the jurisdiction to grant interim relief in this situation, which might take the form of suspending parts of the Decision from publication pending the determination of the appeal. The alternative would appear to require the appellant to make a separate claim for judicial review of the OFT's decision to include the material in question. The CAT has demonstrated an understandable reluctance to find that an appellant is required to commence separate proceedings in relation to issues closely connected with their appeal before the CAT.[26] If the CAT is required in delivering its own decision to have regard to the need to protect confidential information it would be unfortunate if that possibility could effectively be pre-empted by the decision of the OFT before the CAT is in a position to fully consider and determine the matter.[27]

10. DECISION OF THE CAT

4–132 **Delivery.** The decision of the CAT must be delivered in public on the date fixed for that purpose.[28] The CAT's usual practice in relation to more substantial reserved decisions is to send a copy of the decision in draft to the parties' legal representatives in advance of the date fixed for the delivery of the decision subject to an embargo preventing the dissemination of its contents until shortly before the decision is delivered.[29] Any suggested corrections approved by the CAT can then be incorporated as appropriate into the draft that is formally handed down.

---

[25] ss.46 and 47.
[26] See *Bettercare Group Ltd v DGFT (Admissibility of Appeal)* [2001] CAT 6; [2002] Comp. A.R. 9.
[27] Even if the material in question is not confidential, a person affected by a decision should be consulted on matters in the decision before it is finalised: see *Pernod-Ricard v OFT*, n.19, above.
[28] Rule 54(1).
[29] Legal representative will generally cover any lawyer involved in the case who is subject to relevant professional disciplinary arrangements.

Notification. The decision of the CAT will be treated as having been notified on the date on which a copy of the document recording it is sent to the parties.[30] In practice notification will take place when the parties are provided with a copy of the decision at the hearing at which the decision is delivered.[31]   4–133

Publication. The decision of the CAT are published on the CAT's website and published in an official series of reports as approved by the President.[32]   4–134

Decisions as to costs. Generally, written decisions on costs are treated by the CAT as being ancillary to the main decision and are to be delivered at a separate hearing, subject to the observations of the parties on the issue.   4–135

11. COSTS

Introduction. The CAT has delivered a number of judgments on the question of costs (or in Scotland expenses).[33] It is important to bear in mind, as the CAT has pointed out, that experience of the range of different types of appeals which may be brought under the Competition Act 1998 is evolving. The CAT has also now considered on two occasions the question of costs in the context of proceedings under the Enterprise Act. The CAT has been at pains to point out that principles referred to in individual cases should not be allowed to harden into rigid rules. The facts of particular cases are crucial to understanding the particular result achieved.   4–136

No presumption that the loser pays. The starting point under the CAT Rules in relation to costs is that there is no presumption that costs should generally be awarded to a successful appellant as there is in civil litigation.[34] Equally, however, there is no presumption that costs should only be awarded where a party has behaved unreasonably, frivolously or vexatiously.[35]   4–137

GISC: costs. In *Institute of Independent Insurance Brokers and Association of British Travel Agents v DGFT*[36] the CAT allowed appeals by the IIB and ABTA that the Director had been wrong to grant negative clearance to the   4–138

---

[30] Rule 54(3).
[31] This is important for the purposes of calculating the time within which a request for permission to appeal must be made. See paras 4–148–4–162, below.
[32] Rule 54(4). The official reports of the CAT's decisions are the Competition Appeal Reports published by Jordans.
[33] The CAT's jurisdiction to award costs is set out in Rule 55(2) of the Tribunal Rules. Rule 55 is in materially the same terms as Rule 26 of the Competition Commission Appeal Tribunal Rules 2000 under which a number of the cases referred to were decided.
[34] See Civil Procedure Rule 44.3(2)(a) for the position in England and Wales.
[35] As was the case under Rule 58(1) of the Restrictive Practices Court Rules 1976.
[36] [2001] CAT 4; [2001] Comp. A.R. 33.

rules of the General Insurance Standards Council ("GISC") which had been notified to him under the Competition Act for a decision as to their compatibility with the Chapter I prohibition.[37] IIB and ABTA sought their costs of the successful appeal. In its judgment the CAT set out a wide number of factors which may be relevant to the question of costs. A number of these, depending on the circumstances, have featured more or less prominently in subsequent cases[38]:

- A general or rigid rule that a losing appellant should normally be liable for a respondent's costs in the absence of unreasonable conduct could tend to deter appeals especially by smaller companies.[39]

- The cost to the public purse as a reason for not awarding costs against an unsuccessful respondent cannot be decisive when fairness indicates otherwise, even where the Director is not guilty of unreasonable conduct. Case management powers better address concerns regarding costs in future cases *e.g.* in relation to disclosure or multi-party appeals.[40]

- The CAT doubted that the challenged decision could be said to have been taken on "grounds that reasonably appeared to be sound."[41]

- The significant financial expense and significant financial detriment incurred in bringing an appeal by the IIB relative to its size was a factor in awarding costs against the respondent.[42]

- Although ABTA was not so seriously affected as the IIB it had succeeded on the basis of a relatively clear-cut point of law on which the respondent had fallen into error.[43]

- GISC should pay the extra costs incurred by the applicants of its intervention following the practice of the CFI. There was force in the argument that the costs of intervention should be born by the intervener irrespective of the outcome of the appeal but in this case it was appropriate to make an order that GISC pay 15 per cent of the applicants' costs.[44]

- Costs should be assessed in summary fashion wherever possible.[45]

---

[37] s.14 has since been repealed.
[38] See *Institute of Independent Insurance Brokers and Association of British Travel Agents v DGFT (GISC: costs)* [2002] CAT 2.
[39] *ibid.*, at para.54.
[40] *ibid.*, at paras 57–61.
[41] *ibid.*, at para.67 *per* Bingham L.C.J. in *Booth v Bradford MBC* (164 J.P. 485).
[42] *ibid.*, at para.68.
[43] *ibid.*, at para.73.
[44] *ibid.*, at para.75–82.
[45] *ibid.*, at para.86.

Penalty appeals. In relation to appeals against penalties the CAT has stated that[46]:   **4–139**

"In general, we would lean against costs orders against unsuccessful appellants in cases involving penalties unless there were particular exceptional circumstances justifying such orders. The appellant, in such cases, has already suffered the penalty, and possibly further directions, as well as having to bear its own costs. To make a further order for costs may well be excessive in many cases."

The CAT qualified those remarks in a later case where it referred to the fact that experience showed that defending such appeals imposed a significant cost on the public purse and that it might well in future be appropriate to award costs against unsuccessful appellants where cases are not kept within "manageable bounds".[47]

Interveners' costs. The general position as far as the CAT is concerned, is that the costs of an intervention will very often in justice be allowed to lie where they fall.[48] In some cases however it will be proper to make orders either in favour of or against interveners but the CAT has said that there should be no general expectation that a successful intervener is necessarily entitled to its costs.[49]   **4–140**

As to a successful intervener's costs in a penalty appeal, in *Aberdeen Journals* the CAT awarded the intervener 60 per cent of its costs of a first appeal and all of its costs in relation to a second appeal.[50] The CAT justified

---

[46] *Napp Pharmaecutical Holdings Ltd v DGFT (Costs and interest)* [2002] CAT 3; [2002] Comp. A.R. 160 at para.6. The CAT dismissed Napp's appeal against the Director's decision that it had infringed the Chapter II prohibition but reduced the penalty by approximately £1 million. The CAT rejected the Director's application that Napp should pay 50 per cent of his costs and ordered both parties to bear their own costs.

[47] *Aberdeen Journals Ltd v DGFT (No.2)* [2003] CAT 11 at para.20. The CAT dismissed an appeal by Aberdeen Journals against the OFT's decision that it had abused its dominant position in the market for the supply of advertising space in free and paid for local newspapers in the Aberdeen area contrary to the Chapter II prohibition. The CAT, however, reduced the penalty from £1,328,060 to £1,000,000. The costs incurred in the proceedings included the reserved costs of an earlier appeal in which the CAT set aside the OFT's decision and remitted the question of market definition to it. Aberdeen Journals and the OFT agreed that the costs of the first and second appeals should lie where they fell and that neither would make an application for costs against the other. As to the intervener's costs: see para.4–140, below.

[48] See *Freeserve v DGFT* [2003] CAT 6.

[49] In *Bettercare Group Ltd v DGFT* [2002] Comp. A.R. 299 the CAT said that it had "some sympathy with the Director's observation that in general it is not appropriate to give costs of interveners against the Director unless there are particular circumstances which justify the award of such costs in a particular case."

[50] A particular feature of this case was that it was conducted before a tribunal in Scotland. As such, the question of what costs would be recoverable was governed by the rules of the Court of Session. The tribunal noted that the rules of the Court of Session do not provide a process for the summary assessment or interim award of expenses (the Scottish term for costs). The tribunal noted that work done by English solicitors in connection with litigation in Scotland, although subject to the jurisdiction of the Auditor of the Court of Session, would

the award of a significant proportion of its costs to the intervener on the following grounds:

- the intervener had been the complainant and target of the abusive conduct;

- it had successfully supported the substantive case being made to the CAT;

- its submissions had been of assistance to the CAT, notably on the issues of market definition and abuse and questions relating to newspaper production costs;

- its submissions did not merely duplicate those of the OFT;

- significantly, the appellants' defence had consisted in part of an attack on the integrity of the intervener's entry into the market and of its proprietor, allegations against which it was entitled to defend itself and which the CAT had comprehensively rejected;

- the fact that Aberdeen Journals and the OFT had reached agreement on the question of costs was not relevant to the costs which the intervener should receive.

However, even where an intervener is successful it by no means follows that a costs order will be made in their favour.[51] While in many cases the costs of an intervention should remain "cost neutral" the CAT has ordered an unsuccessful intervener to pay a proportion of the appellant's costs attributable to an intervention in support of a respondent.[52]

4–141   **Costs in cases involving the regulated sectors.** The CAT has stated that particular considerations may apply in considering the question of costs in appeals under the Competition Act against the decisions of the sectoral regulators.[53] In an appeal against a decision of the Director General of Water Services to reject a complaint the CAT explained the position as follows[54]:

"As the CAT's previous judgments on costs ... explain, there is no general rule in appeals before the CAT under the Competition Act that costs should be borne by the losing party. In the CAT's view, such a rule would run the serious risk of frustrating the objectives of the Act by

---

nevertheless be assessed by the Auditor according to the relevant English rules, it being within his discretion to hear evidence as to the content of those rules. At para.29 referring to *Wimpey Construction (UK) Ltd v Martin Black & Co (Wire Ropes) Ltd* 1988 S.L.T. 637.

[51] *Freeserve v DGFT*, n.48 above, a case decided in the "specific" context of telecommunications (see para.4–141, below.)

[52] *Institute of Independent Insurance Brokers and Association of British Travel Agents v DGFT (GISC: costs)* [2002] CAT 2; [2002] Comp. A.R. 141.

[53] *ibid.*

[54] *Aquavitae v DGWS* [2003] CAT 17 at paras 31 to 32.

deterring appeals by smaller companies, representative bodies and consumers, as the CAT made clear in *GISC costs* at paragraph 54. It seems to us that these policy considerations apply in cases such as the present. In particular it seems to us that potential new entrants to regulated sectors, such as Aquavitae, which do not appear to command substantial financial resources, are liable to be deterred from bringing appeals if the CAT were regularly to order that such appellants should normally be liable for the Director's costs as well as their own, in the absence of unreasonable conduct or some other exceptional factor.

We understand the Director's concern that in the end the costs that he incurs in such appeals have to be borne in one way or another by the industry and, ultimately, its customers. However, looked at more generally, the system of regulation in the water industry, as in other regulated sectors, exists to protect a wide range of different interests, including those of the general public. In our view, the system as a whole will function more effectively if complaints can be brought and the regulator's decision can be challenged on appeal if necessary. The costs incurred in a case such as the present are miniscule by comparison with the total revenues of the water industry taken as a whole, whereas the burden of costs falling on a small complainant, acting reasonably if unsuccessfully, is likely to be disproportionately heavy. We have already indicated that we consider this appeal was reasonably brought albeit not ultimately successful and in the particular circumstances of this case we consider that the Director's costs of the appeal should be regarded as part of the general costs of regulation in this area."

Particular factors may also apply to certain classes of intervener in a regulated sector. In the telecommunications sector the CAT has said:

"In expressing views on the position of BT [the intervener], we are not allowing the indications we are about to give to harden into a rule, but they do express our view in general on interveners in the situation of BT. In the specific case of a sector such as telecommunications, where there may be interveners who are likely to be regularly appearing before the CAT, we think the general practice is likely to be to allow the costs of the intervention to lie where they fall. We can see that if costs were awarded in every case where a complaint was brought against the dominant enterprise and there was later an unsuccessful appeal, the constant risk of having to pay the costs of the dominant enterprise could affect the balance of the system of appeal under the Act."[55]

Costs in cases under the Enterprise Act 2002. In an application for a review **4–142** of the OFT's decision not to refer a merger for investigation by the

---

[55] *Freeserve v DGFT*, n.48, above.

Competition Commission the CAT has held that its "flexible approach" to costs in appeals under the Competition Act should equally be applied to applications for review under the Enterprise Act.[56] Thus, as in the case of appeals under the Competition Act, there is no presumption that costs should necessarily be borne by the losing party in applications for review of a decision by the OFT to clear a merger. In particular the CAT has pointed out that to do so might frustrate the objects of the Enterprise Act by deterring potential applicants who may be much smaller than the parties to the merger.[57] Different considerations are likely to apply where an unfounded application is brought by a corporate appellant with significant financial resources at its disposal.[58] The CAT has signaled its awareness that the costs of litigation in this area can be high and that the objects of the Enterprise Act could also be frustrated if the OFT were routinely liable for large costs orders when it defends an application for review "reasonably albeit unsuccessfully".[59] The CAT will seek to use its case management powers to ensure that proceedings are kept within reasonable bounds. The appropriate order for costs may depend on a variety of factors including whether the applicant has succeeded to a significant extent on the basis of new material introduced after the OFT's decision, whether resources have been devoted to particular issues on which the appellant has not succeeded, or which were not germane to the solution of the case, whether there is unnecessary duplication or prolixity, whether the evidence adduced is of peripheral relevance or the conduct of the successful party has been unreasonable.[60]

4–143   Costs on withdrawal.   Where a party unilaterally decides to withdraw an appeal under the CAT Rules the CAT has stated that the general principle is that the withdrawing party should pay at least a proportion of the respondent's costs.[61] The full costs may not be payable by the withdrawing party because there is an interest in encouraging litigation to be avoided. However, in the "unusual" circumstances of that case no costs were awarded. This was because the appellant had been justified in starting a "protective" appeal against the penalty awarded in one case in circumstances where it was unable to consider its overall position because of a pending second decision in another investigation which had not been made prior to the deadline for lodging an appeal against the first decision.

In respect of an earlier application by the appellant to extend the time for filing the notice of appeal pending the decision relating to a second investigation being issued the CAT ordered the appellant to pay the costs of that application. The circumstances were not exceptional within the meaning of Rule 6(3) of the CCAT's Rules (now 8(2) of the CAT's Rules) and even if

---

[56] *IBA Health v OFT (Costs)* [2004] CAT 6.
[57] *ibid.*, at para.36.
[58] *ibid.*, at para.38.
[59] *ibid.*, at para.41.
[60] *ibid.*, at para.42. *GISC: Costs* [2001] CAT 4; [2001] Comp. A.R. 33 at para.60.
[61] *Hasbro UK Ltd v DGFT* [2003] CAT 2 at para.6.

they had been the CAT would not have exercised its discretion in Hasbro's favour. Although the application was not "frivolous" it was sufficiently "unfounded" to justify an order for costs.[62]

In another case involving the withdrawal of an application for a review of an OFT decision not to refer a merger to the Competition Commission the CAT applied ordered the applicant to pay 25 per cent of the OFT's costs.[63]

In the unusual situation where a respondent decided not to contest an appellant's notice of appeal the CAT ordered the respondent to pay all the appellant's costs.[64]

Timing of applications for costs. The CAT's practice to date has demon-   **4–144**
strated a marked reluctance to determine applications for costs an an interim stage. "[A]s in all interim applications it is difficult to reach a concluded view on costs at the interim stage until one has arrived at a decision on the main appeal unless exceptional circumstances exist."[65]

(a) Interest

Appeals against penalties. If the CAT confirms or varies any penalty it   **4–145**
may, in addition, order that such interest as it considers appropriate is to be payable on that amount from any date not earlier than the date on which the appeal was made. The rate of interest shall not however exceed the judgment rate set by Order under s.44 of the Administration of Justice Act 1970 (currently 8 per cent). It should be noted that bringing an appeal automatically suspends the obligation to pay the penalty until the appeal has been finally determined. The CAT has held that the relevant principle in determining what interest is payable is to ensure that an appellant does not benefit financially from the delay in paying the penalty arising from the appeal. The measure of that benefit will normally be the appellant's cost of borrowing. In that regard a rebuttable presumption of 1 per cent above the Bank of England Base Rate should apply.[66] Such interest forms part of the penalty and may be recovered as a civil debt.[67]

---

[62] See [2003] CAT 1; [2003] Comp. A.R. 47.

[63] This was calculated as approximately the amount of the OFT's external disbursements. The OFT's internal costs being treated as "part of the general costs of the system." See *Federation of Wholesale Distributors v OFT* [2004] CAT 11.

[64] See *ABI v OFT*, order of July 30, 2004. The unusual nature of such an application is highlighted by the fact that Rule 10 of the Tribunal Rules (withdrawal) does not envisage a withdrawal by a Respondent.

[65] *Genzyme v OFT (Costs)* [2003] CAT 9 (re an application for interim measures). See also *Aberdeen Journals v OFT (No.1)* [2002] CAT 4; [2002] Comp. A.R. 167 at para.196 (original decision set aside on procedural grounds need to await any further action by OFT before determining costs); *Bettercare Group Ltd v DGFT* [2002] CAT 7, [2002] Comp AR 299 (preliminary issue as to whether OFT had made an appealable decision).

[66] See *Napp Pharmaceutical Holdings Ltd v DGFT (Costs and interest)* [2002] CAT 3; [2002] Comp. A.R. 160 at para.13. This mirrors the practice of the Commercial Court.

[67] s.36 of the Competition Act 1998.

4–146 **Damages claims.** If it makes an award of damages the CAT may include in any sum awarded interest on all or any part of the damages in respect of which the award is made, for all or any part of the period between the date when the cause of action arose, and

- in the case of any sum paid before the decision making the award, the date of the payment[68];
- in the case of the sum awarded, the date of that decision.[69]

As in penalty cases, the rate of interest shall not exceed the rate specified in any Order made under s.44 of the Administration of Justice Act 1970.[70]

(b) Consent orders

4–147 **Rule 57 of the CAT Rules.** Where the parties agree the terms on which to settle all or any part of the proceedings, they may request the CAT to make a consent order.[71] Despite its wording, compliance with this rule is mandatory as it is effectively a request to withdraw the appeal, a step which can only be effected with the permission of the CAT.[72] In *Napp* the CAT indicated that the requirement to submit a consent order for its approval also applies to the settlement of requests for interim relief.[73] The rule does not apply to claims for damages.[74]

A request for a consent order must be made by sending to the Registrar a draft consent order, a consent order impact statement and a statement signed by all the parties to the proceedings or their legal representatives, requesting that an order be made in the terms sought.[75] The consent order impact statement must provide an explanation of the draft consent order, including an explanation of the circumstances giving rise to the draft order, the relief to be obtained if the order is made and the anticipated effects on competition of that relief.[76]

If the CAT considers that a proposed consent order may have a significant effect on competition it shall direct the Registrar, as soon a practicable following receipt of the application, to publish a notice on the CAT website or in such other manner as the CAT may direct.[77] The notice must specify in particular the name of each party to the proceedings, the relief sought by the parties and include a statement that the impact statement may

---

[68] Rule 56(2)(a).
[69] Rule 56(2)(b).
[70] Currently 8%.
[71] Rule 57(1).
[72] Rule 12, and see para.21(1) of Sch.4 to the Enterprise Act 2002.
[73] *Napp Pharmaceutical Holdings Ltd v DGFT(No.1)* [2001] Comp. A.R. 1.
[74] Rule 57(10).
[75] Rule 57(2)(a) to (c).
[76] Rule 57(3).
[77] Rule 57(4).

be inspected at the Registry or such other place as may be specified in the notice.[78] Comments must be submitted to the CAT within one month of publication of the notice. They must be in writing, signed and stating the name and address of the commentator and the title of the proceedings to which they relate.[79] Comments received will by sent by the Registrar to the parties who have 14 days from receipt in which to send a response to the Registrar in respect of the comments.[80] The CAT, after hearing the parties and considering the comments of third parties, may either make the order in the terms requested, invite the parties to vary its terms or refuse to make any order.[81]

12. APPEALS FROM THE CAT

Competition Act. Under the Competition Act an appeal lies to the "appropriate court" from a decision of the CAT[82]:   **4–148**

- as to the amount of a penalty imposed under s.36 of the Competition Act 1998;

- as to the award of damages or other sum in respect of a claim made in proceedings under s.47A of the Competition Act 1998 or as to the amount of any such damages or other sum;

- on a point of law arising from any other decision of the CAT on an appeal under ss.46 or 47 of the Competition Act 1998.

Under the Competition Act an appeal may be brought by a party to the proceedings before the CAT or by a person who has a sufficient interest in the matter. An appeal from the CAT requires the permission of the CAT or the appropriate court.[83]

Enterprise Act. Under the Enterprise Act an appeal lies to the appropriate court from a decision of the CAT: **4–149**

- on a point of law arising from a decision of the CAT on an appeal under ss.120 or 179 (merger and market investigation decisions).[84]

- on a point of law or the amount of the penalty arising from a decision

---

[78] Rule 57(5).
[79] Rule 57(7).
[80] Rule 57(8).
[81] Rule 57(9).
[82] s.49 of the Competition Act, as substituted by s.21, Sch.5 paras 1, 4, of the Enterprise Act 2002.
[83] s.49(2)(a) of the Competition Act.
[84] ss.120(6) and 179(6) of the Enterprise Act.

of the CAT on an appeal under ss.114 or 176(1) (imposition of penalties by the Competition Commission).[85]

Under the Enterprise Act an appeal from a decision of the CAT requires the permission of the CAT or the appropriate court.[86]

4–150 **Appropriate court.**   The "appropriate court" means the Court of Appeal, or in the case of an appeal from the CAT proceedings in Scotland the Court of Session, or in the case of an appeal from CAT proceedings in Northern Ireland, the Court of Appeal of Northern Ireland.[87]

4–151 **Request for permission.**   A request to the CAT for permission to appeal from a decision of the CAT may be made, orally at any hearing at which the decision is delivered by the CAT; or in writing to the Registrar within one month of the notification of that decision.[88] Requests for permission to appeal are generally made in writing. In the absence of special circumstances the CAT will determine a written application for permission on the papers without a hearing.[89]

Where a request is made in writing it must comply with the following requirements[90]:

- state the name and address of the party and of any representative of the party;

- identify the CAT decision to which the request relates;

- state the grounds on which the party intends to rely in his appeal; and state whether the party requests a hearing of his request and any special circumstances relied on.

4–152 **Point of law.**   There have as yet been few requests to the CAT for permission to appeal. The CAT has emphasised that "a point of law" will arise where: (i) there is a misdirection on a point of law; (ii) there is no evidence to support a relevant finding of fact; or (iii) the CAT's appreciation of the facts and issues before it is one that no reasonable CAT could reach, that is to say the appreciation in question is outside "the permissible field of judgment". It may well be that the principles to be applied are not significantly different

---

[85] ss.114(10) and 176(1)(f). The latter section simply refers back to s.114.

[86] ss.120(7), 176(7), 114(11) and 176(1)(f).

[87] s.49(3) of the Competition Act; ss.120(8), 179(8), 114(12) and 176(1)(f).

[88] Rule 58(1). "Notification" is defined in Rule 54 as the date on which a signed copy of the decision is "sent" to the parties. In *Chelminski v Gdynia America Shipping Lines (London) Ltd, The Times*, July 21, 2004, CA, it was held that "sent" in Rule 3(3)(a) of the Employment Appeal Tribunal Rules (SI 1993/2854) bore its ordinary and natural meaning and was unaffected by the provision relating to the deemed service of documents in s.7 of the Interpretation Act 1978, which did not bear on the date of sending.

[89] Rule 59(2).

[90] Rule 58(2)(a)–(d).

from those applicable in judicial review proceedings.[91] The CAT is frequently called upon to make a number of more or less complex assessments of such questions as the relevant market,[92] the existence of barriers to entry, whether dominance is established or whether a response by a dominant undertaking is proportionate. In such circumstances to constitute a point of law capable of founding a request for permission to appeal, a manifest error of assessment must be alleged.[93]

Appeals against penalty. A request for permission to appeal against the CAT's decision may be made on the ground that the CAT has committed an error of law in its decision in relation to the penalty.[94] Alternatively, the request may be simply "as to the amount of the penalty".[95] In such circumstances there may not be any error of law alleged merely that taking all the circumstances into account the penalty is excessive. Permission to appeal the amount of a penalty, standing alone, could properly be refused by analogy with the practice of the Court of Appeal (Criminal Division), where there are no grounds for supposing that the penalty is either manifestly excessive or wrong in principle.[96]

4–153

Grounds for granting permission. In *Napp* the CAT applied the provisions of the CPR in considering whether to grant permission to appeal to the Court of Appeal which provide that permission to appeal will only be given where the court considers that the appeal would have a real prospect of success or there is some other compelling reason why permission should be granted.[97]

4–154

Appeals from specialist Tribunals. In relation to applications for permission to appeal from the CAT the Court of Appeal has said in relation to the conclusions of an expert and specialist tribunal, specifically constituted by Parliament to make judgments in an area in which judges have no expertise, is an area in which the Court of Appeal would be very slow indeed to enter.[98]

4–155

---

[91] *Napp Pharmaceutical Holdings Ltd v DGFT (Reasons for refusing permission to appeal)*, March 26, 2002 at para.26. Summarising the effect of *Edwards v Bairstow* [1956] A.C. 14; *Pioneer Shipping Ltd v BTP Tioxide ("the Nema") (No.2)* [1982] A.C. 724 at 752–53; *South Yorkshire Transport v Monopolies and Mergers Commission* [1993] 1 All E.R. 291 at 298 d–f; *O'Kelly v Trusthouse Forte plc* [1984] Q.B. 90 at 122H–123C; *Neale v Hereford & Worcester CC* [1986] I.C.R. 471 at 483; *British Telecommunications Plc v Sheridan* [1990] I.R.L.R. 27 at para.35; *Nipa Begum v Tower Hamlets LBC* [2000] 1 W.L.R. 306 at 312 H–313 F.
[92] *Napp Pharmaceutical Holdings Ltd v DGFT (No.5)* [2002] EWCA Civ 796 at para.35 "... a question of market analysis ... is uniquely a matter for the Tribunal."
[93] *ibid.*
[94] Under s.49(1)(c).
[95] s.49(1)(a).
[96] See *Napp Pharmaceutical Holdings Ltd v DGFT(Reasons for refusing permission to appeal)* [2002] CAT 5 at para.36.
[97] CPR Rule 52.3(6).
[98] *Napp Pharmaceutical Holdings Ltd v DGFT (No.5)* [2002] EWCA Civ 796 at para.34, and see 43; [2002] 4 All E.R. 376, citing *Cooke v Secretary of State for Social Security* [2001] EWCA Civ 734.

4–156   **The CAT's decision on permission.**   The issue has been raised as to whether an appellate court can or should have regard to the CAT's explanations in its decision on permission as to what it intended by statements in its first judgment. The Court of Appeal in England and Wales in one case has said that it saw no reason why it should not have regard to such explanations.[99]

4–157   **Appeals to the appropriate court.**   Where a request for permission to appeal is refused by the CAT, permission must be sought from the appropriate appellate court under the relevant rules of procedure. It should be noted that these provisions are not uniform.

(a) Appeals to the Court of Appeal of England and Wales

4–158   The proposed appellant must satisfy the requirements of the Civil Procedure Rules, namely that the appeal would have a real prospect of success or there is some other compelling reason why permission should be granted.[1] This section merely provides an outline of the procedure which must be followed.[2]

Where the appellant requests but is refused permission to appeal by the CAT, he must file his notice of appeal at the Court of Appeal within 14 days of receipt of the CAT's decision.[3] Where the appellant does not make a request to the CAT for permission to appeal, but wishes to make an application to the Court of Appeal for permission, the appellant's notice must be filed at the court of Appeal within 14 days after the end of the period within which he may make a written application to the Registrar of the CAT.[4] Thus a party would normally have six weeks in the case of appeals to the Court of Appeal. However, it is open to the CAT to abridge the time within which an application for permission to appeal should be filed with the Court of Appeal.[5] An appeal to the Court of Appeal does not operate as a stay unless the CAT or the Court of Appeal so orders.[6]

---

[99] *OFT v IBA Health Ltd* [2004] EWCA Civ 142 at para.20. A differently constituted Court of Appeal had regard to the tribunal's reasons for refusing permission to appeal in *Napp Phamaceutical Holdings Ltd v DGFT (No.5) (Reasons for refusing permission to appeal)* [2002] CAT 5 (the argument that they were not entitled to was not raised by the proposed appellants in that case).

[1] CPR Rule 52.3(6).

[2] For the detailed procedural requirements see CPR Rule 52.

[3] Pt 52 Practice Direction, para.21.10(1) and (2) (52PD.92).

[4] *ibid.*, para.21.10(3). Although not mandatory an application for permission to appeal should generally be made to the tribunal first: see *T (A Child)* [2002] EWCA Civ 1736, at paras 12, 13.

[5] CPR 52.4(a).

[6] CPR 52.7.

(b) Appeals to the Court of Session

Chapter 41 of the Rules of the Court of Session make provision for **4–159** appeals under statute. "Leave" to appeal from the Court of Session is required if leave has been refused by the CAT. An application for leave to appeal shall be made, in the first instance, to the tribunal which made the decision sought to be appealed against unless the enactment allowing the appeal requires the application to be made to the court or there are "special circumstances" which make it impracticable or impossible to apply to the CAT.[7] As there is no obligation requiring an application for permission to appeal to be made to the Court of Session an application to the CAT for leave to appeal is necessary unless there are "special circumstances". Where the CAT grants leave to appeal the appeal must be lodged in the General Department within 42 days after the date on which the decision to grant leave was intimated to the appellant.[8]

Where leave is refused by the CAT and leave is sought from the Court, the application for leave to appeal is to be made to the Inner House of the Court of Session in the appropriate form.[9]

Applications for leave to appeal must be lodged in the General Department within 42 days after the date on which the decision appealed against was "intimated" to the appellant, or where the CAT issues a statement of reasons for its decision later than the decision, the date of intimation of that statement of reasons to the appellant.[10] An application to the court for leave to appeal shall include a statement setting out the proposed grounds of appeal and the grounds on which leave to appeal is sought.[11] The application must also include a process[12] and where applicable[13]:

- evidence that leave to appeal has been refused by the CAT;

- a copy of the grounds of appeal submitted to the CAT;

- any note by the tribunal setting out the reasons for refusing leave;

- a copy of the document issued by the CAT setting out the decision complained of and any reasons for that decision; and

- where the tribunal itself exercised an appellate function, a copy of the decision of the tribunal from which that appeal was taken and any reasons given for that decision.

Upon lodging an application for leave to appeal the applicant shall apply by

---

[7] Rules of the Court of Session, Rule 41.2(1).
[8] *ibid.*, Rule 41.20(2).
[9] *ibid.*, Rule 41.2(2). Form 40.2.
[10] *ibid.*, Rule 41.20(1)(b).
[11] *ibid.*, Rule 41.2(4).
[12] In accordance with Rule 4.4 (steps of process).
[13] Rules of the Court of Session, Rule 41.2(5).

motion to the Inner House for an order for intimation and service.[14] On expiry of the period within which answers may be lodged, the applicant may apply by motion to the Inner House for the application to be granted.[15]

(c) Appeals to the Court of Appeal of Northern Ireland

4–160   Although part of the same jurisdiction, the procedure for appealing to the Court of Appeal of Northern Ireland has a number of features not present in appeals to the Court of Appeal in England and Wales.[16]

4–161   **Leave to appeal.**   Upon refusal of permission to appeal by the CAT, an application for "leave" to appeal to the Court of Appeal must be made to the Court of Appeal within 28 days of the CAT's decision.[17] Such applications must be made *ex parte* by lodging a certified copy of the CAT's decision to refuse to grant permission to appeal; and a statement of the grounds of the application.[18] The proper officer must notify the parties of the determination of the Court of Appeal.[19] Where leave to appeal is granted the applicant must notify the Chairman of the CAT.[20]

4–162   **Appeal by way of case stated.**   The requisition to state the case must be lodged with the CAT within six weeks of the grant of leave to appeal by the CAT or the Court of Appeal as the case may be.[21] The CAT must settle the statement of case within a period of six weeks commencing on the day the requisition was received and send it to the applicant. Upon receipt of the statement of case the applicant must file it in the Court of Appeal's central office within 14 days. Where a CAT refuses or fails to state a case an application may be made to the Court of Appeal by motion within a period of 14 days commencing on the date of the refusal or failure of the CAT to state the case.[22]

---

[14] Rules of the Court of Session, Rule 41.3(1).
[15] *ibid.*, Rule 41.3(2).
[16] It should be noted that at the time of writing Order 61 of the Rules of the Supreme Court of Northern Ireland had not been amended since January 2001 and incorrectly refers to the CAT as being constituted under s.48 of the Competition Act. As Order 61 only refers to appeals under that Act no provision has yet been made for appeals under the Enterprise Act.
[17] Order 61, Rule 17(2).
[18] *ibid.*, Rule 17(3).
[19] *ibid.*, Rule 17(4).
[20] *ibid.*, Rule 17(5).
[21] *ibid.*, Rule 18(1).
[22] *ibid.*, Rule 4.

13. REFERENCES TO THE EUROPEAN COURT

General. The CAT's Rules provide that an order for a reference for a
preliminary ruling by the European Court may be made by the CAT.[23]

4–163

Preliminary rulings. The European Court of Justice ("ECJ") has jurisdiction to give preliminary rulings under Art.234 (formerly Art.177) of the
Treaty Establishing the European Community.[24] Art.234 provides as
follows:

4–164

"The Court of Justice shall have jurisdiction to give preliminary rulings
concerning:

(a) the interpretation of this Treaty;

(b) the validity and interpretation of acts of the institutions of the
Community and of the ECB;

(c) the interpretation of the statutes of bodies established by an act of
the Council, where those statutes so provide.

Where such a question is raised before any court or tribunal of a Member
State, that court or tribunal may, if it considers that a decision on the
question is necessary to enable it to give judgment, request the Court of
Justice to give a ruling thereon.

Where any such question is raised in a case pending before a court or
tribunal of a member State against whose decisions there is no judicial
remedy under national law, that court or tribunal shall bring the matter
before the Court of Justice."

Court or tribunal. The CAT is clearly a tribunal within the meaning of Art.
234 of the Treaty and the court's jurisprudence on this issue.[25]

4–165

Jurisdiction to refer. Since May 1, 2004 National Competition Authorities
such as the OFT have been empowered to apply Arts 81 and 82 of the EC

4–166

---

[23] Rule 60(1). See further, Anderson and Demetriou, *References to the European Court* (2002),
and "Guidance of the Court of Justice of the European Communities on References by
National Courts for Preliminary Rulings" [1999] 1 W.L.R. 260.

[24] Equivalent provisions exist under Treaties establishing the European Atomic Energy
Community (Art.150) and the European Coal and Steel Community (Art.41). It should be
noted that Art.1(31) of the Treaty of Nice amends Art.225 EC to confer jurisdiction on the
CFI to hear and determine preliminary rulings in specific areas laid down by its Statute.
Amendment of the Statute may only be effected by unanimous vote of the Council (Art.245
EC).

[25] Where the status of the body in question is less clear the relevant criteria are set out in Case
C–54/96 *Dorsch Consult Ingenieurgesellschaft mbH v Bundesbaugesellschaft Berlin mbH*
[1997] E.C.R. I–4961; [1998] 2 C.M.L.R. 237.

Treaty.[26] Appeals against the decisions of the national competition authorities under those provisions will clearly raise questions as to the interpretation of Arts 81 and 82 and the acts of the EC Commission in respect of which it may be necessary for the CAT to seek a preliminary ruling. In some cases the situation under consideration by the CAT may come within the scope of both national and Community law. Where in that situation a national court seeks to ensure that national law is interpreted consistently with EC law the ECJ will accept a reference in order to avoid any conflict between the provisions of national and Community law.[27]

At first sight the position is more complicated in cases where there is no effect on interstate trade and only national law is in issue. Generally speaking the ECJ has no power to interpret national legislation even when adopted in order to give effect to Community obligations.[28] Nor will the ECJ ordinarily countenance giving an opinion which would not be binding on the national court in relation to the question referred.[29] Where national legislation requires that the same interpretation be given by the domestic court or tribunal to national legislation as is given to EC legislation it appears that the ECJ will accept jurisdiction.[30] In appeals brought under domestic competition law the CAT is under a duty to act with a view to securing that there is no inconsistency between the principles it applies and decision reached with those principles laid down by the Treaty and decisions of the European Court, in determining any corresponding question arising in Community law.[31] This duty is subject to the requirement to have regard to any relevant differences between the provisions concerned.

Where the CAT decides that it is necessary to make a reference it will necessarily have decided that there is a question of EC law which must be answered by the European Court before it is able to determine the case before it. All things remaining equal the CAT would be bound under s.60 of the Competition Act by the ruling given by the European Court. In those circumstances there seems little doubt that the European Court would

---

[26] See the Competition Act as amended by the Competition Act 1998 and Other Enactments (Amendment) Regulations 2004 (SI 2004/1261).

[27] See Case C–7/97 *Oscar Bronner GmbH & Co KG v Mediaprint Zeitungs und Zeitschriftenverlag GmbH & Co KG* [1998] E.C.R. I–7791. Art.3 of Regulation 1/2003, now requires Arts 81 and 82 to be applied by national competition law authorities to agreements or conduct which comes within the scope of those Arts. Article 3(2) precludes the prohibition by national law of agreements which do not fall within the scope of Art.81(1) or are capable of exemption under Art.81(3), although stricter national laws which prohibit or sanction unilateral conduct by undertakings may continue to be applied.

[28] Case 23/75 *Rey Soda v Cassa Songuaglio Zucchero* [1975] E.C.R. 1279 at para.50.

[29] Case C–346/93 *Kleinwort Benson Ltd v City of Glasgow District Council* [1995] E.C.R. I–615, where the obligation on the domestic court in applying the provisions of Sch. 4 of the Civil Jurisdiction and Judgments Act 1982, was only to "have regard" to the ECJ's caselaw.

[30] Case C–28/95 *A Leur–Bloem v Inspecteur der Belastingdienst/Ondernemingen Amsterdam 2* [1997] E.C.R. I–4161; [1998] 2 C.M.L.R. 157, Case C–130/95 *Bernd Giloy v Hauptzollamt Frankfurt am Main Ost* [1997] E.C.R. I–4295.

[31] s.60 of the Competition Act, which applies to appeals brought under Part I of that Act.

accept a request for a preliminary ruling by the CAT even where the case was a purely domestic one involving no effect on interstate trade.[32]

Uniform application of Community competition law. Regulation 1/2003 requires that when national courts rule on agreements, decisions or practices under Art.81 or 82 of the Treaty which are already the subject of a Commission decision, they cannot take decisions running counter to the decision adopted by the Commission. They must also avoid giving decisions which would conflict with a decision contemplated by the Commission in proceedings it has initiated. To that effect, the national court may assess whether it is necessary to stay its proceedings and, if appropriate, make a reference under Art.234 of the Treaty.[33] The national court may request information from the Commission of a procedural nature to enable it to discover whether a certain case is pending before the Commission, whether the Commission has initiated a procedure or whether it has already taken a position. The national court may also ask the Commission when a decision is likely to be taken, so as to be able to determine the conditions for any decision to stay proceedings or whether interim measures should be adopted.[34]

4–167

Courage v Crehan. In *Courage v Crehan*[35] the English High Court was called upon to decide whether a pub lease containing a beer tie infringed Art.81 EC and, if so, whether damages were recoverable in respect of that breach. As part of its assessment the Court was required to consider whether in 1991 and in subsequent years the structure of beer distribution agreements in the UK was such that the beer ties in Inntrepreneur leases infringed Art.81. The claimant called no factual evidence on this issue but relied on previous decisions of the Commission and reports of the Monopolies and Mergers Commission and the OFT. A previous decision of the Commission had found that leases entered into by Whitbread in the context of the cumulative effect of other networks of such agreements in the UK on-trade beer market had made a significant contribution to the foreclosure of the market and gave rise to an appreciable effect on interstate trade contrary to

4–168

---

[32] Cases decided since *Kleinwort Benson* would also suggest this result: see Case C–1/99 *Kofisa Italia Srl v Ministero delle Finanze, servizio della Riscossione dei Tributi–Concessione Provincia di Genova–San Paolo Riscossioni Genova SpA* [2001] E.C.R. I–207; [2003] 1 C.M.L.R. 29 (where the relevant national provisions did not include a direct and unconditional requirement to apply EC law), Case C–247/97 *Marcel Schoonbroodt, Marc Schoonbroodt and Transports AM Schoonbroodt SPRL v Belgian State* [1998] E.C.R. I–8095, Case C–267/99 *Christiane Adam, épouse Urbing v Administration de l'enregistrement et des domaines* [2000] E.C.R. I–7467.

[33] Art.16(1) of Regulation 1/2003 [2003] O.J. L1/1.

[34] Art.15 of Regulation 1/2003 and see Commission Notice on the co-operation between the Commission and the courts of the EU Member States in the application of Arts 81 and 82 EC [2004] O.J.C101/54, at point 21. These provisions give effect to the judgment of the ECJ in Case C–344/98 *Masterfoods*, December 14, 2000. The Commission will endeavour to provide such information within 1 month of the receipt of the request (point 22).

[35] *Crehan v Inntrepreneur* [2003] EWHC 1510, Ch.D, Park J.

Art.81 EC. Dealing with Inntrepreneur's agreements, rather than the agreements which had been the subject of the Commission's decision, the judge concluded that the UK market was not foreclosed in the way suggested by the Commission's decision in Whitbread.

On appeal the Court of Appeal concluded that if the Commission was to be shown to be wrong in its decision on the applicability of Art.81(1) then that question must be decided not by the national court but by the ECJ or CFI.[36] Accordingly if a national court has doubts about the analysis of the Commission in a decision, the interests of legal certainty and the duty of sincere co-operation require that it should either seek additional information from the Commission or make a reference. In reaching its conclusion the Court of Appeal applied by analogy the approach set out in *Masterfoods* even though in that case the parties conducting the litigation in the national court were the same persons whose conduct was being investigated under Arts 81 and 82 EC.

The effect of *Courage* is that where a court or the CAT considers that the conclusions of the Commission are open to question in a case before it, even though the parties in the litigation before it had no opportunity to mount a direct action against that decision as it was not addressed to them, it should in general make a preliminary reference. A difficulty with this approach is that an Art.234 reference is not particularly suited to determining the sorts of mixed legal and factual issues that may arise in proceedings under Arts 81 and 82.[37] Other drawbacks to the preliminary reference procedure are that it cannot be initiated as of right but depends on the exercise of the national court's discretion in which the proceedings were originally initiated. It is clearly desirable that conflicting decisions between national courts and the Commission should be avoided, but that interest must be weighed against the need for effective judicial protection of the rights of the parties to the particular appeal.[38]

4–169 **Timing of a reference.** An order may be made by the CAT of its own initiative at any stage in the proceedings or on the application of a party before or at the oral hearing.[39] The national court must provide the ECJ with sufficient legal and factual context in order to permit it to answer the questions referred. This may require the CAT to make certain findings of fact before deciding whether or not to refer. The need for a reference may not be apparent to the CAT itself until that is done.

4–170 **Grounds for a reference.** Even though the national court has reached a clear view on the points of European law in issue in the case before it, it

---

[36] [2004] EWCA 637.
[37] See the comments of A.G. Jacobs in Case C–188/92 *TWD Textilwerke Deggendorf GmbH v Germany* [1994] E.C.R. I–833; [1995] 2 C.M.L.R. 145.
[38] On the facts it is apparent that the Court of Appeal was not convinced that the Commission had erred in its conclusions about the foreclosure of the UK beer market as the court at first instance had found.
[39] Rule 60(1).

must be confident that other national courts and the ECJ itself would be likely to reach that conclusion having regard in particular to the fact that the ECJ in particular benefits from a panoramic view of legal developments in the Community. Where the matter is not free from doubt guidance may be needed from the European Court.[39a] There is no necessity to make a reference in interlocutory proceedings where the decision on the point of European law does not bind the court that will hear the substantive issues and either of the parties to the proceedings is in a position to ensure that the main proceedings are instituted.[40]

Duty to make a reference.   As the CAT is not a court from whose decision   **4–171**
there is no judicial remedy there is no duty on the CAT to make a reference.[41] However, given that it is likely to take at least two years to determine an preliminary reference there is much to be said in most cases for making a reference as soon as possible rather than leaving the question to a higher court. The duty to refer does not apply where there is no reasonable scope for doubt about the correct application of European Law ("*acte clair*").[42]

The form of the reference.   The order must set out in a schedule the request   **4–172**
for the preliminary ruling of the European Court and the CAT may give directions as to the manner and form in which the schedule is to be prepared.[43] The proceedings in which an order is made shall, unless the CAT otherwise directs, be stayed (or in Scotland, sisted) until the European Court has given a preliminary ruling on the question referred to it.[44] Once the Order is made the Registrar must send a copy to the Registrar of the European Court.[45]

14. INTERIM ORDERS AND MEASURES

General.   Once an appeal is lodged, the recovery of any penalty imposed by   **4–173**
the OFT is deferred until after the determination of the appeal.[46] Otherwise, the making of an appeal does not suspend the effect of the decision to which the appeal relates. The principal purpose of interim relief is to preserve the integrity of the appeal and to ensure that, subject to the other interests at stake, the appellant does not suffer serious and irreparable damage pending

---

[39a] The circumstances in which an English court other than the House of Lords should make a reference were summarised by Bingham M.R. in *R. v International Stock Exchange Ex p. Else* [1993] Q.B. 534 at 545.

[40] Case 35–36 *Morson and Jhanjan v Netherlands* [1982] E.C.R. 3723; [1983] 2 C.M.L.R. 221, *Garden Cottage Foods v Milk Marketing Board* [1984] A.C. 130, HL.

[41] Art.234(3) EC.

[42] Case 283/81 *CILFIT srl v Ministry of Health* [1982] E.C.R. 3415; [1983] 1 C.M.L.R. 472.

[43] Rule 60(2).

[44] Rule 60(3).

[45] Rule 60(4).

[46] ss.37(1) and 46(4) of the Competition Act 1998.

the determination of the appeal which may succeed.[47] In this sense a request for interim relief is ancillary to the main appeal. Requests under the CAT Rules for interim relief should not be confused with appeals against a decision of the OFT not to grant interim measures pending the completion of an investigation.[48] Such appeals are treated by the CAT as appeals in their own right and are governed by the rules applicable to appeals in Part II of the CAT Rules.

The CAT may make an order on an interim basis under the CAT Rules:

- suspending in whole or part the effect of any decision which is the subject matter of proceedings before it[49];

- granting any remedy which the CAT would have the power to grant in its final decision.[50]

4–174 **Test to be applied.** Where the CAT considers that it is "necessary", as a matter of urgency, for the purpose of preventing serious, irreparable damage to a particular person or category of person or protecting the public interest, the CAT may give such directions as it considers appropriate for that purpose.[51] In exercising its powers to grant interim orders the CAT must take into account "all the relevant circumstances", including (a) the urgency of the matter; (b) the effect on the party making the request if the relief sought is not granted; and (c) the effect on competition if the relief is granted.[52] Any order or direction made is subject to the CAT's further order, direction or final decision.[53]

4–175 **Application for interim relief.** A party must apply for an order or a direction under the CAT Rules by sending a request for interim relief to the Registrar. The request must state:

- the subject matter of the proceedings[54];

- the circumstances giving rise to the urgency[55];

- the factual and legal grounds establishing a prima facie case for the granting of interim relief by the CAT[56];

- the relief sought.[57]

---

[47] *Napp Pharmaceutical Holdings Ltd v DGFT (No.1)* [2001] Comp. A.R. 1 at para.38.
[48] Under s.47(1)(e).
[49] Rule 61(1)(a).
[50] Rule 61(1)(c). Rule 61(1)(b) which empowers the tribunal to vary the conditions or obligations attached to an exemption would also appear to be covered by Rule 61(1)(c) as that is a remedy which the tribunal would have the power to grant in its final decision.
[51] Rule 61(2)(a) and (b).
[52] Rule 61(3).
[53] Rule 61(4).
[54] Rule 61(6)(a).
[55] Rule 61(6)(b).
[56] Rule 61(6)(c).
[57] Rule 61(6)(d).

If no appeal or application has been made in respect of a decision which is the subject of the request for interim relief, the request should contain the matters required by the CAT Rules to be included in the notice of appeal in outline.[58] An applicant will normally be expected to indicate a firm date for the lodging of the main appeal, including full and frank disclosure of all relevant matters regarding the nature of the case to be advanced on the main appeal and to progress it with due expedition.[59]

In most cases, the CAT's necessarily flexible approach to requests for interim relief involves asking five questions[60]:

(1) Are the arguments raised by the applicant as to the merits of its substantive appeal, at least prima facie, not entirely ungrounded, in the sense that the applicant's arguments cannot be dismissed at the interim stage of the procedure without a more detailed examination?[61]

(2) Is urgency established?

(3) Is the applicant likely to suffer serious and irreparable damage if interim relief is not granted?[62]

(4) What is the likely effect on competition, or relevant third party interests, of the grant or refusal of interim relief?

(5) What is "the balance of interests" under heads (iii) and (iv)?

It may be necessary in some cases to go some way into the merits in order to properly appraise the situation before the CAT. The CAT is entitled, if necessary, to make a prima facie assessment of the strength or weakness of the applicant's case on the merits.[63] In most cases, however, this is likely to be undesirable and impracticable.[64]

Serious and irreparable damage. Irrecoverable financial loss does not by itself generally constitute serious and irreparable damage unless the survival of the undertaking is in question.[65] Changes to the structure of a market   **4–176**

---

[58] *i.e.* the matters required by Rule 8(4) including the grounds on which the decision is challenged: see para.4–012, above.

[59] Guide, para.15.6, *Napp Pharmaceutical Holdings v DGFT(No.1)* [2001] Comp. A.R. 1 at para.32.

[60] *Genzyme v OFT (Interim Relief)* [2003] CAT 8 in which the President confirmed its observations previously made in *Napp*.

[61] *Napp*, n.59, above, paras 44 to 46, basing itself on the approach of the CFI, including notably the order of the President of the Court of Justice of July 19, 1995 in Case 149/95P (R) *Commission v Atlantic Container Line AB and others* [1995] E.C.R. I–2165 at paras 26 and 27.

[62] *Napp*, n.59, above, para.38.

[63] *ibid.*, at para.80.

[64] *Napp*, n.59, above, para.38, cited in *Genzyme*, n.60, above, at para.80.

[65] Case T–184/01R *IMS Health v Commission* [2001] E.C.R. II–3193 at paras 120, 121, cited in *Genzyme*, n.60, above, at para.88.

brought about by the imposition of a decision whose effects might be very difficult if not impossible to reverse if the appeal were eventually successful, may constitute serious and irreparable damage.[66] The fact that implementation of the contested decision will restrict an appellant's freedom to define its business policy may also be a relevant consideration.[67]

4–177 **Likely effect on competition and third parties.** In conducting the necessary balancing of interests the CAT is unlikely to give significant weight to the protection of the interests of competing undertakings as such unless those interests cannot be separated from the maintenance of an effective competitive structure on the market in question.[68] That said the balancing of interests may be a complex exercise and it cannot be assumed that even where the appellant can plainly demonstrate serious and irreparable damage that interim relief will be granted if the damage to competition or third party interests would be significant.[69]

4–178 **Cross undertakings and assurances.** Neither OFT nor the CAT have any power to require a cross undertaking in respect of financial loss suffered in connection with the granting of interim relief. Equally, no cross-undertaking can be required of the OFT in the performance of its public functions.[70] Irrespective of whether or not the power to require undertakings exists, the willingness of the party requesting interim relief to give an undertaking in respect of losses which may arise as a result of the non-implementation of a decision may be a factor relevant to the balancing of interests.[71] However, if that undertaking only relates to financial losses it may fail to address the key public interest namely the maintenance of competition.[72]

4–179 **Procedure after the filing of the request.** On receiving a request for interim relief the Registrar must send a copy to all the parties to the proceedings, or where no appeal or application has been made, to the person who made the

---

[66] *ibid.*, where the decision in question required the licensing to rivals of formatted data protected by German copyright law was held to be likely to give rise to irreparable harm.
[67] Case T–184/01R *IMS Health v Commission*, n.65, above at para.130, and Case T–41/96 R *Bayer v Commission* [1996] E.C.R. II–381 at para.54, cited in *Genzyme*, n.60, above, at para.92 (where the requirement in the contested decision to provide an "unbundled" price or "reasonable margin" to third parties in a downstream market by a vertically integrated dominant undertaking was held to involve such a substantial modification. As part of the necessary balancing exercise it was held to be appropriate to require a small margin to be given to the only other competitor in the downstream market).
[68] Case T–13/99R *Pfizer Animal Health v Council* [1999] E.C.R. II–1961; confirmed on appeal to the Court of Justice in Case C–329/99 (P) R [1999] E.C.R. I–8343.
[69] *Napp*, n.59, above, at para.48.
[70] *Genzyme*, n.60, above, at paras 129, 130.
[71] In *Napp Pharmaceutical Holdings Ltd v DGFT (No.4)* [2002] CAT 1; [2002] Comp. A.R. 13, notably at para.510, the CCAT found that the real gain of the company from its conduct was the long term strategic advantage of protecting its market share. As the CCAT noted in its reasons refusing permission to appeal, those effects were not as it turned out adequately addressed by an undertaking given in the context of a request for interim relief at the outset of the case.
[72] *Genzyme*, n.60, above, at para.130.

decision to which the request for interim relief relates, and shall inform them of the date by which they may submit written or oral observations to the CAT.[73]

The CAT must fix a date for the hearing of the request for interim relief and give the parties any directions as may be necessary for disposing of the request for interim relief.[74] The CAT may, for the purposes of a request for interim relief, join any party to the proceedings.[75] An order or direction for interim relief may be made against a person who is not a party to the proceedings provided that that person has been given an opportunity to be heard.[76] This and any other requirement of the CAT Rules may be dispensed with where the urgency of the case so requires.[77]

Unless the context otherwise requires, the CAT Rules apply to requests for interim relief.[78] The exact effect of this rule is necessarily somewhat unclear given the need to be able to deal flexibly with varied nature and urgency of requests for interim relief. In general it will normally be appropriate to publish a summary of the appeal on the CAT website for the purposes of bringing the appeal to the attention of persons potentially having a sufficient interest in the outcome of the proceedings. It has been suggested that that a request to withdraw a request for interim relief may require the permission of the CAT.[79] The provisions on consent orders may also apply.

The CAT Rules relating to interim relief do not apply to claims for damages.[80]

15. ENFORCEMENT OF CAT ORDERS

(a) Recovery of penalties

The OFT may recover from the undertaking as a civil debt due to the OFT any amount payable under the penalty notice which remains outstanding, provided that the date specified in the penalty notice has passed and the period during which an appeal against the imposition, or amount, of the penalty may be made has expired without an appeal having been made, or such an appeal has been made and determined.[81] **4–180**

---

[73] Rule 61(7).
[74] Rule 61(8).
[75] Rule 61(9).
[76] Rule 61(10).
[77] Rule 61(11).
[78] Rule 61(12).
[79] Under Rule 12, see *Napp*, n.59, above, at para.60.
[80] Rule 61(13).
[81] s.37 of the Competition Act.

(b) Payments of damages, costs and expenses

4–181 England and Wales. The Enterprise Act provides for the enforcement of CAT orders requiring payment of damages awarded by the decision, any costs or expenses awarded by the decision and any direction given as a result of the decision.[82] Payments of damages and/or costs and expenses may be enforced as if the damages, costs or expenses were an amount due pursuant to a judgment or order of the High Court. Directions of the CAT are also enforceable as an order or direction of the High Court in accordance with rules of court.[83]

4–182 Scotland. If a decision of the CAT awards damages, costs or expenses, or results in any direction being given, the decision may be recorded for execution in the Books of Council and Session and shall be enforceable accordingly.[84]

4–183 Northern Ireland. Decisions of the CAT may be enforced in the same manner in Northern Ireland as they may be enforced in England and Wales, subject to the requirement that the "leave" of the High Court of Northern Ireland has been obtained.[85]

4–184 Decisions awarding damages. Decisions awarding damages and/or costs and expenses may be enforced by the person to whom the sum was awarded.[86] In the case of a decision to award damages in a consumer claim brought by a specified body the decision may be enforced by the specified body.[87] However, for the decision to be enforced by the specified body the CAT must have ordered that the award is to be recoverable by the specified body.[88] An individual may only enforce an award of damages and/or costs and expenses made in respect of a claim made or continued on his behalf with the permission of the High Court or Court of Session.[89] An award of costs or expenses awarded against a specified body may not be enforced against any individual on whose behalf a claim was made or continued in those proceedings.[90]

---

[82] Para.2 of Sch.4 to the Enterprise Act. "Damages" includes any sum of money recoverable under s.47A of the Competition Act 1998: see para.8 of Sch.4 to the Enterprise Act.

[83] Sch.4, para.2 to the Enterprise Act. For the relevant rules of court: see CPR 70.5 (Enforcement of awards of bodies other than the High Court and county courts) and PD paras 4 (Enforcement of awards of bodies other than the High Court or a county court—Rule 70.5) and 5 (Registration of awards and decisions in the High Court for enforcement—Rule 70.5(8)).

[84] Sch.4, para.3 of the Enterprise Act.

[85] Sch.4, para.5 of the Enterprise Act.

[86] Sch.4, para.4(b)(Great Britain), para.5(b) of the Enterprise Act (Northern Ireland).

[87] Sch.4, para.4(c)(Great Britain), para.5(c) of the Enterprise Act (Northern Ireland).

[88] Under s.47B(6) of the Competition Act. Such an order requires both the consent of the individual concerned and the specified body. Such orders are likely in practice greatly to assist the administration of such claims.

[89] Sch.4, para.6 of the Enterprise Act. In Northern Ireland the "leave" of the Court is required in all cases where enforcement of a decision of the tribunal is sought (para.5).

[90] Sch.4, para.7 of the Enterprise Act.

Directions. A decision of the CAT may also be registered for the purpose of enforcing a direction given as a result of the decision, by the Registrar of the CAT or a person who was a party to the proceedings.[91]   **4–185**

16. SUPPLEMENTARY

Power of the President and Chairmen to exercise the power of the CAT. The President or a Chairman may acting alone exercise any procedural power of the CAT. The following powers are the exception to that general rule: the power to reject, the power to permit withdrawal of an appeal once the hearing has begun; the power to enter summary judgment; the power to determine whether permission to appeal should be granted; the power to make preliminary references.[92] The most important power of the President acting alone is the power to grant interim measures. The President's powers in this respect may be exercised by a chairman of the CAT only where the urgency of an application so requires.[93]   **4–186**

General power of the CAT. Subject to the general provisions of the CAT Rules the CAT may regulate its own procedure. The President in this regard may issue practice directions in relation to the procedures provided for by the CAT Rules.[94]   **4–187**

---

[91] Sch.4, para.4(a) (Great Britain), para.5(a) Northern Ireland of the Enterprise Act.
[92] Rule 62(1).
[93] Rule 62(2).
[94] Rule 68.

CHAPTER 5

THE CARTEL OFFENCE

Clair Dobbin[1] and George Peretz[2]

1. INTRODUCTION

5–001 **Introduction.** This chapter deals with the substantive provisions of the cartel offence created by s.188 of the Enterprise Act 2002. It also deals with investigation and enforcement of the offence and prosecution of the offence in the criminal courts.

5–002 **Position under the Competition Act 1998.** Under the Competition Act, only "undertakings"[3] are capable of infringing the Chapter I or II prohibitions and of being penalised for such infringements. Unless individuals happen to be undertakings themselves—for example if they are self-employed[4]—they cannot themselves be penalised. So individual employees and directors of infringing companies are not themselves liable to penalty for an infringement, since in that capacity they are not undertakings.[5] The Competition Act does create certain offences[6] which can be committed by individuals, relating to such matters as destroying documents sought by the OFT, obstructing OFT investigations, and providing false or misleading information to the OFT, but these offences are ancillary to the OFT's powers of investigation and are not intended to penalise anti-competitive behaviour by individuals.

5–003 **Position generally before enactment of the Enterprise Act 2002.** It is possible that in some circumstances persons involved in anti-competitive agreements could be committing the common law offence of conspiracy to

---

[1] Barrister, 3 Raymond Buildings.
[2] Barrister, Monckton Chambers.
[3] See para.2–009, above for a discussion of the meaning of "undertaking" in competition law.
[4] *e.g.* Case C–35/96 *Commission v Italian Republic* [1998] E.C.R. I–3851; [1998] 5 C.M.L.R. 889 (self-employed customs agents were undertakings).
[5] Cases 40/73 etc. *Suiker Unie v Commission* [1975] E.C.R. 1663 at para.539.
[6] ss.41–44 of the Act.

defraud. A conspiracy to defraud may be committed where two or more persons agree by dishonesty to injure a proprietary right of a person whether or not the fraud amounts to a crime.[7] The essence of the criminality in a conspiracy to defraud lies not in the result of the conspirator's actions but in their agreement to bring about that result. Since the enactment of the Enterprise Act and the introduction of the cartel offence in s.188 thereof, this offence is unlikely to play any significant role in the regulation of anti-competitive behaviour.

A new cartel offence. Shortly after the June 2001 general election, the   5–004
Labour Government announced that it proposed to produce a White Paper including a consultation on the introduction of criminal penalties for those involved in cartels.[8] In July 2001, the Department of Trade and Industry published a White Paper, *Productivity and Enterprise: A World Class Competition Regime*,[9] in which proposals for the introduction of a new criminal offence were set out.[10] The Government stated that:

> "In most cases, the Competition Act 1998 provides a sound basis for deterrence. But for the most damaging form of anti-competitive behaviour—engaging in a 'hard-core' cartel—the Government believes that there is a strong case for strengthening the penalties, with the introduction of criminal sanctions against individuals. A new criminal regime would work alongside the existing civil regime."

"Hard-core cartels". The 2001 White Paper referred[11] to the definition   5–005
of "hard-core cartel" employed by the Organisation for Economic Co-operation and Development (OECD):

> "An anti-competitive agreement, anti-competitive concerted practice or anticompetitive arrangement by competitors to fix prices, make rigged bids (collusive tenders), establish output restrictions or quotas, or share or divide markets by allocating customers, suppliers, territories, or lines of commerce."[12]

The White Paper condemned hard core cartels in the following terms:

> "Hard-core cartels either raise or maintain prices at higher levels than they would be if competition were not distorted. They can restrict the supply of goods and services to consumers and businesses or make them

---

[7] *Scott v Metropolitan Police Commissioner* [1975] A.C. 819.
[8] HM Treasury press release 67/01, June 18, 2001, covering the publication of a joint DTI/Treasury document *Productivity in the UK: Enterprise and the Productivity Challenge*, para.3.23 of which referred to the proposal to introduce an offence punishable by imprisonment.
[9] Cm.5233 (2001): *www.dti.gov.uk/ccp/topics2/pdf2/compwp.pdf.*
[10] *ibid.*, chapter 7.
[11] para.7.4.
[12] OECD: Hard Core Cartels: Meeting of the OECD Council at Ministerial Level, 2000.

unnecessarily expensive. The money that leaves consumers' pockets simply becomes extra profit for the firms involved.

The US competition authorities estimate that cartels, on average, lead to a 10% increase in the price of the goods or services affected. By adversely affecting the efficient running of the economy, the potential harm to society could be much greater—a cartel can affect up to 20% of the volume of commerce."[13]

5–006 Criminal offences in other jurisdictions. The 2001 White Paper referred to a number of other leading industrialised countries that had, at least to some extent, criminalised hard-core cartels: the most well-known example is the US, but the White Paper also noted the existence of criminal offences in Canada, Japan, Austria, France, Norway and Ireland.[14]

5–007 Rationale for introducing a cartel offence. The 2001 White Paper referred to an academic study[15] that suggested that in the US, the probability that a hard-core cartel would be detected was around one in six. Taken together with the assumption that cartels on average led to a 10 per cent increase in prices,[16] the White Paper argued that fines at levels of around 10 per cent of turnover in the affected products would be insufficient to deter companies from involvement in such cartels.[17] The White Paper rejected the option of increasing penalties, on the basis that to increase them to amounts sufficient to act as a proper deterrent would lead to a significant number of corporate insolvencies, damaging a large number of innocent third parties.[18] Rather, it took the view that "The threat of a criminal conviction and the possibility of a prison sentence means that individuals are more likely to think very carefully before engaging in cartels. Or, if they are directed to do so by their managers, they may be far more willing to inform the authorities".[19] The Government also rejected the possibility of introducing an offence punishable only by a fine, on the basis that companies could always find a means of protecting individuals from the effects of a fine.[20]

5–008 The Hammond-Penrose report. After the publication of the White Paper, the OFT commissioned a report from Sir Anthony Hammond QC, a former Treasury Solicitor, and Roy Penrose OBE, a senior police officer, to review the proposed offence and to make recommendations on how prosecutions

---

[13] White Paper, n.9, above, paras 7.5–7.6.
[14] *ibid.*, paras 7.9–7.12.
[15] P.G. Bryant and E.W. Eckhard, "Price Fixing: The Probability of Getting Caught" (1991) *Review of Economics and Statistics* 531.
[16] See para.5–005, above.
[17] White Paper, n.9, above, box 7.3.
[18] *ibid.*, para.7.15.
[19] *ibid.*, para.7.16.
[20] *ibid.*, para.7.17.

for it might best be administered. Their report[21] recommended that the definition of the offence be based on "dishonesty" and should not be linked to the civil prohibitions in the Competition Act and the EC Treaty. It also recommended that the Serious Fraud Office ("the SFO") should either conduct prosecutions itself, or that the OFT should do so under SFO supervision. It further suggested that "no-action letters" be issued to individuals as part of the OFT's leniency programme.

The response to the White Paper.   About 50 per cent of respondents to the consultation initiated by the White Paper favoured the introduction of criminal sanctions, although a minority opposed it.[22] In December 2001, the Government confirmed its intention to proceed to introduce legislation creating the offence when a suitable opportunity arose.[23] The opportunity arose shortly afterwards on the introduction of the Enterprise Bill in March 2002. The offence was created by s.188 of the Enterprise Act 2002, which came into force on June 20, 2003.[24]   **5–009**

2. THE SUBSTANTIVE OFFENCE

The cartel offence.   The definition of the cartel offence is spread over two densely-worded sections,[25] the drafting of which owes little to the drafting of the civil prohibitions in s.2 of the Competition Act and Art.81(1) EC. It is as follows: **5–010**

"**188 Cartel offence**

(1) An individual is guilty of an offence if he dishonestly agrees with one or more other persons to make or implement, or to cause to be made or implemented, arrangements of the following kind relating to at least two undertakings (A and B).

(2) The arrangements must be ones which, if operating as the parties to the agreement intend, would—

(a) directly or indirectly fix a price for the supply by A in the United Kingdom (otherwise than to B) of a product or service,

(b) limit or prevent supply by A in the United Kingdom of a product or service,

---

[21] Reproduced at [2002] U.K.C.L.R. 97.
[22] *"Productivity and Enterprise: A World Class Competition Regime"*: *Government's response to consultation*, December 2001, *www.dti.gov.uk/ccp/topics2/pdf2/responses.pdf*, para.52.
[23] *ibid.*
[24] Enterprise Act 2002 (Commencement No.3, Transitional Provisions and Savings) Order 2003 (SI 2003/1397).
[25] ss.188 and 189.

(c) limit or prevent production by A in the United Kingdom of a product,

(d) divide between A and B the supply in the United Kingdom of a product or service to a customer or customers,

(e) divide between A and B customers for the supply in the United Kingdom of a product or service, or

(f) be bid-rigging arrangements.

(3) Unless subsection (2)(d), (e) or (f) applies, the arrangements must also be ones which, if operating as the parties to the agreement intend, would—

(a) directly or indirectly fix a price for the supply by B in the United Kingdom (otherwise than to A) of a product or service,

(b) limit or prevent supply by B in the United Kingdom of a product or service, or

(c) limit or prevent production by B in the United Kingdom of a product.

(4) In subsections (2)(a) to (d) and (3), references to supply or production are to supply or production in the appropriate circumstances (for which see section 189).

(5) 'Bid-rigging arrangements' are arrangements under which, in response to a request for bids for the supply of a product or service in the United Kingdom, or for the production of a product in the United Kingdom—

(a) A but not B may make a bid, or

(b) A and B may each make a bid but, in one case or both, only a bid arrived at in accordance with the arrangements.

(6) But arrangements are not bid-rigging arrangements if, under them, the person requesting bids would be informed of them at or before the time when a bid is made.

(7) 'Undertaking' has the same meaning as in Part 1 of the 1998 Act.

189 Cartel offence: supplementary

(1) For section 188(2)(a), the appropriate circumstances are that A's supply of the product or service would be at a level in the supply chain at which the product or service would at the same time be supplied by B in the United Kingdom.

(2) For section 188(2)(b), the appropriate circumstances are that A's supply of the product or service would be at a level in the supply chain—

  (a) at which the product or service would at the same time be supplied by B in the United Kingdom, or

  (b) at which supply by B in the United Kingdom of the product or service would be limited or prevented by the arrangements.

(3) For section 188(2)(c), the appropriate circumstances are that A's production of the product would be at a level in the production chain—

  (a) at which the product would at the same time be produced by B in the United Kingdom, or

  (b) at which production by B in the United Kingdom of the product would be limited or prevented by the arrangements.

(4) For section 188(2)(d), the appropriate circumstances are that A's supply of the product or service would be at the same level in the supply chain as B's.

(5) For section 188(3)(a), the appropriate circumstances are that B's supply of the product or service would be at a level in the supply chain at which the product or service would at the same time be supplied by A in the United Kingdom.

(6) For section 188(3)(b), the appropriate circumstances are that B's supply of the product or service would be at a level in the supply chain—

  (a) at which the product or service would at the same time be supplied by A in the United Kingdom, or

  (b) at which supply by A in the United Kingdom of the product or service would be limited or prevented by the arrangements.

(7) For section 188(3)(c), the appropriate circumstances are that B's production of the product would be at a level in the production chain—

  (a) at which the product would at the same time be produced by A in the United Kingdom, or

  (b) at which production by A in the United Kingdom of the product would be limited or prevented by the arrangements."

"Individual". The offence can be committed only by an individual. Bodies corporate remain liable only under the Competition Act regime.   **5–011**

"Agree with one or more other persons to make or implement, or cause to be made or implemented, arrangements". The Hammond-Penrose report recommended that the definition of the offence should not use the word "conspire" (which has an established meaning in English criminal law) but should rather use the word "agree", the meaning of which is more unsettled.   **5–012**

Whether this distinction in terminology ultimately matters is open to question given that an agreement is an intrinsic aspect of a criminal conspiracy. "Agreement" in this context is demonstrated by an intention to play some part in an agreed course of conduct in furtherance of the criminal purpose.

The concept of "agreement" is thus one that the criminal courts are accustomed to applying. The existence of an agreement is an issue of fact that the prosecution will have to prove and it is likely that the term will be afforded its natural meaning. It is unlikely that the criminal courts will treat "agreement" as constituting a technical term by reference to its meaning under Art.81(1) EC.[26]

Individuals commit the offence once the agreement is "made", even if no steps to implement it have been taken.[27] Conversely, the offence also appears to cover an agreement, perhaps between two employees of the same firm, to implement a previously made arrangement. The reference to "cause to be made or implemented. . ." appears to catch a senior manager who instructs a subordinate to enter into or implement prohibited arrangements, although the wording would not appear to catch a senior manager who merely knew what was happening but failed to take any preventive action.[28]

5–013 **Evidence of Agreement.** The Act confers upon the Office of Fair Trading extensive powers of search, seizure and intrusive surveillance (discussed in detail below). Despite these powers it is likely that there will be cases in which there will be little direct evidence that an agreement exists. In those cases the existence of an agreement may be inferred from evidence of concerted practice; patterns of market activity or any other evidence that is suggestive of co-ordination on the part of at least two entities.

---

[26] The extensive jurisprudence as to the meaning of "agreement" and "concerted practice" under Art.81(1) is referred to in para.2–010, above. The criminal courts may, however, have regard to the old jurisprudence as to the meaning of "arrangement" under the (now repealed) Restrictive Trade Practices Acts 1956 and 1976. See, *e.g. British Basic Slag v Registrar of Restrictive Trading Agreements* [1963] 1 W.L.R. 727, where at 747 Diplock L.J. stated that

> "without attempting an exhaustive definition, for there are many ways in which arrangements may be made, . . . it is sufficient [for the purposes of s.6(3) of the Restrictive Trade Practices Act 1956] to constitute an arrangement between A and B, if (1) A makes a representation as to his future conduct with the expectation and intention that such conduct on his part will operate as an inducement to B to act in a particular way, (2) such representation is communicated to B, who has knowledge that A so expected and intended, and (3) such representation or A's conduct in fulfilment of it operates as an inducement, whether among other inducements or not, to B to act in that particular way.".

See also *Re Austin Motor Company's Agreements* [1958] Ch. 61 at 74, *per* Upjohn J.

[27] See also the later wording in subs.(2) "if operating as the parties to the agreement intend, would . . .".

[28] The OFT's July 2002 consultation document on no-action letters, available on the OFT website *www.oft.gov.uk*, indicated that the OFT agrees that an employee who becomes aware of the existence of a cartel and, although not involved in its operation, does nothing to end it, is not guilty of a criminal offence, para.1.7. Note, however, that such a person might well be liable for disqualification as a director under s.204 of the Enterprise Act. See also para.5–023, below on the offence of aiding and abetting the cartel offence.

"Relating to at least two undertakings". This is the only part of the drafting **5–014** of the offence that draws on the terminology of the civil prohibitions; "undertaking" is defined as having the same meaning as in Part I of the Competition Act.[29] The effect is to exclude agreements between entities that are not undertakings (for example, certain public bodies) and also to exclude arrangements between entities that, by reason of common ownership, are to be treated as part of the same undertaking.[30]

Prohibited arrangements. The bulk of the drafting of s.188 is an attempt to **5–015** encapsulate in precise legal terminology the definition of "hard-core cartel" adopted by the OECD.[31] Section 188(2) sets out a number of types of arrangement that are prohibited, that is to say:

(1) Price-fixing agreements[32];

(2) Supply quotas;

(3) Production quotas;

(4) Arrangements dividing markets by the type or nature of products or services supplied;

(5) Arrangements dividing markets by customers;

(6) Bid-rigging arrangements—as defined in s.188(5).

Section 188(3) provides that arrangements in (1) to (3) above (price-fixing and supply and production quotas) are caught only if they are reciprocal, in the sense that the arrangements must involve one or other of these types of restriction for at least two of the undertakings involved.

Vertical arrangements. Section 189, referred to in s.188(4), contains a **5–016** somewhat repetitive series of provisions the effect of which is to exclude from the scope of the offence any vertical arrangements, for example (and notably, given its frequent condemnation under Art.81(1) EC and Chapter I of the Competition Act)[33] resale price maintenance agreements between a supplier and a dealer (although arrangements between dealers that they would comply with RPM imposed by a supplier would potentially fall within the offence).

---

[29] s.188(7).

[30] See para.2–009, above on "undertaking".

[31] See para.5–005, above.

[32] The reference to fixing prices "indirectly" in s.188(2)(a) is apparently intended to catch agreements as to such matters as relative prices, price ranges, discounts, price increases, method of quotation of prices; see Explanatory Notes, para.407.

[33] *e.g. Lladró Comercial SA* [2003] U.K.C.L.R. 652.

5–017 **Dishonesty.** The introduction of the term "dishonesty" was a key recommendation of the Hammond-Penrose report.[34] The need for a fault element is acute because the formalistic drafting of s.188 would otherwise catch a number of innocent commercial agreements between firms. In England and Wales, the concept of what amounts to dishonesty has been the subject of exhaustive analysis and over the years this gave rise to a number of conflicting authorities. The position was finally resolved in *R. v Ghosh*[35] in which the Court of Appeal concluded that a determination as to whether someone acted dishonestly involved a two stage test. The first test, the objective limb, is whether what was done was dishonest according to the ordinary standards of reasonable and honest people. If the act was dishonest according to those standards, the second test, the subjective limb, is whether the defendant himself realised that his acts would be regarded as dishonest according to the standards of reasonable and honest people.

5–018 **"Dishonesty" in practice.** In practice, evidence of dishonesty is likely to consist of such matters as efforts to conceal the arrangements by devices such as code-names and failure to keep records. It remains to be seen whether juries are likely to accept as honest action taken in the belief (whether reasonable or not) that the arrangements could be justified, for example under Art.81(3) EC or s.9 of the Competition Act, or generally in the public interest. The OFT stated in its July 2002 consultation document on no-action letters[36] that an individual who becomes aware of the existence of cartel arrangements and then takes steps to report them to the OFT cannot be said to have behaved dishonestly.

5–019 **Prosecutions.** As the Hammond-Penrose report had recommended, s.190(2) of the Enterprise Act provides that, in England and Wales and Northern Ireland, prosecutions for the cartel offence may only be brought by the SFO or OFT or with the consent of the OFT. In accordance with Scottish constitutional practice, prosecutions in Scotland can be brought only by the Lord Advocate.

5–020 **Penalty.** On conviction on indictment of the cartel offence, an individual is liable to an unlimited fine or imprisonment for up to five years.[37]

5–021 **Territoriality.** The definition of prohibited arrangements in s.188(2) covers only restrictions as to conduct in the UK. Moreover, s.190(3) provides that proceedings may not be brought for the cartel offence in respect of "an

---

[34] para.5–008, above, para.2.5. The report argued that the element of dishonesty would signal the seriousness of the offence and "go a long way to preclude a defence argument to the effect that the activity being prosecuted is not reprehensible or that it might have economic benefits or is an activity which might have attracted exemption domestically or under EC law."

[35] [1983] Q.B. 1053.

[36] n.28 above, para.1.6.

[37] s.190(1).

agreement outside the United Kingdom" unless the agreement has been implemented in whole or in part in the UK. There are no statutory provisions as to the allocation of cases as between the three UK jurisdictions, although the OFT has said that

"Where cross-jurisdictional issues arise, the jurisdiction in which a case will be brought will depend on the outcome of discussions between the OFT, the SFO and the Lord Advocate's office, and will follow the well-established principles that govern other criminal prosecutions."[38]

Extradition. The scheme for extradition to and from the UK is now contained in the Extradition Act 2003. It introduces a fast track system of extradition to countries designated as "Category 1" territories. At present these are the European Union States that have implemented the European Arrest Warrant, namely, Belgium, Denmark, Finland, Ireland, Portugal, Spain, Sweden, Austria, Cyprus, France, Hungary, Latvia, Lithuania, Luxembourg, Malta, The Netherlands, Poland and Slovenia. This list will grow as more EU states adopt the European Arrest Warrant.

5–022

Under the Extradition Act 1989 extradition could only be rendered if the conduct for which the person was sought was an offence in the requesting state and would have constituted an offence had it been committed in the UK. This requirement for "dual criminality" has been abrogated as between the UK and Category 1 territories. The only requirement is that the conduct alleged falls within the European framework list of conduct and is capable of being punished under the law of the Category 1 territory for a term of imprisonment of three years or more.[39] The framework list is not a list of specific offences but rather a list of generic offences. Amongst those offences covered are fraud type offences which may, depending on the circumstances, include the cartel offence. If the cartel offence was deemed to fall outside this type of conduct extradition as between the UK and a Category 1 territory extradition could still take place if it amounted to an offence in both territories and was capable of punishment by one year's imprisonment or more.

The second category of territories is described as "Category 2" and this category is formed by the bulk of other states with which the UK has bilateral extradition relations. Significantly, this includes those EU states yet to implement the European Arrest Warrant and the US. In respect of those EU states and the US the Act permits extradition without the need for those states to demonstrate a prima facie case against the person sought.[40] Extradition between the UK and these States will largely be contingent upon the conduct alleged amounting to an offence in the UK and the other state. In relation to the US, extradition is contingent upon the conduct being

---

[38] *The Cartel Offence: Guidance on the issue of no-action letters to individuals*, OFT 512, para.2.7.
[39] Extradition Act 2003 (Designation of Part 1 Territories) Order 2003 (SI 2003/3333).
[40] Extradition Act 2003 (Designation of Part 2 Territories) Order 2003 (SI 2003/3334).

punishable under the laws of both states for a year or more. Sections 1 and 2 of the Sherman Act 1890 provide that a violation of those antitrust provisions can be punishable with up to three years imprisonment and as such it is likely that the cartel offence will be extraditable as between the US and the UK.

5–023 **Liability for aiding, abetting, counselling, or procuring the cartel offence.** Given that the criminal liability in the cartel offence is predicated on the existence of a dishonest agreement to bring into effect one of the proscribed arrangements it is difficult to foresee circumstances in which secondary liability might arise without the person having become a party to that agreement. A potential circumstance is where a senior management figure becomes aware of an agreement and does nothing to stop it. He may not be criminally liable under the precise terms of the Act but he may be liable as an aider and abettor.[41] Criminal liability might arise in that situation because he is aware of the existence of an agreement; he is in a position to ensure that it does not come to fruition and makes a deliberate decision not to intervene.

The position of a person who "procures" a proscribed arrangement may be covered by the terms of the Act in that it applies to a person who dishonestly agrees with one or more persons to "cause to be made or implemented" a prohibited arrangement.

5–024 **Relationship between the cartel offence and the civil prohibitions.** As has been noted, the cartel offence is not drafted by reference to Art.81 EC or the Chapter I prohibition. Nor—apart from the definition of "undertaking"—does it employ the concepts of those prohibitions. Moreover, the cartel offence applies only to individuals, whereas the civil prohibition applies only to "undertakings". Generally, the civil prohibitions cover much wider ground than does the cartel offence—an obvious example being vertical agreements; and there is no need to establish "dishonesty". However, the cartel offence potentially goes wider than do the civil prohibitions in two respects.

5–025 **No requirement for anti-competitive object or effect.** The requirement that an agreement or concerted practice have the object or effect of preventing, distorting or restricting competition is a fundamental element of the civil prohibitions that must be established by the competition authority concerned to the appropriate standard of proof. But in the case of the cartel offence, the prosecution need not prove any object or effect on competition of the arrangement, and, conversely, it is not a defence to show that the arrangement did not have that object or effect. In practice, however, this distinction is more apparent than real. First, in civil cases it is well established that price-fixing and market sharing agreements can be regarded as having at least the object of preventing, distorting or restricting competition

---

[41] See *R. v JF Alford Ltd* [1997] 2 Cr.App.R. 326, CA.

without further evidence.[42] Secondly, the requirement of "dishonesty" is likely as a matter of practice to exclude from the offence those who make agreements which do not have an anti-competitive object. Thirdly, agreements with a limited impact or potential impact on competition are in practice unlikely to result in a prosecution, since prosecutions will be reserved for serious cases falling within the SFO's criteria for accepting cases, one of which criteria is that the value of the case exceeds £1 million.[43]

No defence that the arrangement complies with Article 81(3) EC or section 9   5–026
of the Competition Act.   The Enterprise Act does not provide that it is any defence to the cartel offence that the agreement in question complies with Art.81(3) EC or s.9 of the Competition Act.[44] Again, this difference between the offence and the civil prohibitions may be more apparent than real, since: (i) an honest belief that Art.81(3) EC or s.9 applied is likely in practice to be inconsistent with a finding of dishonesty; (ii) prosecution is unlikely in any case where those provisions arguably applied; and (iii) in practice, it is unlikely that any "hard-core" cartel could satisfy the various requirements of those provisions. Nonetheless, any agreement is in principle capable of satisfying the requirements of Art.81(3) EC, no matter how anti-competitive its object or effect may be.[45]

Further, Art.3(2) of Regulation 1/2003 ("the Modernisation Regulation") precludes Member States from applying "national competition law" so as to "lead to the prohibition of agreements ... which may affect trade between Member States, but ... which fulfil the conditions of Article 81(1) of the Treaty." If the cartel offence is part of "national competition law" (and the facts that it is part of a competition statute, and that it is largely enforced by the principal UK competition authority would appear to lead to that conclusion), then Art.3(2) would appear at least in theory to provide a defence to a charge under s.188,[46] although, as noted above, it may be doubted that any prosecution would be brought in a case where exemption was arguable.

3. INVESTIGATION AND ENFORCEMENT

The OFT and the SFO.   The scheme of the Enterprise Act provides a   5–027
statutory footing for the involvement of the Serious Fraud Office in the prosecution of the cartel offence. The centrality of the role of the SFO is

---

[42] *e.g.* Case 41/69 *ACF Chemiefarma v Commission* [1970] E.C.R. 661.
[43] The SFO's criteria are set out in *Memorandum of Understanding between the OFT and the SFO*, OFT 547, p.5, available at *www.oft.gov.uk*.
[44] For a discussion of those provisions, see paras 2–016–2–017, above.
[45] Case T–17/93 *Matra Hachette v Commission* [1994] E.C.R. II–595 at para.85.
[46] It should be noted that Art.3(3) of the Modernisation Regulation provides that Art.3(2) does not preclude the application of national law that "predominantly pursue[s] an objective different from that pursued by Articles 81 and 82 of the Treaty", but again it appears difficult to argue that the cartel offence has, predominantly, a different objective from that pursued by Art.81.

apparent from s.188 which enables proceedings to be instituted by the Director of the SFO or by or with the consent of the OFT.[47] The involvement of the SFO in the prosecution of the offence is unsurprising given the overlap that will arise between the cartel offence and the SFO's statutory remit to investigate serious or complex fraud.[48] The Enterprise Act confers upon the OFT its own extensive powers of criminal investigation whilst the Criminal Justice Act 1987 provides the SFO with its own separate powers of investigation. As such, cartel investigations may be subject to two distinct legislative regimes.[49]

The Enterprise Act does no more than to identify the SFO as a potential prosecutor of the offence and does not provide any framework for the respective functions that the SFO and the OFT will exercise in the investigation and prosecution of the cartel offence. To that end they have drawn up a Memorandum of Understanding[50] that sets out the expected delineation in their roles.

The Memorandum starts from the position that the OFT will be the initiator of an investigation and that it will carry out any preliminary investigations into cartel activity. Therefore if the SFO becomes aware of potential cartel activity it is to refer that information on to the Cartel Investigations Branch ("the CIB") of the OFT. Thereafter the OFT will consider whether the activity falls into the acceptance criteria for the SFO.

5–028 **The SFO acceptance criteria.** The factors taken into account by the SFO when determining acceptability are primarily indictors of seriousness coupled with whether its specialist investigation skills are required. Thus the value of the fraud (usually in excess of £1 million); whether the fraud will give rise to public concern; whether its investigation and prosecution requires specialist knowledge; whether this will require a combination of legal, accountancy and investigatory skills; whether there is a significant international dimension and whether the SFO's special powers of investigation are required[51] are all relevant.

5–029 **The initial conduct of the investigation.** As an alternative to accepting a case for investigation the SFO may ask the OFT to undertake further investigations before a decision to accept is made. These further investigations are expected to be undertaken by the CIB utilising the investigatory powers conferred by the Enterprise Act.

5–030 **Joint teams.** According to the Memorandum of Understanding where the SFO accept a cartel case the SFO and the OFT will form a joint criminal

---

[47] Enterprise Act, s.190.
[48] Criminal Justice Act 1987, s.1.
[49] The fact that the SFO is the prosecuting authority may also have important implications for the procedure adopted upon a trial on indictment (see para.5–054, below).
[50] *Memorandum of Understanding between the OFT and the SFO*, n.43, above.
[51] As set out in the Background note to the *Memorandum of Understanding between the OFT and the SFO*, n.43, above.

case team to further investigate and prosecute the matter. The SFO often work in conjunction with the police and it is envisaged that this will be a feature of cartel investigations also.

Investigations after acceptance by the SFO.   Where the SFO accept a case it is expected that they will use the powers of investigation available to them under the Criminal Justice Act 1987. The Memorandum of Understanding thus anticipates that the powers provided by the Enterprise Act will be used in the early stages of an investigation whereas the SFO will utilise its own powers of investigation upon acceptance of an investigation.

5–031

Investigatory powers available to the OFT under the Regulation of Investigatory Powers Act 2000.   The Enterprise Act amends the Regulation of Investigatory Powers Act 2000 ("the RIPA") to add the OFT to the list of public authorities authorised to use wide ranging powers of covert surveillance. The types of surveillance that RIPA authorises the OFT to carry out are "directed surveillance", "intrusive surveillance" and the use of "covert human intelligence sources".

5–032

"Directed intelligence".   "Directed intelligence" is defined as being covert (in that the subject of the surveillance is unaware of it) but not intrusive, undertaken for the purposes of a specific investigation, done in a manner that is likely to result in the obtaining of private information about a person and undertaken otherwise than by way of an immediate response to circumstances whereby it would not be reasonably practicable for an authorisation to be sought.[52] Covert surveillance undertaken in an office or a warehouse would fall within directed intelligence.

5–033

"Intrusive surveillance".   "Intrusive surveillance" is defined as being covert and is carried out in relation to anything that takes place on residential premises or in any private vehicle and involves the presence of an individual on the premises or in the vehicle or is carried out by way of a surveillance device.[53] Surveillance is also intrusive where it consists of a remote device that is not present in the premises or in a vehicle but conveys information of the same quality as might be expected from a device on the premises.[54] An example of surveillance that would fall into this category would be covert surveillance within the home or a hotel room.[55]

5–034

"Covert human intelligence sources".   "Covert human intelligence sources" are persons who establish or maintain relationships with a person for the purposes of obtaining information from that person or to gain access to information from that person. It also applies where a person discloses

5–035

---

[52] RIPA, s.26(2).
[53] RIPA, s.26(3).
[54] RIPA, s.26(5).
[55] RIPA, s.48(1).

information already obtained by virtue of such a relationship.[56] An example of the latter would be an employee who informs the OFT of a prohibited agreement and discloses details of such an agreement. The Enterprise Act gives a statutory footing to the issuance of a no-action letter to an individual who actively informs upon a cartel and therefore the handling of covert human intelligence sources will be of particular importance in cartel investigations.

5–036   How RIPA operates.   RIPA was enacted in order to provide a statutory footing for the use of covert surveillance by public authorities. In essence it provides a statutory criteria for the use of covert surveillance and a framework for the authorisation of such surveillance. The requirements for the use of intrusive surveillance are the most rigorous and its employment is also subject to the greatest level of supervision and scrutiny. As will be noted, intrusive surveillance is confined to that carried out in residential premises or in the car (clearly where the expectation of privacy is greatest). A private office will therefore fall within the ambit of directed surveillance despite the likely expectation of its occupier that it is a place of privacy.

5–037   Authorisation of directed surveillance.   The Director of Cartel Investigations is the person designated to grant authorisations for the use of directed surveillance.[57] Directed surveillance can be carried out for the purposes of preventing or detecting the cartel offence and in respect of investigations under the Competition Act. Whilst RIPA sets out seven grounds upon which such an authorisation may be granted, the Director may only do so on the basis of his belief that it is necessary for the purpose of preventing or detecting crime or of preventing disorder or that it is necessary in the interests of the economic wellbeing of the UK.[58] It is the latter criteria that must be satisfied before directed surveillance can take place pursuant to a Competition Act investigation. He must also believe that the surveillance is proportionate to the object to be achieved by carrying the surveillance out.[59] According to the Code of Practice issued by the OFT in respect of their powers of covert surveillance[60] the OFT will limit authorisations for the use of directed surveillance in its Competition Act investigations to those where it is investigating a suspected cartel agreement to fix prices, limit production or supply, share markets or rig bids.

5–038   Authorisation of covert human intelligence sources.   The Director of Cartel Investigations is the designated person for authorising the conduct or the

---

[56] RIPA, s.26(8).
[57] The Regulation of Investigatory Powers (Directed Surveillance and Covert Human Intelligence Sources) Order 2003 (SI 2003/3171).
[58] RIPA, s.28(3)(b) and (c).
[59] RIPA, s.28(2)(b).
[60] *Covert surveillance in cartel investigations, Code of Practice*, OFT 738.

use of a covert human intelligence source ("CHIS").[61] He may only grant such an authorisation where he believes it is necessary for the purpose of detecting or preventing crime or of preventing disorder or necessary in the interests of the economic well being of the UK.[62] He must believe that the authorisation sought is proportionate to the object to be achieved by the use of the CHIS.[63] He must also believe that arrangements exist for the handling of the CHIS.[64] This latter requirement is a significant one and the handling of a source is subject to detailed regulation.[65] It is critical that informants are handled properly as ultimately a failure to do so may give rise to an application for a trial to be stayed as an abuse of process or render the source unusable.[66] Thus, for example, records must be kept of payments or rewards offered to a source and of the tasks he is assigned and demands made of him. Other necessary arrangements include that there will be an officer charged with day to day responsibility for dealing with the source; that there will be an officer who will have general oversight for the use made of the source and that there will be an officer responsible for maintaining a record of the use made of the source.[67] There will be dedicated officers within the Cartels Investigation Branch ("the CIB") responsible for maintaining such records.[68] The power to utilise a CHIS also applies to Competition Act investigations insofar as it can be demonstrated that such an authorisation is necessary in the interests of the economic well being of the UK.

Authorisation for the use of intrusive surveillance. The use of intrusive surveillance may only be authorised by the Chairman of the OFT.[69] He may only grant such an authorisation where he believes it is necessary for the purpose of preventing or detecting a cartel offence.[70] He must also be satisfied that it is proportionate to what is sought to be achieved by carrying it out.[71] In measuring whether it is necessary and proportionate he should have regard to whether the information could be obtained by other means.[72] Unless it is a case of emergency, an authorisation granted by the Chairman of the OFT will have no effect until it has been approved by a Surveillance Commissioner from the Office of Surveillance Commissioners ("the   **5–039**

---

[61] The Regulation of Investigatory Powers (Directed Surveillance and Covert Human Intelligence Sources) Order 2003 (SI 2003/3171).

[62] RIPA, s.29(3).

[63] RIPA, s.29(2)(b).

[64] RIPA, s.29(2)(c).

[65] The Regulation of Investigatory Powers Act (Source Records) Regulations 2000 (SI 2000/2725).

[66] As to the consequences this had in respect of the handling of informants by HM Customs and Excise see *Review of Criminal Investigations and Prosecutions Conducted by HM Customs and Excise* by Hon Mr Justice Butterfield.

[67] RIPA, s.29(5).

[68] See further *Covert human intelligence sources in cartel investigations, Code of practice*, OFT 739.

[69] RIPA, s.32(6)(n).

[70] RIPA, s.32(3A).

[71] RIPA, s.32(2)(b).

[72] RIPA, s.32(4).

OSC").[73] The OSC is the statutory body responsible for supervising the use of covert surveillance by public authorities. Where the case is one of emergency, the authorisation takes effect from the time of grant but may be quashed by a Surveillance Commissioner if he is of the view that there were no reasonable grounds for viewing the situation as urgent.[74]

5–040 **Failure to comply with RIPA.** RIPA thus provides the framework by which surveillance can be conducted in accordance with law but it does not prescribe what the consequences might be in a criminal trial where such evidence has been obtained in a manner that does not comply with the requirements of RIPA. Surveillance evidence obtained in circumstances that contravene RIPA will not be rendered automatically inadmissible. Rather the issue will be a matter of judicial discretion under s.78 of the Police and Criminal Evidence Act 1984 whereby the court may exclude evidence if its admission would have such an adverse effect on the proceedings that the court ought not to admit it. In exercising that discretion the court must have regard to all the circumstances in which the evidence was obtained. The fairness of the trial may be compromised where the evidence was obtained by unfair means.[75]

5–041 **Interference with property or wireless telegraphy.** The Police Act 1997 allows the Chairman of the OFT to authorise interference with property or with wireless telegraphy. An example of where such a need might arise is where it is proposed to plant a listening device in someone's home pursuant to the power to use intrusive surveillance. The Chairman is confined to authorising such an interference where he believes that it is necessary for the purposes of preventing or detecting the cartel offence and that it is proportionate to the aim of the interference.[76] It is likely that many investigations involving covert surveillance will require an authorisation for entry on or interference with property or wireless telegraphy given the prevalence of the use of listening devices. It is possible to combine authorisations under Part II of RIPA with an authorisation under Part III of the Police Act 1997. This is permissible as long as the separate provisions for each authorisation are complied with.

5–042 **Non-criminal investigations.** It is likely that any criminal investigation into a cartel offence will begin life as an investigation under s.25 of the Competition Act. It is critical however that where a criminal offence is suspected that the investigation is conducted having regard to the rules of admissibility in criminal proceedings. A failure to do so may render any evidence gathered as a result inadmissible in a future cartel offence trial. Where there are grounds to suspect a person of a cartel offence they must be cautioned

---

[73] RIPA, s.36.
[74] RIPA, s.37(4).
[75] *R. v Loosely* [2001] UKHL 53.
[76] Police Act 1997, s.93.

before any questions are put to them about that activity in accordance with the requirements of Code C of the Police and Criminal Evidence Act 1984.[77]

Powers of compulsion. The OFT may compel a person to whom they have given notice in writing to: answer questions; provide information pursuant to an investigation into a cartel offence; or to produce documents relevant to such an investigation. These powers of compulsion are not confined to the subject of an investigation but extend to anyone believed to have information relevant to an investigation.[78]   **5–043**

Use of information obtained under compulsory powers. Where an individual is compelled to make a statement pursuant to a requirement under s.193 or 194 of the Enterprise Act it can only be used against him either where he is prosecuted for making a false or misleading statement or where upon a prosecution for another offence he makes a statement that is inconsistent with it.[79] The statement cannot be used against the individual unless evidence relating to it is adduced or a question relating to it is asked by or on behalf of that person in proceedings arising out of the prosecution. The Enterprise Act thus complies with the ruling by the European Court of Human Rights in *Saunders v United Kingdom*[80] in that the prosecution cannot seek to introduce evidence obtained by virtue of compulsory questioning in the context of a prosecution for the cartel offence (except where the defendant makes a statement inconsistent with it). The same applies to those statements required under the Competition Act.[81]   **5–044**

Powers of search and seizure. Where a person fails to comply with a requirement to produce a document under s.193 of the Enterprise Act the OFT may apply to the High Court for a warrant authorising them to enter premises and take possession of the documents required.[82] The OFT may also make such an application where it is not practicable to serve a notice requiring the documents or where it would seriously prejudice the investigation if such a notice was to be served.[83] A warrant issued under this section also authorises an officer of the OFT to require any person to provide an explanation of any document appearing to be relevant or to state where it may be found.[84]   **5–045**

Effect of a failure to comply. A failure to comply with a requirement under s.193 or 194 of the Enterprise Act, in the absence of a reasonable excuse, is a   **5–046**

---

[77] Code of Practice for the Detention, Treatment and Questioning of Persons by Police Officers, Code C. See Zander, *The Police and Criminal Evidence Act 1984* (4th ed.).
[78] Enterprise Act, s.193(1).
[79] s.197(a)–(b).
[80] [1997] 23 E.H.R.R 313.
[81] s.198.
[82] s.194(1)(b)(i).
[83] s.194(1)(b)(ii)/(iii).
[84] s.194(2)(c).

summary offence and punishable for a term of up to six months imprisonment or a fine (not exceeding level 5 on the standard scale) or both.[85] A person who purports to comply with either section but in fact makes a statement that is false or misleading or recklessly makes such a statement is liable upon conviction on an indictment to a maximum of two years' imprisonment, a fine, or both.[86] It is also an offence to intentionally obstruct a person exercising his powers under s.194. The maximum punishment available for this offence is two years upon conviction on an indictment, a fine or both.[87]

5–047 **Destruction or disposal of documentation.** It is also an offence to falsify, conceal, destroy or otherwise dispose of documents (or to cause or permit such a course of action) which may be relevant to a cartel investigation. An individual must know or suspect that a cartel investigation is being or is likely to be carried out and it will be a defence if he can prove that he had no intention of concealing the facts disclosed by the documents.[88] The maximum sentence available upon a conviction on indictment is five years imprisonment or a fine or both.[89]

5–048 **Compulsory powers exercisable by the SFO.** Under s.2(3) of the Criminal Justice Act 1987 the Director of the SFO has an identical power to that contained in s.193 of the Enterprise Act to require by notice in writing a person under investigation to attend for interview or produce specified documents. It should also be noted that the SFO does not have to give a person compelled to attend for such an interview advance information as to what he will be interviewed about.[90] Failure to comply with such a requirement, in the absence of a reasonable excuse, is a criminal offence.[91] Under s.14 of the Criminal Justice Act 1987 it is also a criminal offence to purport to comply with a requirement and to make a statement that is false or misleading in a material particular or to recklessly make a statement that is false or misleading in a material particular. Any statement made by a person in the context of such a compulsory interview cannot be used against him except in a prosecution for an offence under s.14 or on a prosecution for a different offence where he makes a statement inconsistent with it.[92] Where the latter applies such a statement may again only be used where evidence of it is adduced or a question related to it is asked by or on behalf of the defendant in those proceedings.

---

[85] s.201(1).
[86] s.201(2).
[87] s.201(6).
[88] s.201(4).
[89] s.201(5).
[90] *R. v Serious Fraud Office Ex p. Maxwell (Kevin), The Times*, October 9, 1992.
[91] Criminal Justice Act 1987, s.2(13).
[92] Criminal Justice Act 1987, s.8.

4. "NO ACTION" LETTERS

Immunity from prosecution for individuals.   The OFT is of the view that,   **5–049**
owing to the highly secretive nature of cartels, it is justified in operating
a scheme whereby individuals who inform the OFT of cartel activity may
be granted immunity from prosecution. This immunity from prosecution
will take the form of a "no-action" letter and is enshrined in s.190(4) of
the Enterprise Act. The issuing of a no-action letter is contingent upon the
individual admitting their participation in the cartel offence; providing
the OFT with information about the activities of the cartel; providing consistent co-operation throughout the investigation; not coercing another
undertaking to take part in a cartel and refraining from participating further
in the cartel (except as directed by the investigating authority).[93] Such a
person will in all likelihood fall within the definition of a "covert human
intelligence source" for the purposes of the Regulation of Investigatory
Powers Act 2000 and ought to be managed accordingly. Where the OFT is
of the view that sufficient information exists to bring a successful prosecution, without the information that could be provided by the informant, it
will not issue a no-action letter. Clearly therefore the rationale of the no-
action letter is to encourage individuals to inform at as early a stage as is
possible.

Procedure.   The Chairman of the OFT will give a primary indication as to   **5–050**
whether the OFT might issue a no-action letter in respect of the individual.
The individual will then be interviewed. It is important to note that at this
point the individual has not been granted immunity and that according to
the OFT guidance what is said by the individual in interview may be used
against them subsequently in criminal proceedings (it is presumed therefore
that the individual will be cautioned prior to this interview). The circumstances in which the OFT may seek to use the interview in criminal proceedings are where a no-action letter is not issued and the individual
knowingly or recklessly provided false or misleading information or where a
no-action letter is issued and subsequently revoked.[94] Decisions as to the
issuance of no-action letters are a matter for the OFT and not the SFO.
However, where the issuance of a letter may impact upon an existing SFO
led cartel investigation, then the OFT will consult the SFO.[95]

Revocation.   A no-action letter may be revoked upon the failure of the   **5–051**
individual to comply with the conditions of issuance or where they have
knowingly or recklessly provided false or misleading information. Revocation will be given in notice in writing and an opportunity will be afforded for

---

[93] *The cartel offence, Guidance on the issue of no-action letters for individuals*, OFT 512.
[94] Para.3.7.
[95] *Memorandum of understanding between the OFT and the SFO*, October 2003, n.43, above.

the individual to make representations[96]. The guidance is silent as to the procedure for making representations and does not state who will consider such representations. According to the draft no-action letter annexed to the guidance upon revocation "any" information provided by the informant may be used in evidence against him. This may well give rise to issues under s.78 of the Police and Criminal Evidence Act 1984 (which confers upon the court the discretion to exclude evidence on the basis that it would have such an adverse effect on the fairness of the proceedings that it ought not be admitted).

5. CRIMINAL PROCEDURE

5–052 **Commencement of prosecution.** The cartel offence is triable either in the Magistrates Court or upon an indictment at the Crown Court.[97] Triable either-way offences commence at the Magistrates Court although there is provision for serious or complex frauds to be transferred to the Crown Court. This procedure, by which the SFO serves a notice of transfer, is considered in para.5–054, below. If no such notice is served by the SFO then the accused will be subject to the ordinary process by which mode of trial is determined.

5–053 **Mode of trial.** The preliminary procedure in the Magistrates Court is that the accused will be served either with a copy of parts of every written statement which contain information as to the facts and matters upon which the prosecutor proposes to rely, or a summary of the facts and matters of which the prosecutor proposes to adduce evidence in the proceedings.[98] This frequently amounts to very little except a bare outline of the facts.

The accused will be expected to indicate whether, if the matter was to proceed to trial, he would plead guilty or not guilty.[99] If the accused indicates a plea of not guilty then the court will determine whether the case is suitable for summary trial or whether it should be tried on indictment.[1] Irrespective of the view of the court the accused has the right to elect trial upon indictment. In reality it is highly unlikely given the complex nature of the cartel offence and the limitations of the Magistrates Court in terms of sentence that the cartel offence will be tried anywhere other than the Crown Court.

The matter will be committed to the Crown Court without a consideration of the evidence unless the defence request that the Court consider a submission that there is insufficient evidence upon which the defendant

---

[96] Para.3.13.
[97] Enterprise Act 2002, s.190.
[98] Magistrates' Courts (Advance Information) Rules 1985 (SI 1985/601).
[99] Magistrates' Courts Act 1980, s.17A.
[1] Magistrates' Courts Act 1980, s.19.

could be tried.[2] Such a consideration will be on paper only and no live witnesses will be called.

If the accused pleads guilty at the Magistrates' Court and the court is of the view that owing to the seriousness of the offence a greater sentence than the Magistrates Court can impose should be inflicted then the matter will be committed to the Crown Court for sentence.[3]

Notice of transfer.   In a case of serious or complex fraud the Director of the SFO may serve a notice of transfer. This essentially has the effect of transferring the management of the case to the Crown Court at an early point and of avoiding protracted committal proceedings in complex cases. The procedure at the time of writing is governed by ss.4–6 of the Criminal Justice Act 1987 but these have been repealed by the Criminal Justice Act 2003[4] which amends the Crime and Disorder Act 1998. Those provisions have yet to be commenced but the procedure will in future be governed by s.51B of the 1998 Act. Under s.51B, the Director of the SFO must certify that the case is one of such seriousness or complexity that its management ought, without further delay, be taken over by the Crown Court. Upon service of such a notice the Magistrates' functions in respect of that prosecution cease forthwith. It is likely that the Director of the SFO will serve a notice of transfer in any cartel offence prosecution.

5–054

Application for dismissal.   Where a case is transferred to the Crown Court the defence may (prior to arraignment) make an application to have the charge dismissed.[5] Upon such an application the judge shall dismiss a charge (and quash any count relating to it in any indictment preferred against the applicant) if it appears to him that the evidence against the applicant would not be sufficient for a jury properly to convict him.[6] In *R. (Inland Revenue Commissioners) v Crown Court at Kingston*[7] the Divisional Court set out the judge's function under s.6 of the Criminal Justice Act 1987 (which sets out the same basis for dismissal). The court found that s.6 required the judge to take into account the totality of the evidence against the defendant and to decide whether he was satisfied that it was sufficient for a jury properly to convict the defendant. It was not appropriate for the judge to view any evidence in isolation from its context. The judge's function was not to substitute himself for the jury as the issue was not whether the defendant should be convicted but whether there was sufficient evidence upon which he could be convicted. Where the evidence was largely documentary, and the case depended on the inferences or conclusions to be drawn from it, the

5–055

---

[2] Magistrates' Courts Act 1980, s.17A.
[3] Powers of Criminal Courts (Sentencing) Act 2000, s.3.
[4] Criminal Justice Act 2003, Sch.3, para.18.
[5] Crime and Disorder Act 1998, Sch.3. At the time of writing these arrangements had yet to be commenced.
[6] Crime and Disorder Act 1998, Sch.3, para.2(2).
[7] [2001] 4 All E.R. 721, DC.

judge had to assess the inferences or conclusions that the prosecution proposed to ask the jury to draw from the documents, and decide whether it appeared to him that the jury could properly draw those inferences and come to those conclusions. The judge's assessment as to weight or sufficiency could only be interfered with where no reasonable judge could have reached that conclusion.

5–056   **Preparatory hearings in serious or complex fraud.**   Section 7(1) of the Criminal Justice Act 1987 (as amended by the Criminal Justice Act 2003)[8] enables a judge to conduct preparatory hearings before the time when the jury is sworn. The purpose of any such hearing is: to identify issues which are likely to be material to the determinations and findings which are likely to arise during the trial; if there is to be a jury, to assist their comprehension of those issues and expedite the proceedings before them; to determine an application under s.45 of the Criminal Justice Act 2003 (prosecution application for a trial without a jury); to assist the judge's management of the trial; or to consider questions as to the severance or joinder of charges.[9] It is likely that such hearings will be held in cartel offence cases.

5–057   **Trial without jury.**   Part 7 of the Criminal Justice Act 2003[10] paves the way for a radical overhaul of how serious or complex fraud trials are conducted by enabling such trials to be conducted without a jury. Such a trial would take place before a judge alone as opposed to a judge and a lay panel or a panel of assessors. This provision applies only to those cases where notice has been given under s.51B of the Criminal Justice Act 1998 (notice of transfer to the Crown Court in cases of serious or complex fraud). Under s.43 of the Criminal Justice Act 2003 such an application must be made by the prosecutor to a judge of the Crown Court. The conditions to be met before a judge can order a trial without a jury are either that the complexity of the trial or the length of the trial or both are so burdensome that it is in the interests of justice to consider trial without a jury.[11] In determining whether these conditions are met the judge must consider any steps that could be taken to reduce the complexity or the length of the trial.[12] Both the defence and the prosecution can appeal any decision made pursuant to an application under s.43.

5–058   **Plea and directions hearing.**   In those cases which are not the subject of an application for transfer, the defendant upon a not guilty plea will be committed from the Magistrates Court to the Crown Court for trial. The initial hearing at the Crown Court is the "plea and directions" hearing. At this

---

[8] At the time of writing these amendments had not been commenced.
[9] Criminal Justice Act 1987, s.7.
[10] As at the time of writing, this provision had not yet commenced.
[11] Criminal Justice Act 2003, s.43(5).
[12] Criminal Justice Act 2003, s.43(6).

hearing the defendant will be arraigned and there will be a preliminary identification of the issues anticipated at the trial.

Disclosure. The Criminal Justice Act 2003 amends the Criminal Procedure **5–059** and Investigations Act 1996 in relation to the rules governing disclosure.[13] In particular it requires more extensive disclosure than previously as to the nature of the accused's defence.

The prosecution duty of disclosure. Section 3 of the Criminal Procedure and **5–060** Investigations Act 1996 (as amended by the Criminal Justice Act 2003) provides that the prosecutor must disclose any prosecution material, not previously disclosed, that might reasonably be capable of undermining the prosecution case or of assisting the case of the defence. Whereas prior to amendment this test was based on the subjective opinion of the prosecutor (as to whether or not the material might undermine the prosecution case) as amended the test is objective. It is an ongoing duty that extends to the point at which the accused is acquitted, convicted or a decision is taken not to proceed with the case.[14] The prosecution must keep the issue of disclosure under review throughout this period and in particular have regard to the issues disclosed in the defence statement.

Defence disclosure. Defence disclosure does not arise until the prosecutor **5–061** complies or purports to comply with s.3. Where the matter has been transferred from the Magistrates Court it will not apply until a copy of the notice of transfer and copies of the documents containing the evidence have been given to the accused.[15] As amended, the Criminal Procedure and Investigations Act 1996 requires that the accused sets out his defence in more detail than simply stating the general nature of the defence (as was previously the case). Section 6A[16] requires: that a defence statement sets out the nature of the accused's defence, including any particular defences on which he intends to rely; that the accused indicates the matters of fact on which he takes issue with the prosecution; that the accused sets out, in particular, why he takes issue with the prosecution on those matters; and that any point of law (including any point as to the admissibility of evidence or an abuse of process) to be taken is indicated. Information as to any alibi evidence to be relied upon is also required.[17]

Further defence statement. Section 6(B) of the Criminal Procedure and **5–062** Investigations Act 1996 (as inserted by the Criminal Justice Act 2003) also makes provision for the service of a further defence statement. This requires the defence to update the defence statement if there are changes to that

---

[13] At the time of writing these amendments had yet to be commenced.
[14] Criminal Procedure and Investigations Act 1996, s.7A(b).
[15] Criminal Procedure and Investigations Act 1996, s.5.
[16] Yet to be commenced.
[17] Criminal Procedure and Investigations Act 1996, s.6A(2).

statement or to provide a statement notifying the prosecution that there are no changes to be made.

5–063 **Defence experts.** The Criminal Procedure and Evidence Act 1996 (as amended by the Criminal Justice Act 2003) will make it a requirement[18] that the defence notify the court and the prosecutor of the name and address of any expert that they have instructed with a view to providing an opinion at trial.[19] This requirement puts the prosecutor on notice that the defence have instructed an expert. This is of significance because if the defence decide not to use an expert (perhaps because his opinion is unhelpful to the defence) the prosecutor will have sufficient information to contact the expert and to consider whether he could be called as a witness for the prosecution.

5–064 **Other defence witnesses.** The 1996 Act is also amended to require the defence to notify the prosecution of the names, addresses and dates of birth of any witness that he intends to call at trial.[20] If the defence do not know these details they must provide any information that might materially assist in identifying or finding the proposed witness. This is as far as the obligation goes. The defence are not required to detail what issue the witness goes to or in respect of what they might give evidence.

5–065 **Public interest immunity.** Public interest immunity ("PII") may attach to material where the public interest in non-disclosure outweighs the public interest in the full disclosure of the facts before the court. The balancing exercise in criminal proceedings is distinct from that in civil proceedings where, by virtue of the fact that the accused's liberty is at stake, the public interest in the administration of justice weighs more heavily.

An area where PII is frequently claimed in criminal proceedings is where it is relevant to the prevention, detection or investigation of crime. This may arise in the context of a prosecution for the cartel offence because of the OFT's powers of covert surveillance under the Regulation of Investigatory Powers Act 2000. The prosecution may make an application for PII where, for example, the defence seek disclosure of the circumstances in which surveillance was authorised. Applications for PII also commonly arise in order to maintain the anonymity of informants.

5–066 **Application for PII.** Where an application for PII is to be made the prosecution should serve notice upon the defence specifying the nature of the material to which the application relates.[21] This does not apply where the prosecutor has reason to believe that revealing the nature of the material

---

[18] At the time of writing these amendments had yet to be commenced.
[19] Criminal Procedure and Investigations Act 1996, s.6D.
[20] Criminal Procedure and Investigations Act 1996, s.6C (yet to be commenced at time of writing).
[21] The Crown Court (Criminal Procedure and Investigations Act 1996) (Disclosure) Rules 1997 (SI 1997/698).

would have the effect of disclosing what it is that PII is sought in respect of. In those circumstances a notice may be served omitting the nature of the material.[22] Where the prosecutor is of the view that disclosure of the fact that an application for PII is to be made would in effect disclose that in respect of which PII is sought, notice does not have to be served.[23] Such cases should arise only rarely.[24] Where notice is given to the defence of the fact of the application and of the nature of the material the application will be *inter partes* and the defence will be able to make representations to the court.[25] The prosecutor may however apply for leave to make representations in the absence of the accused.[26] Where the nature of the material has not been disclosed or where no notice has been served on the defence the hearing shall be *ex parte* and only the prosecutor is entitled to make representations.[27]

In *Jasper v United Kingdom*[28] the European Court of Human Rights found that the *ex parte* procedure complied with Art.6 of the European Convention on Human Rights. Relevant considerations included that the defence had been able to outline the defence case to the trial judge and that the need for disclosure was at all times under assessment by the trial judge in that it was his duty to monitor throughout the trial the fairness or otherwise of the evidence being withheld.

Sentencing.   The maximum sentence available upon a trial on indictment for the cartel offence is five years or an unlimited fine or both.[29] Where an accused person enters a guilty plea it is usual that this will result in a reduction in the sentence that would have been passed had the accused been convicted by a jury. It is a matter of discretion for the judge as to whether or not the discount should be applied. However the benefits that accrue from guilty pleas in terms of saving court time, preserving public funds and freeing witnesses from court attendance means that such pleas are encouraged by the application of a discount in most cases. This may be particularly relevant in the context of a complex fraud case which will inevitably require a lengthy trial at considerable expense to the public purse. The application of the discount is not always inevitable and may for example be withheld where the prosecution case is overwhelming.[30]

5–067

Procedure on sentencing.   Where sentence follows a protracted trial the judge will not usually require the facts to be re-opened upon a sentencing hearing. The court should order a pre-sentence report except where the

5–068

---

[22] Para.2(3).
[23] Para.2(4).
[24] *R. v Davies, Johnson and Rowe* [1997] Cr.App.R 110.
[25] Para.3(3).
[26] Para.3(4).
[27] Para.3(5).
[28] 30 E.H.R.R 441.
[29] Enterprise Act 2002, s.188.
[30] *R. v Hastings* [1996] 1 Cr.App.R(S.) 167, CA.

court is of the view that it is unnecessary.[31] The court also has the power to require an individual to give a statement as to his financial circumstances,[32] Where an accused enters a guilty plea at an earlier stage this will normally be on the basis of the Crown's case. This is except where the accused has pleaded on a written basis of plea and the Crown has accepted that plea. Thus for example an accused might plead on the basis that his involvement is lesser than that alleged by the Crown or that his involvement was for a lesser time than that alleged in the indictment. Where an accused seeks to be sentenced on a basis different from that asserted by the prosecution this must be made clear. Where the prosecution do not accept this basis and the difference in the two accounts is such that it may materially affect the sentence imposed then it may be resolved by a *Newton* hearing.[33]

5–069   **Confiscation.**   A detailed treatment of the provisions of the Proceeds of Crime Act 2002 is outside the scope of this work. However where a defendant has been convicted of an offence in the Crown Court or committed for sentence to the Crown Court he may be subjected to proceedings for confiscation.[34] The first issue for the court to determine is whether the defendant has a "criminal lifestyle". In relation to the cartel offence the defendant may be said to have a criminal lifestyle where the offence concerned has been committed over a period of at least six months and the defendant has benefited from that conduct.[35] A defendant will also have a criminal lifestyle if the offence concerned constitutes conduct forming part of a course of criminal activity.[36] If the court determines that a defendant has a criminal lifestyle then it will apply a set of presumptions in determining whether the defendant has benefited from his criminal conduct.[37] If the court decides that the defendant does not have a criminal lifestyle it must determine whether he has benefited from his particular criminal conduct.[38] The issue as to whether or not a defendant has benefited from his involvement in a cartel offence may well raise interesting issues where for example he is an employee and any financial benefit that arose from a prohibited agreement was primarily that of the company's. In such circumstances the court may examine whether the defendant was the recipient of a financial incentive or a bonus owing to his activities. Where a court determines the benefit from the defendant's conduct it will then specify the recoverable amount and make an order requiring the defendant to pay that amount.[39]

---

[31] Powers of Criminal Courts (Sentencing) Act 2000, s.81.
[32] Powers of Criminal Courts (Sentencing) Act 2000, s.126.
[33] *R. v Newton* (1983) 77 Cr.App.R 13, CA.
[34] Proceeds of Crime Act 2002, s.6.
[35] s.75(2)(c).
[36] s.75(2)(b).
[37] s.10.
[38] s.6(4)(c).
[39] s.6(5).

Conclusion. The extent to which the OFT will exercise its prosecutorial 5–070 function in respect of cartels is as yet unknown. The prosecution of individuals for offences predicated upon dishonesty, within a commercial context, has historically been beset by difficulties for prosecuting authorities in the management and presentation of trials. Those difficulties stem from a number of factors including the complexity of the circumstances, the likely reliance on voluminous documentary evidence and proving dishonesty to the requisite degree on the part of individuals. It is foreseeable that these difficulties could be amplified in cartel prosecutions where the prosecution must prove to the criminal standard that the agreement would (if operating as the parties intended) have the prescribed effect. Besides the inherent problems in proving intent on the part of individuals, this requirement will, it seems, necessitate complex economic evidence as to the relevant market and whether the effect has been or would be realised. A prosecution for the cartel offence will therefore give rise to a complex interplay between the acts and mindsets of individual actors and the economic context of their behaviour. How this will translate in a criminal trial and what difficulties it will give rise to remain to be seen.

CHAPTER 6

JUDICIAL REVIEW IN A COMPETITION LAW CONTEXT

Christopher Vajda QC and Julian Gregory[1]

1. GENERALLY

6–001   **The role of judicial review.**   The competition law landscape has been transformed by recent legislation. Recent legislative changes are likely, among other things, to increase the possibilities for judicial review challenges in a competition law context. The possibility has always existed to bring an application for judicial review in the High Court to challenge decisions taken by competition and regulatory authorities. Previously, though, such challenges have been relatively infrequent, and largely unsuccessful. The Enterprise Act, however, has introduced some significant changes. First, as a result of the new merger and market reference regime introduced by Parts 3 and 4 of the Enterprise Act, more decisions subject to the principles of judicial review will be taken in a competition law context. Secondly, those decisions are increasingly likely to be based on economic and legal, as opposed to political, considerations. Thirdly, a considerable number of those decisions will be reviewed by a specialist tribunal, namely the CAT, as opposed to by the High Court. It is highly likely that these changes will result in a greater number of judicial review challenges to competition law decisions.

6–002   **The structure of the chapter.**   After this introductory section, this chapter is broken down into six more sections. The following section provides a brief introduction to the jurisdiction of judicial review. Section 3 then attempts to summarise the grounds of judicial review. This is a huge topic, and Section 3 makes numerous references to four of the leading text books on Administrative Law and Judicial Review where further information may be sought, namely: (i) De Smith, Woolf and Jowell, *Judicial Review of Administrative*

---

[1] Barristers, Monckton Chambers.

Action[2]; (ii) Craig, *Administrative Law* (5th ed.)[3]; (iii) Fordham, *Judicial Review Handbook* (4th ed.)[4]; and (iv) Wade & Forsyth, *Administrative Law* (8th ed.).[5] The principles of judicial review are summarised primarily because they are adopted by the statutory review procedures introduced by ss.120 and 179 of the Enterprise Act, but they will continue to apply to challenges brought in the High Court outside of that context (for example, against many decisions taken by regulatory bodies). Section 4 introduces the statutory review procedures, and explains a few procedural aspects relating to them. Section 5 attempts to set out the considerations likely to affect the intensity with which the judicial review principles will be applied in a competition law context, and in particular in applications under ss.120 and 179. Finally, Sections 6 and 7 provide a brief summary of the substantive provisions in Parts 3 and 4 of the Enterprise Act relating to mergers and market investigations, and provide a few comments as to how the principles of judicial review may be applied in challenges to decisions taken under those parts.

2. INTRODUCTION TO JUDICIAL REVIEW

Definition of judicial review. Part 54.1 of the CPR defines a claim for judicial review as "a claim to review the lawfulness of an enactment or a decision, action or failure to act in relation to the exercise of a public function". The procedure of judicial review is that by which the courts have traditionally exercised a supervisory jurisdiction over the acts and omissions of public bodies. The purpose of the supervisory jurisdiction has variously been described as "to secure that decisions are made by the executive or by a public body according to the law",[6] "to ensure that the rights of citizens are not abused by the unlawful exercise of executive power",[7] and to act as "a positive encouragement to maintain high standards in public administration or by public bodies".[8] The courts have developed various grounds on which applications for judicial review must be based. Those grounds, and the way in which they are applied, are considered further below.

6–003

The remedies of judicial review. For many years, judicial review was effectively defined by reference to the three prerogative remedies of certiorari (now quashing order), mandamus (now mandatory order) and prohibition

6–004

---

[2] (5th ed., Sweet & Maxwell, 1995) (hereafter "De Smith").
[3] (5th ed., Sweet & Maxwell, 2003) (hereafter "Craig").
[4] (4th ed., Hart Publishing, 2004) (hereafter "Fordham").
[5] (8th ed., Oxford, 2004) (hereafter "Wade").
[6] *Mercury Energy Ltd v Electricity Corporation of New Zealand Ltd* [1994] 1 W.L.R. 521 at 526A *per* Lord Templeman.
[7] *R. v Ministry of Defence Ex p. Smith* [1996] Q.B. 517 at 556D–E *per* Sir Thomas Bingham M.R.
[8] *Council of Civil Service Unions v Minister for the Civil Service* [1985] A.C. 374 at 408E *per* Lord Diplock.

(now prohibiting order). From 1977 onwards, the remedies of declaration, injunction and damages have also been available. The remedies are described and provided by CPR Rules 54.2 and 54.3, and an explanation of the historical development of judicial review remedies and procedures can be found in De Smith. It should be noted that judicial review remedies are discretionary, and are not available as of right.[9] Although the review provisions of the Enterprise Act adopt the principles that would be applied on an application for judicial review, they do not adopt the traditional judicial review remedies. Rather, ss.120(5) and 179(5) of the Enterprise Act specify the remedies that the CAT may adopt when determining an application for a review under those provisions.

6–005 **Permission.** The procedure for applications for judicial review is set out in CPR Rule 54, and is further elucidated by the Part 54 Practice Direction. The effect of CPR Rule 54(4) is that, in order to proceed with a claim for judicial review, a claimant must first apply to the court for permission to bring the claim. The purpose of the requirement of permission is to prevent from proceeding claims that are weak, frivolous or vexatious. It is not considered to be in the public interest that public bodies should be put to the trouble of defending such claims in a full substantive hearing. The test for permission is whether there is an arguable ground for judicial review, on which there is a realistic prospect of success.[10] In most cases, the court will consider the application for permission on the papers.[11] If permission is refused, or is granted subject to conditions or on certain grounds only, the claimant may request the decision be reconsidered at an oral hearing.[12] As shall be explained, there is no requirement to obtain permission before bringing a judicial review challenge under the Enterprise Act 2002.

6–006 **The scope of judicial review.** The scope of judicial review is effectively determined by the answers to the following three questions. Who may bring an application for judicial review? What measures, acts or omissions may be challenged by way of an application for judicial review? Against what persons or bodies may an application for judicial review be brought? These questions are considered in the paragraphs below.

6–007 **Standing.** The issue of who may bring an application for judicial review is also referred to as the issue of who has "standing"[13] to bring an application for judicial review. Section 31 of the Supreme Court Act 1981 provides that a court shall not grant leave (now permission) for judicial review unless it considers that the applicant has a "sufficient interest" in the matter to which the application relates. The correct application of the sufficient interest test

---

[9] Subject to the requirements of EC or ECHR law, in relation to which, see below.
[10] Fordham, para.21.1.
[11] Pt 54 Practice Direction, para.8.4.
[12] CPR Rule 54.12.
[13] Or *locus standi*.

is the subject of much debate, and considerable case law. Prima facie, the question of standing falls to be addressed at the permission stage. However, the issue is complicated by the fact that the courts have made it clear that the question of standing is not divorced from the context and merits of the substantive claim.[14] For this reason, the standing test is often left to be considered at the substantive hearing. An applicant that has a direct personal interest in the outcome of a claim will normally be regarded as satisfying the sufficient interest test. Beyond that, Fordham identifies the following principal themes from the case law on standing: (i) that the general approach of the courts to standing is a liberal one; (ii) that financial interest may be sufficient but will seldom ever be necessary; (iii) that public interest considerations favour the testing of the legality of executive action; (iv) that it would be against the public interest if there were a "vacuum" (or lacuna) of unchecked illegality for want of a challenger with standing; (v) that the courts seek to strike a balance, distinguishing broadly between busybodies and those with a legitimate grievance or interest; and (vi) that one factor which may in some situations count against the claimant is where there is an obviously better-placed challenger who is not complaining.[15] There are specific rules which deal with the issue of standing in respect of judicial review appeals under the Enterprise Act.[16]

Acts subject to judicial review.   In addition to the ability to challenge the   **6–008**
legality of enactments, CPR Rule 54.1 defines the scope of judicial review by reference to challenges to decisions, acts and failures to act "in relation to the exercise of *a public function*" (emphasis added). As in the case of standing, there is a degree of uncertainty and considerable case law in relation to the issue of which acts may the subject of judicial review. However, by way of a summary, De Smith states:

"A body is performing a 'public function' when it seeks to achieve some collective benefit for the public or a section of the public and is accepted by the public or that section of the public as having authority to do so. Bodies therefore exercise public functions when they intervene or participate in social or economic affairs in the public interest...

Public functions need not be the exclusive domain of the state. Charities, self-regulatory organisations and other nominally private institutions (such as universities, the Stock Exchange, Lloyd's of London, churches) may in relation also provide some types of public function. As Sir John Donaldson M.R. urged, it is important for the courts to 'recognise the realities of executive power' and not allow 'their vision to be clouded by the subtlety and sometimes complexity of the way in which it can be

---

[14] See, for example, *R. v Monopolies Commission Ex p. Argyll Plc* [1986] 1 W.L.R. 763 at 773, CA (Civ Div).
[15] Fordham, para.38.2.
[16] See paras 6–041 and 6–057, below.

exerted'. Non-governmental bodies such as these are just as capable of abusing their powers as is government."[17]

In some cases, the scope of judicial review has been defined as much by what is excluded than as by what is included. In particular, a person may not seek judicial review of a decision when he has consensually submitted to be bound by the decision maker.[18] The OFT, Competition Commission and sectoral regulators will almost certainly be subject to judicial review when exercising their statutory competition and regulatory functions, save where judicial review is excluded by the availability of alternative remedies, as further considered below.

6–009   **Bodies subject to judicial review.**   As the primary test determining the scope of judicial review relates to the function of the challenged act, the nature of the challenged body is not determinative. Consequently, a body may be subject to judicial review in respect of some of its acts, but not others, and the boundary between the two will not always be clear. For example, where a public body enters into a contract with a third party, a decision by that body in relation to the rights and duties under the contract is likely to be determined by the law of contract. On the other hand, a decision by a public body to enter, or not to enter, into a contract might be subject to judicial review, and the issue may depend on whether it was purely commercial or more political considerations that governed the decision.[19] Similarly, private bodies such as the privatised utilities may not be subject to public law in relation to the vast majority of their activities, but may be subject to judicial review in relation to acts and decisions that are taken pursuant to a statutory power or subject to a statutory duty. A relevant consideration in determining whether an act is subject to judicial review is whether some other area of law more appropriately governs the dispute between the parties. Thus, when considering whether a decision of the Jockey Club was subject to review, the Court of Appeal concluded that judicial review would not be available where the source of the body's power was contractual, and the claimant had private rights that could be used to protect his position in a private claim.[20] De Smith identifies other relevant considerations as follows[21]: (i) the "but for" test—whether, but for the existence of a non-statutory body, the government would itself have intervened to regulate the activity in question; (ii) whether the government has acquiesced or encouraged the activities of the body under challenge by providing "underpinning" for its work, has woven the body into the fabric of public regulation or that the body was established "under the authority of

---

[17] De Smith, para.3–024.
[18] See, for example, *R. v Take-over Panel Ex p. Datafin Plc* [1987] Q.B. 815 at 838, CA (Civ Div).
[19] De Smith, para.3–042.
[20] *R. v Jockey Club Ex p. Aga Khan* [1993] 1 W.L.R. 909, CA (Civ Div).
[21] para.3–027.

government"; (iii) whether the body was exercising extensive or monopolistic powers, for instance by effectively regulating entry to a trade, profession or sport; and (iv) whether the aggrieved person has consensually submitted to be bound by the decision maker.

The relationship between claims for judicial review under Part 54 and the statutory review procedures of sections 120 and 179 of the Enterprise Act. The right to bring a claim for judicial review against a decision or act of a public body is a right that has existed in the common law for hundreds of years. The introduction of the statutory review procedures in ss.120 and 179 of the Enterprise Act does not undermine that right. While it is true that a court is likely to refuse permission to bring a claim for judicial review under Part 54 in respect of a decision falling within the scope of s.120 or 179, that result is a function of the doctrine of alternative remedies, long accepted by the courts, and recently affirmed by the Court of Appeal in *Sivasubramaniam v Wandsworth County Court*.[22] Where, however, a decision or act of a public body falls outside the scope of ss.120 and 179 (and other statutory appeal and review procedures), claims for judicial review will continue to be available. Consequently, a large number of decisions and acts of public bodies in the competition and regulatory field will continue to be subject to the possibility of being judicially reviewed under Part 54 in the usual way.

6–010

3. THE GROUNDS OF JUDICIAL REVIEW

(a) Introduction

Classification of grounds. The grounds of judicial review are the basis on which a claim for judicial review may be brought. The references in ss.120 and 179 of the Enterprise Act to the "principles as would be applied by a court on an application for judicial review" are primarily references to the grounds of review. In a frequently cited passage, Lord Diplock stated that the grounds upon which administrative action is subject to control by judicial review could conveniently be classified under three heads, namely "illegality", "irrationality" and "procedural impropriety",[23] although he noted that further development could lead the addition of further grounds, such as proportionality. Lord Donaldson M.R. subsequently commented that Lord Diplock was "providing three chapter headings for review of the grounds upon which, in the reported cases, judicial review has been granted", and was not suggesting that there were only three grounds of review.[24]

6–011

---

[22] [2003] 1 W.L.R. 475.
[23] *Council of Civil Service Unions v Minister for the Civil Service*, n.8, above, at 410.
[24] *R. v Secretary of State for the Home Department Ex p. Brind* [1991] A.C. 696 at 722.

The different grounds are not entirely separate "watertight compartments", but rather "have blurred edges and tend to overlap".[25] It is therefore not generally possible mechanistically to assign any particular administrative error exclusively to a particular ground, as a single decision can often appropriately be analysed in the light of more than one ground of review.

6–012 **"Soft" and "hard" review, and the flexible nature of review principles.** The process of judicial review is one in which a court reviews the decision of an original decision maker. Fordham draws a useful distinction between "soft" and "hard" review. Soft review may be regarded as the "normal" type of review, in which the court leaves the original decision-maker with a "latitude", or area to exercise its discretion and judgment. When applying soft review, it is often said that the court is concerned with the process followed by the decision maker, rather than with the merits of the decision, and that the court should not substitute its decision for that of the original decision maker, which would have the effect of transforming the review into an appeal. However, the application of the grounds of review will vary according to the subject matter of the case and the specific administrative function under review.[26] Consequently, the principles of review may be applied with greater or lesser intensity, as the situation demands. Soft review is therefore itself capable of varying from something akin to a "quick look" at a decision to a detailed consideration of the procedures, approach and reasoning adopted by a decision maker. In contrast, a handful of grounds involve "hard" review, involving "hard-edged" questions in respect of which the court is entitled simply to substitute its judgment for that of the original decision maker. In these areas, the review is effectively indistinguishable from a full appeal. Hard review arises, in particular, in respect of review for error of law, error of precedent fact, and for breach of procedural fairness, all of which are considered further below.

(b) Procedural fairness

6–013 **Introduction.** The essence of the right to procedural fairness is to have a decision-maker follow a fair procedure. In many instances, a statutory procedure will be laid down, and a failure to comply with the statutory procedure will constitute a ground of review. In some cases, and in particular where the statutory procedure is comprehensive, it may be possible to argue successfully that Parliament intended the statutory scheme to be exhaustive, and that the court should not introduce additional requirements. In most cases, however, the court will determine what it regards as the basic requirements of fairness in any particular context, and will readily imply

---

[25] *Boddington v British Transport Police* [1999] 2 A.C. 143 at 152E–F *per* Lord Irvine L.C.; 170E *per* Lord Steyn.
[26] *R. v Secretary of State for Health Ex p. London Borough of Hackney*, unreported, April 25, 1994.

whatever additional procedural safeguards above those of the statutory scheme that it considers necessary to satisfy them (thereby remedying the "legislative omission").[27] Procedural fairness therefore constitutes hard review to the extent that the basic requirements of fairness are regarded as objective requirements, suitable for the primary judgment of the court, which set minimum standards that must be met by public decision makers.[28] However, the principles of procedural fairness are flexible, and the objective requirements demanded by them will vary from context to context. As stated by Lord Bridge: "what the requirements of fairness demand when any body, domestic, administrative or judicial, has to make a decision which will affect the rights of individuals depends on the character of the decision-making body, the kind of decision it has to make and the statutory or other framework in which it operates".[29] The principles of procedural fairness have traditionally been said to have two pillars, namely the rule against bias and the right to a fair hearing.

The rule against bias.   Procedural fairness requires that decision makers   **6–014**
should not be biased or prejudiced in any way that precludes fair and genuine consideration being given to the arguments advanced by the parties. Actual bias will be shown, for example, if the decision maker has a direct personal interest in the outcome of a decision. However, an application for judicial review will also succeed where the claimant can show a "real danger" of bias. The "real danger" test was originally laid down by the House of Lords in *R. v Gough*.[30] However, the initial test has subsequently been glossed by the Court of Appeal in *Re Medicaments and Related Classes of Goods (No.2)*[31] in order to bring it into line with Strasbourg jurisprudence in relation to Art.6 ECHR. The Court of Appeal set out the following approach to be followed by a court when considering a claim based on a "real danger" of bias.

"The Court must first ascertain all the circumstances which have a bearing on the suggestion that the Judge was biased. It must then ask whether those circumstances would lead a fair-minded and informed observer to conclude that there was a real possibility, or a real danger, the two being the same, that the tribunal was biased. The material circumstances will include any explanation given by the Judge under review as to his knowledge or appreciation of those circumstances. Where that explanation is accepted by the [claimant] for review it can be treated as accurate. Where it is not accepted, it becomes one further matter to be considered from the viewpoint of the fair-minded observer. The Court does not have to rule whether the explanation should be accepted or

---

[27] See, for example, *Wiseman v Borneman* [1971] A.C. 297 at 317G *per* Lord Wilberforce.
[28] Fordham, para.16.5.
[29] *Lloyd v McMahon* [1987] A.C. 625 at 702H.
[30] [1993] A.C. 646.
[31] [2001] 1 W.L.R. 700.

rejected. Rather it has to decide whether or not the fair-minded observer would consider that there was a real danger of bias notwithstanding the explanation advanced."[32]

That formulation by the Court of Appeal was subsequently considered by the House of Lords in *Porter v Magill*.[33] Lord Hope, whose judgment attracted the support of a majority of their Lordships, stated his approval for the Court of Appeal's formulation, subject to the following caveat:

"I would however delete from it the reference to 'a real danger'. Those words no longer serve a useful purpose here, and they are not used in the jurisprudence of the Strasbourg court. The question is whether the fair-minded and informed observer, having considered the facts, would conclude that there was a real possibility that the tribunal was biased".

6–015   **A fair hearing.**   A claimant's right to a fair hearing is a right to be informed of the case against him and the right to be given a reasonable opportunity of putting forward his own case. In terms of the right to be informed of the case against, it is often said that the right is merely to be informed of "the gist" of the case which has to be answered,[34] although "what is sufficient to constitute the gist for one purpose may not be sufficient for another".[35] In *Interbrew*,[36] an application for judicial review against the Competition Commission was allowed on the basis of a failure adequately to inform the claimant of the case against it. Under the regime in place prior to the Enterprise Act, the Competition Commission had reported to the Secretary of State that Interbrew's merger with Bass was liable to operate against the public interest, and had recommended as a remedy that Interbrew should be ordered to divest itself of the entire UK beer business of Bass Brewers. Although Interbrew had been given considerable opportunities to make representations to the Competition Commission, the court allowed its application for judicial review because it had not been informed of, and had therefore not had an opportunity to respond to, an important aspect of the thinking of the Competition Commission that ultimately proved crucial in its assessment of the appropriate remedy. What will be required in order to allow a person affected by a decision to put forward his or her own case is also capable of varying significantly from case to case. The following requirements have in different contexts been deemed to be appropriate, but will not always be required:

---

[32] paras 85–86.
[33] [2002] 2 A.C. 357, at para.103.
[34] *R. v Secretary of State for the Home Department Ex p. Doody* [1994] 1 A.C. 531 at 560F–G.
[35] *R. v Secretary of State for the Home Department Ex p. Harry* [1998] 1 W.L.R. 1737 at 1748B–D *per* Lightman J.
[36] *R. (On the application of Interbrew SA) v Competition Commission* [2001] EWHC Admin 367; [2001] U.K.C.L.R. 954.

(1) time for preparation;

(2) an oral hearing;

(3) the right to call witnesses;

(4) the right to legal representation or to be otherwise assisted with the preparation of a case; and

(5) the right to cross-examine witnesses.

Procedural protection of legitimate expectations.[37]   The need for procedures   **6–016**
to protect legitimate expectations is an aspect of the right to a fair hearing, and can arise in two distinct ways. The first is where a decision-maker leads a person legitimately to expect that a hearing or other procedural safeguards will be afforded before the decision is made. The expectation may be generated from either an express promise or a representation implied from the established practice or settled conduct of the decision maker.[38] In such cases the court may decide that the decision-maker cannot make the decision without affording the procedural safeguards that have legitimately come to be expected.[39] The other way in which legitimate expectations can arise is where a decision maker has previously led a person legitimately to expect a certain substantive outcome or the receipt of a substantive benefit. Here, there are various ways in which the court can seek to protect the expectation, one of which is by requiring the decision-maker, before it takes a decision defeating the expectation, to grant the interested person a hearing.[40] In such cases, the effect of the legitimate expectation may be to require the decision maker to afford a greater degree of procedural rights than would otherwise have been required.

(c) Reasons

A duty to provide reasons.   Often, statutory provisions will require certain   **6–017**
decision-makers to provide reasoned decisions. Traditionally, though, there has been no common law duty to provide reasons. However, the judgment of the House of Lords in *R. v Secretary of State for the Home Department Ex p. Doody*,[41] discussing the exceptions to the general rule where reasons are required, may subsequently come to be seen as a turning point. It has recently been noted that "[t]he trend of the law has been towards an increased recognition of the duty upon decision-makers of many kinds to give reasons", and that "[t]here is certainly a strong argument for the view

---

[37] The possibility of protecting legitimate expectations substantively is considered below, in relation to *Wednesbury* unreasonableness.
[38] De Smith, para.8–053.
[39] See, for example, *Attorney-General of Hong Kong v Ng Yen Shiu* [1983] 2 A.C. 629.
[40] *R. v Secretary of State for the Home Department Ex p. Khan* [1984] 1 W.L.R. 1337.
[41] [1994] 1 A.C. 531.

that what were once seen as exceptions to a rule may now be becoming examples of the norm, and the cases where reasons are not required may be taking on the appearance of exceptions".[42] As elsewhere in the law of procedural fairness, where reasons are required, the level of detail that must be provided will vary with the circumstances.[43] However, the general position is that reasons need not be over-elaborate,[44] so long as they are provided in sufficient detail as to enable the reader to know what conclusion has been reached on the principal important controversial issues.[45]

(d) Error of law

6–018   **Introduction.**   Judicial review will generally lie where the decision maker has made a material error of law, *i.e.* a relevant error of law made in the actual making of the decision which affected the decision itself.[46] An important exception is where the decision maker would inevitably have reached the same decision even if it had correctly directed itself in law.[47] Craig notes that all "grants of authority may be expressed in the following manner: if X exists the tribunal may or shall do Y".[48] The meaning of X (and Y) is generally considered to be a question of law, while the question of whether the requirements of X are satisfied on the facts is generally considered to be a question of fact, or of mixed law and fact.[49]

6–019   **Hard-edged questions of law.**   A question of law is a hard-edged question in the sense that it is for the courts to determine what the law is, and a court will simply substitute its judgment if it disagrees with the decision-maker's assessment of the law.[50] A court will determine the meaning of the law in accordance with the principles of statutory construction.[51] A court may attempt to explain that meaning by providing alternative or additional wording to that used in the statute, or by setting out the considerations which it considers should be taken into account in determining whether the

---

[42]   *Stefan v General Medical Council* [1999] 1 W.L.R. 1293 at 1300G and 1301A–B.
[43]   *R. v Immigration Appeal Tribunal Ex p. Jebunisha Kharvaleb Patel* [1996] Imm. A.R. 161 at 167.
[44]   *Bolton MBC v Secretary of State for the Environment* [1995] 3 P.L.R. 37 at 43C.
[45]   Lord Brown provided a broad summary of the authorities governing the proper approach to a reasons challenge in the planning context in *South Bucks DC v Porter (No.2)* [2004] 1 W.L.R. 1953 at para.36. Although expressly stated to be concerned with challenges in the planning context, the general thrust of his summary is likely to be equally applicable outside of that context.
[46]   *R. v Hull University Visitor Ex p. Page* [1993] A.C. 682 at 702C–D.
[47]   *Kalra v Secretary of State for the Environment* [1996] 1 P.L.R. 37 at 45A.
[48]   Craig, at p.475.
[49]   It should be noted that this area of law is theoretically complex. As explained in Chapter 15 of Craig, the case law has been influenced by theories of jurisdiction which have now been abandoned, and disagreements exist as to precisely when an issue is an issue of law and when it is an issue of fact.
[50]   *R. v Central Arbitration Committee Ex p. BTP Tioxide Ltd* [1981] I.C.R. 843 at 856B–D.
[51]   As to which, see Bennion, *Statutory Interpretation* (4th ed.).

statutory test is met, or by providing examples of how it considers that the statutory provision would apply in relation to certain hypothetical sets of facts. Alternatively, where the wording of the statutory provision is made up of ordinary words of the English language, the court may determine that the correct interpretation of the provision is in accordance with the plain meaning of those ordinary English words, and will not attempt further to elaborate. However, even in that latter instance, it is important to note that the fact that the correct interpretation of the provision is in accordance with the plain meaning of the ordinary English words used, as opposed to in accordance with some more sophisticated interpretation,[52] is a question of law for the court,[53] even if the application of that ordinary meaning to the facts of the case is a question of fact.

Meaning of a statute.   Normally, it appears that courts take the view that a   **6–020** statutory provision has a single correct meaning. A decision maker that bases its decision on an interpretation of a provision that differs from that determined by a court will generally be overturned, however reasonable its interpretation may have been. As has been stated: "In this field there are no marks for trying hard but getting the answer wrong".[54] On the other hand, the courts have also warned of the dangers of taking an inherently imprecise word and, by redefining it, thrusting on it a spurious degree of precision.[55] Consequently, when the provision in question has contained an inherently imprecise word or phrase, courts have in a handful of cases adopted a different approach. In *R. v Monopolies and Mergers Commission Ex p. South Yorkshire Transport*,[56] the House of Lords considered the approach of the Monopolies and Mergers Commission ("the MMC") to the meaning of the phrase "a substantial part of the United Kingdom" in s.64(3) of the Fair Trading Act 1973. In assessing whether the MMC's interpretation of the phrase disclosed an error of law, Lord Mustill, delivering an unanimous judgment, restricted himself to considering whether the interpretation adopted by the MMC was "in broadly in the right part of the spectrum of possible meanings".[57] A similar approach was adopted by Moses J. in the High Court when considering the correct meaning of the phrase "all reasonable demands" in s.3 of the Telecommunications Act 1984:

"113. The question whether a demand is reasonable depends, as it seems to me, on many factors. I reject the notion that it has one particular

---

[52] Necessary to take into account, for example, the broader statutory context.
[53] *Moyna v Secretary of State for Work and Pensions* [2003] 1 W.L.R. 1929 at 1935 *per* Lord Hoffman, explaining the often quoted but frequently misunderstood remarks of Lord Reid in *Cozens v Brutus* [1973] A.C. 854 at 861.
[54] *R. v Central Arbitration Committee Ex p. BTP Tioxide Ltd* [1981] I.C.R. 843 at 856B–D *per* Forbes J.
[55] *R. v Monopolies Commission Ex p. South Yorkshire Transport Ltd* [1993] 1 W.L.R. 23 at 29, HL.
[56] [1993] 1 W.L.R. 23.
[57] *R. v Monopolies Commission Ex p. South Yorkshire Transport Ltd*, n.55, above, at 30F.

meaning, namely to maximise economic efficiency. In particular I reject the notion that the question as to whether a demand is reasonable, can be answered by the application of a definition applicable in every case. In short, the question is not 'hard-edged'. It seems to me that there is a 'range of possible criteria' about which opinions might legitimately differ in deciding whether a demand is reasonable. The statutory criterion is not clear-cut and is sufficiently broad to allow of different conclusions by different decision-makers, each acting rationally.

114. This approach to the meaning of 'all reasonable demands' will strike a chord in all those familiar with the speech of Lord Mustill in *R. v Monopolies & Mergers Commission Ex p. South Yorkshire Transport and another* [1993] 1 W.L.R. 23 at 32. In the same way as the meaning of 'a substantial part of the United Kingdom' was broad enough to call for the exercise of judgment in that case, so is the meaning to be attached to all 'reasonable demands' ".[58]

(e) Questions of fact, and the dividing line between questions of fact and questions of law

6–021   **An important distinction.**   In contrast to the position in relation to questions of law, and subject to certain limited circumstances discussed below, the principles of judicial review do not allow a court to overturn a decision simply because it disagrees with the decision-maker on a question of fact. Consequently, the distinction between questions of law and questions of fact therefore has significant implications for the jurisdiction of the court.[59]

6–022   **The application of law to fact as a question of fact.**   The establishment of primary facts, such as that X did Y on date Z, are obviously matters of fact. However, the application of law to primary facts is also generally considered to be a question of fact. As Lord Hoffman has stated in the recent case of *Moyna v Secretary of State for Work and Pensions*:

"There is a good deal of high authority for saying that the question of whether the facts as found or admitted fall one side or the other of some conceptual line drawn by the law is a question of fact: see, for example, *Edwards v Bairstow* [1956] A.C. 14 and *O'Kelly v Trusthouse Forte plc* [1984] Q.B. 90. What this means in practice is that an appellate court will

---

[58] *T–Mobile v Competition Commission* [2003] EWHC Admin 1566; [2003] U.K.C.L.R. 819.
[59] The distinction has been the subject of considerable academic discussion, including, in particular, an article by Timothy Endercott entitled "Questions of law" (1998) 114 L.Q.R. 292, with which Lord Woolf M.R. has expressed his approval (see *Medicines Control Agency Ex p. Pharma Nord Ltd* (1998) 10 Admin. L.R. 646 at 659C).

not hear an appeal against such a decision unless it falls outside the bounds of reasonable judgment."[60]

Consequently, where a decision-maker that was properly instructed as to the relevant law could reasonably have come to more than one determination, the court will generally regard the question of whether or not the statutory provision is satisfied to be a question of fact, and will not intervene.[61] Such questions are also referred to as questions of "fact and degree". Where, however, the court considers that the application of the correct legal meaning of a provision could only reasonably produce one result on the facts, the court will regard the question as being one of law, and will be prepared to substitute its judgment for that of the decision-maker.[62] In *Moyna*, Lord Hoffman went on to emphasise that the degree to which the court will be prepared to substitute its own judgment for that of the original decision-maker will vary with the nature of the question.[63] The vaguer the relevant standard and the greater the number of factors which the court has to weigh up in deciding whether or not the standard has been met, the less likely it is that the court will conclude that the decision-maker could only reasonably have reached one result.[64] A review court is also less likely to interfere where the original decision-maker, but not the court, has heard witness evidence relevant to the question of whether the statutory standard has been met. The application of these principles undoubtedly provides the court with a degree of "room for manoeuvre". It is likely that, when deciding whether or not to classify the question as one of fact or law, the court will take into account the same sort of considerations that determine whether it adopts a more or less intensive level of review when reviewing the exercise of discretionary powers, such as the importance of the interests affected by the decision, and the extent to which the assessment requires specialist knowledge possessed by the decision-maker but not the court.

Uncertainty. However, in reality, a decision-maker may not always set out in its reasoning precisely what interpretation of a statutory provision it has adopted. In such cases, if a reviewing court disagrees with the decision reached by a decision-maker, a degree of uncertainty may exist as to whether what the court regards as the "wrong" decision was reached because the decision-maker made an error of law, or simply because, although it adopted the same (correct) legal interpretation as the court, the decision-makers' application of the law to the facts reasonably differed from that of the court. In such cases, the review court will have to form a judgment as to

6–023

---

[60] [2003] 1 W.L.R. 1929 at para.24.
[61] *Medicines Control Agency Ex p. Pharma Nord Ltd* (1998) 10 Admin. L.R. 646 at 659C *per* Lord Woolf M.R.
[62] *ibid.*
[63] *Moyna v Secretary of State for Work and Pensions*, n.53, above, at para.27, HL citing *Re Grayan Ltd*, [1995] Ch. 241 at 254–255.
[64] *Re Grayan Ltd*, n.63, above, at 254H.

which explanation is more likely, and either intervene or exercise self-restraint accordingly.

(f) Precedent fact

6–024 **The nature of a precedent fact.** A precedent fact is a fact the existence of which it is necessary to establish in order for a body to have jurisdiction.[65] A court will not usually substitute its judgment for that of a decision-maker on a question of (non precedent) fact. However, if a body exercises jurisdiction on the basis of a precedent fact which does not actually exist, it exercises jurisdiction beyond its powers: powers which will typically have been conferred and determined by Parliament. That consideration is sometimes said to justify a review court investigating for itself whether the precedent fact exists and, if necessary, substituting its judgment for that of the court. However, if, as suggested by Craig, all grants of authority may be expressed as "if X exists, the tribunal may or shall do Y",[66] the existence of X ought always to constitute a precedent fact, in relation to which the court should substitute judgment not only as to the legal meaning of X, but also as to whether the statutory requirement of X is satisfied on the facts of the case. However, as discussed in the two previous paragraphs, that does not represent the traditional approach of the courts. Rather, although a court will substitute judgment as to the correct legal meaning of "X", it will normally substitute its judgment in relation to the application of that meaning to the facts only where it considers that only one reasonable conclusion may be drawn (and therefore to draw any other conclusion would be perverse).

6–025 **A limited class of cases.** Courts have tended to find the existence of precedent facts only in limited classes of case. In *R. v Secretary of State for the Home Department Ex p. Khawaja*,[67] the House of Lords held that whether a person was an "illegal immigrant" for the purposes of the Immigration Act 1971 was a precedent fact. However, the effect of a person being an illegal immigrant for those purposes was to render that person liable to arrest and expulsion from the country by immigration officials, and the House of Lords judgments placed emphasis on the fact that the classification of a person as an illegal immigrant had potentially serious consequences affecting the liberty of the subject.[68] Subsequently, the Court of Appeal, in declining to apply the *Khawaja* judgment, stated that it was "not of universal application

---

[65] It is not sufficient that the fact in question is an important consideration for the decision-maker in exercising its discretion: in order to be a precedent fact the decision-maker must be entirely unable to exercise its discretion absent the existence of that fact (see *R. v Home Secretary Ex p. Bugdaycay* [1987] A.C. 514 at 522.

[66] Craig, p.475.

[67] [1984] A.C. 74.

[68] See, for example, at 125E, *per* Lord Bridge.

and significantly has only so far been applied in immigration matters where the liberty of the person was involved".[69] Similarly, the Divisional Court stated that it is very seldom that a statutory requirement will fall into the precedent fact category, and that it is difficult to think where it might apply outside the sphere of individual liberty and where the court is determining whether proper procedures have been followed.[70] However, since those two statements, the *Khawaja* approach has been applied by courts in other contexts. One example is its application by Sullivan J. in *R. v Secretary of State for the Environment Ex p. Alliance against the Birmingham Northern Relief Road*,[71] in relation to whether information related to the environment for the purposes of the Environmental Information Regulations 1992, implementing Council Directive 90/313 on the freedom of access to information on the environment. Another is the judgment of the Court of Appeal in *R. v Customs and Excise Commissioners Ex p. Lunn Poly Plc*,[72] holding that whether a measure constituted state aid for the purposes of Art.93(3) EC was a precedent fact. It is possible that the decisions in those cases were influenced by the fact that the relevant provision was either a provision of EC law or a domestic provision implementing EC law. Nonetheless, in the light of these developments, it is not possible to state that the doctrine of precedent fact is limited to statutory provisions the satisfaction of which is capable of having an impact on individual liberty, and the precise sphere of application of the doctrine remains to be determined.

(g) Mistake of fact giving rise to unfairness

E v Secretary of State for the Home Department: recognition of a new ground 6–026
of review. Aside from the category of precedent facts, courts have not traditionally granted applications for judicial review simply because a decision disclosed a factual mistake. However, a growing line of academic

---

[69] *Re S (Minors)* [1995] E.L.R. 98 at 105B, CA.
[70] *R. v Secretary of State for Employment Ex p. National Association of Colliery Overmen, Deputies and Shotfirers* [1994] C.O.D. 218 at 220. The Divisional Court also set out three considerations to which the court should inevitably have regard in determining the scheme of the legislation and the level of review appropriate, namely:

  (1) the nature and complexity of any facts to be found and judgment to be formed before the power is exercisable;

  (2) whether any consultation procedure is provided for as a pre-condition to the exercise of the power; and

  (3) the consequences of exercising the impugned power.

[71] [1999] Env. L.R. 447 at 466–467.
[72] [1999] S.T.C. 350.

writing[73] and case law[74] had begun to suggest that review might be granted in respect of a misunderstanding or ignorance of an established and relevant fact. This line of academic writing and case law was reviewed in *E v Secretary of State for the Home Department*,[75] in which the Court of Appeal recognised the existence of a distinct ground of review of a mistake of fact giving rise to unfairness. The criteria which must be ordinarily be shown for the ground to be made out were set out by the Court of Appeal, which stated its conclusions as follows:

> "In our view, the time has now come to accept that a mistake of fact giving rise to unfairness is a separate head of challenge in an appeal on a point of law, at least in those statutory contexts where the parties share an interest in co-operating to achieve the correct result ... Without seeking to lay down a precise code, the ordinary requirements for a finding of unfairness are apparent from the above analysis of *CICB*. First, there must have been a mistake as to an existing fact, including a mistake as to the availability of evidence on a particular matter. Secondly, the fact or evidence must have been 'established', in the sense that it was uncontentious and objectively verifiable. Thirdly, the appellant (or his advisers) must not have been responsible for the mistake. Fourthly, the mistake must have played a material (not necessarily decisive) part in the Tribunal's reasoning."[76]

(h) The failure to exercise and the fettering of discretion

6–027   **The requirement to exercise discretion.** If discretion has been vested in a certain person it must be exercised by that person.[77] A body may unlawfully fail to exercise or fetter its discretion in various ways. First, although bodies are entitled to developed policies or rules governing the exercise of their discretion,[78] they must not develop rigid policies which prevent them from considering the individual merits of each case.[79] Secondly, a body may not unlawfully delegate the exercise of discretion vested in it to another body.[80]

---

[73] In particular; Timothy Jones, "Mistake of fact in Administrative Law" [1990] P.L. 507; and Michael Kant QC, "Widening the scope of review for error of fact" [1999] J.R 239.

[74] In particular two judgments of Lord Slynn, first in *R. v Criminal Injuries Compensation Board Ex p. A* [1999] 2 A.C. 330, and secondly in *R. v Secretary of State for the Environment Ex p. Alconbury* [2003] 2 A.C. 295.

[75] [2004] EWCA Civ 49.

[76] At para.66.

[77] Craig, p.522.

[78] Indeed, the development of such policies or rules will often have a positive impact insofar as they contribute to consistent and efficient decision-making and assist those potentially affected by the exercise of discretion to predict how it will be exercised.

[79] Craig, pp.530–540; Fordham, para.50.4; Wade, pp.328–333.

[80] De Smith, pp.357–374; Craig, pp.523–530; Wade, pp.315–327; Fordham, para.50.3.

Thirdly, a body must not unlawfully fetter its discretion through the entering into of legally binding contracts.[81]

(i) Improper purpose

The requirement to follow the legislative purpose. Statutory powers are   6–028
conferred for certain limited purposes, and the body on which the power is
conferred must exercise it to promote the policy and objects of the conferring act.[82] The courts will determine the purpose of a particular statute as
a matter of construction. However, in some cases, the purposes of a statute
will be far from transparent and/or be set out in very general terms. In such
cases, determination of the precise purposes of a statute may inevitably
require the application of normative judgments relating to issues of policy.[83]
Where that is the case, the court may in some circumstances be prepared to
defer to the judgment of an expert decision-making body. One such occasion
was where the High Court reviewed various decisions of the Rail Regulator,
who was required by statute to exercise his powers in a way that furthered
the national and public interest in having an efficient and effective railway
system. There, the High Court justified its conclusion that it ought to
intervene only in limited circumstances on the basis that the Rail Regulator
was better placed than the court to make an overall assessment of what was
in the interest of the rail network.[84] Difficult issues arise where a decision
was influenced by several purposes, some of which were proper and some of
which were improper, and a variety of different tests have been developed by
the courts in an attempt to deal with them.[85]

(j) Relevancy of considerations

Relevant and irrelevant considerations. If, when exercising a discretionary   6–029
power, a body has taken into account irrelevant considerations, or dis-
regarded considerations required to be taken into account, a court may
grant an application for judicial review on the basis that the body has not
validly exercised the power. Occasionally, the empowering statute will
expressly set out considerations that must and/or must not be taken into
account by the decision-maker. However, in the absence of such considerations, or in addition to them, the court may conclude that certain
other considerations are relevant or irrelevant on the basis of the purpose

---

[81] Wade, pp.333–338; Craig, pp.540–549.
[82] See, for example, *Smith v East Elloe Rural DC* [1956] A.C. 736 at 767 *per* Lord Radcliffe, and
    R. v Secretary of State for the Home Department Ex p. Brind, n.24, above, at 756G *per* Lord
    Ackner.
[83] As was the case in *Bromley LBC v GLC* [1983] Q.B. 484, discussed by Craig at p.555–559.
[84] *R. (on the application of London and Continental Stations and Property Limited) v The Rail
    Regulator* [2003] EWHC Admin 2607 at paras 27–29.
[85] Craig, p.559; Fordham, para.52.2.6.

and scheme of the statute. This ground of review is similar to and overlaps with review on the basis of improper purposes.

6-030 **Three categories of consideration.** A court may place a consideration into one of three distinct categories,[86] namely:

    (i)   considerations that must be taken into account;

    (ii) considerations that must not be taken into account; and

    (iii) considerations that may or may not be taken into account.

The issue of into which category considerations fall is a hard-edged question for the court.[87] Where a decision-maker has failed to take into account a consideration in category (i), a court's decision as to whether to interfere will normally depend on its assessment of the significance of the overlooked factor, *i.e.* it will not automatically grant an application for review simply on the basis of a failure to take into account a trivial consideration.[88] Where a decision-maker has taken into account a consideration in category (ii), the court will normally grant an application for review where that consideration appears to have had an influence on the decision, and it is not necessary for a claimant to show that the consideration was the sole or dominant factor.[89]

6-031 **Avoiding substitution of judgment.** In relation to category (iii), considerations that may or may not be taken into account, the court will not interfere simply because a decision-maker has not taken into account a consideration which, on the basis of the court's construction of the statute, it had a discretion as to whether or not to take into account, even if it is one which many people, including the court itself, would have taken into account for the purposes of reaching the decision.[90] Were the court to interfere in such circumstances, it would be going a long way towards substituting its judgment for that of the original decision-maker. For the same reason, a court will not interfere simply because it disagrees with the weight that a decision-maker has accorded to a particular consideration, unless it considers that the weight given to a particular consideration was perverse.[91] In these areas, the court's review is "soft", and it will normally interfere only where the requirements of *Wednesbury* unreasonableness (or proportionality, if it is applicable) are satisfied.

---

[86] *Re Findlay* [1985] A.C. 318 at 33H–334C *per* Lord Scarman.
[87] *Tesco Stores Ltd v Secretary of State for the Environment* [1995] 1 W.L.R. 759.
[88] De Smith, para.6–087.
[89] De Smith, para.6–086.
[90] And vice versa.
[91] *Tesco Stores Ltd v Secretary of State for the Environment* [1995] 1 W.L.R. 759 at 764G–H; *R. v Director General of Telecommunications Ex p. Cellcom Ltd* [1999] C.O.D. 105 at para.28.

(k) Wednesbury unreasonableness

The basic test. A court will grant an application for judicial review of the 6–032
exercise of a discretion where, even though the decision-maker has not
pursued improper purposes or taken into account irrelevant considerations,
it has reached a decision that it could not reasonably have reached. The
ground was originally set out by Lord Greene M.R. in the seminal case of
Associated Picture Houses Ltd v Wednesbury Corporation,[92] and is known as
"*Wednesbury* unreasonableness". In part because of the similarity between
Wednesbury unreasonableness and the more sophisticated doctrine of proportionality, considered further below, some have suggested that there is no
longer any need to retain *Wednesbury*. However, although it stated that it
had difficulty in seeing what justification there was for retaining the *Wednesbury* test, the Court of Appeal in *R. (ABCIFER) v Secretary of State for
Defence*[93] declined to "perform its burial rights", on the basis that that was a
task that could be carried out only by the House of Lords. For the time
being, therefore, the test continues. A vast array of phrases have been used
by the courts in order to describe what will make conduct or a decision
Wednesbury unreasonable. The ground has been said to apply in respect of
"conduct which no sensible authority acting with due appreciation of its
responsibilities would have decided to adopt",[94] a "decision which is so
outrageous in its defiance of logic or of accepted moral standards that no
sensible person who had applied his mind to the question could have arrived
at it",[95] and decisions that are "bizarre"[96] or containing reasons that are
without foundation or do not "stack up".[97]

A flexible standard. However, while it is correct that the application of 6–033
Wednesbury unreasonableness constitutes soft review, and the courts will
always seek to avoid stepping over the line into the substitution of judgment,
the intensity of review varies with the context. The *Wednesbury* principle has
been described as a sliding scale of review, the intensity of which will be
dependent on the nature and gravity of what is at stake.[98] The flexible nature
of *Wednesbury* review explains why in some circumstances courts have
sought to explain the standard in slightly colourful terms suggesting that the
ground will virtually never be satisfied, whereas in other cases the way in
which the ground has been applied clearly indicates that the courts do not
regard its application to be so limited.

---

[92] [1948] 1 K.B. 223.
[93] [2003] Q.B. 1397 at para.34.
[94] *R. v Chief Constable of Sussex Ex p. International Traders Ferry Ltd* [1999] 2 A.C. 418 at
452B–F.
[95] *Council of Civil Service Unions v Minister for the Civil Service*, n.8, above, at 410.
[96] *R. v Parliamentary Commissioner for Administration Ex p. Balchin* [1998] 1 P.L.R. 1 at 13E–
F.
[97] *R. (on the application of Interbrew SA) v Competition Commission* [2001] EWHC Admin 367.
[98] *R. v Department for Education and Employment Ex p. Begbie* [2000] 1 W.L.R. 1115 at 1130B.

6–034 **Considerations affecting the intensity of review.** A variety of considerations affect the intensity with which the courts will apply the *Wednesbury* doctrine. The following considerations have all pushed the court towards adopting a less intensive level of review: (i) where the decision determined controversial issues of economic or social policy[99]; (ii) where the decision had been approved by Parliamentary resolution[1]; (iii) where the decision was appropriate for the judgment of those who are politically accountable[2]; and (iv) where the decision[3] related to a specialist area in respect of which the original decision-maker but not the court was expert.[4] Conversely, the more important the interest affected by a decision, the greater the intensity of review that is likely to be adopted. In particular, the *Wednesbury* principle is been applied with greater intensity in cases in which human rights are affected. As was stated in *R. v Ministry of Defence Ex p. Smith*:[5] "[t]he more substantial the interference with human rights, the more the court will require by way of justification before it is satisfied that the decision is reasonable". The intensity of review will also be greater where the reviewed decision has the effect of defeating a substantive legitimate expectation. Indeed, in *R. v North and East Devon Health Authority Ex p. Coughlan*,[6] the Court of Appeal stated that substantive legitimate expectation cases could be placed into three categories, with review on *Wednesbury* grounds being appropriate only in respect of one category, and an intensity of review greater than the *Wednesbury* level being appropriate in respect of the other two. Considerations that are specifically relevant to the intensity of review in a competition law context are discussed further below.

(1) Proportionality

6–035 **When proportionality is available.** Proportionality has not traditionally been a common law ground of judicial review.[7] However, domestic courts are required to apply the principle of proportionality in two important categories of case outside of the common law. The first is where principles of EU law are involved, and the EU principles themselves require the application of the principle of proportionality.[8] Secondly, courts are now required to apply the principle of proportionality in cases falling within the scope of the Human Rights Act 1998, discussed further below. Additionally,

---

[99] *R. v Secretary of State for the Environment Ex p. Hammersmith and Fulham LBC* [1991] 1 A.C. 521.

[1] *R. v Secretary of State for the Environment Ex p. Nottinghamshire CC* [1986] A.C. 240.

[2] *Secretary of State for Education and Science v Tameside MBC* [1977] A.C. 1014.

[3] *R. v Director General of Telecommunications Ex p. Cellcom Ltd* [1999] C.O.D. 105 at para.26.

[4] See also the discussion of Laws L.J. in *International Transport Roth GmbH v Home Secretary* [2002] 3 W.L.R. 344 at paras 80–87, which although directed primarily at the intensity of review in cases involving Convention rights, are also of interest more generally.

[5] *R. v Ministry of Defence Ex p. Smith*, n.7, above, at 554G.

[6] [2001] Q.B. 213.

[7] *R. v Secretary of State for the Home Department*, n.24, above.

[8] As in *R. v Chief Constable of Sussex Ex p. International Traders Ferry Ltd* [1999] 2 A.C. 428.

it has been suggested that, even within the common law, the courts effectively apply a proportionality doctrine when reviewing acts or decisions restricting constitutional common law rights, imposing penalties or disappointing substantive legitimate expectations.[9] Several commentators have therefore proposed that proportionality be openly accepted as a common law ground of review, a view which appeared to be endorsed by comments of Lord Slynn in his speech in *Alconbury*.[10] However, in *R. (ABCIFER) v Secretary of State for Defence*,[11] the Court of Appeal stated that, notwithstanding such comments, the effect of authority, and in particular the judgment of the House of Lords in *R. v Secretary of State for the Home Department Ex p. Brind*,[12] was that the door was currently closed to the application of proportionality in domestic law where no human rights or Community Law issues were raised. The Court of Appeal's view was that the adoption of proportionality as a principle of domestic law, and its possible replacement of the *Wednesbury* test, was something that could be done only by the House of Lords.

The nature of the proportionality test. The difference between the principles of proportionality and *Wednesbury* unreasonableness was discussed by Lord Steyn in *R. (Daly) v Home Secretary*.[13] Lord Steyn noted that, although the intensity of review was greater under proportionality than that under *Wednesbury* review, there was a considerable degree of overlap between proportionality and common law principles. That overlap is evident from the fact that proportionality does not entail substitution of judgment, but continues to allow the decision-maker a degree of latitude, or discretionary area of judgment, and because, as in the case of *Wednesbury*, it is a flexible principle that is capable of being applied more or less intensively depending on the circumstances. However, what is distinct about proportionality, in addition to the greater intensity of review, is the idea of a principled template of analysis to be carried out by the court. Fordham states that the proportionality template consists of four questions that can be identified in EU and ECHR proportionality cases.[14] The four questions are:

6–036

(1) whether there is a legitimate objective;

(2) whether the measure is suitable for achieving it;

(3) whether it is necessary (the least intrusive means) for achieving it; and

(4) whether the ends justify the means viewed overall.

---

[9] Michael Fordham, "Common Law Proportionality" [2002] J.R. 110.
[10] *R. (on the application of Alconbury Developments Ltd) v Secretary of State for the Environment, Transport and the Regions* [2001] 2 W.L.R. 1389 at para.51.
[11] [2003] Q.B. 1397 at para.35.
[12] [1991] 1 A.C. 696.
[13] [2001] 2 A.C. 532 at 547.
[14] Fordham, para.58.1.4.

Fordham notes that the fourth question is often implicit and left unstated. The first three questions were clearly identified and endorsed by the House of Lords in *Daly*, currently the leading domestic authority on the nature of the proportionality test.

(m) The Human Rights Act 1998

6–037　**Overview.** In addition to the common law grounds of review discussed above, the Human Rights Act 1998 incorporated into domestic law the rights enshrined in the European Convention on Human Rights. The law of human rights, as that of judicial review, is an entire area of law in itself, and a full discussion is outside the scope of this chapter. Further information may be sought in specialist human rights law textbooks, such as *Human Rights Law and Practice* by Lord Lester QC and David Pannick QC[15] Nonetheless, by way of a very brief and selective summary, one of the key provisions in the Act is s.6, which places a duty on public authorities to act in a manner compatible with the Convention rights.[16] The rights that are most likely to be in issue in a competition and regulatory context are those set out in Art.6 (the right to a fair trial), Art.8 (the right to respect for private and family life)[17] and Art.1 of the First Protocol (the right to peaceful enjoyment of possessions). Bodies such as the Office of Fair Trading, the Competition Commission and the sectoral regulators are almost certainly public authorities for the purpose of s.6 when carrying out their competition and regulatory functions. However, a potential claimant may bring a claim under s.6 only if he or she is a victim of the unlawful act. While the subjects of competition and regulatory decisions may generally be able to satisfy this test, the same will not necessarily be true of interested third parties, such as competitors. One obvious incentive for bringing a claim under the Human Rights Act is the possibility of damages if a breach of a Convention right can be shown, although it should be noted that the circumstances in which damages will be awarded are restricted.[18]

4. THE STATUTORY REVIEW PROCEDURES IN SECTIONS 120 AND 179 OF THE ENTERPRISE ACT 2002

6–038　**Sections 120 and 179 of the Enterprise Act.** Section 120 of the Enterprise Act provides for reviews of decisions taken under Part 3 of the Act, relating

---

[15] (2nd ed., Lexis Nexis Butterworths, 2004).
[16] Save in certain specified circumstances.
[17] For the application of which in a competition law context, see Case C–94/00 *Roquette Freres* [2002] E.C.R. I–9011; [2003] 4 C.M.L.R. 1.
[18] *Anufrijeva v London Borough of Southwark* [2004] 2 W.L.R. 603.

to mergers, and s.179 provides for reviews of decisions taken under Part 4 of the Act, relating to market references. Persons aggrieved by such decisions are able to apply to the CAT for a review. The principles to be applied by the CAT in determining a review under the Enterprise Act are set out in ss.120(4) and 179(4), the terms of which are identical and as are as follows:

"In determining such an application the Competition Appeal Tribunal shall apply the same principles as would be applied by a court on an application for judicial review."

Thus, although the judicial review principles were and continue to be developed by the courts in the exercise of their inherent supervisory jurisdiction, they are expressly adopted by the Enterprise Act as the principles to be applied by the CAT in the statutory review procedures created by ss.120 and 179.[19]

IBA Health **and the principles of review.**   That the principles to be applied in   **6–039**
reviews under ss.120 and 179 must be the same as those that are applied in judicial review applications in the High Court was confirmed by the Court of Appeal in *OFT v IBA Health*,[20] an appeal against the first decision of the CAT on a review under s.120. In its judgment, the CAT had stated that, because it was a specialist tribunal, it was "unpersuaded that there is a necessarily a direct 'readover' to s.120 from cases such as *Cellcom, Interbrew, T-Mobile*, and the *Rail Regulator*",[21] in which High Court had indicated that it ought in applications for judicial review to show considerable deference to the decision of a specialist decision-maker. The appellants argued that those comments reflected the fact that the CAT had in fact departed from the ordinary principles of judicial review. The Court of Appeal stated: "if and in so far as CAT did not apply the ordinary principles of judicial review as would be applied by a court whether on the ground that the CAT is a specialist tribunal or otherwise then they failed to observe the mandatory requirements of s.120(4)".[22] The Court of Appeal went on to reject the arguments of the appellants that the CAT's approach constituted a misapplication of those ordinary principles on the facts. The considerations that are capable of affecting the intensity with which the principles of judicial review are applied are considered in the following section.

Schedule 4 and the CAT Rules.   Although the basic provisions relating to   **6–040**
the statutory review procedures are set out in ss.120 and 179, Sch.4 to the Act makes provision for certain aspects of the procedure before the CAT in such reviews, and also provides for the CAT to produce rules making provision in relation for different kinds of proceedings. The most recent

---

[19] See para.284 of the Explanatory Notes to the Enterprise Act.
[20] [2004] EWCA Civ 142; [2004] U.K.C.L.R. 683.
[21] [2003] CAT 27.
[22] para.53.

Tribunal Rules are "The Competition Appeal Tribunal Rules 2003", a copy of which may be found on the CAT's website.[23] Part III of the Rules makes provision for proceedings under the Enterprise Act. Paragraph 25 provides that Parts I, II and V of the Rules, which are intended primarily to apply to appeals under the Competition Act 1998, also apply to proceedings brought under the Enterprise Act. Paragraphs 26 to 29 make certain specific provision relating to Enterprise Act proceedings.[24]

6–041 **Permission and standing.** Sections 120 and 179 both provide that "any person aggrieved" by a specified decision may apply to the CAT for a review.[25] Applicants are not therefore limited to those that have been the direct subject of a decision: for example, a decision by the OFT not to refer a merger to the Competition Commission may be challenged by a third party competitor if it could satisfy the statutory test. Further, permission is not required in order to bring an application under ss.120 and 179. However, as is envisaged by Sch.4 to the Enterprise Act, the CAT Rules provide that the tribunal may, after giving the parties an opportunity to be heard, reject an application in whole or in part at any stage in the proceedings in certain circumstances. The effect of paras 10 and 28(4) of the Rules is that the CAT may reject applications if:

(1) it considers that the notice of application discloses no valid ground of review;

(2) it considers that the applicant does not have (or represent those who have) a sufficient interest in the decision in respect of which the appeal is made;

(3) it considers that the applicant is not a person aggrieved by the decision in respect of which the review is sought;

(4) the applicant has failed to comply with any rule, direction, practice direction or order of the tribunal; or

(5) it is satisfied that the applicant has habitually and persistently and without any reasonable ground: instituted vexatious proceedings, whether against the same person or different persons; or made vexatious applications in any proceedings.[26]

6–042 **Evidence.** Paragraph 17 of Sch.4 to the Enterprise Act provides, among other things, that the CAT Rules may make provision "as to the evidence which may be required or admitted". Paragraphs 22(1) and (2) of the CAT Rules[27] accordingly provide:

---

[23] *www.catribunal.org.uk/default.asp.*
[24] See Chapter 4, above, for a more general consideration of the CAT's Rules.
[25] ss.120(1) and 179(1).
[26] See para.4–096, above for consideration of the power to reject.
[27] See paras 4–057–4–067, above for evidence in the CAT generally.

"(1) The Tribunal may control the evidence by giving directions as to—

(a) the issues on which it requires evidence;
(b) the nature of the evidence which it requires to decide those issues; and
(c) the way in which the evidence is to be placed before the Tribunal.

(2) The Tribunal may admit or exclude evidence, whether or not the evidence was available to the respondent when the disputed decision was taken."

However, the principles of judicial review themselves make provision for the extent to which new evidence that was not before the original decision-maker may be placed before the review court. Those principles were set out by the Court of Appeal in *R. v Secretary of State for the Environment Ex p. Powis*[28] as follows:

"What are the principles on which fresh evidence should be admitted on judicial review? They are (1) that the court can receive evidence to show what material was before the minister or inferior tribunal ... (2) where the jurisdiction of the minister or inferior tribunal depends on a question of fact or where the question is whether essential procedural requirements were observed, the court may receive and consider additional evidence to determine the jurisdictional fact or procedural error ...; and (3) where the proceedings are tainted by misconduct on the part of the minister or member of the inferior tribunal or the parties before it. Examples of such misconduct are bias by the decision making body, or fraud or perjury by a party. In each case fresh evidence is admissible to prove the particular alleged conduct."

The *Powis* test was applied by the High Court in *Cellcom*, which stated: "[a] party can in judicial review proceedings adduce evidence to show what material was before the decision-maker, but not fresh material not available to the decision-maker designed to persuade the Court that the decision-maker's decision was wrong".[29] Consequently, in the light of ss.120 and 179, the apparent width of para.22(2) of the CAT Rules relating to new evidence needs to be read subject to the general principles that would be applied by the High Court in relation to the admissibility of new evidence in judicial review proceedings.[30]

Further appeals. Subparagraphs (6) and (7) of ss.120 and 179 provide: **6–043**

---

[28] [1981] W.L.R. 584 at 595G–H.
[29] para.28.
[30] Although note that, in its judgment on costs in *IBA*, the CAT expressed the view that s.120(4) did not extend to questions of costs—see *IBA Health v OFT (Costs)* [2004] CAT 6 at para.37.

"(6) An appeal lies on any point of law arising from a decision of the Competition Appeal Tribunal under this section to the appropriate court.

(7) An appeal under subsection (6) requires the permission of the Tribunal or the appropriate court."

Paragraphs 58 and 59 of the CAT Rules make provision in respect of appeals from decisions of the CAT. In particular, para.58 provides that requests to the CAT for permission to appeal may be made orally at any hearing or in writing within one month of the notification of the decision concerned. If the CAT refuses permission to appeal, an application for permission may also be made to the Court of Appeal.[31]

5. THE INTENSITY WITH WHICH THE PRINCIPLES OF JUDICIAL REVIEW ARE APPLIED UNDER SECTIONS 120 AND 179

(a) Introduction

6–044   **The intensity with which these principles will be applied.**   Although in *OFT v IBA Health*,[32] the Court of Appeal confirmed that it is the ordinary principles of judicial review that should be applied in reviews under ss.120 and 179, as was recognised by Carnwath L.J. in his judgment in *IBA*,[33] those principles are flexible and are capable of being applied with greater or lesser intensity depending on the context. A crucial issue for those concerned with decisions taken under Parts 3 and 4 of the Act will be how the principles of judicial review are likely to be applied in the context of reviews under ss.120 and 179. Whether those principles are to be applied with greater or lesser intensity will significantly affect the likelihood of successfully challenging such decisions. The considerations that are likely to affect the intensity of review under ss.120 and 79 are discussed in the following paragraphs.

6–045   **Domestic case law providing an indication of how the ordinary principles of judicial review should be applied under sections 120 and 179.**   The cases of most obvious relevance to the way in which the principles of review should be applied under ss.120 and 179 are those in which the High Court has

---

[31] Or, in the case of Tribunal proceedings in Scotland, to the Court of Session (s.120(8)).
[32] [2004] EWCA Civ 142.
[33] *ibid.*, at paras 90–92.

determined applications for judicial review in a competition law context pursuant to its inherent supervisory jurisdiction. Several of those cases[34] were cited to the CAT in *IBA*.[35] In addition, cases in which the High Court has applied the judicial review principles in other specialised areas may also be of relevance. However, in both cases, careful thought should be given as to the extent to which different considerations apply as a result of the specific statutory context of ss.120 and 179.

The potential significance of European principles and case law. In its judg-   **6–046** ment in *IBA*, the CAT stated that it need not decide the question of the relevance of principles of European law to the way in which the CAT should carry out review under s.120.[36] The Court of Appeal made no reference at all to the potential relevance of principles of European law. However, in the light of the emphasis that the Court of Appeal placed on the need for the CAT to apply the ordinary domestic principles of judicial review, it would be surprising if it subsequently took the view that European law principles or cases were of significant persuasive authority for the purpose of determining how those domestic principles ought to be applied. It seems far more likely that the Court of Appeal would choose to justify its conclusions as to how the principles of judicial review should be applied predominantly, if not exclusively, by reference to domestic considerations. Indeed, such an approach is supported by the fact that ss.120 and 179 incorporate the domestic, and not European, principles of judicial review. To the extent that they are different, for example, because European principles result in a greater intensity of review, Parliament could have based review under ss.120 and 179 on those European principles, but choose not to do so. Nonetheless, European case law may still be of some relevance because, even if domestic courts are unlikely to treat European principles and precedents as being determinative, it cannot be ruled out that it might be possible successfully to argue that they should be treated as persuasive authority for the purposes of determining the position in relation to ss.120 and 179. That may particularly be the case where the European principles and/or precedents are cited in order to support a conclusion based primarily on the domestic principles of judicial review. Finally, European law principles may be of particular relevance to mergers that have been referred back from the European Commission to the UK authorities to the UK under Art.9 of the EC Merger

---

[34] *R. v Director General of Telecommunications Ex p. Cellcom* [1999] COD 105; *R. (on the application of London and Continental Stations and Property) v Rail Regulator* [2003] EWHC Admin 2607; *T–Mobile v The Competition Commission* [2003] EWHC Admin 1566; [2003] U.K.C.L.R. 819; *R. (on the application of Interbrew SA) v Competition Commission* [2001] EWHC Admin 367; [2001] U.K.C.L.R. 954.

[35] *OFT v IBA Health* [2003] CAT 27 at para.220.

[36] In relation to the underlying merger provisions, it should be noted that the Enterprise Act does not include a provision equivalent to s.60 of the Competition Act 1998 (which requires that the Chapter I and Chapter II prohibitions be applied in a way that is consistent with the application of Arts 81 and 82).

Regulation.[37] Although Art.9 states that, on such referrals, the relevant national authority shall apply national competition law, that is subject to the requirement in Art.9(8) that "the Member State concerned may take only the measures strictly necessary to safeguard or restore effective competition on the market concerned". That provision has the effect of introducing the European law principle of proportionality, particularly in relation to an assessment of the appropriateness of remedies.[38]

6–047 **European law principles and case law: a brief introduction.** It is not possible here to provide a detailed explanation of the European law grounds of review, which are described in the major European law textbooks.[39] Article 230 of the EC Treaty sets out four grounds of review, namely:

(1) lack of competence;

(2) infringement of an essential procedural requirement;

(3) infringement of the Treaty or any rule of law relating to its application; and

(4) misuse of power.

There is an obvious overlap between those grounds of review and the domestic grounds of review. The EC grounds are applied by the Court of First Instance ("the CFI"), and on appeal by the European Court of Justice ("the ECJ"), in relation to appeals on a point of law against decisions of the European Commission as to whether there has been an infringement of Arts 81 or 82 of the EC Treaty, or as to whether a merger is contrary to the European Community Merger Regulation. Although both the provisions themselves and the context in which they are applied differ from those in ss.120 and 179, those decisions of the CFI and ECJ may nonetheless be capable of providing some guidance as to how the principles of judicial review will be applied in a competition law context in relation to some of the decisions under Parts 3 and 4 of the Enterprise Act.

6–048 **The relationship between the intensity of review and the standard of proof.** A decision-maker's conclusion as to whether a statutory requirement is satisfied, or as to how it ought to exercise its discretion will often be heavily influenced by its findings of fact. On an application for review, a court may therefore be concerned with whether the decision-maker has adequately

---

[37] Regulation 139/2004 on the control of concentrations between undertakings [2004] O.J. L24/1.

[38] As was taken to be the case in *Interbrew v Competition Commission* [2001] U.K.C.L.R. 954; [2001] EWHC Admin 367 in relation to a merger referred back to the UK and dealt with under the previous UK merger regime.

[39] Such as Craig & De Burca, *EU Law* (3rd ed., Oxford); Weatherill & Beaumont, *EU Law* (3rd ed., Penguin); and Schermers and Waelbroeck, *Judicial Protection in the European Union* (6th ed., Kluwer Law International).

proved a fact, or the adequacy of its reasons in support of a factual conclusion. The type of facts concerned will vary from primary facts, such as
that the price of X on date Y was Z, to more complex factual findings, such
as that an undertaking had considerable market power, and conclusions as
to causality and the likelihood of an event or pattern of behaviour occurring
in the future. Factual findings are therefore relevant not only in the context
of review for failure to establish the existence of a precedent fact, or on the
basis of an incorrect finding of fact leading to unfairness, but are likely to be
relevant also in relation to other grounds of review, such as for error of law,
relevancy of considerations, *Wednesbury* unreasonableness and proportionality. As and when the courts have to consider whether the decision-
maker has adequately proved the existence of some fact, they will do so
according to a standard of proof. The higher the standard of proof adopted
by the court, the more likely it is to find that the decision-maker has not
adequately proved the existence of the fact. The standard of proof and
intensity of review are therefore closely linked, as one will tend to be
determined by the court's conclusion as to the appropriate level of the
other.[40]

(b) Considerations affecting the intensity of review

The specialist nature of the CAT. While the following paragraphs identify   6–049
various other context-specific considerations that are likely to influence the
intensity of review from case to case, a major consideration capable of
affecting the intensity of review in all cases under ss.120 and 179 is the extent
to which the fact that the CAT is a specialist tribunal should cause it to
apply the principles of review more intensively than would be done by the
High Court in the same circumstances. As the same issue does not arise in
judicial review proceedings before the High Court, which by its nature is not
a specialised tribunal, there is no clear authority on the point. The CAT, in
contrast, is required by Sch.2 to the Enterprise Act to be presided over by a
President with appropriate experience and knowledge of competition law
and practice, and will generally contain wing members with specialist
knowledge in areas such as industrial economics, accountancy and business.
The CAT in *IBA* clearly considered that its specialist expertise should affect
the intensity with which it applied the principles of judicial review, com-
menting that it did not consider there to be a direct "readover" to s.120
from judicial review decisions in the High Court in which the need for
deference to specialist decision-makers had been stressed.[41] However, while
the leading judgment of the Vice Chancellor in the Court of Appeal clearly
stated that the CAT's specialist nature did not justify it applying principles
different to the ordinary judicial review principles, it provided no clear

---

[40] See in relation to standard of proof more generally, David Bailey, "Standard of proof in EC
merger proceedings: a common law perspective" (2003) 40 C.M.L.R. 845–888.
[41] *OFT v IBA Health*, n.35, above, at para.220.

comments on whether the CAT's specialist nature should affect the intensity with which it should apply those ordinary principles. The comments of the Court of Appeal that came closest to addressing this issue were provided by Carnwath L.J., who stated as follows:

"[The ordinary principles of judicial review], whether applied by a court or specialised tribunal, are flexible enough to be adapted to the particular statutory context. No doubt the existence of such a special jurisdiction will help to ensure consistency from case to case; and the expertise of the Tribunal will better fit it to deal with such cases expeditiously and with a full understanding of the technical background. However, the essential question was no different from that which would have faced a court dealing with the same subject matter."[42]

The general tenor of Carnwath L.J.'s comments supports the position that the CAT should apply the review principles in the same way, and with the same intensity, as would the High Court. However, even if the appropriate intensity of review for the CAT under ss.120 and 179 was subsequently held to be the same as would be appropriate for the High Court in the same circumstances, the fact that the specialised nature of the CAT will allow it to "deal with cases ... with a full understanding of the technical background" is nonetheless likely, in practice, to result in some applications before it being successful that would not have been successful before the High Court. This result is likely to follow from the fact that the specialist CAT may be better placed than the High Court to comprehend the details and subtleties of some of the decisions under Parts 3 and 4 of the Enterprise Act, with the result that, in some circumstances, the CAT is likely to be able to identify errors in the approach and reasoning of a decision that the High Court would not have been able to identify.

6–050 **The nature of the decision under review.** A large variety of different decisions may be taken under Parts 3 and 4 of the Enterprise Act, by a variety of different bodies and individuals, and under a variety of different statutory provisions. The appropriate intensity of review will vary with the applicable ground of review, which will in turn depend on the nature of the challenged decision. Thus, in *IBA* the CAT suggested that the intensity with which it would review a decision of the Secretary of State under s.58 that the interests of national security were involved would vary considerably from a case in which it was alleged that the turnover had been wrongly calculated for the purposes of the £70 million turnover test under s.23.[43] Similarly, in the Court of Appeal, Carnwath L.J. indicated that the appropriate intensity of review under ss.120 and 179 would be less in relation to decisions depending on

---

[42] At para.100.
[43] At para.221.

administrative or political judgment than in relation to an assessment of the fairness of the procedures followed by the decision-maker.[44]

Economic facts requiring the exercise of judgment. In a competition or regulatory context, many of the conclusions under review will be of an economic nature, such as, for example, the definition of the relevant market, or the extent to which two products are substitutes. These may be questions to which there is no clear answer, requiring the exercise of expert judgment. The courts have traditionally been slow to interfere with the conclusions of decision-makers on such issues, and the High Court in *Cellcom* and the Court of Appeal in *IBA* both cited the warning of Lord Brightman in *R. v Hillingdon BC Ex p. Pulhofer*, that: **6–051**

> "Where the existence or non-existence of a fact is left to the judgment and discretion of a public body and that fact involves a broad spectrum ranging from the obvious to the debatable to the just conceivable, it is the duty of the court to leave the decision of that fact to the public body to whom Parliament has entrusted the decision-making power save in a case where it is obvious that the public body, consciously or unconsciously, is acting perversely."[45]

The extent to which the specialised nature of the CAT should affect the intensity with which it applies the principles of judicial review was discussed above.[46] The way in which that issue is resolved will have a significant impact on the likelihood of the CAT overturning conclusions of an economic nature drawn, in particular, by the OFT and the Competition Commission under Part 4 of the Act.[47]

The inherent plausibility of conclusions. An important consideration likely to affect a court's assessment of the appropriate standard of review is the inherent plausibility of the factual finding in issue. As Lord Hoffmann has stated: "some things are inherently more likely than others. It would need more cogent evidence to satisfy one that the creature seen walking in   **6–052**

---

[44] At para.92.

[45] [1986] A.C. 484 at 518B–F.

[46] para.6–049, above.

[47] In the context of appeals against decisions of the OFT under the Competition Act 1998, the CAT has taken into account the economic nature of certain facts in determining how the appropriate standard of proof should be applied in relation to certain issues. In particular, at para.125 of its judgment in *Aberdeen Journals (No.2)* [2003] CAT 11, the CAT stated:

> "We bear in mind, however, that an issue such as the relevant product market may require a more or less complex assessment of numerous interlocking factors, including economic evidence. Such an exercise intrinsically involves an element of appreciation and the exercise of judgment. On such issues it seems to us that the question whether the Director has 'proved' this case involves asking ourselves: Is the Tribunal satisfied that the Director's analysis of the relevant product market is robust and soundly based?"

Regent's Park was more likely than not to have been a lioness than to be satisfied to the same standard of probability that it was an Alsatian".[48] This consideration appears to have had an important influence on the approach of both the CAT and the Court of Appeal in *IBA*. One of the issues in *IBA* related to the OFT's decision not to refer to the Competition Commission a merger between iSoft and Torex on the basis that the statutory test in s.33(1) of the Enterprise Act was not satisfied. The s.33(1) test, considered further below, required that the OFT make a reference if it believed that it may be the case that the merger may be expected to result in a substantial lessening of competition. The CAT concluded that it was not satisfied as to the OFT's reasoning in that respect, a conclusion which the Court of Appeal declined to overturn. The merger in issue was between two companies that were the largest two companies in the market with a combined market share in the 45 to 55 per cent range, competed horizontally, and benefited from a network effect and information asymmetry. The merger also took place in a market in which supply substitutability was limited and the next competitor had a market share well below that enjoyed by the merging companies. Both the CAT and Court of Appeal appear to have taken the view that, in order to justify what in those circumstances was the rather surprising conclusion that the s.33(1) test was not met, the OFT would have had to produce clear and compelling reasoning, which it had failed to do.[49] In addition to the inherent plausibility of a conclusion, the cogency of any alternative explanations put forward by an applicant is also likely to have an impact on the court's assessment as to how much is required of the decision-maker by way of explanation. However, one of the subtle ways in which a court can effectively adopt a low standard of proof is by requiring an applicant to put forward convincing evidence in support of its case before the court will consider the burden of proof as having shifted onto the decision-maker.[50]

6–053 **Existing facts and predictions of the future.** Other things being equal, the standard of proof adopted by a court in relation to existing facts relied on by the decision-maker is likely to be higher than the standard of proof adopted in relation to predictions for the future made by the decision-maker. That distinction was acknowledged by President Vesterdorft of the CFI when explaining the approach taken by the CFI in appeals from Commission merger decisions,[51] and also reflects the approach taken by the High Court

---

[48] *Home Secretary v Rehman* [2001] 3 W.L.R. 877 at para.55, HL.
[49] *OFT v IBA Health* [2004] EWCA Civ 142 at paras 65–75 of the Court of Appeal's judgment, setting out the relevant passages from the decision of the CAT in addition to the Court of Appeal's conclusions.
[50] David Bailey, "Standard of proof in EC merger proceedings: a common law perspective" (2003) 40 C.M.L.R. 862.
[51] David Bailey, "Standard of proof in EC merger proceedings: a common law perspective", n.50, above, at 865.

in judicial reviews against the Director General of Telecommunications[52] and the Rail Regulator.[53] In part this reflects the obvious point that it is impossible to predict the future with absolute certainty, and it would therefore be unrealistic to set a very high standard of proof. Additionally, it reflects the fact that predictions as to the likelihood of an event occurring often require the exercise of specialist judgment, which the original decision-maker may be in a better position to carry out than the court.

Predicted future changes to the competitive position. However, at least in relation to merger decisions, a tension exists between the tendency of courts not to require as high a standard of proof in respect of future events as is required for past events, and the view that the more remote the anti-competitive effects of a merger the more persuasive should be the evidence to predict them.[54] In merger decisions, the analysis is inevitably prospective, as the decision-maker has to analyse how the competitive position will change as a result of the merger. In some cases, the competitive effects with which the decision-maker is concerned may be immediate and inevitable, such as where the merger results in a single company with a very high market share. In other cases, however, the decision-maker may be concerned with potential effects that are temporally remote and less certain. If a decision turns on such effects, a court is likely to require that the decision-maker's conclusion as to the likelihood of such effects be supported by compelling evidence and cogent reasoning.

6–054

    (i) *Airtours v Commission.*[55] This case involved a merger decision by the Commission that was appealed to the CFI. The Commission had concluded that, although this had not previously been the case, the merger would create a position of oligopolistic dominance in which the three largest undertakings in the market would not have an incentive to compete with each other, but would have every interest to adopt parallel conduct so far as the decision as to how many package holidays to put onto the market was concerned, reducing capacity below what was required as a result of market trends.[56] The CFI subjected the Commission's reasoning in that regard to detailed analysis, ultimately concluding that the Commission's analysis was vitiated by a series of errors of assessment.[57] It seems likely that the intensity with which the Commission reviewed the Commission's decision was influenced by the remoteness and inherent uncertainty of the potential harm

---

[52] *R. v Director General of Telecommunications Ex p. Cellcom Ltd* [1999] C.O.D 105 at para.26.
[53] *R. (on the application of London and Continental Stations and Property Limited) v The Rail Regulator* [2003] EWHC Admin 2607 at para.30.
[54] That tension has also been recognised by President Vesterdorf—see David Bailey, "Standard of proof in EC merger proceedings: a common law perspective", n.50, above, at 865.
[55] Case T–342/99 [2002] E.C.R. II–2585; [2002] 5 C.M.L.R. 7.
[56] At para. 67.
[57] At para.294.

to competition that the Commission had identified, namely the possibility of a position of oligopolistic dominance emerging.

(ii) **IBA**[58] Above,[59] it was suggested that the approach taken by both the CAT and the Court of Appeal in *IBA* may be explained by the fact a court will require greater evidence to justify a conclusion that is inherently implausible that it will to justify one that it more plausible. However, the OFT's conclusion that it did not believe that it may be the case that the merger may be expected to result in a substantial lessening of competition was based on the view that, although the merger would create an entity with a large market presence, it was unlikely to confer significant market power as a result of changes to the market that would be introduced by an upcoming National Programme for IT, proposed by the Department of Health.[60] Although accepting that the introduction of the new programme would change the competitive landscape, the Court of Appeal did not accept that that was sufficient to overcome the anti-competitive features which would immediately and inevitably result from the merger to such an extent as to remove the requisite likelihood of a significant lessening of competition.[61] The judgment in *IBA* may therefore also be seen as an example of how, when the immediate and inevitable consequences of a merger point clearly in favour of one outcome, the court will require compelling evidence and cogent reasons to justify the conclusion that more temporally remote and inherently uncertain competitive effects are of sufficient likelihood and significance such as to justify the contrary result.

(iii) **Tetra Laval.**[62] In *Tetra Laval*, also an appeal before the CFI of a Commission merger decision, considerations arose relating both to the "inherent plausibility" of the Commission's analysis and the temporally remote nature of the anti-competitive effects with which the Commission was concerned. The merger was conglomerate in nature, *i.e.* it was a merger of undertakings that did not have a pre-existing competitive relationship, either as competitors or as supplier and customer. However, the Commission nonetheless concluded that the merger could create a dominant position in markets in which the undertakings were not dominant pre-merger, on the basis that such dominance could be created over time by the merged entity leveraging its dominant position in one market into those other markets.[63] It is clear that the CFI took

---

[58] *OFT v IBA Health*, n.49, above.
[59] para.6–052.
[60] *OFT v IBA Health*, n.49, above, at para. 4.
[61] *ibid.*, at para.73.
[62] Case T–5/02 *Tetra Laval BV v Commission* [2002] E.C.R. II–4381; [2002] 5 C.M.L.R. 28.
[63] [2002] E.C.R. II–4381 at paras 39–58.

these considerations into account when determining the appropriate intensity of review:

> "155 ... Since the effects of a conglomerate-type merger are generally considered to be neutral, or even beneficial, for competition on the markets concerned ... the proof of anti-competitive conglomerate effects of such a merger calls for a precise examination, supported by convincing evidence, of the circumstances which allegedly produce those effects (see, by analogy, *Airtours v Commission*, para.63).
>
> ...
>
> 162. It follows from the foregoing that it is necessary to examine whether the Commission based its analysis of the likelihood of leveraging from the aseptic carton markets, and of the consequences of such leveraging by the merged entity, on sufficiently convincing evidence ... In addition, since the anticipated dominant position would only emerge after a certain lapse of time, by 2005 according to the Commission, its analysis of the future position must, whilst allowing for a certain margin of discretion, be particularly plausible."

Subsequently, having subjected the Commission's analysis to detailed scrutiny, the CFI concluded that the Commission had failed to provide sufficient evidence that it was likely that, following the merger, the merged entity would through leveraging achieve a dominant position in the markets identified by the Commission.[64] However, the Commission appealed the CFI's decision to the ECJ.[65] The ECJ rejected the Commission's appeal from the CFI's judgment, stating[66]:

> "39. Whilst the Court recognizes that the Commission has a margin of discretion with regard to economic matters, that does not mean that the Community Courts must refrain from reviewing the Commission's interpretation of information of an economic nature. Not only must the Community Courts, *inter alia*, establish whether the evidence relied on is factually accurate, reliable and consistent but also whether that evidence contains all of the information which must be taken into account in order to assess a complex situation and whether it is capable of substantiating the conclusions drawn from it. Such a review is all the more necessary in the case of a prospective analysis required when examining a planned merger with conglomerate effect.
>
> ...

---

[64] See, in particular, paras 235, 251, 253, 254, 283 and 307.
[65] Case C–12/03.
[66] *ibid.*

43. . . . such an analysis makes it necessary to envisage various chains of cause and effect with a view to ascertaining which of them are the most likely.

44. The analysis of a 'conglomerate-type' concentration is a prospective analysis in which, first, the consideration of a lengthy period of time in the future and, secondly, the leveraging necessary to give rise to a significant impediment to effective competition means that the chains of cause and effect are dimly discernable, uncertain and difficult to establish. That being so, the quality of the evidence produced by the Commission in order to establish that it is necessary to adopt a decision declaring the concentration incompatible with the common market is particularly important, since that evidence must support the Commission's conclusion that, if such a decision were not adopted, the economic development envisaged by it would be plausible".

6–055 **Questions of policy.** As noted above, the courts will tend to adopt a lower intensity of review in respect of decisions significantly influenced by consideration of policy. That is particularly the case in the case of decisions concerned with economic or regulatory policy.[67] At a time when he was a member of the CFI, Sir Christopher Bellamy QC, the current President of the CAT, stated that the CFI adopted a similar approach when hearing appeals from competition decisions of the European Commission, in particular by according "a considerable margin of appreciation" to the competition authority in respect of questions of policy.[68] These considerations are likely to apply in particular in the context of traditional judicial reviews of regulatory decisions. Because one of the objectives of the reforms leading to the Enterprise Act was to reduce the political element present in the UK's competition regime, many of the most important and frequently-taken decisions within Parts 3 and 4 of the Act will be taken predominantly if not exclusively on the basis of "competition", as opposed to "policy" considerations. Nonetheless, certain decisions within those Parts will continue to contain substantial elements of policy, such as, for example, decisions by the Secretary of State to intervene in a merger case under s.42 of the Act on the basis that one or more one public interest consideration is relevant to consideration of the merger.

6–056 **Human rights.** As noted above, if a decision impacts on a right of the applicant enshrined in the European Convention on Human Rights, the provisions of the Human Rights Act 1998 will apply, and the principles of

---

[67] See, in particular, *R. (on the application of London and Continental Stations and Property) v The Rail Regulator* [2003] EWHC Admin 2607 at paras 27 to 34.
[68] In a seminar entitled "Judicial Enforcement of Competition Law", co-ordinated by the OECD in October 1996, details of which are available on the OECD's website: *www.oecd.org*.

judicial review will be applied with greater intensity than would otherwise be the case. The provision of the Convention that is likely most often to be relevant to the substance of decisions in a competition and regulatory context is Art.1 of the First Protocol, which provides:

"Every natural or legal person is entitled to the peaceful enjoyment of his possessions. No one shall be deprived of his possessions except in the public interest and subject to the conditions provided for by law and by the general principles of international law.

The preceding provisions shall not, however, in any way impair the right of the State to enforce such laws at it deems necessary to control the use of property in accordance with the general interest or to secure the payment of taxes or other contributions or penalties."

The article may be engaged not merely by outright deprivations of property, but also by state measures which control the use of property. The extent to which decisions in a competition or regulatory context, and in particular decisions under Parts 3 and 4 of the Enterprise Act, engage Art.1 of the First Protocol may be controversial. The High Court found that the Article was engaged by a decision of the Rail Regulator,[69] but that decision turned on the specific facts of the case. In *Interbrew*,[70] the High Court found it unnecessary to decide whether the Article was engaged by the Secretary of State's implementation of the Competition Commission's recommendation that the applicant, Interbrew, be required to divest itself of brewing interests that it had acquired in a merger. However, where Art.1 of the First Protocol, or any of the other rights of the ECHR, is engaged, the principle of proportionality, will be applicable (although the European Court of Human Rights has suggested that Member States have a broad margin of appreciation in relation to taking or placing restrictions on the use of property, in particular in relation to the determination of fair levels of compensation).[71]

6. THE REVIEW OF MERGER DECISIONS UNDER PART 3 OF THE ENTERPRISE ACT 2002

(a) Introduction

Challengeable decisions within Part 3. The scope of s.120(1) of the Enterprise Act is broad, in that it allows any decision taken by the OFT, the   6–057

---

[69] *R. (on the application of London and Continental Stations and Property Ltd) v The Rail Regulator* [2003] EWHC Admin 2607 at paras 27–29.
[70] *R. (On the application of Interbrew SA) v Competition Commission* [2001] EWHC Admin 367; [2001] U.K.C.L.R. 954.
[71] See, for example, *James v United Kingdom* (1986) 8 E.H.R.R. 123 at para.54.

Secretary of State or the Competition Commission under Part 3 of the Enterprise Act 2002 to be challenged by any person aggrieved by it before the CAT. Part 3 puts in place a process to be followed in relation to merger decisions. A detailed description of the Part 3 process itself is beyond the scope of this chapter, the focus of which is on the considerations that will be relevant as and when decisions under Part 3 are reviewed under s.120. However, Guidelines relating to the Part 3 procedures are available on the websites of both the OFT[72] and the Competition Commission,[73] and the procedures are described in detail in other competition law texts.[74] The process will normally involve only the OFT and the Competition Commission, with the Secretary of State becoming involved only in cases which raise exceptional public interest considerations. In overview, the process will usually be as follows. Although there is no requirement for parties to notify mergers, parties to a merger will usually make a statutory voluntarily notification and/or make informal submissions to the OFT.[75] The OFT's role is to carry out a preliminary analysis of the merger. It has a duty to refer some mergers to the Competition, but has a discretion in other instances. Some mergers are incapable of being referred. The OFT may also accept legally binding undertakings to modify a merger in lieu of making a reference. Following a statutory voluntary notification, the OFT has a relatively short period in which to assess whether or not to refer a merger (20 working days, with a maximum extension of a further 10 working days). If the OFT refers a merger, the Competition Commission will carry out a more detailed investigation, generally within a 24 week period (with a maximum extension of eight weeks). The Competition Commission procedure will generally involve gathering documentary evidence, hearing witnesses, producing a statement of issues and provisional findings, considering the responses of the parties, notifying and considering possible remedies, and publishing its report.

6–058   **The substantial lessening of competition test.**   At the heart of the new merger regime introduced by Part 3 is the question of whether a merger has or may be expected to result in a "substantial lessening of competition". This is the question at the heart of the assessments that have to be made by the OFT and the Competition Commission. Both the OFT[76] and the Competition

---

[72] *www.oft.gov.uk.* In particular, *Mergers: procedural guidance.*
[73] *www.competition-commission.org.uk.*
[74] See, for example, Whish, Chapter 22.
[75] A merger may also come before the OFT as a result of it being referred back to it by the European Commission. See, in that respect, Art.9 of Regulation 139/2004 on the control of concentrations between undertakings (the EC Merger Regulation). Where mergers are referred back, the relevant national authority is to apply national competition law, subject to the provision in Art.9(8) that: "In applying the provision of this Article, the Member State concerned may take only the measures strictly necessary to safeguard or restore effective competition on the market concerned".
[76] *Mergers: substantive assessment guidance,* available on the OFT's website, n.72, above.

Commission[77] have produced guidance as to how they are likely to apply the test, including the approach that they are likely to take to market definition. Nominally, at least, the substantial lessening of competition test represents a change from the test applied by the Monopolies and Mergers Commission (the predecessor to the Competition Commission) under the previous regime which asked whether a merger might be expected to operate against the public interest. In practice, however, the Monopolies and Mergers Commission had for several years adopted a substantial lessening of competition test in all but name. Consequently, reports of the Monopolies and Mergers Commission under the previous regime may continue to be of some relevance to new cases arising under Part 3. However, it should be noted that, as explained in more detail below, as a result of the different roles played by the OFT and Competition Commission, the courts have indicated that it is appropriate for the two bodies to apply the substantial lessening of competition test in slightly different ways.

Completed and anticipated mergers. Part 3 contains provisions dealing with both anticipated and completed mergers. For example, while ss.33 (relating to the OFT) and 36 (relating to the Competition Commission) contain provision relating to anticipated mergers, ss.22 and 35 deal with completed mergers. The wording of the two sets of provisions are equivalent. For the purpose of brevity, the following sections refer primarily to the provisions of Part 3 relating to anticipated mergers (with which, in reality, the OFT and the Competition Commission are likely more frequently to be concerned). However, unless expressly stated, the considerations set out below in relation to anticipated mergers are equally applicable to the equivalent provisions dealing with completed mergers.
6–059

(b) Preliminary decisions of the OFT

The OFT's assessment process. A merger may fall to be considered by the OFT either after its completion, or before its completion following voluntary statutory notification or an informal approach by the parties. Prior to making its decision as to whether or not to refer the merger to the Competition Commission, the OFT will carry out an assessment process, and may be involved in informal discussions with the parties. The OFT's assessment process is set out in Chapter 6 of its guidance *Mergers: procedural guidance*, and Chapter 3 of the same guidance summarises the informal discussions that may take place. An issue arises as to whether any steps taken by the OFT in this preliminary period are capable of constituting a decision falling within the scope of s.120 in relation to which the CAT,
6–060

---

[77] *Merger references: Competition Commission guidelines*, available on the Competition Commission's website, n.73, above.

applying the principles of judicial review, would entertain an application for review prior to the substantive OFT reference decision.

6–061 **A "decision"?** The Enterprise Act does not define the meaning of "a decision" for the purposes of s.120. In another context, the CAT has stated:

> "On the ordinary meaning of words, to take 'a decision' in a legal context means simply to decide or determine a question or issue. Whether such a decision has been taken for the purposes of the Act is, in our view, a question of substance, not form, to be determined objectively".[78]

It is clear from the ordinary meaning of the word "decision" that several acts that the OFT could take prior to its reference decision would clearly not fall within the scope of s.120. For example, the OFT's procedural guidance clearly states that any informal or confidential guidance is not capable of binding the OFT. The position in relation to certain other acts, however, could be more uncertain. For example, prior to making its reference decision, it is possible that the OFT could:

(1) in the process of inviting comments from third parties, determine to publish certain information relating to the merger;

(2) select a group from within the relevant OFT Branch to assess the merger; and/or

(3) require the parties to provide a response in relation to an issue within a specified period.

It is possible to imagine circumstances in which such acts could be challenged on the following grounds:

(1) that the OFT would be publishing confidential information contrary to Part 9 of the Enterprise Act;

(2) that a person selected to assess the merger was biased; and

(3) that the time period within which the parties had been required to respond was too short and contrary to the requirements of procedural fairness.

In such instances, it may be less clear whether such acts constitute a decision for the purpose of s.120.

6–062 **Prematurity/ripeness.** It is unlikely that the CAT will determine such questions solely by reference to the ordinary meaning of the phrase "a

---

[78] *Bettercare v DGFT* [2001] CAT 7 at para.62; [2002] Comp. A.R. 299. See more generally paras 3–042–3–045, above.

decision", and without reference to the "principles that would be applied by a court on an application for judicial review". In an application for judicial review, the court may consider whether the application is "ripe", or has been brought prematurely.[79] Where an application is brought in respect of an act or decision taken during a procedure leading up to a final determination, the issue may be whether the court should determine the applicant's complaint in respect of the preliminary matter, or refuse the application on the basis that, if the alleged error affects the final determination, the applicant will be able to bring a challenge at that stage. It is clear that a court may quash some procedural decisions even if it would not subsequently be prepared to quash the final decision solely on that ground.[80] However, it has also been stated that the courts will not "generally" intervene to regulate procedures in advance of a substantive decision.[81] The issue will often be whether any unfairness would be caused by requiring the applicant to wait until a final decision has been taken to bring a challenge. Obviously, if it will be too late by the time of the final decision to protect the interest on which the applicant relies, allowing the challenge at the preliminary stage may well be appropriate. Thus, in relation to example (1) above, relating to the alleged proposed disclosure of confidential information, it may be that the only way to protect the applicant's interest would be to allow a challenge prior to publication. The position in relation to the other two examples is less clear cut and might well turn on the precise facts of each case. In general, however, it is possible that, in the light of the fact that one of the objectives of the new regime is that the OFT decision whether or not to make a reference should be taken quickly, the CAT will be reluctant to encourage challenges to the OFT procedure prior to its reference decision.

(c) Decisions of the OFT to refer a merger

The duty on the OFT to refer mergers.   Section 33 of the Enterprise Act, 6–063
relating to anticipated mergers, provides that the OFT is under a duty to refer a merger to the Competition Commission if the conditions set out in subs.(1) of each section are met. Section 33(1) provides as follows:

"(1) The OFT shall, subject to subsections (2) and (3), make a reference to the Commission if the OFT believes that it is or may be the case that—

(a) arrangements are in progress or in contemplation which, if carried into effect, will result in the creation of a relevant merger situation; and

(b) the creation of that situation may be expected to result in a

---

[79] See, for example, *R. v Hammersmith & Fulham LBC Ex p. Burkett* [2002] 1 W.L.R. 1593.
[80] *R. v Lord Saville of Newdigate* [2000] 1 W.L.R. 1855 at para.43.
[81] *R. v Secretary of State for the Home Department Ex p. Hickey (No.2)* [1995] 1 W.L.R. 734 at 757H.

substantial lessening of competition within any market or markets in the United Kingdom for goods or services."

Subsection (2) sets out situations in which, notwithstanding the fact that the conditions of subs.(1) are met, the OFT has a discretion whether or not to refer. Subsection (3) provides that no reference may be made under certain specified circumstances.

6–064 **Challenging a decision to refer on the basis that no relevant merger situation has been created: error of law.** Section 23 of the Enterprise Act makes express provision in relation to relevant merger situations. A relevant merger situation will be created when two or more enterprises "have ceased to be distinct", and either the turnover test or the share of supply test is met. Other provisions of Part 3 make further provision as to the precise meaning of these tests and how they are to be applied. Further explanation is provided in the OFT's guideline *Mergers: substantive assessment guidance*. It is therefore possible that an OFT decision to refer a merger could be challenged on the basis that no relevant merger situation had been created. In terms of the most appropriate ground of review in this situation, the starting point is likely often to be error of law. Obviously, the precise meaning of "a relevant merger situation" is a hard-edged question of law for the court, and the CAT will substitute its judgment as the meaning of that term if it considers that the OFT adopted the wrong legal interpretation. As explained above, though, the court will not normally substitute its judgment for that of the decision maker on questions of fact, and the application of law to findings of fact is normally considered to be a question of fact.[82] However, the exception to that approach is where the review court considers that the application of the correct legal meaning of a provision could only reasonably produce one result on the facts. In such cases, the court will regard the question as being one of law, and will substitute its judgment for that of the decision maker. This may often be the case in relation to the "relevant merger situation" test, several aspects of which are relatively "open and shut" (for example, in relation to the question of whether the value of the turnover in the UK of the enterprise being taken over exceeds £70 million).[83]

6–065 **Challenging a decision to refer on the basis that no relevant merger situation has been created: error of precedent fact and mistake of fact giving rise to unfairness.** Where an applicant considers that the OFT has made a reference to the Competition Commission where no relevant merger situation exists, it is clearly arguable that it could base its challenge on the ground of either error of precedent fact and/or mistake of fact giving rise to unfairness. Whether a relevant merger situation exists is a classic example of a fact

---

[82] para.6–022, above.
[83] s.23(1)(b).

going to the jurisdiction of the decision-making body: if one did not exist, the OFT would be acting outside of the powers conferred on it by Parliament by making a reference. However, as noted above, the courts have tended to apply the doctrine only in limited circumstances, and it is unclear whether the CAT will seek to apply the doctrine in this context. Alternatively, however, if the CAT considers that the OFT made a factual mistake which caused it incorrectly to conclude that a relevant merger situation existed, it seems likely that the criteria for the newly recognised doctrine of review for mistake of fact giving rise to unfairness will often be satisfied. It should be noted that, in addition to potentially delaying an intended merger, the making of a reference to the Competition Commission is likely to impose a considerable administrative burden on and create a significant degree of uncertainty for the parties concerned. Those considerations may be considered to militate in favour of the application of the heightened intensity of review accompanying the doctrines of precedent fact and mistake of fact giving rise to unfairness in this context. The only situations in which a heightened intensity of review would obviously not be appropriate is where the specific part of the "relevant merger situation" test that is in issue is not "open and shut" in nature, but is more open-ended and/or it is apparent that the OFT has or ought to have a degree of discretion as to how it is applied. The most obvious example is in relation to the share of supply test, in respect of which s.23(5) expressly provides that the criterion or criteria to be applied by the OFT shall be such that the OFT considers appropriate.

The nature of the substantial lessening of competition test when it is applied by the OFT. The meaning of the substantial lessening of competition test, which has to be applied by the OFT in determining whether to make a reference under ss.22(1)(b) and 33(1)(b) of the Enterprise Act, fell for consideration by the Court of Appeal in the case of *IBA*.[84] Unlike the Competition Commission, the question that the OFT has to ask itself contains a "double may", namely: "whether the OFT believes that it is or *may* be the case that the [merger] *may* be expected to result in a substantial lessening of competition . . .". The Court of Appeal overturned the CAT's interpretation of that test, which had referred to the need for the OFT to take into account what view might subsequently be taken by the Competition Commission, and emphasised that it is the OFT's own beliefs that are relevant.[85] The

6–066

---

[84] [2004] EWCA Civ 142; [2004] U.K.C.L.R. 683.

[85] The CAT had held that, in the grey area in which there was room for more than one view as to whether a merger would lead to a substantial lessening of competition, the OFT must satisfy itself of the following two-part test, namely.

(i) that as far as the OFT is concerned there is no significant prospect of a substantial lessening of competition; and

(ii) there is no significant prospect of an alternative view being taken in the context of a fuller investigation by the Commission.

Court of Appeal stated that the words in s.33(1) were ordinary English words and should be applied in accordance with their ordinary meaning.[86] However, the Court of Appeal added the following comments. First, that the requirement of a belief required some form of mental assent which was a more positive frame of mind that a suspicion.[87] Secondly, that the OFT's belief must be reasonable and objectively justified by the relevant facts, in accordance with Lord Wilberforce's comments in *Education Secretary v Tameside BC*.[88] Thirdly, that the role of the OFT was that of a first screen and that, accordingly, and in the light of the different wording of the provisions applicable to the different stages of the process, the degree of likelihood of a substantial lessening of competition required to justify the OFT making a reference under s.33(1) was lower than the degree of likelihood required to justify the equivalent conclusion by the Competition Commission under s.36(1). As explained by the Court of Appeal:

> "That lower degree of likelihood might, for example, exist in circumstances where the work done by the OFT did not justify any positive view, but left some uncertainty, and where the OFT therefore believed that a substantial lessening of competition might prove to be likely on further and fuller examination of the position (which could only be undertaken by the Competition Commission".[89]

At the other end of the scale, the Court of Appeal stated that the statutory language precluded the possibility of a reference on the basis of purely fanciful considerations. In between the fanciful and a degree of likelihood less than 50 per cent, however, there was a wide margin in which the OFT was required to exercise its judgment.[90]

6–067   **Challenging a decision to refer on the basis that the substantial lessening of competition test is not met.**   There will normally be two aspects to the OFT's reasoning that will fall to be considered in references under s.33 of the Enterprise Act. The first is the interpretation of the wording of s.33(1)(b) adopted by the OFT. Clearly, if the OFT interprets the provision incorrectly, and applies the wrong test, a review will lie on the basis of error of law. Indeed, in *IBA*, the Court of Appeal stated that in its view, one possibility was that the OFT had applied the wrong test by adopting too high a test of likelihood.[91] The second aspect is whether, "in the OFT's belief", the statutory test is satisfied on the facts. In relation to this aspect, the relevant ground of appeal is one based on the test set out by Lord Wilberforce in *Education Secretary v Tameside BC*, namely:

---

[86] At para.43.
[87] At para.44.
[88] [1977] A.C. 1014 at 1047.
[89] At para.47.
[90] At para.48.
[91] At para.75.

"If a judgment requires, before it can be made, the existence of some facts, then, although the evaluation of those facts is for the Secretary of State alone, the court must inquire whether those facts exist, and have been taken into account, whether the judgment has been made upon a proper self-direction as to those facts, whether the judgment has not been made upon other facts which ought not to have been taken into account."[92]

Review under this head is capable of being applied with a greater or lesser intensity, and the CAT's approach is likely to vary in accordance with the considerations set out above. However, although the CAT's two-stage test was overturned by the Court of Appeal, some of its other comments in *IBA* suggest that, in its view, borderline cases should be referred to the Competition Commission. The CAT reasoned that Parliament's intention in the Enterprise Act was that mergers potentially leading to a substantial lessening of competition should be scrutinised closely, and that there was therefore little room for a presumption that doubtful or borderline cases should "get the benefit of the doubt".[93] It also stated that, because of the short timescales and its reliance to a significant extent on the submissions of the parties, it was inherently difficult in complex "grey area" cases for the OFT to be able to explore the matter in sufficient depth to be able to decide not to make a reference with the necessary degree of certainty.[94] Finally, the CAT was concerned that in complex cases it would not, in a review from an OFT decision, be provided with all the material necessary for it properly to assess the situation.[95] These comments suggest that, in borderline cases, the CAT's starting position may well be that the merger ought to be referred, with the consequence that it will regard arguments that a merger ought not to be referred with a degree of scepticism, and will not subject the OFT's reasoning in support of its decision to refer to an intense level of scrutiny.

Challenging a decision to refer on the basis that the OFT ought to have exercised its discretion not to refer. Even if the "relevant merger situation" and "substantial lessening of competition" tests are met, s.33(2) of the Enterprise Act provides the OFT with a discretion not to refer the merger in the following three situations: 6–068

    (i)   the merger in process or in contemplation is insufficiently advanced to warrant reference;[96]

    (ii) the market or markets in question are not of sufficient importance to warrant the making of a reference; or

---

[92] [1977] A.C. 1014 at 1047.
[93] At para.200.
[94] At para.204.
[95] At paras 207–213.
[96] This scenario obviously does not apply in the case of completed mergers.

(iii) the customer benefits of a merger would outweigh its adverse effects.

It is therefore possible that a party could seek to challenge a decision by the OFT to refer a merger on the basis that the facts of the case fell within the scope of one of the limbs of s.33(2) and the OFT should have exercised its discretion not to refer. As and when it is faced with such a challenge, the CAT may well have regard to the guidance in relation to these three possibilities provided by the OFT in Chapter 7 of its *Mergers: substantive assessment guidance* document. If the OFT denied that any of the three limbs applied, the applicant would first have to show that the facts of his case fell within the scope of s.33(2). As to the legal meaning of s.33(2), the wording of each of the three limbs is to a degree imprecise, raising the possibility that the CAT might consider the approach of Lord Mustill in *R. v Monopolies and Mergers Commission Ex p. South Yorkshire Transport* to be applicable, with the consequence that it would overturn the OFT's legal interpretation only if it did not fall "broadly in the right part of the spectrum of possible meanings".[97] Secondly, it is clear from the wording of each of the three limbs, and the opening wording of subs.(2) (namely, "the OFT *may* decide not to make a reference"), that s.33(2) confers a discretion on the OFT. As the exercise of that discretion will involve considerations of policy, the CAT is likely to be wary of reviewing the OFT's exercise of its discretion intensively.

6–069   **Challenging a decision to refer on the basis that the terms of sections 22(3) or 33(3) are satisfied.**   Sections 22(3) and 33(3) of the Enterprise Act provide that the OFT shall not make a merger reference in certain specified circumstances. The specified circumstances cover a diverse range of possibilities, and a description of them is outside of the scope of this chapter. Nonetheless, once the facts have been determined, the question of whether any of the limbs of ss.22(3) or 33(3) are satisfied is likely to be relatively uncontroversial, and a matter in relation to which a decision-maker properly instructed as to the relevant law could reasonably reach only one conclusion.

(d) Decisions of the OFT not to refer a merger

6–070   **Decisions not to refer a merger.**   It is also possible for third parties, such as competitors of the merging companies, to challenge a decision of the OFT not to refer a merger. As in respect of OFT decisions to refer a merger, OFT decisions not to refer a merger are capable of being based on various different reasons. In particular, the OFT may decide not to make a reference because it:

---

[97] [1993] 1 W.L.R. 23 at 30F.

(1) does not consider that a relevant merger situation has been or will be created;

(2) does not consider the substantial lessening of competition test to be satisfied;

(3) considers that the terms of s.22(2) or 33(2) of the Enterprise Act are satisfied and has exercised its discretion not to make a reference; or

(4) considers that it is precluded from making a reference by the terms of s.22(3) or 33(3).

The considerations relevant to challenges to such decisions will generally be the same as those discussed above in relation to where the OFT has decided to make a reference. However, as discussed above,[98] in *IBA* the CAT appears to have attached considerable importance to the need to scrutinise closely mergers potentially leading to a substantial lessening of competition, and expressed the view that the OFT should generally refer borderline cases to the Competition Commission.

(e) Decisions taken by the Competition Commission

Procedural decisions of the Competition Commission. The procedure of the 6–071 Competition Commission following a merger reference is longer and involve several more steps than the procedure of the OFT in deciding whether to make a reference decision. Details of the Competition Commission's procedures are set out in its guidelines, *General advice and information*, and *rules of procedure*. In the light of its greater length and complexity, more opportunities to challenge the Competition Commission procedure are likely to arise than in relation to the OFT procedure. It was noted above that one of the considerations militating against the CAT being receptive to challenges to the OFT procedure prior to its final reference decision was the fact that one of the objectives of the Part 3 regime was that the OFT decision should be taken within a very tight timeframe. That consideration does not apply to the same extent in relation to the Competition Commission procedure which, although still tight in terms of what has to be done, is considerably longer at 24 weeks. It is also costly, and the OFT has stated that it would expect the Competition Commission procedure to cost around £400,000.[99] On one view, therefore, it would be preferable for any complaints relating to the procedure to be resolved immediately, in order to ensure that the procedure is correct "first time around", rather than generally allowing challenges only following the publication of the final report, and raising the possibility that certain aspects of the procedure would then have to be repeated. However, where a preliminary decision also has

---

[98] para.6–067, above.
[99] OFT publication *Mergers: substantive assessment guidance*, OFT website, n.72, above, s.7.5.

substantive aspects, and is merely intended to pave the way for a final decision, a court may be reluctant to allow challenges to it, in order to avoid having to attempt to anticipate what final view will be adopted.[1] In terms of the intensity with which the CAT is likely to review procedural decisions of the Competition Commission, it was noted above that the principles of procedural fairness are generally regarded as being hard-edged, in the sense that the basic requirements of fairness are regarded as objective standards, suitable for the primary judgment of the court. On the other hand, there are also certain indications in the case law that it may be appropriate, in certain circumstances, for the review court to give some weight to the Competition Commission's own view as to what is fair. For example, in *R. v MMC Ex p. Stagecoach Holdings*, Collins J. stated:

"I entirely accept that the Court will be slow to intervene (in procedural matters). This is because regard must be had to the nature of the MMC and the knowledge that having directed itself properly on the requirements of fairness it will be unlikely that nonetheless it will be unfair. As Lloyd LJ said at page 184D (of *R. v Take-over Panel Ex p. Guinness PLC* [1991] Q.B. 146) the Court will give great weight to the tribunal's own view of what is fair. No doubt, this will mean that in the vast majority of cases the Court will be unlikely to regard what the MMC has reasonably believed to be fair as unfair ..."[2]

At the very least, when assessing the fairness of a particular aspect of the Competition Commission's procedure, the CAT should obviously have regard to how that aspect fits into the procedure as a whole, and take into account, for example, the additional opportunities that the parties will have to respond to the case against it.

6–072 **Whether a relevant merger situation has or will be created.** Sections 35(6) and 36(5) of the Enterprise Act expressly provide that references under ss.22 or 33 may be framed so as to exclude the need for the Competition Commission to consider whether a relevant merger situation has or will be created. It may be that, in relation to many mergers, that issue is uncontroversial, and the reference will be worded accordingly. In any event, it seems unlikely that this issue is likely to lie at the heart of many applications for review brought against the Competition Commission. If there is an issue in relation to this criterion, it is far more likely that a challenge would be brought at an earlier stage against the OFT's reference.

---

[1] See, for example, in a European context, case 60/81 *IBM v Commission* [1981] E.C.R. 2639 at 2651–2655.
[2] *The Times*, July 23, 1996, QBD.

The nature of the substantial lessening of competition test as applied by the   6–073
Competition Commission.   In relation to anticipated mergers, s.36(1) of the
Enterprise Act provides as follows:

> "(1) Subject to subsections (5) and (6) and section 127(3), the Commis-
> sion shall, on a reference under section 33, decide the following
> questions—
>
> > (a) whether arrangements are in progress or in contemplation
> > which, if carried into effect, will result in the creation of a
> > relevant merger situation; and
> > (b) if so, whether the creation of that situation may be expected to
> > result in a substantial lessening of competition within any
> > market or markets in the UK for goods or services.

The wording of the question in subs.(b) relating to a substantial lessening of
competition differs subtly from that which the OFT has to ask under s.33,[3]
as the latter refers to the OFT's belief and includes the "double may"
referred to in the *IBA* case.[4] In *IBA,* the Court of Appeal referred to the test
that the Competition Commission had to apply by way of contrast to that
facing the OFT, and two things are clear from its comments. First, that,
unlike the OFT, the Competition Commission is not concerned with its
belief, but rather simply has to decide the matter.[5] Secondly, that the term
"may be expected to result" involves a degree of likelihood amounting to an
expectation, which may crudely be expressed as a more than 50 per cent
chance.[6] That is the position reflected in the Competition Commission
Guidelines, which state that: ". . . it will not be sufficient for the Commission
to believe that an SLC is possible: for the Commission to reach an adverse
decision either the merger must have resulted in an SLC or the Commission
must expect such a result. The Commission will usually have such an
expectation if it considers that it is more likely than not that the SLC will
result".

Challenging a report of the Competition Commission on the basis that it   6–074
incorrectly applied the substantial lessening of competition test.   Application
of the substantial lessening of competition test will require the Competition
Commission to ask itself several different questions and carry out several
different types of analysis. The appropriate ground of review for an applicant challenging the Competition Commission's conclusions in relation to
the substantial lessening of competition test, and the intensity with which
the court will apply the review principles, will depend on the nature of the
reasoning being attacked and the considerations affecting the intensity of

---

[3] See para.6–063, above.
[4] See para.6–066, above.
[5] At paras 47 and 82.
[6] At paras 46 and 81.

review set out above.[7] If, however, the CAT accepts that the Competition Commission did not make an error of law, and the sole issue is whether the Competition Commission erred in applying the law to the facts, it is arguable that the appropriate intensity of review ought not to be high. This in part follows from the proposition set out by Lord Hoffman in *Moyna v Secretary of State for Work and Pensions* that the question of whether the facts as found fall one side or the other of some conceptual line drawn by the law is generally considered to be a question of fact.[8] Also, many of the relevant questions are likely to be of an economic nature, requiring the exercise of expert judgment, and in relation to which there is no clear answer. Finally, and unlike the OFT, which has to make its reference decision in a very short timeframe and rely to a considerable extent on the submissions of the parties, the Competition Commission ought, assuming that it has satisfactorily followed its own procedures, to have gathered and analysed a great deal of evidence and had the opportunity to give its full attention to the various competition issues arising. All of those reasons suggest that the CAT may be reluctant to overturn the conclusions of the Competition Commission unless they are outside the bounds of reasonable judgment.

6–075 **Challenging the Competition Commission's conclusions as to remedies.** In addition to deciding the substantial lessening of competition issue, the Competition Commission also has to decide various questions in relation to remedies. In relation to anticipated mergers, ss.36(2) to (4) of the Enterprise Act provide as follows:

> "(2) The Commission shall, if it has decided on a reference under section 33 that there is an anti-competitive outcome (within the meaning given by section 35(2)(b)), decide the following additional questions—
>
> (a) whether action should be taken by it under section 41(2) for the purpose of remedying, mitigating or preventing the substantial lessening of competition concerned or any adverse effect which may be expected to result from the substantial lessening of competition;
>
> (b) whether it should recommend the taking of action by others for the purpose of remedying, mitigating or preventing the substantial lessening of competition concerned or any adverse effect which may be expected to result from the substantial lessening of competition; and
>
> (c) in either case, if action should be taken, what action should be taken and what is to be remedied, mitigated or prevented.

---

[7] paras 6–044–6–056, above.
[8] [2003] 1 W.L.R. 1929 at para.24.

(3) In deciding the questions mentioned in subsection (2) the Commission shall, in particular, have regard to the need to achieve as comprehensive a solution as is reasonable and practicable to the substantial lessening of competition and any adverse effects resulting from it.

(4) In deciding the questions mentioned in subsection (2) the Commission may, in particular, have regard to the effect of any action on any relevant customer benefits in relation to the creation of the relevant merger situation concerned."

As was recognised by the High Court in *Interbrew*,[9] the issue of whether a particular remedy would be effective in the post-merger market may be a matter upon which more than one view could be held, with the consequence that the court should not be quick to overturn the Competition Commission's assessment. As was also recognised by the court in *Interbrew*, where only one remedy is capable of remedying or preventing the identified competitive harm, the position is likely to be straightforward. Where, however, more than one remedy may be suitable, questions of proportionality are likely to arise, in particular where Art.1 of the First Protocol is engaged (*e.g.* where the Competition Commission decides in favour of divestment), or the merger has been referred back to the UK under Art.9 of the EC Merger Regulation.[10] The potential relevance of the principle of proportionality in this context is acknowledged by the Competition Commission in its merger reference guidelines, which state:

"The Commission will aim to ensure that no remedy is disproportionate in relation to the SLC or other adverse effect. If the Commission is choosing between two remedies which it considers would be equally effective, it will choose the remedy that imposes the least cost or that is least restrictive."[11]

Finally, as was the case in *Interbrew*, decisions as to the appropriate remedy will also be capable of being challenged on the basis of a failure to respect the applicant's rights to a fair procedure.

(f) Decisions taken by the Secretary of State

Limited role. One of the objectives of the new merger regime is to make the   6–076
process more objective, and to limit the potential for political influence.
Consequently, the role for the Secretary of State in the Part 3 process is

---

[9] *R. (on the application of Interbrew SA) v Competition Commission* [2001] U.K.C.L.R. 954; [2001] EWHC Admin 367.
[10] As to which, see para.6–046, above.
[11] *Merger references: Competition Commission guidelines*, n.73, above, para.4.9.

limited. The main way in which the Secretary of State could become involved is based on the possibility that he or she could intervene in relation to mergers raising public interest considerations. Sections 42 to 58 of the Enterprise Act deal with public interest cases. It may be noted, however, that although the possibility exists for specifying additional considerations, the only public interest consideration currently specified in s.58 is the interests of national security. However, if and when intervention by the Secretary of State is challenged by an applicant, it seems likely that the intensity of the CAT's review will be relatively low. This is in part because of the wording of the relevant sections, which is generally in terms of whether the Secretary of State believes that it is or may be the case that a public interest consideration is relevant to consideration of the relevant merger situation.[12] Additionally, however, a decision to intervene will inevitably be driven by policy considerations (indeed, as it currently stands, by considerations of national security), in relation to which the Secretary of State has a margin of discretion.

7. THE REVIEW OF MARKET INVESTIGATION REFERENCES UNDER PART 4 OF THE ENTERPRISE ACT 2002

6–077 **Overview.** Part 4 of the Enterprise Act provides for a system of market references allowing for the investigation of markets in which it appears that competition is prevented, restricted or distorted, but where there has been no obvious breach of Chapters I or II of the Competition Act or Arts 81 or 82 of the EC Treaty. As in the case of Part 3 of the Enterprise Act, it is the OFT[13] that will normally make a decision to refer a market investigation, with the reference being investigated in depth by the Competition Commission. Provision is also made for the possibility of references being made by Ministers, but it is intended that such cases will be rare. A detailed discussion of the relevant provisions is outside the scope of this chapter, but the following sections make a few brief comments on the core provisions in the light of the fact that it is possible for parties to bring an application under s.179 for a review of decisions taken under Part 4 in connection with a reference or possible reference by the CAT. As to the likely approach of the CAT on review, much will depend on the nature of the decision or issue under challenge. The factors set out above in relation to the intensity with which the principles of judicial review are applied are likely to be relevant,[14] as are many of the considerations set out in relation to reviews of decisions taken under Part 3. As to further information about how the Part 4

---

[12] Although such belief will obviously be subject to scrutiny along the lines of the approach in the *Tameside* case; see para.6–067, above.
[13] Or the sectoral regulators.
[14] See paras 6–044–6–056, above.

provisions are likely to be operated, the following are helpful sources of information:

(1) the Explanatory Notes to the Enterprise Act 2002[15];

(2) the OFT publication *Market investigation references: guidance about the making of references under Part 4 of the Enterprise Act*[16]; and

(3) the Competition Commission publication *Market investigation references: Competition Commission Guidelines.*[17]

OFT reference decisions. The basic provision is found in s.131(1) of the Enterprise Act, which provides: **6–078**

"(1) The OFT may, subject to subsection (4), make a reference to the Commission if the OFT has reasonable grounds for suspecting that any feature, or combination of features, of a market in the United Kingdom for goods or services prevents, restricts or distorts competition in connection with the supply or acquisition of any goods or services in the United Kingdom or a part of the United Kingdom."

For those considering challenging a reference decision, it should be noted that, in order for it to have the power to make a reference, the OFT merely needs to have "reasonable grounds for suspecting" that the terms of the provision are satisfied. The "reasonable grounds for suspecting" requirement is a less stringent requirement than one to "believe" that a certain situation exists. Consequently, the OFT may make a reference even if it cannot be said that it is more likely than not that competition is prevented, restricted or distorted (*i.e.* the relevant percentage is less than 50 per cent). The OFT's guidelines set out in considerable detail how the OFT intends to interpret the statutory test. On the basis of s.131(1), even if the OFT has reasonable grounds to suspect that the test is met, it has a discretion as to whether or not to make a reference. The OFT's guidelines state it will not make a reference unless each of the following four criteria are met:

"(i)   it would not be more appropriate to deal with the competition issues identified by applying CA98 or using other powers available to the OFT, or, where appropriate, to sectoral regulators;

(ii)   it would not be more appropriate to address the problem identified by means of undertakings in lieu of a reference;

(iii) the scale of the suspected problem, in terms of its adverse effect on

---

[15] Available on the HMSO website, *www.hmso.gov.uk.*
[16] Available on the OFT website, n.72, above.
[17] Available on the Competition Commission website, n.73, above.

competition, is such that a reference would be an appropriate response to it; and

(iv) there is a reasonable chance that appropriate remedies will be available."[18]

6–079 **Competition Commission reports.** Once a reference is made, s.134(1) of the Enterprise Act provides:

"(1) The Commission shall, on a market investigation reference, decide whether any feature, or combination of features, of each relevant market prevents, restricts or distorts competition in connection with the supply or acquisition of any goods or services in the United Kingdom or part of the United Kingdom."

The Competition Commission must normally publish its report within two years of the date of the reference.[19] The Commission's guidelines set out how the Commission will normally approach market investigation references, including that it will normally frame the reference in terms of two related issues, namely identification of the relevant market, and assessment of competition in the market.[20] Following its assessment of competition in the market, s.134(4) provides:

"(4) The Commission shall, if it has decided on a market investigation reference that there is an adverse effect on competition, decide the following additional questions—

(a) whether action should be taken by it under s. 138 for the purpose of remedying, mitigating or preventing the adverse effect on competition concerned or any detrimental effect on customers so far as it has resulted from, or may be expected to result from, the adverse effect on competition;

(b) whether it should recommend the taking of action by others for the purpose of remedying, mitigating or preventing the adverse effect on competition concerned or any detrimental effect on customers so far as it has resulted from, or may be expected to result from, the adverse effect on competition; and

(c) in either case, if action should be taken, what action should be taken and what is to be remedied, mitigated or prevented."

As in the case of merger references, issues may arise in respect of the appropriateness of remedies.[21]

---

[18] *Market investigation references: guidance about the making of references under Part 4 of the Enterprise Act*, para.2.1.
[19] s.137(1).
[20] para.1.21.
[21] In relation to which, see para.4.10f of *Market investigation references: Competition Commission Guidelines*.

CHAPTER 7

DAMAGES IN COMPETITION LAW LITIGATION

Daniel Beard[1]

1. BACKGROUND

The desire for damages.   It is often more than just the $64,000 question: can   **7–001**
we get damages? If you are a company who feels that you have suffered
because of somebody else's anti-competitive behaviour, it will be good that a
regulator intervenes to stop the infringing conduct. It may be even more
satisfying to see the infringer suffer a swingeing fine. But that sort of
schadenfreude does not show up on the balance sheet. It is no financial
consolation to you to see a rival paying money to the Treasury or the EC
Commission. What would be a much more substantial direct benefit would
be if you could recover money from the infringer.

No specific competition law provisions on damages.   Nothing in the EC   **7–002**
Treaty specifies that damages should be available to those who suffer
because of breaches of competition law. Similarly, no specific provision was
inserted in the Competition Act 1998 giving a right to damages or imposing
an obligation to make reparation on those in breach. This position is in
stark contrast to that prevailing in the US where private damages claims
play a key part in the enforcement of US antitrust (competition) rules. The
availability of treble damages there indicates just how seriously anti-trust is
taken by law makers.

The end of (an) argument.   For years many practitioners and academics   **7–003**
have argued that damages should be available to right the wrongs of anti-
competitive behaviour. Many referred to the judgment of Lord Diplock in
Garden Cottage Foods Ltd v Milk Marketing Board[2] where his Lordship
indicated that a breach of Art.86 EC should sound as a breach of statutory
duty in domestic law and that, as such, an action for damages should be

---

[1] Barrister, Monckton Chambers.
[2] [1984] 1 A.C. 130 especially at 141 and 144.

available. However, until the European Court of Justice's judgment in *Crehan v Courage*[3] there was no ruling of a Community or domestic court that stated definitively that competition damages should be available.

7–004 **Crehan.** *Crehan* concerned a claim by a pub tenant that the agreement he had concluded with his brewery landlord was anti-competitive and contrary to Art.81 of the EC Treaty. He alleged that the terms on which he had to deal with the brewery were too onerous and, in particular, tied him into buying expensive beer. Not only did he dispute the validity of the agreement but he also wanted damages.

7–005 **Previous English authority.** The difficulty for Mr Crehan was that in a series of previous cases, including proceedings before the Court of Appeal,[4] these types of claims had failed. The courts had held that as a party to the anti-competitive agreement people like Mr Crehan had acted unlawfully and were not entitled to rely on their own illegality to claim damages. But despite the overwhelming domestic authority against him Crehan's claim was not dismissed. The Court of Appeal was persuaded that the English courts' rulings may have been in breach of Community law. And so the Court of Appeal sought the advice of the ECJ.

7–006 **The conclusion of the ECJ.** The European Court concluded that the previous Court of Appeal judgments had been wrong. It held that English courts must protect an individual's rights derived from Community competition law. It also emphasised the importance of private actions in enforcing competition law. Making damages available to a party to a prohibited and illegal agreement gives an incentive for it to go to court to stop the anti-competitive arrangements.

7–007 **Effect in domestic law.** Section 60 of the Competition Act requires UK courts and authorities to follow decisions of the ECJ. As a result, although there has not to date been a judgment confirming the availability of damages in respect of infringements of the Chapter I and Chapter II prohibitions, it is generally accepted that as a matter of principle damages are also available in respect of such infringements. In the remainder of this chapter, comments relating to the EC law prohibitions should be treated as equally applicable to the domestic law prohibitions unless otherwise indicated.

2. WHERE TO BRING THE CLAIM

7–008 **Use national courts.** Even if you are concerned with breaches of Community law, damages claims must be brought in the domestic courts of the Member States. Although EC law provides rights and protection, remedies

---

[3] Case C–453/99 [2001] E.C.R. I–6297; [2001] 5 C.M.L.R. 28.
[4] *Gibbs Mew v Gemmell* [1998] Eu. L.R. 588, CA (Civ Div).

must be provided by and under national law. That means you do not try to bring competition law damages claims against other private parties in the Community courts: the European Court of Justice or the Court of First Instance. If you are dealing with domestic competition law, any damages claims should be brought in the national courts.

England and Wales: Chancery division. In England and Wales, the relevant court is the High Court. CPR Practice Direction B12 requires that any party whose statement of case raises or deals with an issue relating to the application of Art.81 or Art.82 of the EC Treaty must either commence proceedings in or apply for their transfer to the Chancery Division of the High Court.[5] There has been a programme of judicial training undertaken by Chancery Division judges in order to enable them to gain experience of competition law matters and indeed they are now permitted to sit in the CAT. Although there is no specific practice direction governing the listing of competition claims brought in relation to domestic competition law, given the similarities between the domestic and EC regimes, it is expected that listing of such cases will also be most appropriate in the Chancery Division. — 7–009

UK: "follow on claim"—CAT after infringement decision. Following the Enterprise Act, a damages claim may be brought not only in the High Court but also in the CAT if there has already been an infringement decision by the OFT or the European Commission. Section 47A of the Competition Act provides that the CAT is able to hear damages claims in cases where an adverse finding has been made under the Chapters I or II prohibitions or Arts 81 or 82 EC and the claim arises from that infringement. — 7–010

Other jurisdictions and consolidation in the UK. Of course, if you are concerned with an infringement which involves or has affected parties in a number of jurisdictions questions as to the most appropriate jurisdiction in which to bring any claim will arise. The possibility of bringing claims outside England and Wales and, in particular, the conflicts of laws rules which might be applicable are outside the scope of this chapter. It is to be noted, however, that in *Provimi v Aventis*[6]—an interim application relating to a damages claim brought in the High Court following a decision by the EC Commission that various vitamins producers were part of a cartel contrary to Art.81 EC—parties which were based overseas (in particular in Germany) and had bought from German subsidiaries of the cartel members were allowed to consolidate their claims with those of UK buyers who had purchased vitamins from UK based cartel subsidiaries. This approach makes a great deal of sense in terms of reducing costs and minimizing the risk of inconsistent judgments. Nonetheless, it may surprise many that — 7–011

---

[5] B12, Rule 2.1.
[6] [2003] EWHC 961 (Comm).

companies based outside the UK and dealing outside the UK can have their damages claims heard in the UK.[7]

3. WHEN TO BRING THE CLAIM

7–012   **Limitation:**   Undertakings will need to be aware that the time limits for bringing claims for damages differ depending on whether the proceedings are commenced in the CAT or in the Chancery Division of the High Court.

Damages claims to the CAT under s.47A of the Competition Act must be brought within two years of the expiry of the period for appealing the OFT/EC Commission decision relied upon.[8] Otherwise, the time limit in which to institute proceedings is determined by the limitation period of six years for tort damages determined by s.2 of the Limitation Act 1980. The time limit starts on the date the wrongful act caused the damage in issue, subject to fraudulent concealment.[9]

4. BASIS OF A CLAIM IN THE UK COURTS

7–013   **Breach of statutory duty.**   The fact that damages may, in principle, be claimed in respect of infringements of competition law does not resolve the question of how such claims are to be brought. Although the matter has been the subject of some debate, it now appears clear that a claim can be brought as a breach of statutory duty claim in tort.[10] However, it is noted that in the first damages claim to come before the CAT,[11] Sir Christopher Bellamy QC, President of the CAT, questioned whether:

"claims arising from infringement of the 1998 Act, or of Community Law are strictly speaking in the nature of damages in a way analogous to an action for tort or whether they can be looked at in some other way, for example, as some kind of claim that could perhaps go under the general heading of " 'unjust enrichment'...".

7–014   **Ingredients.**   In claims for breach of statutory duty it is necessary first to establish that the breach of a statutory standard gives rise to an action in private law. If that can be shown, a claimant must show that:

---

[7] See also, Mark Furse "Provimi v Aventis: damages and jurisdiction" [2003] Comp. Law 119. The ruling is also of particular interest in relation to the extent to which exclusive jurisdiction clauses operate *vis-à-vis* competition damages claims.

[8] s.7A(6). See paras 4–083–4–108, above.

[9] s.32 of the Limitation Act 1980.

[10] See *Crehan v Inntrepreneur* [2004] EWCA Civ 637 at para.156. This had previously been thought to be the case following *Garden Cottage Foods Ltd v Milk Marketing Board* [1984] A.C. 130.

[11] *BCL Old Co Ltd v Aventis* and *Deans Foods v Roche Products Ltd* Cases 1028/5/7/04 & 1029/5/7/04, judgment of July 26, 2004. The claims were subsequently settled.

(a) the damage suffered falls within the ambit of the statute;

(b) the statutory duty was breached;

(c) the breach caused the loss; and

(d) there are no applicable defences.

(a) EC law

Breach of Articles 81 or 82 EC. In assessing whether the breach of a   **7–015**
particular statutory standard gives rise to a private law claim it is ordinarily
necessary to consider what the intention of parliament was in respect of the
breach of the duty. However, in the light of the ECJ judgment in *Crehan* it is
unnecessary to consider the nature of parliamentary intent in enacting the
European Communities Act 1972 (which brought into English law the
competition law provisions of the EC Treaty). Since the ECJ has concluded
that persons who have suffered loss by reason of the breach of Community
law must, in principle, be able to claim compensation means that domestic
procedure—whether using the mechanism of breach of statutory duty or
otherwise—must permit such a claim.

Modification of the ingredients. It is notable that when, following the   **7–016**
decision of the ECJ in the matter, Mr Crehan's case came back before the
English courts, the Court of Appeal found that the ordinary constraints of
the breach of statutory duty tort could not confound a claim for damages
(see *Crehan v Inntrepreneur*[12] at para.167). It was argued for Inntrepreneur
that even if Crehan had shown a breach of Art.81 EC it was at the distribution level of trade, not the retail level, at which Mr Crehan operated
and in respect of which he claimed losses. The court recognised that as a
matter of English law a claimant for damages for breach of statutory duty
had to show, not only that a duty was owed to him, but also that it was a
duty in respect of the kind of loss he has suffered.[13] It was contended that
since the only unlawful distortion of competition occurred at the distribution level, loss at a retail level was not loss against which Mr Crehan was
protected by Art.81 EC. Thus damages for breach of statutory duty could
not be claimed by him. The Court of Appeal rejected that suggestion.
Although it was recognised that this analysis was correct as a matter of
English law, to apply the English requirements for a breach of statutory
duty would be contrary to the principle of effectiveness in Community law
i.e. domestic procedure must not render the vindication of Community
rights practically ineffective. So Mr Crehan could make his claim.[14]

---

[12] n.10, above.
[13] See para.156 of *South Australia Asset Management v Milk Marketing Board* [1984] A.C. 130
at 141 *per* Lord Diplock.
[14] At the time of writing, the case is on appeal to the House of Lords.

7-017   **Effect of _Crehan_.** The European Court's judgment in _Crehan_ (and its application in the domestic courts) makes it clear that two of the essential requirements of the tort are satisfied: any loss suffered is within the scope of the statute; and the statute[15] gives rise to a civil cause of action. In each case it will therefore remain necessary for a claimant to establish that there has been a breach of statutory duty and that the breach caused the loss complained of, that is, the damage would not have occurred but for the breach.

(b) Domestic law

7-018   **Availability of claims intended.** In respect of domestic competition law, there is no real doubt that Parliament intended there to be available an actionable right of damages in respect of the Chapter I and II prohibitions in a form analogous to that in respect of Arts 81 and 82 EC. At the time the Competition Bill was passing through Parliament, the promoter of the Bill, Lord Simon said:

> "[I]t is an important part of the new regime that businesses and consumers who have been seriously harmed by anti-competitive behaviour should be able to seek redress. To that end, we are including provisions to facilitate rights of private action in the courts for damages."[16]

In addition, the drafters of the Competition Act left what have been referred to as "footprints" in the text indicating the expectation that damages claims could be brought in respect of infringements of the prohibitions. These footprints have become rather clearer indications since the amendment of the Act by the Enterprise Act so that s.47A specifically countenances such claims. In any event, there would have been a strong argument that the effect of s.60 of the Competition Act was to ensure that damages claims should be available if they were available in respect of breaches of EC competition law.[17]

7-019   **Modification of the ingredients?** There is an interesting point as to whether an argument such as that rejected by the Court of Appeal in _Crehan_ about the extent to which a defendant could rely on the formal constraints of the breach of statutory duty cause of action could be run in a purely domestic law claim. To put the argument another way: does s.60 mean that the criteria for obtaining damages in domestic law are conditioned by a "principle of effectiveness" as they will be in relation to EC law even though no such principle exists or is necessary in domestic law? If different criteria

---

[15] In this case Art.81 EC incorporated into UK law by virtue of s.2 of the European Communities Act 1972.
[16] HL 2R 30, col.1148 (October 1997).
[17] Note in this context the reasoning of the CAT in _Pernod-Ricard v OFT_ [2004] CAT 10 at paras 229–238 relating to the scope and impact of s.60 of the Competition Act.

applied to domestic law claims, it would create the anomalous situation that claims for damages on certain bases (such as those brought by Mr Crehan) would not succeed at a domestic level in respect of provisions which were identical in terms to those under which the claim could succeed at Community level. That would seem to run contrary to the spirit of the Competition Act and the modernised, decentralised EC competition enforcement regime.[18]

Availability of the claim only the start.   The fact that damages claims can be brought by way of breach of statutory duty claims is, of course, only the start of the process of obtaining damages. It is necessary still to prove infringement, loss and causation of loss apart from considering certain of the public policy issues discussed below.

7–020

EC law in national courts: equivalence and effectiveness

Articles 81 and 82 EC are directly effective: individuals can rely upon them directly in proceedings. The principle of direct effect enables individuals to protect the rights they are given by Community law in national proceedings. It encourages the enforcement of Community law in national courts. The domestic courts are obliged to apply effective provisions of Community law and must give them precedence over conflicting rules of domestic law: Community law is supreme.

But, even if substantive Community law rights are "trumps", how, in practice, are they to be vindicated in domestic proceedings? The starting point is that national courts are to use national procedural tools to protect the Community law rights. This is known as the principle of "national procedural autonomy".[19] However, it can easily be foreseen that this principle could be problematic since different procedural regimes in different Member States could potentially result in vastly differing levels of protection of the Community rights.[20]

As a result, the European Court of Justice has ruled that there are two important limitations upon the principle of national procedural autonomy[21]:

- the principle of equivalence: national rules governing the application of EC rules must not be less favourable than those relating to similar claims of a domestic nature; and

---

[18] The reasoning of the CAT in *Pernod-Ricard v OFT*, n.17, above, at paras 229–238 of its judgment would militate in favour of the same approach being adopted in relation to the Competition Act as in relation to EC law.

[19] See, for example, Case C–33/76 *Rewe-Zentral Finanz eg and Rewe-Zentral AG v Landwirtscheftskammer fur das Saarland* [1976] E.C.R. 1989 at 1997.

[20] For an assessment of the current position, see the survey commissioned by the EC Commission on private enforcement in Member States at *http://europa.eu.int*.

[21] *ibid.*

- the principle of effectiveness: national procedural rules may not make it virtually impossible or excessively difficult to exercise the EC right that the national courts are obliged to protect.

The second principle in particular has been of great significance in ensuring that claimants with bona fide EC claims are not stymied in their attempts to bring such claims by national procedures which were not developed with such claims in mind.

5. WHO CAN CLAIM?

7–021 **Two categories of potential claimant.** There are, broadly, two categories of potential claimants who could allege actionable damage against infringing undertakings: third parties and parties to the infringing anti-competitive behaviour.

(a) Third parties

7–022 **Potential third party claimants *vis-à-vis* Chapter I or Article 81 EC.** A third party who has not been party to the infringing agreement or concerted practice but has suffered due to undertakings entering into anti-competitive arrangements may be able to bring a claim against the infringing parties under either the Chapter I prohibition or Art.81 EC, depending upon the extent of the effects of the infringement. Where there is some issue as to whether the infringement involves an effect on interstate trade it will be sensible to plead each in the alternative.[22] If we take the simple example of a price-fixing cartel, we can identify at least five categories of persons who might potentially claim that they have suffered loss which should be compensated. The diagram illustrates those categories:

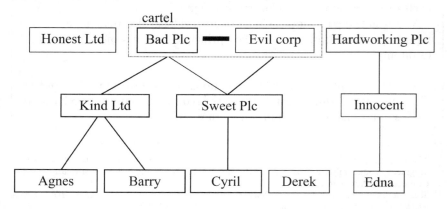

---

[22] This may also be the case if different exemption or exclusion provisions might apply under the domestic and EC regimes.

Direct purchasers. It is clear that direct customers of the cartel who paid   **7–023**
the inflated prices—Kind and Sweet—would have a claim against the cartel
members. The injury they would appear to suffer is the difference between
what they actually paid for the products and what they would otherwise
have paid if the unlawful behaviour had not occurred. In addition, if, as a
result of the inflated purchase prices, these direct customers sold on at
higher prices than they otherwise would have sold on at, they may have
suffered an additional loss of profit due to loss of additional sales to price
sensitive customers of theirs.

Indirect purchasers. As well as direct purchasers from the cartel members,   **7–024**
it is possible that so-called "indirect purchasers"—Agnes, Barry and Cyril
may also have suffered injury because of the cartel's behaviour. Because the
cartel charged higher prices to its direct purchasers, they, in turn, may have
increased their prices to their own customers who therefore bore or shared
the injury that would otherwise be suffered exclusively by the direct purchaser. The implications of these sorts of injury and the scope for claiming
damages in respect of them are considered further below.

Potential purchasers. There is, of course, another category of persons who   **7–025**
may have suffered loss because of the higher prices. Those are the potential
customers who would have bought the goods had they been sold at a
competitive price but did not do so because they considered them too
expensive—Innocent and, possibly, Derek. They will either have bought less
desirable substitute goods or simply reduced their total purchases.

Competitors. Apart from customers, competitors to infringing under-   **7–026**
takings—Honest and Hardworking—may also suffer losses. Obviously,
where the cartel is a price fixing cartel, non-participating competitors might
struggle to show any loss but other forms of infringing behaviour (in particular, exclusionary conduct) may well cause injury to competitors both
actual and potential.

Purchasers from non-conspirators. On the other hand, if the effect of the   **7–027**
cartel is to raise prices such that non-conspirator competitors such as
Honest and Hardworking also raise their prices above that which would
exist in a competitive market, it may be that their customers (such as Edna)
may want to make a claim against the cartel member companies.

Suppliers. In addition, moving further back up the supply chain, suppliers   **7–028**
to cartel members (not illustrated) may suffer loss by reason of the cartel
because they may lose sales or income due to the artificial reduction in
output caused by the cartel.

Similar range of potential claimants re: Chapter II and Article 82 EC. The   **7–029**
range of potential third party claimants against a dominant undertaking (or
jointly dominant undertakings) is similar to that who might contend that
they have suffered loss by reason of the operation of a cartel.

(b) Parties to anti-competitive arrangements

7–030   *In pari delicto?*   A far more vexed question is whether a party to an anti-competitive arrangement can bring a claim against another party to the same arrangement. In a series of cases,[23] principally concerning exclusive beer supply agreements, the English courts (both at first instance and, in some cases, on appeal) had held that a party to an agreement contrary to Art.81(1) EC could not sue the other party for loss that the first party had sustained due to the inclusion of the infringing provisions. Broadly, the courts held that a party could not rely on its own illegality (the participation in the unlawful anti-competitive arrangement) in bringing its claim. To use the oft-cited Latin tag, the parties were considered by the courts to be *in pari delicto* and therefore neither could claim against the other.

7–031   **ECJ reference in *Crehan*.**   However, in the ECJ decision in *Crehan v Courage*, which related to five appeals against findings that claims could not be brought by parties to exclusive beer supply agreements, the Court of Appeal concluded that the following questions of EC law needed to be referred to the ECJ under the Art.234 (ex Art.177) procedure:

"1.   Is Article 81 EC (ex Article 85) to be interpreted as meaning that a party to a prohibited tied house agreement may rely upon that article to seek relief from the courts from the other contracting party?

2.   If the answer to Question 1 is yes, is the party claiming relief entitled to recover damages alleged to arise as a result of his adherence to the clause in the agreement which is prohibited under Article 81?

3.   Should a rule of national law which provides that Courts should not allow a person to plead and/or rely upon his own illegal actions as a necessary step to recovery of damages be allowed as consistent with Community law?

4.   If the answer to Question 3 is that in some circumstances such a rule may be inconsistent with Community law, what circumstances should the national court take into consideration?"[24]

---

[23] *Inntrepreneur Estates plc v Milne*, unreported, July 30, 1993, High Ct; *Inntrepreneur Estates plc v Smythe*, unreported, October 14, 1993, High Ct; *Greenalls Management Ltd v Canavan* [1998] Eu. L.R. 507, CA; *Matthew Brown plc v Campbell* [1998] Eu. L.R. 530, QBD; *Parkes v Esso Petroleum Co Ltd* [1998] EuLR 550, Ch D; *Trent Taverns v Sykes* [1998] EuLR 571, QBD; *Passmore v Morland plc* [1998] EuLR 580, Ch D; *Gibbs Mew v Gemmell* [1998] Eu. L.R. 588, CA.

[24] [1999] U.K.C.L.R. 407 at 412.

Perma Life Mufflers.   Crucial to the Court of Appeal's decision to refer the   **7–032**
questions was the US case of *Perma Life Mufflers Inc v International Parts
Corp.*[25] In that case, the Supreme Court held[26]:

> "There is nothing in the language of the Anti Trust Acts which indicates
> that Congress wanted to make the Common Law in *pari delicto* doctrine
> a defence to treble damages actions, and the facts of this case suggest no
> basis for applying such a doctrine even if it did exist. Although in *pari
> delicto* literally means 'of equal fault' the doctrine has been applied,
> correctly or incorrectly, in a wide variety of situations in which a plaintiff
> seeking damages or equitable relief is himself involved in some sort of
> wrong doing. We have often indicated the inappropriateness of invoking
> broad common law barriers to relief where a private suit serves important
> public purposes ... [past decisions] were premised on a recognition that
> the purposes of the Anti Trust laws are best served by ensuring that the
> private action will be an ever-present threat to deter any one con-
> templating business behaviour in violation of the Anti Trust Laws. The
> plaintiff who reaps the reward of treble damages may be no less morally
> reprehensible than the defendant, but the law encourages his suit to
> further the over-riding public policy in favour of competition."

In other words, enabling parties to anti-competitive arrangements to sue one
another is in the public interest because it encourages competition to be
maintained through a system of private policing and attendant deterrence. It
is notable, however, that the US courts have not ruled out the possibility of
in pari delicto operating as a defence (or, more accurately, a defense) where
the parties to the arrangement are equally culpable.[27]

ECJ reply.   The Opinion of A.G. Mishco in *Crehan* concluded that the UK   **7–033**
courts are mistaken in finding that, as a matter of principle, damages cannot
be available to parties to an anti-competitive agreement. The ECJ gave
judgment in the case on September 20, 2001 and followed the approach of
the Advocate General.[28] Damages are, therefore, available in principle even
to those who are parties to unlawful agreements. However, in reaching this
conclusion the ECJ made it clear that where a party bore "significant
responsibility" for the infringement it would not be entitled to claim
damages.

(c) Significant responsibility

ECJ criteria.   Precisely what constitutes "significant responsibility" is not   **7–034**

---

[25] 392 U.S. 134 (1968).
[26] At 138 *per* Black J. as cited in the order for reference in *Crehan v Courage* [1999] U.K.C.L.R. 407 at 411.
[27] See, for example, *Sullivan v Tagliabue* 34 F.3d 1091 (1st Cir. 1994).
[28] n.3, above.

something which the ECJ commented upon in any detail although it indicated that the economic and legal context in which the parties to an unlawful anti-competitive arrangement found themselves, their respective bargaining power and conduct will be relevant.[29]

7–035 **Relevant considerations.** It would seem that any party that encourages the agreement and the unlawful terms within it will have significant responsibility for the breach. If, for example, an agreement is reached on the standard terms of a party which is in a strong bargaining position and includes unlawfully restrictive provisions, that party would appear to bear significant responsibility for the infringement. Conversely, a party in an economically weaker bargaining position, particularly one which objected to the restrictive terms but reluctantly accepted them, would seem not to bear significant responsibility for the infringement.

7–036 **Assessment in *Crehan*.** In the case of Mr Crehan, the Court of Appeal concluded that he did not have significant responsibility for the unlawfully restrictive provisions of the beer tie arrangement to which he was a party.[30] Although Mr Crehan was free to enter into the tied house agreement—and, to that extent, had bargaining power—he was dealing with the single largest tied house owner in the UK who had made it clear that the offending terms of the agreement were not negotiable. The court concluded that "[t]here was no equality of bargaining power in any real sense" and that Mr Crehan was in a markedly weaker position than Inntrepreneur.

7–037 **Horizontal v vertical arrangements.** Although no specific distinction is made in the reasoning of the ECJ, the concept of "significant responsibility" would appear to be more likely to be of relevance in cases involving vertical agreements. In other words, where the parties to the arrangement are at different levels of the supply chain, *e.g.* manufacturer-wholesaler or distributor-retailer. In cases where parties are at the same level in the supply chain and are competitors (horizontal agreements), it would appear less likely that any party to an agreement will be able to contend that it did not bear significant responsibility for any restrictive provisions. In particular, it is to be expected that courts (including the Community courts) would be less likely to conclude that members of a cartel are entitled to bring claims for damages against one another on the basis that the claimant cartel member did not have significant responsibility for the unlawful restrictions.

---

[29] See paras 32–35 of the judgment.
[30] *Crehan v Inntrepeneur*, n.10, above, at para.153.

6. PROVING THE INFRINGEMENT

The basis for showing an infringement of one of the relevant provisions of competition law is considered in Chapter 2. Those issues are not rehearsed here.

"Piggy back" on a domestic infringement decision: section 58A. It is **7–038** important to note, however, that if the OFT has made a finding of infringement following an investigation, for the purposes of the damages claim that decision can be relied upon to prove the infringement pursuant to s.58A of the Competition Act. Such decisions can only be relied upon once the period for appealing them has lapsed or the appeal process has been completed.[31]

"Piggy back" on an EC Commission infringement decision. Although no **7–039** similar legislative provision is made in relation to Commission decisions, in the light of the decision of the ECJ in *Masterfoods*,[32] it is clear that the same rule applies in respect of Commission decisions. In that case the ECJ concluded:

"Where a national court is ruling on an agreement or practice the compatibility of which with Articles [81(1) and 82] of the EC Treaty is already the subject of a Commission decision, it cannot take a decision running counter to that of the Commission, even if the latter's decision conflicts with a decision given by a national court of first instance."

In the absence of any capacity to take a differing decision there seems no basis for contending that the Commission's finding of infringement should be diverged from by domestic courts. That it should not be open to a defendant to challenge in national damages proceedings the findings of infringement by the Commission was accepted by the High Court in *Iberian (UK) Ltd v BPB*[33] where Laddie J. stated, *inter alia*:

"... Of course due regard has to be paid to the interests of justice to the parties. But where, as here, the parties have disputed the same issues before the Commission and have had real and reasonable opportunities to appeal from an adverse decision, there is no injustice in obliging them to accept the result obtained in Europe. The position is a fortiori when, as here, the opportunities of appeal have been used to the full."

---

[31] s.58A(4).
[32] Case 344/98 *Masterfoods* [2000] E.C.R. I–11369; [2001] 4 C.M.L.R. 14.
[33] [1996] 2 C.M.L.R. 601.

The facts found by the Commission in its decision are not merely admissible but in these circumstances must be binding on the domestic court.

7. CAUSATION AND QUANTUM

7–040   **National procedural autonomy.** It is one thing for a person to consider that they have suffered by reason of the action of an infringer of competition law; it is another for a court to consider that that indignation should be recompensed. The principle of national procedural autonomy means that in considering issues of causation and quantum, it is appropriate first to apply the ordinary domestic rules applicable to claims of breach of statutory duty. Indeed, it has been accepted in cases where competition damages claims have been brought that "[i]t is common ground that questions of causation and remoteness of loss are governed by principles of English law."[34]

7–041   *Arkin.* That approach was adopted by the High Court in *Arkin v Borchard Lines Ltd (No.4)*[35] which concerned allegations that the operation of liner conferences (agreements between sea going cargo carriers as to uniform terms and rates) caused the collapse of a shipping group by acting in breach of Arts 81 and 82 EC. Although the comments of Coleman J. were, strictly, *obiter* since he had decided that there had been no infringement of competition law, he went on to consider the appropriate approach for causation and, in particular, whether the actions of the claimant were such as to prevent any putative infringement being causative of damage. The judge emphasised that the burden lay upon the claimant to prove that the defendant's unlawful conduct caused the claimed loss[36] and went on to say:

> "Where the issue is whether there was a break in the chain of causation by conduct on the part of the claimant, that is to say whether the effect of the defendant's conduct was more than to provide the opportunity for the claimant by his own deliberate act to cause himself loss, the approach must be one of commonsense, there being in each case an overarching concept that the chain of causation can be broken only if it is concluded that the claimant's own conduct displace that of the defendant *as the predominant cause of the claimant's loss.*"[37] [emphasis added]

7–042   **Traditional domestic analysis.** Domestic tort law analysis of causation has tended to focus on a two stage test: establishing factual causation and then considering whether the damage caused is too "remote" from the causative

---

[34] *Society of Lloyd's v John Stewart Clementson (No.2)*, unreported judgment of Cresswell J., May 7, 1996 at para.14, QBD.
[35] [2003] EWHC 687 (Comm).
[36] At para.536.
[37] At para.536.

action to warrant protection or, more particularly, recompense. Clerk and Lindsell[38] describes the application of this two stage approach as follows:

"the first stage looks to see what concrete evidence exists to link the defendant's wrongdoing to the harm of which the claimant complains. ... The second stage ... is not strictly concerned with causation but with the limits of legal responsibility for damage which has undoubtedly been caused by the defendant. Even where it is patent that the defendant's conduct caused the claimant's loss the question remains whether the defendant should be held responsible for all the consequences flowing from his wrongdoing."

Applying the two stage test in competition cases. Whether and, if so, to what extent the second limb of the traditional causation test—remoteness—will be relevant or add to causation analysis in the context of competition law damages claims is unclear. If factual causation of loss by reason of infringement can be made out, it might appear from the reasoning of the ECJ in *Crehan*[39] that enabling compensation for such loss is an appropriate and necessary part of domestic procedure; it is necessary to ensure the vindication of directly effective rights. However, such reasoning might be criticised since (a) it is unclear that what the ECJ envisaged was that national procedure should ensure that any loss—however small—should potentially found a claim for compensation; and (b) allowing such recovery might appear to reduce the deterrent effect of private enforcement—an important consideration for the ECJ in its reasoning in *Crehan*. **7–043**

8. PASSING ON AND INDIRECT PURCHASERS

The diagram below illustrates how passing on operates and the nature of indirect purchasers. Gigantic Plc is dominant and has abused its dominance by charging excessive prices to Onthechin Ltd and Throughput Ltd. Onthechin, lives up to its name and takes a hit on the high prices, it maintains its prices to its own customers (Agnes and Barry) whilst losing profitability. Throughput acts differently, it passes the price increase straight on to its customers. In doing so, it charges higher prices, maintains its profits on each sale (for example, to Cyril) but loses customers (such as Derek) who are not willing to pay the high prices. **7–044**

Onthechin Ltd and Throughput Ltd are direct purchasers from the infringer. Agnes, Barry and Cyril are indirect purchasers. Derek would have been an indirect purchaser if the price had been lower. Agnes and Barry have not lost out by reason of the higher prices and cannot have any claim. Their supplier, Onthechin, may have a claim for loss of profit against

---

[38] *Clerk and Lindsell on Torts* (18th ed., Sweet & Maxwell, London), paras 2–03–2–04.
[39] See above paras 7–006 and 7–031–7–033, above.

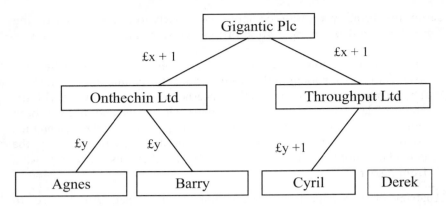

Gigantic. More interesting is the situation involving Throughput. Throughput has had to pay the higher price and so has, on the face of it suffered loss. However, it has, at least notionally, recovered that loss insofar as the sales it makes are concerned—its profits remain the same. Can Throughput claim damages against Gigantic in relation to the purchases it sells on or can Gigantic plead in its defence to any claim that Throughput has "passed on" the loss to its customers? Equally, can Cyril claim damages against Gigantic because he (and all of Throughputs other customers) paid higher prices because of Gigantic's conduct, *i.e.* can they claim for their losses as indirect purchasers from Gigantic?

(a) The US Federal Approach

7–045   *Illinois Brick.*   In US Federal anti-trust law the Supreme Court has stated in *Illinois Brick Co v Illinois*[40] that claims brought by *indirect* purchasers, *i.e.* purchasers who did not buy directly from the infringer, should generally be refused.[41] Although this general prohibition may seem harsh, it has a range of public policy benefits.

7–046   **Reasons for precluding indirect purchaser claims.**   First, it avoids a number of complex practical questions about "tracing" loss through transactions down the supply chain. Secondly, it avoids any difficult arguments about a criterion of remoteness being applied to damages claims, *i.e.* there is no discussion equivalent to the application of the traditional second stage in the English law causation inquiry. Further, it reduces the prospect of a defendant facing a multiplicity of claims and duplicate recovery. This latter issue must, however, be seen in the context of the fact that the US anti-trust enforcement system enables the recovery of treble damages, *i.e.* damages

---

[40] 431 U.S. 720 (1977).
[41] It should be noted, however, that certain exceptions to the *Illinois Brick* rule are recognised, for example, where there is a pre-existing, fixed-quantity, cost-plus contract between the first purchaser and the indirect purchaser.

three times the size of loss.[42] In other words, built into the system is a strong incentive for private parties to bring claims and a punitive dimension to awards against a defendant which go beyond a simple mechanism for the compensation of loss. In addition, any system that constrains claims can also reduce the process costs of litigation as well as reducing the risk of inconsistent judgments.

Hanover Shoe.   Alongside the rule that indirect purchasers should not be   7–047
able to sue in US Federal anti-trust law is the principle that defendants are not entitled to argue that a claimant does not have good claim because he has passed his loss on to his own customers. In *Hanover Shoe Inc v United Shoe Machinery Corp*,[43] the Supreme Court ruled that a direct purchaser from a monopolist is allowed to claim as damages the entirety of the unlawful overcharge which has been imposed no matter whether or not that overcharge has been passed on to others further down the value chain. The court recognised the problems and complexities of tracing the overcharge down the chain. It was explicitly acknowledged that to allow the operation of the passing on defence would reduce the deterrent effect of the private enforcement remedy.

Symmetry.   Thus, a certain symmetry is produced: the fact that loss has   7–048
been passed on to third parties may not be taken into account "defensively" in a claim between a seller and the purchaser and, generally, it should not be open to the indirect purchaser to use the passing on principle "offensively" in damages proceedings by making a claim for his loss.[44] Of course, the operation of the *Illinois Brick* and *Hanover Shoe* rules is to deprive indirect purchasers of a right to compensation whilst conferring a potential windfall on direct claimant purchasers. But could the UK courts adopt such an approach for similar policy reasons?[45]

(b) Passing on and indirect purchasers: approach of the UK courts

Reasons for allowing passing on defence.   There are a number of reasons   7–049
which might militate in favour of the UK courts accepting the passing on defence.

---

[42] Albeit that costs are not awarded in the US in the same way as they awarded to victorious parties in the UK and it is understood that pre-judgment interest is not awarded as a matter of routine.

[43] 392 U.S. 481 (1968).

[44] There are commentators who consider that this symmetry is not necessary in competition damages rules, *e.g.* a system could properly apply the Hanover Shoe rule but not Illinois Brick so that indirect purchasers could sue but no defensive use of passing on could be permitted. See Clifford Jones, *Private Enforcement of Antitrust Law in the EU, UK and USA* (OUP), especially Chapter 16.

[45] See also Mark Brealey QC, "Adopt Permalife but follow Hanover Shoe to Illinois?" [2002] Comp. Law 127.

7–050 **Nature of passing on "defence".** First, the defensive use of passing on, *i.e.* where a defendant contends that a claimant has passed his loss on to other customers, may be seen less as a defence in the strict sense and more as a part of the exercise of quantification of loss. In other words, it may be seen not as an impediment to the success of a claim so much as a measure of the claim itself. If, as indicated by the ECJ in *Crehan*,[46] the rationale for competition law damages claims is to provide compensation to those who have suffered loss due to infringement, it might be argued that, in principle, failing to recognise that someone has not lost a certain sum (because they have passed that loss on) would not be consistent with the underlying rationale for such claims in the first place. You cannot claim compensation for a loss that does not lie with you.

7–051 **Recognition in tax law.** Secondly, the passing on defence as such has been recognised in other areas of domestic law, in particular in relation to taxation. Where the state has imposed an unlawful tax on a person the courts have allowed the tax authorities to raise the passing on defence in the face of claims for repayment.[47]

7–052 **EC law approach.** Thirdly, it is clear from the case law, that EU law does not preclude the operation of a passing on "defence". More precisely, the ECJ has recognised that national rules which allow for such a defence to operate do not fall foul of the principles of effectiveness or equivalence.[48] In *Hans Just* the ECJ held:

> "25 ... In the absence of Community rules concerning the refunding of national charges which have been unlawfully levied, it is for the domestic legal system of each Member State to designate the courts having jurisdiction and to determine the procedural conditions governing actions at law intended to ensure the protection of the rights which subjects derive from the direct effect of Community law, it being understood that such conditions cannot be less favourable than those relating to similar actions of a domestic nature and that under no circumstances may they be so adapted as to make it impossible in practice to exercise the rights which the national courts are bound to protect.
>
> 26. It should be specified in this connection that the protection of rights guaranteed in the matter by Community law does not require an order for the recovery of charges improperly made to be granted in conditions

---

[46] n.3, above.
[47] See, for example, *Marks & Spencer v Commissioners for Customs & Excise* [1999] S.T.C. 205, (appeal [2000] 2 C.M.L.R. 256—issue not considered) and *CCE v National Westminster Bank* [2003] S.T.C. 1072.
[48] See, for example, Case 68/79 *Hans Just I/S v Danish Ministry for Fiscal Affairs* [1980] E.C.R. 501; [1981] 2 C.M.L.R. 714 and Case 199/82 *Amministrazione delle Finanze dello Stato v SpA San Georgio* [1983] E.C.R. 3595; [1985] 2 C.M.L.R. 658.

which would involve the unjust enrichment of those entitled. There is nothing, therefore, from the point of view of Community law, to prevent national courts from taking account in accordance with their national law of the fact that it has been possible for charges unduly levied to be incorporated in the prices of the undertaking liable for the charge and to be passed on to the purchasers...."

Effective compensation. Fourthly, if prohibiting a passing on defence was seen as the natural counterpart to a prohibition on indirect purchasers being able to bring claims, that might, itself, undermine the operation of the principle of effectiveness in relation to those potential claimants. In other words, a group of persons who suffered due to the infringement could not obtain compensation.

7–053

Against passing on. There are, however, a number of countervailing considerations which might militate against the domestic courts accepting a passing on defence:

7–054

Kleinwort Benson. First, there is very significant doubt that the availability of a passing on defence is recognised in domestic law outside the scope of tax cases or, perhaps more broadly, cases where there has been an unlawful imposition of a charge by the state.[48a] The Court of Appeal has explicitly rejected the existence of such a defence in the context of a claim for restitution of sums paid under a void contract. In *Kleinwort Benson v Birmingham City Council*[49] it was argued by the local authority (who had been the net beneficiary of a swap transaction) that the counterparty bank was not entitled to any money back once the swap deal was held to be void because the bank had taken specific steps to hedge against any loss which it might suffer under the swap contract. In other words, the bank had passed on any losses it might incur by entering into further hedging contracts. The court rejected this argument and held, *per* Evans L.J.[50]:

7–055

"If the payment was made for valuable consideration, then the payer did not suffer 'loss' even though the payment was made by him. But if it appears, as it did in the present case, that in law there was no consideration for it, then in that sense the payer has suffered loss. His pocket is emptier than it would have been if the money, or its value, was still there. But I would not give 'loss' any wider meaning than that. In particular, it seems to me that it would be inconsistent with the principle of repayment that 'loss' should be given some wider meaning equivalent to 'overall losses on the transaction', even if 'the transaction' could be sufficiently identified, or that the right to recover restitution should be

---

[48a] See para.7–051, above.
[49] [1997] Q.B. 380.
[50] At 393.

limited to the amount of 'loss' in that sense, though never increased above the amount of the payment.

. . .

If the claim is treated as limited to compensation for loss in fact suffered, taking account of related transactions which are not too remote from it, then in my judgment such hedge contracts as were entered into by the bank in the normal course of its business were 'too remote' to be taken into account. Market rates are taken into account when assessing damages because the plaintiff comes under a duty to mitigate his loss and it is presumed that he has done so by entering the market for that purpose. It is only in special cases that actual transactions are taken in to account: *R. Pagnan & Fratelli v. Corbisa Industrial Agropacuaria Limitada* [1970] 1 W.L.R. 1306. But here, there was no duty on the bank to hedge the risks to which it was exposed under the swaps contract, and its claim for restitution is not based on any wrongdoing or breach of contract by the authority."

Furthermore, the court reached its conclusions having regard to the tax cases and the EC jurisprudence available at that date. Evans L.J. stated[51]:

"In my judgment, the taxation cases are of limited assistance in addressing the question of general principle which is raised by the present appeal. There is a public law element involved in them (see *Air Canada v. British Columbia*, 59 D.L.R. (4th) 161, 170, per Wilson J.) and a further question, akin to agency, which is whether the taxpayer should be regarded as having collected tax from his customers on behalf of the taxing authority. Conversely, it may appear that any tax recovered by him will be held by him as a fiduciary for his customers: *123 East Fifty-Fourth Street Inc. v. United States* (1946) 157 F.2d 68, per Learned Hand J."

7–056   **Limited fields considered in EC case law.**   The rulings of the ECJ have been limited to cases where there has been an unlawful imposition of a charge by the state—in particular in relation to VAT—and have indicated that a passing on defence may be permissible.[51a] However, in *Weber's Wine World v Abgabenberufungskommission Wien*,[52] the ECJ emphasised that the existence of such a defence does not mean that a Member State can just presume that it applies in a particular case:

---

[51] At p.389.
[51a] See para.7–052, above.
[52] Case C–147/01 *Weber's Wine World v Abgabenberufungskommission Wien* [2004] 1 C.M.L.R. 7.

"101. ... Community law precludes a Member State from refusing to repay to a trader a charge levied in breach of Community law on the sole ground that the charge was included in that trader's retail selling price and thus passed on to third parties, which necessarily means that repayment of the charge would entail unjust enrichment of the trader.

102. It must therefore be concluded on this point that the rules of Community law on the recovery of sums levied but not due are to be interpreted as meaning that they preclude national rules which refuse—a point which falls to be determined by the national court—repayment of a charge incompatible with Community law on the sole ground that the charge was passed on to third parties, without requiring that the degree of unjust enrichment that repayment of the charge would entail for the trader be established...

110. It is clear from the case-law of the Court ... that the authority cannot merely establish that the charge was passed on to third parties and presume from that fact alone, or from the fact that the national legislation requires that the charge be incorporated in the selling price to consumers, that the economic burden which the charge represented for the taxable person is neutralised and that, consequently, repayment would automatically entail unjust enrichment of the trader."

Conflict with the "effective compensation principle".   Insofar as the rejection   **7–057**
of the passing on defence may be seen as running contrary to the reliance upon the "effective compensation principle" articulated by the ECJ in its reasoning in *Crehan*,[53] that criticism[53a] might be met with the following arguments: first, the ECJ did not explicitly consider these issues; secondly, the "deterrence principle" which also formed part of the ECJ's reasoning might militate in favour of such a rule since it would give greater incentives for claimants to bring claims; thirdly, it would, accordingly, reduce the risk that infringers would be able to retain any of their ill-gained profits; and fourthly, the scope of national procedural autonomy might be argued to cover such a rule.

Duplicate recovery.   If the passing on defence were not to be allowed *and*   **7–058**
indirect purchasers were entitled to make claims in addition to direct purchasers who had suffered loss, there would be a risk of defendants having to pay damages twice over for the same loss caused. This could, of course, be prevented by precluding such claims as being too remote (applying a *Hanover Shoe* type rule). But that approach might appear both to be in tension with the compensation principle articulated by the ECJ and to require

---

[53] n.3, above.
[53a] See paras 7–050 and 7–053, above

significant judicial intervention in the absence of any statutory framework constraining such claims.

7–059 **Practical considerations.** Two further considerations which might be relevant to a court's consideration of whether a passing on defence should be permitted (and whether indirect purchasers should be entitled to sue) are: (a) the practicality of proving the passing on or otherwise; and (b) the practical impact upon deterrence. It may be possible for economists to make predictions based on a generalised analysis of the market, for example, if all the competitors on a competitive downstream market are affected by an abuse by a dominant supplier, it is likely that passing on by those competitors to their customer will be significant.[54] However, the Court of Appeal in *Kleinwort Benson* highlighted the practical considerations outlined in the opinion of the Advocate General, Sir Gordon Slynn, in the *Bianco and Gerard* case[55] which show the difficulties that can arise when it becomes necessary to inquire whether the burden of the overpayment has been passed on to customers in the form of increased charges for the taxpayer's goods or services. It was recognised that difficult economic questions arise such as: has the taxpayer by raising his prices reduced the demand for what he supplies, so that he has not benefited overall? And, why should it be assumed that a repayment of tax will not be passed on to future customers in the form of reduced prices? Thus the effectiveness and practical usefulness of the defence might be questioned. The effect of its existence may simply serve to complicate and extend proceedings and, concomitantly, to raise their costs. Given the costs of litigation in the UK, that alone may mean that potential claimants will be more reluctant to bring claims against defendants with deep pockets.

7–060 **Burden of proof.** Of course, it might be argued that since the primary burden of proving the defence appears to fall upon the defendant, the complexity of the defence might reduce its chances of success and, thereby, reduce the extent to which valid claims are stifled by the fear of incurring high costs. However, although, in principle, the burden of making out the defence might lie upon the defendant, since the passing on defence refers to and relies upon the actions of the claimant, in practice, if the defendant can make out a prima facie case that all or part of the excess price charged has been passed on by the direct purchaser to others further down the supply chain, it may be that greater scrutiny will fall upon the behaviour of the claimant. Thus, whilst a court may not be seeking formally to transfer the burden of proof, significant questions may be asked (and, potentially, wide-ranging disclosure demanded) of the claimant.

---

[54] See Ben Dubow "The passing on defence: an economist's perspective" [2003] E.C.L.R. 238.
[55] Joined Cases 331/85, 376/85, 378/85 *Les Fils de Jules Bianco SA and J Girard Fils SA v. Directeur Général des Douanes et Droits Indirects* [1988] E.C.R. 1099; [1989] 3 C.M.L.R. 36.

Deterrence and range of claimants. Apart from the complexity of the 7–061 defence reducing the deterrent effect[56] of private actions, there is also the practical problem that if the direct purchaser is not able to claim the entirety of, for example, the excess price charged, it will have less of an incentive to bring a claim at all. Of course, if the defendant were to face claims from indirect purchasers just as much as from direct purchasers, this might not undermine the overall deterrent effect of the possibility of claims being brought; the fact that different people would recover different components of the overcharge would not reduce the overall deterrent effect. However, it should be noted that in many circumstances, those who have suffered eventual loss may be many and their individual losses small. This is often the case where anti-competitive behaviour increases the retail prices of goods or services. In those circumstances the loser is, in particular, the end consumer, or, more accurately, all the actual and potential end consumers. Each of those end consumers will have suffered a small loss which would never justify their taking the risk of bringing an action. In practice, therefore, whilst many parties may have good claims against infringing parties, they will not ever enforce them.

(c) Class actions

Class action claims in the UK. That situation might be different if the UK 7–062 had a system equivalent to the US "opt-out" class action system *i.e.* a class action claim can be brought on behalf of all of the members of a defined class unless the particular individuals within the class opt-out of participation in the group. The UK has no equivalent of that type of rule (or the attendant provisions relating to remedies which may be ordered if the class action suit is successful). Many think that this approach to civil procedure reflects an important issue of public policy, *i.e.* the desire to reduce the extent of litigation. Others have suggested that, in fact, this precludes the proper operation of Community law because it infringes the principle of effectiveness by rendering difficult, often to the point of impossibility, to bring a claim on behalf of those who have suffered loss. Such an approach has not attracted sympathy in any recent amendments to the legislative scheme of competition law. Although a discussion of the availability of class actions in the UK is outside the scope of this chapter, three matters warrant particular note:

"Consumer claims" under section 47B. First, the legislative scheme of the 7–063 Competition Act does envisage civil actions by representative "super complainants" under s.47B. In practice, there are few outside the major consumer representative organisations such as the National Consumer Council and the Consumers' Association who are likely to qualify as representative

---

[56] Deterrence in the sense of deterring infringement rather than deterring claims for damages.

bodies. In addition, the consumer claim must specify the consumers on behalf of whom the claim is brought. It is also unclear quite what remedies could be ordered by any court or tribunal hearing any claim on behalf of such a body which would have any greater effect than recompensing the particular consumers on behalf of whom the claim is brought.

7–064   **Development of class claims.**   Secondly, creative use of funding arrangements and group litigation orders in civil proceedings may enable class actions to become a type of procedure with which both courts and litigants are more familiar in the UK.

7–065   **Impact of UK costs rules.**   However, thirdly, the rules on costs in domestic civil proceedings mean that the risks for individual consumers are likely to outweigh the potential benefits of claims. The fact that the general rule that costs follow the event is likely to apply to any group claims is, notwithstanding the various qualifications to the rule under the Civil Procedure Rules, sufficient to deter any such group claims. The existence of litigation insurance might, of course, change the manner in which these issues are to be considered.

9. QUANTUM

"Ah, solving that question
Brings the priest and the doctor
In their long coats
Running over the fields."

From *Days* by Philip Larkin

7–066   **Complexity.**   Potential claimants often see the quantification of competition damages as an inordinately complex process using increasingly sophisticated economic techniques. The words of Larkin when facing moral or existential doubt might seem to have certain relevance, though for the purposes of competition damages claims we might replace the priests and doctors with economists and accountants. In Chapter 12 a more detailed analysis of the application of economics in competition litigation is provided. Here some more basic observations about quantification are made.

7–067   **Compensatory principle.**   The loss which can be claimed in an action for damages is the difference between the profits (losses) made and the greater profits (smaller losses) which would have been made in the absence of the infringing conduct. This is the same question which a court asks itself in the context of any inquiry into tortious damages. Such a counterfactual analysis ("if ... the infringement had not happened ... then ... we would have made X ...") is easy to set out in these very basic terms but the application of the principle may be complex and the relevant considerations will vary from case to case and infringement to infringement. Indeed, in practice it can be artificial to divorce the quantification exercise from that of causation, the same factual matters will be often to be relevant to both questions.

Quantification evidence.   The sorts of evidence that may be relied upon to   **7–068**
prove the extent of loss is, as with any other type of claim, not a closed set. For example, if you are assessing what quantum of damage is caused by a price fixing cartel, the key question you will be asking is what would have happened to the claimant if the cartel had not operated as it did. In order to prove that price was in fact higher during the course of the cartel, price data from periods of the alleged cartel and prior (and, if possible, subsequent) to the alleged cartel might be sought as comparators. That data which might be used to identify the "competitive price" of the product in question, *i.e.* the price which might be assumed in the absence of the cartel which would be used as the basis for the quantification of damage. Alternatively, it may be possible to obtain cost of production data from the cartel members and, with addition of a reasonable profit margin a figure for competitive pricing may be ascertained. A further alternative method might be rather than trying to benchmark against prices of the cartellised good or service over time thus comparing cartel prices with non-cartel prices, to compare the prices of the cartellised product in other geographically markets: an international comparison.

One method may not be sufficient.   Depending upon the nature of the   **7–069**
infringement at issue and the extent of the data available, it may be preferable to try to approximate competitive prices and concomitant losses using a number of different methods. In practice, an econometric analysis which tries to control for various factors may be employed. So, for example, changes in prices of raw materials, inflation and even regulatory costs may need to be controlled of in considering what the competitive price might have been absent the infringing activity.

This is all too difficult.   The temptation to use ever more sophisticated   **7–070**
techniques of analysis can, however, be both dangerous and counter-productive. In the reference of the Premier League to the then Restrictive Practice Court[57] which was concerned with the terms of sale of rights to televise Premier League football matches, Ferris J., having heard prolonged econometric evidence on the effect of televising matches upon live attendance intervened and said: "At the moment, I am firmly of the school which says, 'This is all too difficult, we had better give up'." and, later "I am thinking of buying a little flag which I can raise when we get to a part of the case that I just do not understand, but perhaps a notional flag will do. It is up at this part of the case."

---

[57] *Re Televising Premier League Football Matches* [2000] E.M.L.R. 78.

7–071   **Damages assessed at date of loss.** It is notable that the Court of Appeal in *Crehan*[58] was reluctant to engage in a long a speculative exercise about the extent of Mr Crehan's profits had he been able to continue running his pubs absent the restrictive beer ties which had put him out of business. Instead they emphasised that the calculation of damages was to be made when the losses were incurred[59] and so, apart from a small amount relating to losses incurred during the currency of the beer ties, the principal measure of recovery was the difference in value of pub leases at the time of surrender as compared with their value absent the unlawful ties. This was a matter of expert evidence upon which the court clearly felt well able to rule.

(a) Impact of fines

7–072   **Fines to be discounted?** Claims for damages in respect of infringements of competition law may be unusual in the sense that an infringer may have been the subject of an adverse decision of a public authority in relation to the conduct in question. That decision may have imposed a financial penalty. The calculation of that financial penalty may have included some consideration of the damage caused to others. A defendant faced with the prospect of civil damages actions following on from an adverse regulatory decision which imposed a fine may feel as if it is paying twice for the same offence. It is doubtful, however, that that sense of grievance could or should impact upon the quantum of damages to be awarded to a claimant. This is for three interrelated reasons:

- first, if damages can be claimed for losses caused, it is of little consolation that the state has received the payment of a fine. As indicated at the outset of this chapter, the cash value of schadenfreude would seem to be zero;

- secondly, apart from the compensatory function of private damages actions, the deterrent function of private enforcement might be undermined if, once a public authority had acted, any claims could be significantly reduced by reason of a decision. Indeed, on the assumption that public authorities were most interested in the most serious infringements of competition law, the result could be perverse in that the most serious infringers were proportionately the least at risk of facing private claims;

- thirdly, the imposition of fines is not an exact science[60] although the authorities might try to assess the nature of the losses caused by an

---

[58] n.10, above.
[59] n.10, above, at para.173.
[60] See, in particular, *Napp Pharmaceutical Holdings Ltd v OFT (No.4)* [2002] CAT 1, especially at para.535 where the CAT accepted that it was necessary to adopt a "broad brush" approach and that each case turned on its facts.

infringement, that may be difficult, it is a part of the fine setting exercise but is not the sole or key component. Furthermore they will rarely have very detailed data from other parties regarding loss and any such data will almost certainly not be comprehensive.

(b) Mitigation

Application of mitigation principle. There seems no doubt that the domestic 7–073 courts will require claimants or potential claimants to mitigate their losses insofar as it is reasonable to expect them to do so in accordance with ordinary principles of mitigation. It may be somewhat artificial to try to consider the degree of mitigation required apart from questions of causation (and indeed quantum, see above). In *Arkin v Borchard Lines Ltd (No.4)*,[61] Coleman J. stated[62]:

> "The claimant's so-called 'duty' to mitigate is a misnomer rendered respectable only by age. In reality the concept is that, if the claimant's conduct is such that it breaks the chain of causation between the claimed breach of duty on the part of the defendant and the loss, the claimant is not entitled to be compensated, for the claimant has failed to discharge the legal burden of proving the essential causal link between his loss and the defendant's breach of duty. There has been an intervening dominant cause engendered by the claimant himself."

Thus, in that case, the claimant's continuing participation in the market was found to be the predominant cause of his losses (not the alleged infringing activity) and, as such precluded recovery.

(c) Exemplary damages

> "an award of exemplary damages can serve a useful purpose in vindicating the strength of the law..."[63]

Restriction on exemplary damages. Notwithstanding this general statement 7–074 in the seminal case on exemplary damages, it has historically been considered that exemplary damages should rarely be awarded and that the categories of cases in which they should be awarded was closed. Although the measure is not extensively employed in the provision of remedies under English law, it is clear from *Rookes v Barnard* itself that exemplary damages may be claimed in three types of situation:

---

[61] n.35, above.
[62] At para.536.
[63] *Rookes v Barnard* [1964] A.C. 1129.

- where the damage in question has been caused by the oppressive action of government servants;

- where the damage has been caused by an action calculated to make a profit, *i.e.* it was calculated that it would be more profitable to take the action and incur the risk of an ordinary damages claim;

- where there is express statutory authorisation for such a claim.

7–075   Competition claims under the second head. Clearly competition law damages claims do not fall within the first or third of these categories. The second is of greater interest. In *Rookes*, the House of Lords held *per* Lord Devlin that:

"Where a defendant with cynical disregard for a plaintiff's rights has calculated that the money to be made out of his wrongdoing will probably exceed the damages at risk, it is necessary for the law to show that it cannot be broken with impunity."[64]

That might be thought precisely to cover the sorts of situation where competition law is infringed. Furthermore, in the case of *Kuddus v Chief Constable of Leicestershire*[65] the House of Lords made it clear both that the categories of case in which exemplary damages might be awarded was not closed and, more particularly, stressed *per* Lord Nicholls:

"National and international companies can exercise enormous power. So do some individuals. I am not sure it would be right to draw a hard and fast line which would always exclude such companies and persons from the reach of exemplary damages."[66]

Although these comments specifically related to Lord Devlin's first category (oppressive government action) they were made in a passage reaffirming the importance and relevance of the second category.

7–076   Benefits of availability of exemplary damages. In addition to giving potentially significant incentives to claimants (and deterrents to infringers) the availability of exemplary damages might significantly impact upon the principles of remoteness discussed above especially in relation to the operation of the passing on defence and/or the availability of indirect purchaser claims. It has been suggested[67] that were exemplary damages to be available, this would militate in favour of permitting the operation of the passing on defence and allowing indirect purchaser claims. If such damages are available even to those who have only suffered limited losses *e.g.* end

---

[64] n.63, above, at 1226.
[65] *Kuddus v Chief Constable of Leicestershire* [2002] 2 A.C. 122.
[66] At 145, para.66.
[67] See Brealey, n.45, above.

consumers, then they may have sufficient incentive (alone, or in a group) to bring a claim to vindicate their rights and strip the defendant of his ill-gotten gains. It is not necessary, therefore, to prohibit indirect purchaser claims on grounds of practicality or reduced deterrence.

Opposition to exemplary damages. However, it should be noted that there   **7–077** remains strong judicial and other[68] opposition to the award of exemplary damages and their extension into new areas of law. In particular, in *Kuddus*, Lord Scott stated:

"119. ... the exemplary damages principle is itself an anomaly in civil law ...

121. My Lords, I view the prospect of any increase in the cases in which exemplary damages can be claimed with regret. I have explained already why I regard the remedy as no longer serving any useful function in our jurisprudence. Victims of tortious conduct should receive due compensation for their injuries, not windfalls at public expense.

122. Faced with the unattractive alternatives of leaving the cause of action test in place or removing it, I would, for my part, favour a pragmatic solution under which, on the one hand, the cause of action test were removed but, on the other, exemplary damages were declared to be unavailable in cases of negligence, nuisance and strict liability, and also for breach of statutory duty except where the statute in question had expressly authorised the remedy...."[69]

The declaration wished for by his Lordship at para.122 was not made by the House of Lords.

(d) Restitutionary measures

Meaning of "restitution". In the context of competition claims a restitu-   **7–078** tionary measure might be read as having two meanings: in circumstances where the claim is between parties to a void contract, it may mean that restitution of sums paid should be made. Alternatively, it may refer to a "disgorgement"[70] measure of damages: the stripping of profits unlawfully made.

Monies paid under a void contract. On the first meaning of the term, if an   **7–079** agreement contrary to Art.81 EC is entered into which, as a result of its

---

[68] See *McGregor on Damages* (17th ed.), Chapter 11.
[69] *Kuddus v Chief Constable of Leicestershire*, n.65, above, at 159.
[70] See James Edelman, *Gain Based Damages* (Hart Publishing), especially Chapter 3.

restrictive terms, is entirely void, could one party which has, incidentally, paid significant sums to the other pursuant to the void contract before having received his benefits in return, recover those sums? There is no clear authority on this point. The principle of national procedural autonomy would suggest that specific limitation by the ECJ of the heads of damage/ recovery available would be inappropriate and there is nothing in the case law which requires the availability of such a claim in addition to or alongside the compensatory claim. Nonetheless, the constraints on such claims in domestic law—in particular the application of public policy to any form of recovery under void contracts—mean that if EC law did not require such a claim to be available, it is difficult to envisage when it would be of any use aside from a "straightforward" damages claim. The analysis of the ECJ in *Crehan*[71] in respect of the operation of the *in pari delicto* rule in respect of a co-contractor's damages claim suggests that such a restitutionary claim may in practice add nothing. After all, if a party is "significantly responsible" for the restrictive provisions which render the contract void and so is not entitled to damages, it is unclear whether the courts should otherwise intervene to provide any sort of restitutionary remedy. Indeed, although a damages claim between co-contractors might include heads of claim relating to further resultant losses, the primary claim is, in fact, likely to be restitutionary in nature, *i.e.* "I have paid you too much, that is my loss, can I have it back?"

7–080 Terms of section 47A. It is noted, however, that s.47A of the Competition Act which provides for the CAT to be able to hear damages actions specifically refers to monetary claims being "(1)(a) any claim for damages, or (b) any other claim for a sum of money". Subsection (1)(b) might be read, therefore, to refer to the specific possibility of restitutionary awards which, strictly speaking, should not be considered damages claims. Of course, the possibility that such claims may be brought before the CAT if they are available in domestic law, does not, itself, make such claims available.

7–081 Disgorgement. The second sense of "restitution" which may be employed is that relating to a claim which is intended to strip an infringer of their profits. The infringer has been unjustly enriched to the tune of those profits by its unlawful action and should not be entitled to retain them. Again, this is not a topic upon which either the domestic or European courts have clearly commented in any case to date. The principle of national procedural autonomy would, again, appear to leave the question of the measure of damages (aside for the need to enable compensation) for the national courts. Whilst a "disgorgement" remedy is found in domestic law (see, for example, *Attorney-General v Blake*)[72] it is generally seen as the exception rather than the rule. Given the approach of the domestic and European courts and,

---

[71] n.3, above.
[72] [2001] 1 A.C. 268.

subject to the considerations set out above, their emphasis upon the compensatory nature of competition law claims, it seems that a "gain based" claim for damages might not be attractive to courts considering competition claims. However, in a developing area of law such as this, there remains scope for argument whether and in what circumstances such claims can be brought in relation to competition law damages claims.[73]

10. COUNTERCLAIMS FOR DAMAGES AND SET OFF

Last refuge of the damned? The use of European competition law in   7–082
commercial litigation in the UK has, in the past, had something of a dubious reputation. When a party sought to avoid liability under a contract and all else had failed, it might turn its mind to Art.81 EC to see if, by reliance upon it it could treat the contract in question as void and thereby escape its obligations. Such Euro-defence arguments became known as "the last refuge of the damned". As familiarity of courts and lawyers with European and competition law has grown, these types of arguments have been more adeptly deployed and have thus been more effective.[73a] A variation on the theme of the traditional Euro-defence of voidness under Art.81 is to seek to meet a claim for debt (or damages) with a counterclaim for damages under competition law (whether under Art.81 or 82). Usually, the argument is couched in terms of a set-off defence, *i.e.* the counterclaim should be set-off against any debt or damages claim. Such an approach can be tactically advantageous (if successful) since it can be used to rebut any application for summary judgment on the basis that dealing with the competition issues is a complex issue requiring evidence. Thus the evil day of payment is at least postponed and often, by dint of delay and expense, the debtor is able to avoid paying the entirety of the debt and can negotiate a more favourable level of repayment.

Set off. In competition claims where damages are not liquidated the   7–083
defence/counterclaim can only be set off *in equity* against any claim. The necessary requirements for making out an equitable set off were considered in *Esso Petroleum v Milton*[74] where Simon Brown L.J. stated:

"For equitable set-off to apply it must ... be established: first, that the counterclaim is at least closely connected with the same transaction as that giving rise to the claim; and second, that the relationship between the

---

[73] The comments of the CAT President in the *BCL* case management conference referred to above at para.7–013 are noted.

[73a] *Intel Corporation v Via Technologies Inc* [2003] U.K.C.L.R. 106; see also Anneli Howard, "Competition law defences in commercial litigation: *Intel v Via*" [2003] Comp. L.J. 36.

[74] [1997] 1 W.L.R. 938.

respective claims is such that it would be manifestly unjust to allow one to be enforced without regard to the other...."[75]

7–084 *Esso Petroleum v Milton.* In that case the defendant occupied and managed two petrol service stations under licence agreements with the claimant whereby he agreed to buy from them his entire requirements of petrol and to pay for deliveries by direct debit. The claimant made various deliveries and the defendant cancelled his direct debit. The claimant sued for the price of the petrol delivered and sought summary judgment. The defendant contended that he had an equitable set off. In simple terms, the defendant's counterclaim was that there was to be a term implied into the agreements that the shop rents and licence margins should not be reduced to such a level as would prejudice his ability to operate and manage the garages at a reasonable profit. The defendant alleged that the claimant breached that term and that he was driven out of business. The Court of Appeal concluded that notwithstanding the close relationship between the claim and counterclaim, there was no basis for set off. Simon Brown L.J. emphasised:

"...the fact that both claim and counterclaim arise out of the same trading relationship is wholly insufficient to provide a sufficiently close link between the claims to support an equitable set off."[76]

7–085 **"Umbrella" contracts.** In cases where competition damages are sought to be used as a counterclaim and set off defence in circumstances where individual deliveries have been made by the claimant and not paid for by the defendant, it will be difficult to contend that the requirements for equitable set off are made out. Courts have tended to analyse the arrangements between the parties as being an "umbrella" contract which sets the general terms of dealing and individual orders and deliveries under those terms. Even if it could be said that the umbrella contract was void as being contrary to competition law, that does not avoid the enforceability of the individual delivery arrangements nor is it sufficiently closely related to enable an equitable set off to operate.

7–086 *Crehan* **and set off.** In *Crehan v Courage*[77] equitable set off was considered in the context of Art. 81 as it applied to the beer tie arrangements under scrutiny. Morritt L.J. said:

"60. It was also suggested that if the tie is illegal and void because it infringes Article [81] then the individual contracts for the supply of the beer and other products entered into pursuant to the tie are likewise

---

[75] *ibid.*, at 951.
[76] *ibid.*, at 951.
[77] [1999] U.K.C.L.R. 407, the Court of Appeal hearing when the ECJ reference was made, *not* the subsequent hearing following the ECJ decision at which damages were granted (*Crehan v Inntrepreneur*, n.10, above).

illegal and void. . . . First we have to assume that the principles of illegality applied by the courts in England and exemplified in *Gibbs Mew* are displaced or superseded by the requirement of European Community Law that the rights conferred by Art [81] are of direct effect and to be protected by national courts.[78] Without that assumption there can be no cross liability capable of set-off. In our view there is no scope within that assumption for a finding that the individual supply contracts are themselves illegal and void. Further in *Kerpen*[79], to which we have referred, one of the questions referred to the European Court of Justice was whether, if the umbrella contract was void under Art [81(2)], individual contracts of sale made in performance of that contract were likewise to be regarded as void. The Court answered this by holding that the consequences for any orders or deliveries made on the basis of the umbrella contract of the nullity of contractual provisions in the umbrella contract were not a matter for Community Law. Community law does not provide that those who have taken deliveries under the individual contracts do not have to pay for them. Nor in our judgment does English law. Second, as we have already pointed out the vice at which Art [81] is, in the circumstances of beer ties, aimed is that identified by the European Court of Justice in *Delimitis*[80] at page 987 para. 27. . . . it is the cumulative effect of all the ties in foreclosing the relevant market and the contribution to that effect made by the individual agreement which is to be considered. In that context individual contracts for the supply of beer pursuant to a single tie cannot be illegal and void in their own right. Nor, in our view can such a contract be considered to be so closely connected with the breach of Art [81] so that it should be regarded as springing from or founded on the agreement rendered illegal by Art [81]."

Pay now, sue later? Thus, although it might at first appear that transac- 7–087
tions carried out on agreed terms which were void and subject to a damages claim might be impugned by reason of that voidness and, therefore, attendant claims in relation to those individual transactions subject to set off, that is not the way in which the courts have approached these matters. There is a distinct reluctance to give defendants "a free lunch" in the sense of allowing them to avoid paying for goods they have received (at least until final trial of the issues). In the words of Master Yoxall in *3Com v Medea*[81] the defendant must "pay now and sue later". Apart from there remaining questions as to the proper interpretation of the contractual arrangements between parties and the application of *Kerpen & Kerpen* to them, it may be that different types of competition law challenge to overarching agreements will enable set off defences to operate even in relation to umbrella contracts. For example,

---

[78] This was, of course, precisely the result of the ECJ reference.
[79] Case 319/82 *Societe de Vente de Ciments et Betons de l'Est v Kerpen & Kerpen GmbH & Co KG* [1983] E.C.R. 4173; [1985] 1 C.M.L.R. 511.
[80] Case 234/89 *Delimitis v Henniger Brau AG* [1991] E.C.R. I–935; [1992] 5 C.M.L.R. 210.
[81] [2004] U.K.C.L.R. 356 at 363.

if the challenge to the umbrella contract is not that it is restrictively exclusive but sets prices which are excessive and these prices apply in relation to each delivery, there might be different arguments to be deployed as to the extent which the *Esso v Milton* formula applied.

CHAPTER 8

STATE AID LITIGATION IN DOMESTIC COURTS

Tim Ward[1]

1. INTRODUCTION

The rules on State aid. The rules on State aid serve to "prevent trade **8–001** between Member States from being affected by advantages granted by public authorities which, in various forms, distort or threaten to distort competition by favouring certain undertakings or certain products."[2] As the Commission has explained:

> "The elimination of internal frontiers between Member States enables undertakings in the Community to expand their activities throughout the internal market and consumers to benefit from increased competition. These activities must not be jeopardized by distortions of competition caused by aid granted unjustifiably to undertakings."[3]

The substantive rules on State aid are to be found solely within EC law, principally Arts 87–89 of the EC Treaty. There is no substantive domestic law of State aids. Principal responsibility for the enforcement of State aid law falls upon the Commission,[4] subject of course to the supervision of the European Courts. Nevertheless, as the Court of Justice has explained, the "national courts and the Commission fulfil complementary and separate roles" as regards the supervision of Member States' compliance with their obligations under Arts 87 and 88 of the Treaty.[5] As shall be explained, whilst

---

[1] Barrister, Monckton Chambers.
[2] Case C–387/92 *Banco Exterior de España SA v Anyuntamiento de Valencia* [1994] E.C.R. I–0877 at para.12.
[3] Commission Notice on co-operation between national courts and the Commission in the State aid field [1995] O.J. C312/8, para.1.
[4] Case C–354/90 *Fédératation Nationale du Commerce Extérieur des Produits Alimentaires and Syndicat National des Négotiants et Transformateurs de Saumon v France* [1991] E.C.R. I–5505 at para.14.
[5] Case C–39/94 *Syndicat français de l'Express international (SFEI) and Ors v La Poste and Ors* [1996] E.C.R. I–3547 at para.41.

the question of the compatibility of aid with the common market falls exclusively within the competence of the Commission, the national courts have an important role in the recovery of aid which is paid unlawfully.

8–002　**The scope of this chapter.**　This chapter begins with a brief explanation of the substantive law of State aids, and the role of the Commission and the Council in the assessment of the compatibility of aid with the common market.[6] It then considers the role of both the Commission and the national authorities in the enforcement of State aid law, and the extent to which remedies are available to those who have suffered economic harm as a result of the grant of unlawful State aid to competitors.

2. AID

8–003　**The Article 87(1) prohibition.**　The substantive prohibition upon the grant of State aid is set out in Art.87(1) EC:

> "Save as otherwise provided in this Treaty, any aid granted by a Member State or through State resources in any form whatsoever which distorts or threatens to distort competition by favouring certain undertakings or the production of certain goods shall, insofar as it affects trade between Member States, be incompatible with the common market."

A measure only falls to be categorised as aid if all the conditions set out in that provision are fulfilled.[7] As the Court of Justice has explained, there are essentially four conditions:

> "First, there must be an intervention by the State or through State resources. Second, the intervention must be liable to affect trade between Member States. Third, it must confer an advantage on the recipient. Fourth, it must distort or threaten to distort competition."[8]

8–004　**Intervention by the State or through State resources.**　Not all advantages granted by the State fall to be considered to be aid: only advantages granted directly or indirectly through State resources are caught.[9] There must be a transfer of State resources to an undertaking, or a relief from financial

---

[6] For a detailed account, see Bellamy & Child, *European Community Law of Competition* (5th ed., Sweet & Maxwell, London, 2001), Chapter 19; D'Sa, *European Community Law on State Aids* (Sweet & Maxwell, 1988); Quigley & Collins, *EC State Aid Law and Policy* (Hart, 2003). For State aids litigation before the Community Courts, see Quigley & Collins, Chapters 7 & 8.

[7] Case C–345/02 *Pearle BV & Ors v Hoofdbedrijfschap Ambachten*, July 15, 2004 at para.32.

[8] *ibid.*, para.33; Case C–280/00 *Altmark Trans und Regierungspräsidium Magdeberg* [2003] E.C.R. I–7747 at para.74.

[9] Case C–379/98 *PreussenElektra AG and Schleswag AG v Land Schleswig-Holstein* [2001] E.C.R. I–2099 at para.58.

obligations towards the State, such as tax or social security charges.[10] Thus, neither the fixing of minimum prices[11] nor an obligation imposed upon private electricity supply undertakings to purchase electricity produced from renewable energy sources at fixed minimum prices from other private undertakings constituted State aid: there was no direct or indirect transfer of State resources.[12] The resources in question need not be granted directly by the State. Advantages granted by a public or private body designated or established by the State[13] so that its actions are "imputable"[14] to the State, fall within this definition. A measure taken by the State, but funded through a levy imposed by the State on private undertakings may also be State aid.[15]

Liable to affect trade between Member States. Aid only falls within the **8–005** scope of Art.87(1) EC to the extent which it affects trade between Member States. As already observed,[16] there is no domestic substantive law of State aids in the UK and measures with purely internal effects are outside the scope of State aids supervision. Effect on trade between Member States, is, however, easy to establish. The Court of Justice has repeatedly made clear that where aid strengthens the position of an undertaking *vis-à-vis* other undertakings competing in intra-Community trade, the latter must be regarded as affected by that aid.[17] Thus, in the *Altmark*[18] case, which concerned subsidies for regional transport, the Court of Justice observed that "it is not impossible that a public subsidy granted to an undertaking which provides only local or regional transport services and does not provide any transport services outside its State of origin may none the less have an effect on trade between Member States."[19] The court concluded:

"there is no threshold or percentage below which it may be considered that trade between Member States is not affected. The relatively small amount of aid or the relatively small size of the undertaking which

[10] Joined Cases C–52/97, C–53/97 and C–54/97 *Viscido & Ors v Ente Poste Italiane* [1998] E.C.R. I–2629, Opinion of A.G. Jacobs at para.9; case C–174/02 *Streekgewest Westelijk Noord-Brabant v Staatssecretaris van Financiën*, unreported, January 13, 2005 at paras 25 and 26.

[11] Case 82/77 *Ministère public du Kingdom of the Netherlands v Jacobus Philippus van Tiggele* [1978] E.C.R. 25 at 52.

[12] Case C–379/98 *PreussenElektra AG*, n.9, above, at para.59.

[13] *ibid.*, at para.58.

[14] Case C–126/91 *Ministre de l'économie, des finances et de l'industrie v GEMO SA*, November 20, 2003 at para.23.

[15] *e.g.* Case 78/76 *Steinike & Weinlig v Germany* [1977] E.C.R. 595 at para.22. Contrast, however, *Pearle BV*, n.7, above, at para.38: levy collected by a public body but not "made available to the State" or used as a "vehicle for the implementing of a policy determined by the State" not aid.

[16] para.8–001, above.

[17] Case 730/79 *Philip Morris Holland BV v Commission* [1980] E.C.R. 2671 at para.11; Case C–126/91 *Ministre de l'économie, des finances et de l'industrie v GEMO SA*, n.14, above, at para.41.

[18] *Altmark Trans GmbH & Anr v Nahverkehrsgesellschaft Altmark GmbH & Anr*, n.8, above at para.81.

[19] *ibid.*, at para.77.

receives it does not as such exclude the possibility that trade between Member States might be affected."

The requirement that there should be an effect on trade between Member States is accordingly easy to satisfy.

8–006 **Confer an advantage upon the recipient.** State aid must confer an advantage upon its recipient, by "favouring certain undertakings or the production of certain goods." Article 87(1) EC does not distinguish between State interventions by reference to their causes or objectives, but by reference to their effects.[20] The concept of aid is accordingly "an objective one, the sole test being whether a State measure confers an advantage on one or more undertakings."[21] Advantages falling with the definition of "aid" are not restricted to positive benefits such as subsidies, or preferential terms for loans or guarantees. The definition extends to:

"interventions which, in various forms, mitigate the charges which would normally be included in the budget of an undertaking and which, without therefore being subsidies in the strict meaning of the word, are similar in character and have the same effect."[22]

Thus, a property tax exemption granted to "public credit institutions" has been held to be a State aid.[23] A supply of goods or services on preferential terms which has the same effect as a subsidy may constitute aid.[24] There may, however, be no "advantage" for these purposes where the State resources provided to the recipient amount to no more than the annual uncovered costs actually recorded by the undertakings taking into account a reasonable profit for the discharge of a public service obligation.[25]

8–007 **Selectivity.** A State measure which benefits all undertakings in national territory, without distinction, does not favour "certain undertakings" or the production of "certain goods". It therefore lacks "selectivity" requirement,

---

[20] Case C–482/99 *France v Commission* [1996] E.C.R. I–4551 at para.19–20.

[21] Cases T–228/99 and T–233/99 *Westdeutsche Landesbank Girozentrale & Anr v Commission* [2003] E.C.R. II–435 para. 180.

[22] Case 30/59 *De Gezamenlijke Steenkolenmijnen in Limburg v High Authority* [1961] E.C.R. 1, 19; recently reaffirmed in Case C–126/91 *Ministre de l'économie, des finances et de l'industrie v GEMO SA*, n.14, above, at para.28.

[23] Case C–387/92 *Banco Exterior de España SA v Anyuntamiento de Valencia*, n.2, above, at para.14. See also Case C–6/97 *Italy v Commission* [1999] E.C.R. I–2981; [2002] 2 C.M.L.R. 919; Case C–200/97 *Ecotrade Srl v Altiforni e Ferriere di Servola SpA* [1998] E.C.R. 7907; [1999] 2 C.M.L.R. 804.

[24] Case C–126/91 *Ministre de l'économie, des finances et de l'industrie v GEMO SA*, n.14, above, at para.29.

[25] Case 240/83 *Procureur de la République v Association de défense des brûleurs d'huiles usagées (ADBHU)* [1985] E.C.R. 531 at paras 3, 18; Case C–53/00 *Ferring SA v Agence centrale des organismes de sécurité sociale* [2001] E.C.R. I–9067 at para.27; Case C–280/00 *Altmark Trans GmbH & Anr v Nahverkehrsgesellschaft Altmark GmbH & Anr*, n.8, above, at paras 87–93; Case T–274/01 *Valmont Nederland BV v Commission*, September 16, 2004, at paras 130, 131.

and cannot therefore constitute State aid.[26] The requirement of selectivity is not satisfied where a "measure which, although conferring an advantage on its recipient, is justified by the nature or general scheme of the system of which it is part".[27]

Distort, or threaten to distort competition. Distortion of competition is relatively easy to establish where the foregoing criteria for the existence of an aid are met. The ECJ has observed that: "[w]here financial aid granted by a State or from State resources strengthens the position of an undertaking compared with other undertakings competing in intra-Community trade the latter must be regarded as affected by that aid."[28] The Commission is not required to demonstrate the "real effect of that aid on competition and trade between Member States". If it were required to do so, that would "ultimately favour Member States which pay aid without complying with the duty to notify ... to the detriment of those which notify the aid at the proposal stage".[29] In reaching a decision as to the existence of aid, the Commission must set out the circumstances which entail that the aid is liable to affect trade between Member States and so distort competition, even where it is clear from the circumstances that this will be so.[30] An extremely detailed economic analysis is not necessary where the effects on competition and on trade between Member States are manifest.[31]

8–008

De minimis. Even very small amounts of aid may be held to have distorted competition where profit margins in a sector are very narrow,[32] or where the market is comprised of a large number of small-scale undertakings.[33] The Commission has, however, issued a regulation on the application of the *de minimis* rule in State aid.[34] It provides that, subject to certain conditions and exceptions, the Art.88(1) EC prohibition may be deemed not to apply to grants of aid up to a maximum amount of 100,000 over a three year period beginning when the first *de minimis* aid is granted.[35]

8–009

---

[26] Case C–143/99 *Adria–Wien Pipeline and Wietersdorfer & Peggauer Zementwerke* [2001] E.C.R. I–8365 at para.35.

[27] *ibid.*, paras 42–45; Case 308/01 *Gil Insurance Ltd & Ors v Commissioners of Customs & Excise*, April 29, 2004, paras 72–75. See also: Case C–75/97 *Belgium v Commission* [1999] E.C.R. I–367 at para.33.

[28] Case 730/79 *Philip Morris Holland BV v Commission*, n.17, above, at para.11.

[29] *ibid.*, at para.296. See also Joined Cases T–116/00 and T–118/01 *P & O European Ferries (Vizcaya) SA v Diputación Foral de Vizcaya*, August 5, 2003, at para.113; Case C–301/87 *France v Commission* [1990] E.C.R. I–307 at para.33.

[30] Cases T–228/99 and T–233/99 *Westdeutsche Landesbank Girozentrale & Anr v Commission*, n.21, above, at para.292.

[31] *ibid.*, at para.295.

[32] Case 259/85 *France v Commission* [1987] E.C.R. 4393 at para.24.

[33] Case T–288/97 *Regione Autonoma Friuli Venezia Giulia v Commission* [2001] E.C.R. II–1169 at para.46.

[34] Commission Regulation 69/2001 on the application of Arts 87 and 88 of the EC Treaty to *de minimis* aid [2001] O.J. L10/30.

[35] *ibid.*, at para.2.

8–010 **Market economy investor principle.** There is no grant of State aid where assistance is provided in accordance with the "market economy investor principle". There is no aid where the State has acted in the same way as a private investor of comparable size to public sector bodies operating under normal market economy conditions.[36] As the ECJ explained in *SFEI*,[37] a case concerning logistical and commercial assistance to an express delivery service by the French State, the question is:

> "whether the recipient undertaking receives an economic advantage that it would not have obtained under normal market conditions.
>
> In examining that question, it is for the national court to determine what is normal remuneration for the services in question. Such a determination presupposes an economic analysis taking into account all the factors which an undertaking acting under normal market conditions should have taken into consideration when fixing the remuneration for the services provided."

In order to rely upon the market economy investor principle, it is not sufficient that the terms of the transaction would have been accepted by a private investor "if it turns out that the State did not have an actual need for those goods and services."[38]

3. COMPATIBILITY WITH THE COMMON MARKET

8–011 **The role of the Commission.** The question whether an aid is "incompatible with the common market" is the exclusive responsibility of the Commission, subject to the supervision of the Court of Justice,[39] and save for an exceptional power on the part of the Council, considered further below.[40] The

---

[36] Joined Cases T–116/00 and T–118/01 *P & O European Ferries (Vizcaya) SA v Diputación Foral de Vizcaya*, n.29, above, at para.113.

[37] Case C–39/94 *Syndicat français de l'Express international (SFEI) and Ors v La Poste and Ors*, n.5, above, at para.60; see Joined Cases C–83/01 P, C–93/01 P and C–94/01 P *Chronopost SA & Ors v Union Française de l'Express & Ors* [2003] E.C.R. I–6993; [2003] 3 C.M.L.R. 11, for guidance as to how this test should be applied where the situation cannot be compared to any private sector transaction. The test was considered by the Court of Appeal in *BT3G Ltd & Ors v Secretary of State for Trade and Industry* [2001] EWCA Civ 1448 at paras 65–77, CA.

[38] Joined Cases T–116/00 and T–118/01 *P & O European Ferries (Vizcaya) SA v Diputación Foral de Vizcaya*, n.29, above, at para.117.

[39] Case C–354/90 *Féderatation Nationale du Commerce Extérieur des Produits Alimentaires and Syndicat National des Négotiants et Transformateurs de Saumon v France*, n.4, above, at para. 14.

[40] See para.8–026, below.

nature of the assessment of compatibility with the common market was explained by the Court of Justice in the *Steinike*[41] case:

> "The prohibition in Article [87(1)] is neither absolute nor unconditional since Article [87(3)] and Article [88(2)] give the Commission a wide discretion and the Council extensive power to admit aids in derogation from the general prohibition in Article [87(1)].
>
> In judging these cases whether State aid is compatible with the common market complex economic factors subject to rapid change must be taken into account and assessed."

The criteria upon which the Commission conducts this assessment are briefly considered further below.

The role of the national courts.   The question of compatibility of an aid with the common market cannot be raised before the national courts. As the Court of Justice explained in *Steinike*:   **8–012**

> "The parties concerned cannot therefore simply, on the basis of Article [87] alone, challenge the compatibility of an aid with Community law before national courts or ask them to decide as to any incompatibility which may be the main issue in actions before them or may arise as a subsidiary issue."[42]

There are, however, circumstances in which the national court must "interpret ... and apply the provisions contained in Article 87",[43] although not in order to determine whether the grant of aid is compatible with the common market. As shall be explained, this question may arise where the national court is called upon to decide whether aid has been granted in breach of the procedural requirements of Art.88(3) EC and must be repaid.[44]

Assessment of compatibility: Articles 87(2) and (3) EC.   The Commission's assessment of the compatibility of aid with the common market is governed by Arts 87(2) and (3) EC and guidelines it has adopted as to their application.[45] A detailed explanation of their application is beyond the scope of this book.[46] Briefly, Art.87(2) EC provides that three types of aid are compatible with the common market: **8–013**

> "(a) aid having a social character, granted to individual consumers,

---

[41] Case 78/76 *Steinike & Weinlig v Germany*, n.15, above, at paras 8–9; Case 74/76 *Ianelli & Volpi SpA v Ditta Paolo Meroni* [1977] E.C.R. 557 at para.11.

[42] Case 78/76 *Steinike & Weinlig v Germany*, n.15, above, at para.10; Case 74/76 *Ianelli & Volpi SpA v Ditta Paolo Meroni*, n.41, above, at paras 11–12.

[43] Case 78/76 *Steinike & Weinlig v Germany*, n.15, above, at para.14.

[44] See paras 8–034–8–039, below.

[45] Such guidelines cannot derogate from the provisions of Arts 87 and 88: Case 310/85 *Deufil v Commission* [1987] E.C.R. 901 at para.22.

[46] See Bellamy & Child, paras 19–029–19–048; D'Sa, *European Community Law on State Aids* (Sweet & Maxwell, 1988).

provided that such aid is granted without discrimination related to the origin of the products concerned;

(b) aid to make good the damage caused by natural disasters or exceptional occurrences;

(c) aid granted to the economy of certain areas of the Federal Republic of Germany affected by the division of Germany, insofar as such aid is required in order to compensate for the economic disadvantages caused by their division."

Aid which falls into any of these categories is deemed to be compatible with the common market. As such it qualifies for "automatic approval" by the Commission.[47] There is no element of discretion. Art.87(3) EC identifies five types of aid that "may be considered to be compatible with the common market":

"(a) aid to promote the economic development of areas where the standard of living is abnormally low or where there is serious underemployment;

(b) aid to promote the execution of an important project of common European interest or to remedy a serious disturbance in the economy of a Member State;

(c) aid to facilitate the development of certain economic activities or of certain economic areas, where such aid does not adversely affect trading conditions to an extent contrary to the common interest;

(d) aid to promote culture and heritage conservation where such aid does not affect trading conditions and competition in the Community to an extent that is contrary to the common interest;

(e) such other categories of aid as may be specified by decision of the Council acting by a qualified majority on a proposal from the Commission."

It is a matter for the discretion of the Commission whether to authorise aid under Art.87(3) EC. In exercising that discretion it seeks to strike a balance between the degree of distortion of competition caused by the aid and its contribution to Community objectives. As the Commission has explained:

"if the Commission has to use its discretionary power not to raise objection to an aid proposal, it must contain a compensatory justification which takes the form of a contribution by the beneficiary of aid over and

---

[47] Commission Notice on co-operation between national courts and the Commission in the State aid field [1995] O.J. C312/8, para.45.

above the effects of normal play of market forces to the achievement of Community objectives as contained in derogations of Article [87(3)]."[48]

The Commission is bound in the exercise of its discretion by the guidelines and notices it issues in the area of supervision of State aid, at least in so far as they do not depart from the rules contained in the Treaty.[49]

3. COMPATIBILITY: PROCEDURE BEFORE THE COMMISSION

Assessment by the Commission.   The Commission must assess any proposed   8–014
grant of new aid and decide whether it is compatible with the common market. It must also consider the compatibility of existing aid with the common market. The procedural rules governing the exercise of the Commission's powers and duties are set out in Regulation 659/99[50] laying down detailed rules for the application of Art.93 [now Art.88] of the EC Treaty ("the Procedural Regulation"). It is considered and explained below.

Existing aid: Article 88(1) EC.   Article 88(1) of the EC Treaty places the   8–015
Commission under an obligation to keep existing State aid under review:

"The Commission shall, in co-operation with Member States, keep under constant review all systems of aid existing in those States. It shall propose to the latter any appropriate measures required by the progressive development or by the functioning of the common market."

"Existing aids" are those which were in existence when the Treaty came into force, or those which have since been authorised, or deemed to have been authorised.[51] The Procedural Regulation requires the Commission to obtain from the Member States all necessary information for the review of existing aid schemes.[52] If the Commission decides that an existing aid is not, or is no longer compatible with the common market, it must inform the Member State concerned of its preliminary view and give the Member State the opportunity to submit comments.[53] Where the Commission concludes that the aid is not compatible with the common market, it must issue a recommendation to the Member State, which may propose substantive

---

[48] Xth Report on Competition Policy, para.213.
[49] Case C–91/00 *Italy v Commission*, July 29, 2004, para.45. For the scope of review by the Community Courts of the exercise of this discretion, see *ibid.*, para.43; Case C–351/98 *Spain v Commission* [2002] E.C.R. I–8031 at para.74; Case C–409/00 *Spain v Commission* [2003] E.C.R. I–1487 at para.93.
[50] [1999] O.J. L83/1.
[51] See para.8–021, below for the circumstances in which aid can be deemed to be authorised.
[52] Art.17(1) of the Procedural Regulation.
[53] Art.17(2) of the Procedural Regulation. Comments must be submitted within one month, although the Commission has the power to extend this period in "duly justified cases": *ibid.*

amendment, introduction of procedural requirements or abolition of the aid scheme.[54] If the Member State informs the Commission of its acceptance of the proposed measures, it becomes bound to implement them.[55] If the Member State does not accept them, and if the Commission (having taken into account the arguments of the Member State) still considers them to be necessary, it must initiate the formal investigation procedure pursuant to Art.88(2) EC which is applicable to the grant of new aid,[56] and is explained in further detail below.[57]

8–016   **Misuse of aid.**   Misuse of aid arises where aid which has been held to be compatible with the common market by the Commission, is used in contravention of the terms of the decision of the Commission holding it to be so.[58] In such a case, the Commission may open the formal investigation procedure pursuant to Art.88(2) EC.[59] By way of interim measures, it may order the suspension of the aid, but not its interim recovery.[60] If it concludes that the misused aid is incompatible with the common market, it must decide that the Member State shall take all necessary measures to recover the aid.[61]

8–017   **New aid: Article 88(3) EC.**   Control of the grant of new aid is governed by Art.88(3) EC. It provides:

"The Commission shall be informed, in sufficient time to enable it to submit its comments, of any plans to grant or alter aid. If it considers that any such plan is not compatible with the common market having regard to Article 87, it shall without delay initiate the procedures provided for in paragraph 2. The Member State concerned shall not put its proposed measures into effect until this procedure has resulted in a final decision."

8–018   **The duty to notify.**   The first sentence of Art.88(3) EC obliges the Member State to notify the Commission of "any plans to grant or alter aid". The purpose of this requirement is "to provide this institution with sufficient time for consideration and investigation to form a prima facie opinion on

---

[54] Art.18 of the Procedural Regulation.
[55] Art.19(1) of the Procedural Regulation.
[56] Art.19(2) of the Procedural Regulation.
[57] paras 8–022–8–025.
[58] Art.1(g) of the Procedural Regulation.
[59] See further para.8–022, below.
[60] See further para.8–029, below.
[61] See further para.8–032, below.

the partial or complete conformity with the Treaty of the plans which have been notified to it."[62] The notification must contain "all necessary information to enable the Commission to take a decision"[63] as to whether, on preliminary examination, the measure is State aid, if so, whether it is compatible with the common market.[64] In particular, the notification must cover the proposed method of financing the aid in as much as that method is an integral part of the planned measure: in assessing the compatibility of the aid, the Commission cannot isolate it from the method by which it is financed.[65] The Commission may not permit any derogation from this requirement.[66] Once an aid scheme has been authorised by the Commission, individual awards of aid under the scheme do not normally have to be notified.[67] A Member State may withdraw such a notification at any time before the Commission has taken either a preliminary[68] or final decision[69] on the notification.[70] The implications of a failure to notify are considered below.[71]

Exemption from the duty to notify.   Article 89 EC provides the Council with   **8–019** power to make regulations for the application of Arts 87 and 88 EC and in particular, to exempt categories of aid from the notification procedure. Pursuant to this provision, the Council has adopted an enabling regulation, granting power to the Commission to declare certain categories of aid to be compatible with the common market and exempting them from the requirement to notify pursuant to Art.88(3) EC.[72] The Commission has

---

[62] Case 120/73 *Gebruder Lorenz GmbH v Federal Republic of Germany and Land Rhine Palatinate* [1973] E.C.R. 1471 at para.3.

[63] Art.2(2) of the Procedural Regulation. If the Commission considers the information provided to be incomplete it can request further information from the Member State: Art.5(1). The Member State may provide the Commission with a "duly reasoned statement" that the information requested is not available or has already been provided. If it does not do so, and if, following a reminder, the requested information is not provided within the prescribed period, the notification shall be deemed to be withdrawn: Art.5(3).

[64] *i.e.* a decision pursuant to Arts 4 and 7 of the Procedural Regulation; see Art.2(2).

[65] Joined Cases C–261/01 and C–262/01 *Belgium v Calster & Ors* [2004] 1 C.M.L.R.18, paras 41–51; Case C–345/02 *Pearle BV & Ors v Hoofdbedrijfschap Ambachten*, n.7, above, at para.30.

[66] Joined Cases T–116/00 and T–118/01 *P & O European Ferries (Vizcaya) SA v Diputación Foral de Vizcaya*, n.29, above, at para.70.

[67] This principle is subject to certain important qualifications: Commission Notice on co-operation between national courts and the Commission in the State aid field [1995] O.J. C312/8 para.15.

[68] *i.e.* pursuant to Art.4 of the Procedural Regulation.

[69] *i.e.* pursuant to Art.7 of the Procedural Regulation.

[70] Procedural Regulation, Art.8(1). If the Commission has initiated the formal investigation procedure (see para.8–022, below) the Commission must close that procedure: Art.8(2).

[71] paras 8–029–8–051, below.

[72] Regulation 994/98 on the application of Arts 87 and 88 of the Treaty establishing the European Community to certain categories of horizontal State aid [1998] O.J. L142/1.

subsequently adopted regulations concerning training aid,[73] *de minimis* aid,[74] and aid to small and medium-sized enterprises.[75]

8–020 **Standstill on the grant of aid.** The Procedural Regulation expressly affirms the principle set out in the final sentence of Art.88(3) EC, namely that aid which ought to be notified to the Commission "shall not be put into effect before the Commission has taken, or is deemed to have taken a decision authorising such aid."[76] The consequences of a breach of this requirement are considered further below.

8–021 **Preliminary examination.** The Commission must examine a notification of proposed aid as soon as it is received[77] and conduct a preliminary examination. If it concludes that the measure does not constitute State aid, it must reach a decision to that effect.[78] Similarly, if, following preliminary examination, the Commission concludes there are no doubts as to the compatibility with the common market of a notified measure it must reach a "decision not to raise objections", specifying which Treaty exception[79] has been applied.[80] Subject to legal challenge, such a decision brings State aid supervision of a measure to an end. Where, however, the Commission finds that doubts are raised as to the compatibility with the common market of a notified measure it must reach a "decision to initiate the formal investigation procedure" pursuant to Art.88(2) of the Treaty.[81] The Commission must reach a decision on the basis of its preliminary investigation within two months.[82] Should it fail to do so, the aid will be deemed to have been authorised.[83] If the Member State then wishes to implement the measure in question it must first give the Commission prior notice. The Commission then has 15 working days from receipt of the notice in which to reach a decision, failing which the Member State is free to adopt the measures.[84]

8–022 **Formal investigation procedure: Article 88(2) EC.** The formal investigation procedure provides an opportunity for the Member State, and other

---

[73] Regulation 68/2001 on the application of Arts 87 and 88 of the EC Treaty to training aid [2001] O.J. L10/20.
[74] Regulation 69/2001, n.34, above.
[75] Regulation 70/2001 on the application of Arts 87 and 88 of the EC Treaty to small and medium-sized enterprises [2001] O.J. L10/33.
[76] Procedural Regulation, Art.3(1).
[77] Procedural Regulation, Art.4(1).
[78] Procedural Regulation, Art.4(2).
[79] See para.8–013, above.
[80] Procedural Regulation, Art.4(3).
[81] Procedural Regulation, Art.4(4).
[82] Time begins to run on the day after receipt of a complete notification. The notification will be considered to be complete if, within two months from its receipt, or from the receipt of any additional information requested, the Commission does not request any further information. The two month period may be abridged by the Commission, or extended with the consent of both the Commission and the Member State concerned: Procedural Regulation Art.4(5).
[83] Procedural Regulation, Art.4(6).
[84] Procedural Regulation, Art.4(5).

interested parties to make submissions as to the proposed measure. The basis for it is to be found in the first paragraph of Art.88(2) EC:

> "If, after giving notice to the parties concerned to submit their comments, the Commission finds that aid granted by a State or through State resources is not compatible with the common market having regard to Article 87, or that such aid is being misused, it shall decide that the State concerned shall abolish or alter such aid within a period of time to be determined by the Commission."

A decision to initiate the formal investigation procedure must contain a statement of the Commission's preliminary assessment as to the measure's character as aid its doubts as to the measure's compatibility with the common market, a decision to initiate the formal investigation procedure. The decision must also call upon the Member State concerned and upon other interested parties to submit comments within a prescribed period.[85] "Interested parties" are:

> "any Member State and any person, undertaking or association of undertakings whose interests might be affected by the granting of aid, in particular the beneficiary of the aid, competing undertakings and trade associations."[86]

Any interested party may submit comments.[87] There is no requirement on the part of the Commission to individually notify the recipient of the aid, or other interested parties. The Court of Justice has ruled that publication of a notice in the Official Journal is an appropriate means of informing all the parties concerned that a procedure has been initiated,[88] and this approach is now mandated by the Procedural Regulation.[89] The "sole aim of this communication is to obtain from persons concerned all information required for the guidance of the Commission with regard to its future action."[90] Thus "far from enjoying the same rights of defence as those which individuals against whom a procedure been instituted are recognised as having, the parties concerned have only the right to be involved in the administrative procedure to the extent appropriate in the light of the circumstances of the case."[91] The Member State concerned is then given an

---

[85] That proscribed period should not normally exceed one month, but may be extended by the Commission: Procedural Regulation, Art.6(1). An interested party which submits comments and any beneficiary of the aid have a right to receive a copy of the final decision taken by the Commission under Art.7 of the Procedural Regulation: Art.20(1).

[86] Art.1(h) of the Procedural Regulation.

[87] Art.20(1) of the Procedural Regulation.

[88] Case 323/82 *SA Intermills v Commission* [1984] E.C.R. 3809 at para.17.

[89] Art.26(1) of the Procedural Regulation.

[90] Case 70/72 *Commission v Germany* [1973] E.C.R. 813 at para.19.

[91] Cases T–228/99 and T–233/99 *Westdeutsche Landesbank Girozentrale & Anr v Commission*, n.21, above, at para.125; case T–176/01 *Ferriere Nord SpA v Commission*, November 18, 2004.

opportunity to reply to the comments submitted.[92] By contrast to the proposed recipient, "the Member State's right to be heard ... constitutes an essential procedural requirement and ... failure to comply with that requirement entails the nullity of a Commission decision ordering that aid be abolished or altered."[93]

8–023 **Closure of the formal investigation procedure.** There are four ways in which the Commission may bring the formal investigation procedure to a close: a decision that the notified measure does not constitute aid[94]; a "positive decision" that the aid is compatible with the common market[95]; a "conditional decision" that the measure is compatible with the common market, subject to certain obligations which will enable compliance with the decision to be monitored[96]; or a "negative decision" that the measure is not compatible with the common market.[97] A decision bringing the formal investigation to a close must be taken as soon as the Commission's doubts as to the compatibility of the measure with the common market are removed. The Procedural Regulation requires the Commission "as far as possible" to endeavour to adopt a decision within a period of 18 months from the opening of the procedure, although this time limit may be subject to extension by agreement with the Member State concerned.[98] In practice, the Member State has little choice but to consent to the extension of this period where it still considers there to be a prospect that the proposed grant of aid will be approved. There is no deeming provision under which the aid will be approved by default of the kind which operates at the stage of preliminary examination. Once time has expired under the formal investigation procedure, the Member State may request the Commission to take a decision take a decision within two months on the basis of the information available to it. The Procedural Regulation specifically provides, however, that if the information provided is not sufficient to establish compatibility, the Commission shall take a negative decision. In substance, therefore, the default position is not approval, but refusal of authorisation for the proposed aid.

8–024 **Failure to comply with the Commission's decision.** Where the State fails to comply with a decision of the Commission taken pursuant to Art.88(2) EC within the prescribed time, the Commission or any other interested State

---

[92] The period for such a reply is prescribed by the Commission. It should not normally exceed one month, but may be extended by the Commission. An interested party may request that its identity should be withheld from the Member State on grounds of potential damage: Procedural Regulation, Art.6(2).

[93] Cases T–228/99 and T–233/99 *Westdeutsche Landesbank Girozentrale & Anr v Commission*, n.21, above, at para.141. The beneficiary of the aid may plead such a defect: *ibid.*, para.142.

[94] Procedural Regulation, Art.7(2). Such a decision may be taken following modification of the measure by the Member State concerned.

[95] Procedural Regulation, Art.7(3). Such a decision may be taken following modification of the measure by the Member State concerned.

[96] Procedural Regulation, Art.7(4).

[97] Procedural Regulation, Art.7(5).

[98] Procedural Regulation, Art.7(6).

may refer the matter to the Court of Justice. The right to make such a reference is expressly stated to be in derogation from Arts 226 and 227 of the EC Treaty. A Member State which disputes such a decision must challenge it within two months, pursuant to Art.230 EC. If it fails to do so, it may not subsequently call the decision into question in subsequent proceedings.[99] Its only defence to an action by the Commission for a declaration that it has failed to comply with its obligation in this regard is to plead that it was "absolutely impossible for it to implement the decision properly".[1]

Revocation of a decision. The Commission may revoke a decision taken either at the stage of preliminary examination[2] or following formal investigation,[3] but only where the decision was "based on incorrect information provided during the procedure which was a determining factor for the decision". Before revoking a decision, the Commission must open the formal investigation procedure.[4] **8–025**

5. COMPATIBILITY: ROLE OF THE COUNCIL

Application to the Council. The third paragraph of Art.88(2) of the EC Treaty for the Council to grant approval for State aid in "exceptional circumstances": **8–026**

"On application by a Member State, the Council may, acting unanimously, decide that aid which the State is granting or intends to grant shall be considered to be compatible with the common market, in derogation from the provisions of Article 87 or from the regulations provided for in Article 89, if such a decision is justified by exceptional circumstances. If, as regards the aid in question, the Commission has already initiated the procedure provided for in the first subparagraph of this paragraph[5], the fact that the State concerned has made its application to the Council shall have the effect of suspending that procedure until the Council has made its attitude known."[6]

Application to the Council under this paragraph has the effect of suspending any action by the Commission under the first paragraph of Art.88(2) EC. If,

---

[99] Case 52/84 *Commission v Belgium* [1986] E.C.R. 89 at para.13.
[1] *ibid.*, at para.14. See further para.8–036, below.
[2] *i.e.* a decision pursuant to Arts 4(2) or (3) of the Procedural Regulation.
[3] *i.e.* a decision pursuant to Arts 7(2), (3) or (4) of the Procedural Regulation.
[4] *i.e.* pursuant to Art.4(4) of the Procedural Regulation: Art.9. If a decision is re-opened Arts 6 and 7 (above) and Arts 13, 14 and 15 (below) apply: Art.9.
[5] *i.e.* the formal investigation procedure pursuant to Art.88(2) of the EC Treaty; see para.8–022, above.
[6] In reviewing the exercise of this power, the Court of Justice is confined to examination of whether the Council's decision contains a manifest error or constitutes a misuse of power or whether it clearly exceeded the bounds of its discretion: Case C–122/94 *Commission v Council* [1996] E.C.R. I–881 at para.18.

however, the Council has not made its attitude to such an application known within three months of such an application, the Commission must give its decision on the case.[7] The Council has no power to rule on the compatibility of aid which the Commission has already ruled to be incompatible with the common market.[8] Thus, where aid has been ruled to be incompatible by the Commission, the Council cannot subsequently authorise the grant of a new aid of an equivalent amount in order to compensate for the repayment of that first aid.[9]

6. UNLAWFUL AID

8–027 **Unlawful aid.** The last sentence of Art.88(3) EC expressly precludes a Member State from putting proposed aid measures into effect until the Commission has reached a final decision on the compatibility of the aid. Aid which is granted in breach of this provision is "unlawful".[10] The obligation to notify the aid includes an obligation to notify any alteration to the proposed aid.[11] Where aid is notified to the Commission, but the Member State concerned subsequently makes alterations to the plan of which the Commission has not been informed, the prohibition precludes the putting into effect of the aid programme in its entirety.[12]

(a) Powers of the Commission

8–028 **The basis for action.** The Commission may first become alerted to the existence of non-notified aid as a result of information received from an interested party such as a competitor.[13] The Procedural Regulation provides that where the Commission has in its possession information from whatever source regarding alleged unlawful aid, it must examine that information without delay.[14] If necessary, it must request information from the Member

---

[7] Fourth paragraph of Art.88(3).
[8] Case C–110/02 *Commission v Council*, June 29, 2004, para.33.
[9] *ibid.*, para.43.
[10] Procedural Regulation, Art.1(f).
[11] Joined Cases 91 and 127/83 *Heineken Brouwerijen BV v Inspecteur der Vennootschapsbelasting, Amsterdam and Utrecht* [1984] E.C.R. 3435 at para.18.
[12] *ibid.*, at para.21. The position may be different only where the alteration in question amounts to a separate aid measure which falls to be assessed separately. The notification of alterations to aid which was previously unlawful may not suffice to render that aid lawful; see Joined Cases T–116/00 and T–118/01 *P & O European Ferries (Vizcaya) SA v Diputación Foral de Vizcaya*, n.29, above.
[13] Procedural Regulation, Art.20(2).
[14] Procedural Regulation, Art.10(1).

State concerned.[15] Failure to provide such information may result in a decision requiring the information to be provided, known as a "recovery injunction".[16]

Suspension injunction. By way of interim measure, the Commission may grant a "suspension injunction" requiring a Member State to suspend any unlawfully granted aid pending its decision on compatibility with the common market.[17] The power of a national court to grant interim relief is considered below.[18]

8–029

Recovery injunction. As the Commission explained in its Notice on co-operation between national courts and the Commission in the State aid field[19]:

8–030

"in some cases an order requiring the suspension of which has been unlawfully granted will not go far enough: such an order will not always counteract the infringements of procedural rules which may have been committed, particularly where all or part of the aid has already been paid out."

The Procedural Regulation accordingly provides the Commission with power to grant a "recovery injunction" requiring the Member State to make provisional recovery of unlawful aid, pending a decision by the Commission as to its compatibility with the common market.[20] Three criteria must be satisfied before the Commission can order provisional recovery:

(1) according to an established practice there are no doubts about the aid character of the measure concerned,

(2) there is an urgency to act, and

(3) there is a serious risk of substantial and irreparable damage to a competitor.[21]

Before adopting such a "recovery injunction" the Commission must give the

---

[15] Procedural Regulation, Art.10(2). The Member State is then obliged to provide "all necessary information in order to enable the Commission to take a decision: *ibid.*, applying Art.2(2). If the Commission considers the information provided is incomplete, it must request all necessary additional information, and if necessary, send a further reminder: Art.10(2), applying Arts 5(1) and (2).

[16] Procedural Regulation, Art.10(3). The Commission may only take such a decision if the Member State does not provide the information requested despite a reminder pursuant to Art.5(2): Art.10(3).

[17] Procedural Regulation, Art.11(1). Before adopting such a "suspension injunction" it must give the Member State concerned the opportunity to submit its comments: see above.

[18] See para.8–047, below.

[19] [1995] O.J. C 312/8, para.10.

[20] Procedural Regulation, Art.11(2).

[21] Procedural Regulation, Art.11(2).

Member State concerned the opportunity to submit its comments.[22] The effect of such an order may, potentially, be catastrophic for the recipient of such unlawful aid. Where an order for interim recovery is made, it may be academic whether or not the aid is ultimately held to be compatible with the common market. The Procedural Regulation offers a form of solution to this problem: it specifically provides that the Commission may authorise the member State to couple the refunding of the aid with the payment of rescue aid to the firm concerned.[23]

8–031 **Compatibility with the common market of unlawful aid.** The fact that aid has been granted unlawfully does not relieve the Commission of its obligation to consider whether that aid is compatible with the common market. As the Court of Justice explained in *Boussac*,[24] the Commission must consider the question of compatibility even in respect of an unlawful aid. A finding that the aid is compatible with the common market does not, however, retrospectively validate the grant of unlawful aid; "any other interpretation would have the effect of according a favourable outcome to the non-observance by the Member State concerned of the last sentence of Article [88(3)] and would deprive that provision of its effectiveness."[25]

8–032 **Final recovery of aid by the Commission.** Where the Commission ultimately decides that unlawful aid is not compatible with the common market, it must take a "recovery decision", save if this would be contrary to a general principle of Community law. The Community Courts have held that:

> "the elimination of an illegal aid through recovery of the amount of aid disbursed plus interest is the logical consequence of a finding that this aid is incompatible with the common market, its sole purpose being to restore the previously existing situation, that obligation cannot in principle be disproportionate to the objectives of Articles [87],[88] and [89]."[26]

Such a decision requires the Member State to take "all necessary measures to recover the aid from the beneficiary"[27] and must include interest at an

---

[22] *ibid.*
[23] Procedural Regulation, Art.11(1). The grant of rescue aid is governed by Community guidelines on State aid for rescuing and restructuring firms in difficulty (2004/C 244/02) [2004] O.J. C244/2.
[24] Case C–301/87 *France v Commission ("Boussac")* [1990] E.C.R. I–307 at paras 21, 22.
[25] Case C–354/90 *Fédératation Nationale du Commerce Extérieur des Produits Alimentairs and Syndicat National des Négotiants et Transformateurs de Saumon v France* [1991] E.C.R. I–5505 at para.16.
[26] Joined Cases T–298/97, T–312/97, T–313/97, T–315/97, T–600/97 to 607/97, T–1/98, T–3/98 to T–6/98 and T–23/98 *Alzetta Mauro & Ors v Commission* [2002] E.C.R. II–2319 at para.169; Case C–142/87 *Belgium v Commission ("Tubemeuse")* [1990] E.C.R. I–959 at para.66.
[27] Procedural Regulation, Art.14(1).

appropriate rate fixed by the Commission.[28] The Commission is not, however, required to calculate the precise sum to be recovered.[29]

Limitation period. The power of the Commission to order recovery of aid **8–033**
is subject to a limitation period of 10 years, beginning on the day on which
the unlawful aid is awarded to the beneficiary.[30] Any action taken by the
Commission or by a Member State, acting at the request of the Commission,
with regard to the unlawful aid has the effect of interrupting the limitation
period; each such interruption starts time running afresh. The mere fact that
the recipient of aid is unaware of such action is immaterial to the operation
of this rule in respect of that undertaking.[31] The running of time is also
suspended where any decision of the Commission is the subject any proceedings pending before the ECJ.

(b) Obligation of the State to recover aid

Obligation of the Member State to make recovery. Where the Commission **8–034**
orders recovery of aid, the decision is addressed to the Member State which
granted the aid, not the recipient.[32] The effect is to place the Member State
under an obligation to take all measures necessary to ensure implementation
of that decision.[33] Article 14(3) of the Procedural Regulation provides that it
must do so:

"without delay and in accordance with the procedures under the national
law of the Member State concerned, provided that they allow the
immediate and effective execution of the Commission's decision. To this
effect, and in the event of a procedure before national courts, the Member
States concerned shall take all necessary steps which are available in their
respective legal systems, including provisional measures, without prejudice to Community law."

As the recovery is the "logical consequence" of a finding that aid has been
granted unlawfully, the Commission is not obliged to provide specific reasons for the exercise of that power.[34] Where a Member State fails to make
recovery, the Commission is entitled to seek a declaration from the Court of

---

[28] Procedural Regulation, Art.14(2).
[29] Case T–67/94 *Ladbroke Racing Ltd v Commission* [1998] E.C.R. II–1 at para.189.
[30] Procedural Regulation, Arts 15(1), (2).
[31] Case T–366/00 *Scott SA v Commission* [2003] E.C.R. II–1763 at para.60.
[32] Procedural Regulation, Art.25.
[33] Case C–404/00 *Commission v Spain* [2003] E.C.R. I–6695 at para.21.
[34] Joined Cases T–116/00 and T–118/01 *P & O European Ferries (Vizcaya) SA v Diputación Foral de Vizcaya*, August 5, 2003, para.224.

Justice that the Treaty has been infringed, pursuant to either Arts 226 or 88(2) EC.[35]

8–035 **Recovery under the procedures provided for by national law.** As there are no Community provisions on the procedure for recovery of wrongly paid amounts, illegal aid must be recovered in accordance with the relevant procedural provisions of national law.[36] As a result, a Member State is free to chose the means of fulfilling this obligation. The court has, however, imposed minimum requirements that such measures must meet. The measures chosen must not adversely affect the scope and effectiveness of Community law[37]; they must not render recovery practically impossible[38]; they must "have the same effect as that of repayment by way of transfer of funds"[39]; they must be suitable to re-establish the normal conditions of competition which were distorted by the grant of the illegal aid and capable of being identified as such by the Commission and other interested parties[40]; they must be unconditional and immediately applicable.[41] Thus, for example, the court held that a measure under which the State had the right to receive a share of surpluses generated by an aid recipient company in the event of its liquidation or a change in its shareholders' holdings related to an uncertain future event and did not suffice to implement a recovery decision.[42]

8–036 **Impossibility of recovery.** As has already been noted,[43] where a Member State has failed to challenge a recovery decision, it must make recovery unless it is absolutely impossible for it to do so.[44] The mere "apprehension of insuperable internal difficulties" or the fact that "repayment would be complicated and hard to verify" are not sufficient.[45] Nor may the State complain that the Commission has initiated legal action against it "within an unusually short time after notification of the decision".[46] The ECJ has made clear that this rule:

"does not prevent a State which, in giving effect to a Commission

---

[35] Case C–404/00 *Commission v Spain*, n.33, above, at para.25. The burden of proof in establishing such an infringement lies upon the Commission: *Commission v Spain*, para.26.

[36] Case C–404/00 *Commission v Spain*, n.33, above, at para.21. See also Art.14(3) of the Procedural Regulation.

[37] *ibid.*, at para.21.

[38] Case 142/87 *Belgium v Commission ("Tubemeuse")*, n.26, above, at para.61, applied in Case C–480/98 *Spain v Commission* [2000] E.C.R. I–8717 at para.37: inability to recover interest from insolvent recipient of aid not sufficient render recovery "practically impossible."

[39] Case C–209/00 *Commission v Germany* [2002] E.C.R. I–11695 at para.57.

[40] *ibid.*, at para.58.

[41] *ibid.*, at para.58.

[42] *ibid.*, at para.60.

[43] para.8–024, above.

[44] Case C–404/00 *Commission v Spain*, n.33, above, at para.30.

[45] Case C–99/02 *Commission v Italy*, April 1, 2004, para.22.

[46] *ibid.*, para.24. As the court observed in that case, where action is brought pursuant to Art.88(2) EC, rather than Art.226 EC, there is no provision for a pre-litigation phase, or requirement of a reasoned opinion: see above.

decision on State aid, encounters unforeseen and unforeseeable difficulties or becomes aware of consequences overlooked by the Commission, from submitting those problems to the Commission for consideration, together with proposals for suitable amendments to the decision in question. In such cases, the Commission and the Member State must, by virtue of the rule imposing on the Member States and the Community institutions a duty of genuine co-operation which underlies, in particular, Article 10 EC, work together in good faith with a view to overcoming the difficulties whilst fully observing the Treaty provisions, and, in particular, the provisions on aid".[47]

What the State cannot do is merely inform the Commission of the difficulties involved in implementing the decision, "without taking any real step to recover the aid from the undertakings concerned, and without proposing to the Commission any alternative arrangements".[48]

Recipient of aid unable to pay. The fact that the recipient of the aid is in no position to pay it back does not absolve the Member State from its obligation to seek recovery. Thus, where the Belgian government had granted aid in the form of the purchase of a holding in a company, it argued that as the company was unable to redeem the aid, the government could not implement the recovery decision without winding up the company.[49] The Court of Justice held:

> "The fact that, on account of the undertaking's financial position, the Belgian authorities could not recover the sum paid does not constitute proof that implementation was impossible, because the Commission's objective was to abolish the aid, and, as the Belgian Government itself admits, that objective could be attained by proceedings for the winding up of the company, which the Belgian authorities could institute in their capacity as shareholder or creditor."[50]

In *Tubemeuse*[51] the Belgian government brought unsuccessful proceedings to annul a recovery decision in respect of another measure which the Commission had held to be unlawful aid which was incompatible with the common market. The government argued that the recovery decision was "without purpose" because, by the time it was adopted, the recipient undertaking was subject to judicial composition proceedings and had "ceased to exist in economic terms."[52] Consequently, it was argued, intra-Community trade could no longer be affected or competition distorted. The

8–037

---

[47] Case C–404/00 *Commission v Spain*, n.33, above, at para.46.
[48] *ibid.*, at para.47.
[49] Case 52/84 *Commission v Belgium* [1986] E.C.R. 89; [1987] 1 C.M.L.R. 710. See also Case C–349/93 *Commission v Italy* [1995] E.C.R. I–343.
[50] Case 52/84 *Commission v Belgium*, n.49, above, at para.14.
[51] Case C–142/87 *Belgium v Commission ("Tubemeuse")*, n.26, above.
[52] *ibid.*, at para.49.

argument failed, but only on the facts. The court noted that in fact, the recipient had continued its economic activities throughout the composition proceedings, and had not ceased to exist in economic or legal terms. The court accordingly concluded that it could not be argued that the contested decision had no purpose.[53]

8–038   **The position of other creditors.**   The requirement that the Member State should make recovery save in cases of "absolute impossibility" raises a question as to whether the claim of the State should take priority over other creditors. On the face of it, it would be anomalous if the State, which has acted unlawfully, should recoup its funds ahead of a third party which had traded lawfully with the recipient of the aid, in ignorance of the unlawful grant of aid. In *Tubemeuse*[54] the Court of Justice rejected an argument that the requirement to recover aid would cause serious damage to other creditors. It explained, however, that the recovery decision at issue did not require the recovery of the aid in question on a "privileged basis".[55] Community law required only that recovery should take place in accordance with the relevant provisions of national law, provided that those provisions were applied in such a way that recovery was not rendered practically impossible. But the requirement that recovery should be "possible" did not extend to a requirement that the government's claim to recover the aid should rank ahead of other creditors. On the facts, the government was held to have fulfilled its obligations by seeking to have its debt registered as one of the recipient's unsecured liabilities and then, when that application was refused, lodging an appeal.[56]

8–039   **Legitimate expectations.**   The recipient of unlawful aid may, in exceptional circumstances, resist the repayment of aid on the basis of a legitimate expectation that the aid had been lawfully granted. Thus, in *RSV v Commission*,[57] the Court of Justice held that an unjustified 26 month delay on the part of the Commission in adopting a decision on the legality of the aid conferred a legitimate expectation on the recipient of the aid which prevented the Commission from requiring the State to order repayment. Nevertheless, in general, the position is that:

"undertakings to which an aid has been granted may not, in principle, entertain a legitimate expectation that the aid is lawful unless it has been granted in compliance with the procedure laid down in that article. A diligent businessman should normally be able to determine whether that procedure has been followed."[58]

---

[53] Case C–142/87 *Belgium v Commission ("Tubemeuse")*, n.26, above. at para.51.
[54] *ibid.*
[55] *ibid.*, at para.60.
[56] *ibid.*, at para.66.
[57] Case 223/85 *Rijn-Schelde-Verlome v Commission* [1987] E.C.R. 4617 at para. 17.
[58] Case 5/89 *Commission v Germany* [1990] E.C.R. I–3437 at para.14.

A Member State which granted unlawful aid is not itself entitled to invoke the legitimate expectations of the recipient in order to justify a failure to implement a Commission decision instructing it to recover unlawful aid. As the Community Courts have explained "[i]f it could do so, Arts 87 and 88 EC would be deprived of all practical force, since national authorities would thus be able to rely on their own unlawful conduct in order to render decisions taken by the Commission under those provisions of the Treaty ineffectual."[59]

(c) Right of third parties to seek recovery

Rights of third parties. The grant of unlawful aid is likely to have implications for third party competitors of the recipients—by definition, such aid is liable to distort competition. There is no obligation upon the Member State to make known to any interested parties that it has notified the Commission of a plan to grant such State aid.[60] But when competing undertakings[61] become aware of the grant of unlawful aid, or the misuse of aid, they are entitled to pursue certain Community law rights and remedies in respect of the grant of unlawful aid through the national courts.[62] **8–040**

Direct effect of the Article 88(3) prohibition on implementation. The object of the requirement to notify State aid is to prevent implementation of aid contrary to the rules of the Treaty.[63] Thus, as early as 1973 the Court of Justice decided, in the *Lorenz* case[64] that: **8–041**

"the prohibition on implementation referred to in the last sentence of Article [88(3)] has a direct effect and gives rise to rights in favour of individuals, which national courts are bound to safeguard."

The direct effect of this prohibition extends to all aid which has been implemented without being notified and, in the event of notification, until the Commission reaches a final decision.[65]

---

[59] Joined Cases T–116/00 and T–118/01 *P & O European Ferries (Vizcaya) SA v Diputación Foral de Vizcaya*, n.34, above, at para.202; Case I–67/94 *Ladbroke Racing v Commission*, n.29, above, at para.183; Case C–99/02 *Commission v Italy*, n.45, above, at para.21. Joined cases C–183/02 P and C–187/02 P *Daewoo Electronics Manufacturing España SA (Demesa) v Commission*, November 11, 2004, para.44.

[60] Joined Cases 91 and 127/83 *Heineken Brouwerijen BV v Inspecteur der Vennootschapsbelasting, Amsterdam and Utrecht* [1984] E.C.R. 3435 at paras 14–15.

[61] Case C–39/94 *Syndicat français de l'Express international (SFEI) and Ors v La Poste and Ors* [1996] E.C.R. I–3547, Opinion of A.G. Jacobs, para.72.

[62] Interested parties may also inform the Commission of any alleged unlawful aid or misuse of aid: Art.20(2) of the Procedural Regulation.

[63] Case 120/73 *Gebrüder Lorenz GmbH v Federal Republic of Germany and Land Rhine Palatinate* [1973] E.C.R. 1471 at para.3.

[64] *ibid.*, at para.8.

[65] *ibid.*

8–042 **Role of the national court in ordering recovery of the aid.** The involvement of national courts is the result of the direct effect of the last sentence of Art.88(3) EC.[66] As the Court of Justice explained in *FNCE*, national courts must offer to individuals in a position to rely upon a breach of that provision:

> "the certain prospect that all the necessary inferences will be drawn, in accordance with their national law, as regards the validity of measures giving effect to the aid, the recovery of financial support granted in disregard of that provision and possible interim measures." [67]

As has already been observed, the Commission also has the power to order recovery of unlawful State aid on an interim basis, pending its determination of the merits. As the ECJ observed in *SFEI*, the power of the Commission to order such repayment is subject to conditions, laid down in the Procedural Regulation. It may not act to order immediate recovery. It must give the Member State concerned the opportunity to submit its comments, and may only make such an order if certain criteria are established.[68] The Commission itself has observed: "[w]hile the Commission is not always in a position to act promptly to safeguard the interests of third parties in State aid matters, national courts may be better placed to ensure that breaches of the last sentence of Article [88(3)] are dealt with and remedied."[69] By contrast, the national courts are under a "duty" to safeguard the rights of individuals in the event of a breach of the requirement to give prior notification, notwithstanding the existence of a parallel power on the part of the Commission.[70] The obligatory nature of this duty was emphasised by the Commission in its Notice on co-operation between national courts and the Commission in the State aid field:

> "The [national] court should use all appropriate devices and remedies and apply all relevant provisions of national law to implement the direct effect of this obligation placed by the Treaty on the Member States. A national court must, in a case within its jurisdiction, apply Community law in its entirety and protect rights which that law confers on individuals; it must therefore set aside any provision of national law which may conflict with it, whether prior or subsequent to the Community rule."[71]

---

[66] Case C–39/94 *Syndicat français de l'Express international (SFEI) and Ors v La Poste and Ors*, n.61, above, at para.39.

[67] Case C–354/90 *Fédératation Nationale du Commerce Extérieur des Produits Alimentairs and Syndicat National des Négotiants et Transformateurs de Saumon v France*, n.25, above, at para.12.

[68] Procedural Regulation, Art.11. See para.8–030, above.

[69] Notice on co-operation between national courts and the Commission in the State aid field [1995] O.J. C312/8, para.3.

[70] Case C–39/94 *Syndicat français de l'Express international (SFEI) and Ors v La Poste and Ors*, n.61, above, at para.44.

[71] [1995] O.J. C312/8, para.10.

The fact the Commission may be in the course of examining the measure and may not yet have given a decision does not deprive the national courts of their jurisdiction to consider whether there has been a breach of the requirement to give prior notification.[72]

Consideration of "aid" by national court. As has already been explained,[73] the Commission has exclusive competence in respect of the question of compatibility of aid with the common market. The national court may not engage this question when seeking to determine whether to order recovery. Its role is to do:

8–043

"no more than preserve, until the final decision of the Commission, the rights of individuals faced with a possible breach by State authorities of the prohibition laid down in Article 88(3) of the Treaty. When those courts make a ruling in such a matter, they do not thereby decide on the compatibility of the aid with the common market, the final determination on that matter being the exclusive responsibility of the Commission, subject to the supervision of the Court of Justice."[74]

In carrying out this assessment, the national court must, of course, determine whether or not the measure at issue is in fact State aid. In *R. v Commissioners of Customs & Excise Ex p. Lunn Poly*[75] the Court of Appeal held that even where the question whether there had been a contravention of Art.88(3) EC arises in the course of judicial review proceedings, that issue is one of precedent fact.[76] The court must accordingly decide the question for itself; its function is not confined to one of review. In a suitable case, this may require oral evidence and cross-examination, even in judicial review proceedings. Such questions can give rise to great difficulty.[77] Both the Court of Justice[78] and the Commission[79] have encouraged national courts to seek clarification from the Commission on this question, where doubts are

---

[72] Case C–39/94 *Syndicat français de l'Express international (SFEI) and Ors v La Poste and Ors*, n.61, above, at para.44.

[73] para.8–011, above.

[74] Case C–354/90 *Fédératation Nationale du Commerce Extérieur des Produits Alimentaires and Syndicat National des Négotiants et Transformateurs de Saumon v France*, n.25, above, at para.14.

[75] [1999] S.T.C. 330 at 358, CA.

[76] See *R. v Secretary of State for the Home Dept Ex p. Khawaja* [1984] A.C. 74.

[77] See Notice on co-operation between national courts and the Commission in the State aid field [1995] O.J. C312/8, para.23. By way of example, the Divisional Court and Court of Appeal in *R. v Commissioners for Customs and Excise Ex p. Lunn Poly* [1990] S.T.C. 350 and the VAT and Duties Tribunal in *GIL v Commissioners for Customs and Excise* [2001] Eu. L.R. 401 all expressed the view that higher rate Insurance Premium Tax was a State aid; the ECJ subsequently reached the opposite conclusion: Case C–308/01 *GIL Insurance v Commissioners of Customs & Excise*, April 29, 2004. See also *BT3G Ltd & Ors v Secretary of State for Trade and Industry* [2001] EWCA Civ 1448, CA.

[78] Case C–39/94 *Syndicat français de l'Express international (SFEI) and Ors v La Poste and Ors*, n.61, above, at para.50.

[79] Notice on co-operation between national courts and the Commission in the State aid field, n.77, above, para.9, and in respect of co-operation more generally, paras 26–32.

entertained. Where such a request is made, the Commission is obliged to respond as quickly as possible.[80]

8–044   The duty to order repayment. Where an order for the recovery of unlawful aid is sought from a national court, it is under a strict, but not absolute, duty to order repayment. In the *SFEI* case, the ECJ explained:

> "a finding that aid has been granted in breach of the last sentence of Article [88(3)] must in principle lead to its repayment in accordance with the procedural rules of domestic law."[81]

The reason for this strict rule is that, as the court went on to explain, any other interpretation would encourage Member States to disregard the prohibition laid down in Art.88(3) EC.[82] It is nevertheless clear that the duty to order repayment is subject to important qualifications. In *SFEI*, the court accepted that there may be "exceptional circumstances" in which it would be inappropriate to order repayment of the aid.[83] The court did not define those circumstances, but referred to a passage of the Opinion of A.G. Jacobs in *SFEI*. [84] The only example the Advocate General gave of such exceptional circumstances was derived from the ECJ's case law concerning recovery of aid by the Commission, namely the possibility that a legitimate expectation on the part of the recipient of the aid might preclude recovery, which is considered above.[85] It is quite clear, however, that neither the language of the Advocate General, nor that of the court's judgment is exhaustive.[86] *SFEI* leaves entirely open the possibility that there may be other "exceptional circumstances" in which repayment would be precluded. It may be that other general principles of Community law, such as would justify the Commission in declining to order recovery from the Member State,[87] would defeat an action for recovery. Where the recipient of aid seeks to rely upon such exceptional circumstances to decline to refund unlawful aid in a case before a national court, it is for that court to assess the material circumstances, if necessary after obtaining a preliminary ruling from the Court of Justice.[88]

8–045   Prior compatibility decision. By the time the national court reaches a

---

[80] Case C–2/88 *JJ Zwartveld & Ors* [1990] E.C.R. I–3365 at paras 17–18, applied in *SFEI* at para.50.
[81] *SFEI*, n.78, above, at para.68.
[82] *ibid.*, at para.69.
[83] *ibid.*, at para.70.
[84] paras. 73–77 of the Opinion of A.G. Jacobs.
[85] para.8–039, above.
[86] Contrast the approach of the CFI in Case T–55/99 *Confederacion Española de Transporte de Mercancías (CETM) v Commission* [2000] E.C.R. II–3207 at paras 115–131: exceptional circumstances did not suffice to preclude repayment as did not justify any legitimate expectation.
[87] Art.14(1) of the Procedural Regulation.
[88] Case 5/89 *Commission v Germany* [1990] E.C.R. I–3437 at para.16.

decision as to whether aid has been granted unlawfully, the Commission may have reached a decision that the aid, although unlawful, is compatible with the common market.[89] In *FNCE*,[90] Mr A.G. Jacobs expressed the view that in those circumstances, the national court may still be required to order repayment; otherwise, Member States would have an incentive not to await the outcome of the Commission's investigation. He concluded:

> "In principle, therefore, the national courts must ensure the recovery of all aid paid prematurely. If it is necessary to allow an undertaking to retain any aid paid prematurely, such aid being set off against aid payable subsequently under a plan found compatible with the common market, then an adjustment may have to be made to offset any competitive advantage that would otherwise accrue to the undertaking concerned by reason of early payment."[91]

In its judgment in *FNCE*, the Court of Justice did not expressly endorse this approach, but observed that the Commission's final decision "does not have the effect of regularizing *ex post facto* the implementing measures which were invalid because they had been taken in breach of the prohibition laid down by the last sentence of Art. 93(3) of the Treaty".[92]

Repayment from a successor.   Where the recipient of unlawful aid has been subsequently sold to another undertaking, the purchaser may not be required to make repayment of unlawful aid. In *Banks v Coal Authority*,[93] the ECJ found that a coal industry levy which Banks, a coal mining company, was required to pay, but which British Coal, and certain State-owned coal companies which succeeded it, did not have to pay, amounted to unlawful aid to those competitors. The State-owned companies had subsequently been sold to private undertakings and not received further aid. The ECJ concluded that the purchasing undertakings could not be required to repay the aid: **8–046**

> "Since those undertakings bought the companies in question under non-discriminatory competitive conditions and, by definition, at the market price, that is to say at the highest price which a private investor acting under normal competitive conditions was ready to pay for those companies in the situation they were in, in particular after having enjoyed State aid, the aid element was assessed at the market price and included in the purchase price. In such circumstances, the undertakings to which the

---

[89] See para.8–031, above.
[90] Case C–354/90 *Fédératation Nationale du Commerce Extérieur des Produits Alimentairs and Syndicat National des Négotiants et Transformateurs de Saumon v France*, n.25, above.
[91] *ibid.*, at para.28.
[92] *ibid.*, at para.16.
[93] Case C–390/98 *HJ Banks & Co Ltd v The Coal Authority and Secretary of State for Trade and Industry* [2001] E.C.R. I–6117; [2001] 3 C.M.L.R. 51.

tenders were granted cannot be regarded as having benefited from an advantage in relation to other market operators."[94]

The effect of such a transaction is, however, that the seller of the recipient company in effect retains the benefit of the aid, as the court went on to note. On the facts of *Banks*, the State was both the provider of the aid, and the recipient; in those circumstances, ordering the State to repay the aid to itself would be nonsensical.

8–047   **Interim relief.**   The national court is under a duty to grant interim measures in an appropriate case.[95] In its Notice on co-operation between national courts and the Commission in the State aid field[96] the Commission suggested by way of example that that the judge may "as appropriate" order "the freezing or return of monies illegally paid".

8–048   **Recovery of charges.**   It is well established that as a principle, the State is in principle required to repay charges levied in breach of Community law.[97] Thus, where unlawful aid has been financed by a levy which forms an "integral part" of that aid, "national courts must in principle order reimbursement of charges or contributions levied specifically for the purpose of financing that aid".[98] In *Banks v Coal Authority*,[99] the facts of which are summarised above,[1] the ECJ accepted that the situation which existed prior to the grant of the contested aid could not be restored by ordering repayment[2] but nevertheless concluded that "[p]ersons liable to pay an obligatory contribution cannot rely on the argument that the exemption enjoyed by other persons constitutes State aid in order to avoid payment of that contribution".[3] In that case, the contributions paid by Banks did not finance the grant of aid; rather, the aid was comprised of the exemption itself.

8–049   **Action for damages by competitors.**   The grant of unlawful aid may cause

---

[94] *ibid.*, [2001] E.C.R. I–6117 at para.77.

[95] C–354/90 *Fédératation Nationale du Commerce Extérieur des Produits Alimentairs and Syndicat National des Négotiants et Transformateurs de Saumon v France*, n.25, above, at para.12; Case C–39/94 *Syndicat français de l'Express international (SFEI) and Ors v La Poste and Ors*, n.61, above, at para.40.

[96] [1995] O.J. C312/8, para.10.

[97] Joined Cases C–192/95 to C–218/95 *Comateb & Ors v Directeur général des douanes et droits indirects* [1997] E.C.R. I–165 at para.20.

[98] Joined Cases C–261/01 and C–262/01 *Belgium v Calster & Ors* [2004] 1 C.M.L.R. 18, para.54. This is so whether or not the person seeking the refund was affected by the distortion of competition caused by the measure: case C–174/02 *Streekgewest*, n.10, above, para.21.

[99] Case C–390/98 *HJ Banks & Co Ltd v The Coal Authority and Secretary of State for Trade and Industry*, n.93, above.

[1] para.8–046, above.

[2] See para.8–046, above.

[3] Case C–390/98 *HJ Banks & Co Ltd v The Coal Authority and Secretary of State for Trade and Industry*, n.93, above, at para.80. In reaching this view, the court invoked its earlier judgments in Case C–437/97 *EKW and Wein & Co* [2000] E.C.R. I–1158 at paras 51–53 and Case C–36/99 *Idéal Tourisme v Belgium* [2000] E.C.R. I–6049 at paras 26–29.

harm to a competitor of the recipient of the aid. The aid may, for example, allow that competitor to lower prices and capture additional market share. Harm may be done even where the recipient of the aid ultimately repays the aid. In *Banks v Coal Authority*,[4] the Court of Justice said:

> "restoring the situation prior to the payment of aid which was unlawful or incompatible with the common market is a necessary requirement for preserving the effectiveness of the provisions of the Treaties concerning State aid and the national court must examine, in the light of the circumstances, whether it is possible to uphold the individuals' claims so as to help restore the previous situation."

That suggests that compensation ought to be available to the injured party, as does the Commission's Notice on co-operation between national courts and the Commission in the State aid field.[5] In *Banks*, the Court of Justice made clear that whilst Banks could not avoid the obligation to pay the contested royalty on grounds that it gave rise to an unlawful State aid, this was

> "without prejudice to any action which it, or other competitors of the undertakings which British Coal's former competitors might bring, if the conditions were met, for compensation for any damage caused to them by the competitive advantage enjoyed by British Coal and State companies which succeeded it."[6]

But this may not always be the case. It is clear that in such circumstances, the injured party can in principle claim damages from the State which awarded the aid.[7] The English High Court[8] has indicated that to make good such a claim it would be necessary to satisfy the restrictive criteria for the award of damages set down by the Court of Justice in the *Francovich*[9] line of cases, namely that the rule of law infringed was intended to confer rights on individuals, that the breach is sufficiently serious to sound in damages and that there is a direct causal link between the breach and the damage sustained.[10]

Damages from the recipient of aid.   There is, as yet, no Community remedy   **8–050**

---

[4] Case C–390/98 *HJ Banks & Co Ltd v The Coal Authority and Secretary of State for Trade and Industry*, n.93, above, at para.75.
[5] [1995] O.J. C312/8, para.13.
[6] Case C–390/98 *HJ Banks & Co Ltd v The Coal Authority and Secretary of State for Trade and Industry*, n.93, above, at para.80.
[7] Case C–39/94 *Syndicat français de l'Express international (SFEI) and Ors v La Poste and Ors* [1996], n.61, above, at para.75.
[8] *Betws Anthracite Ltd v DSK Anthrazit Ibbenburen GmbH* (2004) 1 All E.R. 1237 at para.75.
[9] Cases C–6 and 9/90 *Francovich and Bonifaci v Italy* [1991] E.C.R. I–5357; [1993] 2 C.M.L.R. 66.
[10] Cases C–46 and 48/93 *Brasserie du Pêcheur and Factortame* [1996] E.C.R. I–1029 at para.51.

in damages against the recipient of aid. In *SFEI*, the Court of Justice ruled that "Community law does not provide a sufficient basis for the recipient to incur liability where he has failed to verify that the aid received was duly notified to the Commission."[11] The reason is that the EC Treaty does not impose any "specific obligation on the recipient of the aid". The duty to notify under Art.88(3) lies upon the Member State; it is the Member State, not the recipient of the aid which is the addressee of a decision as to the compatibility of the aid.[12] Whilst the Court of Justice made plain in SFEI that Community law did not *preclude* the possible use of a national law remedy in respect of such liability, no such remedy arose solely as a matter of Community law.[13] In *SFEI*,[14] Advocate General Jacobs expressed the view that effective remedies existed in the form of an action for recovery and a claim for damages against the State.

8–051 **Misuse of aid.** The English High Court has rejected an attempt to claim damages by a competitor against the recipient of the aid itself, in circumstances where the recipient had been found by the Commission to have misused aid. In the *Betws* case[15] the claimant produced anthracite coal in South Wales. The defendant, Preussag, produced anthracite coal in Germany and imported it to the UK. The defendant had received lawful State aid, but the Commission had subsequently decided that the aid had been misused. It ordered the German state to require the company to repay part of the aid. Betws argued that the misuse of aid had distorted competition between it and Preussag, by allowing it to engage in predatory and discriminatory pricing. It argued that unlike *SFEI*, Preussag was responsible for the unlawfulness: it had an obligation to its competitors use the aid conferred upon it properly. It invoked the subsequent decision of the Court of Justice in the more recent case of *Courage v Crehan*[16] in which it had held that a party to a contract which was in breach of Art.81 could in some circumstances sue the other party for damages for loss caused by performance of the contract. Morison J. rejected the argument. He concluded that the fact that Preussag had used the aid unlawfully did not suffice to distinguish the case from *SFEI*. The duty to comply with the State aid rules lay upon the State; the only possible target for a claim for damages was the State itself.

---

[11] Case C–39/94 *Syndicat français de l'Express international (SFEI) and Ors v La Poste and Ors*, n.61, above, at para.74.
[12] *ibid.*, at para.73.
[13] *ibid.*, at para.75.
[14] *ibid.*, Opinion of A.G. Jacobs, para.82.
[15] *Betws Anthracite Ltd v DSK Anthrazit Ibbenburen GmbH*, n.8, above.
[16] Case C–453/99 [2001] E.C.R. I–6297; [2001] 5 C.M.L.R. 28. See paras 7–031–7–033, above.

CHAPTER 9

PRACTICE AND PROCEDURE IN EUROPE

Anneli Howard[1]

1. INTRODUCTION

Modernisation. On May 1, 2004, Council Regulation 1/2003[2] ("the Modernisation Regulation") came into force which revolutionises the enforcement of Community competition law in the European Union and the relationship between the Commission and the national competition authorities ("NCAs") and national courts. These reforms, together with a new Commission Regulation 773/2004,[3] repeal Regulation 17/62 and amend the Commission's practices and procedures so that it can concentrate its administrative resources on investigating serious cartel offences and abuses of dominant position.[4]

9–001

The European Competition Network. The Modernisation Regulation establishes a network of public authorities (the "European competition network" or "ECN") comprised of the Commission and the competent authorities of each of the 25 Member States.[5] The Modernisation Regulation sets out the administrative framework for the Commission and the NCAs to apply the Community competition rules in close co-operation.

9–002

Judicial review before the Community Courts. The decentralisation of competition law enforcement to the national courts will also underpin the influence of the Community institutions. Commission decisions in a specific

9–003

---

[1] Barrister, Monckton Chambers and former référendaire to Judge David Edward at the ECJ.
[2] Council the Modernisation Regulation on the implementation of the rules on competition laid down in Arts 81 and 82 of the Treaty [2003] O.J. L1/1.
[3] Commission Regulation 773/2004 relating to the conduct of proceedings by the Commission pursuant to Arts 81 and 82 of the EC Treaty [2004] O.J. L123/18.
[4] See the 3rd recital to the Modernisation Regulation.
[5] The competent authorities are designated by the Member States under Art.35 of the Modernisation Regulation.

case will be binding upon NCAs and national courts in all Member States.[6] There will therefore be a greater incentive for accused undertakings to challenge Commission findings via judicial review to the Court of First Instance.[7] The anticipated increase in private litigation before national courts can be expected to produce an initial stream of preliminary references to the European Court of Justice.[8] These judicial pronouncements will help to secure the consistent application of Community competition law across the Union.

9–004 **Plan of this chapter.** Section 2 of this chapter sets out a brief overview of the co-operation mechanisms between the Commission and the NCAs and the extent to which they may impact on the wider interests of participants in the Commission's investigations. Section 3 deals with the procedures for seeking informal guidance from the Commission and for submitting complaints, whistle-blowing or applying for immunity from fines. Section 4 analyses the procedural and tactical implications of the Commission exercising its powers to grant interim relief, make findings of non-applicability and accept binding commitments. Section 5 deals with the Commission's investigatory powers. Section 6 covers the undertakings' participation in and procedural rights during the Commission's investigation and sets out the process for access to the file, written submissions and oral hearings. Section 7 deals with the adoption of the Commission's formal decision. Section 8 describes the procedural steps for challenging a Commission decision before the Court of First Instance. Section 9 explains the relationship between national courts and the European Court of Justice and sets out the various stages of the preliminary reference procedure.

2. CO-OPERATION BY THE COMMISSION WITHIN THE EUROPEAN COMPETITION NETWORK

9–005 **Generally.** Detailed information on the extent of co-operation between the Commission, the NCAs and the national courts as a result of modernisation is set out in Chapter 10. This section is confined to describing the extent to which such co-operation has been built into the Commission's administrative procedures. The exchange of information and consultation between

---

[6] Case C–344/98 *Masterfoods* [2000] E.C.R. I–11369 at para.58 and paras 8, 11–14 of the Commission Notice on the co-operation between the Commission and courts of the EU Member States in the application of Arts 81 and 82 EC [2004] O.J. C101/54 ("the Notice on co-operation with national courts"). For co-operation between the Commission and national courts generally, see paras 10–057—10–072, below.

[7] The extent to which the Commission's findings in one case will be binding in a similar or related case pending at national level, is not clear. Undertakings may want to resist findings of dominance or appreciability being extended to other cases.

[8] This is especially so in view of the potential risk of Member State liability in damages if national supreme courts refuse to refer questions for preliminary reference; Case C–224/01 *Gerhard Köbler v Austria* [2003] E.C.R. I–10239; [2003] 3 C.M.L.R. 28.

the various enforcement authorities will have practical implications for private parties (*e.g.* complainants, whistleblowers or undertakings suspected of committing an infringement). There may be particular concerns for the protection of the parties' business secrets, other confidential information and, potentially, their rights of defence.

Investigation procedures. The Commission and the NCAs will work closely together when conducting inspections. The NCA officials may actively assist the Commission with obtaining judicial warrants and conducting "dawn raids" or may even, in an appropriate case, carry out the inspections on behalf of the Commission. Further details are set out at paras 9–045–9–051, below.

9–006

Consultation procedures. The Modernisation Regulation sets up framework arrangements for the exchange of information and consultation between the members of the ECN. The mechanics have been fleshed out in various Commission Notices[9] and guidance, which have been drafted and will be revised, from time to time, in close co-operation with the Member State authorities.[10] The Commission must, pursuant to Art.11(2) of the Modernisation Regulation, transmit copies of the most important documents on its files to the NCAs before it takes a formal decision on interim relief, non-applicability or commitments, withdrawal of a block exemption in a particular case, or a final infringement decision imposing behavioural or structural remedies. If the NCA requests, the Commission shall provide it with a copy of any other documents before taking any formal decision.

9–007

The Advisory Committee. The Commission is assisted by the Advisory Committee on Restrictive Practices and Dominant Positions ("the Advisory Committee") which, may discuss general issues of Community competition law or the proposed treatment of individual cases by the Commission or, where appropriate, the NCAs. For discussions of individual cases, the Advisory Committee is composed of representatives from the NCAs. Where wider issues are being discussed, additional Member State representatives or experts who are competent in competition matters may be appointed.[11] Meetings need not be quorate. The Commission must consult the Advisory Committee before it takes any formal decision on interim relief, non-applicability or commitments, withdrawal of a block exemption in a particular case, the imposition of periodic penalties or a final infringement decision imposing behavioural or structural remedies.[12] Consultation can take place through meetings or via a written procedure, as follows:

9–008

---

[9] See the Notice on co-operation with national courts, n.6, above and the Commission Notice on co-operation within the network of competition authorities [2004] O.J. C101/43 ("the ECN co-operation notice").

[10] Recital 15 and Art.33(1) of the Modernisation Regulation.

[11] Art.14(2) of the Modernisation Regulation.

[12] Art.14(1) of the Modernisation Regulation.

(a)   Under the *written procedure*, the Commission will invite the NCAs to circulate their observations to all other Member States within a 14 day period.[13] If a Member State objects to the use of the written procedure, the Commission has to convene a meeting.

(b)   *Meetings of the Advisory Committee* will be convened by the Commission dispatching a notice, including a summary of the case, an indication of the most important documents and a preliminary draft decision. The meeting will be held no earlier than 14 days after dispatch.[14] The Advisory Committee will provide a written opinion on the draft decision ("the advisory opinion"), which will be delivered and discussed at the meeting and appended to the draft decision. The advisory opinion will only be reasoned (in part) in appropriate cases and need not be published.[15] The Commission is not bound by the advisory opinion but is required to take "the utmost account" of it. The Commission must explain to the Advisory Committee the manner in which it has taken the advisory opinion into account.

Members of the Advisory Committee are bound by the obligations of professional secrecy laid down in Art.28 of the Modernisation Regulation. The publication of any advisory opinions will protect undertakings' legitimate business secrets.

9–009   **Exchange of information.**   Article 12(1) of the Modernisation Regulation provides for extensive disclosure of any information that has been collected by the Commission within the European competition network. The exchange is reciprocal so the Commission will receive information from the NCAs.[16] Disclosure extends to "any matter of fact or of law, including confidential information". It will therefore cover business secrets, commercially sensitive or legally privileged information provided in complaints, applications for informal guidance or leniency applications. Disclosure to

---

[13]   Reduced to seven days for decisions on interim relief.

[14]   For decisions on interim relief, the meeting may be held seven days after dispatch.

[15]   Query, however, whether a copy of the advisory opinion or a summary of its contents could be obtained through the Community's Access to Information regime in Regulation 1049/2001 of the European Parliament and of the Council regarding public access to European Parliament, Council and Commission documents [2001] O.J. L145/43.

[16]   Note that NCAs only have a power, as opposed to a duty, to disclose such information to the Commission and make exercise some discretion over the extent to which they make particular information available to the European Community network: see paras 6.11 and 6.13 of the draft OFT guideline on *Powers of Investigation* (404), which reserves the right of the OFT to assess:

(1)   the public interest;

(2)   the confidential nature of the information; and

(3)   the necessity for its disclosure for the purpose of a Community obligation under Art.11 or 18(6) of the Modernisation Regulation.

the European Community network is automatic in the sense that there is no opportunity for the undertakings concerned to object or submit observations.

Use of information exchanged. Members of the ECN will be entitled to use exchanged information "as evidence" to establish an infringement of Community competition law "in respect of the subject-matter"[17] for which it was collected by the transmitting authority. Moreover, NCAs can use it as evidence for establishing a parallel infringement of their own national competition law in the same case, provided the parallel application of such law does not lead to a different outcome.[18]   9–010

Protection of confidential information. The extent to which NCAs can disclose such information to third parties is also unclear and may be determined by national law, which will vary from Member State to Member State.[19] Exchanges within the ECN could lead to sensitive information being revealed to third parties, such as competitors or important trading partners, with ramifications for the undertaking's market or commercial bargaining position. Such disclosure could a proliferation of private damages claims from disaffected suppliers or customers before the national courts. Further, some NCAs may choose to disclose the information to other sectoral regulators who may arguably use it as a basis for a separate regulatory investigation.[20] In light of the potential repercussions of disclosure to the NCAs in all 25 Member States, undertakings should take extreme caution to control and protect the extent of confidential information that is set out in   9–011

---

[17] As interpreted by the ECJ, "subject matter" refers to the factual circumstances of the suspected infringement, such as the alleged restriction or distortion of competition, the mechanics of the agreement, concerted practice or abuse and the products affected. See Case 85/87 *Dow Benelux v Commission* [1989] E.C.R. 3137.

[18] From the scheme of the Modernisation Regulation as a whole, "different outcome" does not appear to be confined to the uniformity of any sanctions imposed (in terms of custodial sentences versus fines). The author suggests that the term is read in the light of the NCAs' duties of consistency set out in Arts 3 and 16(2) of the Modernisation Regulation so that the application of national competition law cannot run counter to the decision eventually reached by the Commission. National competition law cannot permit agreements, decisions or practices which would be prohibited under Arts 81 or 82 of the Treaty or, so far as the Chapter I infringement is concerned, prohibit agreements that would be permitted under Art.81. NCAs are allowed to impose stricter sanctions under national law prohibiting unilateral conduct even if it does not fall foul of Art.82 EC.

[19] Note that NCAs are bound by Art.28 of the Modernisation Regulation and cannot disclose information acquired or exchanged by them that is subject to "professional secrecy" obligations. However, there is no uniform definition of professional secrecy across the Community and, as shown by Case 155/79 *AM&S v Commission* [1982] E.C.R. 1575; [1982] 2 C.M.L.R. 264, the legal systems of the various Member States respect differing standards of legal privilege. The OFT has stated that UK rules on legal professional privilege will apply when it investigates on its own initiative or on behalf of another NCA or the Commission. This means it will not transmit in-house legal communications to the ECN. However, the OFT will receive and use such communications from other NCAs in Member States that do not confer privilege: see paras 6.2 and 6.3 of the OFT Guideline on Powers of Investigation, OFT 404.

[20] In the UK and Ireland, there will be particular concern about using exchanged information for the purpose of prosecuting criminal cartel offences against the company directors.

any submissions to the Commission. Such information may be submitted in the form of written representations on the statement of objections or as arguments against the rejection of a complaint.

9–012 **Best practice for protecting confidential information.** Regulation 773/2004 clearly places the burden of identifying confidential information on the parties rather than on the Commission services.[21] Recommended best practice is for the parties to submit a clean and redacted version of their submissions. In the "clean" version, information should be clearly marked as confidential by adopting the now standard practice of surrounding enclosing it with square brackets followed by a confidentiality sign as follows: [*confidential information*] [**C**]. In the redacted version, the confidential passages will be deleted. An accompanying annex should set out a table identifying the precise passage and paragraph location of the information that is sought to be protected together with a brief description of the deleted information and reasons in support of its confidential status. The reasons should demonstrate how disclosure of such information would significantly damage the undertaking's interests or the individual's reputation or private life. Business secrets are confined to a narrow field of industrial property rights. Typical justifications for other confidential information include sales figures, costs information, market share information, customer lists, commercial strategy, etc.[22] Parties may be called upon to substantiate their claim for confidentiality with regard to each statement identified in a particular document. Failure to comply with such a request within the specified time-limit (at least two weeks) will entitle the Commission to assume that the documents or statements concerned do not contain confidential information.[23]

9–013 **Commission practice.** It is common practice for the Commission to ask the parties to review the Commission's statement of objections, case summaries, notices or final decision in advance to identify any information that should not be published. The Commission will take care not to disclose confidential information as part of the access to the file procedure. However, this is without prejudice to the extensive provision for the exchange of information (including confidential information) with the NCAs. As an additional precaution, undertakings should reserve the right to make further submissions should the NCAs wish to use such information for wider purposes or to disclose the information to a wider circle.

---

[21] Art.16 of Regulation 773/2004.
[22] See the definitions contained in paras 17–18 of the Commission draft notice on access to the file ([2004] O.J. C259/8).
[23] Art.16(3) of Regulation 773/2004.

3. INFORMAL GUIDANCE, COMPLAINTS AND WHISTLE-BLOWING

(a) Requests for informal guidance

Abolition of notification.   A major reform introduced by the Modernisation   **9–014**
Regulation is that the Commission will no longer accept notifications or
applications for negative clearance or grant informal comfort letters.
Agreements which fall under Art.81(1) but which fulfil the conditions in
Art.81(3) are valid and enforceable without a prior decision by a competition authority.[24] Undertakings are expected to conduct their own self-
assessment of the legality of their commercial agreements and practices, by
reference to the block exemptions, Commission guidelines and notices and
case law of the Community courts.[25]

Informal guidance.   Notwithstanding this general position, the Commission   **9–015**
will issue informal guidance in cases that raise novel or unresolved questions
for the application of the Community competition rules.[26] The Commission
has a wide discretion whether to issue such guidance, depending on the
appropriateness of the request and the Commission's wider enforcement
priorities.[27]

Formalities of the request.   Undertakings can apply for informal guidance   **9–016**
by sending a detailed reasoned request to the Competition DG. There is no
prescribed form. The request can be submitted before or after the agreement
or practice has been put into effect.[28] In addition to setting out the factual
background and enclosing all relevant documentation, the request will need
to provide:

(1) an explanation of the novelty of the legal issue regarding the
      application of Arts 81 and 82 EC, which has not been settled by
      previous decisions, guidance or case law;

(2) an explanation of the utility of the informal guidance for the market
      sector concerned, in view of the importance of the products or ser-
      vices for consumers, the common trade usage of the commercial
      practice, or the economic investments linked to the proposed
      transactions;

---

[24] Art.1 of the Modernisation Regulation.
[25] Commission Notice on informal guidance relating to novel question concerning Arts 81 and
      82 of the EC Treaty that arise in individual cases [2004] O.J. C101/78 ("the Guidance
      Notice"), para.3.
[26] Recital 38 of the Modernisation Regulation.
[27] Guidance Notice, paras 5 and 7.
[28] *ibid.*, paras 10 and 12.

(3) a declaration that the agreement or practice is not subject to proceedings pending before a NCA or national court or the Community courts.

If these conditions are not met, the Commission will reject the request as inappropriate.[29] The Commission is also entitled to reject hypothetical or obsolete questions or requests that are factually imprecise.[30]

9–017 **Effect of informal guidance.** Guidance letters are informal and will not bind NCAs, the national or Community courts or even the Commission in subsequent proceedings. The Commission may use the information contained in the request as the basis for starting its own investigation or exchange it with NCAs from other Member States. As guidance letters will be published on the Commission's website, the request should clearly identify and request protection for all confidential information.[31]

(b) *Complaints*

9–018 **Generally.** The Commission has set up two mechanisms for consumers and undertakings to inform it about suspected infringements:

(1) Informants may post or email market information to the Antitrust Registry's mailbox on an informal basis.[32] The information does not have to comply with any specific formalities. Although the Commission will handle such correspondence in line with good administrative practice, the informants will not be entitled to the same procedural safeguards as complainants.

(2) Complainants may lodge a formal complaint with the Commission under Art.7(2) of the Modernisation Regulation. Provided the complaint satisfies certain requirements, the complainant will be entitled to participate in the Commission's investigation.

The rest of this chapter will deal with the procedural and formal requirements for formal complaints.

9–019 **Choice of forum.** There are considerable advantages in consumers, competitors and affected trading partners making a direct complaint to the Commission rather than starting proceedings before a NCA or national

---

[29] *ibid.*, paras 8–9.
[30] *ibid.*, para.10.
[31] See para.9–012, above.
[32] See link at *www.europa.eu.*

court. In addition to cost considerations, any eventual Commission decision will have binding status on all NCAs and national courts in all 25 Member States.[33] This will mean that the complainant is saved the uncertainty and expense of proving dominance or the distortion of competition and can restrict the issues of any private litigation to causation and quantum of loss. However, as set out in more detail below, the Commission is not required to accept all complaints submitted to it and will take account of the alternative enforcement options available to the complainant as part of its admissibility assessment. At the outset, the complainant should address the respective merits of a complaint to the Commission *vis-à-vis* complaining to one or more NCAs or lodging a claim for injunctive or monetary relief before the national courts and be prepared to justify its position.

Formalities. Complaints must comply with the formalities set out in Art.5 **9–020** of Regulation 773/2004 and should follow the guidance in the Commission's complaints notice.[34] Complaints must provide the information set out in the model "Form C"[35] and attach any supporting information or documents. If the complainant cannot reasonably get hold of such documentation, it should inform the Commission where it can be obtained. The Form C information includes:

(1) detailed information about the complainant, its corporate group and business activities and its relationship to the undertaking(s) whose conduct the complaint relates to ("the accused");

(2) all available information regarding the accused, its corporate group and business activities;

(3) the facts establishing the existence of an infringement with full details of the alleged anti-competitive agreements, decisions or practices;

(4) tull details regarding the products or services affected, the relevant geographic market, the relative market positions of the undertakings concerned and any other relevant market data or statistics;

(5) explanation of any documentary evidence (*e.g.* texts of agreements, minutes, notes of telephone calls, business documents and correspondence). Identity of witnesses willing to testify or other persons who may be affected by the infringement;

---

[33] Case C–344/98 *Masterfoods*, n.6, above. Moreover, in the UK, by virtue of ss.47A and B of the Competition Act 1998, the Commission's infringement decision will bind the Competition Appeal Tribunal in any subsequent proceedings for monetary compensation.

[34] Commission Notice on the handling of complaints to the Commission under Art 81 and 82 of the EC Treaty [2004] O.J. C101/65 ("the Complaints Notice").

[35] A copy of Form C, annexed to Regulation 773/2004, is appended to this chapter. An electronic version is at *www.europa.eu.int/dgcomp/complaints-form*.

(6) details of the Member States affected and any effect on inter-state trade;

(7) details of the complainant's participation in any concurrent proceedings before NCAs or national courts regarding the same or closely related subject;

(8) the complainant's legitimate interest[36]; and

(9) the findings sought from the Commission.[37]

Although, in certain cases, the Commission may not insist on full compliance with these formalities, the general position is that a defective document may not be regarded as a "complaint" for the purposes of the Modernisation Regulation.[38] Even if the Commission takes account of the allegations by way of general information,[39] the informant will not be entitled to any procedural safeguards and will not be able to actively participate in the investigation.

9–021 Practicalities. The complaint should be submitted, in any one of the Community's official languages, in three hard copies plus an electronic version. If confidentiality is claimed, a non-confidential redacted version of the complaint, which can be released to third parties, should be provided in hard and soft format.[40] Complainants and informants can request that their identity remains anonymous and unless such request is manifestly unjustified, the Commission is obliged not to disclose their identity to the accused.[41] Note that complainants are expected to "cooperate diligently" throughout the Commission's investigation and update the Commission on recent developments.[42]

9–022 Legitimate interest. Member States will be deemed to possess a legitimate interest for the purposes of any complaint.[43] A private complainant, whether an individual or a company, must show that it has a legitimate interest in making the complaint and in seeking the termination of the alleged anti-

---

[36] See para. 9–022, below.
[37] Although contrary to the wording of Art.8 of the Modernisation Regulation and the Complaints Notice, it is also advisable to include submissions on interim relief, where appropriate: see para.9–037, below.
[38] Complaints Notice, para.32.
[39] See the first informal mechanism described at para. 9–018, above.
[40] Art.5 of Regulation 773/2004.
[41] Case 145/83 *Adams v Commission* [1985] E.C.R. 3539; [1986] 1 C.M.L.R. 506.
[42] Case T–77/94 *VGBO v Commission* [1997] E.C.R. II–759 at para.75.
[43] Complaints Notice, para.33.

competitive conduct.[44] Normally, the complainant must be directly and adversely affected by the alleged infringement; that criterion will usually be met if the complainant is a competitor or commercial trading partner of the accused.[45] The Commission may, at any stage in the investigation, reject the complaint as inadmissible if this criterion is not met.[46]

Administrative priorities. The Commission is entitled to allocate different priorities to the complaints brought before it and cannot be required to pursue a complaint to a final decision.[47-48] It may reject complaints that do not fit with the Community interest or its enforcement priorities.[49] Such a decision can be taken at any time, even after the Commission has taken investigative measures.[50] In light of these grounds of rejection, it is advisable to frame the complaint in terms that will anticipate and resolve any concerns that the Commission may have.

9–023

(1) *Community interest*: The Commission will assess the factual and legal aspects of the complaint to assess whether a further investigation furthers the Community interest.[51] There is no exhaustive list of the criteria that the Commission may take into account as part of this exercise and it deploys considerable discretion as to the weight to be attributed to each element in the circumstances of the particular case. Examples of such criteria include:

(a) whether the complainant can enforce its rights before the national courts;

(b) the seriousness and duration of the alleged infringement(s) and their effect(s) upon competition in the Community[52];

(c) whether the anti-competitive practice still persists[53] or can be negated by an offer of commitments about the undertaking(s)' future conduct[54];

(d) the probability of establishing the infringement, the scope of

---

[44] See Regulation 5(1) of Regulation 773/2004 and Art.7(2) of the Modernisation Regulation.
[45] Complaints Notice, paras 34–39. Trade associations and consumer associations can come forward if their members are directly and adversely affected. Individual consumers will be able to lodge complaints. Local and regional public authorities have standing to the extent that they purchase goods and services affected by the alleged infringement but cannot complain in order to protect the wider general interest.
[46] See paras 9–023 and 9–025, below.
[47-48] Case C–344/98 *Masterfoods*, n.6, above, at para.46 and Case C–119/97 P *Ufex v Commission* [1999] E.C.R. I–1341 at para.88.
[49] Case T–24/90 *Automec v Commission* [1992] E.C.R. II–2223 at para.76.
[50] Complaints Notice, para.45.
[51] Case C–119/97 P *Ufex v Commission*, n.47, above, at paras 79–80.
[52] *ibid.*, at paras 92–93.
[53] *ibid.*, at para.95.
[54] Case T–110/95 *IECC v Commission* [1998] E.C.R. II–3605 at para.56, affirmed by the ECJ in Case C–449/98 P *IECC* [2001] E.C.R. I–3875, at paras 44–47.

investigation required and the stage of investigation conducted to date[55];

(2) *Enforcement priorities*: the Commission will tend to focus on complaints about serious infringements where it is "well-placed to act".[56] That will normally be where the agreement(s) or practice(s) have effects on competition in more than three Member States or where the case raises new matters of Community competition law or policy that need uniform definition to ensure their consistent application in all Member States.[57]

9–024   Re-allocation of complaints.   The Commission is entitled to reject a complaint if another NCA is already dealing with the case or has already dealt with the agreement or practice.[58] In such circumstances, the Commission will inform the complainant without delay of the NCA concerned[59] so that the complainant can participate in the local investigation instead. However, the Commission may decide to pursue a complaint even though the same case is being handled by one or more NCAs under the Community or domestic law regime. The NCAs will only lose their competence to apply Arts 81 and 82 EC once the Commission has initiated its own investigation.[60] The re-allocation will only take place following consultation between the Commission and the NCA concerned.

9–025   Assessment Procedure.   As a matter of principle, the Commission will inform the complainant about its proposed course of action within four months of receipt.[61] Although this is not a binding time-limit, the complainant can seek judicial review if the Commission fails to act within a reasonable time.[62] The Commission's assessment procedure follows several stages. On receipt of the complaint, the Commission will run a preliminary examination of the factual and legal issues raised to see if there are sufficient grounds to start an investigation. At this preliminary stage, it may revert to the complainant for further clarification or to indicate its initial informal reaction. At the next stage, the Commission may consider that the information provided does not raise sufficient grounds for it to act. In such case, it must inform the complainant of its reasons for rejecting the complaint on this basis and impose a time-limit (of at least four weeks) for the complainant to submit its views in writing.[63] The complainant can request access, to

---

[55] Case T–24/90 *Automec v Commission*, n.49, above, at para.86.
[56] Complaints Notice, paras 8–11.
[57] ECN Co-operation Notice, paras 14–15.
[58] Art.13 of the Modernisation Regulation.
[59] Art.9 of Regulation 773/2004.
[60] Art.11(6) of the Modernisation Regulation.
[61] Complaints Notice, para.61.
[62] Art.232 of the EC Treaty as discussed in Case C–282/95 P *Guerin v Commission* [1997] E.C.R. I–1503 at paras 37–38.
[63] Arts 7(1) and 17(2) of Regulation 773/2004.

the Commission's file, subject to redaction of third party confidential information.[64] If the complainant fails to respond within the time-limit, the Commission is not obliged to take account of any late submissions and the complaint will be deemed to have been withdrawn.[65] If the complainant submits its observations but does not persuade the Commission to change its provisional assessment, the Commission will reject the complaint by formal decision.[66] This decision is subject to judicial review before the Court of First Instance.[67] If the complaint is adequately substantiated, the complaint will pass to the third substantive stage. At this stage, the Commission may consult with third parties, including the accused and other interested parties. The Commission will, most likely, disclose the complaint to the NCAs at an early stage as part of its co-operation within the network and consultation regarding case allocation.[68] At the end of the third stage, the Commission may decide to reject the complaint. This may be because the conduct does not fall within the scope of or does not infringe Arts 81 or 82.[69] In such case, the Commission must adopt a definitive reasoned decision rejecting the complaint, which may be challenged before the Court of First Instance.[70] Another potential ground for rejection is that another NCA is already dealing with the case or has already dealt with the agreement or practice.[71] It is not clear from the Modernisation Regulation whether or not the Commission must adopt a formal rejection decision or allow access to the case file. If not, the judicial review of case allocation before the Court of First Instance may be more problematic. A rejection decision means that the complainant cannot re-open the complaint unless it submits significant new evidence to the Commission.[72] However, as the rejection decision does not have the same binding status as an infringement decision, there is nothing to prevent the complainant from bringing subsequent proceedings before a NCA or national court.[73] If, at the third stage, the Commission decides to open an investigation, it will inform the complainant, who will be entitled to participate in the investigation. The initiation of proceedings will be made public.[74]

---

[64] Art.8 of Regulation 773/2004.
[65] Arts 7(1) and 7(3) of Regulation 773/2004.
[66] Art.7(2) of Regulation 773/2004.
[67] See paras 9–069–9–072, below.
[68] Art.11(2) of the Modernisation Regulation.
[69] The rejection may be accompanied by a formal finding of inapplicability under Art.10 or the acceptance of commitments under Art.9 of the Modernisation Regulation: see Section 4 of this chapter.
[70] Case 210/81 *Demo Studio Schmidt v Commission* [1983] E.C.R. 3045; [1984] 1 C.M.L.R. 63.
[71] Art.13 of the Modernisation Regulation and Art.9 of Regulation 773/2004.
[72] Complaints Notice, para.78.
[73] *ibid.*, para.79.
[74] Art.2(2) of Regulation 773/2004.

(c) Whistle-blowing and leniency applications

9–026 Generally. Whistle-blowing occurs when cartel participants want to terminate the anti-competitive agreement and minimise their exposure to fines. It frequently occurs when a minor player no longer wants to "toe the party line" or when a purchaser of one of the cartelists discovers skeletons in the corporate cupboard and wants to make a clean breast of the company's past trading activities. In highly concentrated markets, it can even be used against rivals for tactical advantage. There are considerable benefits in being the first to inform the Commission of a cartel or concerted practice as it can result in 100 per cent. immunity from any fines.[75] Applicants who are second or third past the post may still secure a significant reduction of up to 50 per cent of their fine, depending on whether the Commission has started its investigation.[76] An application for total immunity should be made at the same time as whistle blowing or, where the Commission is already aware of the existence of the cartel, the undertaking should apply for a significant reduction of its fine as soon as it can. Applications for total immunity from fines will only be successful where the undertaking was not a ringleader in the cartel and stops its involvement in the cartel as soon as it makes contact with the Commission.[77]

9–027 Initial contact. In view of the "race against time", informal contact should be made with the Commission immediately without waiting to submit a formal written application. Initial contact with the Commission on leniency matters can be made directly or through a legal advisor on the dedicated fax line: +32 2 299 45 85. This route records the precise time and date of the contact (which is important for leniency purposes) and ensures that the information is treated with the utmost confidentiality within the Commission. In exceptional cases, telephone contact may be made by on the dedicated numbers: +32 2 298 41 90 or +32 2 298 41 91. The initial leniency application can be made on a hypothetical basis by providing the Commission with a descriptive list of the evidence that the whistle-blower proposes to disclose at a later agreed date. This list should accurately reflect the nature and content of the evidence.[78] The Commission may reject the application outright if it is already aware of the infringement from another source. If the application is accepted, the Commission will provide a written acknowledgement of the application and confirm the date on which the undertaking provided or has to provide evidence of the cartel.

9–028 Submission of evidence. Once the Commission has been informed, the process can move at a rapid pace. The undertaking will be expected either to

---

[75] Pt A of the Commission notice on immunity from fines and reduction of fines in cartel cases [2002] O.J. C45/03 ("the Immunity Notice"), para.8.
[76] Pt B of the Immunity Notice.
[77] Pt B of the Immunity Notice, para.11.
[78] Immunity Notice, para.13(b).

provide the Commission with all the evidence relating to the suspected infringement available to it at that time or disclose, within a specified deadline, the evidence described in its list. Documentary evidence may be provided in redacted form to exclude sensitive or irrelevant matters. Business secrets and confidential information should be marked as confidential using the standard procedure.[79] If time allows, the best procedure is to conduct an internal investigation, collecting all the information available that may be relevant to the suspected infringement. Evidence may include personal data such as diaries, emails and telephone records. Company representatives and staff should be interviewed to probe their knowledge of the cartel, the extent of their participation, their memories of the key events and conversations and their understanding of the context of and statements in the documentary evidence. The content of the interviews should be submitted in the form of witness statements and exhibits.

Form of application. There is no set format for a formal leniency appli-   9–029
cation. A starting point would be the lay-out established for complaints in Form C.[80] The application should contain a comprehensive section on the factual events giving rise to the infringement, cross-referenced to an annex of documentary and witness evidence. The undertaking should also make extensive representations in mitigation, justifying its case for a reduction in the fine.

Leniency conditions. Leniency will only be awarded if the whistle-blower   9–030
provides the Commission with sufficient evidence which enables the Commission: (i) to adopt a decision to carry out an investigation; or (ii) to find an infringement of Art.81 EC.[81] The sufficiency of the evidence will be determined by the Commission in its own opinion. If, at the time of the application, the Commission already possesses sufficient information, the leniency application will be immediately refused. If the application is rejected for any reason, the undertaking may either withdraw the evidence disclosed or request the Commission to consider it by way of general co-operation outside the immunity regime.[82] This does not prevent the Commission from using its normal powers of investigation to obtain the information from the suspected cartel participants.

Grant of immunity. If after assessing the evidence that has been submitted,   9–031
the Commission is satisfied that it is sufficient for its purposes, it will make a formal written offer of "conditional" immunity from fines.[83] Immunity will be granted at the end of the administrative procedure only if the undertaking has:

---

[79] See para.9–012, above.
[80] See the Annex to this chapter.
[81] Immunity Notice, paras 8(a) and (b).
[82] Pt B of the Immunity Notice.
[83] *ibid.*, paras 15 and 16.

(1) co-operated fully, on a continuous basis and expeditiously throughout the Commission's administrative procedure;

(2) provides the Commission with all evidence that comes into its possession or is available to it relating to the suspected infringement;

(3) ends its involvement in the suspected infringement no later than the time at which it submits evidence;

(4) refrained from taking steps to coerce other undertakings to participate in the infringement.[84]

The obligation of full and continuous co-operation continues throughout the investigation and even during any subsequent appeal. The whistleblower must be prepared to answer swiftly any of the Commission's enquiries or requests for information and may be asked to comment on the substance of the responses submitted by the accused. Failure to comply may result in the withdrawal of immunity.[85]

9–032   Reduction in the level of the fine.   Even if an undertaking has coerced others to participate in the cartel or applies late when the Commission already has sufficient evidence, it may still submit evidence in support of an application for a significant reduction in its fine. The undertaking must terminate its involvement in the cartel before it contacts the Commission.

9–033   Reduction in the level of the fine: procedure and requirements.   The application procedure is the same as for immunity applications. The Commission will not assess any evidence submitted by way of general co-operation until it has taken a position on any existing application for immunity in relation to the same suspected infringement.[86] To obtain a reduction, the information must add "significant added value" over and beyond the evidence already in the Commission's possession. Direct or contemporaneous evidence will, by its very nature and/or its level of detail, strengthen the Commission's ability to prove the existence of the infringement.[87] The parties will not know whether their application has been successful until the Commission issues its final decision. Successful applicants will be banded, according to the timing and value of their evidence and the extent of their continuing co-operation, as follows:

(1) the first undertaking past the post will obtain a reduction of 30–50 per cent;

(2) the second undertaking will obtain a reduction of 20–30 per cent;

---

[84] Pt B of the Immunity Notice, paras 11 and 19.
[85] *ibid.*, para.30.
[86] *ibid.*, para.25.
[87] *ibid.*, paras 21–22.

(3) subsequent undertakings will merit a reduction of up to 20 per cent.[88]

Confidentiality of the fact of co-operation. Undertakings may be concerned   **9–034**
about their commercial position if it becomes known that they have whistle-
blown or otherwise cooperated with the Commission's investigation. The
Commission will respect the undertaking's request for anonymity during the
administrative procedure and will treat any documents submitted as part of
a leniency application as one of its internal documents. Although the
documents form part of the Commission's investigation file, it will not
disclose them even if the accused requests their disclosure as part of the
access to the file or under the freedom of information regime.[89] The Commission will, however, exchange such information with NCAs in the competition network, who will be able to use it as evidence of an infringement
under Art.81 or their national competition law.

Extent of protection. The protection from identification only extends   **9–035**
during the administrative phase. The Commission will indicate the fact of an
undertaking's co-operation in its formal decision, so as to explain the reason
for the immunity or reduction of the fine and to forestall accusations of
discrimination. Further, the immunity from fines cannot protect an undertaking from liability in damages to co-contractors or third parties for losses
caused from its participation in an infringement of Art.81 EC.[90]

4. INTERIM MEASURES, NON-APPLICABILITY AND COMMITMENTS

Generally. The Modernisation Regulation formalises the powers of the   **9–036**
Commission to grant interim measures and increases the flexibility of its
procedures so that it can bring an end to an investigation where the alleged
competition concerns are not actually engaged or can be resolved by
appropriate behavioural commitments. The Commission's exercise of these
powers will have important tactical implications for the accused and complainants alike.

(a) Interim Measures

Interim Measures. Complainants are not supposed to request interim   **9–037**
measures as part of a formal complaint under Art.7(2) of the Modernisation

---

[88] *ibid.*, para.23.
[89] The Commission's refusal is justified on the public policy concern that disclosure would
undermine the efficacy of its investigations and deter leniency applicants: see Art.4(2) of
Regulation 1049/2001.
[90] Immunity Notice, para.31.

Regulation.[91] The complainant will therefore need to consider whether it would be more appropriate, depending on the applicable national rules of procedure, to address such requests to the national court or a well-placed NCA instead. The Commission will only award interim measures acting on "its own initiative" where the following conditions are met:

(a) there is a case of urgency;

(b) there is a prima facie finding of infringement; and

(c) there is a risk of serious and irreparable damage to competition (not competitors or consumers).[92]

In practice, notwithstanding the phrasing of Art.8 of the Modernisation Regulation, it would be advisable to include submissions on these aspects as part of any complaint. The Commission must consult and take account of any opinion of the Advisory Committee before it adopts interim measures.[93] Interim measures will only be ordered for a specific period of time, subject to renewal. They may be reinforced by periodic penalty payments of up to 5 per cent of the undertakings average daily turnover in the preceding business year.[94] Contravention of an interim order may attract fines of up to 10 per cent of the undertaking's turnover in the preceding business year.[95] The award of or failure to grant interim measures is subject to judicial review before the Court of First Instance.[96]

(b) Findings of non-applicability

9–038   **Basis of non-applicability.**   The Commission may, at any stage in the investigation, find that Art.81 or 82 of the Treaty are not applicable in a particular case.[97] This may be because the particular agreement, decision or concerted practice falls outside Art.81(1) under the "rule of reason", ancillary restraints doctrine or for wider public interest reasons.[98] Alternatively, the agreement or practice may satisfy the conditions in Art.81(3) and be covered by a block or individual exemption. As regards Art.82 of the

---

[91] Complaints notice, para.80.
[92] Art.8 of the Modernisation Regulation.
[93] Art.14(1).
[94] Art.24(1)(b) of the Modernisation Regulation.
[95] Art.23(2) of the Modernisation Regulation.
[96] Case T–184/01 R *IMS Health v Commission* [2001] E.C.R. II–3193; [2002] 4 C.M.L.R. 2.
[97] Art.10 of the Modernisation Regulation.
[98] See Case 255/78 *Nungesser* [1982] E.C.R. 2015; Case 42/84 *Remia* [1985] E.C.R. 2545; [1987] 1 C.M.L.R. 1; Case 161/84 *Pronuptia* [1986] E.C.R. 353; [1986] 1 C.M.L.R. 414 and Case C–309/99 *Wouters* [2002] E.C.R. I–1577; [2002] 4 C.M.L.R. 27 discussed in Bellamy & Child, *European Community Law of Competition* (5th ed., Sweet & Maxwell, London, 2001) at paras.2–082 *et seq.*

Treaty, the behaviour complained of may not amount to an "abuse" because of some objective justification.[99]

Non-applicability decision. A non-applicability decision will only be made in exceptional cases where the public interest where the Community public interest so requires.[1] The formal decision will be declaratory in nature and will be issued where the Commission considers it expedient to clarify the law and ensure its consistent application throughout the Community. By "exceptional cases", the procedure is most likely to be confined to cases that raise new types of agreements or practices that have not been previously addressed by Community case law or practice. Before it adopts the formal decision, the Commission will transmit copies of the key documents supporting its proposed conclusions to the NCAs for consultation.[2] The Commission will also consult the Advisory Committee.[3] It will also publish a notice containing a concise summary of the case and the main content of its proposed course of action. Interested third parties, including any complainants, must be allowed a reasonable opportunity (at least one month) to comment.[4] The Commission appears to have a wide discretion to determine whether the public interest merits such a finding in the circumstances of each particular case. It will reach its decision on its own initiative; the parties or other NCAs cannot require it to make such a finding. Due to the discretionary nature of the decision, the prospects of a successful challenge via judicial review before the Court of First Instance will be slim.[5]

9–039

Effect of a non-applicability decision. Owing to its status as a Commission decision, decisions of non-applicability will have binding effect for NCAs and national courts dealing with the same or a related case.[6] They will not be allowed to reach an infringement decision under Art.81 or 82 as such conclusion would run counter to the Commission's findings of non-applicability. Moreoover, so far as Art.81 EC is concerned, at least, the Commission's decision will impact upon the application of national competition law. NCAs and national courts will not be able, when applying their domestic legislation, to prohibit agreements, decisions or concerted practices (to the extent that they may affect inter-state trade) which are covered by a

9–040

---

[99] Cases C–241/91 P a.o.*RTE and ITP v Commission* ("*Magill*") [1995] E.C.R. I–743 at para.55, affirmed in Case C–418/01 *IMS Health GmbH & Co OHG v NDC Health GmbH & Co KG* [2004] (not yet published) at para.51.
[1] Recital 14 of the Modernisation Regulation.
[2] *ibid.*, Art.11(2).
[3] *ibid.*, Art.14.
[4] Art.27(4) of the Modernisation Regulation.
[5] For the principles governing judicial review of the Commission's exercise of its discretion, see para.9–073, below.
[6] Art.16 of the Modernisation Regulation and Case C–344/98 *Masterfoods* [2000] E.C.R. I–11369. Query, however, its status in other cases that involve different parties but involve similar facts.

non-applicability decision.[7] In view of these tactical advantages, it is to be expected that, notwithstanding the fact that the Commission will only take such decision on its own initiative, the accused will press its case for a non-applicability decision from the Commission at an early stage in any investigation. In effect, the non-applicability decision will function as a powerful "trump card" in all 25 Member States.

(c) Commitments

9–041   **Power to accept commitments.**   The Modernisation Regulation introduces a new power for the Commission to accept binding commitments from the accused about its future behaviour instead of proceeding to issue an infringement decision.[8] In theory, the accused can make an offer of commitments at any stage in the proceedings, even before the Commission has formally accepted the complaint. However, it is likely that in most cases, the accused will not be aware of the allegations made against it until the Commission informs it of its preliminary assessment and of its intention to adopt an infringement decision.[9]

9–042   **Procedure.**   Before the Commission accepts an offer of commitments, it must publish a notice containing, subject to any necessary redactions to protect confidentiality, a concise summary of the case and the text of the proposed commitments. Interested third parties, including any complainants, must be allowed a reasonable opportunity (at least one month) to comment on the proposed course of action.[10] The Commission will also consult and take account of any opinion of the Advisory Committee before it accepts any commitments.[11] A copy of the final commitments will be published in the Official Journal and on the Commission's website.[12]

9–043   **Acceptance of commitments.**   Commitments may be behavioural or structural and may be limited in time. They will only be accepted if they meet three conditions.[13] First, the commitments must remove the Commission's initial competition concerns as expressed in a preliminary assessment so that there are no longer any grounds for the Commission to act.[14] Secondly, the Commission will not accept commitments where it intends to impose a fine.

---

[7] Art.3(2) of the Modernisation Regulation: in contrast, NCAs are allowed to adopt stricter national laws which prohibit or sanction unilateral conduct that is not caught by Art.82 EC.

[8] Art.9 of the Modernisation Regulation.

[9] *ibid.*

[10] *ibid.*, Art. 27(4).

[11] *ibid.*, Art.14(1).

[12] At the time of writing, the Commission has accepted commitments in its investigations into the central marketing of Bundesliga rights (see IP/04/1110 of September 17, 2004) and in its antitrust probe into Coca-Cola's practices in Europe (see IP/04/1247 of October 19, 2004).

[13] See the Commission's Memorandum MEMO/04/217 on commitment decisions of September 17, 2004.

[14] The Modernisation Regulation, Recital 13.

As a matter of deterrence policy, it will not be prepared to accept commitments in cases involving hard-core cartels or serious abuses of dominant position.[15] Thirdly, the Commission decision to accept binding commitments binding rather than issuing a formal prohibition decision must be justified by efficiency reasons.

Commitments are not fixed in stone but may be adapted to reflect changes in market circumstances. The Commission can reassess the situation if a material change takes place in any of the facts on which the decision was based. It is also possible for the accused to ask the Commission to lift a commitment that is no longer appropriate.

There is an important tactical advantage for the accused in offering commitments as their acceptance means that the Commission will not go on to issue an infringement decision, which would otherwise be binding on NCAs and national courts throughout the Union.[16] Article 9 decisions are silent on whether there was or still is a breach of the EU competition rules. However, nothing prevents the NCAs or national courts from determining whether or not there has been an infringement of Art.81/82 in a particular case.[17] However, a claimant (whether a customer or a competitor) will still need to prove the illegality of the former behaviour from scratch in order to obtain compensation for damages.

Binding nature of commitment decisions. Commitment decisions will be binding on the accused for a specified period and may be enforced by periodic penalty payments of up to 5 per cent of the undertakings average daily turnover in the preceding business year.[18] If the accused breaches the commitments or provides incomplete or misleading information in its request to the Commission, the Commission will be entitled to re-open the proceedings.[19] Contravention of the commitments may attract fines of up to 10 per cent of the undertaking's turnover in the preceding business year.[20] National courts will also be expected to enforce the commitments by any means provided for by national law, including the adoption of interim measures.[21]

9–044

5. COMMISSION'S INVESTIGATIVE POWERS

Generally. The Modernisation Regulation has increased the Commission's investigatory powers to enable it to detect cartels and serious abuses more effectively. Acting in co-operation with the NCAs, the Commission may

9–045

---

[15] See, by analogy, the OFT's position at para.4.4 of its Notice on Enforcement, OFT407.
[16] Case C–344/98 *Masterfoods*, n.6, above.
[17] Recitals 13 and 22 of the Modernisation Regulation.
[18] The Modernisation Regulation, Art.24(1)(c).
[19] *ibid.*, Art.9(2).
[20] *ibid.*, Art.23(2).
[21] See MEMO 04/217, answer to the second question.

conduct inspections, interviews or request information from undertakings. Those powers can be exercised before the Commission formally takes a decision to initiate proceedings[22] and may be used as a form of *ex ante* control to oversee the achievement of effective competition in a particular market sector.

(a) General market inquiries

9–046 **Article 17 of the Modernisation Regulation.** The Commission may, following a complaint or on its own initiative, conduct an inquiry into a particular sector of the economy or into a particular type of agreements across that sector. In order to start an investigation, the Commission does not have to establish a reasonable suspicion that an infringement has been committed. It is sufficient that trends in inter-state trade, price rigidity or other circumstances suggest that competition is being restricted or distorted.[23] The Commission can exercise its powers to conduct inspections, interviews or request information from undertakings in the context of its market inquiries. An intentional or negligent failure to comply with or provide complete and accurate information in response to a Commission's request for information about agreements, decisions or concerted practices will attract fines of up to 1 per cent of the undertaking's total turnover in the preceding business year.[24] The Commission may consult the Advisory Committee and invite comments from interested third parties before publishing the results of its inquiry in a report.

(b) Requests for Information

9–047 **Article 18 of the Modernisation Regulation.** More often than not, Commission investigations are initiated by unpublicised requests for information rather than high-profile dawn raids. The Commission may request information from undertakings by: (i) a simple request; or (ii) a formal decision. In both cases, the Commission must specify the legal basis and purpose of the request, the information required and the time-limit for the response. The Commission will forward a copy of the request to the NCA of the Member State where the undertaking is headquartered and whose territory is affected.[25] Owners, representatives, legally authorised representatives and legal advisors are entitled to answer the request on behalf of the undertaking. The intentional or negligent supply of incomplete, incorrect, misleading or out-of-time information can attract fines of up to 1 per cent of the undertaking's

---

[22] Art.2(3) of Regulation 773/2004.
[23] Art.17(1) of the Modernisation Regulation.
[24] The Modernisation Regulation, Art.23(1)(a) and (b).
[25] *ibid.*, Art.18(5).

total turnover in the preceding business year.[26] Where the Commission requests information by formal decision, it may compel the provision of complete and accurate information by imposing a daily penalty payment of up to 5 per cent of the undertaking's average daily turnover in the preceding business year.[27] Note that information requests can be addressed to undertakings only and not private individuals. A limited privilege against self-incrimination may be asserted in the face of such a request, derived from Art.6 ECHR[28]: undertakings cannot be forced to admit that they have committed an infringement. However, they can be obliged to answer factual questions, provide documents and explain statements in documents. Such information can be used against them or against another undertaking to establish the existence of an infringement.[29] A request by formal decision is subject to judicial review before the Court of First Instance.

(c) Interviews

Article 19 of the Modernisation Regulation. With the consent of the person **9–048** concerned, the Commission may now interview a private individual or the representatives of an undertaking to collect additional information. At the start of the interview, the Commission official must state the legal basis and purpose of the interview and inform the interviewee that the interview will be recorded.[30] A copy of the transcript will be made available to the interviewee for his approval.[31] The interviewee is given the opportunity to submit corrections within a time-limit of at least two weeks.[32] Such interviews are voluntary and the interviewee cannot be compelled to answer any incriminatory questions.[33] Article 19 makes clear that interviews can only be conducted for the purpose of collecting information that relates to the subject matter of the investigation.[34] Thus the Commission can rely on information gathered from the interview "as evidence of an infringement" only to the extent that it falls within the four corners of the factual matters alleged by the Commission. Interviews may be conducted by telephone, video

---

[26] *ibid.*, Art.23(1)(a) and (b).

[27] *ibid.*, Art.24(1)(d).

[28] Case T–112/98 *Mannesmannröhren–Werk v Commission* [2001] E.C.R. II–729 at para.62; Cases C–204/00 P etc. *Aalborg Portland v Commission*, judgment of January 7, 2004 at para.65; Case T–236/01 etc. *Tokai Carbon v Commission*, April 29, 2004 at para.402.

[29] Modernisation Regulation, Recital 23 and Case C–94/00 *Roquette Frères* [2003] E.C.R. I–9011; [2003] 4 C.M.L.R. 1.

[30] Art.3(1) of Regulation 773/2004.

[31] *ibid.*, Art.3(3).

[32] *ibid.*, Art.17(3).

[33] In Strasbourg jurisprudence on the freedom from self-incrimination, there may be a distinction between documents that have been compulsorily seized (which have an independent existence of the individual's will) and providing entirely voluntary statements: see *Saunders v United Kingdom* (1997) 23 E.H.R.R 313; although contrast *Funke v France* (1993) 16 E.H.R.R. 297 and *JB v Switzerland*, No.31827/96, May 3, 2001.

[34] For an explanation of the purpose and subject matter of the investigation, see Case 85/87 *Dow Benelux v Commission* [1989] E.C.R. 3137.

conference or other electronic means. Where the interview is to be conducted in person at the undertaking's premises, the Commission must notify the NCA of that Member State and, if the latter requests, permit the NCA's officials to attend the interview and assist the Commission's representatives to conduct the interview.

9–049 **Exchange of information.** Information obtained from the interview may be exchanged with NCAs under Art.12 of the Modernisation Regulation and used by them as evidence for applying their national competition law in parallel to the same case. However, such information can only be used to impose sanctions on individual persons where the Commission's interview methods respects the same level of protection for the individual's rights of defence as the laws of the receiving NCA. It cannot be used to impose custodial sanctions against the individual.[35]

(d) Inspections or "dawn raids"

9–050 **Articles 20 and 21 of the Modernisation Regulation.** Before exercising its inspection powers, the Commission must give advance notice "in good time" to the NCA of the Member State in whose territory the inspection is to be conducted ("the local NCA"). The Commission will consult the local NCA before it takes any formal decision to conduct the inspection and, if necessary, co-ordinate with it on obtaining a precautionary judicial warrant in advance of the dawn raid. At the request of the Commission or the local NCA, the authorised officials of the local NCA may actively assist the Commission's officials with the inspection and will exercise the same inspection powers during the raid.[36] Alternatively, the local NCA may conduct the inspections on the Commission's behalf according to the national rules of procedure.[37] The Commission must issue a written decision authorising its officials to conduct the inspection. That authorisation must be produced to the undertaking at the start of the inspection. The authorisation must state the purpose and subject matter of the investigation, its commencement date and any sanctions that could be imposed for obstructing the investigation.[38]

9–051 **Inspection powers.** Authorised Commission officials have power to enter the undertaking's premises, land or vehicles and examine and take copies from any books and records that relate to the business.[39] The inspection powers extend to all paper and electronic forms of records, including searching through email archives and computer hard disks. The

---

[35] Art.12(3) of the Modernisation Regulation.
[36] the Modernisation Regulation, Art.20(5).
[37] *ibid.*, Art.22(2).
[38] *ibid.*, Art.20(3).
[39] *ibid.*, Art.20(2).

Commission has powers to take protective measures to preserve evidence by sealing premises and books to the extent necessary to finish its inspection.[40] Seals will normally be applied for a maximum of 72 hours.[41] The Commission officials may also, during the course of an inspection, ask the undertaking's representatives or staff to explain any facts or statements in documents.[42] It is expected that such questioning will be conducted on similar lines to Art.19 interviews. The accused has the right to refuse to answer an illegitimate question where the response would be tantamount to self incrimination.[43] Should he unwittingly answer such an illegitimate question, the accused can seek relief from the Court of First Instance to prevent the Commission from relying upon that answer in proving its case.[44] The undertaking will be entitled to a copy of the recording of the answers provided. If the member of staff is not authorised to provide explanations on behalf of the undertaking, the company may amend or supplement the explanations given within a time limit of at least two weeks.[45] The Modernisation Regulation confers on the Commission a new power to inspect non-business premises, land and vehicles.[46] These include the homes and cars of company directors, managers and members of staff where the Commission suspects that books or other records are being stored.

Co-operation or objection? Given that information gathered from the inspection can be exchanged with NCAs and may be used as evidence for the application of national competition laws in multiple Member States without, necessarily, the benefit of any leniency regime, the accused will want to make a tactical decision about the level of co-operation it wishes to offer the investigating authorities. Co-operation with the Commission's investigation may be taken into account as a mitigating factor to reduce the amount of any penalty that may be imposed should the Commission issue an infringement decision at the end of its investigation. Should an undertaking wish to object to the inspection and challenge the validity of the Commission's authorisation, it will seek judicial review of the Commission's inspection decision before the Court of First Instance. National courts have no competence to assess the Commission's competence or the need for or lawfulness of the exercise of its powers.[47]

9–052

Refusal of entry. Refusing entry is likely to be treated as an aggravating factor in the calculation of any penalty. In such case, the local NCA will assist the Commission by calling the police to force entry or by applying to the national courts for a warrant. In issuing a warrant, the national court's

9–053

---

[40] *ibid.*, Art.20(2).
[41] *ibid.*, Recital 25.
[42] *ibid.*, Art.20(2)(e).
[43] See para.9–048, above.
[44] Case T–112/98 *Mannesmannröhren-Werk v Commission* [2001] E.C.R. II–729.
[45] Arts 4(3) and 17(3) of Regulation 773/2004.
[46] *ibid.*, Art.21(1).
[47] Case C–94/00 *Roquette Frères*, n.29, above.

task is to check that the authorisation decision is authentic and does not amount to an arbitrary or excessive interference with the undertaking's rights. It cannot question the necessity for the coercive measures or demand access to the Commission's file. The local NCA may assist the Commission by providing the national court with an explanation of the grounds for the Commission's suspicions, the seriousness of the suspected infringement and the extent of the undertaking's involvement.[48]

6. INITIATION OF PROCEEDINGS

9–054   **Initiation decision.** The Commission may decide to initiate infringement proceedings at any point in time, but will be obliged to open proceedings as soon as it[49]:

(a)   informs the accused of its preliminary assessment of the conduct in the context of an offer of commitments;

(b)   issues a statement of objections; or

(c)   publishes a notice of its intention to accept commitments or adopt a non-applicability decision;

Before the Commission opens proceedings, it must inform the parties concerned (including any complainants) and, in an appropriate case, publish its initiation decision.[50] Publication may be effected in "any appropriate way", which may include press coverage or posting on the Commission's website. Publication is important, as the Commission's initiation of proceedings will relieve NCAs of their competence to apply Arts 81 and 82. National courts must also be made aware of the investigation so that they can suspend their proceedings or avoid adopting a judgment that would conflict with any decision envisaged by the Commission in the same case.

9–055   **Statement of objections.** The statement of objections marks the transition from the Commission's investigative phase to the infringement stage. It is a key procedural safeguard as it provides the means for the Commission to inform the accused of the "case" against it and for the accused to exercise its right to be heard. The statement of objections is a preliminary document that identifies the allegations made against each party subject to the investigation and the evidence in support of those allegations.[51] It must set out clearly the facts upon which the Commission relies and its classification of

---

[48] Art.20(8) and Case C–94/00 *Roquette Frères*, n.29, above.
[49] Art.2(1) of Regulation 773/2004.
[50] Art.2(2) of Regulation 773/2004.
[51] See, in particular, Case C–62/86 *AKZO* [1991] E.C.R. I–3359 at para.29.

those facts.[52] It does not have any binding status as such and cannot be the subject of judicial review before the Court of First Instance.[53] Each party must be given the opportunity to state its views on the truth and relevance of all the factual and legal allegations which the competition authority intends to raise against it in the final decision.[54] The Commission will notify the statement of objections to each of the parties concerned and specify a time limit of at least four weeks for the receipt of the parties' written representations.[55] Written submissions received after the expiry of that time-limit may not be taken into account.

Right to be heard. All addressees of the statement of objections must be given an opportunity to be heard (either through written or oral representations) before the Commission consults the Advisory Committee on its proposed decision.[56] The right to be heard is administered by the hearing officer, who although attached to the Commission is completely independent.[57] If a particular allegation is not included in the statement of objections, the Commission will not be able to rely on it unless the accused has been notified of the change in the Commission's case and given an opportunity to comment.[58] If there is any inconsistency between the allegations in the statement of objections and the findings in the decision, the Commission's findings and any relevant parts of the decision may be set aside if the allegation cannot be sustained on the basis of other legitimate evidence.[59]

9–056

Access to the file. After notification of the statement of objections, the parties should submit a request for access to the Commission's file.[60] The accused is entitled to comment on the documents relied upon by the Commission and only the documents cited or mentioned in the statement of objections will be admissible evidence as against the addressee of the statement of objections.[61] The file may contain copies of documents seized during inspections, the parties' responses to information requests, transcripts of interviews and background documents submitted as part of a complaint or leniency application. Only documents cited or mentioned in

9–057

---

[52] Case C–89/85 *Ahlström (A) OY v Commission ("Woodpulp II")* [1993] E.C.R. I–1307; [1993] 4 C.M.L.R. 407.

[53] Case 60/81 *IBM v Commission* [1981] E.C.R. 2639 at para.21.

[54] Case T–7/89 *Hercules* [1991] E.C.R. II–1711 at para.51.

[55] Regulation 773/2004, Art.10(2) and Art.17(2): where the Commission intends to award interim relief, the time limit may be reduced to one week.

[56] *ibid.*, Art.11(1).

[57] The terms of reference of hearing officers is laid down in Commission Decision 2001/462 [2001] O.J. L162/21 ("Hearing Officers terms of reference").

[58] Regulation 773/2004, Art.11(2) and Case 41/69 *ACF Chemiefarma v Commission* [1970] E.C.R. 661 at para.94 and Joined Cases T–39/92 and T–40/92 *CB and Europay v Commission* [1994] E.C.R. II–49 at para.47.

[59] Case T–86/95 *Compagnie générale maritime (FEFC)* [2002] E.C.R. II–1011 at para.447.

[60] Art.15(1) of Regulation 773/2004 and the Commission's new draft notice on access to the file ([2004] O.J. C259/8) which is currently open to consultation.

[61] Case C–62/86 *AKZO*, n.51, above, at para.21 and Case T–13/89 *ICI v Commission* [1992] E.C.R. II–1021 at para.34.

the statement of objections will be admissible evidence. The parties may either inspect the file at DG Comp's offices or request copies of the file or a CD-Rom to be sent to them for inspection. Documents obtained through the access to the file process may only be used for the purpose of judicial or administrative proceedings for the application of Arts 81 or 82.[62] The accused is entitled to inspect the documents relied upon by the Commission so that it can assess their evidential strength and make useful comments on the inferences drawn from them in the statement of objections.[63] In line with the equality of arms, the Commission is not allowed to limit disclosure to the documents that it considers to be relevant for the undertaking's defence.[64] The accused's rights of access extend not just to incriminatory evidence but to all neutral or exculpatory documents that may useful for its defence. The Commission's failure to disclose "incriminatory" documents will mean that such documents are excluded as evidence in support of the Commission's findings.[65] If access to "exculpatory" documents is denied despite a request to see them, the accused will be able to set the Commission's findings aside if it can prove that the administrative procedure would have had a different outcome if it had had access.[66] If the accused has reason to believe that the Commission has not disclosed all the documents that are necessary for it to be properly heard, it must submit a reasoned request for access to those documents. The hearing officer will be responsible for overseeing the request and taking a reasoned decision. The decision is communicated to the accused as well as any other person or undertaking concerned.[67]

9–058   **Documents withheld.**   The parties will not have an absolute right to see all the documents on the Commission's file. The Commission is entitled to withhold its internal and/or policy documents from inspection, *e.g.* communications between DG Comp and the Commission Legal Service.[68] Likewise, the parties will not be able to examine communications between the Commission and the NCAs or copy correspondence between the various NCAs held on the Commission's file,[69] as well as certain confidential documents.

---

[62] Art.15(4) of Regulation 773/2004: query whether, post *Crehan v Courage*, co-contractors to an anti-competitive agreement can use such information for the purpose of private claims for damages before the national courts.

[63] Joined Cases 43/82 and 63/82 *VBVB and VBBB v Commission* [1984] E.C.R. 19 at para.25. Case C–185/95 P *Baustahlgewebe v Commission* [1998] E.C.R. I–8417 at para.89 and Case C–51/92 P *Hercules Chemicals v Commission* [1999] E.C.R. I–4235 at para.75.

[64] Case T–30/91 *Solvay v Commission* [1995] E.C.R. II–1775 at para.81 and Case T–36/91 *ICI v Commission* [1995] E.C.R. II–1847 at para.93.

[65] Case T–10/92 *Cimenteries CBR SA v Commission* [1992] E.C.R. II–2667 at para.382.

[66] Case T–7/89 *Hercules* [1991] E.C.R. II–1711 at para.56 and T–12/89 *Solvay v Commission* [1992] E.C.R. II–907 at para.98.

[67] Art.8 of the Hearing Officers' terms of reference.

[68] Case T–175/95 *BASF v Commission* [1999] E.C.R. II–1581 at para.45.

[69] Art.15(2) of Regulation 773/2004.

Confidential documents and business secrets. When granting access to the   **9–059**
file, the Commission will not disclose information that contains business
secrets or confidential information whose disclosure would significantly
harm the undertaking or person concerned.[70] Access to the file is organised
so that business secrets and confidential information are protected via
redaction so that only non-confidential versions of the document will be
available for inspection. Where appropriate, the entire document may be
removed from the file. The parties' representatives will be provided with a
list of the documents on the file, which will be coded to indicate whether
each particular document is: (1) fully available; (2) redacted in part; or (3)
entirely confidential.

Reliance by the Commission on confidential material or business secrets.   **9–060**
Notwithstanding this protection, the Commission is entitled to disclose
information on which it relies as evidence of the infringement.[71] Such disclosure is necessary to ensure the protection of the accused's rights of
defence as it is entitled to know the evidence against it. Failure to disclose
material evidence will prevent the Commission from being able to rely on it
in support of its eventual findings in the decision and may lead to the
decision being set aside in whole or in part. The Commission will therefore
have to assess each individual statement or document to determine whether
the accused's need for disclosure is greater than the harm that might result
to third parties from disclosure.[72] If the Commission intends to disclose
material to the accused that has been identified as confidential by the provider, the hearing officer will inform the undertaking concerned of the
Commission's reasons. The provider will have an opportunity to make
submissions and object to the disclosure. If the Commission finds that the
information is not protected, it must notify the provider by reasoned decision and allow one week before the information is disclosed.[73]

Written representations. The parties' written representations afford them   **9–061**
an opportunity to correct the Commission's version of events, put forward
their defence and provide additional information by way of mitigating co-
operation. Parties should include a formal request for an oral hearing in the
written representations.[74] Written representations and annexed documents
should be submitted in hard copy original as well as in electronic version.[75]
There is no set format for written representations. Some parties prefer to
comment on the Commission's allegations on a line by line basis. Others
prefer to simply set out their version of the events and highlight the

---

[70] Art.16(1) of Regulation 773/2004.
[71] Art.15(3) of Regulation 773/2004.
[72] Recital 14 of Regulation 773/2004.
[73] Art.9 of the Hearing Officers' terms of reference.
[74] Art.12 of Regulation 773/2004.
[75] If an electronic version is not available, the accused will need to provide 28 paper copies of
the representation and annexed documents.

inconsistencies and weaknesses of the various elements in the Commission's case. The parties are advised to set out all facts known to them which are relevant to their defence and to attach any documentary evidence in support.[76] They may also wish to enclose witness statements from the protagonists providing detailed explanations of the statements contained in any documents or the background circumstances of any anti-competitive meetings or discussions.

9–062 **Representations as to penalty.** The Commission will often expressly indicate in its statement of objections whether it intends to impose fines on the undertakings and, if so, the main factual and legal criteria that it will take into account, such as the gravity and the duration of the alleged infringement and whether that infringement was committed "intentionally or negligently". The statement of objections does not have to set out the precise level of any eventual fine.[77] It is therefore important that the accused comments on the appropriateness of a penalty in the particular circumstances of the case and makes a plea in mitigation for a reduction of the fine, either by challenging the Commission's assessment of its specified criteria or by active co-operation with the Commission's investigation.[78] To merit a reduction in any eventual fine, the written representations must "add value" to the Commission's investigation in the sense that they must provide evidence or information beyond that which the Commission has managed to compile through its investigative procedures to date.[79] The information must facilitate the Commission's investigation in the sense of helping the Commission to establish the existence of an infringement more easily and, where relevant, to bring it to an end.[80] One way is to offer to make witnesses available for questioning by the Commission. Admissions of liability or the provision of additional information about the participation of other undertakings in the infringement will count towards a reduction of the fine.[81]

9–063 **Oral hearings.** There is no automatic right to an oral hearing—the parties must make a formal request in their written representations.[82] The Commission cannot refuse such requests. Oral hearings are arranged and conducted by the hearing officer, who may decide to hold a preliminary meeting with the parties to prepare for the meeting. The hearing officer may prepare a list of questions and circulate them to the parties in advance for them to consider and reply to during the hearing.[83] She may ask the parties to provide an advance summary of the main elements of the submissions they

---

[76] Art.10(3) of Regulation 773/2004.
[77] Joined Cases 100/80 to 103/80 *Musique diffusion française v Commission* [1983] E.C.R. 1825 at para.21, and Case 322/81 *Michelin v Commission* [1983] E.C.R. 3461 at para.19.
[78] Immunity Notice, Pt B.
[79] *ibid.*, para.18 and Case T–12/89 *Solvay v Commission*, n.70, above, at para.341.
[80] Case C–297/98 P *SCA Holding v Commission* at para.36.
[81] Case T–230/00 *Daesang Corporation v Commission* [2003], E.C.R. II–2733.
[82] Art.12 of Regulation 773/2004.
[83] Art.11 of the Hearing Officers' terms of reference.

intend to make at the oral hearing.[84] NCAs and other Member State officials will now be invited to take part in oral hearings[85] and may ask questions.[86] The hearing officer will determine whether the parties are to be heard separately or together and whether they can put forward witnesses or fresh documents.[87] Oral hearings are not public and, for reasons of confidentiality, may be segregated so that business secrets and other confidential information are not disclosed to other parties, complainants or interested third parties. The parties and their authorised representatives may either appear in person or be legally represented at oral hearings. The parties and other attendees may ask questions during the hearing and may be expected to answer questions posed by the Commission services or the NCAs. Points may arise that require clarification and the parties may be invited to make further written submissions after the hearing.[88] A transcript of the oral hearing will be recorded and, subject to redaction for confidentiality reasons, will be circulated to the attendees on request.[89]

Impact of the right to be heard. The hearing officer will report to the Commission on the conduct of the hearing and his conclusions on the right to be heard. In addition to procedural issues, the hearing officer will recommend whether there is any need to obtain further information, to withdraw certain allegations or to re-formulate objections in a further statement of objections.[90] The Commission must take account of the evidence and arguments put forward by the undertakings in their written and oral representations. In some instances, these may absolve the accused of all liability or compel the Commission to re-assess its initial findings. Until a final decision has been adopted, the Commission may alter its case, by abandoning some or even all of the allegations initially and thus alter its position in the undertakings' favour.[91] Conversely, it may decide to add new complaints, provided that it affords the undertakings concerned the opportunity of being heard on those new points.[92] Sometimes, the undertaking's observations may cast doubt on the Commission's evaluation of the evidence or the inferences it has drawn. There is nothing stopping the Commission from re-opening its investigative fact-finding phase and issuing further requests for information to clarify the arguments and version of events evidence put forward by the accused in response to the statement of

9–064

---

[84] *ibid.*
[85] Art.14(3) of Regulation 773/2004.
[86] *ibid.*, Art.14(7).
[87] Art.12 of the Hearing Officers' terms of reference.
[88] *ibid.*
[89] Art.14(8) of Regulation 773/2004.
[90] Art.14 of the Hearing Officers' terms of reference.
[91] Case 60/81 *IBM v Commission*, n.53, above, at para.18 and Cases T–191/98 *Atlantic Container Line* [2003] E.C.R. 0000, judgment of September 30, 2003 at para.115.
[92] Case 107/82 *AEG v Commission* [1983] E.C.R. 3151 at para.29 and Case T–16/99 *Lögstör Rör v Commission* [2002] E.C.R. II–1633 at para.168.

objections.[93] If the requests raise fresh evidence or implicate new participants, the Commission must set out the new allegations in a supplementary statement of objections and give the undertakings concerned an opportunity to comment.

9–065   **Participation by complainants.**   Complainants are automatically entitled to a non-confidential version of the statement of objections relating to the matters raised by the complaint.[94] The statement of objections will be redacted to protect the business secrets and confidential information supplied by the accused and other participants in the investigation. The complainant will be able to submit any written representations that it may wish to make regarding the statement of objections of at least four weeks.[95] There is no provision for complainants to have access to the Commission's file for the purpose of responding to the statement of objections. This is in line with Community case law which holds that complainants are not entitled to the same rights of access as the accused.[96] However, it is hard to see how the right to be heard can be exercised in any meaningful way if the complainant has not read the statement of objections in context, with the background supporting documents. The refusal of complainants' access to the file also sits uneasily with the right of access they have been given when their complaint has been rejected.[97] The author takes the view that complainants should be entitled to a non-confidential (redacted) version of the file, where that information is necessary for them to make effective representations. The complainant should, however, be subject to a condition that it can only use such information for the purposes of judicial or administrative proceedings concerning the application of Arts 81 and 82 of the Treaty.[98] Access should not descend into a "fishing expedition" to further the complainant's commercial interests. Should complainants wish to participate in any oral hearings and submit oral observations, they should make a formal request in their written representations. This request will be dealt with by the hearing officer.[99] Complainants have no automatic right to attend the hearings; the Commission will only accede to such request where it considers their attendance is appropriate.[1] In previous cases, it has been possible for complainants and whistle-blowers to attend separate hearings so that they can respond to the oral submissions made by the accused whilst preserving their anonymity.

---

[93] Cases T–191/98 *Atlantic Container Line*, n.91, above, at paras 116–121.

[94] Art.6(1) of Regulation 773/2004.

[95] *ibid.*, Art.17(2).

[96] Case T–65/96 *Kish Glass* [2000] E.C.R.II–01885 affirmed by the ECJ in Case C–241/00 P1 *Kish Glass Co Ltd* [2001] E.C.R. I–7759.

[97] Art.8(1) of Regulation 773/2004.

[98] *ibid.*, Art.8(2). Query the extent to which this should cover the use of such materials in private damages claims before the national courts rather than merely judicial review of the Commission's eventual decision. Access to the file on a wider basis will afford complainants extensive pre-action information, far beyond the scope of ordinary disclosure.

[99] Art.6 of the Hearing Officers' terms of reference.

[1] Art.6(2) of Regulation 773/2004.

Participation by other interested persons.   Often the Commission may want   **9–066**
to seek the views of interested third parties, such as consumer associations,
who are not complainants or addressees of a statement of objections.
Interested third parties, assuming they have been made aware of the
investigation through the published initiation decision, can apply to the
Commission and ask for an opportunity to be heard.[2] Provided they
establish that they have a sufficient interest in the proceedings,[3] the hearing
officer will inform them in writing of the nature and subject matter of the
procedure[4] and ask them to submit written representations within a given
period. In an appropriate case, in response to a request in their written
representations, the Commission may invite such interested third parties to
attend the oral hearing and submit oral arguments.

The Commission may invite any other person to submit written observations and to attend and express its views at the oral hearing.[5] This invitation can be made in cases where the interested person lacks sufficient
interest and/or has not taken the initiative to request permission to participate in the proceedings.

7. INFRINGEMENT DECISIONS

Issuing an infringement decision.   If, at the end of the administrative phase,   **9–067**
the Commission concludes that there is an infringement of Art.81 or 82, it
will publish a formal decision, requiring the undertakings to bring the
infringement to an end.[6] The decision does not have to be an exact replica of
the statement of objections.[7] As long as it does not alter the nature of its
case, the Commission may alter its assessment and withdraw certain complaints if necessary, in particular in the light of the responses to the statement of objections.[8] The Commission must consult with the Advisory
Committee before it takes a formal infringement decision[9] and must take
utmost account of its advisory opinion.[10] A copy of the draft decision will
also be circulated to the hearing officer who will produce a final report,
checking the consistency of the proposed decision with the original allegations in the statement of objections and the observance of the parties' right

---

[2] Art.13 of Regulation 773/2004.
[3] There is no definition of "sufficient interest" in Regulation 773/2004 but, by analogy with the
test for intervention, competitors, suppliers and customers of the accused will have sufficient
interest even though they may not be directly implicated in the Commission's investigation.
[4] Note that this summary does not equate to a right to receive a non-confidential copy of the
statement of objections.
[5] Art.13(3) of Regulation 773/2004.
[6] Art.7 of the Modernisation Regulation.
[7] Cases 209/78 *Van Landewyck v Commission* [1980] E.C.R. 3125 at para.68.
[8] Case T–228/97 *Irish Sugar v Commission* [1999] E.C.R. II–2969 at paras 34 and 36.
[9] Art.14(1) of the Modernisation Regulation.
[10] See para.9–008, above.

to be heard.[11] The hearing officer's report is attached to the final decision and notified to the addressees of the decision before it is published in the Official Journal. All infringement decisions are published, subject to redaction of confidentiality issues.[12]

9–068 **Remedies.** The Commission has power to impose any behavioural or structural remedies that it considers necessary to bring the infringement to an end. Structural remedies must be proportionate to the infringement committed and will only be acceptable where there is a substantial risk of a lasting or repeated infringement that derives from the very structure of the undertaking.[13] They can be imposed only where there is no equally effective behavioural remedy or where a behavioural remedy would be more onerous for the undertaking that a structural remedy.[14] As part of the behavioural remedies, the Commission may impose fines of up to 10 per cent of the undertaking's turnover in the preceding business year.[15] There is a limitation period of five years from the date on which the infringement was first committed, unless the infringement is of continuing or repetitive nature, in which case time will run from the date of its cessation.[16] The Commission's investigation is deemed to interrupt this limitation period and it will be suspended during any appeal to the Court of First Instance.

8. JUDICIAL REVIEW BEFORE THE COURT OF FIRST INSTANCE

9–069 **Article 230 and 232 EC.** The legality of a Commission decision can be challenged by judicial review before the CFI under Art.230 of the EC Treaty. Only decisions that produce binding legal effects by altering the appellant's position are susceptible to review. Purely preliminary or preparatory acts, such as opening the investigation procedure or issuing the statement of objections, are not reviewable.[17] Examples of competition decisions that can be challenged include:

(a) rejection of a complaint;

(b) authorisation of an inspection or information request;

(c) award or refusal of interim relief;

(d) decision of non-applicability;

---

[11] Art.15 of the Hearing Officers' terms of reference.
[12] Art.30 of the Modernisation Regulation.
[13] *ibid.*, Recital 12.
[14] Art.7 of the Modernisation Regulation.
[15] Art.23(2) of the Modernisation Regulation.
[16] Art.25(1)(b) of the Modernisation Regulation.
[17] Case 60/81 *IBM v Commission*, n.48, above.

(e) acceptance of commitments;

(f) finding of infringement;

(g) imposition of structural remedies; and

(h) imposition of financial penalties.

Undertakings can also challenge the Commission's wrongful failure to act within a reasonable time under Art.232 EC. This is a potential route for challenging the Commission's failure to address a complaint or award interim measures within two months of a request calling upon the Commission to take specific action. However, as an undertaking cannot oblige the Commission to issue a formal decision in competition proceedings[18] and the Commission's administration procedures prompt timely clarification of its position at various stages, resort to Art.232 EC is comparatively rare.

Locus standi. Natural and legal persons have standing to bring proceedings under Art.230 EC if they are: **9–070**

(a) addressees of the decision[19]; or

(b) directly and individually concerned by a decision addressed to another undertaking.

The Community courts have interpreted the requirements of direct and individual concern narrowly which operates to reduce considerably the opportunity for third parties to challenge Commission decisions directly before the CFI, particularly where they have not been involved in the administrative procedure.[20] The third party customer or competitor must show that: (i) the measure has a direct impact upon him; and (ii) he is affected as an individual. The appellant must demonstrate that he has unique attributes or that other factual circumstances differentiate him from all other persons so that he is affected in the same way as if he were an addressee of the decision.[21] The ECJ has held that complainants,[22] competitors and upstream or downstream trading parties may have standing to challenge Commission competition decisions. The extent to which ordinary consumers or even national competition authorities can challenge acts is

---

[18] Case 125/78 *GEMA v Commission* [1979] E.C.R. 3173; [1980] 2 C.M.L.R. 177 and Case C–282/95 P *Guerin v Commission* [1997] E.C.R. I–1503; [1997] 5 C.M.L.R. 447.

[19] See, *e.g.* Case 56/64 *Consten & Grundig v Commission* [1966] E.C.R. 299 and Case 6/72 *Continental Can v Commission* [1973] E.C.R. 215; [1973] C.M.L.R. 199.

[20] For instance, the third party may want to challenge the Commission's market findings which, by virtue of *Masterfoods*, may be persuasive authority in a related or similar case pending before a national court.

[21] Case 25/62 *Plaumann v Commission* [1963] E.C.R. 95; [1964] C.M.L.R. 29 and Case C–50/00P *Union des Pequeños Agricultores* [2002] E.C.R. I–6677; [2002] 3 C.M.L.R. 1.

[22] Case 26/76 *Metro v Commission* [1977] E.C.R. 1875; [1978] 2 C.M.L.R. 1 and Case 210/81 *Demo Studio Schmidt v Commission* [1983] E.C.R. 3045; [1984] 1 C.M.L.R. 63.

unclear.[23] These rigorous standing requirements are likely to have an increased impact post-modernisation as third parties will be confined to challenging the validity of Commission decisions through the national courts, with a mandatory reference to the ECJ.[24]

9–071   **Time limits.**   Actions for annulment must be brought within two months of notification of the decision.[25] The deadline cannot be extended, even by consent. If an undertaking fails to challenge the decision within this time limit, not only will the action for annulment be declared inadmissible but he will also lose the right to challenge its validity indirectly in the national courts.[26] This limit will have severe ramifications post-modernisation as Commission decisions that are not challenged are binding on NCAs and national courts throughout the Union.

9–072   **Procedure.**   The appellant must submit a written application to the Court of First Instance, setting out the names of the parties, the subject matter of the dispute, a summary of the pleas in law relied on and the forms of order sought.[27] The Commission's decision must be included in an annex of supporting documents and listed in a schedule of annexes. The pleading must be dated and signed by the appellant's lawyer.[28] The original and five certified copies of the application must be lodged at the Registry of the Court of First Instance,[29] with an additional copy for the Commission. Appellants should produce evidence of their corporate incorporation, a power of attorney conferring authority to act on their legal advisor and evidence that the signatory of the power of attorney is authorised to act on behalf of the company. The legal advisor must submit his practising certificate, showing that he has rights of audience before the courts of a Member State. Within one month of service of the application, the Commission will file its defence,[30] which the Registry will serve on the appellant. Unless the appellant submits a reasoned request for the opportunity to submit

---

[23] There is no provision for class actions in the Court's procedure although the merits of private enforcement through class actions has recently been welcomed by A.G. Jacobs in Case C–195/98 *Österreichischer Gewerkschaftsbund, Gewerkschaft öffentlicher Dienst v Austria* [2000] E.C.R. I–1497 at paras 47–48.

[24] See para.9–079, below.

[25] Art.230(5) EC.

[26] Case C–188/92 *TWD* [1994] E.C.R. I–833; [1995] 2 C.M.L.R. 145.

[27] Rules of Procedure of the Court of First Instance, Art.44 and the Practice Direction issued by the Court of First Instance [2002] O.J. L87/48.

[28] Rules of Procedure of the Court of First Instance, Art.43.

[29] Pleadings can be submitted by hand or post to the Registry of the Court of First Instance of the European Communities, L–2925 Luxembourg or by fax (the dedicated fax number is 00 352 4303 2100) or by email (the dedicated mail box is *cfi.registry@curia.eu.int* : Art.43(6). If distant communication methods are used, a scanned version of the signed original should be sent and the signed original must be sent to the Registry within 10 days. The Registry will effect service on the Commission or create copies for any interveners.

[30] Art.46(1) of the Rules of Procedure.

supplementary pleadings or has requested measures of preparatory inquiry,[31] the court will open the oral procedure and fix a date for the hearing. Third parties, *e.g.* complainants or interested parties, may apply to intervene in the proceedings, in support of the appellant or the Commission.[32] Several appeals against the same decision may be consolidated or heard together.

Grounds of review of the Commission's findings. Under Art.230(2) EC, **9–073** Commission decisions can be challenged on the following, often overlapping, grounds:

(a) *Lack of competence*: This is equivalent to lack of *vires* and can be used to challenge Commission decisions authorising inspections or awarding interim relief where the conditions for such action have not been met.

(b) *Infringement of an essential procedural requirement*: Appeals asserting breaches of fundamental procedural rights during the investigation and administrative procedure are the most common grounds of appeal. Rights to a fair hearing, access to the file, freedom from self incrimination, privacy, and to a reasoned decision[33] are guaranteed by Arts 6 and 8 ECHR and have been recognised by the ECJ as fundamental principles of EC law.[34] Challenges on these grounds may succeed in excluding evidence or eliminating the Commission's findings on a particular aspect of the decision. However, they rarely lead to annulment of the entire decision unless there is no other legal or evidential basis underpinning the Commission's conclusions.[35]

(c) *Infringement of the Treaty or other rule of law*: This ground asserts that the Commission has misapplied or misconstrued its powers in the Treaty or secondary legislation, such as the Modernisation Regulation and Regulation 773/2004. It also covers breach of the fundamental principles of Community law, such as human rights, proportionality,[36] equal treatment[37] and legitimate expectations.[38]

---

[31] *ibid.*, Arts 52(1) and 64. A request for measures of organisation of the procedure (such as discovery, inspection of records, witness examination or an expert opinion) should be made by separate application.

[32] Protocol on the Statute of the Court of Justice, Art.40(4).

[33] Art.253 of the EC Treaty.

[34] See also Arts 2 and 7 of the European Constitution and Arts II–81,101, 102, 107–110 of the Charter of Fundamental Rights.

[35] Case T–86/95 *Compagnie générale maritime and Others v Commission (FEFC)* [2002] E.C.R. II–1011 at para.447.

[36] Case C–94/00 *Roquette Frères v Commission* [2003] E.C.R. I–9011.

[37] Case T–311/94 *BPB de Eendracht v Commission* [1998] E.C.R. II–1129 at para.309.

[38] Case C–152/88 *Sofrimport v Commission* [1990] E.C.R. I–2477; [1990] 3 C.M.L.R. 80.

(d) *Misuse of powers*: This ground is rarely successful as it involves allegations that the Commission has used its powers inappropriately or for an illegitimate purpose other than that for which they were intended. Even if misuse is established, the decision will not be set aside unless the improper purpose has some effect on the substance of the decision.

Judicial review by the CFI is confined to errors of law not fact. However, the assessment of the Commission's application of the law may involve inherent issues of fact. As part of that legal assessment, the court will assess whether the Commission's material findings of fact are correct.[39] In practice, the court has tended to show a degree of deference to the Commission's expertise, particularly in competition cases which involve complex economic factors and an element of discretion. In such cases, the court's review will be limited to ensuring that the Commission has complied with its rules of procedure and correctly stated the facts without any manifest error in their appraisal.[40]

9–074 **Appeals against fines.** The CFI has "unlimited jurisdiction" in appeals against penalties imposed by the Commission.[41] Challenges against fines are subject to a full appeal on the merits rather than judicial review. This means that the Court is not confined to the limited grounds of review in Art.230(2), but may inquire into the Commission's findings of fact and economic appraisals that underpin its conclusions on penalties and oversee the exercise of the Commission's discretion. It can substitute its assessment for that of the Commission, by reducing or increasing the level of the fine imposed or even cancelling it outright.[42]

9–075 **Annulment.** Aside from fines, the CFI has no power to substitute its assessment of the merits for that of the Commission. It the challenge is successful, the CFI will declare the decision void, in whole or in part. The case will be remitted to the Commission who must take any necessary steps to comply with the court's judgment, if necessary, by issuing a fresh decision within a reasonable time. It will be unable to enforce the decision against the appellant; it will, however, be able to enforce it against any other addressees that have not challenged it before the CFI.[43] The contested decision will be void and of no legal effect and, to the extent that it has been annulled, will not bind the NCAs and national courts throughout the Union.

---

[39] Case 40–48/73 *Suiker Unie v Commission* [1975] E.C.R. 1663; [1976] 1 C.M.L.R. 295.
[40] Case C–7/95P *Deere v Commission* [1998] E.C.R. I–1311; [1998] 5 C.M.L.R. 311.
[41] Art.229 of the EC Treaty and Art.31 of Regulation 1/2000.
[42] Case 27/76 *United Brands* [1978] E.C.R. 207; [1998] 1 C.M.L.R. 429.
[43] Case C–310/97P *Commission v AssiDoman* [1999] E.C.R. I–5363; [1999] 5 C.M.L.R. 1253.

Appeals to the ECJ.   Judgments of the CFI are subject to appeal on points   **9–076**
of law only, asserting the lack of competence of or an infringement of
Community law or a breach of procedure by the CFI.[44] Only unsuccessful
parties, Member States or interveners that are directly affected by the
judgment, are entitled to appeal.[45] The appeal must be lodged within two
months of notification of the judgment.[46] The ECJ is becoming increasingly
robust at rejecting appeals (often by reasoned order at an early stage in the
proceedings) that are inadmissible or unfounded in whole or in part.[47] The
ECJ's remit is to review arguments originally put forward before the CFI;
appellants will not be allowed to raise new pleas in law. The appeal will not
have suspensory effect unless the court orders interim relief.[48] If the appeal is
successful, the ECJ will annul the first instance judgment and may either
give final judgment itself or, in cases involving complex issues of fact or
economic assessment, remit the case back to the CFI. The CFI will give the
parties an opportunity to submit written arguments before it decides on the
case again, in the light of the legal position set out by the ECJ.[49]

9. REFERENCES FOR A PRELIMINARY RULING FROM THE EUROPEAN COURT OF JUSTICE

Generally.   Issues concerning the application or interpretation of Com-   **9–077**
munity competition law or the validity of a Commission decision that are
raised in disputes pending before national courts may be referred to the
European Court of Justice for preliminary ruling. The binding nature of
rulings from the Court of Justice will help to secure consistency in the
application and enforcement of Arts 81 and 82 across all 25 Member States.

Interpretation of Community competition law.   Under Art.234 EC, the ECJ   **9–078**
has competence in the competition field to interpret Arts 81 and 82 of the
EC Treaty and the provisions of secondary legislation, such as the Modernisation Regulation and 773/2004. As national courts are subject to duties
of loyal co-operation[50] and of protecting substantive rights under Community law,[51] questions may extend beyond to mere application of Arts 81
and 82 to the particular facts of the case and raise issues about the appropriate procedure to be adopted, the inter-relationship between Community

---

[44] Protocol on the Statute of the Court of Justice, Art.58.
[45] *ibid.*, Art.56.
[46] Appeals against a refusal to allow intervention must be brought within two weeks: Art.59.
[47] Rules of Procedure of the Court of Justice, Art.119. See the orders in the Cement Appeals
cases C–204/00 P *Aalborg Portland v Commission* which dismissed a large part of the appeals
as inadmissible.
[48] Protocol on the Statute of the Court, Art.60.
[49] Rules of Procedure of the Court of First Instance, Art.119.
[50] Art.16 of Regulation 1/2000.
[51] Art.10 of the EC Treaty and Recital 7 of Regulation 1/2000.

law and national procedural law and/or the adequacy and availability of the remedies under national law.

9–079   **Indirect Assessment of the legality of Commission decisions.**   The ECJ also has jurisdiction, under Art.234 of the EC Treaty, to assess the validity of any final decisions or acts taken by the EC Commission. National courts have no power to declare the Commission's acts invalid[52] as the Community Courts have exclusive competence for assessing their legality.[53] Direct challenges of Commission decisions before the national courts are likely to be rare as the parties directly involved in the Commission's decision-making process will have to appeal directly to the CFI rather than bring proceedings in the national courts.[54] Accordingly, in the majority of cases before national courts, Commission decisions are most likely to be challenged indirectly where a third party seeks to enforce its rights flowing from that same decision in a private damages action or where one party seeks to transpose the Commission's findings in one decision to the facts in a similar or related case. The accused will seek to contest the Commission's findings on similar grounds to those in Art.230 EC.[55]

9–080   **National Procedure.**   A question regarding Community competition law may be raised by the written or oral application of one of the parties to the dispute or by the national court of its own motion at any stage.[56] In competition cases in the UK, references will normally be sent from the Competition Appeal Tribunal or from the Chancery Division of the High Court or the appellate courts. Unless the national court is a court of last resort from which there is no possibility of appeal,[57] it has a wide discretion whether to refer the case to Luxembourg, depending on whether it considers that the court's ruling is necessary to enable it to give judgment.[58] In cases raising an arguable case that a Commission decision is invalid, the national court must refer.[59] However, on issues of interpretation, it may refuse to refer if it considers that the issue has already been resolved by a previous preliminary ruling[60] or where the answer is so obvious as to leave no scope for reasonable doubt.[61] With the recent modernisation reforms, that is

---

[52] Case 314/85 *Foto–Frost* [1987] E.C.R. 4199; [1988] 3 C.M.L.R. 57.
[53] Case C–94/00 *Roquette Frères*, n.36, above.
[54] Case C–188/92 *TWD*, n.26, above.
[55] See para.9–073, above.
[56] Case 126/80 *Salonia v Poidomani* [1981] E.C.R. 1563; [1982] 1 C.M.L.R. 64 and RSC Order 114, Rule 2.
[57] Art.234(3) EC and Case C–224/01 *Gerhard Köbler v Austria* [2003] E.C.R. I–10239; [2003] 3 C.M.L.R. 28.
[58] Art.234(2) EC.
[59] Case 314/85 *Foto–Frost*, n.52, above. See also the Commission's notice on co-operation with the national courts [2004] O.J. C101/54, para.13, which states that national courts can only avoid the binding nature of a Commission decision by seeking a reference to the European Court.
[60] Case 28–30/62 *Da Costa* [1963] E.C.R. 1; [1963] C.M.L.R. 224.
[61] Case *CILFIT v Ministry of Health* [1983] E.C.R. 3415; [1983] 1 C.M.L.R. 472.

unlikely to be the case for some time to come. The national court will issue a formal order for reference with a schedule setting out an account of the salient facts of the dispute, the rules of national law which may apply, a summary of the parties arguments, the reasons for making the reference and a formulation of the question(s) to be answered.[62] In practice, in the UK, the parties' lawyers tend to draft an agreed version of the schedule which is adopted by the court. On issuing the order for reference, the domestic proceedings will be suspended pending the resolution of the reference procedure[63] and the national court must consider whether it is necessary to order interim measures to safeguard the interests of the parties.[64] The national court remains seised of the dispute and may be called upon by the ECJ to provide additional information or to answer specific questions that the Court considers necessary to resolve the issue of law.[65]

Procedure before the ECJ. Once the order for reference is transmitted to the Registry of the Court of Justice, it will be registered, translated into the official languages of the Community and notified to the parties, the Member States and the Commission. The parties to the national proceedings (including any interveners) will be entitled to submit written observations[66] and attend any oral hearing.[67] There may also be interventions by the Member States and the Commission. Interested third parties that are not enjoined in the national proceedings will not be allowed to participate.[68]   **9–081**

Written observations. Within two months of the notification of the order for reference, the parties must submit their written observations.[69] All written observations are put in "blind" without an opportunity to review the arguments of the other side. There is no set form.[70] Although the court will be bound by the facts as set out in the order for reference, the pleading should highlight any important factual circumstances and applicable provisions of national law. It should also provide detailed reasoned legal arguments in support of the proposed answer to the questions suggested by the party. An annex of supporting documents should be attached.   **9–082**

---

[62] See, the European Court of Justice Information Note on References by National Courts at *www.curia.eu.int* and the Queens's Bench Practice Guide at White Book, 1A–90.

[63] Protocol of the Statute of the Court, Art.23.

[64] Case C–344/98 *Masterfoods* [2002] E.C.R. I–11369 at para.58.

[65] Rules of Procedure of the Court of Justice, Art.104(5).

[66] Protocol of the Statue of the Court, Art.20.

[67] Rules of Procedure of the Court of Justice, para.104(4).

[68] Order in Case 6/64 *Costa v ENEL* [1964] E.C.R. 1141; [1964] C.M.L.R. 425.

[69] Protocol on the Statute of the Court, Art.23 and Rules of Procedure of the Court of Justice, Art.103(3). There is an additional allowance of ten days for distance: Rules of Procedure, Art.80(2).

[70] See, however, the Notes for the Guidance of Counsel, published in February 2001 at *www.curia.eu.int*.

Written observations can be lodged by hand, post, fax[71] or email to the Registry of the Court.[72] They must be dated and signed by the party's lawyer. If distant communication methods are used, a scanned version of the signed original should be sent and the signed original must be sent to the Registry within 10 days. The Registry will effect service on the other parties, the Commission or other interveners. The Court now has power to ask questions of the parties or the Member State interveners[73] or to request supplementary information from the national court to clarify the questions referred or the factual background to the case.[74]

9–083   **Oral hearing.**   There is no automatic right or obligation to attend an oral hearing. The court may dispense with the hearing altogether unless the parties or the interveners submit a reasoned request for an opportunity to be heard within one month of service of the written observations.[75] Parties will have a maximum of 30 minutes[76] to make their oral observations to the court followed by the Member States and the Commission, who will have 15 minutes each. In many cases, the Advocate General or the Reporting Judge will have additional questions at the end of submissions.

9–084   **Opinion of the Advocate General.**   The court may, in certain circumstances, decide that there is no need for an opinion from the Advocate General.[77] This is unlikely to be so in competition cases that raise novel questions about Arts 81 and 82 or the mechanics of the modernisation regime. Where the Advocate General produces an opinion, it will be delivered in open court and a translation into the language of the case will be sent to the parties. The parties do not have the right to submit observations on the opinion.[78] The opinion is not binding on the ECJ or on the national court.

9–085   **Judgment.**   Unless the opinion raises a new issue which necessitates a further hearing, the Reporting Judge will produce a draft judgment which will be deliberated in secret by the formation of judges who attended the hearing.[79] The eventual judgment will set out a summary of the facts and an answer to the questions referred, according to its interpretation of Community law. It will not seek to comment on national law or to apply the law to the facts of the case as that is a matter for the national court. The judgment is delivered in open court and published on the court's website.

---

[71] The dedicated fax number is 00 352 433 766.
[72] The dedicated mail box is *ecj.registry@curia.eu.int*.
[73] Rules of Procedure of the Court of Justice, Art.54(a).
[74] *ibid.*, Art.104(5).
[75] *ibid.*, Art.104(4)
[76] Reduced to 15 minutes if the cases before a small chamber.
[77] Art.222 of the EC Treaty, Art.20(4) of the Protocol on the Statute of the Court of Justice.
[78] Case 17/98 *Emesa Sugar (Free Zone) NV v Aruba* [2000] E.C.R. I–665.
[79] Protocol on the Statute of the Court, Art.27(2).

The parties and the national court will receive a certified copy of the judgment.[80]

Resumption of the national proceedings. The judgment of the ECJ will be   **9–086**
binding on the referring court (and any appellate courts), who must apply it
to the facts of the case pending before it.[81] Often the judgment will resolve
the case in its entirety or lead to the parties settling their dispute. In other
cases, the referring court will hear legal argument concerning the application
of the court's interpretation of the law to the facts of the case before proceeding to judgment. The extent to which the ECJ's ruling binds other
national courts and NCAs in other Member States is a matter of some
debate. The aim of the preliminary reference procedure is to secure the
uniform application of Community law throughout all 25 Member States.
The suggested approach is as follows:

(1) As regards rulings on the legality or otherwise of Commission's acts
    and decisions, national courts and NCAs should respect the Eur-
    opean Court's declaration of invalidity and treat the act as void.[82]
    The court's ruling has the effect of releasing national courts from
    their obligations under Art.16(2) of Regulation 1/2000. If possible,
    the national court should follow the ECJ's re-statement of the law
    or, if there is some uncertainty, seek a preliminary reference on the
    consequences of such invalidity for the particular case before them.

(2) As regards rulings which interpret the application of Community
    competition law, the author takes the view that NCAs and national
    courts should, pursuant to their duty of loyal co-operation under
    Art.10 of the EC Treaty, be obliged to follow the *dispositif* in the
    court's judgment. In absence of any temporal restrictions imposed
    by the ECJ in its judgment, national courts can also apply the ruling
    to situations that arose before the date of the judgment.[83]

That approach is necessary, not just because of the need to provide legal
certainty for undertakings operating in the Union, but also, in the words of
the first recital of Regulation 1/2000, to "ensure that competition is not
distorted [and that] Articles 81 and 82 of the EC Treaty are applied effectively and uniformly in the Community." Those objectives are crucially

---

[80] Rules of Procedure of the Court of Justice, Art.64(1).
[81] Case C–320/88 *Staatssecretaris van Financien* [1990] E.C.R. I–285; [1993] 3 C.M.L.R. 547.
   See also the Commission's Notice on co-operation with the national courts [2004] O.J. C101/
   54, para.13. Failure to apply an ECJ judgment could attract State liability in damages for a
   serious breach of Community law—see Case C–224/01 *Gerhard Köbler*, n.57, above.
[82] Case 66/80 *SpA International Chemical Corporation v Amministrazione delle finanze dello
   Stato* [1981] E.C.R. 1191; [1983] 2 C.M.L.R. 593.
[83] Case 61/79 *Amministrazione delle Finanze dello Stato v Denkavit* [1980] E.C.R. 1205; [1981] 3
   C.M.L.R. 694.

important for the success of the newly-established decentralised enforcement network of competition authorities and national courts in the enlarged European Union.

ANNEX TO CHAPTER 9

FORM C

Complaint pursuant to Article 7 of Regulation (EC) No. 1/2003

Information regarding the complainant and the undertaking(s) or association of undertakings giving rise to the complaint

1. Give full details on the identity of the legal or natural person submitting   **9–087**
the complaint. Where the complainant is an undertaking, identify the corporate group to which it belongs and provide a concise overview of the
nature and scope of its business activities. Provide a contact person (with
telephone number, postal and email-address) from which supplementary
explanations can be obtained.

2. Identify the undertaking(s) or association of undertakings whose conduct
the complaint relates to, including, where applicable, all available information on the corporate group to which the undertaking(s) complained of
belong and the nature and scope of the business activities pursued by them.
Indicate the position of the complainant vis-à-vis the undertaking(s) or
association of undertakings complained of (e.g. customer, competitor).

II. Details of the alleged infringement and evidence

3. Set out in detail the facts from which, in your opinion, it appears that
there exists an infringement of Article 81 or 82 of the Treaty and/or Article
53 or 54 of the EEA agreement. Indicate in particular the nature of the
products (goods or services) affected by the alleged infringements and
explain, where necessary, the commercial relationships concerning these
products. Provide all available details on the agreements or practices of the
undertakings or associations of undertakings to which this complaint
relates. Indicate, to the extent possible, the relative market positions of the
undertakings concerned by the complaint.

4. Submit all documentation in your possession relating to or directly
connected with the facts set out in the complaint (for example, texts of
agreements, minutes of negotiations or meetings, terms of transactions,
business documents, circulars, correspondence, notes of telephone conversations?). State the names and address of the persons able to testify to the
facts set out in the complaint, and in particular of persons affected by the
alleged infringement. Submit statistics or other data in your possession
which relate to the facts set out, in particular where they show developments

in the marketplace (for example information relating to prices and price trends, barriers to entry to the market for new suppliers etc.).

5. Set out your view about the geographical scope of the alleged infringement and explain, where that is not obvious, to what extent trade between Member States or between the Community and one or more EFTA States that are contracting parties of the EEA Agreement may be affected by the conduct complained of.

III. Finding sought from the Commission and legitimate interest

6. Explain what finding or action you are seeking as a result of proceedings brought by the Commission.

7. Set out the grounds on which you claim a legitimate interest as complainant pursuant to Article 7 of Regulation (EC) No. 1/2003. State in particular how the conduct complained of affects you and explain how, in your view, intervention by the Commission would be liable to remedy the alleged grievance.

IV. Proceedings before national competition authorities or national courts

8. Provide full information about whether you have approached, concerning the same or closely related subject-matters, any other competition authority and/or whether a lawsuit has been brought before a national court. If so, provide full details about the administrative or judicial authority contacted and your submissions to such authority.

Declaration that the information given in this form and in the Annexes thereto is given entirely in good faith.

Date and signature.

Send by email to COMP-GREFFE-ANTITRUST@cec.eu.int

or to:
European Commission
DG Competition, Antitrust Registry
B - 1049 - Brussels

CHAPTER 10

MODERNISATION: USING EC COMPETITION LAW IN THE UK COURTS

Josh Holmes[1]

1. INTRODUCTION

EC Treaty. This chapter considers the application of Arts 81 and 82 EC, the main substantive rules of Community competition law, in civil litigation before the UK courts. The European Community Treaty contains no direct mention of the possibility of such private enforcement. Articles 83 to 85 EC suggest that the primary responsibility for enforcing Community competition law falls on the European Commission, with an interim role for the Member States until the legislation required to empower the Commission has been adopted.

10–001

Regulation 17/62. The first such enforcement legislation, Regulation 17/62,[2] applicable from 1962 to 2004, gave the Commission the powers to investigate alleged infringements,[3] to require firms to desist from anti-competitive conduct[4] and to impose fines[5] or periodic penalty payments[6] in respect of such conduct. It also provided that the "authorities of the Member States" should remain competent to apply the Community competition rules until the Commission initiated proceedings.[7] Such terminology did not make clear whether the national authorities in question were to be administrative, judicial or both, thereby apparently leaving the choice to the Member States.

10–002

---

[1] Barrister, Monckton Chambers.
[2] Council Regulation 17/62 [1962] O.J. 13/204 (Special English Edition 1959–62, p.87).
[3] *ibid.*, Arts 11–14.
[4] *ibid.*, Art.3(1).
[5] *ibid.*, Art.15.
[6] *ibid.*, Art.16.
[7] *ibid.*, Art.9(3).

10–003 **Direct effect of Community competition law.** In the 1970's, the European Court of Justice held that Arts 81(1) and 82 EC have direct effect: they confer rights and impose obligations upon private parties which national courts are required to protect.[8] The court thereby confirmed that private enforcement is a necessary component of the system of Community competition law, supplementing the public enforcement effected by the Commission and national competition authorities. It has recently been confirmed[9] that such private enforcement of Community competition law may take one of two forms. First, a party may rely upon it defensively (or "as a shield") in order to have a contractual obligation declared void. Secondly, a party may seek to use it offensively (or "as a sword") to claim damages in respect of loss suffered as a consequence of their breach, or to obtain injunctive relief to prevent future harm.[10]

10–004 **Modernisation.** Although it has therefore been apparent for at least three decades that private parties may rely upon Community competition law in proceedings before national courts, offensive claims have rarely been brought in the UK or elsewhere.[11] One of the stated objectives of the recent modernisation of Community competition enforcement is to promote the private enforcement of Community competition law.[12] Regulation 17/62[13] has been replaced with effect from May 1, 2004 by a new Regulation 1/2003 ("the Modernisation Regulation"),[14] which explicitly recognises and codifies the role of national courts as Community competition enforcers.[15] It also confers direct effect on Art.81(3) EC,[16] which allows for the exemption of agreements meeting certain specified criteria from the prohibition contained in Art.81(1) EC, and which under the previous Regulation was applicable only by the Commission following the prior notification of an agreement.[17]

---

[8] Case 127/73 *BRT v Sabam* [1974] E.C.R. 51; [1974] 2 C.M.L.R. 238.

[9] In Case C–453/99 *Courage v Crehan* [2001] E.C.R. I–6297; [2001] 5 C.M.L.R. 1058, the European Court of Justice held that a party can claim damages for a breach of Community competition law in national courts. It had long been assumed that this was the case. In 1983, in the thirteenth Report on Competition Policy, the Commission stated its opinion that both damages and an injunction could be obtained by private parties who were the victim of conduct contrary to Arts 81 or 82 EC (pp.135–136, paras 217–218).

[10] For a detailed consideration of the availability of damages for breach of competition law, see Chapter 7, above.

[11] Two prominent recent attempts in the UK of which the latter was successful were made in *Arkin v Borchard Lines Ltd (No.4)* [2003] EWHC 687 (Comm Ct) and *Crehan v Inntrepeneur* [2003] EWHC 1510 (Ch); [2003] 27 E.G. 138 (CS), Ch D, and now on appeal [2004] EWCA Civ 637. See Holmes, "Public enforcement or private enforcement? Enforcement of competition law in the EC and UK" (2004) 25(1) E.C.L.R. 25–36.

[12] Commission White Paper on modernisation of the rules implementing Articles [81] and [82] of the EC Treaty [1999] O.J. C132/1, paras 3, 8 and 12 of the Executive Summary.

[13] n.2, above.

[14] Council Regulation 1/2003 on the implementation of the rules on competition laid down in Arts 81 and 82 of the Treaty [2003] O.J. L1/1. For the provisions of the Modernisation Regulation which grant powers to the Commission, see Chapter 9, above.

[15] Art.6 provides that "national courts shall have the power to apply Articles 81 and 82 of the Treaty".

[16] Art.1 of the Modernisation Regulation, n.14, above.

[17] Arts 4, 6 and 9(1) of Regulation 17/62, n.2, above.

Remaining barriers to private enforcement. It may be doubted whether the 10–005 enactment of the Modernisation Regulation will dramatically increase the scope for the private enforcement of Community competition law. The traditional reluctance to litigate in the national courts cannot wholly be attributed to the inability of those courts, until recently, to apply Art.81(3) EC, an obstacle which has never existed in relation to Art.82 EC. Instead, the main disincentive to litigation may be its speculative nature, given ambiguities in the applicable Community rules, doubts about the expertise of generalist national courts to apply those rules, uncertainties as to the governing national procedural and remedial principles, difficulties in obtaining the necessary evidence, and (at least in the UK) the fear of having to meet the other party's costs if unsuccessful.[18] A potential litigant will usually prefer to complain either to the European Commission or a national competition authority, and to rely upon their investigative powers to establish an infringement at no cost to it.[19] If a favourable Commission decision can be obtained, it will be binding upon a national court in subsequent litigation,[20] and therefore removes the uncertainties relating to liability if not quantum.

Reform of UK competition law. In any event, litigants now have less reason 10–006 to rely specifically on the Community competition rules. National competition law in the UK, as in other Member States, has been remodelled in the image of the Community provisions. It will rarely make any difference to the legal analysis of a situation whether it is considered through the lens of domestic or Community law. Even when litigation is brought under national competition law, however, Community law has a role to play. National courts are obliged to apply domestic and Community provisions in tandem whenever the jurisdictional criterion for the application of Community competition law is met.[21] A range of substantive, procedural and remedial consequences follow.

Structure. The remainder of the present chapter is divided up as follows: 10–007

(1) The chapter first provides an overview of the legislative and administrative texts which contribute to the system of Community competition law: the relevant provisions of the European Community Treaty; the Modernisation Regulation, which implements the Community competition rules; the block exemption regulations; Commission decisions; and the various other Commission

---

[18] See generally Kon and Maxwell, "Enforcement in national courts of the E.C. and new U.K. competition rules: obstacles to effective enforcement" (1998) 19(7) E.C.L.R 443–454.
[19] See Holmes, n.11, above.
[20] Art.16 of the Modernisation Regulation.
[21] The Modernisation Regulation, Art.3.

documents which may be relevant when interpreting the Community competition rules, in particular the notices and guidelines.[22]

(2) Secondly, the principles governing the applicability of Community competition law in civil proceedings before the national courts are considered. Three such principles may be distinguished. First, national courts have the power to apply Community competition law by virtue of the doctrine of direct effect.[23] Secondly, pursuant to Art.3 of the Modernisation Regulation, they must apply Community competition law whenever they apply domestic competition law and the conditions for its application are met.[24] Thirdly, the same jurisdictional criterion governs the applicability of both Arts 81 and 82 EC: namely, whether the agreement or practice at issue is capable of affecting trade between Member States.[25]

(3) The third part of the chapter examines the substantive consequences if Community competition law is applicable in national civil proceedings, of which there are four. First, according to the doctrine of supremacy, Community law prevails over all inconsistent national law. As a consequence, national competition law clearly cannot exculpate conduct which infringes Art.81 or 82 EC. If national law is less strict, Community law, where applicable, will nonetheless operate to prohibit the agreement or practice in question.[26] Secondly, as regards stricter national rules, Art.3 of the Modernisation Regulation prevents national competition law from prohibiting an agreement or practice to which Art.81 EC applies but which it does not prohibit. No equivalent restraint is imposed upon national competition law in respect of conduct falling within the scope of Art.82 EC.[27] In any event, there are now few substantive differences between UK and EC competition law.[28] Thirdly, Art.16 of the Modernisation Regulation lays down rules to govern situations in which the Commission has taken or is contemplating a decision in relation to conduct which is the subject of national proceedings. A national court must avoid giving a judgment in conflict with the Commission's decision. If the Commission has already decided, the court is bound by the Commission's decision. If the Commission has yet to decide, the court must consider whether to stay proceedings. This it should do unless the legal analysis of the case is clear and the Commission's decision cannot be in doubt.[29] Fourthly, as regards the remedies available for breach of Community

---

[22] paras 10–008–10–017, below.
[23] paras 10–018–10–025, below.
[24] paras 10–026–10–027, below.
[25] paras 10–028–10–036, below.
[26] para.10–038, below.
[27] paras 10–039–10–042, below.
[28] paras 10–043–10–046, below.
[29] paras 10–047–10–053, below.

competition law in the national courts, it is for national law to determine the applicable principles. However, those principles must not impair the effectiveness of Community law. The recent case of *Courage v Crehan*[30] reveals the resultant potential for Community law to require alterations to be made to national remedial rules.[31]

(4) The final part of the chapter considers the procedural consequences for national proceedings if Community competition law is applicable. A range of procedural consequences arises out of the relationship of co-operation between the national courts and the Commission, now codified in Art.15 of the Modernisation Regulation. National courts may seek information or advice from the Commission in national proceedings which involve Community competition law. The Commission and the national competition authority of the Member State where the proceedings take place may make written observations, and may request the permission of the national court to make oral observations. Member States must also transmit to the Commission a copy of any written judgment applying Art.81 or 82 EC.[32] A further procedural consequence for judicial proceedings in which questions of Community law are at issue is that the court or tribunal hearing the case may (and in some circumstances must) refer those questions to the European Court of Justice. That facility probably also exists in cases which involve purely domestic competition provisions where those provisions are modelled on Community law.[33]

2. OVERVIEW OF EC COMPETITION LAW

(a) Relevant treaty provisions

Competition provisions of the EC Treaty. The European Community[34] was established by the Treaty of Rome in 1957. Article 3(1)(g) identifies one of the activities of the Community as being to institute a "system ensuring that competition in the internal market is not distorted". Although that EC Treaty has since been amended on a number of occasions, the rules on competition have remained basically unchanged in their substance. Since the

10–008

---

[30] n.9, above.
[31] paras 10–054–10–056, below.
[32] paras 10–057–10–072, below.
[33] paras 10–073–10–075, below.
[34] The European Community was originally known as the European Economic Community but was renamed following the Treaty of Maastricht, 1992. That Treaty also established the European Union, an overarching structure which includes the Community as one of its three pillars.

renumbering effected by the Treaty of Amsterdam in 1999,[35] they are contained in Arts 81 to 89 EC, which make up Chapter 1 of Part III of the Treaty.[36]

10–009   **Article 81 EC.**   Article 81 EC is the provision upon which the Chapter I prohibition[37] in UK competition law is based. It prohibits certain "agreements between undertakings, decisions by associations of undertakings and concerted practices which may affect trade between Member States and which have as their object or effect the prevention, restriction or distortion of competition within the common market". Its provisions are explained elsewhere in this work.[38]

10–010   **Article 82 EC.**   Article 82 forms the basis for the Chapter II prohibition.[39] It prohibits the abuse of a dominant position by one or more undertaking and is explained elsewhere in this work.[40]

10–011   **Article 83 EC.**   The Treaty does not specify in any detail how Arts 81 and 82 EC are to be enforced. Instead, Art.83 confers authority on the Council, acting by a qualified majority on a proposal from the Commission and after consulting the European Parliament, to adopt "the appropriate regulations or directives to give effect to the principles set out in Articles 81 and 82".

10–012   **Articles 84 to 89 EC.**   Articles 84 and 85 EC deal with the respective roles of the Member States and the Commission in enforcing Community competition law prior to the adoption of an implementing regulation pursuant to Art.83 EC. In most cases, those provisions are no longer of any application.[41] Article 86 contains specific rules directed at more heavily regulated sectors of economic activity. Articles 87 to 89 provide for the control of State aid.[42] Articles 86 to 89 are beyond the scope of the present chapter.

10–013   **Article 10 EC.**   Also relevant to the application of Community competition law in the national courts is Art.10 EC, which provides as follows:

---

[35] Prior to the renumbering, the competition rules were found in Arts 85 to 94 of the Treaty. Arts 81 and 82 EC were previously Arts 85 and 86 of the Treaty.

[36] The European Constitution, if it is adopted in accordance with the draft submitted by the Convention, would not alter the substance of the provisions relating to competition law, but would result in further changes of form. The distinction between Community and Union would be abolished, and the competition rules would henceforward form part of a single corpus of European Union law. The relevant provisions, which would fall within Pt III of the Constitution, would again be renumbered.

[37] See Competition Act 1998, ss.1 to 16.

[38] See paras 2–008–2–020, above.

[39] See Competition Act 1998, s.18.

[40] See paras 2–021–2–029, above.

[41] They will apply only to those sectors in respect of which implementing regulations have yet to be adopted, in particular air transport between Member States of the Community and third countries.

[42] For the application of the State aid rules in domestic courts, see Chapter 8, above.

"Member States shall take all appropriate measures, whether general or particular, to ensure fulfilment of the obligations arising out of this Treaty or resulting from action taken by the institutions of the Community. They shall facilitate the achievement of the Community's tasks.

They shall abstain from any measure which could jeopardise the attainment of the objectives of this Treaty."

Article 10 EC applies to all institutions of the Member States, including the national courts. It supplies the basis for the provisions of the Modernisation Regulation concerning co-operation between the Commission and the national courts in proceedings which involve the Community competition rules.[43]

(b) Community legislation

The Modernisation Regulation. Regulation 17/62[44] was the first regulation implementing the competition rules of the Treaty. It entered into force on March 13, 1962, and laid down rules regarding the application of Arts 81 and 82 EC. It reserved to the Commission the power to authorise agreements pursuant to Art.81(3), a process commonly referred to as "exemption". It could only do so, however, in respect of agreements which had been notified to it in advance. The period of exemption could commence, at earliest, from the date when the notification was received. The consequences for litigation in the national courts are described below.[45] In April 1999, the Commission published a White Paper on the modernisation of the rules implementing Arts 81 and 82 of the EC Treaty.[46] Its reform proposals were embodied in a new Modernisation Regulation[47] which replaced Regulation 17/62 with effect from May 1, 2004. The Modernisation Regulation abolishes both the Commission's exclusive competence to apply Art.81(3) EC and the possibility for prior notification.[48] **10–014**

The block exemption regulations. The block exemption regulations specify generalised exemptions under Art.81(3) EC. An agreement falling within the terms of those regulations has traditionally enjoyed the benefit of Art.81(3) without the need for it to have been notified and individually exempted by the Commission. Although the Modernisation Regulation abolishes the system of prior notification and individual exemption, it leaves intact the **10–015**

---

[43] See paras 10–056 *et seq.*, below.
[44] n.2, above.
[45] paras 10–020–10–022, below.
[46] n.12, above.
[47] n.14, above. For the powers of the Commission under the Modernisation Regulation, see Chapter 9, above.
[48] Art.1.

block exemptions,[49] which still therefore guarantee exemption to any agreement falling within their ambit.

(c) Decisions and statements of the Commission

10–016   **Commission decisions.**   Commission decisions are binding in their entirety on those to whom they are addressed. National courts may not reach any conclusion which is directly contrary to a Commission decision concerning the specific agreement or conduct to which that decision relates. Otherwise, whilst supplying useful guidance to national courts, Commission decisions are "not law creating".[50]

10–017   **Other statements of the Commission.**   The Commission has issued various documents, recording its understanding of the correct interpretation of the Community competition rules, and indicating the policy which it intends to adopt when applying those rules. As interpretations of Community law, such documents are not legally binding, but they do provide a useful resource upon which national courts may draw.[51] They include the Commission's annual reports on competition policy, as well as various notices and guidelines. To coincide with the entry into force of the Modernisation Regulation, the Commission issued a number of new notices.[52] The following general notices may, in particular, be of relevance in litigation involving Community competition law before the national courts:

- Commission Notice on the co-operation between the Commission and the courts of the EU Member States in the application of Articles 81 and 82 EC (hereafter, the "Notice on co-operation with national courts")[53];

- Commission Notice—Guidelines on the effect on trade concept contained in Articles 81 and 82 of the Treaty (hereinafter, the "Guidelines on the effect on trade concept")[54];

---

[49] Despite the fact that the Commission was apparently solely empowered by Art.9(1) of Regulation 17/62, (n.2, above) to adopt block exemption regulations as well as individual exemption decisions, the Commission in fact proceeded on the basis of later Council Regulations, such as Regulation 19/65 ([1965] O.J. 36/533) and Regulation 2821/71 ([1971] O.J. L285/46) when adopting block exemption regulations. As recital 10 and para.40 of the Modernisation Regulation make clear, those Council Regulations remain in force and so do the block exemptions enacted pursuant to them.

[50] See Opinion of A.G. Warner in Case 19/77 *Miller v Commission* [1978] E.C.R. 131 at 161; [1978] 2 C.M.L.R. 334 at 346.

[51] Case 66/86 *Ahmed Saeed Flugreisen* [1989] E.C.R. 803 at para.27; Case C–234/89 *Delimitis* [1991] E.C.R. I–935 at para.50.

[52] See Chapter 9, above.

[53] [2004] O.J. C101/54.

[54] [2004] O.J. C101/81.

- Communication from the Commission—Notice—Guidelines on the application of Article 81(3) of the Treaty[55];

- Commission Notice on agreements of minor importance which do not appreciably restrict competition under Article 81(1) of the Treaty (*de minimis*)[56];

- Commission Notice on the definition of the relevant market for the purposes of Community competition law.[57]

A complete and updated list of Regulations, Notices and Guidelines can be found on the website of the Directorate General for Competition of the European Commission.[58]

3. APPLICABILITY OF COMMUNITY COMPETITION LAW IN NATIONAL PROCEEDINGS

(a) The direct effect of Community competition law

The doctrine of direct effect. Early in the history of the Community legal order, the ECJ established the related doctrines of the direct effect and supremacy of Community law. The former concerns the applicability of Community law norms, and is considered here. The latter concerns the substantive consequences for the national legal order of a finding that such norms are applicable, and is dealt with below.[59] Under the doctrine of direct effect, rules of Community law which are sufficiently clear and unconditional may be invoked in proceedings before a national court.[60] Provided that the court has jurisdiction, it must give effect to them. Treaty Articles, legislation in the form of regulations or directives, as well as decisions are all capable of direct effect.[61] Other types of Community act, such as recommendations or opinions, which are not intended to produce binding legal consequences, are not capable of direct effect. National law supplies the applicable framework of procedural, evidential and remedial rules governing the application of directly effective Community law in the national courts.[62] However, those rules must not make it impossible or excessively

10–018

---

[55] [2004] O.J. C101/97.
[56] [2001] O.J. C368/13.
[57] [1997] O.J. C372/5.
[58] *http://europa.eu.int/comm/competition/antitrust/legislation/*.
[59] See para.10–038, below.
[60] Case 26/62 *Van Gend en Loos* [1963] E.C.R. 1; [1963] C.M.L.R. 105.
[61] Directives, however, are only capable of directly imposing obligations upon Member States (so-called vertical direct effect) and not private parties (so-called horizontal direct effect).
[62] National rules in the UK require claims involving Community and national competition law to be commenced in the High Court, Chancery Division. See Practice Direction—Competition law—Claims relating to the Application of Articles 81 and 82 of the EC Treaty and Chapters I and II of Part I of the Competition Act 1998, para.2.

difficult to bring a claim. They must also apply in the same way in proceedings which involve Community law as they would in equivalent domestic proceedings.

10–019 **The direct effect of Articles 81 and 82 EC.** In the 1970's, the ECJ held that Arts 81(1) and 82 EC have direct effect,[63] and may therefore be relied upon by private parties in proceedings before the national courts. A broad distinction can be drawn between the defensive assertion of those provisions, normally in the context of a contractual dispute (use "as a shield") and their offensive invocation in order to obtain damages or an injunction (use "as a sword"). In the former case, the party wishing to escape from its obligations under a contract argues that those obligations are contrary to Community competition law and therefore void. The voidness of an agreement which is prohibited under Art.81 EC is expressly stipulated by Art.81(2) EC. Similarly, it is generally assumed that a contractual provision amounting to an abuse of a dominant position by one of the parties to the contract under Art.82 could not be enforced by the dominant party. Articles 81 and 82 EC may also be used offensively in order to claim damages[64] and probably also an injunction.[65] The remedial consequences for national proceedings in which Community competition law is at issue are considered below.[66]

10–020 **Previously no direct effect for Article 81(3) EC.** Under Regulation 17/62, the Commission had sole power to apply Art.81(3) EC to an agreement.[67] It could only do so in respect of an agreement which had previously been notified to it.[68] Any exemption granted could not commence prior to the date of notification. That system had mixed consequences for litigation involving Art.81 EC before the national courts.[69]

10–021 **Use of Article 81(1) EC as a shield.** This system of enforcement encouraged the use of Art.81(1) EC as a shield by parties seeking to escape from their contractual obligations. Assuming that no block exemption was applicable, a national court had no choice but to apply Art.81(2) EC and to declare void all or part of an agreement at least for the period prior to notification, regardless of whether it met the conditions for an individual exemption under Art.81(3) EC.

10–022 **Use of Article 81(1) EC as a sword.** As regards the use of Art.81(1) EC as a sword, in proceedings for damages or an injunction, the Commission's exclusive competence to apply Art.81(3) EC served as an impediment to

---

[63] Case 127/73 *BRT v SABAM*, n.8, above, at para.16.
[64] See Case C–453/99 *Courage v Crehan*, n.9, above.
[65] See the Opinion of A.G. Jacobs in joined Cases C–246/01, C–306/01, C–354/01 and C–355/01 *AOK Bundesverband* [2004] 4 C.M.L.R. 22 at para.104.
[66] See paras 10–054–10–056, below.
[67] Art.9(1), Regulation 17/62.
[68] Arts 4 and 6(1), Regulation 17/62.
[69] See Commission White Paper, n.12, above, paras 99 to 100.

private enforcement through litigation.[70] A national court, when considering an agreement which had been notified, or which was notified during the course of proceedings, was in most cases obliged to order a stay and to await a decision from the Commission as to whether Art.81(3) EC was applicable. The national court could only proceed to judgment if completely satisfied that Art.81(3) EC was clearly inapplicable. The Commission's exclusive competence in relation to Art.81(3) EC therefore had the effect of hampering the application of the Community competition rules by the national courts. It had similar consequences for enforcement by national competition authorities. It also created a significant volume of work for the Commission, thereby preventing the Commission from concentrating its resources on the most serious infringements.

Modernisation. The main argument in favour of an exclusive competence on the part of the Commission was to ensure that Community competition law was correctly and uniformly applied at a time when there was little experience of such law in the Member States and perhaps also some risk of national bias. However, by the end of the 1990s, it was apparent that a competition culture was well established in the Member States. There was therefore less need for a centralised system of enforcement.[71] As a result, Regulation 17/62 has been replaced by the Modernisation Regulation. **10–023**

Article 81(3) EC now directly effective. The Modernisation Regulation removes the Commission's monopoly on the application of Art.81(3) EC. Since May 1, 2004, Arts 81 and 82 EC have therefore both become directly effective in their entirety. Article 1 of the Modernisation Regulation states that: **10–024**

"1. Agreements, decisions and concerted practices caught by Article 81(1) of the Treaty which do not satisfy the conditions of Article 81(3) of the Treaty shall be prohibited, no prior decision to that effect being required.

2. Agreements, decisions and concerted practices caught by Article 81(1) of the Treaty which satisfy the conditions of Article 81(3) of the Treaty shall not be prohibited, no prior decision to that effect being required.

3. The abuse of a dominant position referred to in Article 82 of the Treaty shall be prohibited, no prior decision to that effect being required."

Article 6 of the Modernisation Regulation confirms that "national courts shall have the power to apply Articles 81 and 82 of the Treaty". The Modernisation Regulation also abolishes the system of prior notification

---

[70] See, to that effect, recital 3 of the preamble to the Modernisation Regulation.
[71] See, to that effect, recitals 1 and 2 of the preamble to the Modernisation Regulation.

and of exemption decisions. Undertakings no longer have the security which could previously be gained by notifying an agreement to the Commission. As a result of the Modernisation Regulation, the defensive assertion of Art.81(1) EC in litigation before the national courts by a party seeking to avoid a contractual obligation has been curtailed in cases where Art.81(3) EC applies. A national court may now itself apply Art.81(3) EC to rescue an agreement even if no block exemption is available. At the same time, the offensive deployment of Art.81 EC, as a basis for claiming damages or injunctive relief, has been rendered somewhat more attractive. There is no longer now the delay and uncertainty which previously resulted from the need for the national court in all but the clearest of cases to await a Commission decision on any notified agreement.

10–025 **The direct effect of Community competition legislation.** The Modernisation Regulation is itself capable of direct effect, and most of its provisions are sufficiently clear and unconditional to allow for their application in national proceedings without the need for any further national implementing legislation. Undoubtedly, however, many Member States will wish to take steps to adapt their national legal frameworks in accordance with the terms of the Regulation.[72] For instance, it may be appropriate to amend the rules of procedure of national courts to accommodate the various types of co-operation envisaged between such courts and the Commission, which are discussed below. In the UK, a new practice direction (hereafter, "the EU Competition Law practice direction") makes provision for such co-operation.[73] The block exemption regulations, which remain in place after the Modernisation Regulation, are also directly effective and must be applied where relevant by national courts hearing cases which involve Art.81 EC.

(b) The rule of concurrent application under the Modernisation Regulation

10–026 **Article 3(1) of the Modernisation Regulation.** The relationship between Community and national competition law is now also governed by Art3 of the Modernisation Regulation. The second and third paragraphs of Art.3 lay down rules for resolving any difference of substance between domestic and Community rules. Those paragraphs are considered below.[74]

---

[72] Member States are not permitted under Community law to adopt measures to implement Regulations which are described in Art.249 EC as "directly applicable in the Member States". See Case 39/72 *Commission v Italy* [1973] E.C.R. 101 at paras 17–18. However, such implementing measures are permissible where they are explicitly or implicitly authorised by a Regulation. See *e.g.* Case 128/78 *Commission v United Kingdom* [1979] E.C.R. 419; [1979] 2 C.M.L.R. 45.

[73] Practice Direction—Competition law—Claims relating to the application of Articles 81 and 82, n.62, above.

[74] See paras 10–039–10–042, below.

Article 3(1) is relevant to the applicability of Community competition law before the national courts. It provides as follows:

"Where the competition authorities of the Member States or national courts apply national competition law to agreements, decisions by associations of undertakings or concerted practices within the meaning of Article 81(1) of the Treaty which may affect trade between Member States within the meaning of that provision, they shall also apply Article 81 of the Treaty to such agreements, decisions or concerted practices. Where the competition authorities of the Member States or national courts apply national competition law to any abuse prohibited by Article 82 of the Treaty, they shall also apply Article 82 of the Treaty."

Concurrent application of national and Community competition law. Article 3(1) of the Modernisation Regulation therefore lays down a rule of concurrent application: whenever a national court or competition authority applies domestic competition law to an agreement or practice, it must at the same time also apply Art.81 or 82 EC, provided that the agreement or practice in question is capable of affecting trade between Member States. The rule in Art.3(1) of the Modernisation Regulation supplements the doctrine of direct effect, by virtue of which national courts with jurisdiction may still apply Community competition law independently of national competition law.[75]   **10–027**

(c) The effect on trade test

A common jurisdictional criterion. Articles 81 and 82 EC apply to agreements, decisions and concerted practices which "may affect trade between Member States". That criterion supplies a basis for determining the jurisdiction of Community law.[76] Agreements and practices which have such an effect are subject both to national and Community competition law. Those which have no such effect are subject only to national competition law. In the case of Art.81 EC, Art.3(1) of the Modernisation Regulation explicitly recognises the jurisdictional role of the effect on trade criterion. In the case of Art.82 EC, Art.3(1) states only that national courts and competition authorities should apply Art.82 EC whenever they apply national rules to "any abuse prohibited by" that Article. In practice, however, with Art.82 EC as with Art.81 EC, the capacity to affect trade is the decisive criterion.[77] A number of judgments of the Court of Justice deal with the concept of an   **10–028**

---

[75] The point is made by the Commission in its Guidelines on the effect on trade concept, n.54, above, at point 9.

[76] On the jurisdictional function of the criterion, see *e.g.* Joined Cases 56/64 and 68/64 *Consten and Grundig v Commission* [1966] E.C.R. 429; [1966] C.M.L.R. 418, and Joined Cases 6/73 and 7/73 *Commercial Solvents* [1974] E.C.R. 223; [1974] 1 C.M.L.R. 309.

[77] The Commission Guidelines on the effect of trade concept, n.52, above, acknowledges at point 8 that the effect on trade criterion determines the scope of application of Community competition law, without distinction between Arts 81 and 82 EC.

effect on trade.[78] To coincide with the introduction of the Modernisation Regulation, the Commission has also issued guidelines.[79] Those guidelines summarise the Court of Justice's case law to date. They also introduce a rule which the Commission intends to use when applying Art.81 EC to assist it in determining when agreements, decisions and concerted practices are in general unlikely to be capable of appreciable affecting trade between Member States (the so-called non-appreciable affectation of trade rule or NAAT rule). Despite the clarification supplied by the Court of Justice and the Commission, the effect on trade criterion remains a vague and uncertain basis for allocating jurisdiction.

10–029   **Pattern of trade test.**   According to the classic test laid down by the Court of Justice in *Société Technique Minière*, for the Community competition rules to apply, "it must be possible to foresee with a sufficient degree of probability on the basis of a set of objective factors of law or fact that the agreement or practice may have an influence, direct or indirect, actual or potential, on the pattern of trade between Member States".[80]

10–030   **Increases in trade.**   The Court of Justice has held that the term pattern of trade is neutral: trade will be affected when an agreement or practice causes an increase in trade. Any difference in the manner in which trade between Member States is likely to develop will be sufficient to establish Community law jurisdiction.[81]

10–031   **Test applies to whole agreement.**   Under Art.81 EC, it is not necessary to show that the specific provision of an agreement which is under challenge is capable of affecting trade between Member States. It is sufficient to show that the agreement as a whole is capable of that effect.[82]

10–032   **Potential and indirect effects.**   It is clear from its face that the pattern of trade test is a broad one. It is not necessary to show that an agreement or practice has had any actual effect on trade, only that it is reasonably fore-seeable that it might have such an effect.[83] The effect may be indirect as well as direct. Indirect effects may be felt in relation to products related to those covered by an agreement or practice, where, for example, the agreement or practice concerns an intermediate product which is not itself the subject of trade between Member States, but is used in the supply of a final product

---

[78] See the cases cited in n.80–n.84, below.
[79] n.54, above.
[80] Case 56/65 *Société Technique Minière v Maschinenbau Ulm* [1966] E.C.R. 235 at 249; [1966] C.M.L.R. 357 at 375.
[81] Joined Cases 56/64 and 68/64 *Consten and Grundig v Commission* [1966] C.M.L.R. 418 at 472.
[82] Case 194/83 *Windsurfing International Inc v Commission* [1986] E.C.R. 611; [1986] 3 C.M.L.R. 489 at paras 95–97.
[83] Case 19/77 *Miller v Commission*, n.50, above.

which is traded.[84] Such effects may also occur in relation to products covered by the agreement or practice, where, for example, the terms on which those products are supplied within a Member State make them less attractive for subsequent export.[85]

Appreciability. The Court of Justice has held that the ability to affect trade between Member States must be "appreciable".[86] The effect on trade criterion therefore "incorporates a quantitative element, limiting Community law jurisdiction to agreements and practices which are capable of having effects of a certain magnitude".[87] The need for the effect on trade to be appreciable is separate and distinct from the requirement under Art.81(1) EC that an agreement, decision or concerted practice appreciably affect competition (the so-called *de minimis* rule).[88]

10–033

The NAAT rule. In its guidelines on the effect on trade concept, the Commission offers a standard defining the absence of an appreciable effect on trade between Member States, which it calls the NAAT rule.[89] The Commission intends, when applying Art.81 EC, to consider that standard as a negative rebuttable presumption applicable to all agreements within the meaning of Art.81(1) EC irrespective of the nature of the restrictions which they contain, and therefore including hardcore restrictions. The NAAT rule represents a statement of Commission policy and is not binding upon national courts or competition authorities when assessing the appreciability of an agreement. In practice, however, such bodies may choose to rely on it to add a quantitative element when assessing their jurisdiction to apply Community as well as national competition law. The NAAT rule holds that agreements are in principle not capable of appreciably affecting trade between Member States when they meet the following two cumulative conditions:

10–034

(1) The aggregate market share of the parties on any relevant market[90] within the Community affected by the agreement must not exceed 5 per cent[91];

---

[84] Case 123/83 *BNIC v Clair* [1985] E.C.R. 391; [1985] 2 C.M.L.R. 430 at para.29.

[85] Commission decision in *Zanussi* [1978] O.J. L322/36 at para.11.

[86] Case 22/71 *Béguelin* [1971] E.C.R. 949 at para.16.

[87] Guidelines on the effect on trade concept, n.54, above, point 44.

[88] See, as regards the *de minimis* rule, the Commission notice on agreements of minor importance which do not appreciably restrict competition under Article 81(1) of the Treaty, n.56, above.

[89] Guidelines on the effect on trade concept, n.54, above, points 50 to 57.

[90] The determination of market share obviously requires the relevant market to be defined, and is to be calculated on the basis of sales value date or, where appropriate, purchase value data. If such data are not available, other reliable market information, such as volume data, may instead be used. See guidelines on the effect on trade concept, n.54, above, point 55.

[91] See Guidelines on the effect on trade concept, n.54, above, point 52(a).

(2) In the case of horizontal agreements, the aggregate annual Community turnover[92] of the undertakings concerned in the products covered by the agreement must not exceed 40 million euro.[93] In the case of vertical agreements, the aggregate annual Community turnover of the supplier in the products covered by the agreement should not exceed 40 million euro.[94]

Agreements which cannot gain the benefit of the NAAT rule may nonetheless lack appreciability: a case by case analysis remains necessary.[95] However, the Commission intends to apply a rebuttable "positive" presumption, in the case of agreements which are by their very nature capable of affecting trade between Member States, for example, because they concern imports and exports or cover several Member States, that the effects on trade are appreciable whenever the turnover thresholds specified by the NAAT rule are exceeded. Such agreements can also often (although apparently not in all cases) be presumed to have appreciable effects on trade where the threshold specified in the market share condition is exceeded.[96]

10–035 **Agreements likely to affect inter-State trade.** The Commission argues in its guidelines on the effect on trade concept that agreements or practices covering or implemented in several Member States will almost always be capable of affecting trade between Member States without the need to conduct any detailed qualitative assessment.[97] It refers in that regard to agreements concerning imports and exports, cartels covering several Member States, horizontal co-operation agreements covering several Member States, vertical agreements implemented in several Member States, and abuses of dominance covering several Member States.

10–036 **Agreements requiring more careful analysis.** More detailed analysis may be necessary in relation to agreements and abuses covering a single Member State or only a part of a Member State.[98] Cartels and abuses of dominance covering a single Member State will ordinarily be capable of affecting trade

---

[92] Turnover is calculated on the basis of total Community sales excluding tax during the previous financial year by the undertakings concerned of the products covered by the agreement, excluding intra-group transfers. See Guidelines on the effect on trade concept, n.54, above, point 56.

[93] In the case of agreements concerning the joint buying of products the relevant turnover shall be the parties' combined purchases of the products covered by the agreement. See Guidelines on the effect on trade concept, n.54, above, point 52(b).

[94] In the case of licence agreements, the relevant turnover is the aggregate turnover of the licensees in the products incorporating the licensed technology and the licensor's own turnover in such products. In cases involving agreements concluded between a buyer and several suppliers the relevant turnover is the buyer's combined purchases of the products covered by the agreements. See Guidelines on the effect on trade concept, n.54, above, point 52(b).

[95] See Guidelines on the effect on trade concept, n.54, above, point 51.

[96] *ibid.*, point 53.

[97] *ibid.*, points 61 to 76.

[98] *ibid.*, points 77 to 99.

between Member States. By contrast, horizontal co-operation agreements or vertical agreements which cover a single Member State are unlikely to be capable of affecting trade between Member States unless they give rise to foreclosure effects, rendering it more difficult for undertakings from other Member States to penetrate the national market in question. The same is true of agreements covering only part of a Member State.

4. SUBSTANTIVE CONSEQUENCES OF APPLICABILITY

Summary. If Community competition law does apply to proceedings before a national court, the following consequences ensue for the substantive analysis of the case. First, Community competition law enjoys supremacy over inconsistent national law: it applies regardless of whether national law would also prohibit the agreement or conduct in question, or of any exemptions available as a matter of national law. Secondly, under the Modernisation Regulation, national competition law may not penalise an agreement which is subject to Art.81 EC but which is not prohibited by it. There is no similar rule in relation to conduct falling within Art.82 EC. Thirdly, under the Modernisation Regulation, a national court may not reach a decision contrary to an actual or contemplated Commission decision relating to the same agreement or conduct. Finally, whilst the remedies available are governed by national law, the applicable national rules must not impair the effectiveness of Community law. They may not make it impossible or excessively difficult to exercise rights conferred by directly effective Community law.   10–037

(a) The doctrine of supremacy

National law may not exclude the application of Community competition law.   10–038
According to the doctrine of supremacy, directly effective Community law prevails over all inconsistent national law.[99] As a consequence, if Community competition law is applicable in national proceedings and requires the prohibition of a given agreement or practice, its effect cannot be blocked by any more generous approach adopted under the applicable national rules.[1] Member States remain free to adopt national competition rules which are less stringent than those enshrined in Community law, but their application will be limited, by operation of the doctrine of supremacy,

---

[99] Case 6/64 *Costa v ENEL* [1964] E.C.R. 1141; [1964] C.M.L.R. 425; Case 35/76 *Simmenthal v Italian Minister of Finance* [1976] E.C.R. 1871; [1977] 2 C.M.L.R. 1.

[1] See *e.g.* Case 14/68 *Walt Wilhelm* [1969] E.C.R. 1; Joined Cases 253/78 and 1 to 3/79 *Giry and Guerlain* [1980] E.C.R. 2327 at paras 15–17.

to cases in which Community law is not applicable because of the lack of any potential effect on trade between Member States.

(b) The scope for substantive divergence under the Modernisation Regulation

10–039   **Article 3(2) of the Modernisation Regulation.** The doctrine of supremacy thus prevents national competition law from imposing a less stringent solution than that required by Community competition law in cases where the latter is applicable. The second paragraph of Art.3 deals with situations in which national law purports to be stricter than applicable Community competition law. It provides as follows:

> "The application of national competition law may not lead to the prohibition of agreements, decisions by associations of undertakings or concerted practices which may affect trade between Member States but which do not restrict competition within the meaning of Article 81(1) of the Treaty, or which fulfil the conditions of Article 81(3) of the Treaty or which are covered by a Regulation for the application of Article 81(3) of the Treaty. Member States shall not under this Regulation be precluded from adopting or applying on their territory stricter national laws which prohibit or sanction unilateral conduct engaged in by undertakings."

10–040   **No stricter national rules where Article 81 EC applies.** Article 3(2) of the Modernisation Regulation provides that, when applying their national competition rules, national courts may not arrive at an outcome different from that applicable under Art.81 EC. Any agreement which would not be prohibited under Art.81(1) EC may not be prohibited under the applicable national rules. Similarly, any agreement to which Art.81(3) EC is directly applicable, or which enjoys the benefit of a block exemption, may not be prohibited by national law. The combined effect of Art.3(2) and the doctrine of supremacy is that national competition law cannot treat differently from Community competition law any agreement which may affect trade between Member States, and to which Community competition law is therefore applicable.[2]

10–041   **Stricter national rules permissible where Article 82 EC applies.** Article 3(2) of the Modernisation Regulation does not impose any comparable prohibition upon national courts applying domestic competition law to prohibit or sanction the kind of unilateral conduct of undertakings at which Art.82 EC is aimed. The doctrine of supremacy would, however, prevent more

---

[2] See Notice on co-operation with national courts, n.53, above, point 6.

permissive national competition rules regulating unilateral conduct from interfering with the application of the Community rules.[3]

Other types of national law not affected. Article 3(3) provides that: **10–042**

"Without prejudice to general principles and other provisions of Community law, paragraphs 1 and 2 do not apply when the competition authorities and the courts of the Member States apply national merger control laws nor do they preclude the application of provisions of national law that predominantly pursue an objective different from that pursued by Articles 81 and 82 of the Treaty."

Article 3(3) of the Modernisation Regulation confirms that national courts may apply rules regulating contracts which pursue objectives not directly related to those of Community competition law, such as legislation regulating unfair terms in consumer contracts.

(c) Remaining differences of substance between Community and UK competition law

Recent amendments. Since the enactment of the Competition Act 1998, the **10–043** domestic system of competition law applicable in the UK is very closely modelled on the Community system. The UK law has been further amended to coincide with the introduction of the Modernisation Regulation. The possibility for the notification and exemption of agreements by the OFT has been abolished in parallel with the removal of the equivalent arrangements at Community level.[4] Similarly, the general exclusion from the Chapter I prohibition of vertical agreements other than those for the maintenance of resale prices has been removed.[5] This was not strictly required by modernisation: EC competition law would simply have applied in parallel to such agreements as were capable of affecting trade between the Member States. However, the UK government considered it preferable to avoid having two different sets of legal provisions applying simultaneously to the same agreements.[6] Finally, the OFT has issued guidance in December 2004 on a

---

[3] See Notice on co-operation with national courts, n.53, above, point 6.
[4] Those amendments were effected by the Competition Act 1998 and Other Enactments Amendment Regulations (SI 2004/1261).
[5] That amendment was effected by the Competition Act 1998 (Land Agreements Exclusion and Revocation) Order 2004 (SI 2004/1260), which comes into operation on May 1, 2005.
[6] See the Government response to the consultations on giving effect to Regulation 1/2003 and aligning the Competition Act 1998 including exclusions and exemptions, April 2004, at pp.9–10.

range of aspects of EC and UK competition law, emphasising a concurrent approach with the Commission.[6a] Despite such amendments, some differences nonetheless remain between the two systems. Several of those differences are briefly considered below.

10–044 **Market investigations.** Under the Enterprise Act 2002, the OFT may refer a market for investigation to the Competition Commission, and the Commission is empowered to adopt remedies to deal with any adverse effects on competition which its investigation brings to light.[7] The Commission lacks any equivalent power. That difference clearly relates to public rather than private enforcement. Under Art.3(2) of the Modernisation Regulation, it would be permissible to take stricter action under the market investigation provisions against unilateral behaviour than would be possible under Art.82 EC.[8]

10–045 *De minimis* **rules.** Until recently, different combined market share thresholds have been applied by the Commission and the OFT in order to determine whether horizontal agreements other than hard core cartels have an appreciable effect on competition. The former ordinarily applied a 10 per cent threshold,[9] whereas the latter fixed upon the higher figure of 25 per cent.[10] However, in its Guidance on agreements and concerted practices, published in December 2004, the OFT signaled a change of policy. Henceforward, it will apply the same thresholds as the Commission. The same is true in the case of vertical agreements; to which UK competition law now applies. This difference between EC and UK competition law has therefore been eliminated. In any event, the thresholds are discretionary and are not binding upon national courts when determining whether an agreement appreciably restricts competition.

10–046 **Parallel exemptions.** Under s.10 of the Competition Act 1998, provision is made for so-called parallel exemptions, exempting from the Chapter I prohibition agreements which fall within a Community block exemption or would do so if it affected trade between Member States. Section 10(5) empowers the OFT to impose, vary or remove conditions or obligations subject to which a parallel exemption is to have effect, or to cancel the exemption in its entirety. There is clearly a risk of incompatibility with Art.3(2) of the Modernisation Regulation if the OFT were to attempt to exercise its powers under s.10(5) in respect of any agreement capable of

---

[6a] The relevant guidance documents relate to modernisation; agreements and concerted practices; abuse of a dominant position; market definition; powers of investigation; assessment of conduct; assessment of market power and as to the appropriate amount of remedy.

[7] Pt 4 of the Enterprise Act 2002.

[8] See Whish, *Competition Law* (5th ed., Butterworths, 2003), p.77.

[9] OFT Guideline on *The Chapter I prohibition*, OFT 401, paras 2.18–2.22.

[10] The Commission Notice on agreements of minor importance which do not appreciably restrict competition under Art.81(1) of the Treaty (*de minimis*), n.56, above.

affecting trade between Member States.[11] Under Art.29(2) of the Modernisation Regulation, a Member State may withdraw the benefit of a block exemption in respect of a given part of its territory but only where the agreements which would otherwise have the benefit of that exemption have effects which are incompatible with Art.81(3) of the Treaty within that territory, which must have "all the characteristics of a distinct geographical market".

(d) The effect of an existing or contemplated Commission decision

Article 16(1) of the Modernisation Regulation. The rules governing the   **10–047**
parallel or consecutive application of EC Competition rules to a given agreement or conduct by both the Commission and the national courts are set out in Art.16(1) of the Modernisation Regulation, under the heading, "Uniform application of Community competition law". It provides:

> "When national courts rule on agreements, decisions or practices under Article 81 or Article 82 of the Treaty which are already the subject of a Commission decision, they cannot take decisions running counter to the decision adopted by the Commission. They must also avoid giving decisions which would conflict with a decision contemplated by the Commission in proceedings it has initiated. To that effect, the national court may assess whether it is necessary to stay its proceedings. This obligation is without prejudice to the rights and obligations under Article 234 of the Treaty."

Article 16(1) effectively codifies the guidance on the issue given by the Court of Justice.[12]

Binding effect of a prior Commission decision. As Art.16(1) of the Mod-   **10–048**
ernisation Regulation makes clear, a national court may not take any decision contrary to a prior decision of the Commission. The Commission decision is binding upon the national court by virtue of the doctrines of direct effect and supremacy. As the Commission states in its notice on co-operation with national courts, a national court which doubts the legality of the Commission's decision can only avoid the binding effects of that decision in the event of a ruling to the contrary from the Community Courts.[13] Two possible situations can be distinguished in that regard.

Appeal brought under Article 230 EC. First, the Commission's decision   **10–049**
may already be the subject of a challenge before the Community Courts

---

[11] See Whish, *op cit.*, n.8, p.340.
[12] See, in particular, Case C–344/98 *Masterfoods* [2000] E.C.R. I–11369; [2001] 4 C.M.L.R. 449.
[13] Notice on co-operation with national courts, n.53, above, point 13.

pursuant to Art.230 EC. If that is the case, the normal course for the national court will be to stay its proceedings pending final judgment in the action for annulment by the Community courts, unless it considers that, in the circumstances of the case, a reference to the Court of Justice for a preliminary ruling on the validity of the Commission decision is warranted. A reference would most obviously be appropriate if for any reason there are relevant questions of Community law which arise in the national proceedings which are unlikely to be fully ventilated in the action for annulment.

10–050 **Preliminary reference.** If there is no action under Art.230 EC, the national court has no choice but to stay proceedings and refer a question or questions to that court for a preliminary ruling pursuant to Art.234 EC. The latter will then decide on the compatibility of the Commission's decision with Community law. Where proceedings are stayed pending judgment by the Community courts, the national court must consider whether to order interim measures in order to safeguard the parties' interests.[14]

10–051 **Section 47A of the Competition Act 1998.** In UK law, s.47A of the Competition Act 1998, as inserted by s.18 of the Enterprise Act 2002, provides for damages actions to be brought before the CAT where there has been a finding of an infringement of European Competition law by the Commission, or of domestic competition law by the OFT or the CAT. The rules governing such an action are given detailed consideration in Chapter 4, above.

10–052 **The effect on national proceedings of a parallel Commission investigation.** Article 16(1) of the Modernisation Regulation imposes a further obligation upon national courts to avoid giving decisions which would conflict with a decision contemplated by the Commission in proceedings which it has initiated. It suggests, to that effect, that national courts may assess whether it is necessary to stay their proceedings. The Notice on co-operation with national courts notes that, in order to assist them in determining whether a stay in proceedings would be appropriate, national courts may ask the Commission whether it has initiated proceedings regarding the same agreements or conduct, and, if so, about the progress of proceedings and the likelihood of a decision in that case.[15] The Commission indicates that it will endeavour to give priority to cases for which it has decided to initiate proceedings and that are subject of national proceedings stayed in this way. A national court which grants such a stay must again assess the need for

---

[14] Notice on co-operation with national courts, n.53, above, point 14, citing Case C–344/98 *Masterfoods* [2000] E.C.R. I–11369, [2001] 4 C.M.L.R. 449 at para.58.
[15] Point 12, citing Case C–234/98 *Delimitis* [1991] E.C.R. I–935; [1992] 5 C.M.L.R. 210 at para.53 and joined Cases C–319/93, C–40/94 and C–224/94 *Dijkstra* [1995] E.C.R. I–4471; [1995] C.M.L.R. 178 at para.34. Such an enquiry by a national court could now be made pursuant to Art.15(1) of the Modernisation Regulation, a possibility which is acknowledged at point 21 of the Notice on co-operation with national courts, n.53, above.

interim measures.[16] There are, however, some circumstances in which the national court may decide on the case pending before it prior to a Commission decision. This will be the case, in particular, where the national court cannot reasonably doubt the outcome of the Commission's investigation or where the Commission has already decided on a similar case.[17]

National obligation to notify court.   In the UK, the EU Competition law practice direction[18] requires every party to a claim, and any national competition authority which has been served with a copy of a party's statement of case, to notify the court at any stage of the proceedings if they are aware that the Commission has adopted, or is contemplating adopting, a decision which has or would have legal effects in relation to the particular agreement, decision or practice in issue before the court.[19] The provision reduces the risk of a national court giving judgment in ignorance of the existence of parallel or prior Commission proceedings relating to the same subject matter.

10–053

(e) Impact on remedies

Limits of national remedial autonomy.   Where Community law confers rights which are directly effective, it is in general for national law to specify the rules governing remedies for any breach of those rights. However, the remedial autonomy of national legal orders is subject to two limitations. First, the applicable national rules must not make it impossible or excessively difficult to exercise rights deriving from directly effective Community law (the "principle of effectiveness"). Secondly, the national rules applicable in respect of Community legal rights must not be less favourable than those applicable in respect of equivalent provisions of national law (the "principle of equivalence").

10–054

Damages remedy must be available.   For many years, it has been assumed that those two principles required national legal orders to make available damages and injunctive relief to a private party suffering harm as a consequence of a breach of Art.81 or 82 EC. In 2001, the European Court of Justice held, in *Courage v Crehan*,[20] that the full effectiveness of Art.81 of the Treaty would be put at risk if it were not open to any individual to claim damages for loss caused to him by a contract or by conduct liable to restrict or distort competition.[21] The court noted that "the action for damages before the national courts can make a significant contribution to the

10–055

---

[16] *ibid.*, point 12.
[17] *ibid.*
[18] Practice Direction—Competition law—Claims relating to the application of Article 81 and 82, n.62, above.
[19] Practice Direction—Competition Law—Claims relating to the application of Article 81 and 82, n.62, above, para.5.
[20] Case C–453/99 *Courage v Crehan* [2001] E.C.R. I–6297; [2001] 5 C.M.L.R. 1058.
[21] *ibid.*, para.26.

maintenance of effective competition in the Community" because it acts as a disincentive to anti-competitive agreements or practices.[22] It is therefore clear that Community law requires that national legal orders make available a damages remedy for breach of the Community competition rules.[23] The same is almost certainly also true in respect of injunctive relief.[24]

10–056 **Potential of EC law to modify domestic remedial rules.** *Courage v Crehan* also reveals the potential of the principle of effectiveness to require changes to be made to the UK's domestic remedial rules as they apply to claims brought under Community competition law. The Court of Justice held that any absolute bar under domestic rules on the recovery of damages by a party to an anti-competitive agreement, based on the principle *in pari delicto*, would be incompatible with Community law. The case is discussed in detail in Chapter 7, above.

5. PROCEDURAL CONSEQUENCES OF APPLICABILITY

(a) The relationship of co-operation between the Commission and national courts

10–057 **Article 15 of the Modernisation Regulation.** Article 15 of the Modernisation Regulation contains rules regulating co-operation between the Commission,[25] the national competition authorities of a Member State and the national courts of that State. Those rules are explained in recital 21 of the Regulation as being necessary in order to ensure consistency in the application of the competition rules across the Community. As the notice on co-operation with national courts states, they derive of the more general obligation of loyal co-operation which Art.10 EC imposes on both Member States and European institutions with a view to attaining the objectives of the EC Treaty.[26] Against that background, it cannot be assumed that Art.15 is necessarily exhaustive of the mutual rights and obligations associated with the relationship of co-operation between the Commission and national courts.[27] Article 15 provides:

"1. In proceedings for the application of Article 81 or 82 of the Treaty,

---

[22] *ibid.*, para.27.

[23] See more generally Chapter 7, above.

[24] See the Opinion of A.G. Jacobs in joined Cases C–246/01, C–306/01, C–354/01 and C–355/01 *AOK Bundesverband*, n.65, above, at para.104.

[25] For the role of the Commission under the Modernisation Regulation more generally, see Chapter 9, above.

[26] Notice on co-operation with national courts, n.53, above, point 15.

[27] The Notice on co-operation with national courts, n.53, above, suggests as much, at point 17, when it states that Art.15 "refers to the most frequent types of assistance" which the Commission offers to national courts.

courts of the Member States may ask the Commission to transmit to them information in its possession or its opinion on questions concerning the application of the Community competition rules.

2.   Member States shall forward to the Commission a copy of any written judgment of national courts deciding on the application of Article 81 or Article 82 of the Treaty. Such copy shall be forwarded without delay after the full written judgment is notified to the parties.

3.   Competition authorities of the Member States, acting on their own initiative, may submit written observations to the national courts of their Member State on issues relating to the application of Article 81 or Article 82 of the Treaty. With the permission of the court in question, they may also submit oral observations to the national courts of their Member State. Where the coherent application of Article 81 or Article 82 of the Treaty so requires, the Commission, acting on its own initiative, may submit written observations to courts of the Member States. With the permission of the court in question, it may also make oral observations.

For the purpose of the preparation of their observations only, the competition authorities of the Member States and the Commission may request the relevant court of the Member State to transmit or ensure the transmission to them of any documents necessary for the assessment of the case.

4.   This Article is without prejudice to wider powers to make observations before courts conferred on competition authorities of the Member States under the law of their Member State."

Direct effect of Article 15.   As indicated above,[28] the Modernisation Regulation is directly effective as such, and the provisions of Art.15 are arguably not dependent upon implementing measures on the part of Member States. As the notice on co-operation with national courts states, however, "to the extent that they are necessary to facilitate the ... forms of assistance [specified in Art.15], Member States must adopt the appropriate procedural rules to allow both the national courts and the Commission to make full use of the possibilities the Regulation offers".[29] In the UK context, reference is made below to the relevant provisions of the EU competition law practice direction.[30]   **10–058**

The Commission or NCA as *amicus curiae*.   National courts may request   **10–059**

---

[28] See para.10–025, above.
[29] Notice on co-operation with the national courts, n.53, above, point 17.
[30] Practice Direction—Competition law—Claims relating to the application of Articles 81 and 82, n.62, above.

information or an opinion of the Commission. The Commission may also, and of its own motion, make written observations to a national court, as may the national competition authority of the same Member State. Oral observations may also be made, but only with the permission of the court in question. In exercising its role as *amicus curiae* in proceedings before a national court, the Commission has emphasised that it must safeguard its own functioning and independence. Accordingly, any assistance offered will be neutral and objective. It refuses to serve the private interests of the parties involved in the case pending before the national court. As a consequence, it will not hear any of the parties about its assistance to the national court. In case the Commission has been contacted by any of the parties in the case pending before the court on issues which are raised before the national court, it will inform the national court, independent of whether these contacts took place before or after the national court's request for co-operation.[31] Requests by the national court may be sent to the Commission either by post (European Commission, Directorate General for Competition, B–1049 Brussels, Belgium) or in electronic form (to the email address: *comp-amicus@cec.eu.int*).[32]

10–060 Commission's duty to transmit information to national courts. Pursuant to Art.15(1), national courts may ask the Commission to transmit information in its possession. The Commission states in the notice on co-operation with national courts that it will endeavour to accede to such a request within one month. That period will only start to run after any necessary clarification has been sought and received from the national court and any parties directly affected by the transmission of the information in question have been consulted by the Commission.[33] The information requested by a national court is likely to fall into one of two categories.

10–061 Procedural information. A national court may seek information of a procedural nature to enable it to decide upon whether it is necessary to stay the proceedings before it in accordance with Art.16(1) of the Modernisation Regulation, to grant interim measures, or to refer a question or questions to the European Court of Justice pursuant to Art.234. It might for example ask whether the Commission has initiated a procedure in relation to a given agreement or practice. If so, it may ask when the Commission is likely to reach a decision.

10–062 Substantive information and the obligation of professional secrecy. A national court may also request information of a more substantive nature. It might for example request documents which are in the Commission's possession. The Commission's capacity to respond to such a request is limited

---

[31] Notice on co-operation with the national courts, n.53, above, point 19.
[32] *ibid.*, point 18.
[33] *ibid.*, point 21.

by its obligation under Art.287 EC not to disclose information covered by the obligation of professional secrecy. In accordance with the case law of the European Court of Justice, the Commission may only communicate information covered by professional secrecy to a national court if the court has first guaranteed that it can and will protect any confidential information or business secrets contained therein.[34] The Commission will then indicate which parts of the information transmitted are covered by professional secrecy and which parts are not and may therefore be disclosed.[35]

Other grounds for refusing to supply information.   The Commission also has   **10–063**
the right to refuse to transmit information to national courts for overriding reasons relating to the need to safeguard the interests of the Community or to avoid any interference with its functioning and independence, in particular by jeopardising the accomplishment of the tasks assigned to it.[36] On that basis, the Commission claims the right not to transmit to national courts information voluntarily submitted by a leniency applicant without the consent of that applicant.[37]

Request for an opinion on questions concerning the application of EC com-   **10–064**
petition rules.   Article 15(1) of the Modernisation Regulation also provides that courts of the Member States may ask for the Commission to transmit its opinion on questions concerning the application of the Community competition rules. Whilst the Commission acknowledges in its notice on co-operation with national courts that it is under an obligation to respond to requests for information, it avoids using the same language with regard to requests for an opinion. It is noteworthy that in each case, Art.15 of the Modernisation Regulation states only that national courts "may ask" for information or an opinion. It remains to be seen whether the Commission could refuse to accede to a request for an opinion, and, if so, upon what grounds.[38] The Commission has indicated that it will endeavour to respond to such a request within four months from the date of receipt. The Commission may need to seek further information from the national court in order to be able to give a useful opinion. In that case, time will run from the moment when the additional information is received.[39]

Impartiality of the Commission.   The Commission emphasises that it cannot   **10–065**
offer a view on the merits of the case pending before the national court. It

---

[34] Case C–2/88 *Zwartveld* [1990] E.C.R. I–4405; [1990] 3 C.M.L.R. 457 at paras 10–11, Case T–353/94 *Postbank* [1996] E.C.R. II–921; [1997] 4 C.M.L.R. 33 at para.93.
[35] Notice on co-operation with national courts, n.53, above, point 25.
[36] Case C–2/88 *Zwartveld*, n.34, above, [1990] 3 C.M.L.R. 457 at paras 10–11, Case C–275/00 *First and Franex* [2002] E.C.R. I–10943 at para.49; Case T–353/94 *Postbank*, n.34, above.
[37] Notice on co-operation with national courts, n.53, above, point 26.
[38] Also unclear is how such a refusal could be brought before the Community courts. It is questionable whether the parties to national proceedings would have standing to proceed under Art.230 EC, as the opinion is for the benefit of the national court.
[39] Notice on co-operation with national courts, n.53, above, point 28.

suggests however that the opinion sought by the national court may relate to other than strictly legal points, encompassing also economic issues.[40] Similarly, the Commission states that it will not hear the parties before formulating its opinion. However, it also states that the procedures before the national court when applying Community law must respect the general principles of Community law.[41] On that basis, it is arguable that the parties should be given an opportunity to make observations on the Commission's opinion before the national court reaches its judgment.

10–066   **Commission opinion not binding.**   Unlike a ruling given by the European Court of Justice in response to a preliminary reference under Art.234 EC, a Commission opinion pursuant to Art.15(1) of the Modernisation Regulation is not binding on the court which requested it. It is also without prejudice to the right of the national court to make a preliminary reference at any stage of its proceedings.

10–067   **The submission of observations by the Commission.**   Article 15(3) of the Modernisation Regulation empowers the Commission to submit observations on issues relating to the application of Arts 81 or 82 EC to a national court which is called upon to apply those provisions. Written submissions may be made by the Commission as of right, but oral observations require the national court's consent. Observations may only be made by the Commission where the coherent application of the Community competition rules so requires. The Commission has indicated that it will limit its observations to an economic and legal analysis of the facts underlying the case pending before the national court.[42]

10–068   **Submission of observations by an NCA.**   Article 15(3) also empowers a national competition authority to make observations before a national court of the same Member State. As with the Commission, oral observations require the permission of the court. Article 15(4) expressly preserves the right for national systems of competition law to confer a broader power to intervene upon their national competition authority.

10–069   **Request for documents.**   Under the second subparagraph of Art.15(3), the Commission or a national competition authority may also request the national court to transmit documents needed in order to assess the case and prepare observations. It is explicitly stated that such documents may be requested only for the purpose of preparing observations. They could not be used, for example, to assist in the separate investigation of a case by the Commission or a national competition authority.

---

[40] *ibid.*, point 29.
[41] *ibid.*, point 30.
[42] Notice on co-operation with national courts, n.53, above, point 32.

Applicable procedural rules. It is left to national procedural rules to determine the framework within which observations are to be submitted. Those rules must respect the general principles of Community law and must not impede the effective submission of observations or make such submission more difficult than the submission of observations in court proceedings where equivalent national law is applied.[43] As regards the UK, para.4 of the EU competition law practice direction specifies how case management is to proceed when either the Commission or one of the designated national competition authorities in the UK wishes to intervene in judicial proceedings.[44] If the Commission or an NCA intends to make written observations to the court, it must give notice of its intention to do so by letter to Chancery Chambers at the Royal Courts of Justice at the earliest reasonable opportunity.[45] The court may then give case management directions, including directions about the date by which any written observations are to be filed.[46] Similarly, if either body wishes to make oral representations, it must apply for permission in writing at the earliest reasonable opportunity, stating why it wishes to make such representations.[47] The other parties must be served with the notice or application.[48] Any request by the Commission or NCA for the court to send it documents relating to the claim should be made when the notice or application is filed.[49]

10–070

The transmission of national courts' judgments applying Articles 81 and 82 EC. The Commission's power to make observations in national proceedings obviously depends upon its acquiring knowledge of those proceedings. The obligation upon the Member States to transmit judgments of the national courts which apply the Community competition rules provide it with a means of becoming aware of proceedings, and may allow it to intervene should an appeal be brought.[50]

10–071

Obligation to notify the OFT. Paragraph 3 of the EU competition law practice direction concerning claims under Community and national competition law[51] requires any party to civil proceedings whose statement of case raises or deals with an issue relating to the application of Art.81 or 82 EC, or Chapter I or II, to serve a copy of the statement of case on the OFT at the

10–072

---

[43] Notice on co-operation with national courts, n.53, above, point 35.
[44] Similar provisions have also been inserted in a new rule 21.10A in Practice Direction 52— Appeals.
[45] Practice Direction—Competition law—Claims relating to the Application of Articles 81 and 82, n.62, above, para.4.2. The letter should include the claim number, and be addressed to the Court Manager, Room TM 6.06, Royal Courts of Justice, Strand, London WC2A 2LL.
[46] *ibid.*, para.4.6.
[47] *ibid.*, para.4.3.
[48] *ibid.*, para.4.4.
[49] *ibid.*, para.4.5.
[50] *ibid.*, point 37.
[51] *ibid.*

same time as it is served on the other parties to the claim.[52] By that means, the OFT, which in most cases will be the relevant national competition authority for the purposes of Art.15 of the Modernisation Regulation, is kept informed of judicial proceedings in relation to which it may wish to submit observations.

(b) Preliminary references to the European Court of Justice

10–073 **Article 234 EC.** National courts or tribunals may seek the guidance of the European Court of Justice on questions of Community law which are relevant to the proceedings before them.[53] The preliminary reference procedure is laid down in Art.234 EC. The jurisdiction of the European Court of Justice under that Article is limited to the interpretation of Community law. It may not make the factual determinations involved which are involved, for example, in determining the relevant geographical and product markets or ascertaining whether a given practice is capable of affecting trade between Member States.[54] However, it is not always easy to demarcate issues of law from those of fact, and the European Court of Justice has on occasion been prepared to supply guidance as to how Community law might apply to a given fact situation.[55]

10–074 **Bodies which may refer.** The concept of "court or tribunal" under Art.234 EC is autonomous to Community law. A reference may therefore be considered as admissible by the European Court of Justice despite coming from a body which is not recognised as a court within its own domestic legal order. There can be no doubt that the ordinary courts—the High Court, Court of Appeal and House of Lords—constitute "courts or tribunals" within the meaning of Art.234. The CAT almost certainly also amounts to a court or tribunal, and provision is made in its rules for the making of a reference.[56] It is less likely that any of the national competition authorities in the UK would be able to make a reference, should they wish to make the attempt.

10–075 **References in purely domestic proceedings.** A reference may probably be made not only in a case which involves Community law directly, but also where purely national legal provisions have been invoked which (as in the

---

[52] The statement of case should be addressed to the Director of Competition Policy Co-ordination, OFT, Fleetbank House, 2–6 Salisbury Square, London EC4Y 8JX.

[53] See more generally paras 9–077–9–086, above.

[54] See Case 311/84 *CBM v CLT and IPB* [1985] E.C.R. 3261; [1986] 2 C.M.L.R. 558, where the European Court of Justice emphasised that such matters as market definition, dominance, and effect on trade were all for the national court alone to assess.

[55] See Cases C–215 and 216/96 *Bagnasco v BPN and Carige* [1999] E.C.R. I–135; [1999] 4 C.M.L.R. 624, in which the European Court of Justice itself concluded that there was no appreciable effect on trade between Member States.

[56] See more generally Chapter 4, above.

case of the Competition Act 1998) are based upon Community law provisions. In *Oscar Bronner*,[57] for example, the European Court of Justice responded to questions concerning Art.82 EC which were referred to it by an Austrian court which was applying domestic competition law. The court considered that "the fact that a national court is dealing with a restrictive practices dispute by applying national competition law should not prevent it from making a reference ... on the interpretation of Community law ... when it considers that a conflict between Community law and national law is capable of arising".[58] It is therefore likely that a court in the UK could refer a question regarding the interpretation of Art.81 or 82 EC in a case which fell to be decided only on the basis of the equivalent provisions of the Competition Act 1998, the agreement or practice at issue lacking the potential to affect trade between Member States.

---

[57] Case C–7/97 *Oscar Bronner GmbH v Mediaprint* [1998] E.C.R. I–7791; [1999] 4 C.M.L.R. 112.
[58] *ibid.*, at para.20.

CHAPTER 11

ARBITRATION AND COMPETITION

Michael Bowsher[1]

1. TWO CONTRASTING REGIMES

11–001   **Nature of commercial arbitration.**   Commercial Arbitration is a contractual process by which parties to a dispute agree to have that dispute resolved by a third party tribunal.[2] Arbitrators establish the private law rights and obligations of the parties to the dispute referred to them. It is a process in which the arbitrator owes direct obligations to the parties for the resolution of their dispute. The parties' dispute is normally resolved in private and the proceedings and their outcome remains, subject to certain specific reservations, confidential.

11–002   **Nature of competition law.**   Competition law is a system of public law governing the private commercial relations between economic entities. By its nature it asserts some measure of primacy over the parties' own provisions. Further, EC competition law by virtue of its supranational character demands primacy over the largely national laws that govern the parties' respective private law rights. For the purposes of this chapter, reference is made to EC competition law (or EEA competition law)[3] although the issues considered below would be similar whether EC or UK competition law is engaged.

11–003   **Potential for tension between the approaches taken by practitioners in these fields.**   These different perspectives have led to concern by practitioners in

---

[1] Barrister, Monckton Chambers.

[2] Such tribunals usually comprise one or three arbitrators.

[3] Although reference is made throughout to EC competition law, that must also encompass the law applicable throughout the EEA. For a full discussion of the issues regarding the application of competition law in the EEA and EFTA, and its impact in arbitration see Baudenbacher, "Enforcement of EC and EEA Competition Rules by Arbitration Tribunals Inside and Outside the EU" in *European Competition Law Annual 2001: Effective Private Enforcement of EC Antitrust Law* (Ehlermann & Atansiu ed., Hart, 2003).

each of these areas regarding the impact of the other upon the proper operation of the law with which they are concerned. Practitioners and academics continue to express remarkably divergent views regarding the tension between these areas of law. At the risk of oversimplification, lawyers practicing in commercial arbitration have been concerned about the impact of public law altering the parties' private resolution of their own affairs, while competition lawyers have expressed concerns that the general and uniform application of competition law will be adversely affected by the resolution of matters of competition policy resolved in a private and generally confidential process.

The scope of this chapter. This chapter considers this tension between commercial arbitration and competition law. It considers certain key practical issues that arise when competition law issues are raised in the context of commercial arbitration.[4] Competition law issues may arise in an arbitration within the EU (whether that be a domestic arbitration or an international arbitration involving parties from two EU states) and in an arbitration outside the EU where the subject matter has effects on the EU market. EC and national competition law are likely to have a similar impact in arbitration. Accordingly the discussion considers the position of EC law and the assumption is made that the impact of domestic law will usually be similar. Each Member State (and any other arbitral location) will have its own arbitration law. This chapter takes English arbitration law as its point of reference, but addresses both the international and domestic situation. The special situation of Switzerland is considered at various points as its significance as a seat of arbitrations and geographical and commercial relationship with the EU make this a particularly interesting jurisdiction.

    11–004

The chapter addresses first certain introductory matters, and then deals in turn with the following topics:

(1) What sorts of private dispute resolution procedures may be invoked to aid resolution of disputes involving competition law?

(2) Can an arbitral tribunal apply competition law to the dispute referred to it?

(3) Must an arbitral tribunal apply competition law to the dispute referred to it?

(4) To what extent can or should the Community institutions (or analogous national bodies) supervise or support the application of competition law within arbitration?

---

[4] Given the very broad range of topics affected by the intersection of these areas of law, it is not proposed to overburden the chapter with comprehensive footnotes. It is anticipated that by referring to principal legislation and authorities, and providing selective references to other literature the basis for the reader's further investigation is provided. For further material in this area see Shelkoplyas, *The Application of EC Law in Arbitration Proceedings* (Europa Law Publishings, Groningen, 2003); Nazzini, *Concurrent Proceedings in Competition Law: Procedure, Evidence and Remedies* (OUP, 2004), Chs 10 and 11.

(5) How should an arbitral tribunal apply competition law to the dispute referred to it? In particular, should an arbitral tribunal dealing with a private dispute between two parties try to take account of wider policy issues, and if so how should it do so?

This chapter focuses on commercial arbitration rather than the use of arbitration in the application of merger control and in disputes in regulated sectors.

2. ARBITRATION LAW AND PRACTICE

11–005   **Common standards of arbitration law.**   Jurisdictions worldwide increasingly share similar laws and principles in the field of commercial arbitration. In many cases the national law regarding international commercial arbitration involves direct implementation of the UNCITRAL Model Law on International Commercial Arbitration and this legislation has also had considerable influence over the reform of domestic arbitration legislation. Even in those countries that have not adopted the UNCITRAL Model Law, its provisions provide an important international standard on a number of key issues. UNCITRAL has also produced a set of arbitration rules that are often used as the procedural basis for international arbitration.

11–006   **English Arbitration Act 1996.**   The English legislation (unlike that in Scotland) does not follow the Model Law in all respects.[5] English arbitration law is based on statutory underpinning provided by the Arbitration Act 1996. This legislation provides a comprehensive code for both domestic and international arbitration in England and Wales.

11–007   **New York Convention.**   English arbitration law is also affected by the need to comply with obligations pursuant to the various international conventions relating to the enforcement of foreign awards. The most important of these is the 1958 New York Convention on the Recognition and Enforcement of Foreign Arbitral Awards. This convention provides an effective means of enforcement of arbitration awards in other Convention countries. In order for an award to be enforceable it must fulfil the standards of that convention. (There are earlier conventions that may be relevant with regard to some jurisdictions.)

11–008   **Role of arbitral institutions.**   While parties can establish a valid arbitration by means of an appropriate "ad hoc" agreement, many arbitrations are administered by an arbitration institution selected by the parties. Institutions involved in domestic, international arbitration, or in arbitration in

---

[5] A summary of the key differences is set out in Merkin, *Arbitration Act 1996* (2nd ed., Informa), p.10.

specific sectors are to be found in most commercial centres of importance. These institutions provide procedures for the appointment of arbitral tribunals, and some are active in overseeing the arbitration procedure. Some, such as the International Chamber of Commerce review draft awards in arbitrations proceeding under their auspices. It is quite common for changes to be made to the drafts by the arbitral tribunal following this review. Albeit that arbitration is a private process, these institutions (and organisations such as the International Bar Association) provide a substantial degree of coordination of arbitral practice through the rules and guidelines[6] that they produce, and the opportunities for education and exchange of views that they provide to arbitrators.

Role of the courts. National courts have an important, albeit limited role in shaping arbitration law. There are a number of circumstances in which national courts may be called upon to support the arbitral process in the appointment of arbitrators, or grant of supporting injunctive relief. There are only limited circumstances in which the arbitral process and award will be the subject of direct judicial supervision.

11–009

Legal Review. In some jurisdictions there is a process of appeal from arbitral awards on points of law. The international trend has been to limit the scope of such appeals as the conventional view has been that those arbitration locations at which appeal is impossible or very limited are more attractive to parties. English law does provide for appeal from an award on a point of law,[7] albeit that access to this process is tightly controlled. Even in jurisdictions that provide for appeals on points of law, most will also provide for the exclusion of that right by agreement of the parties.[8] Provision is also made in the English Arbitration Act 1996 for the parties and tribunal to agree to refer a question of law for determination by a court.[9]

11–010

Procedural review. National courts will also have a role in protecting the impartiality of the tribunal, and protecting the parties' various procedural rights. In England for example, an arbitrator can be removed for various matters including failure properly to conduct the proceedings or failure to use all reasonable dispatch in conducting the proceedings or making the award.[10] The English courts may also remit an award to the tribunal, or

11–011

---

[6] The Court of Arbitration of the International Chamber of Commerce in Paris, the London Court of International Arbitration and the American Arbitration Association are particularly prominent in this regard. There are arbitration institutions, some addressing specialist areas, in many of the important commercial cities worldwide. The IBA, for instance, has produced the *IBA Rules on the taking of evidence in International Commercial Arbitration* and *IBA Guidelines on conflicts of interest in international arbitration*.

[7] s.69 of Arbitration Act 1996.

[8] See further para.11–014, below, regarding the differences between domestic and international arbitration.

[9] s.45 of Arbitration Act 1996.

[10] s.24 of Arbitration Act 1996.

have it set aside or declare it ineffective if there has been serious irregularity affecting the tribunal, the proceedings or the award.[11] National courts may also entertain challenges made to the jurisdiction of the tribunal.

11-012   **Enforcement.**   National courts will also enforce awards. In the case of domestic awards this can be done either by action on the award, or pursuant to statute.[12] A separate statutory regime applies to enforcement of international awards pursuant to the New York and other conventions.[13]

3. THE VARIOUS SYSTEMS OF LAW RELEVANT TO ARBITRATION IN THE INTERNATIONAL CONTEXT

11-013   **The seat of arbitration.**   Any arbitration has a seat. This is its juridical location. The local arbitration legislation of the seat will apply to the arbitration and the award is deemed to be made at the seat. The provisions for judicial control of arbitration at the seat will be applicable to the arbitration. The seat is designated by the parties by agreement, by the person appointing the arbitral tribunal, or by the tribunal itself. If it is to be determined by the tribunal, it will have regard to the surrounding circumstances in making that determination. The seat provides the legal focus of the arbitration, albeit that it is not necessarily the case that hearings must take place at the seat. On the contrary it is sometimes necessary or appropriate to conduct the arbitration elsewhere. The English Arbitration Act 1996 makes no assumption that there is a necessary connection between the seat and the location of the arbitration. There is some discussion in international arbitration literature of truly delocalised arbitrations with no seat. Except where an arbitration is proceeding but the seat is yet to be chosen, English law does not recognise this as a possibility.[13a]

11-014   **The distinction between domestic and international arbitration.**   If both parties to an English arbitration are UK nationals, incorporated in or resident in the UK, that arbitration is a domestic arbitration. In an English domestic arbitration, the parties can only contract out of their rights to appeal on a point of law, or to have the arbitrator make a reference to the courts on a point of law where the parties agree to oust this jurisdiction after the arbitration is commenced. In international cases, standard institutional rules applicable to arbitrations are likely to provide for such exclusion. The only judicial control will be on the basis that there has been a serious

---

[11] s.69 of Arbitration Act 1996.
[12] s.66 of Arbitration Act 1996.
[13] ss.99–104 of Arbitration Act 1996.
[13a] Investment treaty arbitrations under ICSID or bilateral treaties may be exceptions to this proposition. Such arbitrations are between investor and host state and are therefore of a different nature to commercial arbitration between the parties to a contract.

irregularity affecting the proceedings, the tribunal or the award. This is a remedy focusing on compliance with normal standards of fairness and impartiality and the specific procedural requirements of arbitration.

Application of law in domestic arbitration. In a domestic English arbitration (in which the right of appeal is not excluded), an award can be the subject of an appeal or reference on a point of law. It would usually be the case that arbitrators must determine the disputes referred to them in a domestic English dispute in accordance with English law as a failure to do so could lead to an appeal. Even the generality of this proposition must be qualified by the fact that s.46(1)(b) of the Arbitration Act 1996 provides that if the parties agree, the tribunal may decide the dispute in accordance with such considerations as agreed by them or determined by the tribunal. There is therefore the possibility of an award being made other than on the basis of law if the parties so agree.

11–015

Application of various legal systems to an international arbitration. The situation is rather different in an international context. It is sometimes said that all law is foreign law to an arbitrator.[14] In an international context an arbitral tribunal must have regard to all of the following different legal systems:

11–016

- the law governing the substance of the dispute—the substantive law which will usually be the applicable law of the contract;

- the law governing the arbitration agreement;

- the law governing the conduct of the arbitration—this is usually the law of the seat and is sometimes referred to as the curial law or *lex arbitri*;

- the law governing enforcement of the arbitral award, which clearly depends on where it is likely that the award will have to be enforced;

---

[14] Pinsolle, "Private enforcement of European Community competition rules by arbitrators" (2004) 7(1) Int. A.L.R. 14:

"Arbitrators have no forum, and they are not the guardians of any legal order. To them, any legal system is foreign. Their main duties are to apply the law chosen by the parties and to render an enforceable award".

Radicati di Brozolo, "Antitrust: a paradigm of the relations between mandatory rules and arbitration—a fresh look at the 'second look'" (2004) 7(1) Int. A.L.R. 23:

"... since their brief derives from the will of the parties, arbitrators have no lex fori. They thus lack the main pivot for any decision of a national judge relating to the application of any type of rule, including competition and other mandatory rules. Therefore, as regards the choice of the applicable substantive rules, especially mandatory and competition rules, arbitration so to speak floats above, or outside, national legal systems until the moment when its final product, i.e. the award, is brought before a national court (or possibly more than one of them) in an action to set aside or enforce".

- the conflict of law rules applicable to selection of the above laws—it has become established practice that arbitrators are not bound to follow the conflict of law rules of the country in which the arbitration has its seat, and they may apply such conflicts rules are more appropriate for other reasons.[15]

Of course, depending on the circumstances, some of these laws may be the same.

11–017   **Jurisdiction of performance.**   It may also be relevant to take account of the mandatory rules of a jurisdiction where performance of the agreement has an effect. Taking competition law as an example, it may be that the effect of an award would be affected by action of a local court or competition authority regarding the effects of an agreement in that jurisdiction. The law of that jurisdiction need not be any of the laws otherwise described above.

11–018   **Rome Convention.**   This practical consideration is reflected in the express provision in the Rome Convention[16] that requires a tribunal to have regard to the mandatory rules of other systems with which the case has a close connection. Clearly a tribunal will have to have regard to difficulties that would arise with enforcement if mandatory rules in the place of enforcement are not taken into account. Account must also be taken of the possibility that the overall outcome of the dispute will be affected if mandatory rules were invoked in the courts of yet another jurisdiction by one of the parties. The outcome of the arbitration could be altered or nullified.[17] Even though tribunals will normally apply the system or systems of law that they regard as appropriate, it does not follow that they will apply the law in the same manner as a national judge.

4. RELEVANT ATTRIBUTES OF ARBITRATION

11–019   **Generally.**   The following attributes of arbitration are particularly relevant to the challenges posed by the application of competition law within commercial arbitration. Given the number of similar arbitration laws in the EU, no attempt is made in this chapter to address the differences that arise from the details of particular legislation. Save where noted particularly to the

---

[15] See Art.28(2) of the Model Law and s.46 of Arbitration Act 1996; Art.17(1) of ICC Rules (1998 version) and Redfern and Hunter, *Law and Practice of Commercial Arbitration* (3rd ed., Sweet & Maxwell, London, 1999), paras 2–80 and 2–81. The complexity involved in choosing these various systems of law is explored in Chow, "Issues in International Arbitration: Application of 'Foreign' Legislation" (2004) 20(5) Const. L.J. 262.

[16] Art.7 (1) of the Convention on the Law Applicable to Contractual Obligations ("the Rome Convention") [1980] O.J. L266/1.

[17] See Chow, *op. cit.*, which considers how claims under Australian trade practices legislation may have to be entertained in a Singapore arbitration.

contrary, the issues raised are addressed by reference to the position that pertains in England and Wales.

Party autonomy. Arbitrators take on an obligation to the parties and the **11–020** parties only to resolve their dispute. The process is "owned" by the parties, and party autonomy is regarded as paramount, at least in classical arbitration analysis. The importance of party autonomy is derived from the fact that this method of dispute resolution is a product of the free choice of parties. Insofar as the adoption of arbitration as a means of dispute resolution is not the product of the parties' choice,[18] party autonomy might not be so decisive a factor.

Enforceability of arbitration agreement. An agreement requiring that a **11–021** dispute of a particular type be referred to arbitration is capable of enforcement by the courts. In England the court will stay its own proceedings if the relevant criteria are fulfilled[19] while the UNCITRAL Model Law requires the matter to be referred on to arbitration by the court.

Formulated dispute. An arbitration for the purposes of national legislation **11–022** and international conventions regarding arbitration will involve the making of a decision on a dispute which is already formulated at the time when the tribunal is appointed.

Privacy and confidentiality. The process is conducted subject to strict **11–023** obligations of privacy and confidentiality.[20] Indeed, it is often the confidential characteristic of arbitration that causes parties to choose this method of dispute resolution. One aspect of this of potential interest to parties to competition law related disputes in the UK is that while any statement of case in litigation relating to the application of competition law must be served on the Office of Fair Trading,[21] that requirement would not apply to arbitration.

---

[18] For example, the parties' consent to arbitration in investment arbitration is generally imputed by reference to the terms of the relevant investment treaty. Where parties to an agreement are required to arbitrate certain disputes in order to meet the requirements of a block exemption regulation (see further below), it might be argued that the parties' consent has been procured by a measure of compulsion. Does this raise issues regarding the parties' rights under Art.6 ECHR or does it open the way for an argument that in such situation the "agreement" to arbitrate does not necessarily involve a waiver of the right to particular procedural safeguards such as the right to call or challenge evidence and to have sufficient time to prepare for that process (see for example, *Dombo Beheer BV v Netherlands* (1993) 18 E.H.R.R. 213, ECtHR, *Mantovanelli v France* (1997) 24 E.H.R.R. 370, ECtHR).

[19] s.9 of Arbitration Act 1996.

[20] See Mustill & Boyd, *Commercial Arbitration* (2nd ed., LexisNexis, 2001 companion), p.112; *Associated Electric and Gas Insurance Services Ltd v European Reinsurance Co of Zurich UKPCII* [2003] 1 W.L.R. 1041; and a fuller review of the authorities in Rawding and Seeger, "*Aegis v European Re* and the Confidentiality of Arbitration Awards" (2003) *Arbitration International* 483.

[21] See Practice Direction—Competition Law—Claims relating to the application of Arts 81 and 82 of the EC Treaty and Chapters I and II of Part I of the Competition Act 1998, White Book, 1st supplement, B12–001.

11–024 **Publication of awards and information about the process.** As a consequence of the confidentiality attached to the arbitration process, awards would not normally be published. There are however a number of works in which awards are published on an anonymised basis, but publication is dependent on the parties' consent which is often lacking. Few awards involving competition law issues have been published.

11–025 **Finality of awards.** While there is express power in English law for the making of a provisional award (with the agreement of the parties)[22] the normal position is that an award must be final on all matters to which it relates.

11–026 **Completeness of awards.** A valid arbitration award must deal with all the issues that were put to the tribunal. Failure to do so amounts to serious irregularity[23] in English law which may lead to remission or setting aside of the award, or in extreme cases the removal of the arbitrator pursuant to s.24 of the Arbitration Act 1996. An arbitrator can however decide to make awards on different aspects of the case at different times. Such awards are sometimes called interim or partial awards. These terms are potentially confusing, however, as such an award is final and determinative of the matters to which it relates.

11–027 **Requirement of enforceability.** It is the primary aim of arbitration to provide an enforceable determination of the dispute involved,[24] and in the international context the award should be one that can be enforced pursuant to the relevant international conventions on enforcement. In some circumstances it may be impossible to produce an award that is universally enforceable and the tribunal must take such steps as it can to provide for effective enforcement in an appropriate jurisdiction. Arbitration awards are readily enforced worldwide pursuant to the New York Convention. There are well understood but very limited standards by which the enforcement of awards may be resisted.

A particularly relevant provision for current purposes is Art.V.2 which provides that:

> "Recognition and enforcement of an arbitral award may also be refused if the competent authority in the country where recognition and enforcement is sought finds that:
>
> (a) the subject matter of the difference is not capable of settlement by arbitration under the law of that country; or

---

[22] s.39 of the Arbitration Act 1996.
[23] s.68(2)(d) of the Arbitration Act 1996; for a recent example see *Ronly Holdings Ltd v JSC Zestafoni G Nikoladze Ferroalloy Plant* [2004] EWHC 1354 (Comm).
[24] See ICC Rules of Arbitration, Art.35; LCIA Rules, Art.32.2.

(b) the recognition or enforcement of the award would be contrary to the public policy of that country."

Further useful explanation of this provision is provided by ILA Resolution on Public Policy as a Bar to Enforcement of International Arbitral Awards, and the interim and final reports relating to that resolution.[25]

Limited scope of judicial supervision.   As the finality of awards is treated as a core requirement of effective arbitration, the process of judicial review of arbitration awards and procedures are generally subject only to a narrow basis of judicial review. The availability of challenge on legal grounds is limited or non-existent. The provision in England for challenge on grounds of law is unusually permissive by international standards as it provides for appeal on points of law, challenges for serious irregularity affecting the tribunal, proceedings or award and certain other means of recourse. However in most international arbitrations in England (certainly those under institutional rules such as the ICC and the LCIA) there will be no possibility of any appeal on a point of law from the award. **11–028**

Confidentiality of judicial supervision.   In English courts, appeals and other challenges to the arbitral process are generally heard in private. The judgments are, however, published unless an order is made to the contrary.[26] **11–029**

Separability of arbitration agreement.   An arbitration agreement is not normally to be regarded as invalid because the agreement of which it forms part is invalid.[27] Thus, the fact that an agreement is void pursuant to Art.81(2) EC would not normally have the necessary consequence that the arbitration agreement within that agreement was itself invalid. **11–030**

Arbitration and illegal agreements: arbitrator's capability of determining illegality.   It is a natural consequence of the separate nature of the arbitration agreement that an arbitral tribunal should be capable of determining an issue as to the validity and even the legality of the agreement to which the arbitration agreement relates, unless the illegality strikes at the agreement to arbitrate itself. **11–031**

Tribunal's obligation to raise issues of illegality of its own motion (as a matter of English law).   It may become apparent during proceedings that the contract or performance of the contract is or may be illegal, even though neither of the parties has raised this issue. The tribunal must consider a number of factors. The tribunal owes contractual obligations to the parties, **11–032**

---

[25] All to be found in (2003) *Arbitration International*, pp.213 *et seq.*
[26] CPR Pt 62.10, and note at 2E–16.1 of White Book; see also, *Department of Economic Policy and Development of the City of Moscow v Bankers Trust Co* [2003] 1 W.L.R. 2885; [2004] B.L.R. 229.
[27] s.7 of Arbitration Act 1996; Art.16(1) of UNCITRAL Model Law.

and some might argue that it is in breach of those obligations in taking steps to invalidate their agreement. On the other hand, the tribunal may be failing in its duty to the parties and may even commit a serious irregularity if it fails to deal with an issue critical to the outcome of the dispute. The express statutory provision dealing with this class of serious irregularity only requires that all issues put to the tribunal be dealt with, not that all issues that it occurs to the tribunal may arise should be determined.

It would also be relevant for the tribunal to consider that it may be failing in its duty to the parties if it were to make an unenforceable award.

11–033 **Comparison with the duties of an English court to raise illegality of its own motion.**[27a] The procedural law of the arbitration will be a relevant consideration. In England there seems no particular reason why the approach of a tribunal should be different from that taken by a court in a similar situation.[27b] The appropriate judicial approach was described by Colman J. in *David Birkett v Acorn Business Machines Ltd*:

> "If a transaction is not on its face manifestly illegal but there is before the court persuasive and comprehensive evidence of illegality, the court may refuse to enforce it even if illegality has not been pleaded or alleged. The principle behind the court's intervention of its own motion in such a case is to ensure that its process is not being abused by inviting it to enforce sub silentio a contract whose enforcement is contrary to public policy."[28]

Colman J. relied particularly upon the following passage from the decision in *Re Mahmoud and Ispahani*.[29]

> "In my view the court is bound, once it knows that the contract is illegal, to take the objection and to refuse to enforce the contract, whether its knowledge comes from the statement of the party who was guilty of the illegality, or whether its knowledge comes from outside sources. The court does not sit to enforce illegal contracts. There is no question of estoppel. It is for the protection of the public that the court refuses to enforce such a contract."

The court must, however, exercise care in exercising its jurisdiction as it may not have access to all the relevant information and may on the basis of partial information take an incorrect and unfair decision. In *Edler v*

[27a] For general discussion see Enonchong, *Illegal Transactions* (Informa, 1998) at p.22 *et seq.*
[27b] It is for domestic law to establish whether national courts should raise EC competition law matters of their own motion; Cases C–430/93 and C–431/93 *Van Schijndel* [1995] E.C.R. I–4705.
[28] [1999] 2 All E.R. (Comm) 429; this approach was approved by the Court of Appeal in *Pickering v McConville* [2003] EWCA Civ 554.
[29] [1921] 2 K.B. 716 at 729.

Auerbach[30] Devlin J. considered the approach the court should take when considering a case of possible illegality. He summarised four propositions drawn from earlier authorities, in particular *North Western Salt Company Limited v Electrolytic Alkali Company Ltd*:

"First that, where a contract is ex facie illegal, the court will not enforce it whether the illegality is pleaded or not. Secondly, that where, as here, the contract is not ex facie illegal, evidence of extraneous circumstances tending to show that it has an illegal object should not be admitted unless the circumstances relied on are pleaded. Thirdly, that where unpleaded facts, which taken by themselves show an illegal object, have been revealed in evidence (because perhaps no objection was raised or because they were adduced for some other purpose) the court should not act on them unless it is satisfied that the whole of the relevant circumstances are before it but, fourthly, that were the court is satisfied that all the relevant facts are before it and it can see clearly form them that the contract had an illegal object, it may not enforce the contract whether the facts were pleaded or not."[31]

It seems likely that a tribunal in an arbitration with its seat in England can and should adopt a similar approach. It is necessary to consider particularly though whether and if so how that general approach might apply in the setting of competition law.

5. ARBITRATION CONTRASTED WITH OTHER FORMS OF DISPUTE RESOLUTION

Nature of arbitration. Commercial arbitration is a private procedure for obtaining a final, binding and enforceable determination of a dispute between two, or perhaps more parties.   **11–034**

Other forms of dispute resolution. There are many other forms of private commercial dispute resolution that have there own distinct characteristics. The following terms are commonly encountered. The terms are not always used consistently. Commercial courts do however make a clear distinction between the different processes by reference to both the differences in process and outcome.[32]   **11–035**

- Expert Determination/Adjudication—This usually refers to a process in which the "tribunal" is asked to answer a specific question which is

---

[30] [1950] 1 Q.B. 359 at 371.
[31] [1914] A.C. 461.
[32] *David Wilson Homes Ltd v Survey Services* [2001] B.L.R. 267; *Cable & Wireless plc v IBM UK Ltd* [2002] 2 All E.R. (Comm) 1041; *Flight Training International v International Fire Training Equipment Ltd* [2004] EWHC 721.

in dispute. This might be, for instance, the price to be paid for a particular service. The outcome of the process is contractually binding on the parties in that it defines the parties' contractual rights henceforward.

- Conciliation—This usually refers to a process that involves some measure of discussion regarding settlement of the case followed by the production by the conciliator of an opinion regarding the likely outcome or outcomes in the case.

- Mediation—This is a process in which the parties seek a settlement with the assistance of one or more mediators. It is a purely consensual process in which an agreed outcome is sought with the aid of a mediator.

- Mini-trial—In this process there is an abbreviated trial of the dispute before, say, senior management of both parties so that they can gain a better picture of likely outcomes.

- Neutral evaluation—In this process an appropriate individual, such as a retired judge, indicates what the likely outcome would be if the trial were to proceed.

Only arbitration has all the relevant attributes identified in the previous section. These other ADR processes (and others not named here) are each distinct from commercial arbitration.

6. INTERFACE BETWEEN COMPETITION AND PRIVATE DISPUTE RESOLUTION METHODS

11–036 **Practical significance of arbitration for application of competition law.** Many agreements raising competition law issues will include compulsory arbitration clauses.[33] Issues of competition law, in particular disputes as to whether the contract in question is void pursuant to Art.81(2) EC, or should be subject to individual exemption pursuant to Art.81 (3) EC may often arise in arbitration.

11–037 **Attitude of EU Commission to arbitration.** The Commission has been historically mistrustful of arbitration, perhaps suspicious that it could be a vehicle for facilitating clandestine activity. In recent years, though, DG Comp has begun to make use of arbitration in resolving issues arising from its decisions or legislation. For instance, reference is made to arbitration of certain matters in the field of merger control and in early patent and know-

---

[33] Indeed, it is suggested by Idot that most contractual disputes of the type likely to be affected by application of Art.81(3) end up before arbitrators rather than national courts, see contribution to panel discussion in Ehlermann & Atansiu, n.3, above, p.285.

how licensing block exemption regulations. However, as appears from the following examples, the references made to arbitration and private dispute resolution methods sometimes suggest a confused view of these different processes.

Recent references to "Arbitration" and other forms of dispute resolution in EC competition legislation: block exemption provisions.   Block exemption regulations concerning maritime transport (Regulation 4056/86)[34] and liner shipping companies (Regulation 823/2000)[35] demonstrate a cautious approach to arbitration. Under these regulations, parties to contracts covered by the block exemption must notify the Commission of any award or conciliated outcome to any dispute between them.[36] Perhaps this is symptomatic of the Commission's suspicion that the clandestine nature of arbitration might undermine the effect of the block exemption.

11–038

Motor vehicle block exemption.   A more enthusiastic approach to alternative dispute resolution has been taken in the recent motor vehicle block exemption regulation, Regulation 1400/2002.[37] Recital 11 of that Regulation provides:

11–039

> "In order to favour the quick resolution of disputes which arise between the parties to a distribution agreement and which might otherwise hamper effective competition, agreements should only benefit from exemption if they provide for each party to have a right of recourse to an independent expert or arbitrator, in particular where notice is given to terminate an agreement."

This is reflected in Art.3(6) of the Regulation which provides for the referral of contractual disputes to an independent expert or arbitrator. That right is said, however, to be without prejudice to each party's right to make an application to a national court. This provision is confusing in a number of respects. Apparently the provision for arbitration or expert determination must not provide for mandatory arbitration or expert determination. In particular, it is not clear what "application to a national court" is contemplated. This might mean that any dispute was to be referable to litigation or whatever private dispute resolution process is selected. This would seem to confirm that the arbitration provision should not be a mandatory arbitration clause. The explanatory guidance notes to the Regulation indicate that the Commission, contrary to normal usage, regards its reference to expert determination as including mediation. There must also be some doubt as to whether the term "arbitration" is intended to refer to commercial arbitration properly so called. While most language versions of the

---

[34] [1986] O.J. L378/4.
[35] [2000] O.J. L100/24.
[36] Art.4 of Regulation 4056/86; Art.9(4) of Regulation 823/2000.
[37] [2002] O.J. L203/30.

regulation refer to the relevant word for arbitrator, the Spanish language version says that the dispute is to be referred to a "*mediador*" which would seem to be a reference to a distinctly different form of dispute resolution.

11–040   Arbitration/ADR and monitoring of remedies: merger control.   In a number of cases the Commission has imposed arbitration-related measures as part of the remedies it imposes. The detailed analysis of these procedures falls outside the scope of this work,[38] but it is notable again that the term "arbitration" seems to be used in many cases to cover dispute resolution procedures that would not be regarded as arbitration for the purposes of the relevant conventions, or national arbitration law.[39] In outline the remedies fall into three categories: general arbitration clauses imposed as part of the dispute resolution provision in respect of disposals or licensing or access remedies; expert determinations used usually to deal with valuation disputes likely to arise in due course and finally the imposition of an obligation on a party to insert into its contracts with other parties (customers, suppliers, etc.) a right to arbitrate or participate in some other dispute resolution procedure, albeit that it is not always clear what the content of that right is intended to be.

11–041   Arbitration/ADR and monitoring of remedies: competition or regulatory cases.   The policing of any remedy in a competition or regulatory case could be the subject of a similar procedure. Comparison may be made with the various systems required to resolve disputes in the telecommunications sector pursuant to the 2002 package of telecommunications directives.[40] In the UK, specific provision has been made to deal with certain categories of dispute in the telecommunications adjudication scheme for local loop unbundling established by OFCOM.[41] Similarly, any remedy imposed as a consequence of the operation of the new cartel procedure under Art.9 of

---

[38] A comprehensive summary of these cases up to 2001 is provided in Blessing, *Arbitrating Antitrust and Merger Control Issue*s (Helbing & Lichtenhahn, Basel, 2003).

[39] An extreme example of confusion can be seen in the decision of the Commission in Case M.3225 *Alcan/Pechiney* II (Decision of September 29, 2003) in which some disputes are referred to a "licensing trustee" who can "arbitrate", and other disputes go to another tribunal. By contrast the adjudication remedy required following clearance of the Carlton/ Granada merger in *Re UK* involves determination of contract rights issues by an adjudicator who is expressly not to be treated as an arbitrator. That remedy is implemented by the "Office of the Independent Adjudicator" within OFCOM. A more coherent bifurcated dispute system is provided for in Case M.3280 *Air France/KLM* (Decision of February 11, 2004) which provides for a process of "expert determination" by a monitoring trustee in respect of certain specific issues, and requires that the merging parties make available an arbitration procedure to third parties affected by any failure to comply with commitments undertaken to the Commission by the parties. But see Radicati di Brozolo, n.14, above, who takes the view that arbitrations relating to EC merger control are no different from other commercial arbitrations.

[40] Framework Directive 2002/21 Authorisation Directive 2002/20. Access and Interconnection Directive 2002/19, Universal Service Directive 2002/22, Privacy Directive 2002/58 EC.

[41] For details see *www.ofcom.org.uk/ind_groups/ind_groups/telecommunications/telecoms_adj_sch/*.

Regulation 1/2003 might also have incorporated into it a clause providing for resolution or determination of any subsequent disputes.

Points of difficulty. Some general points of difficulty arise in any use of arbitration/ADR as an adjunct to remedies:

11–042

- Should the tribunal be able to receive submissions or evidence from the competition enforcement authority in a private dispute?

- Is the tribunal in a case such as this a true arbitrator, or other private dispute resolver, or is the tribunal the delegate of the enforcement authority?

- Have the parties truly consented to the process, and if not how does this affect their due process rights in this process?[41a] For instance, while "arbitration" is often put forward as a sensible procedure for these purposes because it can be relatively fast, it may be that the nature of the issues involved are such that it is not possible or practical to achieve a fair determination within the limited time allowed. In many technical areas it might take some time for an appropriately qualified and available expert to be engaged and for that expert to prepare the necessary evidence.

There has been little detailed consideration of these issues. It may be that the timing advantage is illusory if a dispute can only properly be dealt with if the tribunal has access to expert evidence and the process of finding an appropriate expert and having the evidence prepared cannot be completed within the limited time available.

7. CAN AN ARBITRAL TRIBUNAL APPLY COMPETITION LAW TO THE DISPUTE REFERRED TO IT? ARBITRABILITY OF COMPETITION LAW

Arbitrability of competition law: power to apply Article 81(2) EC. There is considerable literature regarding the arbitrability of competition law issues, albeit that there is no decision directly on this point in English law.[42] While the issues raised are far from straightforward it seems that in general terms it is now uncontested that issues of competition law are capable of being resolved in arbitration.

11–043

The objection to arbitrability. Even though the consideration of this question has moved on to consider when an arbitrator is obliged to consider

11–044

[41a] See para.11–020, above.
[42] For a relatively early analysis see Hochstrasser, "Choice of Law and 'Foreign' Mandatory Rules in International Arbitration" (1994) Jnl. of Intl. Arb. 57.

a question of competition law, there still remains a live debate as to the proper extent to which competition disputes are capable of being resolved in arbitration. This is considered further below. In that context it is relevant to note the basis upon which arbitrability has been resisted in principle. This was summarised by the US Supreme Court in *American Safety Equipment Corp v JP Maguire & Co*[43] as follows:

> "A claim under the antitrust laws is not merely a private matter ... Antitrust violation can affect hundreds of thousands, perhaps millions, of people and inflict staggering economic damage. We do not believe Congress intended such claims to be resolved elsewhere than in the Courts."

11–045   **Arbitrability in principle: *Mitsubishi Motors v Soler*.**   The conventional view has now changed and the decision generally taken by the international arbitration community as establishing the arbitrability of competition issues is a decision of the US Supreme Court in *Mitsubishi Motors Corp v Soler Chrysler Plymouth*.[44] In that judgment the court held that a Japanese arbitral tribunal in considering a contract expressly governed by Swiss law had to take into account, on the grounds of international public policy, the antitrust law of the US.

11–046   **The "second look" doctrine.**   The *Mitsubishi* decision has given rise to a concept referred to as the "second look" doctrine. The content of this concept is not always consistently described. It appears to be derived from the following comment of the court:

> "Having permitted the arbitration to go forward, the national courts of the United States will have the opportunity at the award enforcement stage to ensure that the legitimate interest in the enforcement of the antitrust laws has been addressed. The [New York Convention] reserves to each signatory country the right to refuse enforcement of an award where the 'recognition or enforcement of the award would be contrary to a public policy of that country'"

The practical difficulty with this doctrine is that in arbitration in general, and international arbitration in particular, the scope for judicial interference is intentionally limited. Many if not most awards will be honoured without the need for enforcement through the judicial process, and the scope for substantive legal review is limited or almost non-existent in many jurisdictions.

---

[43] 391 F.2d 821 (2d Cir. 1968).
[44] 105 S.C. 3346 (1985).

Other jurisdictions.   It has been accepted that antitrust issues are arbitrable   **11–047**
in France,[45] in Switzerland[46] and by statutory amendment in Germany.[47] In
fact, and despite earlier decisions discouraging this, arbitrators have been
applying for Arts 81 and 82 EC for years.[48]

Arbitrability in practice.   It does not of course follow that all issues will fall   **11–048**
naturally within the scope of an arbitration. Where competition law issues
are raised by the effect of a number of agreements with different parties, it
may not be possible to resolve all the competition issues involving each such
party in arbitration. Other types of issue are unlikely to arise in the context
of arbitration at all. In particular, some Art.82 issues are unlikely to arise in
arbitration unless the parties entered into an ad hoc agreement particularly
in connection with this dispute. In each case it would be necessary to
establish not only whether the competition law issue is arbitrable but
whether it falls within the scope or the arbitration agreement.

Factors indicating that EC competition law should be taken into account.   **11–049**
Taking account of their obligations towards the parties, some arbitration
practitioners have suggested that there should be a graduated approach to
deciding whether they can or should apply EC competition law in international proceedings. It has been suggested[49] that arbitrators may take account
of at least the following three factors:

(1)   Whether the law chosen by the parties, or the law applicable to the
merits, is that of a Member State.

(2)   Whether the seat of the arbitration is located in one of the Member
States so that the award would be subject to an action to set aside
before the national courts of this state.

(3)   Whether the award is likely to be enforced in a Member State.

It has been suggested that the more these factors come into play, the more
European competition law should be taken into consideration.

Can EC competition law be applied in arbitrations with their seat in England   **11–050**
(or elsewhere in the EU) regardless of the law of the contract?   Although
there is no directly relevant decision, it seems that a tribunal in an

---

[45]   Decision of the Cour d'appel de Paris of May 19, 1993 [1993] Rev. Arb. 645; Decision of the
Cour de Cassation, January 5,1999.
[46]   Decisions of the Tribunal Fédéral, April 28, 1992 [1992] A.S.A. Bull 368; November 13, 1998
[1999] A.S.A. Bull. 529 and 455.
[47]   Revision of Art.91 of Act against Restraints on Competition (GWB); Baron & Liniger, "A
Second Look at Arbitrability" (2003) *Arbitration International* 27.
[48]   Derains, "Arbitrage et droit de la concurrence" (1982) 14 *Revue Suisse du Droit International
de la Concurrence* 39.
[49]   Pinsolle, "Private Enforcement of European Competition Rules by Arbitrators", n.14,
above.

arbitration with a seat in England should follow the *Mitsubishi* approach. As a matter of principle, there can be little doubt that where the law of the contract is that of an EC Member State, EC competition law must be applied as part of that law.

11–051   **Application of EC competition law in arbitrations with seat outside the EC or EEA.** For many years arbitrations were held outside the EC on the basis that it was supposed that courts and arbitrators would not apply EC competition law.[50] That was seen as an advantage by some. In deciding whether to apply EC competition law in an arbitration with a seat outside the EU, it will be for the tribunal to consider the impact on the validity and enforceability of the award of its failure to do so. In many cases the tribunal is likely to consider whether attempts are likely to be made to enforce the award inside the EU, and what the impact of failure to deal with this issue would have on the enforceability of the judgment in the relevant state.

11–052   **Arbitrations in which the seat is not in a Member State and the applicable law is not that of a Member State.** In practice many tribunals outside the EC would expect to apply EC competition law where appropriate. An example of such application is provided by an ICC award[51] in a case in which a tribunal sitting in Geneva applied Art.85 EC (now Art.81 EC) to a licence agreement executed between a US licensor and a German licensee, although the contract was governed by New York law. A non-competition clause in the contract was declared to be illegal. In a situation such as this it is probably necessary to have regard not just to the enforcement of the award, but whether the effect of the award would be altered by regulatory action in a Member State, such as a decision of a national competition authority that effectively reverses part of the award.

8. MUST AN ARBITRAL TRIBUNAL APPLY COMPETITION LAW TO THE DISPUTE REFERRED TO IT?

11–053   **Must a tribunal with its seat in the EU raise a competition law issue of its own motion?** There is no clear authority bearing on this question, although it seems likely that a tribunal with its seat in England would usually apply the same procedure as a national court.[52] On this basis, English law would indicate that the tribunal should apply a competition law prohibition of its own motion if it has received persuasive and comprehensive evidence of

---

[50] As an example, see the ICC Award rendered in Case No.6503 in (1995) *Journal de Droit International* 1022, note by Y. Derains.

[51] Award No.8626 in (1999) *Journal de Droit International* 1073, note by Arnaldez.

[52] See para.11–013, above.

illegality.[52a] The tribunal must exercise care in exercising its jurisdiction as it may not have access to all the relevant information and may on the basis of partial information take an incorrect and unfair decision. The following paragraphs consider how EC law might affect that position.

Eco Swiss v Benetton: **must the Member State court called upon to enforce an arbitration award raise and determine issues of competition law of its own motion?** One of the few decisions of the ECJ considering the interplay of competition and arbitration is Case C–126/97 *Eco Swiss China Time v Benetton International*.[53] This decision arose on a preliminary reference to the European Court of Justice in proceedings brought to enforce an arbitration award. This decision was directed to the nature of the obligation of the court to consider the competition law issues that arise when called upon to enforce that award and involves, in effect, the ECJ's approach to the "second look" referred to in *Mitsubishi*. In *Eco Swiss*, the ECJ decided that a Member State court is required to take account of compliance with EC competition law when enforcing (or considering annulment of) an arbitration award. It was said that EC competition law rules are mandatory rules of EC member state law and that this is so even though national competition law may not necessarily be regarded as a matter of public policy in each Member State. The court stated that:

> "it is in the interest of efficient arbitration proceedings that review of arbitration awards should be limited in scope and that annulment of or refusal to recognise an award should be possible only in exceptional circumstances ... Because of the fundamental character of Article 81 the judge's review must extend to Community public policy."

This review must be "effective" according to the Advocate General.

11–054

Finality of awards. This decision may be regarded as unremarkable to competition lawyers, but it does raise difficulties with regard to the finality of awards. Not all arbitrators would regard the *Eco Swiss* as a fair approach to the resolution of an essentially commercial dispute. One commentator has been highly critical of Benetton's position.[54] He has noted, with some force, that Benetton should surely be expected to have had access to legal advice that took account of competition law yet it failed to raise the supposed violation of competition law throughout two phases of extended, and no doubt costly arbitration. Further, Benetton only raised the issue as a defence to enforcement of an award of damages. Perhaps it was content with the agreement. It is unclear what the wider economic impact of the agreement was. Whatever the policy issues involved, it has been suggested that

11–055

[52a] See paras 11–032–11–033, above.
[53] [1999] E.C.R. I–3055; [2000] 5 C.M.L.R. 816.
[54] Radicati Di Brozolo, "Antitrust: a paradigm of the relations between mandatory rules and arbitration—a fresh look at the 'second look'", n.15, above.

Benetton should not benefit from what can have only been either an incompetent or cynical defence in the arbitration, a procedural tactic aimed at preventing enforcement of the eventual award, or just an attempt to conceal a violation of competition law, the unveiling of which it feared could lead to proceedings before the competition authorities. Indeed even *Eco Swiss* does nothing to challenge the proposition that the finality of the award must be respected even in the face of failure by arbitrators to address the issue.

11–056 **Application of *Eco Swiss* to the position of the arbitral tribunal considering whether to raise competition law issues of its own motion?** Nothing is said in *Eco Swiss* about the ability of the arbitrator to raise competition law issues of its own motion. It is said by some competition lawyers that this is so because within the EU it is so clear that arbitrators must do so. Dolmans and Grierson[55] read Art.1 of Regulation 1/2003 as making it even clearer that arbitrators are obliged to take account of EC competition law of their own motion. This seems, however, an unduly extensive reading of the provision as there seems no reason why arbitrators should act beyond the limits of the civil procedure rules that govern them, any more than should a national court (see *Van Schijndel*[56]). On this basis the English law position summarised above is not altered by EC law. If a tribunal sitting in England and applying the law of an EC Member State fails to deal with the potential invalidity of an agreement pursuant to Art.81(2) EC, it might have failed to deal with an issue that is critical to the determination of the dispute and have committed a serious irregularity.[57] Certainly by not raising the issue the tribunal exposes the award to challenges.[57a] However, in considering the circumstances in which the point must be raised by a tribunal regard must be had to the separate considerations that apply when a court has to decide whether to raise a point of illegality of its own motion.[58] An over enthusiastic application of competition law beyond the circumstances provided for in that case law may itself constitute serious irregularity. The tribunal's finding may, for instance be based on insufficient evidence.[58a]

11–057 **Due process concerns.** In considering whether it should introduce an issue, a tribunal will be particularly concerned to address any relevant due process

---

[55] Dolmans & Grierson, "Arbitration and Modernization of EC Antitrust Law: New Opportunities and New Responsibilities" (2003) 14(2) ICC Bull. 37.

[56] Cases C–430/93, 431/93 [1995] E.C.R. I–4705; [1996] 1 C.M.L.R. 801. For a critique of *Eco Swiss* and *Van Schijndel* see Prechal & Shelkoplyas, "National Procedures, Public Policy and EC Law. From *Van Schijndel* to *Eco Swiss* and Beyond" (2004) (5) *European Review of Private Law* 589.

[57] See para.11–026, above.

[57a] Mehrens, "The Eco Swiss Case and International Arbitration" (2003) *Arbitration International* 465.

[58] See para.11–033, above.

[58a] In the absence of some clear evidence of anti-competitive object or intent it is unlikely that the tribunal will have sufficient material to establish a breach of competition law if neither party presents it.

concerns. Most arbitrations raising a competition law issue will be concerned with a reference to potential Art.81(2) EC invalidity. If the validity of the contract is challenged in whole or in part it may be said that that underlying issues of validity are also raised implicitly, but otherwise arbitrators in a jurisdiction such as England where tribunals do not typically raise matters of their own motion may well regard any action of this type as contradictory to their understanding of the rules of natural justice. Thus, arbitrators in England may be concerned that in some circumstances an award made on the basis of issues not raised by the parties themselves might be set aside for serious irregularity.[59] Certainly a tribunal would feel it necessary to give the parties an opportunity to address it on the issues that it wished to raise so as to ensure that the parties' due process rights had been protected. The practical issues raised by this are considered further below.

Judicial review of the award. Even if the award does address the appropriate competition law issues, the award may apply the law incorrectly and as already explained the scope for review of findings of law is very limited in most jurisdictions. While *Eco Swiss* guarantees that no award that upholds a transaction contrary to EC antitrust law should be enforced, it does not follow that an award that incorrectly applies EC antitrust law will also be denied enforcement. On the contrary, as discussed further below, one of the unsatisfactory aspects of the intersection between competition law and arbitration is the fact that the consequences of arbitral error are asymmetric.　　11–058

Application of competition law as a mandatory rule. An arbitral tribunal must also consider which system of law's mandatory rules are to be applied:　　11–059

- **Substantive or procedural.** Both the substantive law of the contract, and the procedural law of the seat will be relevant to determining when a tribunal must raise a competition law point that has not been raised by the parties.

- **Law of place of enforcement.** Taking account of the *Eco Swiss* decision, the ultimately decisive factor for a tribunal considering whether to raise and determine a competition law issue of its motion may often be the achievement of the primary goal of producing an enforceable award. For instance, in order to ensure that the award is fully effective the tribunal may need to have regard to the effects of the award in jurisdictions in which it is to be enforced rather than that of the seat, or the place of performance or the law of the contract.

Impact of regulatory or other proceedings in other jurisdictions. The tribunal will also have to have regard to the fact that the effect of an award may be undermined by action of a competition authority (or court) that changes　　11–060

---

[59] s.68 of the Arbitration Act 1996.

or reverses its effect in the jurisdiction in question. Quite apart from questions of comity it may be that in making an arbitration award a tribunal must consider where any anti-competitive agreement or conduct relating to that award may have an effect.

11–061   **Practical limits on the ability of tribunal to raise issue if outside its own knowledge.**   On the other hand, arbitrators may not be lawyers, and even if they were it would be surprising if in an international case they could be aware of all the possible public policy issues that the parties have concealed (or failed to discover) relating to all jurisdictions to which the agreement might relate. There are many prominent lawyer arbitrators in the EU whose practice has not led them to acquire a detailed knowledge of competition law.

11–062   **In practice tribunals do raise competition law issues of their own motion.** Arbitral tribunals have applied competition law in circumstances where no such issue has been raised by the parties. Blessing[60] cites ICC awards in which the tribunal has taken just this step. In practice, it seems likely that tribunals will have regard to the need to produce an award that is enforceable and not subsequently undermined by regulatory action, and act accordingly. The practical constraint is likely to be that not all arbitrators are aware of the detail of EC competition law, particularly where the issues do not concern restraints that do not have an anti-competitive object, or are not "hardcore" so that any proper analysis is likely to depend on economic issues that the tribunal may not be equipped to deal with alone.

9. NON-EU STATES AND SWITZERLAND IN PARTICULAR

11–063   **EC Commission's historic suspicions of Swiss arbitration.**   Historically there has been concern that Switzerland was a haven for anti-competitive conduct. Arbitration was thought by some to be implicated in that environment. This was exemplified by the classic, or perhaps apocryphal case concerning an arbitration in Switzerland over an agreement governed by Swiss law of which only one copy is kept in a bank vault in Switzerland. The document is taken out and studied at the arbitration hearing, but is then replaced and the panel of three Swiss arbitrators are asked to make an enforceable award by reference to the obligations imposed by the contract

---

[60] Blessing, "Impact of Mandatory Rules, Sanctions, Competition Laws" in *International Arbitration in Switzerland* (Berti ed., Aspen), p.234.

without explicitly referring to it.[61] Baudenbacher summarises[62] four reasons for the historic suspicions held by the Commission regarding Switzerland:

(1) Switzerland is perceived as having a tradition of hosting cartels operating in the EC market.

(2) Switzerland has tried to avoid the extraterritorial effect of EC competition law.

(3) Switzerland is a traditional host of numerous arbitration tribunals which were themselves suspected of helping companies to avoid the application of EC competition rules.

(4) In 1974 the Swiss Federal Supreme Court ruled that the competition provision in the bilateral Free Trade Agreement between Switzerland and the EC did not have direct effect.

It is perhaps understandable that in these circumstances the impact of arbitration in Switzerland upon EC competition law issues was regarded as a matter of concern.

Switzerland: arbitrators may apply competition law of their own motion but are not required to do so.   It seems that by now, at least, many of these fears are misplaced. It has become clear that Switzerland is not necessarily a safe haven for EC competition law avoidance. This is of significance not only because of Switzerland's geographic and economic relationship with the EU but also because of its relative importance as a site for international commercial arbitration. The tension between the various issues raised concerning the application of competition law by the tribunal of its own motion are illustrated by recent cases in Switzerland.   **11–064**

Swiss award set aside for failure to apply competition law as part of applicable law.   In 1992 the Swiss Federal Tribunal set aside a Swiss award for failure to assess the validity of an agreement whose applicable law was Belgian law by reference to EC competition law. This decision demonstrated that there was nothing in principle inimical to Swiss law in enforcing EC competition law.[63]   **11–065**

Swiss tribunal permitted, but not required to take into account EC competition law in case affecting EC market but subject to Swiss substantive law.   There still remains some scope, though, for incomplete application of competition law in Swiss awards. A decision of the Swiss Federal Tribunal in 1998   **11–066**

---

[61] Werner, "Application of Competition Laws by Arbitrators: The Step too Far" 12 *Jnl. of Intl. Arb.* 23.

[62] Baudenbacher, n.3, above.

[63] Decision of April 28, 1992 cited in Blessing, n.60, above, para.734, p.232.

concerning a cover bid agreement is particularly relevant.[64] A consortium C had been awarded the concession to build and operate some works by the government of an EC Member State. The consortium initiated a tender process for the carrying out of the construction. Three construction companies X, Y & Z (which were all based in another Member State) entered into an agreement. Z would submit a bid to C in terms determined by X and Y. In exchange X and Y would pay 5 million FF to Z if they were awarded the works contract, albeit that payment of half of that sum could be substituted by the award of a sub-contract (presumably of equivalent value). The agreement also provided that it would terminate if the project were cancelled. C's concession was then cancelled by the Member State and the tender process fell by the wayside. A new concession was awarded to a consortium K. A tender procedure was initiated by K for a different scope of works, and Z were not invited to bid. The works contract was awarded to a consortium of four contractors that included X and Y. The works were carried out and X and Y did not enter into any sub contract with Z. Z brought a claim for recovery of its 5 million FF. The arbitration clause provided for arbitration under Swiss law in Switzerland. A Geneva advocate was appointed as arbitrator. X and Y resisted the claim on the basis that the cancellation of C's concession was to be treated as cancellation of the project and did not give rise to termination of the agreement between them and Z. They did not raise any issue of competition law (either Swiss or EC). The arbitrator found that the award of the new contract was to be treated as an award of a contract covered by the original arrangement and made an award for payment of 5 million FF together with interest was made in favour of Z. The "cover bid" arrangement was thus enforced. X and Y then challenged the award on the grounds that it was contrary to Swiss public order in that it was in breach of EC competition law. The court found that the Swiss arbitrator or judge will examine the compatibility of an agreement with Art.81 where the agreement is subject to EC competition law regardless of the applicable law of the agreement. An award that fails to take account of a relevant plea of invalidity based on Art.81 can therefore be challenged. Compliance with EC competition law was not however a question of public order—there is no obligation on an arbitrator to raise the issue of his or her own motion. The court stated that it could not require the arbitrator to be aware of or systematically search for mandatory rules of law in each of the legislations showing signs of significant points of contact with the relationship in dispute. Accordingly, the award was upheld. It is not recorded whether, or where it was enforced. In principle it ought to have been difficult to resist enforcement under the New York Convention outside the EU, the challenge to the award already having been made, and failed in Switzerland.

---

[64] Decision of November 13, 1998 (1999) A.S.A. Bull. 529.

EC competition law not part of Swiss public policy? The Swiss Federal   **11–067**
Tribunal confirmed in a further decision in 2002[65] that it was doubtful
whether domestic or EC competition law formed part of public policy. The
court stated that "it appears doubtful that national or European competition law are part of the fundamental legal or moral principles recognised by
all civilised nations to such an extent that their breach should be regarded as
contrary to public policy." In practice therefore arbitrators in Switzerland
may apply European competition law of their own motion, but the resulting
award will not be annulled if they fail to do so.

No universal application of competition law by arbitrators. It seems likely,   **11–068**
but not necessary that a similar approach would be taken in other jurisdictions with sophisticated competition/antitrust regimes of their own. The
situation may be quite different in arbitrations held in countries with no
competition law, or only recent introduction of such law. Such states will
often have different traditions of political economy and competition policy
imperatives may seem very much less important than other aspects of policy.

Practical implications. While competition lawyers may all agree that an   **11–069**
arbitration outside the EU regarding an agreement with anti-competitive
effects within the EU should apply European competition law, from an
arbitration perspective this raises many difficulties. Why should a non-EC
tribunal apply EC law of its own motion when it has no knowledge of this
law? How many other mandatory rules, or public policy issues must the
international arbitrator take account of "of his own motion"—in other
words without any one else's help or training? Competition law is another
set of mandatory rules to set alongside money laundering regulations, anti-
corruption laws or laws in some Islamic countries forbidding payment of
interest. These last might certainly be regarded in other Muslim countries as
self-evidently the product of international public policy. It is not self-evident
that competition law is a requirement of all civilised or commercial societies.
Hong Kong, for example, has no such general competition law. Countries
that are only now introducing their own competition laws[66] may pursue very
different goals with that competition law, and achieve very different results.
The goals of EC competition law may not be shared or even understood by
arbitrators in all other jurisdictions.

---

[65] Decision of February 1, 2002 (2002) 2 ASA Bull. 337.
[66] *e.g.* Singapore where the Competition Act 2004 comes into force on January 1, 2006.

10. TO WHAT EXTENT CAN OR SHOULD THE COMMUNITY INSTITUTIONS (OR NATIONAL COMPETITION AUTHORITIES) SUPERVISE OR SUPPORT THE APPLICATION OF COMPETITION LAW WITHIN ARBITRATION?

11–070 **From Commission (or NCA): oversight of arbitration awards.**   There is an inequality inherent in any arbitration involving a potentially decisive issue of competition law. Where one party seeks to contend that there is an infringement and the other takes a contrary position, the party that contends for validity or non-infringement only has recourse to the usually limited or non-existent domestic appellate remedies available. The party taking the contrary view can always "appeal" to the Commission or relevant NCA. There are at least four categories of award over which the Commission might exercise some degree of control after the award has been made:

(1) Awards in which agreements that might have benefited from exception under Art.81(3) EC are held invalid under Art.81(1) EC without consideration of the application of that exception.

(2) Awards with an anti-competitive effect contrary to Art.81 or Art.82 EC.

(3) Awards made outside the EC with an anti-competitive effect contrary to Art.81 or 82 EC. On an application to enforce the agreement within the EC, the national court should raise the competition law issue of its own motion.

(4) Awards that make erroneous findings of breach of Art.82 EC.

11–071 **Support for arbitrators from the EEA Courts and Commission.**   The relationship, or lack of it, between the institutions and arbitration has been the subject of much comment. The ECJ has decided that arbitrators may not make a reference to the ECJ under Art. 234.[67] Curiously, Judge Baudenbacher has indicated extra-judicially that the EFTA court might not feel bound by that decision.[68] This raises the prospect that an arbitral tribunal might seek authoritative guidance from the EFTA court if an arbitration were to involve an issue of competition law that arose in both an EC and EFTA context.

11–072 **References to the ECJ.**[69]   References may however be made to the ECJ by national courts exercising a supervisory judgment. Many commentators

---

[67] Case 102/81, *Nordsee Deutsche Hochseefisherei GmbH v Reederei Mond Hochseefischerei Nordstern AG* [1982] E.C.R. 1095.
[68] Baudenbacher, n.3, above.
[69] See more generally paras 9–077–9–086, above.

outside England have noted particularly the unusual provision in s.45 of the English Arbitration Act 1996 which enables an arbitrator to raise a point of law with the Commercial Court. That court could then make a reference on the relevant point of law. That reference would probably have to be transferred to the Chancery Division pursuant to CPR 30.8 for that court to address the question itself, or to make the necessary reference.

Support from the Commission.   A tribunal in a case involving competition   11–073
law issues will discuss with the parties how issues of competition are to be resolved. The tribunal may wish to obtain assistance from the Commission as it has on occasion responded positively to such approaches. The tribunal should probably not approach the Commission without consulting with the parties and obtaining their consent.

Joint approach to Commission.   A more effective route is likely to be for the   11–074
parties and the tribunal to agree at a certain point to make certain requests of the Commission for assistance in agreed terms. Depending on the impact of the matters on which guidance is sought on other issues in the case, it may be necessary to stay the proceedings while this guidance is obtained.

Course to adopt if one or both parties reluctant.   Many arbitrators[70] would   11–075
take the view that even if they wished to seek competition policy guidance from the Commission, to do so would infringe their agreement with the parties under which they are obliged to resolve all questions of law, and to do so in private and subject to obligations of confidentiality and that they could not do so without both parties' agreement. Indeed formally speaking such action might give rise to a serious irregularity in an arbitration governed by the English Arbitration Act 1996 as an arbitrator can only rely upon the assistance of a third party with the knowledge and consent of the parties. That knowledge and consent would normally require also complete transparency in the process between the arbitrator and the third party so that the parties can see how the award is being affected by the third party's involvement.

Material submitted to the Commission.   A related concern is that insofar as   11–076
communications between tribunal and Commission inform the outcome of the arbitration, the parties may have had insufficient knowledge about, and ability to comment on the substance of that procedure, the material submitted to the Commission for its view and its response. Some of these objections might be met by the tribunal ordering that the input of the Commission be treated in a manner akin to the tribunal appointed expert permitted by many sets of rules and procedural laws. This does not, however, seem to be a promising basis upon which to proceed. If the Commission's contribution is to be of any value it is likely to affect one or more

---

[70] Blessing, n.60, above.

important issues in the case and there is likely to be a reasonable ground for supposing that its advice is more than merely the contribution of an expert witness.

11–077 **Arbitrator's duties.** Further, some arbitrators would find it inconsistent with their duties to seek assistance from a body that fuses both law enforcement and decision-making roles. For similar reasons most arbitrators would be reluctant to put any party in a position in which it had to seek guidance.

11–078 **Suggested approach.** There seems to be no current basis to compel the reluctant party's participation in the process and the safer approach may be not to seek that guidance and to make the award without that assistance. It may be appropriate to draw then the parties' attention to the fact that if the outcome of the competition law issue is controversial, one or other party may have the opportunity to attack the award through the Commission or NCA.

11. HOW SHOULD AN ARBITRAL TRIBUNAL APPLY COMPETITION LAW TO THE DISPUTE REFERRED TO IT?

11–079 **The tribunal's approach to competition law.** It seems likely that arbitrators will take a flexible approach to competition law, as they often do to aspects of the law that they regard as unduly restrictive. This is particularly so in the case of international arbitrations where there will be little or no opportunity for a "second look" before enforcement proceedings. For all the discussion above about application of competition law as a matter of public policy, and arbitrators raising competition law points of their own motion, these policy concerns are likely to turn almost entirely around questions of invalidity and (perhaps) severance. It seems unlikely that arbitrators will be required to raise the prospect of a *Crehan*[71] damages claim of their own motion.[72] Further, arbitrators are likely in reality to take a graduated approach to competition law. While some might feel obliged to avoid taking any step that validated a price fixing cartel, it seems unlikely that many would feel it necessary to raise a point that can only be brought on the basis of complex legal, factual or economic analysis.

11–080 **The arbitrator and Article 81(3) EC.** This graduated approach to enforcement of competition law would be particularly applicable in cases in which reliance is placed on Art.81(3) EC to avoid invalidity.

---

[71] Case C–453/99 *Courage v Crehan* [2001] E.C.R. I–6297; [2001] 5 C.M.L.R. 28.
[72] See more generally Chapter 7, above.

Practical and legal difficulties in applying Article 81(3) EC.   The application   11–081
of Art.81(3) EC involves carrying out a balancing exercise between the anti-
competitive effects of a restraint and its pro-competitive benefits. This
involves an analysis of a broad span of policy issues far beyond the interests
of the parties themselves.[73] As we have already seen, an arbitrator may not
get any help from either Commission or ECJ in carrying out this exercise.

Application of Article 81(3) EC by some tribunals before the Modernisation   11–082
Regulation.   As suggested above, even if help were available, many arbitrators would probably regard it as contrary to their engagement to leave
exemption issues to be left to others. Even before the adoption of Regulation 1/2003 ("the Modernisation Regulation"), it seems that some arbitrators applied themselves Art.81 (3) EC "with a distant look".[74] It is
difficult to obtain reliable indications as to how extensive this practice was,
or what its effect was. Certainly, competition law would have been applied
without the sort of analysis the Commission might usually have expected.

Approach in Switzerland.   As already indicated, many agreements of the   11–083
type typically notified to the Commission have typically provided for disputes to be resolved in arbitration in Switzerland. Some of the arbitrators
dealing with these matters have regarded themselves as prevented from
doing anything to encourage or require the parties to seek direction from the
Commission regarding the impact of Art.81(1) or Art.81(3) EC in the event
that a competition law issue is raised in a dispute before them. They have
regarded such acts as inconsistent with the obligations of privacy that they
owe to the parties that appoint them. At least some arbitrators in Switzerland have clearly regarded themselves as obliged to resolve any dispute
regarding Art.81(3) if possible. It has been argued that arbitrators are not
obliged to apply competition law in the same fashion as would DG Comp.
The arbitrators do not pretend to have the wider public issues before them
in the same way that the regulator would. Their obligations are only to the
parties before them.

> "An arbitral tribunal must sit back and reflect on the solution (or
> application) which does justice to the very particular parties, and which is
> the most appropriate under the prevailing circumstances ... arbitral tri-
> bunals should consider (or apply) competition laws (such as Arts 81 and
> 82 EC, etc) with a "distant look" which respects the objectively fair and
> the subjectively reasonable expectations of the parties; no more, no
> less."[75]

---

[73] An extensive discussion of the evidence which the Commission indicates should be adduced
to justify a finding that Art.81(3) applies is set out in paras 51 to 58 of the Guidelines on the
application of Article 81(3).
[74] Blessing, "Introduction to Arbitration—Swiss and International Perspectives" in *International Arbitration in Switzerland* (Berti ed., Aspen), pp.241–2.
[75] Blessing, n.74, above.

Under this approach the wider public interests provided for under Art.81(3) might be given little weight. The impact of competition policy on the particular agreement may therefore be materially different from that that would have applied if DG Comp had been considering the matter. This must affect the overall impact of competition policy upon the economy.

11–084 **Arbitral application of Article 81(3) and the Modernisation Regulation.** Some have been highly critical of the failure to address arbitration in the new system of competition law enforcement under Regulation 1/2003. Others regard this as a stroke of masterly inactivity. On the latter view the silence may reflect the position that there is no duty of loyalty or co-operation as between Commission and arbitration. Alternatively, it may be that there were so many difficulties in achieving adoption and implementation of the modernisation package that this additional difficulty had to be put to one side.

11–085 **Non-application by arbitrators.** As neither the Modernisation Regulation nor the accompanying guidance makes any reference to arbitration, it has been argued by some that Art.81(3) EC cannot be applied by arbitrators[76] as it raises matters of policy that arbitrators ought not to address. As already noted, this argument is redolent of the pre-*Mitsubishi* argument for denying the arbitrability of competition law as expressed in *American Safety Equipment Corp v JP Maguire & Co*[77] The procedural impact of this conclusion would be to produce bifurcated application of Art.81 in which the application of Art. 81(1) could be considered in arbitration, while any claim for individual exception under Art. 81(3) would have to be considered by a national court. That court would necessarily decide issues relating to contractual validity, even if such matters would normally be regarded as falling within the scope of the arbitration agreement. It is submitted, however, that if it had been intended to exclude competition law, or any part of it from the jurisdiction of arbitrators, some clear language would have had to have been used. The normal position is that legal disputes are resolved by courts, or arbitrators where the parties to the dispute have given them jurisdiction. In a claim concerning a contract in which its validity is in issue, that issue must be for the tribunal in the absence of an exceptional provision. The provisions of Regulation 17/62[78] were indeed such an exception from the normal approach of civil and arbitral procedure and with the removal of that procedure some clear means would have to be provided to keep any part of the dispute out of the jurisdiction of a validly appointed arbitrator.

11–086 **Analogy to restraint of trade.** In the English context, a comparison may be made with application of the restraint of trade doctrine which since the

---

[76] Lomas, "Arbitration: Jurisdiction over EC competition law issues" PLC, May 2004, p.12
[77] 391 F.2d 821 (2d Cir. 1968); see para.11–044, above.
[78] [1962] O.J. L13/204.

leading decision in *Nordenfelt v Maxim Nordenfelt Guns and Ammunition*[79] has justified restrictions in restraint of trade only if the restriction is reasonable by reference to both the interests of the parties concerned and by reference to the interests of the public. In judicial decisions the public interest, has often been neglected, conflated with the interests of the parties or dealt with superficially.[80] That element has remained, however, an element of the test that courts and arbitrators have been obliged to apply and there has been no suggestion that an arbitral tribunal seised of a dispute involving this issue would not have to determine both elements of the test. If the public interest issue has been dealt with superficially or inadequately in a case, it may be that the responsibility for this lies with the parties or their representation. It may be also that courts have been limited by the scope of evidence that might be regarded as admissible as to what constitutes the public interest.[81] In that regard, the more flexible approach of arbitration to admission of evidence may give it a distinct advantage over litigation in resolution of these issues.

Application of Article 81(3).   Some arbitrators have already treated themselves as being responsible for determining the applicability of Art.81(3) EC without any notification to the Commission. They have treated themselves as being required to resolve all such issues, albeit that they are not able to take advantage of the Commission's powers to take on board comments from others so as to establish take account of the wider impact of the agreement affected, whether that be by investigation or by seeking comments (for instance by advertisement under Art.19(3) of Regulation 17/62 in the former notification procedure).   **11–087**

Judicial review of decisions on Article 81(3).   As already noted, the scope for appeal on purely factual grounds from any arbitral award is either limited or non-existent in most jurisdictions. Given that any decision under Art.81(3) EC is likely to raise questions of fact and policy rather than law, it is difficult to see how any tribunal that takes a procedurally correct, but substantively erroneous approach to these matters can be corrected.   **11–088**

Certainty and Article 81(3) EC: validity and severance.   The procedural differences between the operation of an individual exemption application under Regulation 17/62 and the resolution of such issues in arbitration must have a number of other practical effects on the legal outcomes. One of the purposes of that procedure was to achieve a measure of comfort as to the validity of a contract. That can now only be achieved through a determination by a court, or an arbitrator. Arbitration raises an interesting route by   **11–089**

---

[79] [1894] A.C. 535.
[80] No doubt courts have been and remain concerned about the legitimacy of their role as interstitial legislator when applying policy concerns. Courts may therefore prefer to address public interest issues as if they were purely issues between the parties.
[81] *Mogul SS Co Ltd v McGregor, Gow & Co* [1892] A.C. 25 at 45.

which parties may be able to obtain some measure of the security that Regulation 17/62 once afforded. This is a particular opportunity for those who have regretted the passing of the individual exemption system. There are those who have expressed concern that in areas such as maritime law where London is an important centre for arbitration, that position may be jeopardised by the lack of any regulatory procedure for individual exemption under either UK or EC competition law. It is suggested that parties with maritime disputes will prefer to litigate them in locations in which the local NCA can grant, at least, a national exemption. It seems to me however that a more potent forum shopping factor may be the ability to obtain either a court order conferring validity upon an agreement for the entirety of its term, or perhaps better still an arbitration award from a panel of appropriate experts.

11–090   **Individual exemption.**   Individual exemption was previously granted for a limited period, and it was normal for there to be negotiations between the parties to a contract and the Commission as to the terms that would be acceptable. Under the notification procedure an agreement entered into for a term of say, 10 years, might be found to benefit from an exemption for only five years and altered accordingly. In the new regime, under English rules of severability of contracts it is unlikely that the valid five years could be severed from the invalid period. The invalidity over part of the term would probably cause the entire agreement to fail. Of course, some boiler plate severability clauses do try to save a contract to the extent that it is valid, but I doubt whether even the most careful drafting would be able to help here.[82]

11–091   **Possible solutions.**   If two parties to an agreement wish to bind each other to an agreement, the best they may be able to do now to achieve some measure of certainty as between each other is to refer the applicability of Art.81(3) EC to their agreement to arbitration. At least as between themselves there will be a final and binding award as to the validity of the contract. It might be possible in a dispute over the validity of a contract to seek a declaration in respect of its entire term. Alternatively, if there is difficulty as to the term to which an exemption is applicable, or regarding the provisions of some other potentially objectionable conditions, the arbitrator could be asked to determine the applicability of Art.81(3) EC to a range of alternative terms, or on the basis of various altered contractual arrangements.

11–092   **Transience of an award.**   Regardless, however, of how the dispute was referred to the arbitration, the award applying Art.81 (3) EC may only be

---

[82] See Whish, "The Enforceability of Agreements under EC and UK Competition Law" in *Lex Mercatoria: Essays on International Commercial Law in Honour of Francis Reynolds* (LLP Professional Publishers, London, 2000).

binding as a snapshot stating that at a particular time a contract was or was not valid. The decision of the court of Appeal in *Passmore v Morland*[83] which establishes that an agreement may only be transiently void applies also, presumably, to the impact of Art.81(3) EC on the validity of an agreement. The transience of the award is likely to depend to a great degree, though, on the quality of the analysis in the original decision. Perhaps it is appropriate to devise arbitration rules specifically for competition disputes and a panel of appropriate arbitrators to address just these types of issues so that the award that is produced can be seen to address all the relevant Art.81(3) issues appropriately and be treated as conclusive for all practical purposes for the entirety of the term of the contract, despite the threat of transient voidness. Arbitration could provide a form of privatised exemption (and negative clearance) system.

---

[83] [1999] 3 All E.R. 1005; although this decision is controversial, similar issues about changes in the validity of an agreement over time are raised in the Commission Guidelines on the application of Article 81(3) EC [2004] O.J. C101/97 (especially paras 44 and 45).

CHAPTER 12

UNDERSTANDING ECONOMIC EVIDENCE

Meredith Pickford[1] and Paul Reynolds[2]

1. INTRODUCTION

12–001   **Purpose of the chapter.**   This chapter introduces key economic concepts and tools relevant to competition law. Its purpose is to provide practical assistance to the non-economist reader when working with economic evidence in:

- understanding the underlying approach typically[3] taken by economists to competition issues;

- focusing on what issues are critical to an economic appraisal of a competition case; and

- understanding key theoretical and empirical tools that economists often use to assess these issues.

12–002   **Scheme of the chapter.**   The chapter is arranged as follows:

- Section 2 introduces key economic issues which arise when considering competition cases:

  (a) it introduces key areas which are required for a full understanding of competition: (i) core concepts and objectives of competition policy; and (ii) models of how firms behave. The concepts introduced in this first subsection may appear somewhat abstract, but they are intended to provide a (highly condensed) guide to the economics which underpins the analysis which follows. Reader's who, however, wish to avoid this more abstract section should skip to paras 12–003–12–018.

---

[1] Barrister, Monckton Chambers.
[2] Principal, Charles River Associates.
[3] The authors present their view of the orthodox economic approach; clearly, this view may not necessarily be shared by every practising economist.

(b) it then builds on the concepts considered in (a) to introduce an analytical framework for assessing the economic questions which arise in competition cases: (i) describing the concepts of effective competition and market power; (ii) explaining how economists go about defining markets; and (iii) explaining various extensions to the basic concepts of market analysis.

(c) finally, it explains the analytical tools which economists use to assess market power and competition including: (i) market shares and concentration; (ii) barriers to expansion, entry and exit; (iii) buyer power; (iv) collective dominance; and (v) what may be learnt from the actual conduct of undertakings.

- Section 3 then examines the empirical tools which economists use in understanding key theoretical issues and examines the main quantitative techniques currently employed by professional economists.

2. KEY ECONOMIC ISSUES UNDERLYING COMPETITION CASES

(a) Understanding competition

(i) Core concepts and objectives of competition policy

Competition: rivalry versus outcomes. Competition law is fundamentally about the protection of competition. In a general sense, competition is a *process of rivalry*[4] between firms as they strive to achieve their particular business objectives, such as higher profits or sales. However, the development of competition law has shown that there is often a need to go beyond competition viewed merely as a process and to focus also on *outcomes*. This is necessary to prevent competition law being applied too broadly so as to prohibit behaviour[5] that, whilst changing the form of competition, would leave customers unaffected or, indeed, make them better off. For example, a key benefit of competition is that it leads to production being undertaken by only the most efficient firms that are capable of producing the good or service in question. Thus the exit of an inefficient producer, which may have the effect of lowering industry costs, can be considered as a natural outcome of competition and need not be viewed as being inimical to the competitive process.

12–003

Tests for promoting competition: maximising welfare. The above discussion prompts consideration of what outcomes competition can be expected to

12–004

---

[4] See, for example, Competition Commission Guidelines on Merger References (June, 2003) CC2 at para.1.20.

[5] Unless otherwise indicated "behaviour" is used very broadly in this chapter to include any actions, agreements, practices or other arrangements which may be under consideration from an economic perspective.

achieve and what can provide a meaningful test of whether particular behaviour promotes or harms competition. Particular consumer benefits generated by firms competing may include lower prices, higher quality products and a greater range of products on offer. More generally, competition is desirable to the extent that it promotes the *maximisation of welfare*.

12–005 **Social welfare versus consumer welfare.** While economists tend to focus on *social* welfare (that is, overall living standards, including firms' profits), Community and UK competition law has instead tended to give primacy to *consumer* welfare[6] (that is, the sum of benefits to consumers).[7] For example, s.33(2) of the Enterprise Act allows for the possibility of customer benefits potentially outweighing concerns that a merger would lead to a substantial lessening of competition; but it does not allow for a more general efficiency criterion which also takes account of higher firms' profits arising, for example, from cost savings.

12–006 **Key cost concepts.** Before examining how economists generally assess the effects of economic behaviour on welfare, it is helpful to introduce core cost concepts which permeate the following discussion:

- *Marginal cost*: the cost of producing an additional unit of output;

- *Variable cost*: any cost that varies with changes in output (for example, raw material costs may be variable);

- *Average variable cost*: total variable costs per unit of output; this is equal to total variable costs divided by total output;

- *Fixed cost*: a cost that does not change with changes in output (for example, the cost of building plant will be fixed in the short run)[8];

- *Common cost*: a cost which is incurred in the production of two or more products and that does not vary with changes in output of any one product (for example, general investment in a company's brand may support the sales of a range of products supplied by the company).

---

[6] The adoption of a consumer welfare standard, rather than a general social welfare standard, represents a strong distributional judgment that attaches full weight to, say, the welfare of the customers of two companies proposing to merge and attaches no weight to the welfare of those who have a claim on the future income of those companies.

[7] A further specific feature of Community competition law has been its objective in achieving market integration: see for example, Cases 56/64 and 58/64 *Consten and Gundig v Commission* [1966] E.C.R. 299 at 340.

[8] The "short run" is that period in which at least one cost is fixed. The "long-run" is that period long enough to enable all costs to be varied. Understanding firm behaviour frequently requires taking into account the time period in which the business decision is being made. For example, in the short-run a firm may be prepared to keep operating even if market prices only enable it to cover its variable costs as it will incur its fixed costs even if it ceased production. However, in the long-run, a firm can only be expected to want to stay in business if it is able to recover all its costs.

- *Sunk costs*: the proportion of costs that are not recoverable if a firm exits an industry (such as advertising spent on a product that is withdrawn).

Assessing welfare: three types of economic efficiency. In considering effects on welfare, three elements of economic efficiency can be distinguished: "allocative", "productive" and "dynamic" efficiency. Examining the impact of the matter being investigated on each of the three elements of efficiency provides the basis for an assessment of the overall effect on competition. **12–007**

Allocative efficiency. Allocative efficiency requires that the resources in an economy are allocated to the production of the mix of goods and services that provides maximum benefit to society. Economic theory shows that this is achieved under certain assumptions where the price of each product equals its marginal cost. The assumptions that are required for this result include that there are no fixed or common costs or externalities,[9] consumers have perfect information about products, and there are no public goods[10] being considered. Where these assumptions do not hold, then the simple relationship between price and marginal cost breaks down: **12–008**

- Where firms have significant fixed and/or common costs (as they often do) in the long run they must recover these costs in addition to their marginal costs. The manner in which these costs are recovered in individual prices will have important implications for allocative efficiency. In particular, the theory of "Ramsey pricing" shows that allocative efficiency will be maximised where a greater proportion of fixed and common costs are recovered from the products for which demand is relatively unresponsive to price ("price inelastic"). Thus both cost and demand factors will often be relevant to determining efficient prices.

- Further, the production or consumption of a product may also give rise to externalities which need to be taken into account in determining the allocatively efficient outcome. For example, there may be benefits to existing subscribers to a telecommunications network from another subscriber's decision to join the network. These may require subscriptions to be priced below marginal cost to achieve maximum allocative efficiency.

Productive efficiency. Productive efficiency refers to the goods and services in an economy being produced at the least possible cost. This concept **12–009**

---

[9] Externalities are effects on other individuals that are not party to the particular transaction in issue.

[10] A public good is a good such as national defence which is "non-excludable" in the sense that once it is provided to one consumer it is provided to all, and is "non-rival" in the sense that one person's consumption does not reduce the consumption available to other consumers.

captures gains both from production being undertaken by the most efficient firms and from individual firms minimising their own production costs. The economic notion of productive efficiency coincides with the non-technical use of the word efficiency such as used in reference to the "efficiencies", or cost savings, created by a merger.

12–010 **Dynamic efficiency.**   Dynamic efficiency refers to the maximisation of welfare over the long run and requires that firms have the right incentives to invest and innovate so as to improve the quality and range of products and increase productivity and lower costs through time.

12–011 **Tensions between the types of efficiency.**   There can be tensions between these three types of efficiency. For example, the prices that are required to achieve dynamic efficiency in terms of providing a sufficient incentive for risky investments may be greater than marginal cost and therefore involve some allocative inefficiency. The existence of such tensions requires judgements in relation to the likely magnitude of the differing effects of behaviour so that the overall impact on competition and welfare can be determined. Economists often attach particular significance to the promotion of dynamic efficiency in raising living standards because it can engender a stream of innovations that give rise to entirely new products and that lower costs and prices through time. In contrast, an improvement in allocative efficiency may be limited to the benefit of a one-off alignment of prices with the current level of costs. A key problem with focussing on dynamic efficiency, however, is that it is often difficult to measure in practice.

(ii) Models of firm behaviour

12–012 **Two paradigms: perfect competition and monopoly.**   A number of economic models exist which provide insights into how changes in competitive conditions affect efficiency and welfare. At the two extremes are the models of perfect competition and monopoly. The model of perfect competition assumes that there are a sufficiently large number of buyers and sellers in a market so that no one buyer or seller can influence the market price.[11] Perfect competition can be shown to lead to prices being set in line with marginal costs and with the industry operating at the lowest point of its average cost curve and thus achieves the key conditions required to attain allocative and productive efficiency. At the other extreme is a monopoly, where there is only one seller of the good or service (or a monopsony where there is only one buyer of the good or service). A monopoly is the quintessential example of a firm with "market power".[12]

---

[11] Other key assumptions of the model are that there are no barriers to entry (see paras 12–037–12–039, below), the firms sell a homogeneous product and that all buyers and sellers have perfect information.

[12] See paras 12–022–12–023, below.

Monopoly inefficiency.   Monopolies can involve substantial inefficiency.   **12–013**

- *Allocative efficiency*: In particular, monopolies may seek to maximise their profits by generating a higher price through restricting output (compared with the competitive output level). A key consequence is that some consumers who would be prepared to pay the lower competitive price for the product would not be able to acquire the product and thus they lose the "consumer surplus"[13] they would otherwise have gained on consuming those products; other consumers who continue to consume but at a higher price will also lose some consumer surplus. The loss in "total surplus"[14] as a result of a monopolist restricting supply is known as the "deadweight loss" and formally represents a loss in allocative efficiency. (In addition to this effect on allocative efficiency, monopoly pricing also has a distributional impact, in that it gives rise to a transfer of benefits from consumers to producers; that is, for the products that are sold, consumers pay a higher price than they would in a competitive market, and the firm makes correspondingly higher profits.)

- *Productive inefficiency*: The relationship between competition and productive efficiency is less clear-cut. The owners of all firms, including a monopoly, generally have the incentive for their firm to operate at least cost. Thus it might be thought that the degree of competition would have little impact on the achievement of productive efficiency. However, owners need the means by which to know if their firm is operating as efficiently as possible so as to avoid managerial slack. In such a case, the existence of competitors can be important to provide a "yardstick" with which to measure the firm's performance. Competitors can also provide extra discipline on a firm's management and workforce to keep down costs so that the firm, and their own jobs, remain viable. The underlying technology of the industry will also be relevant to achieving productive efficiency. For example, some products may only be efficiently supplied by a small number of firms[15] and thus accommodation of additional firms within a market may lead to productive inefficiency with a consequent loss in consumer welfare.

- *Dynamic efficiency*: The relationship between particular competitive conditions and the promotion of dynamic efficiency is even more

---

[13] Consumer surplus represents the difference between the value that consumers gain from consuming a product (that is, how much they would be willing to pay) and the price that they actually pay for the product.

[14] A transaction may also give rise to producer surplus in terms of the difference that the producer receives and the amount that they would be prepared to sell the good for. The sum of consumer and producer surplus is total surplus.

[15] In the extreme, the lowest cost way of supplying some products may be to have only one firm in the market, that is, a situation economists label "natural monopoly". Industries that involve physical distribution networks to customers' premises, such as water and electricity distribution, tend to be natural monopolies as it will not normally be cost-effective for there to be more than one power line or water pipe to an individual house.

complex. Empirical research has not found a simple relationship between market structure and innovation across industries.[16] Both the level of market concentration and the amount of innovation appear to be driven by more fundamental factors such as innovative opportunities, institutional factors, the characteristics of demand and the historical path of technological innovation. The implications of the research are that in some dynamically competitive industries, a high level of market concentration may be inevitable and should not be taken as implying market power.[17] For example, in industries subject to rapid technological change (such as many consumer electronics industries), a firm that is leading the market at one time may be entirely displaced in the space of a few years by an entrant that develops a superior product. In such dynamic industries, it can be critical to analyse potential competition, taking into account factors such as whether market shares have shifted significantly over time and the rate of technological change.

12–014 **The Structure-Conduct-Performance ("SCP") approach.** Most real-world markets do not match either the textbook models of perfect competition or monopoly. Even in markets with many firms, there may be a degree of product differentiation in the sense that consumers do not regard the products supplied by the different firms as identical (such markets are described by economists as "monopolistically competitive"). Further, there are many markets in which only a few firms supply the bulk of the market (termed "oligopolies"). Economic theory shows that the outcomes of markets that fall between the two extremes of perfect competition and monopoly can vary significantly depending on the particular characteristics of the market and the behaviour of the firms within that market. The SCP approach suggests that market structure (for example concentration, barriers to entry, etc.) determines the conduct of firms (for example their pricing behaviour, marketing activities, investment in research and development, etc.) that, in turn, determine the outcomes of the market as a whole (efficiency, profits, innovation, etc.).[18] However, there is a need to avoid ready presumptions that changes in one aspect of a market's structure must imply a change in outcomes. In particular, empirical research provides little support for the

---

[16] For an overview of the literature, see G. Symeonidis, "Innovation, firm size and market structure: Schumpeterian hypotheses and some new themes" (1996) *OECD Economics Department Working Papers*, No.161.

[17] For a fuller discussion of the exercise of competition law in relation to dynamically competitive markets see OFT Economic Discussion Paper 3, *Innovation and competition policy*, OFT 377, March 2002, prepared by Charles River Associates. A summary of approaches by different competition authorities is provided in OECD, "Merger Review in Emerging High Innovation Markets" (DAFFE/COMP(2002)20), June 24, 2003.

[18] See, for example, F.M. Scherer, *Industrial Market Structure and Economic Performance* (Rand McNally and Co, Chicago, 1970).

view that structure systematically determines conduct and performance.[19] Further, the direction of causation is not one way. For example, a firm may become large if it develops better ways than its competitors at meeting customer demand. In such a case, higher market concentration may reflect better customer outcomes whereas the SCP model may suggest the opposite.

Contestability theory.   Importantly, it is by no means the case that market outcomes become steadily more like those of a monopoly the fewer firms there are in a market. Even a small number of firms may be sufficient to generate competitive outcomes in some markets. "Contestability theory" establishes the conditions under which the *threat of entry* will lead to efficient pricing even when there is only one firm or a few firms in the market.[20] These conditions are that entrants do not suffer any disadvantage relative to existing firms (such as cost or informational disadvantages), there are no sunk costs and that new firms can enter and supply the market before existing firms can adjust their prices. While contestability theory requires that demanding assumptions are fulfilled to ensure competitive outcomes, it has helped to highlight the implications of particular market characteristics, such as the significance of sunk costs in discouraging entry.[21] Another example of a type of market in which only a few firms may be sufficient to generate efficient outcomes is where competition takes place by way of a bidding contest.[22]

12–015

Strategic firm behaviour and game theory.   "Game theory"[23] is an approach to understanding markets in which there is strategic interaction between firms with each firm taking into account the behaviour of its rivals. In practice, assumptions made about the manner in which firms behave strategically may be as significant as structural characteristics in explaining or predicting the outcomes in a market. A central assumption of many economic models is that firms' decisions are determined rationally (that is, no systematic errors) and are aimed at maximising profits and thus firms' behaviour can be predicted by logically following through the implications of the profit maximising assumption in a particular case. Two long-established models examine profit maximising outcomes when the key

12–016

---

[19] A survey of this research is provided in R. Schmalensee, "Inter-industry studies of structure and performance" in *Handbook of Industrial Organization* (R. Schmalensee and R.D. Willig ed., North-Holland, Amsterdam, 1989).

[20] W.J. Baumol, J.C. Panzar and R.D. Willig, *Contestable Markets and the Theory of Industry Structure* (Harcourt Brace Jovanovich, San Diego, 1982).

[21] Competition authorities sometimes used the term contestable more loosely to refer to any market with low barriers to entry. Contestability was taken into account in the OFT's report on the proposed acquisition by EasyJet Plc of NewGo 1 Limited (A report under s.125(4) Fair Trading Act 1973 on the advice given on July 10, 2002 to the Secretary of State for Trade and Industry under s.76 of the Act).

[22] See paras 12–090–12–092, below on bidding studies.

[23] For examples of the implications of game theory in competition policy, see G. Norman and J.F. Thisse ed., *Market structure and competition policy : game theoretic approaches* (Cambridge University Press, Cambridge, 2000).

variable being set by firms is quantity (the *Cournot* model) or price (the *Betrand* model).

12–017 **Further theoretical developments.** More recently, "Experimental Economics" has sought to test how human decision-makers behave in reality, and whether biases may be expected to affect decisions, particularly in relation to risks and uncertainty.[24] Further, "New Institutional Economics" focuses on the implications of the institutional setting in which competition takes place in an industry, such as how transactions occur, the information available to each party and whether supplier/buyer relationships are long-term.[25] Advancements in the understanding of the significance of institutional features have been particularly significant in the recognition that many forms of vertical restraints serve to promote consumer welfare.[26]

12–018 **Conclusion.** With the proliferation of economic models, it might be thought that the value of economic theory in competition law has become debased: that an economic model can be developed to support or condemn any behaviour being investigated. However, it is submitted that the use of economic theory is inescapable because critical questions in competition law relate to hypothetical issues, such as what would have occurred absent the business conduct being investigated or what will occur in the future if a merger is allowed. It is economic theory, used implicitly or expressly, that allows these questions to be answered. However, determining which theory should be relied upon requires a thorough assessment of the potentially applicable theories and their assumptions against the institutional setting and facts of the matter in question. Thus, empirical analysis will often be critical.[27] However, before discussing how empirical techniques can provide answers it is necessary to know what questions to ask. The remainder of this section discusses questions of general relevance relating to market definition and the assessment of market power.

(b) A framework for assessing competition and competitive constraints

12–019 **Introduction.** The previous section outlined some of the key factors influencing consumer welfare and in particular how market structures,

---

[24] An example of the use of experimental economics, in this case to examine how changes in concentration in the US cable industry affect the flow of programming to consumers, is M. Bykowsky, A. Kwasnica & W. Sharkey, "Horizontal Concentration in the Cable Television Industry: An Experimental Analysis", *FCC Office of Plans and Policy Working Paper 35*, June 2002.

[25] For a discussion of some of the implications of New Institutional Economics in competition policy, see P. L. Joskow, "The Role of Transactions Cost Economics in Antitrust and Public Utility Regulatory Policies" (1991) 7 (Special Issue) *Journal of Law, Economics and Organization* 53–82.

[26] See Bellamy & Child, *European Community Law of Competition* (5th ed., Sweet & Maxwell, London, 2001), para.7–005 for a discussion of how economic analysis increasingly pervades the Commission's approach to vertical restraints.

[27] See paras 12–045–12–095, below for a discussion of empirical techniques.

institutional arrangements and firms' strategic behaviour interact to influence economic efficiency. In translating economic theory into competition law, a number of general concepts have proved useful as analytical tools which underpin much competition law.

(i) Concepts of effective competition and market power

Effective competition. It is argued above[28] that the concept of competition needs to be considered not just in terms of a process of rivalry but also in terms of consumer outcomes. Flowing from this, the concept of "effective competition"[29] can usefully be considered as a situation in which it is not possible, in practice, to improve the functioning of the market so that overall consumer welfare would be higher. The objective of competition policy can then be stated as preventing the behaviour of a firm or firms from impeding the attainment of effective competition. Two key concepts related to effective competition are the legal concept of dominance and the economic concept of market power.

12–020

Dominance. The ECJ has characterised dominance in the following way:

12–021

> "The dominant position thus referred to by Article [82] relates to a position of economic strength enjoyed by an undertaking which enables it to prevent effective competition being maintained on the relevant market by affording it the power to behave to an appreciable extent independently of its competitors, customers and ultimately of its consumers."[30]

While different commentators have focused on different aspects of this definition, from an economic perspective the key element is the ability of a firm (or firms) to act sufficiently free from competitive constraints so that effective competition is not attained. This interpretation aligns dominance with the notion of "significant market power".

Significant Market Power ("SMP"). Market power is usually understood to refer to the ability of a firm profitably to raise prices above the competitive level by restricting output for a sustained period of time.[31] As noted

12–022

---

[28] para.12–003.
[29] The concept of effective competition is repeatedly found in competition law. For example, Art.2(3) of the EC's Merger Regulation prohibits concentrations that would significantly impede effective competition, in particular as a result of the creation or strengthening of a dominant position.
[30] Case 27/76 *United Brands v Commission* [1978] E.C.R. 207 at para.38.
[31] See, for example, the Commission guidelines on market analysis and the assessment of significant market power under the Community regulatory framework for electronic communications networks and services [2002] O.J. C165/6, para.73. While we focus the discussion on the ability to raise price, we also note that market power may take other forms, such as the ability of a firm to exclude competitors from the market.

above,[32] the ability to raise prices by restricting output is the key reason why monopoly leads to a loss in welfare compared with competitive markets. Thus, the greater the degree of market power the closer the market outcomes will be to those of a monopoly. Given that a finding of dominance, or even the risk of such a finding, can significantly restrict the conduct of a firm it is desirable that a finding of dominance is only made where firms possess significant market power, that is, where the market power would lead to outcomes significantly different to the outcomes under effective competition, so that intervention would have a reasonable prospect of improving consumer outcomes.

12–023 **Identifying market power.** If market power is interpreted as the ability of a firm to price above the competitive level then it might be thought that identifying the existence of market power would simply involve a comparison of prevailing market prices with those that would be attained under effective competition. However, seeking to identify the effectively competitive price level is generally a substantial and difficult task. The results of analysis tend to be highly sensitive to input assumptions, and factors such as how a "reasonable" return on capital is determined; they therefore involve a significant risk of error.[33] Reflecting these difficulties, market power tends in practice to be identified by reference to a range of indirect indicators, including market concentration, barriers to entry and expansion as well as the actual conduct of firms within the market. However, before discussing how market power can be assessed, the following section first introduces the concept of the relevant market and the role of market definition in competition investigations.

(ii) Defining markets

12–024 **Introduction.** Market definition often assumes a central role in many competition law cases, particularly in considering the effect on competition of a merger, agreement or conduct, and in considering whether a dominant position exists or would come into existence. Competition and dominance are thus both concepts that may be seen as relating to particular markets.[34] The European Commission has explained the general role of market definition as follows:

---

[32] para.12–013.

[33] See, for example, F. M. Fisher and J. J. McGowan, "On the misuse of accounting rates of return to infer monopoly profits" *American Economic Review*, March 1983, p.82–97.

[34] That said, some commentators have criticised the prominence that is often given to market definition, particularly if it comes at the expense of the analysis of the ultimate matter of interest—the effect on competition. For example, see S. Salop, "The first principles approach to antitrust, Kodak and antitrust at the millennium" *Georgetown University Law Center 1999 Working Paper Series in Law in Business and Economics*, No.195490. Nonetheless, whether or not market definition is analytically useful in a particular case, it is often a necessary legal step.

"Market definition is a tool to identify and define the boundaries of competition between firms ... The objective of defining a market in both its product and geographic dimension is to identify those actual competitors of the undertakings involved that are capable of constraining those undertakings' behaviour and of preventing them from behaving independently of effective competitive pressure."[35]

As is clear from the Commission's Notice, market definition in competition law serves a particular purpose and is distinct from more general market concepts such as may be used in business strategy.[36] Market definition is a tool that can aid competition analysis by identifying those products and firms that offer a significant constraint on the products of the firms under investigation. Market definition has been attractive to practitioners wishing to make inferences about market power from market shares. However, as discussed below[37] there are dangers in inferring too much from market shares and the market definition exercise needs to be integrated with the competitive analysis so that they form part of one consistent framework.

Substitutability. At the core of market definition is the concept of "substitutability". A firm will face greater competitive constraints the more readily consumers switch away from its product to other products when the firm raises the price of its product relative to the price of the other products (or reduces the relative quality of its product). If a sufficiently large number of customers switch, the firm will not be able to increase its profits by raising its price; indeed its profits might fall.[38] In addition to demand-side substitutability, supply-side substitutability may also be present. In particular, a firm may be constrained in raising its price if other firms would readily switch their production facilities to supplying products that take demand away from the firm.[39]   **12–025**

The hypothetical Monopolist or "SSNIP" test. Substitutability can be used,   **12–026**
in practice, to delineate the relevant market by means of the "hypothetical monopolist test", also known as the "SSNIP" test, where SSNIP stands for

---

[35] Commission Notice on the definition of the relevant market for the purposes of Community Competition Law (O.J. C372) December 9, 1997, para.2.

[36] It is also the case that a market definition that is used for a product in relation to one competition law case may differ to the market definition used in a case involving a different type of competition issue even when the same product is involved.

[37] para.12–036.

[38] Note that it is changes in relative prices causing changes in demand that acts as the constraint. Even if one product is priced significantly above a lower quality product, the two products may still be in the same market if, say, the effect of the first product becoming relatively more expensive is that there is a significant drop in sales of that product as demand switches to the lower quality product.

[39] Analytically, it is somewhat arbitrary whether the possibility for a firm to switch production to supply competing products should be considered as part of market definition or in the subsequent assessment of market power. However, to the extent that particular significance is attached to market shares then it is important in defining the market to take into account supply-side substitutability that can effectively constrain the behaviour of the firm.

"Small but Significant Non-transitory Increase in Price".[40] The test asks whether a hypothetical monopolist over a particular product or collection of products in a given geographic area could maximise profits by raising prices by 5–10 per cent for a sustained period, assuming the prices of other products remain constant. When conducting the test, the starting point is the smallest conceivable market (often the product and geographic area supplied by the firm under investigation—although a firm might have market power, for example, in a number of discrete geographic markets, thus requiring some care in the choice of starting point). If a hypothetical monopolist supplying only that product in that area could maximise its profits by raising prices by 5–10 per cent, then that product and area constitute a relevant market. If it could not, because of substitution from competing products or the supply of the product from other areas, then the market needs to be widened either by the inclusion of those substitute products or a wider geographic area. The relevant market is the smallest set of products and areas for which the hypothetical monopolist test is met.

12–027 **Applying the hypothetical monopolist test.** The hypothetical monopolist test has proven to be a useful way to organise the analysis of competitive constraints and advances the analysis beyond an ad hoc identification of factors that might make two products substitutes for each other. While the test provides a way to approach the assessment of competitive constraints that can be useful in qualitative analysis, it also leads to the following two key empirical questions: (i) what amount of sales would need to be lost to make the hypothesised price rise unprofitable (this volume is known as the "critical loss")[41]; and (ii) how many sales would actually be lost? Evidence in relation to both questions can then be compared to help delineate the relevant market.[42]

12–028 **Difficulties with the hypothetical monopolist test: the "Cellophane Fallacy".** The hypothetical monopolist test lends itself readily to the assessment of the competitive effects of a merger, where the concern is whether prices post-merger would be raised above the prevailing price level. However, where market definition is being undertaken to determine whether a firm or firms currently face constraints that are effective at preventing prices from rising above competitive levels the test is less useful and, if applied incorrectly, can be highly misleading. All firms can be expected to set prices to maximise

---

[40] The SSNIP test was first deployed by the US Department of Justice and the Federal Trade Commission in their *Horizontal Merger Guidelines* issued in 1982.

[41] The practical application of critical loss analysis is discussed at paras 12–083–12–086, below. For an overview of the current literature on critical loss analysis see B.C. Harris, *Recent Observations About Critical Loss Analysis*, presentation to FTC/DOJ Joint Workshop on Merger Enforcement, February 17, 2004.

[42] Many practitioners incorrectly base market definition on only a partial analysis, such as concluding that two products are in the same market if there is some substitution between them without considering whether the degree of substitution is sufficiently strong to cause a critical loss in sales. An examination of both questions is required.

profits. In the case of a firm with market power, prices can be expected to be set above the competitive level and, in particular, up to the level at which any further price rise would be unprofitable because the margin on lost sales outweighs the additional margin on remaining ones. Examining substitutability at the prevailing price level might lead to the finding that the firm faces competitive constraints from other products and wrongly lead to the inference that the firm does not have market power. This error is referred to as the "Cellophane Fallacy" after a case involving cellophane in which the problem was not recognised by the US Supreme Court in its analysis.[43] The more limited use that can be made of the hypothetical monopolist test in non-merger cases is discussed in Bishop and Walker.[44]

(iii) Extensions to the basic concepts of market analysis

Chains of substitution. In some cases, there may be a "chain of substitution" between products so that two products form part of the same market even when there is no direct competitive interaction between them. For example, the pricing of a firm in area A may competitively constrain the pricing of a firm operating in the margins of areas A and B which, in turn, may constrain the pricing of a firm operating in area B. In such a case, all three firms could be in the same market even though there is no direct demand or supply-substitutability between two of them. The relevant question is whether the extent of the constraint imposed across the chain is sufficient in relation to the products under investigation to justify the inclusion of the products that are not directly substitutable.

Cluster markets. A "cluster market" approach recognises that in some industries, competition takes place in relation to the supply of bundles (or clusters) of products.[45] For instance, banks generally provide retail customers with a group of transaction services through their branch networks. More generally, cluster markets arise where there are complementarities in supply or demand so that it is cheaper to supply the products together or for consumers to purchase the products together. In such cases, a firm attempting to sell one of the products individually may not be able to compete with firms making joint offerings. Consequently, it may be appropriate to define the market in relation to the supply of the bundle of products rather than separate individual product markets.

Aftermarkets. A similar situation may arise where consumers purchase an initial durable product and then acquire complementary products (such as spare parts or consumables) at a later date. The technical specification of the

12–029

12–030

12–031

---

[43] *United States v EI du Pont de Nemour and Co*, 351 U.S. 377 (1956).
[44] S. Bishop and M. Walker, *The Economics of EC Competition Law: Concepts, application and evidence* (2nd ed., Sweet & Maxwell, London, 2002), p.100–104.
[45] For a further discussion, see, I. Ayres, "Rationalizing Antitrust Cluster Markets" (1985) 95 Yale L.J. 109.

primary product may limit the range of secondary products that are compatible with the primary product. In such cases, there may be a need to determine whether it is appropriate to define a market for the system (that is, both primary and secondary products) or a separate "aftermarket" limited to the secondary product(s) that are compatible with each primary product. The analysis would need to consider whether a firm would be constrained from raising prices for the secondary product because a sufficient number of customers would switch away from buying the primary product, thereby reducing sales of the related secondary product. If the firm was so constrained, this would indicate that the market should be a defined for the system as a whole.

12–032 **Two-sided or multi-sided markets.** Two-sided (or multi-sided) markets are markets for platforms that enable interactions between different types of customers and in which the price charged to one side of the market affects the volumes on the other side.[46] Examples include: newspapers—which may be priced low to readers to increase sales and thereby attract more advertisers; credit cards—which may be priced to attract customers to the network to boost merchant acceptance; and mobile phones—where the price of phone subscription may affect the volumes of calls to an operator's network. Competition analysis of such markets can be misleading if it considers only one side of the market and fails to consider the interactions between the two sides.

(c) Assessing competition and market power

12–033 **Introduction.** Market definition lends itself readily to the measurement of market shares which can potentially be used to draw inferences about market power. In this section, we discuss the use (and abuse) of market share information in the assessment of market power as well as other indicators that should also be examined to determine whether a firm has the power to price above the competitive level. Ultimately, the assessment should rest on whether the particular characteristics of the market, and the manner in which they interact, is likely to effectively constrain the behaviour of the firm under investigation.

(i) Market shares and market concentration

12–034 **The SCP approach.** The SCP approach[47] suggests that market structure determines the conduct of firms and conduct, in turn, determines the ultimate market outcomes. When practitioners consider market structure, they tend to look foremost at market shares. For a given market demand and

---

[46] For a fuller discussion, see D. Evans, "The Antitrust Economics of Multi-Sided Platform Markets" (2003) 20(2) *Yale Journal on Regulation* 325 at 325–82.
[47] See para.12–014, above.

elasticity of supply[48] of other firms (and subject to certain assumptions about the nature of competition), the larger a firm's market share, the less elastic will be the demand facing the firm. In other words, a firm with a larger market share will tend to suffer a smaller proportionate loss in sales if it raises its price while the other firms in the market hold their prices constant. The conclusion of this analysis is that a firm with a larger market share is more likely to be able profitably to set a higher price than a firm in the same market with a smaller market share. Under the case law, there is a presumption of single firm dominance where a firm has a market share above 50 per cent,[49] although the Commission has raised concerns where firms have held market shares lower than 40 per cent in a few cases.[50]

Market concentration and the Herfindhal-Hirschman Index. Where the concern is with the competitiveness of a market in general (and particularly the potential for co-ordination amongst firms) then it is useful to consider overall market concentration in addition to individual firms' market shares.[51] The Herfindhal-Hirschman Index ("HHI") provides a measure of market concentration and is defined as the sum of the squared market shares of all firms in the market.[52] The European Commission and US Federal Trade Commission and Department of Justice calculate the HHI post-merger and the change in the HHI ("delta") that would result from the merger as part of the initial determination of the likely effects of a merger.[53] The HHI is superior to simpler measures of concentration based on the shares of only the leading firms in that it takes into account the relative sizes of the leading firms and the position of smaller firms.　　12–035

Problems with the use market shares. There are a number of specific problems with the use of market shares and market concentration:　　12–036

- first, the measurement of market shares and market concentration can be highly dependent on the definition of the relevant market. If a

---

[48] The elasticity of supply of the other firms measures the extent to which they increase the quantity they supply in response to a price rise. See W. L. Landes and R. A. Posner, "Market Power in Antitrust Cases" (1981) 94 Harvard L.R. 937 at 946, n.13.

[49] Case C–62/86 *AKZO Chemie v Commission* [1991] E.C.R. I–3359 at para.60

[50] See Commission Guidelines on the assessment of horizontal mergers under the Council Regulation on the control of concentrations between undertakings [2004] O.J. C31/5, para.17; *Virgin/British Airways* [2000] O.J. L 30/1, dismissed on appeal as Case T–219/1999 *British Airways v Commission* [2004] 4 C.M.L.R. 19.

[51] The factors impacting on the likelihood of tacit collusion are discussed in paras 12–042– 12–043, below. Higher overall market concentration may also imply higher firm margins in *Cournot* models.

[52] For example, a market with three firms with market shares of 50, 30 and 20% will have an HHI of 3800 ($= 50^2 + 30^2 + 20^2 = 2500 + 900 + 400$).

[53] For example, the EC's Guidelines on the assessment of horizontal mergers under the Council Regulation on the control of concentrations between undertakings, n.50, above, note in para.20 that "the Commission is also unlikely to identify horizontal competition concerns in a merger with a post-merger HHI between 1000 and 2000 and a delta below 250, or a merger with a post-merger HHI above 2000 and a delta below 150, except where special circumstances ... are present."

market is defined too broadly then the resulting market shares will underestimate the ability of firms within that market to raise their prices above competitive levels and conversely a market definition that is too narrow will overestimate a firm's market power;

- secondly, the use of historical data may fail to capture foreseeable changes in market conditions that can have large impacts on the competitive dynamics of a market;

- thirdly, focussing on market definition may lead to the false conclusion that all products within the market offer equally significant competitive constraints and that products outside the market make no contribution to the overall constraint on the firm. In many cases, however, the competitive constraint on a product is likely to represent a spectrum with the degree of substitutability generated by other products gradually declining as those other products become more differentiated from the product in question. Thus, in the relatively common case of markets with differentiated products, examining how "close" (or substitutable) the different products are to each other is likely to be necessary while an analysis focused exclusively on market shares can prove highly misleading. Similarly, a firm's current market share may understate its competitive impact if, say, it is an entrant that is expected to disrupt the market equilibrium significantly and generate lower prices to consumers;

- fourthly, the price elasticity facing a firm in relation to its own product[54] also depends on the overall market elasticity[55] and the elasticity of supply of other firms in the market. This implies that even a firm with a high market share may face significant constraints on its pricing if the overall market demand is elastic and/or if the supply of the other firms in the market is elastic;

- fifthly, the absence of the other indicators of market power discussed below[56] may mean that a firm does not have SMP even where it has a relatively large market share.

(ii) Barriers to expansion, entry and exit

12–037 **Expansion and entry.** One of the clearest ways in which a price increase may be made unprofitable is if other firms in the market can readily respond by expanding their output to take market share. Thus, the presence in the market of firms with sufficient existing spare capacity or the ability to

---

[54] The firm own-price elasticity of demand is the percentage change in demand for the firm's product for a percentage change in the price of the product offered by the firm.

[55] The market elasticity of demand is the percentage change in demand for the product across the market for a percentage change in the overall market price level.

[56] paras 12–037–12–041.

expand capacity quickly may ensure that even the prices of firms with existing large market shares are competitively constrained. In addition, reflecting the insight of contestable market theory, the ability of new firms to enter the market quickly and profitably in response to a price rise can also act to constrain the existing firms.[57] As a consequence, the examination of barriers to expansion and entry can be a critical part of the competitive analysis.

Barriers to expansion and entry.   A well-accepted test for whether some‑   **12–038** thing constitutes a barrier to entry is elusive. The OFT has proposed a definition of entry barriers as "factors that allow an undertaking profitably to sustain supra-competitive prices in the long term, without being more efficient than its potential rivals."[58] Barriers to expansion and entry may include absolute barriers such as the inability to obtain scarce inputs (which may be underpinned legally)—for example, a radio spectrum licence, as well as factors that influence the expected profitability of expanding output or entering. Key determinants of expected profitability are: (a) the likely market prices following the decision (particularly, whether the original firm can be expected to reverse its price rise); (b) the level of switching costs faced by customers moving between firms[59]; and (c) the risks for the other firms of investing in new capacity. The risks will be greater where installing capacity involves significant sunk costs. In particular, even if existing firms are earning high profits, a new firm may decide not to enter if to do so would involve large sunk costs for fear that entry would provoke the incumbent firms to cut their prices to a level that left the entrant unable to recover the sunk costs that it has incurred. In some cases, barriers to entry such as the level of sunk costs can be affected by firm behaviour. For example, an incumbent firm may invest heavily in advertising and research and devel‑ opment precisely to reduce other firms' expected profitability of expansion or entry by forcing them to make matching investments which would then become a sunk cost.[60]

Relevance of economies of scale.   It should be noted that economies of scale   **12–039** (which occur when average costs are lower with a larger volume of output) do not of themselves necessarily create a barrier to entry since an entrant may simply be able to enter the market at an appropriate size. However,

---

[57] While practitioners often focus on barriers to entry, examining whether there are barriers to expansion for existing firms will generally be more significant. In particular, if barriers to expansion are low then the firms in a market can be competitively constrained even if there are high barriers to entry.

[58] OFT, *Assessment of market power*, December 2004, para.5.3.

[59] Switching costs can give rise to a number of dynamic effects so that they do not necessarily harm overall competition. A survey of the economic literature on switching costs is presented in a report for the OFT and DTI, *Switching costs—Economic Discussion Paper 5*, April 2003.

[60] The expected profitability of entry could fall because the other firm would now need to incur greater sunk costs to be able to compete with the incumbent or because the incumbent would now be less likely to cede market share following its expenditure.

they may in practice contribute to deterring entry if, for example, a large number of customers would be unlikely to switch to the entrant or the entrant suffers a disadvantage relative to the incumbents in raising finance to build a large plant.

(iii) Buyer power

12–040   **The effect of buyer power.**   A further way in which a firm may be competitively constrained arises where the firm's customers are able to act so that any attempt to raise prices will prove unprofitable. For example, customers accounting for a large proportion of total market demand may be able to switch readily to alternative existing or new suppliers, including by sponsoring entry or supplying the product themselves through vertical integration. Thus powerful buyers may counterbalance powerful sellers.[61] This suggests the need to consider structural and behavioural features on the buyer-side of the market such as the degree of buyer concentration, the costs involved in buyers switching supplier and the scope for buyers to act strategically.

12–041   **The institutional structure underpinning transactions.**   Analysis of buyer power also serves to highlight the importance of the way in which transactions occur in an industry. For example, in some industries there may be protracted negotiations with rounds of offers from each side and threats to walk away. In other industries ("bidding markets"), sales may occur through infrequent tenders and the consequence of failing to win a large tender can effectively discipline firms even when they have historically had a large market share.[62]

(iv) Collective dominance

12–042   **In general.**   The nature of some markets can lead to firms behaving in such a way that the firms collectively share market power, particularly in being able sustainably to maintain their prices above the competitive level. Where firms are able to behave in this way, the situation is referred to as collective dominance or tacit collusion.[63] In essence, the conditions facing the firms are such that they can maximise their individual profits by restricting output to support a higher market price rather than by seeking to take market share by undercutting the prices of their competitors—any attempt to undercut

---

[61] A competition authority may nonetheless also be concerned with the position of smaller buyers. If such buyers are unable to benefit from the buyer power of larger buyers, they may suffer a competitive disadvantage in the downstream market when competing against the larger buyer with its lower input costs.

[62] See paras 12–090–12–092, below.

[63] The collusion is tacit as it requires no formal agreement between the firms but only a mutual recognition of what is in each firm's individual interests.

their competitors would be met by a swift response, such as retaliatory price cuts, so that the attempt would not prove profitable.

The test for collective dominance.   Four necessary conditions are required   **12–043**
for collective dominance to emerge and be sustained:

(1)   the firms must be able to reach a co-ordinated position in the first place;

(2)   the co-ordinating firms must be able to monitor each other's adherence to the co-ordinated position;

(3)   the co-ordination must be sustainable with a credible deterrence mechanism that can be used if deviation is detected; and

(4)   the foreseeable reactions of other firms and customers must not be able to undermine the co-ordination.

The specific market characteristics can thus be examined to see whether each of these four conditions is likely to be met and thus whether collective dominance is likely.[64] In many cases, some market characteristics may tend to support co-ordination while other characteristics would undermine it, so that a reasoned approach may be required to assess which effect is likely to dominate in a particular case.

(v) Actual conduct

In general.   Finally, it should be noted that the analysis of the character-   **12–044**
istics of the market is undertaken because it is often the case that market power and competitive harm cannot be identified directly. However, in some cases there may be direct evidence of actual market power or anti-competitive effects so that (at least as a matter of economics) an analysis of indirect indicators of market power can be dispensed with. As the US Supreme Court has stated:

> "since the purpose of the inquiries into market definition and market power is to determine whether an arrangement has the potential for genuine adverse effects on competition, 'proof of actual detrimental effects, such as a reduction of output,' can obviate the need for an inquiry into market power, which is 'but a surrogate for detrimental effects.'"[65]

---

[64] See, for example, the European Commission's discussion of the four conditions in the Guidelines on the assessment of horizontal mergers under the Council Regulation on the control of concentrations between undertakings, n.50, above, paras 39–57, as well as the judgment of the CFI in Case T–342/99 *Airtours v Commission* [2002] E.C.R. II–2585 at para.62.

[65] *Federal Trade Commission v Indiana Federation of Dentists*, 476 U.S. 450 (1986) at 460–61.

3. EMPIRICAL ANALYSIS AND QUANTITATIVE TOOLS

(a) In general

(i) Introduction

12–045 **Purpose of section.**   This chapter has so far discussed the various economic theories that can help determine the impact on competition of a particular transaction, agreement or business practice. It has been noted that testing whether a particular theory is relevant, and ultimately whether competition is likely to be promoted or hindered, will generally require an analysis of the institutional setting and facts of the case. Empirical analysis can thus be critical to the outcome of many competition cases. This section discusses general economic principles that should govern the use of empirical analysis to help ensure its acceptance by regulators and the courts, as well as out-lining the major types of empirical analysis available.[66]

(ii) General principles for empirical analysis

12–046 **In general.**   Empirical analysis can play an important role in many com-petition law investigations in distinguishing between competing theories or in quantifying the likely magnitude of the overall effect on competition—particularly where there are factors operating in different directions. While all empirical tools have advantages and disadvantages, in general they can provide useful information and are to be preferred to an approach that does not seek to make use of the available information. In its judgment in *Leeds City Council v Watkins*[67] the court was highly critical of the lack of empirical analysis presented on questions such as market definition and competitive effects.[68] Even where a case does not turn on the outcome of empirical analysis alone, such analysis can nevertheless play a useful role in sup-porting the other evidence so strengthening the overall case.

12–047 **Identifying the critical issues.**   There are a number of general principles that can guide the development of empirical analysis to ensure that it is robust and to improve its chances of being accepted by regulators and the courts:

- Prior to undertaking any empirical analysis, it is important to identify clearly the critical empirical issues in the case, such as whether two

---

[66] A fuller discussion of empirical techniques can be found in S. Bishop and M. Walker, n.44, above and OFT Research Paper 17, *Quantitative techniques in competition analysis*, prepared by LECG Ltd, October 1999.

[67] [2003] 14 E.G. 122 (CS).

[68] *ibid.*, at para.103.

products are in the same market, whether a firm has a dominant position or whether the effect of a particular conduct harms competition. In many cases, the empirical analysis will throw up new issues so that a series of analyses may be necessary to present a full explanation of the impact of the matter under investigation;

- Identifying the critical issues is likely to involve the adoption of a particular economic theory and it is important that the theory chosen is consistent with the institutional settings and the facts of the case. For example, whether or not a particular empirical test actually resolves the matter at issue will often depend on explicit and implicit assumptions being made in relation to the manner in which firms compete in the industry or the way consumers behave. Thus it is not only necessary to show that the test is passed but also to explain the economic model used and its assumptions, and that the associated empirical test is the right test to use.

Identifying data.   The next step is to identify the data that can be used and assess the extent to which sufficient data is available to yield reliable results. For example, list prices may be of limited use if prices actually paid in the market are based on customer-specific discounts; and reliable demand elasticities may not be obtainable if there has been little price variability. Assumptions that have a significant impact on the final result should have greater empirical support.   **12–048**

Interpreting results: sensitivity analysis.   The results of the analysis should be subject to sensitivity analysis to provide an indication of how robust the results are to small changes in assumptions. Tests should be conducted in relation to: **12–049**

- the key parameters that are uncertain;

- model specification (for example, the shape assumed for the curve showing how demand varies with price)[69]; and

- the data sample (for example, the consistency of results over different time periods or geographic areas).

Interpreting results: consistency with other evidence.   Results also need to be consistent with other evidence (for example, from customers and company documents); or, at least, the differences must be explained. Further, differences in the results of empirical analysis presented by the other side should also be explained to avoid the risk that both sides' empirical evidence will be rejected. In the *UK Premier League* case,[70] the judge was presented with   **12–050**

---

[69] For example, the results may vary depending on whether linear (that is, a straight line) or non-linear demand is assumed.
[70] *Re Televising Premier League Football Matches* [2000] E.M.L.R. 78.

competing econometric evidence from both the OFT and the Premier League. However, the judge described the evidence as of "limited assistance" as he did "not feel able to prefer the evidence of one of the experts to that of the other".[71] Evidence should be presented as to which results are likely to be most relevant to the particular case. If there remains significant uncertainty, this will affect the weight that can be attached to that particular piece of evidence.

12–051 **Presenting analysis.** More generally, the method, assumptions and results should be set out and presented in a form that is sufficiently clear to enable them to be given weight in decision-making by non-economists. Where possible, the data and the modeling should be made available at an early stage to the other side so that it can replicate the results. A clear intuitive explanation for the result can be useful, although some matters may simply come down to an empirical question of which effect is likely to be stronger given plausible underlying assumptions. Finally, whilst a general discussion of the use of economic witnesses in court is outside the scope of this chapter, it should be borne in mind that evidence provided by economists to a court or tribunal constitutes expert evidence and should comply where appropriate with Part 35 of the CPR and its associated practice direction, and paras 10.4–10.5 of the Competition Appeal Tribunal's Guide to Appeals under the Competition Act 1998,[72] including containing a statement acknowledging the overriding duty of the expert to the court or tribunal.[73]

(iii) Areas of application

12–052 **Market definition and the assessment of market power.** Many of the techniques discussed below can assist in assessing the degree of competitive constraint imposed by one product on another or suppliers in one area in relation to suppliers in another. Shock analysis, price correlation analysis, co-integration and Granger causality tests provide an indication of the extent to which changes in the prices of one product are reflected in changes in the prices of another product or products. Shipment and transport cost studies provide an indication of the extent to which there may be competitive interactions between products from different geographic areas. Econometric estimates of elasticities, diversion ratios and customer surveys provide information on substitutability, while critical loss analysis shows what degree of substitutability would be necessary for a price rise to be unprofitable. In assessing market power, these techniques complement simpler quantitative analysis such as the use of market shares as well as qualitative evidence.

---

[71] *ibid.*, at para.227.
[72] June 2000.
[73] See *Aberdeen Journals Ltd v OFT (No.2)* [2003] CAT 11 at para.288.

The effects of a merger, agreement or behaviour on competition.   In addition   **12–053**
to assisting in market definition, a number of the techniques described below
may be used to address directly competitive effects such as what the impact
of a merger will be or what would have occurred in the absence of particular
behaviour. Techniques that can provide useful information on these questions include shock analysis, econometric estimates (including as part of a
simulation model), diversion ratios, price/margin concentration analysis,
bidding studies and customer surveys.

Estimation of damages.   Many competition cases raise questions about the   **12–054**
actual impact of anti-competitive behaviour, such as by how much a cartel
raised prices or by how much a firm's behaviour harmed the profits of its
competitors. The key challenge in answering such questions is to estimate
what would have been the market outcomes "but for" the behaviour (the
"counterfactual"). For example, market prices and the profits of competitors may reflect not only the alleged anti-competitive conduct, but also the
impact of other factors, such as external changes in costs and demand. In
Arkin v Borchard Lines[74] the court found that the claimant's own irrational
pricing was the cause of his business' failure.[75] Estimating the "but for"
scenario requires information on market outcomes unaffected by the
behaviour, such as prices before the cartel commenced or prices in areas it
which the cartel did not operate. Econometric analysis can be an important
tool in helping to isolate the effects of the allegedly anti-competitive behaviour from the impact of changes in other factors. The econometric results
nevertheless need to be consistent with and considered in light of the market
features and a judgement made as to whether there would have been other
changes in the market structure, such as new entry, or the conduct of the
firms in the absence of the behaviour.

(b) Specific techniques

Introduction.   This section discusses various techniques of empirical ana-   **12–055**
lysis ranging from relatively simple techniques to more sophisticated
econometric[76] statistical analyses. Simple analysis can often prove most
powerful because the results are relatively intuitive, the techniques relatively
easily understood, and the scope for technical disagreements between
competing economists minimised. Nonetheless, it is important to understand the limitations of simple analysis and thus where more complex
analysis is required. To assist in this regard, reference is made to main uses

---

[74] *Arkin v Borchard Lines Ltd and Ors* [2003] EWHC 687.
[75] At para.562.
[76] Econometrics can be defined as "the field of economics that concerns itself with the application of mathematical statistics and the tools of statistical inference to the empirical measurement of relationships postulated by economic theory" (W. H. Greene, *Econometric
Analysis* (4th ed., Prentice-Hall, New Jersey, 2000), p.1).

of each technique, and the constraints on, or difficulties associated with, that use.

(i) Shock analysis

12–056 **General.** Shock analysis, or natural experiments, can be a simple, yet powerful means of gaining information on the nature of competition in an industry. Essentially, shock analysis involves identifying a significant change that has occurred in an industry and seeing what insights can be gained from the way the industry responded to the change. Potentially informative shocks include the launch of a new product or a new production technology, a cut in supply of an existing product such as resulting from a strike or a technical fault, the impact of a promotion, a sudden change in exchange rates or a price cut imposed by regulation. For example, consider the launch of a new product. By examining how the launch affected the prices and quantities sold of other products, an indication can be gained as to which products are competitively constrained by the new product and which products are left unaffected and thus likely to be in separate markets. The behaviour of different firms after the launch can also provide insights, such as whether an existing firm felt the need to increase its marketing to retain customers.

12–057 **Exchange rate shocks.** Exchange rate shocks can be particularly useful in delineating the geographic dimension of the market. A sharp change in the exchange rate between two countries will change the relative prices of the product sold in each country expressed in terms of one currency. If, following the shock, the relative prices quickly return to their previous level, this would suggest there is competitive interaction between the countries and that they form part of one market.

12–058 **Stock market reactions.** The stock market's reaction to the announcement of a merger can also provide information on the expected impact of the merger. Some effects may be ambiguous such as whether higher share prices for the merging companies suggest they will be able to exploit market power to raise prices or whether the merger is expected to generate cost efficiencies. However, changes in the share price of other firms in the industry may be more illuminating. For example, if the share price of other firms remains unchanged or falls as a result of the merger announcement then a conclusion which may be drawn is that the merger is not expected to raise market prices.

12–059 **Considerations as to applicability.** Shock analysis is most useful where a significant shock takes place at a time when other factors determining supply and demand are stable. Where other factors also change, these need to be taken into account. It is also important that the shock is non-transitory as customers and other suppliers may take time to adjust to changed market conditions.[77]

(ii) Price correlation analysis

General.   Where the matter at issue is whether product A is constrained by   **12–060**
product B, one source of information is whether movements in the price of B are reflected in movements in the price of A, that is, whether the two prices move together over time.

The correlation coefficient.   The correlation coefficient provides a standard   **12–061**
statistical measure that can be used to assess the degree to which prices of two products or in two areas move together over time. A correlation coefficient of 1 implies perfect correlation while a coefficient of 0 implies no correlation (a coefficient of -1 implies perfect negative correlation suggesting that the products are complements).

Economic basis and use in determining product markets.   The economic   **12–062**
intuition is that if the price of B were increased, then customers would switch to product A to the extent that the products were substitutes on the demand-side. Higher demand for A would then be expected to increase the price of A as well. If, instead, the products were close substitutes on the supply-side, an increase in the price of B should lead to firms switching away from supplying A and towards supplying B. This would again act to increase the price of A as less of A were supplied. Conversely, if A and B were in separate markets, then if the price of one product were changed significantly without having any impact on the price of the other product, this would suggest that the two products were not part of the same market.

Use in determining geographic markets.   Price correlation can also be useful   **12–063**
in determining the geographic dimension of the market. Where the prices of a product in different geographic areas move together, this suggests that the two areas form part of the same market. Conversely, if the price of a product in one area is able to change significantly without impacting the price of the product in the other area then there may be two distinct geographic markets for the product.

Absolute versus relative price changes.   It should be borne in mind that for   **12–064**
both product and geographic dimensions, it is whether there are changes in relative prices that matters rather than whether one product or area is more expensive than another. For example, a branded product may be more expensive than an unbranded product but they may still impose competitive

---

[77] Rosenzweig and Wolpin provide an overview of the methological issues in the use of shock analysis. Rosenzweig, M. and K. Wolpin, "Natural 'Natural Experiments' in Economics" (2000) 38 *Journal of Economic Literature* 827–874.

constraints on each other so that changes in the prices of one are reflected in changes in the price of the other.

12–065 **Interpretation of results.** Price correlation analysis provides a simple intuitive approach with minimal data requirements and, as such, is used frequently.[78] There remains the question, however, of whether the coefficient is sufficiently high, that is, whether substitution between two products or areas is sufficiently strong for the products or areas to be considered to be part of the same market.[79] In seeking to draw an inference on the basis of the correlation coefficient, it is important to have some understanding of the potential supply response. If supply is able to be changed readily, then even a low correlation coefficient may imply a sufficiently strong competitive constraint. For example, suppose the price of A were increased and this encouraged customers to switch to B. If the producers of B were able to expand the supply of B substantially then a large number of customers could switch to B with relatively little pressure on its price. The ability of the producers of B to accommodate customers switching from A would undermine the profitability of the original increase in A's price, implying a relatively strong competitive constraint even though the correlation coefficient would be relatively small.

12–066 **The use of benchmarks.** Benchmarks are often relied on to assess whether the correlation coefficient is sufficiently high, although such benchmarks tend to be arbitrary in nature, and their use limited. For example, in *Nestlé/Perrier*,[80] the average correlation coefficient between brands of still water was accepted as providing a benchmark for the correlation coefficient consistent with two products being in the same relevant market. This benchmark was then used to assess whether brands of sparkling water were in the same market as brands of still water. The different types of mineral water (that is, still and sparkling) were found to be as sufficiently correlated as different brands of still water, so as to enable a conclusion that they formed part of the same market. However, even if sparkling water had turned out not to be as close a substitute for still water as were different brands of still water for each other, it may still have been in the same market as still water. Thus whilst some results of correlation analysis may be informative, others may not.

12–067 **Difficulties.** Price correlation analysis may also be subject to a number of problems that require adjustments to the analysis or make it inapplicable, including the following:

---

[78] For example, price correlation analysis was used in Case IV/M.190 *Nestlé/Perrier* [1992] O.J. L356/1, Case IV/M.430 *Procter & Gamble/VP Schickedanz* [1992] O.J. L354/33 and Case COMP/M.2187 *CVC/Lenzing* [2004] O.J. L82/20.
[79] See also para.12–067, below in relation to other difficulties.
[80] n.78, above.

- if two products are subject to similar influences, their prices may move together even where the products are in separate markets (for example, inflation or higher fuel costs raising the cost of air and sea transport, or ice cream and sun tan lotion prices both being higher in summer);

- changes in the quality of one product may lead to the relative prices of two products diverging even though they both continue to form part of one market;

- price correlation analysis assessing whether different countries form part of the same geographic market is subject to a more serious problem where it is necessary to convert the prices into a common currency.[81] The problem cannot be readily solved and suggests that price correlation should generally not be used to determine the geographic dimension of a market across areas with variable exchange rates;

- correlation analysis may also be subject to serious statistical problems where the price series are "non-stationary".[82] In this case, the analysis may be applied to the changes in prices rather than absolute prices, although this does lead to a loss of some of the information contained in the original data which might otherwise be useful in the analysis; and

- where a high correlation coefficient is estimated, it is important also to carry out the correlation analysis on the differences in prices (that is, the changes from period to period) as well as the actual price level. This enables trends in the series to be eliminated.

(iii) Co-integration tests

In general. Co-integration tests measure the extent to which there is a stable relationship between two series. The intuition for the use of co-integration tests is similar to price correlation analysis. In particular, testing whether the prices of different products (or prices in different areas) display a stable relationship enables inferences to be made about market definition. If two products are in the same market, the price of one relative to the other would be expected to remain stable in the long run (barring changes in market structure such as the quality of one product increasing relative to the other). Conversely, a finding that relative prices diverge, that is, the

12–068

---

[81] For a discussion of this problem see S. Bishop and M. Walker, *The Economics of EC Competition Law: Concepts, application and evidence*, n.44, above, pp.394 *et seq.*

[82] A stationary series is one which has a constant mean to which it tends to return and a finite "variance" (*i.e.* the standard measure of "variability" or the extent to which a distribution is spread out), that is, shocks to the series only have transitory effects. Prices of close substitutes are viewed as generally being non-stationary.

individual prices vary independently of each other, would suggest that the products are in separate markets.

12–069 **Use.**   Co-integration tests can avoid some of the difficulties associated with correlation analysis, particularly where the price series are "non-stationary" (and thus when correlation analyses are subject to statistical problems).[83] Co-integration tests do not lead to information being lost when the data is converted into differences. Co-integration tests also avoid other key problems of price correlation analysis, such as where two products share common inputs and where the impact of changes in one price on the other price is delayed. Reflecting these considerations, co-integration tests have been used in recent competition law investigations in the UK and Europe.[84]

12–070 **Difficulties.**   Co-integration tests are nevertheless subject to a number of weaknesses:

- a co-integration test may find a stable long-run relationship even where there are significant deviations away from the long-run equilibrium in the medium term (such as for a couple of years); but the ability of a firm to price its products independently of another product's prices for such a period may be a legitimate concern of competition authorities; and

- in common with price correlation, finding that the prices of two products do have some impact upon each other does not answer the question of whether the interaction is sufficiently strong to be able to conclude that the two products are in the same market.

(iv) Granger causality tests

12–071 **In general.**   Granger causality tests seek to determine if changes in one series cause changes in another series. The intuition for the use of the tests in competition law is that if the price of product A is competitively constrained by the price of product B, then changes in the price of product B should lead to changes in the price of product A. Granger causality tests assess the existence of a causal relationship by testing whether past values of product B's price can be used to improve predictions of product A's price compared with using past values of product A's price alone.

---

[83] See para.12–067, above.
[84] For example, see *UK Competition Commission, Nutreco Holding NV and Hydro Seafood GSP Ltd: A report on the proposed merger*, 2000, and Case IV/M.619 *Lonrho/GenCorp* [1997] O.J. L11/30 and Case COMP/M.2187 *CVC/Lenzing*, n.78, above.

Difficulties. While Granger causality tests have been used in competition investigations,[85] they are subject to a number of problems: **12–072**

- as with a number of other tests, Granger causality tests can provide information on whether there is some relationship between two products but not whether the degree of interdependence is sufficiently strong so that the products can be considered to belong to the same market;

- in some cases the test may give a "false negative" suggesting that the past prices of product A do not affect the price of product B when the past price of A lagged by a particular period or periods is nonetheless statistically significant; and

- a further problem arises from the need to deal with factors that are common influences on the price of both products. Adjusting for the impact of these factors can readily become a complex econometric exercise.

(v) Shipment and transport cost tests

In general. Shipment and transport cost tests provide information on the degree of competition between different regions and, in particular, whether they form part of one market.   **12–073**

Use of shipment studies. Shipment tests, such as the *Elzinga-Hogarty* test and the *Shrieves* test,[86] use data on trade volumes between regions, to assess whether the regions impose competitive constraints on each other. If there are large volumes of trade in a product between two regions this suggests that they form part of the same geographic market for that product, that is, that an attempt to raise prices would be defeated by customers switching to non-local suppliers. However, the converse need not apply. In particular, if there is little trade between areas, this need not imply that the suppliers in the different regions do not act as competitive constraints on each other. In particular, there may be few imports into a region precisely because the local firms are pricing competitively so that they do not lose sales to imports or to each other. Thus further information may be required to understand why there is little trade.   **12–074**

Use of transport cost studies. Transport cost studies provide information on the potential for greater trade should prices in a particular region rise   **12–075**

---

[85] For example, evidence based on Granger causality tests was submitted in Case IV/M.315 *Mannesmann/Vallourec/Ilva* [1994] O.J. L102/15.

[86] K. Elzinga and T. Hogarty, "The problem of geographic market definition in antimerger suits" (1973) 18 *Antitrust Bulletin* 45, and R. Shrieves, "Geographic market areas and market structure in the bituminous coal industry" (1978) 34 *Antitrust Bulletin* 291.

and thus can be useful where a shipment test indicates there is little current trade. For example, a merger of two firms in a region may not raise competition concerns if it is found that imports could readily increase should prices rise above current levels. The analysis would need to consider the production costs in other regions and the cost of transporting the product into the local region. A key attraction of transport cost studies is that they provide information on potential constraints and thus can inform the forward-looking analysis required in the assessment of a proposed merger. More formally, the responsiveness of imports to price changes can be estimated as part of an econometric model of supply and demand.

(vi) Econometric estimates of elasticities

12–076   **In general.** Econometric analysis enables elasticities[87] to be estimated directly where there is sufficient time series data on prices and quantities. Essentially, an econometric analysis of demand isolates the impact of different factors on the demand for a product (or the group of products postulated to belong to one market). For example, amongst other factors, the demand for a product may be affected by its own price, the price of substitute products, and income levels. As these factors are all likely to vary over time, it is necessary to undertake an econometric analysis to assess the sensitivity of the demand to any individual factor.

12–077   **Use.** Market elasticities can address the key question in market definition of whether, in response to a rise in the price of a product, there would be sufficient loss in demand for the product through substitution to other products or to other geographic areas to make that price rise unprofitable. The own-price elasticity of demand[88] can be used to answer the question of what the loss in demand for the product would be if its price were to be increased by 5 or 10 per cent. This can then be combined with critical loss analysis to determine whether such a loss in demand would be sufficient to constrain prices to competitive levels.[89]

12–078   **Extensive data requirements.** Econometric estimation of elasticities can be highly powerful in competition law investigations, particularly in mergers in which the matter of interest is the likely impact of price rises from existing levels. However, there are extensive data requirements that can prevent the use of econometric analysis in many cases. For example, private parties may not have access to the price and quantity data from all market participants. Further, available data may not be appropriate, such as where only list price data are available even though customer-specific discounts are common.

---

[87] See n.48, n.54 and n.55 above.
[88] See n.54 above.
[89] See the discussion of critical loss analysis at paras 12–083–12–086, below.

Other considerations and difficulties. The following considerations should   **12–079**
also be borne in mind in using econometric analyses of elasticities:

- as with all econometrics, it is important to ensure the model chosen
  and the results are consistent with other evidence and economic
  theory. It is also important to ensure that the estimates actually
  address the key questions, particularly noting that evidence that one
  product constrains another does not imply the converse;

- basic econometric analysis takes no account of the reactions of other
  firms in the market, such as whether the other firms would be expected
  to respond to a price change by changing their prices as well; this may
  be likely if the initial firm is a price leader. Thus information on the
  nature of competition in the industry is also important in assessing the
  likely competitive impact; and

- merger simulation models can be used to predict the effects of mergers, particularly in oligopolistic markets.[90] These models use own-
  price and cross-price[91] elasticities to estimate the likely overall price
  change. However, these models generally rely on simple assumptions
  about the nature of competition and ignore strategic or dynamic
  reactions that may be critical to the ultimate impact on price. As such,
  the models may be poor predictors of market outcomes both before
  and after the merger. Nonetheless, the models may be useful in a
  limited way in helping to identify more problematic areas and screen
  out areas of less concern.

(vii) Diversion ratios

In general. A diversion ratio between two products measures the propor-   **12–080**
tion of the sales lost by one product to another product when its price rises.
For example, if a 10 per cent price rise for product A causes sales to drop by
100 units, with 20 units going to product B, then the diversion ratio from
product A to B is $20/100 = 0.2$. A high diversion ratio suggests that the
products are close substitutes.

Use. Diversion ratios can be useful in providing information on the likely   **12–081**
effect of a merger. They are intuitively appealing in differentiated product
markets in which market shares fail to capture the "closeness" of the products of the merging firms. Further, while diversion ratios can be based on
own and cross-price elasticity estimates, more readily available company

---

[90] For example, merger simulation analysis was considered in the UK Competition Commission's inquiry into the Centrica/Dynegy acquisition (*Centrica plc and Dynegy Storage Ltd
and Dynegy Onshore Processing UK Ltd: A report on the merger situation*, 2003).
[91] The cross-price elasticity of product A to B is the percentage change in sales for product A
for each percentage change in price of product B.

data on customer switching can also be useful. Under strict assumptions, the diversion ratio between two firms, along with the pre-merger price and marginal cost, can be used to estimate the likely price rise.

12–082   **Constraints on use.** The following should be borne in mind in using diversion rations to estimate post-merger prices:

- the assumptions that are required to hold to estimate the likely price rise by way of a simple formula are that the two merging firms are symmetric, single product firms, and that they face constant elasticity demand curves. In the absence of these assumptions, estimating the likely price effect becomes more complex;

- the use of diversion ratios also assumes that there are no shifts in market positioning[92] following the merger and no new market entry and thus will only be informative where such market changes are unlikely; and

- diversion ratios cannot be estimated from market shares as this assumes that the products are "equally close" in the sense that customers buying one product would as readily switch to any of the other products in the market.

(viii) Critical loss analysis

12–083   **In general.** Critical loss analysis represents the practical application of the hypothetical monopolist test by bringing together the different components that determine whether or not a price rise will be profitable. In particular, a price rise will lead to higher margins on the products that continue to be sold and a loss in margins on the products that are no longer sold because of substitution to other products. The question of how much substitution would need to take place to render a price rise unprofitable can be calculated by means of a simple formula.

12–084   **Formula.** The gross margin (M) can be defined as the percentage difference between price (P) and marginal cost (C)[93]:

$$M = (P-C) / P$$

The critical loss (L) for any percentage price increase (Y) can thus be expressed:

---

[92] That is, changes in the degree to which a firm's products are considered to be close substitutes to those of other products in the eyes of customers.

[93] More accurately, the relevant cost is the average cost of the increment of sales that would be lost; that is, the costs that would be avoided by no longer supplying that increment.

$$L = Y/(Y + M)$$

For example, if the original price equals £100 and the marginal cost is £25 then the gross margin is 75 per cent. Thus for a 5 per cent price rise, the critical loss will be 6.25 per cent.

Use. A key insight of critical loss analysis is that it may take only a rela- **12–085** tively small number of customers in a market to be willing to switch for prices to be competitively constrained. This implies that competitive analysis should focus on the marginal customers whose behaviour is affected by relatively small price changes. Once the critical loss has been calculated, the second step requires the application of the hypothetical monopolist test is to determine how many sales would actually be lost. If the actual loss is larger than the critical loss then the price increase will be unprofitable and thus the products in question would not form part of the same market. This second step requires information on the demand elasticity of the product which can be provided by other tests described in the chapter, such as econometric estimates of demand elasticity and the diversion ratio.

Constraints on use. While critical loss analysis is relatively simple, care **12–086** needs to be taken that the right variables are being compared. For example, in market definition, the required demand elasticity relates to all the pro-ducts in the postulated market; market demand will generally be less elastic than the demand facing a single competitor since competitors face sub-stitution not only from other products but from rivals in the same market. In addition, there may be complications where changes in the supply of one product influence the sales of the firm's other products so that a more elaborate analysis is necessary.

(ix) Price/margin concentration studies

In general. Price concentration studies seek to assess whether geographic **12–087** areas which have higher levels of concentration tend to have higher prices. Where sufficient data is available, a margin concentration study may instead be undertaken that directly assesses the extent to which margins vary between areas with different levels of concentration. Such studies can be useful in competition law investigations in a number of ways:

- most intuitively, concentration studies can provide information directly on whether a higher level of concentration in a particular area should be a concern. For example, if areas with four supermarkets tend to have similar prices/margins to areas with three supermarkets, then a merger that reduces the number of supermarkets in a range of areas from four to three should not be a concern in relation to those areas;

- similarly, if a firm with a large market share in some areas was only earning margins around the level of margins it earned in less concentrated areas this would suggest that the firm was not abusing a dominant position;

- if two firms are alleged to be engaging in price fixing, the prices/margins in the areas in which the firms are present can be compared with prices/margins in other areas.

Forms of price concentration study have been used in a number of UK competition investigations including in relation to pharmacies, the funeral services industry, supermarkets and betting shops.[94]

12–088   **Advantages.**   By providing information directly on potential competition concerns, price/margin concentration studies can generate powerful results. They can also avoid the need to engage in long debates over market definition. If concentration and margins are unrelated, it does not matter if this is because the areas are part of a wider market or because other factors, such as low barriers to entry, are constraining prices. Whichever is the case, a merger that only affected concentration in particular areas would not lead to higher prices.

12–089   **Considerations in application.**   A number of complications may arise in undertaking price/margin concentration studies:

- costs or product characteristics may differ between areas and this may distort the analysis in relation to a price concentration study. Where costs are likely to vary significantly between areas, a margin concentration study can prevent distortions arising from cost differences;

- alternatively, an econometric analysis can be conducted that includes variables for key cost factors that differ between areas or a "hedonic pricing"[95] approach can take account of the impact of differences in product characteristics between areas.

---

[94] *The control of entry regulations and retail pharmacy services in the UK: A report of an OFT market investigation*, OFT, January 2003; *Funerals: A report of the OFT inquiry into the funerals industry*, OFT, July 2001; *Competition Commission, Supermarkets: A report on the supply of groceries from multiple stores in the United Kingdom*, Competition Commission 2000; and *Monopolies and Mergers Commission, Grand Metropolitan plc and William Hill Organisation Limited: A report on the merger situation*, Monopolies and Mergers Commission 1989.

[95] A hedonic pricing approach is an econometric analysis that can identify the impact of particular product attributes on the overall price for the product, such as how much more on average consumers are prepared to pay for cars with air-conditioning compared with cars without air-conditioning, when other differences between car attributes are held constant.

(x) Bidding studies

In general. In some industries, sales take place via tenders with each firm   **12–090**
bidding to be the lowest cost supplier. Tenders are common in the provision
of services to large corporates as well as in industries where the individual
products are very substantial and where individual customers make infrequent purchases (for example, shipbuilding or aircraft manufacture).
Examples of bidding markets that have been subject to competition investigations in the UK include the merger between GEC and VSEL and the
merger between CHC Helicopter Corporation and Helicopter Services
Group ASA.[96]

Economic implications of bidding markets. In bidding markets, only a few   **12–091**
suppliers may be necessary to achieve competitive outcomes as firms are
unaware of what other firms will bid on any particular tender and risk
ending up with no sales if they bid slightly too high. Further, even a firm
with a small existing market share can exert a significant competitive constraint if they can submit credible bids. These considerations imply that
historical market shares are likely to be uninformative as regards future
competitive constraints within the industry. Analysis of past bids can instead
provide a useful source of information on competition in the industry.

Use. Bidding analysis may have the following uses: **12–092**

- analysis of bidding processes can provide information on how the
  number of firms in a market influences outcomes. For example, it may
  be that prices are relatively high in areas in which bidders are only
  able to obtain tenders from one or two suppliers, but that once three
  suppliers are present to provide tenders final prices drop significantly,
  and that having additional suppliers beyond three does not result in
  any lower prices. An analysis of the bidding process can thus provide
  information on the degree of market power of a particular firm, or
  how a merger between two suppliers would affect market outcomes
  depending on the extent to which alternative suppliers were present in
  the areas in which the merging suppliers were present;

- another example of the use of bidding studies is to gain information
  on whether or not two suppliers are close competitors. In particular, if

---

[96] *GEC/VSEL UK Competition Commission, CHC Helicopter Corporation and Helicopter Ser-
vices Group ASA: A report on the merger situation*, 2000. The European Commission has also
investigated a number of bidding markets, including the joint venture between *Group
SNECMA and TI Group* (Case IV/M.368 [1993] O.J. C42/0000 and the mergers between
Mercedes-Benz and Kässbohrer (Case IV/M. 477 [1995] O.J. L211/1), *Boeing and McDonnell
Douglas* (Case IV/M.877 [1994] O.J. C245/9), *MCI Worldcom and Sprint* (Case COMP/
M.1741 [2003] O.J. L300/53), *Price Waterhouse and Coopers & Lybrand* (Case IV/
M.1016,[1999] O.J. L50/27) and *Philips and Agilent* (Case COMP/M.2256 [2001] O.J. C292/
10).

in many of the bids won by one of the suppliers the other supplier was the next lowest bidder, this would suggest that the two suppliers are close competitors and that a merger between them would lead to market prices rising. If the two firms were to merge the combined firm would not need to price as low because the firm that had previously been most likely to undercut it was no longer submitting rival bids. If, instead, other suppliers tended to be the next lowest bidders in the bids that the firms won then the merger might be expected to have little impact on the merged firm's bids and thus on final prices achieved.

(xi) Consumer surveys

12–093   **In general.**   Where the required market data such as on prices and quantities are not available, surveys can be used to obtain data from which inferences can be drawn to assist in estimating demand functions and in market definition.

12–094   **Use.**   Customer surveys are intuitively appealing in market definition as they enable the customers to answer directly the hypothetical monopolist question of what would they do in response to a 5 or 10 per cent price rise. By posing questions in relation to hypothetical price levels, customer surveys can also attempt to avoid the cellophane fallacy[97] if there is a risk that existing prices are already above their competitive level. The key issue to be addressed is the proportion of customers who would change their behaviour in response to a price rise (that is, those with weak preferences) and, in particular, whether they would cause a sufficient loss in demand to make the price rise unprofitable. The market definition guidelines of the OFT and the European Commission recognise customer surveys as a form of evidence for market definition.[98]

12–095   **Difficulties.**   Survey evidence from customers is nonetheless subject to a number of problems and considerations in relation to its use:

- it can be particularly unreliable in addressing hypothetical questions about which the customers have no direct experience. In particular, inferences about demand are likely to be less reliable where customers are asked to estimate the degree to which they would reduce consumption (for example, litres of petrol consumed in a week), rather than whether they would or would not make a discrete purchase (for example, a broadband connection);

---

[97] See para.12–028, above.
[98] *Guidelines on market definition*, OFT 403, March 1999, para.3.6 and Commission Notice on the definition of the relevant market, n.35, above, para.40–41.

- hypothetical questions should reflect actual trade-offs, such as any switching costs[99] involved in changing between products.

- The framing of questions (including the language, presentation, explanation of the context for the question and arrangements of questions within the survey) may have significant influences on responses and lead to biases in results;

- surveys may also be subject to selection bias. For example, if the panel is drawn from the customers of a particular firm under consideration, these may be unrepresentative of the market as a whole and may place disproportionate weight on the importance to competition of the particular firm; and

- the group of respondents to each question must be sufficiently large that the survey has statistical validity. Even where the initial panel of customers is large, if only small numbers are able to answer certain questions (because the question are only applicable to sub-groups within the panel) then the answers to those questions may not have any statistical validity.

---

[99] These may include the cost (in terms of time and effort) associated with finding a new supplier, negotiating a new deal, etc.

APPENDIX

The Competition Appeal Tribunal Rules 2003[1]

(SI 2003/1372)

Made .... *23rd May 2003*
Laid before Parliament .... *27th May 2003*
Coming into force .... *20th June 2003*

ARRANGEMENT OF RULES

PART I

INTRODUCTION

1. Citation and commencement
2. Interpretation
3. Application of rules
4. The Registrar
5. Tribunal address for service
6. Tribunal Website
7. Representation

PART II

APPEALS

Commencing appeal proceedings

8. Time and manner of commencing appeals
9. Defective notices of appeal
10. Power to reject
11. Amendment
12. Withdrawal of the appeal

---

[1] As amended by The Competition Appeal Tribunal (Amendment and Communications Act Appeals) Rules (SI 2004/2068).

PART III

PROCEEDINGS UNDER THE ENTERPRISE ACT 2002

PART IV

CLAIMS FOR DAMAGES

The Secretary of State, after consultation with the President of the Competition Appeal Tribunal and such other persons as she considers appropriate in accordance with section 15(1) of the Enterprise Act 2002, and after consultation with the Council on Tribunals in accordance with section 8(1) of the Tribunals and Inquiries Act 1992,[2] in exercise of the powers conferred by section 15 of and Part 2 of Schedule 4 to the Enterprise Act 2002, hereby makes the following rules:

PART I

INTRODUCTION

Citation and commencement

1. These rules may be cited as the Competition Appeal Tribunal Rules 2003 and shall come into force on 20th June 2003.　　　　　　　　　　　　　　A–001

Interpretation

2. In these rules—　　　　　　　　　　　　　　　　　　　　　　　A–002

"a chairman" means any member of the panel of chairmen;
"the chairman" means the chairman of the Tribunal as constituted for particular proceedings;
"the Competition Service" means the body corporate established by section 13 of the Enterprise Act 2002;
"damages" means any sum which may be claimed under section 47A of the 1998 Act[3];
"the Registrar" means the person appointed to be Registrar of the Tribunal;

---

[2] See Sch.1 to the Act, which is amended by para.27 of Sch.25 to the Enterprise Act 2002.
[3] s.47A is inserted by s.18 of the Enterprise Act 2002.

"the 1998 Act" means the Competition Act 1998;
"the 2002 Act" means the Enterprise Act 2002.

Application of rules

A–003   3. Unless the context otherwise requires—

    (a) Parts I and V of these rules apply to all proceedings before the Tribunal;

    (b) Part II of these rules applies to all proceedings before the Tribunal save as otherwise provided in Part III (proceedings under the 2002 Act) or Part IV (claims for damages);

    (c) Part III of these rules applies to proceedings for a review or an appeal against penalties under the 2002 Act;

    (d) Part IV of these rules applies to claims for damages.

The Registrar

A–004   4.— (1) Any person appointed to be the Registrar under section 12(3) of the 2002 Act must—

    (a) have a seven year general qualification within the meaning of section 71 of the Courts and Legal Services Act 1990, or

    (b) be an advocate or solicitor in Scotland of at least seven years' standing, or

    (c) be—

        (i) a member of the Bar of Northern Ireland of at least seven years' standing, or

        (ii) a solicitor of the Supreme Court of Northern Ireland of at least seven years' standing.

(2) The Registrar shall act in accordance with the instructions of the President and shall, in particular, be responsible for—

    (a) the establishment and maintenance of a register in which all pleadings and supporting documents and all orders and decisions of the Tribunal shall be registered;

    (b) the acceptance, transmission, service and custody of documents in accordance with these rules;

    (c) the enforcement of decisions of the Tribunal pursuant to paragraphs 4 and 5 of Schedule 4 to the 2002 Act;

    (d) certifying that any order, direction or decision is an order, direction or decision of the Tribunal, the President or a chairman, as the case may be.

(3) With the authorisation of the President, the Registrar may consider and dispose of interlocutory matters in accordance with rule 62(3).

(4) A party may within 5 days of any exercise by the Registrar of his functions pursuant to paragraph (3) of this rule request in writing that the exercise of such functions be reviewed by the President. The President may determine the matter acting alone or refer the matter to a chairman or to theTribunal.

(5) Any administrative function of the Registrar may be performed on his behalf by any member of staff of the Competition Service whom the President may authorise for the purpose.

Tribunal address for service

5. The address for service of documents on the Tribunal (referred to in these rules   **A–005** as "the Tribunal address for service") is: The Registrar of the Competition Appeal Tribunal, New Court, 48 Carey Street, London WC2A 3BZ or such other address as may be notified in the London, Edinburgh andBelfast Gazettes and on the Tribunal Website.

Tribunal Website

6. The location of the Tribunal Website is: www.catribunal.org.uk or such other   **A–006** location as may be notified from time to time in such manner as the President may direct.

Representation

7. In proceedings before the Tribunal, a party may be represented by—   **A–007**

   (a)   a qualified lawyer having a right of audience before a court in the United Kingdom; or

   (b)   by any other person allowed by the Tribunal to appear on his behalf.

PART II

APPEALS

Commencing appeal proceedings

Time and manner of commencing appeals

8.— (1) An appeal to the Tribunal must be made by sending a notice of appeal to   **A–008** the Registrar so that it is received within two months of the date upon which the appellant was notified of the disputed decision or the date of publication of the decision, whichever is the earlier.

(2) The Tribunal may not extend the time limit provided under paragraph (1) unless it is satisfied that the circumstances are exceptional.

(3) The notice of appeal shall state—

   (a)   the name and address of the appellant;

   (b)   the name and address of the appellant's legal representative, if appropriate;

   (c)   an address for service in the United Kingdom; and

   (d)   the name and address of the respondent to the proceedings, and shall be signed and dated by the appellant, or on his behalf by his duly authorised officer or his legal representative.

(4) The notice of appeal shall contain—

   (a)   a concise statement of the facts;

   (b)   a summary of the grounds for contesting the decision, identifying in particular:

      (i)   under which statutory provision the appeal is brought;

      (ii)   to what extent (if any) the appellant contends that the disputed decision was based on an error of fact or was wrong in law;

      (iii)   to what extent (if any) the appellant is appealing against the respondent's exercise of his discretion in making the disputed decision;

(c) a succinct presentation of the arguments supporting each of the grounds of appeal;

(d) the relief sought by the appellant, and any directions sought pursuant to rule 19; and

(e) a schedule listing all the documents annexed to the notice of appeal.

(5) The notice of appeal may contain observations on the question in which part of the United Kingdom the proceedings of the Tribunal are to be treated as taking place for all or for any purposes of those proceedings.

(6) There shall be annexed to the notice of appeal—

(a) a copy of the disputed decision; and

(b) as far as practicable a copy of every document on which the appellant relies including the written statements of all witnesses of fact, or expert witnesses, if any.

(7) Unless the Tribunal otherwise directs the signed original of the notice of appeal (and its annexes) must be accompanied by ten copies certified by the appellant or his legal representative as conforming to the original.

Defective notices of appeal

A–009   **9.**— (1) If the Tribunal considers that a notice of appeal does not comply with rule 8, or is materially incomplete, or is unduly prolix or lacking in clarity, the Tribunal may give such directions as may be necessary to ensure that those defects are remedied.

(2) The Tribunal may, if satisfied that the efficient conduct of the proceedings so requires, instruct the Registrar to defer service of the notice of appeal on the respondent until after the directions referred to in paragraph (1) have been complied with.

Power to reject

A–010   **10.**— (1) The Tribunal may, after giving the parties an opportunity to be heard, reject an appeal in whole or in part at any stage in the proceedings if—

(a) it considers that the notice of appeal discloses no valid ground of appeal;

(b) it considers that the appellant does not have (or represent those who have) a sufficient interest in the decision in respect of which the appeal is made;

(c) it is satisfied that the appellant has habitually and persistently and without any reasonable ground—

(i) instituted vexatious proceedings, whether against the same person or different persons; or

(ii) made vexatious applications in any proceedings; or

(d) the appellant fails to comply with any rule, direction, practice direction or order of the Tribunal.

(2) When the Tribunal rejects an appeal it may make any consequential order it considers appropriate.

Amendment

A–011   **11.**— (1) The appellant may amend the notice of appeal only with the permission of the Tribunal.

(2) Where the Tribunal grants permission under paragraph (1) it may do so on such terms as it thinks fit, and shall give such further or consequential directions as may be necessary.

(3) The Tribunal shall not grant permission to amend in order to add a new ground for contesting the decision unless—

(a) such ground is based on matters of law or fact which have come to light since the appeal was made; or
(b) it was not practicable to include such ground in the notice of appeal; or
(c) the circumstances are exceptional.

Withdrawal of the appeal

12.— (1) The appellant may withdraw his appeal only with the permission of the Tribunal, or if the case has not yet proceeded to a hearing, the President.

A–012

(2) Where the Tribunal gives permission under paragraph (1) it may—

(a) do so on such terms as it thinks fit; [...]⁴
(b) instruct the Registrar to publish notice of the withdrawal on the Tribunal website or in such other manner as the Tribunal may direct[; and]⁵
[(c) publish any decision which it would have made had the appeal not been withdrawn.]⁶

(3) Where an appeal is withdrawn—

(a) any interim order of the Tribunal, other than an order made in respect of costs, shall immediately cease to have effect; and
(b) no fresh appeal may be brought by the appellant in relation to the decision which was the subject of the appeal withdrawn.

Response to appeal proceedings

Acknowledgement and notification

13. On receiving a notice of appeal the Registrar shall—

A–013

(a) send an acknowledgement of its receipt to the appellant; and
(b) subject to rules 9(2) and 10 send a copy of the notice of appeal to the respondent who made the disputed decision.

Defence

14.— (1) The respondent shall send to the Registrar a defence in the form required by this rule so that the defence is received within six weeks (or such further time as the Tribunal may allow) of the date on which the respondent received a copy of the notice of appeal in accordance with rule 13(b).

A–014

(2) The defence shall state—

(a) the name and address of the respondent;
(b) the name and address of the respondent's legal representative, if appropriate;

---

⁴ Words repealed by Competition Appeal Tribunal (Amendment and Communications Act Appeals) Rules SI 2004/2068, Sch.1, para.1(b).
⁵ Added by Competition Appeal Tribunal (Amendment and Communications Act Appeals) Rules SI 2004/2068, Sch.1, para.1(b).
⁶ Added by Competition Appeal Tribunal (Amendment and Communications Act Appeals) Rules SI 2004/2068, Sch.1, para.1(b).

(c) an address for service in the United Kingdom, and shall be signed and dated by the respondent, or on his behalf by his duly authorised officer or his legal representative.

(3) The defence shall contain—

(a) a succinct presentation of the arguments of fact and law upon which the respondent will rely;

(b) the relief sought by the respondent and any directions sought pursuant to rule 19; and

(c) a schedule listing all the documents annexed to the defence.

(4) The defence may contain observations on the question in which part of the United Kingdom the proceedings of the Tribunal are to be treated as taking place for all or for any purposes of those proceedings.

(5) There shall be annexed to the defence a copy of every document upon which the respondent relies including the written statements of all witnesses of fact, and where practicable expert witnesses, if any.

(6) The signed original of the defence (and its annexes) must be accompanied by ten copies certified by the respondent or his duly authorised officer or legal representative as conforming to the original.

(7) Rules 9, 10 (except rule 10(1)(b) and (c)) and 11 shall apply to the defence.

(8) On receiving the defence, the Registrar shall send a copy to the appellant.

Intervention, consolidation and forum

Publication of summary of appeal

A–015   **15.**— (1) Subject to rules 9 and 10 of these rules the Registrar shall as soon as practicable upon receipt of an appeal publish a notice on the Tribunal website and in any other manner the President may direct.

(2) The notice referred to in paragraph (1) above shall state—

(a) that an appeal has been received;

(b) the name of the appellant;

(c) the disputed decision to which the appeal relates and the person by whom it was made;

(d) the particulars of the relief sought by the appellant;

(e) a summary of the principal grounds relied on; and

(f) a statement indicating that any person who considers that he has sufficient interest may apply to intervene in the proceedings, in accordance with rule 16, within three weeks of publication of the notice or such other period as the President may direct.

Intervention

A–016   **16.**— (1) Any person who considers he has sufficient interest in the outcome may make a request to the Tribunal for permission to intervene in the proceedings.

(2) The request must be sent to the Registrar within the period referred to in rule 15(2)(f).

(3) The Registrar shall give notice of the request for permission to intervene to all the other parties to the proceedings and invite their observations on that request within a specified period.

(4) A request for permission to intervene must state—

(a) the title of the proceedings to which that request relates;

(b) the name and address of the person wishing to intervene;

(c) the name and address of his legal representative, if appropriate;

(d) an address for service in the United Kingdom.

(5) The request must contain—

(a) a concise statement of the matters in issue in the proceedings which affect the person making the request;

(b) the name of any party whose position the person making the request intends to support; and

(c) a succinct presentation of the reasons for making the request.

(6) If the Tribunal is satisfied, having taken into account the observations of the parties, that the intervening party has a sufficient interest, it may permit the intervention on such terms and conditions as it thinks fit.

(7) On granting permission in accordance with paragraph (6), the Tribunal shall give all such consequential directions as it considers necessary with regard, in particular, to the service on the intervener of the documents lodged with the Registrar, the submission by the intervener of a statement of intervention and, if appropriate, the submission by the principal parties of a response to the statement of intervention.

(8) In making any decision or direction under this rule the Tribunal shall have regard to the matters referred to in paragraph 1(2) of Schedule 4 to the 2002 Act.

(9) The statement of intervention [...][7] shall contain:

(a) a succinct presentation of the facts and arguments supporting the intervention;

(b) the relief sought by the intervener;

(c) a schedule listing all the documents annexed to the intervention and, as far as possible, a copy of every document on which the intervener relies including the written statements of witnesses of fact or expert witnesses, if any.

(10) Rules 9, 10 (except 10(1)(b)) and 11 shall apply to the statement of intervention.

Consolidation

17.— (1) Where two or more proceedings are pending in respect of the same decision, or which involve the same or similar issues, the Tribunal may, on the request of a party or of its own initiative, order that the proceedings or any particular issue or matter raised in the proceedings be consolidated or heard together. **A–017**

(2) Before making an order under this rule, the Tribunal shall invite the parties to the relevant proceedings to submit their observations.

Forum

18.— (1) The Tribunal, after taking into account the observations of the parties, may at any time determine whether its proceedings are to be treated, for purposes connected with— **A–018**

(a) any appeal from a decision of the Tribunal made in those proceedings; or

(b) any other matter connected with those proceedings, as proceedings in

---

[7] Words repealed by Competition Appeal Tribunal (Amendment and Communications Act Appeals) Rules SI 2004/2068, Sch.1, para.2.

England and Wales, in Scotland or in Northern Ireland and shall instruct the Registrar to notify the parties of its determination.

(2) Notwithstanding any determination under paragraph (1), the Tribunal may hold any meeting, case management conference, pre-hearing review or hearing, or give any directions, in such place and in such manner as it thinks fit having regard to the just, expeditious and economical conduct of the proceedings.

(3) In making a determination under paragraph (1), the Tribunal may have regard to all matters which appear to it to be relevant and in particular the part of the United Kingdom where—

(a)　any individual party to the proceedings is habitually resident or has his head office or principal place of business;

(b)　the majority of the parties are habitually resident or have their head offices or principal places of business;

(c)　any agreement, decision or concerted practice to which the proceedings relate was made or implemented or intended to be implemented;

(d)　any conduct to which the proceedings relate took place.

(4) Without prejudice to paragraph (3), in making a determination under paragraph (1) for the purposes of a claim for damages under section 47A of the 1998 Act, the Tribunal—

(a)　may have regard to the law which is applicable to the claim; and

(b)　in the case of claims included in proceedings under section 47B of the 1998 Act, may decide that one or more of the claims is to be treated as included in separate proceedings.

Case management

Directions

A–019　　**19.**— (1) The Tribunal may at any time, on the request of a party or of its own initiative, at a case management conference, pre-hearing review or otherwise, give such directions as are provided for in paragraph (2) below or such other directions as it thinks fit to secure the just, expeditious and economical conduct of the proceedings.

(2) The Tribunal may give directions—

(a)　as to the manner in which the proceedings are to be conducted, including any time limits to be observed in the conduct of the oral hearing;

(b)　that the parties file a reply, rejoinder or other additional pleadings or particulars;

(c)　for the preparation and exchange of skeleton arguments;

(d)　requiring persons to attend and give evidence or to produce documents;

(e)　as to the evidence which may be required or admitted in proceedings before the Tribunal and the extent to which it shall be oral or written;

(f)　as to the submission in advance of a hearing of any witness statements or expert reports;

(g)　as to the examination or cross-examination of witnesses;

(h)　as to the fixing of time limits with respect to any aspect of the proceedings;

(i)　as to the abridgement or extension of any time limits, whether or not expired;

(j) to enable a disputed decision to be referred back in whole or in part to the person by whom it was taken;

(k) for the disclosure between, or the production by, the parties of documents or classes of documents;

(l) for the appointment and instruction of experts, whether by the Tribunal or by the parties and the manner in which expert evidence is to be given;

(m) for the award of costs or expenses, including any allowances payable to persons in connection with their attendance before the Tribunal; and

(n) for hearing a person who is not a party where, in any proceedings, it is proposed to make an order or give a direction in relation to that person.

(3) The Tribunal may, in particular, of its own initiative—

(a) put questions to the parties;

(b) invite the parties to make written or oral submissions on certain aspects of the proceedings;

(c) ask the parties or third parties for information or particulars;

(d) ask for documents or any papers relating to the case to be produced;

(e) summon the parties' representatives or the parties in person to meetings.

(4) A request by a party for directions shall be made in writing as soon as practicable and shall be served by the Registrar on any other party who might be affected by such directions and determined by the Tribunal taking into account the observations of the parties.

Case management conference etc.

20.— (1) Where it appears to the Tribunal that any proceedings would be facilitated by holding a case management conference or pre-hearing review the Tribunal may, on the request of a party or of its own initiative, give directions for such a conference or review to be held.   **A–020**

(2) Unless the Tribunal otherwise directs, a case management conference shall be held as soon as practicable after the filing of an appeal, whether or not the time for service of the defence has expired.

(3) A case management conference or pre-hearing review shall be held in private unless the Tribunal otherwise directs.

(4) The purpose of a case management conference or pre-hearing review shall be—

(a) to ensure the efficient conduct of the proceedings;

(b) to determine the points on which the parties must present further argument or which call for further evidence to be produced;

(c) to clarify the forms of order sought by the parties, their arguments of fact and law and the points at issue between them;

(d) to ensure that all agreements that can be reached between the parties about the matters in issue and the conduct of the proceedings are made and recorded;

(e) to facilitate the settlement of the proceedings.

(5) The Tribunal may authorise a person qualified for appointment to the panel of chairmen to carry out on its behalf a case management conference, pre-hearing review or any other preparatory measure relating to the organisation or disposal of the proceedings.

Timetable for the oral hearing

A–021   **21.** As soon as practicable, the Tribunal shall—

(a)   set a timetable outlining the steps to be taken by the parties pursuant to the directions of the Tribunal in preparation for the oral hearing of the proceedings;

(b)   fix the date for the oral hearing;

(c)   notify the parties in writing of the date and place for the oral hearing and of any timetable for that hearing; and

(d)   if it considers it necessary for the expeditious disposal of the proceedings, send the parties a report for the hearing summarising the factual context of the case and the parties' principal submissions.

Evidence

A–022   **22.—** (1) The Tribunal may control the evidence by giving directions as to—

(a)   the issues on which it requires evidence;

(b)   the nature of the evidence which it requires to decide those issues; and

(c)   the way in which the evidence is to be placed before the Tribunal.

(2) The Tribunal may admit or exclude evidence, whether or not the evidence was available to the respondent when the disputed decision was taken.

(3) The Tribunal may require any witness to give evidence on oath or affirmation or if in writing by way of affidavit.

(4) The Tribunal may allow a witness to give evidence through a video link or by other means.

(5) The Tribunal may dispense with the need to call a witness to give oral evidence if a witness statement has been submitted in respect of that witness.

Summoning or citing of witnesses

A–023   **23.—** (1) Subject to paragraphs (2) and (3) below, the Tribunal may, at any time, either of its own initiative or at the request of any party, issue a summons, (or in relation to proceedings taking place in Scotland, a citation), requiring any person wherever he may be in the United Kingdom to do one or both of the following—

(a)   to attend as a witness before the Tribunal, at the time and place set out in the summons or citation; and

(b)   to answer any questions or produce any documents or other material in his possession or under his control which relate to any matter in question in the proceedings.

(2) A request by a party for the issue of a summons or citation under this rule shall state with reasons—

(a)   upon which facts the witness is to be questioned and the reasons for the examination;

(b)   the documents required to be produced.

(3) No person may be required to attend in compliance with a summons or citation under this rule unless—

(a)   he has been given at least seven days' notice of the hearing; and

(b)   he is paid such sum as would be recoverable by that witness in respect of his attendance in proceedings before the Supreme Court of England and Wales, the Court of Session or the Supreme Court of Northern Ireland.

(4) The Tribunal may make the summoning or citation of a witness in accordance with paragraph (1) conditional upon the deposit with the Registrar of a sum determined by the Tribunal as sufficient to cover—

(a)   the costs of the summons or citation;
(b)   the sum referred to in paragraph (3)(b).

(5) The Registrar shall advance the funds necessary in connection with the examination of any witness summoned by the Tribunal of its own initiative.

Failure to comply with directions

24. If any party fails to comply with any direction given in accordance with these rules, the Tribunal may if it considers that the justice of the case so requires, order that such party be debarred from taking any further part in the proceedings without the permission of the Tribunal.　　　　　　　　　　　　　　　　　　　A–024

PART III

PROCEEDINGS UNDER THE ENTERPRISE ACT 2002

Application of these rules

25. Parts I, II and V of these rules apply to proceedings under sections 114 or 176(1)(f) (appeals against penalties in merger or market investigations), section 120 (review of merger decisions) and section 179 (review of market investigation decisions), save as otherwise provided in this Part.　　　　　　　　　　　A–025

Time for commencing proceedings for a review under section 120 of the 2002 Act

26. An application under section 120(1) of the 2002 Act for the review of a decision in connection with a reference or possible reference in relation to a relevant merger situation or a special merger situation, must be made within four weeks of the date on which the applicant was notified of the disputed decision, or the date of publication of the decision, whichever is the earlier.　　　　　　　　　　A–026

Time for commencing proceedings for a review under section 179 of the 2002 Act

27. An application under section 179(1) of the 2002 Act for review of a decision in connection with a reference or possible reference under Part 4 of that Act (market investigations) must be made within two months of the date on which the applicant was notified of the disputed decision, or the date of publication of the decision, whichever is the earlier.　　　　　　　　　　　　　　　　　　　A–027

Supplementary provisions concerning reviews

28.— (1) In proceedings for a review under sections 120 or 179 of the 2002 Act, rules 8 to 16 shall be construed and applied as if references to "appeal" were references to "application", references to　　　　　　　　　　　　　A–028

"the notice of appeal" were references to "the notice of application", references to the "appellant"
were references to the "applicant", and references to the "grounds of appeal" were references to the "grounds of review".

(2) Rule 8(2) shall apply to the time for commencing proceedings under rules 26 and 27 as it does to the time for commencing an appeal under rule 8(1).

(3) In proceedings for a review under section 120 of the 2002 Act, rule 14(1) shall apply with the substitution of "four weeks" for "six weeks".

(4) The Tribunal's power to reject an appeal under rule 10 includes a power to reject an application for review if it considers that the applicant is not a person aggrieved by the decision in respect of which the review is sought.

Appeals in relation to penalties under sections 114 or 176(1)(f) of the 2002 Act

A–029   **29.**— (1) An appeal against a penalty brought under section 114 or 176(1)(f) of the 2002 Act must be made by sending a notice of appeal to the Registrar so that it is received within the period of 28 days starting with—

    (a)   in the case of an appeal against a penalty imposed by a notice under section 112(1) of that Act, the day on which a copy of the notice was served on the person concerned;

    (b)   in the case of an appeal against a decision on an application under section 112(3), the day on which the person concerned was notified of the decision.

(2) In an appeal against a penalty brought under section 114 or 176(1)(f) of the 2002 Act, rule 14(1) shall apply with the substitution of "three weeks" for "six weeks".

(3) Rules 15 and 16 shall not apply to appeals against penalties under sections 114 or 176(1)(f) of the 2002 Act.

PART IV

CLAIMS FOR DAMAGES

Application of rules to claims for damages

A–030   **30.** The rules applicable to proceedings under sections 47A and 47B of the 1998 Act (claims for damages) are those set out in this Part, and in Part I, Part II (except for rules 8 to 16) and Part V of these rules. In respect of proceedings in Scotland, references in this Part to "claimant" and "defendant" shall be read respectively as "pursuer" and "defender".

Commencement of proceedings

Time limit for making a claim for damages

A–031   **31.**— (1) A claim for damages must be made within a period of two years beginning with the relevant date.

(2) The relevant date for the purposes of paragraph (1) is the later of the following—

    (a)   the end of the period specified in section 47A(7) or (8) of the 1998 Act in relation to the decision on the basis of which the claim is made;

    (b)   the date on which the cause of action accrued.

(3) The Tribunal may give its permission for a claim to be made before the end of the period referred to in paragraph (2)(a) after taking into account any observations of a proposed defendant.

(4) No claim for damages may be made if, were the claim to be made in proceedings brought before a court, the claimant would be prevented from bringing the proceedings by reason of a limitation period having expired before the commencement of section 47A.

Manner of commencing proceedings under section 47A of the 1998 Act

32.— (1) A claim for damages under section 47A of the 1998 Act must be made by   **A–032** sending a claim form to the Registrar within the period specified in rule 31(1).

(2) The claim form referred to in paragraph (1) shall state—

  (a) the full name and address of the claimant;

  (b) the full name and address of the claimant's legal representative, if appropriate;

  (c) an address for service in the United Kingdom; and

  (d) the name and address of the defendant to the proceedings.

(3) The claim form shall contain—

  (a) a concise statement of the relevant facts, identifying any relevant findings in the decision on the basis of which the claim for damages is being made;

  (b) a concise statement of any contentions of law which are relied on;

  (c) a statement of the amount claimed in damages, supported with evidence of losses incurred and of any calculations which have been undertaken to arrive at the claimed amount;

  (d) such other matters as may be specified by practice direction, and its contents shall be verified by a statement of truth signed and dated by the claimant or on his behalf by his duly authorised officer or his legal representative.

(4) There shall be annexed to the claim form—

  (a) a copy of the decision on the basis of which the claim for damages is being made;

  (b) as far as practicable a copy of all essential documents on which the claimant relies.

(5) Unless the Tribunal otherwise directs, the signed original of the claim form (and its annexes) must be accompanied by ten copies certified by the claimant or his legal representative as conforming to the original.

Manner of commencing proceedings under section 47B of the 1998 Act

33.— (1) Where a claim for damages is made under section 47B of the 1998 Act by   **A–033** a specified body on behalf of consumers the claim form shall in addition to the information required by rule 32—

  (a) contain the name and address of the specified body and a concise statement of the object or activities of that body;

  (b) contain the names and addresses of the persons it seeks to represent;

  (c) be accompanied by a document or documents, giving consent to the specified body by each of the individuals listed in the claim form to act on his behalf;

(d) indicate whether each individual listed in connection with the claim is a "consumer" for the purposes of section 47B of the 1998 Act.

(2) A claim for damages commenced under section 47A of the 1998 Act may be continued by a specified body under section 47B of that Act subject to such directions as may be given by the Tribunal.

Amendment

A–034   **34.** A claim form may only be amended—

    (a) with the written consent of all the parties; or
    (b) with the permission of the Tribunal.

Addition of parties

A–035   **35.** The Tribunal may, after hearing the parties, grant permission for one or more parties to be joined in the proceedings in addition or in substitution to the existing parties.

Response to a claim for damages

Acknowledgment and notification

A–036   **36.**— (1) On receiving a claim the Registrar shall send an acknowledgment of receipt to the claimant and send a copy of the claim form to the defendant.

(2) Within 7 days of receipt of the copy of the claim form from the Registrar the defendant shall send to the Registrar an acknowledgment of service of the claim form in such form as the President may direct.

Defence to a claim for damages

A–037   **37.**— (1) Within 28 days of receipt of the copy of the claim form from the Registrar the defendant shall send to the Registrar a defence setting out in sufficient detail which of the facts and contentions of law in the claim form it admits or denies, on what grounds and on what other facts or contentions of law it relies.

(2) The contents of the defence shall be verified by a statement of truth signed and dated by the defendant or on his behalf by his duly authorised officer or his legal representative.

(3) Unless the Tribunal otherwise directs, the signed original of the defence (and its annexes) must be accompanied by ten copies certified by the defendant or his legal representative as conforming to the original.

Additional claims

A–038   **38.**— (1) A defendant may make a counterclaim against a claimant or a claim against any other person—

    (a) without the Tribunal's permission if he includes it with his defence;
    (b) at any other time with the Tribunal's permission.

(2) Rules 31, 32(2), (3), (4) and (5) shall apply to claims or counterclaims under this rule and rules 36 and 37 shall apply to the response to such claims, subject to any direction by the Tribunal to the contrary.

Further pleadings

39. No further pleadings may be filed without the permission of the Tribunal.   **A–039**

Summary disposal

Power to reject

40.— (1) The Tribunal may, of its own initiative or on the application of a party,   **A–040**
after giving the parties an opportunity to be heard, reject in whole or in part a claim
for damages at any stage of the proceedings if—

(a) it considers that there are no reasonable grounds for making the claim;

(b) in the case of proceedings under section 47B of the 1998 Act it considers that
     the body bringing the proceedings is not entitled to do so, or that an indi-
     vidual on whose behalf the proceedings are brought is not a consumer for the
     purposes of that section;

(c) it is satisfied that the claimant has habitually and persistently and without
     any reasonable ground—

    (i) instituted vexatious proceedings, whether against the same person or
     different persons; or

    (ii) made vexatious applications in any proceedings; or

(d) the claimant fails to comply with any rule, direction, practice direction or
     order of the Tribunal.

(2) When the Tribunal rejects a claim it may enter judgment on the claim in whole
or in part or make any other consequential order it considers appropriate.

Summary judgment

41.— (1) The Tribunal may of its own initiative or on the application of a party,   **A–041**
after giving the parties an opportunity to be heard, give summary judgment in a
claim for damages or reject in whole or in part a claim or defence in a claim for
damages if—

(a) it considers that—

    (i) the claimant has no real prospect of succeeding on the claim or issue; or

    (ii) the defendant has no reasonable grounds for defending the claim or
     issue; and

(b) there is no other compelling reason why the case or issue should be disposed
     of at a substantive hearing.

(2) The Tribunal shall not exercise its power under this rule before the filing of the
defence.

(3) The Tribunal shall give such directions as it considers appropriate for dealing
with a request under this rule.

(4) Upon giving summary judgment the Tribunal may make any consequential
order it considers appropriate.

Withdrawal

42.— (1) The claimant may withdraw his claim only—   **A–042**

(a) with the consent of the defendant; or

(b) with the permission of the President or, if the case has proceeded to a hearing, the Tribunal.

(2) Where a claim is withdrawn—

(a) the Tribunal may make any consequential order it thinks fit;

(b) no further claim may be brought by the claimant in respect of the same subject matter.

Offers and payments to settle

Offers and payments to settle

A–043   **43.**— (1) A payment to settle is an offer made by way of payment into the Tribunal in such manner as may be prescribed by practice direction.

(2) A payment to settle the whole or part of a claim may be made by a defendant once a claim for damages has been commenced.

(3) Notification of a payment to settle into the Tribunal must be sent to the Registrar and to the party to whom the payment to settle is made. Such notification must state precisely the basis on which the payment has been calculated.

(4) A payment to settle may be withdrawn or reduced only with the permission of the Registrar.

(5) A payment to settle may be accepted any time up to 14 days before the substantive hearing of the claim.

(6) Where a claimant accepts a defendant's payment to settle the whole or part of the proceedings, he shall be entitled to his costs of the proceedings or such costs relating to the part of the proceedings to which the offer related, up to the date of serving notice of acceptance, unless the Tribunal otherwise directs.

(7) [...][8] where following a substantive hearing a claimant fails to better a payment to settle, the Tribunal will order the claimant to pay any costs incurred by the defendant after the latest date on which the payment or offer could have been accepted unless it considers it unjust to do so. The Tribunal may order such costs to carry interest from that date and to be paid on an indemnity basis.

(8) The fact that a payment to settle has been made shall not be communicated to the members of the Tribunal deciding the case until all questions of liability and the amount of money to be awarded have been agreed between the parties or determined by the Tribunal.

(9) A payment to settle under this rule will be treated as "without prejudice" except as to costs.

(10) This rule does not preclude either party from making an offer to settle at any time or by any other means. In the event that, following a substantive hearing, a claimant recovers less than the amount offered by a defendant other than by way of a payment to settle, the Tribunal may take that fact into account on the issue of costs, notwithstanding the provisions of rule 55(3).

Case management

Case management generally

A–044   **44.**— (1) In determining claims for damages the Tribunal shall actively exercise the Tribunal's powers set out in rules 17 (Consolidation), 18 (Forum), 19 (Directions), 20

---

[8] Words repealed by Competition Appeal Tribunal (Amendment and Communications Act Appeals) Rules SI 2004/2068, Sch.1, para.3.

(Case management conference etc.), 21 (Timetable for the oral hearing), 22 (Evidence), 23 (Summoning or citing of witnesses) and 24 (Failure to comply with directions) with a view to ensuring that the case is dealt with justly.

(2) Dealing with a case justly includes, so far as is practicable—

(a) ensuring that the parties are on an equal footing;
(b) saving expense;
(c) dealing with the case in ways which are proportionate—

    (i) to the amount of money involved;
    (ii) to the importance of the case;
    (iii) to the complexity of the issues; and
    (iv) to the financial position of each party;

(d) ensuring that it is dealt with expeditiously and fairly; and
(e) allotting to it an appropriate share of the Tribunal's resources, while taking into account the need to allot resources to other cases.

(3) The Tribunal may in particular—

(a) encourage and facilitate the use of an alternative dispute resolution procedure if the Tribunal considers that appropriate;
(b) dispense with the need for the parties to attend any hearing;
(c) use technology actively to manage cases.

Security for costs

45.— (1) A defendant to a claim for damages may by request under this rule seek   **A–045**
security for his costs of the proceedings.

(2) A request for security for costs must be supported by written evidence.

(3) Where the Tribunal makes an order for security for costs, it shall—

(a) determine the amount of security; and
(b) direct—

    (i) the manner in which, and
    (ii) the time within which the security must be given.

(4) The Tribunal may make an order for security for costs under this rule if—

(a) it is satisfied, having regard to all the circumstances of the case, that it is just to make such an order; and
(b) one or more of the conditions in paragraph 5 applies.

(5) The conditions are—

(a) the claimant is an individual—

    (i) who is ordinarily resident out of the jurisdiction; and
    (ii) is not a person against whom a claim can be enforced under the Brussels Conventions or the Lugano Convention or the Regulation, as defined by section 1(1) of the Civil Jurisdiction and Judgments Act 1982[9];

---

[9] s.1(1) is amended by para.1 of Sch.2 to the Civil Jurisdiction and Judgments Order 2001 (SI 2001/3929).

(b)   the claimant is a company or other incorporated body—

    (i)   which is ordinarily resident out of the jurisdiction; and

    (ii)   is not a body against whom a claim can be enforced under the Brussels Conventions or the Lugano Convention or the Regulation;

(c)   the claimant is an undertaking (whether or not it is an incorporated body, and whether or not it is incorporated inside or outside the United Kingdom) and there is reason to believe that it will be unable to pay the defendant's costs if ordered to do so;

(d)   the claimant has changed his address since the claim was commenced with a view to evading the consequences of the litigation;

(e)   the claimant failed to give his address in the claim form, or gave an incorrect address in that form;

(f)   the claimant is acting as a nominal claimant, other than under section 47B of the 1998 Act, and there is reason to believe that he will be unable to pay the defendant's costs if ordered to do so;

(g)   the claimant has taken steps in relation to his assets that would make it difficult to enforce an order for costs against him.

Payments of damages

Interim payments on claims for damages

A–046   **46.**— (1) An interim payment is an order for payment by the defendant on account of any damages (except costs) which the Tribunal may hold the defendant liable to pay.

(2) The claimant may not request an order for an interim payment before the end of the period for filing a defence by the defendant against whom the claim is made.

(3) The claimant may make more than one request for an order for an interim payment.

(4) The Tribunal may make an interim payment order if—

(a)   the defendant against whom the order is sought has admitted liability to pay damages to the claimant;

(b)   it is satisfied that, if the claim were to be heard the claimant would obtain judgment for a substantial amount of money (other than costs) against the defendant from whom he is seeking damages.

(5) The Tribunal must not order an interim payment of more than a reasonable proportion of the likely amount of the final judgment.

(6) A request for an interim payment shall include—

(a)   the grounds on which an interim payment is sought;

(b)   any directions necessary in the opinion of the claimant for the determination of the request.

(7) On receiving a request for an interim payment the Registrar shall send a copy to all the other parties to the proceedings and shall inform them of the date by which they may submit written or oral observations to the Tribunal.

Order for payment of damages

A–047   **47.**— (1) If satisfied that the claimant is entitled to an amount of damages, the Tribunal shall order that amount to be paid to the claimant by the defendant.

(2) Where an award is made in respect of a claim included in proceedings brought by a specified body under section 47B of the 1998 Act, the Tribunal may (with the consent of the individual concerned and the specified body) order that the amount awarded is to be paid to the specified body on behalf of the individual.

(3) The Tribunal shall make such consequential orders as may be necessary for the payment of damages awarded in proceedings under section 47B of the 1998 Act.

(4) In making any order for the payment of damages to a claimant the Tribunal may take into account any sums owing from the claimant to the defendant.

Transfers

Transfer of claims from the Tribunal

48. The Tribunal may, at any stage of the proceedings on the request of a party or **A–048** of its own initiative, and after considering any observations of the parties direct that a claim for damages (other than a claim included in proceedings under section 47B of the 1998 Act) be transferred to—

    (a) the High Court or a county court in England and Wales or Northern Ireland; or

    (b) the Court of Session or a sheriff court in Scotland.

Transfer of claims to the Tribunal

49.— (1) A claim which may be made under section 47A of the 1998 Act may be **A–049** transferred to the Tribunal from any court in accordance with rules of court or any practice direction.

(2) The person bringing the claim shall within 7 days of the order of the court transferring the claim or such other period directed by that court, send to the Registrar—

    (a) a certified copy of the order of the court transferring the claim to the Tribunal;

    (b) any pleadings and documents in support of the claim filed with the court in which the claim was begun;

    (c) any directions sought for the further progress of the claim.

(3) As soon as practicable after receipt of the documents referred to in paragraph (2) a case management conference shall be held in accordance with rule 20.

PART V

GENERAL AND SUPPLEMENTARY

The hearing

Hearing to be in public

50. The hearing of any appeal, review or claim for damages shall be in public **A–050** except as to any part where the Tribunal is satisfied that it will be considering information which is, in its opinion, information of the kind referred to in paragraph 1(2) of Schedule 4 to the 2002 Act.

Procedure at the hearing

A–051   **51.**— (1) The proceedings shall be opened and directed by the President or the chairman who shall be responsible for the proper conduct of the hearing.

(2) The Tribunal shall, so far as it appears to it appropriate, seek to avoid formality in its proceedings and shall conduct the hearing in such manner as it considers most appropriate for the clarification of the issues before it and generally to the just, expeditious and economical handling of the proceedings.

(3) Unless the Tribunal otherwise directs, no witness of fact or expert shall be heard unless the relevant witness statement or expert report has been submitted in advance of the hearing and in accordance with any directions of the Tribunal.

(4) The Tribunal may limit cross-examination of witnesses to any extent or in any manner it deems appropriate.

Quorum

A–052   **52.**— (1) If, after the commencement of any hearing, the chairman is unable to continue the President may appoint either of the remaining two members to chair the Tribunal; and in that case the Tribunal shall consist of the remaining two members for the rest of the proceedings.

(2) If the person appointed under paragraph (1) is not a member of the panel of chairmen, the President may appoint himself or some other suitably qualified person to attend the proceedings and advise the remaining members on any questions of law arising.

(3) For the purposes of paragraph (2), a person is "suitably qualified" if he is, or is qualified for appointment as, a member of the panel of chairmen.

(4) If, after the commencement of any hearing, a member of the Tribunal (other than its chairman) is unable to continue, the President may decide that the Tribunal shall consist of the remaining two members for the rest of the proceedings.

(5) Where in pursuance of this rule the Tribunal consists of two members, a decision of the Tribunal must be unanimous.

Confidentiality

Requests for confidential treatment

A–053   **53.**— (1) A request for the confidential treatment of any document or part of a document filed in connection with proceedings before the Tribunal shall be made in writing by the person who submitted the document at the latest within 14 days after filing the document indicating the relevant words, figures or passages for which confidentiality is claimed and supported in each case by specific reasons and, if so directed by the Registrar, the person making the request must supply a non-confidential version of the relevant document.

(2) No request for confidential treatment made in disregard of this rule or outside the period provided under paragraph (1) shall be permitted unless the Tribunal considers that the circumstances are exceptional.

(3) In the event of a dispute as to whether confidential treatment should be accorded, the Tribunal shall decide the matter after hearing the parties, taking into account the matters referred to in paragraph 1(2) of Schedule 4 to the 2002 Act.

Decision of the tribunal

Delivery of the decision

54.— (1) The decision of the Tribunal shall be delivered in public on the date fixed   **A–054**
for that purpose.

(2) The Registrar shall send a copy of the document recording the decision to each
party and shall enter it on the register.

(3) The decision of the Tribunal shall be treated as having been notified on the date
on which a copy of the document recording it is sent to the parties under paragraph
(2).

(4) The President shall arrange for the decision of the Tribunal to be published in
such manner as he considers appropriate.

Costs

55.— (1) For the purposes of these rules "costs" means costs and expenses reco-   **A–055**
verable before the Supreme Court of England and Wales, the Court of Session or the
Supreme Court of Northern Ireland.

(2) The Tribunal may at its discretion, subject to paragraph (3), at any stage of the
proceedings make any order it thinks fit in relation to the payment of costs by one
party to another in respect of the whole or part of the proceedings and in determining how much the party is required to pay, the Tribunal may take account of the
conduct of all parties in relation to the proceedings.

(3) Any party against whom an order for costs is made shall, if the Tribunal so
directs, pay to any other party a lump sum by way of costs, or all or such proportion
of the costs as may be just. The Tribunal may assess the sum to be paid pursuant to
any order under paragraph [(2)][10] or may direct that it be assessed by the President, a
chairman or the Registrar, or dealt with by the detailed assessment of a costs officer
of the Supreme Court or a taxing officer of the Supreme Court of Northern Ireland
or by the Auditor of the Court of Session.

(4) Unless the Tribunal otherwise directs, an order made pursuant to [paragraph
(2) or a direction made pursuant to paragraph (3)][11] may be made in the decision, if
the parties so consent, or immediately following delivery of the decision.

(5) The power to award costs pursuant to paragraphs (1) to (3) includes the power
to direct any party to pay to the Tribunal such sum as may be appropriate in
reimbursement of any costs incurred by the Tribunal in connection with the summoning or citation of witnesses or the instruction of experts on the Tribunal's behalf.
Any sum due as a result of such a direction may be recovered by the Tribunal as a
civil debt due to the Tribunal.

Interest

56.— (1) If it imposes, confirms or varies any penalty under Part 1 of the 1998 Act,   **A–056**
the Tribunal may, in addition, order that interest is to be payable on the amount of
any such penalty from such date, not being a date earlier than the date upon which
the application was made in accordance with rule 8, and at such rate, as the Tribunal
considers appropriate. Unless the Tribunal otherwise directs, the rate of interest shall

---

[10] Words substituted by Competition Appeal Tribunal (Amendment and Communications Act
Appeals) Rules SI 2004/2068, Sch.1, para.4(a).
[11] Words substituted by Competition Appeal Tribunal (Amendment and Communications Act
Appeals) Rules SI 2004/2068, Sch.1, para.4(b).

not exceed the rate specified in any Order made pursuant to section 44 of the Administration of Justice Act 1970. Such interest is to form part of the penalty and be recoverable as a civil debt in addition to the amount recoverable under section 36 of the 1998 Act.

(2) If it makes an award of damages the Tribunal may include in any sum awarded interest on all or any part of the damages in respect of which the award is made, for all or any part of the period between the date when the cause of action arose and—

(a) in the case of any sum paid before the decision making the award, the date of the payment; and

(b) in the case of the sum awarded, the date of that decision. Unless the Tribunal otherwise directs, the rate of interest shall not exceed the rate specified in any Order made pursuant to section 44 of the Administration of Justice Act 1970.

Consent orders

A–057   57.— (1) If all the parties agree the terms on which to settle all or any part of the proceedings, they may request the Tribunal to make a consent order.

(2) A request for a consent order shall be made by sending to the Registrar—

(a) a draft consent order;

(b) a consent order impact statement; and

(c) a statement signed by all the parties to the proceedings or their legal representatives requesting that an order be made in the form of the draft.

(3) A consent order impact statement shall provide an explanation of the draft consent order, including an explanation of the circumstances giving rise to the draft order, the relief to be obtained if the order is made and the anticipated effects on competition of that relief.

(4) If the Tribunal considers that a proposed consent order may have a significant effect on competition, it shall direct the Registrar as soon as practicable following receipt of the application to publish a notice on the Tribunal website or in such other manner as the Tribunal may direct.

(5) The notice referred to in paragraph (4) shall state—

(a) that a request for a consent order has been received;

(b) the name of each of the parties to the proceedings;

(c) the particulars of the relief sought by those parties; and

(d) that the draft consent order and consent order impact statement may be inspected at the Tribunal address for service or such other place as may be mentioned in the notice and shall so far as practicable exclude any information of the kind referred to in paragraph 1(2) of Schedule 4 to the 2002 Act.

(6) Any person may send his comments upon a request for a consent order to the Registrar within one month of the date upon which the notice was published in accordance with paragraph (4).

(7) Comments supplied in accordance with paragraph (6) shall be in writing, signed by the commentator and shall state the title of the proceedings to which the comments relate and the name and address of the commentator.

(8) The Registrar shall send all comments received in accordance with paragraph

(6) to all parties to the proceedings. Any party to the proceedings may within 14 days of receipt of the comments send a response to the comments to the Registrar.

(9) In respect of any request for a consent order the Tribunal may, as it thinks fit, after hearing the parties and considering the comments of third parties—

(a) make the order in the terms requested; or
(b) invite the parties to vary the terms; or
(c) refuse to make any order.

(10) This rule does not apply to claims for damages.

Appeals from the tribunal

Permission to appeal

58.— (1) A request to the Tribunal for permission to appeal from a decision of the Tribunal may be made— **A–058**

(a) orally at any hearing at which the decision is delivered by the Tribunal; or
(b) in writing to the Registrar within one month of the notification of that decision.

(2) Where a request for permission to appeal is made in writing, it shall be signed and dated by the party or his representative and shall—

(a) state the name and address of the party and of any representative of the party;
(b) identify the Tribunal decision to which the request relates;
(c) state the grounds on which the party intends to rely in his appeal; and
(d) state whether the party requests a hearing of his request and any special circumstances relied on.

Decision of the Tribunal on request for permission to appeal

59.— (1) Where a request for permission to appeal is made orally the Tribunal shall give its decision either orally or in writing, stating its reasons. **A–059**

(2) Where a request for permission to appeal is made in writing, the Tribunal shall decide whether to grant such permission on consideration of the party's request and, unless it considers that special circumstances render a hearing desirable, in the absence of the parties.

(3) The decision of the Tribunal on a written request for permission to appeal together with the reasons for that decision shall be recorded in writing and the Registrar shall notify the parties of such decision.

References to the european court

References to the European Court

60.— (1) An order may be made by the Tribunal of its own initiative at any stage in the proceedings or on application by a party before or at the oral hearing. **A–060**

(2) An order shall set out in a schedule the request for the preliminary ruling of the European Court and the Tribunal may give directions as to the manner and form in which the schedule is to be prepared.

(3) The proceedings in which an order is made shall, unless the Tribunal otherwise directs, be stayed (or in Scotland, sisted) until the European Court has given a preliminary ruling on the question referred to it.

(4) When an order has been made, the Registrar shall send a copy of it to the Registrar of the European Court.

(5) In this rule—

"European Court" means the Court of Justice of the European Communities;

"order" means an order referring a question to the European Court for a preliminary ruling under Article 234 of the Treaty establishing the European Community, Article 150 of the Treaty establishing the European Atomic Energy Community or Article 41 of the Treaty establishing the European Coal and Steel Community.

Interim orders and measures

Power to make interim orders and to take interim measures

A–061   **61.**— (1) The Tribunal may make an order on an interim basis—

    (a) suspending in whole or part the effect of any decision which is the subject matter of proceedings before it;

    (b) in the case of an appeal under section 46 or 47 of the 1998 Act, varying the conditions or obligations attached to an exemption;

    (c) granting any remedy which the Tribunal would have the power to grant in its final decision.

(2) Without prejudice to the generality of the foregoing, if the Tribunal considers that it is necessary as a matter of urgency for the purpose of—

    (a) preventing serious, irreparable damage to a particular person or category of person, or

    (b) protecting the public interest, the Tribunal may give such directions as it considers appropriate for that purpose.

(3) The Tribunal shall exercise its power under this rule taking into account all the relevant circumstances, including—

    (a) the urgency of the matter;

    (b) the effect on the party making the request if the relief sought is not granted; and

    (c) the effect on competition if the relief is granted.

(4) Any order or direction under this rule is subject to the Tribunal's further order, direction or final decision.

(5) A party shall apply for an order or a direction under paragraphs (1) and (2) by sending a request for interim relief in the form required by paragraph (6) to the Registrar.

(6) The request for interim relief shall state—

    (a) the subject matter of the proceedings;

    (b) in the case of a request for a direction pursuant to paragraph (2), the circumstances giving rise to the urgency;

    (c) the factual and legal grounds establishing a prima facie case for the granting of interim relief by the Tribunal;

    (d) the relief sought;

    (e) if no appeal or application has been made in accordance with rule 8, in respect of a decision which is the subject of the request for interim relief, an outline of the information required by rule 8(4).

(7) On receiving a request for interim relief the Registrar shall send a copy to all the other parties to the proceedings (and where no appeal or application has been made in accordance with rule 8, to the person who made the decision to which the request for interim relief relates) and shall inform them of the date by which they may submit written or oral observations to the Tribunal.

(8) The Tribunal shall fix a date for the hearing of the request for interim relief and give the parties any directions as may be necessary for disposing of the request for interim relief.

(9) The Tribunal may, for the purposes of this rule, join any party to the proceedings.

(10) Subject to paragraph 11, an order or direction for interim relief may be made against a person who is not a party to the proceedings, provided that no such order may be made unless that person has been given an opportunity to be heard.

(11) If the urgency of the case so requires, the Tribunal may dispense with a written request for interim relief or grant the request for interim relief before the observations of the other parties have been submitted.

(12) Unless the context otherwise requires, these rules apply to requests for interim relief.

(13) This rule does not apply to claims for damages.

Supplementary

Power of President, Chairman and Registrar to exercise powers of Tribunal

62.— (1) Any procedural act required or authorised by these rules, not being one required or authorised by the following rules—   A–062

  (a) rules 10 (Power to reject) and [28(4)][12];
  (b) rule 12 (Withdrawal of the appeal), in the case of a withdrawal during or after the hearing;
  (c) rule 40 (Power to reject);
  (d) rule 41 (Summary judgment);
  (e) rule 42 (Withdrawal), in the case of a withdrawal during or after the hearing;
  (f) [rule 59][13] (Decision of the Tribunal on request for permission to appeal);
  (g) rule 60 (References to the European Court), may be done by the President acting alone.

(2) The powers of the President may be exercised by a chairman provided that the powers conferred by rule 61 may only be exercised by a chairman if the urgency of an application made in accordance with rule 61(7) so requires.

(3) If so authorised by the President, the Registrar may, subject to rule 4(4) and without prejudice to rule 55(3)—

  (a) make any order by consent (except where rule 57(4) applies);
  (b) deal with extensions or abridgments of time limits under rule 19(2)(i), except

---

[12] Figure substituted by Competition Appeal Tribunal (Amendment and Communication Act Appeals) Rules SI 2004/2068, Sch.1, para.5(a).
[13] Figure substituted by Competition Appeal Tribunal (Amendment and Communications Act Appeals) Rules SI 2004/2068, Sch.1, para.5(b).

a request for an extension of time for filing an appeal or application under Part II or Part III of these rules;

(c)   deal with requests for confidential treatment under rule 53;

(d)   exercise the Tribunal's powers in respect of the service of documents under rule 63.

Documents etc.

A–063   **63.**— (1) Any document required to be sent to or served on any person for the purposes of proceedings under these rules may be—

(a)   delivered personally at his appropriate address;

(b)   sent to him at his appropriate address by first class post;

(c)   served through a document exchange;

(d)   where authorised by the Tribunal, sent to him by facsimile or electronic mail or other similar means.

(2) Where—

(a)   a document is to be served by the Tribunal; and

(b)   the Tribunal is unable to serve it, the Tribunal must send a notice of non-service, stating the method attempted, to the other parties to the proceedings.

(3) Where it appears to the Tribunal that there is a good reason to authorise service by a method not permitted by these rules, the Tribunal may of its own initiative or on the request of a party make an order permitting and specifying an alternative method of service, and specifying when the document will be deemed to be served.

(4) The Tribunal may dispense with service of a document if the interests of justice so require.

(5) A document which is sent or served in accordance with these rules shall be treated as if it had been received by or served on that person—

(a)   in the case of personal delivery, on the day of delivery;

(b)   when sent by first class post or through a document exchange, on the second day after it was posted or left at the document exchange;

(c)   in the case of a facsimile transmitted on a business day before 4pm on that day or in any other case on the business day after the day on which it is transmitted;

(d)   in the case of electronic mail or similar means, on the second day after the day on which it is transmitted.

(6) If a document (other than a facsimile) is served [or is treated by virtue of paragraph (5) as having been served][14] after 5pm on a business day, or at any time on a Saturday, Sunday or a Bank Holiday, the document shall be treated as having been served on the next business day.

(7) For the purposes of these rules "business day" means any day except Saturday, Sunday or a Bank Holiday and "Bank Holiday" includes Christmas Day and Good Friday.

(8) A person's appropriate address for the purposes of paragraph (1) is—

---

[14] Words inserted by Competition Appeal Tribunal (Amendment and Communications Act Appeals) Rules SI 2004/2068, Sch.1, para.6.

(a) in the case of a document directed to the Tribunal or to the Registrar, the Tribunal address for service;

(b) in the case of a document directed to the applicant or to his representative, the address stated in the application in accordance with rule 8(3)(c) or such other address as may be subsequently notified to the Tribunal;

(c) in the case of a document addressed to the respondent, the address stated in the defence in accordance with rule 14(2)(c) or such other address as may be subsequently notified to the Tribunal;

(d) in the case of an intervener, the address stated in the request to intervene in accordance with rule 16(4)(d) or such other address as may be subsequently notified to the Tribunal.

(9) Anything required to be sent to or served on a company is duly sent or served if it is sent to or served on the secretary of the company at its principal place of business or registered address for the time being.

(10) Anything required to be sent or delivered to or served on a partnership is duly sent or served if it is sent to or served on any one of the partners for the time being.

(11) The Registrar shall, at the request of the Tribunal, or any party, certify the steps taken to serve a document pursuant to this rule, including the date and manner of service.

Time

64.— (1) Where a period expressed in days, weeks or months is to be calculated   **A–064**
from the moment at which an event occurs or an action takes place, the day during which that event occurs or that action takes place shall not be counted as falling within the period in question.

(2) A period expressed in weeks or months shall end with the expiry of whichever day in the last week or month is the same day of the week or falls on the same date in the month, as the day during which the event or action from which the period is to be calculated occurred or took place. If, in a period expressed in months, the day on which it should expire does not occur in the last month, the period shall end with the expiry of the last day of that month.

(2) "Month"shall mean calendar month.

(3) Where the time prescribed by the Tribunal, the President, a chairman or the Registrar, or by these rules, for doing any act expires on a Saturday, Sunday or Bank Holiday, the act is in time if done on the next following day which is not a Saturday, Sunday or Bank Holiday.

Conditional Fee Arrangements

65. The rules on funding arrangements made under the Civil Procedure Rules 1998   **A–065**
as amended apply to proceedings before the Tribunal.

Enforcement of orders

66. Any order, direction or decision of the Tribunal is enforceable in accordance   **A–066**
with Schedule 4 to the 2002 Act.

Irregularities

67.— (1) Any irregularity resulting from failure to comply with any provision of   **A–067**

these rules before the Tribunal has reached its decision shall not of itself render the proceedings void.

(2) Where any such irregularity comes to the attention of the Tribunal, the Tribunal may, and must if it considers any person may have been prejudiced by the irregularity, give such directions as it thinks just, to cure or waive the irregularity before reaching its decision.

(3) Clerical mistakes in any document recording a direction, order or decision of the Tribunal, the President, a chairman or the Registrar, or errors arising in such a document from an accidental slip or omission, may be corrected by the President, that chairman or the Registrar, as the case may be, by certificate under his hand.

General power of the Tribunal

A–068   **68.**— (1) Subject to the provisions of these rules, the Tribunal may regulate its own procedure.

(2) The President may issue practice directions in relation to the procedures provided for by these rules.

Transitional and revocation

Transitional

A–069   **69.** Proceedings commenced before the Tribunal prior to the coming into force of these rules shall continue to be governed by The Competition Commission Appeal Tribunal Rules 2000[15] as if they had not been revoked.

Revocation

A–070   **70.** Save as provided by rule 69, the Competition Commission Appeal Tribunal Rules 2000 are revoked.

Brian Wilson
Minister of State for Energy and Construction,
Department of Trade and Industry
23rd May 2003

---

[15] As amended by SI 2003/767 which will be treated as having been made under s.15 of the 2002 Act by virtue of para.12(1) of Sch.24 to that Act.

INDEX